P9-CWD-798

France

Vintage	Red Bordeaux		White Bordeaux		Alsace
	Médoc/Graves	Pom/St-Ém	Sauternes & sw	Graves & dry	
2014	7–8	6–8	8–9	8–9	7–8
2013	4–7	4–7	8–9	7–8	8–9
2012	6–8	6–8	6–7	7–9	8–9
2011	7–9	6–9	8–10	7–8	5–7
2010	7–10	6–10	8–10	7–9	8–9
2009	7–10	7–10	8–10	7–9	8–9
2008	6–9	6–9	6–7	7–9	7–8
2007	5–7	6–7	8–9	8–9	6–8
2006	7–8	7–8	8–9	8–9	6–8
2005	9–10	8–9	8–10	8–9	8–9
2004	7–8	7–9	5–7	6–7	6–8
2003	5–9	5–8	7–8	6–7	6–7
2002	6–8	5–8	7–8	7–8	7–8
2001	6–8	7–8	8–10	7–9	6–8
2000	8–10	7–9	6–8	7–9	8–10
1999	5–7	5–8	6–9	7–10	6–8
1998	5–8	6–9	5–8	5–9	7–9
1997	5–7	4–7	7–9	4–7	7–9
1996	6–8	5–7	7–9	7–10	8–10

France continued

Vintage	Burgundy			Rhône	
	Côte d'Or red	Côte d'Or white	Chablis	Rhône (N)	Rhône (S)
2014	6–8	7–9	7–9	7–8	6–8
2013	5–7	7–8	6–8	7–8	7–8
2012	8–9	7–8	7–8	7–9	7–9
2011	7–8	7–8	7–8	7–8	6–8
2010	8–10	8–10	8–10	8–10	8–9
2009	7–10	7–8	7–8	7–9	7–8
2008	7–9	7–9	7–9	6–7	5–7
2007	7–8	7–8	8–9	6–8	7–8
2006	7–8	8–10	8–9	7–8	7–9
2005	7–9	7–9	7–9	7–8	6–8
2004	6–7	7–8	7–8	6–7	6–7
2003	6–7	6–7	6–7	5–7	6–8
2002	7–8	7–8	7–8	4–6	5–5
2001	6–8	7–9	6–8	7–8	7–9

Beaujolais 2014, 11, 10. Crus will keep. **Mâcon-Villages** (white). Drink 14, 12. **Loire** (Sweet Anjou and Touraine) best recent vintages: 10, 09, 07, 05, 02, 97, 96, 93, 90, 89; Bourgueil, Chinon, Saumur-Champigny: 14, 10, 09, 06, 05, 04, 02. **Upper Loire** (Sancerre, Pouilly–Fumé): 14, 12. **Muscadet:** DYA.

Hugh Johnson's Pocket Wine Book 2016

Edited and designed by Mitchell Beazley,
an imprint of Octopus Publishing Group Limited,
Carmelite House, 50 Victoria Embankment
London EC4Y 0DZ
www.octopusbooks.co.uk

An Hachette UK Company
www.hachette.co.uk

Distributed in the US by Hachette Book Group
1290 Avenue of the Americas
4th and 5th Floors
New York, NY 10020
www.octopusbooksusa.com

A CIP record for this book is available from
the British Library.

ISBN (UK): 978-1-845-33987-6

ISBN (US): 978-1-784-72090-2

The author and publishers will be grateful for any
information that will assist them in keeping future editions
up to date. Although all reasonable care has been taken in
preparing this book, neither the publishers nor the author
can accept any liability for any consequences arising from
the use thereof, or from the information contained herein.

General Editor **Margaret Rand**
Commissioning Editor **Hilary Lumsden**
Project Editor **Pauline Bache**
Proofreader **Jamie Ambrose**
Deputy Art Director **Yasia Williams-Leedham**
Designer **Jeremy Tilston**
Assistant Production Manager **Caroline Alberti**

Printed and bound in China

Mitchell Beazley would like to acknowledge and thank the following
for supplying photographs for use in this book:

1 pashapixel/Thinkstock; 4 PHB.cz (Richard Semik)/ Shutterstock; 6 John
Kasawa/ Thinkstock; 7 S Photo/Shutterstock; 11 Julian Elliott Photography/
Getty Images; 14 Inti St Clair/Getty Images; 16 sarra22/Shutterstock; 321
Christian Mueringer/Alamy; 322-3 LaineM/Shutterstock; 325 © Maximin
Grünhaus Schlosskellerei C von Schubert; 326 Mick Rock/Cephas; 329 Per
Karlsson, BKWine 2/Alamy; 330-1 Herbert Lehmann/Cephas; 333 Kevin
Argue/Cephas; 334-5 Thierry Grun/Alamy; 336 Viel/SoFood/Corbis.

HUGH JOHNSON'S

JOHNSON'S

POCKET WINE BOOK

GENERAL EDITOR

MARGARET RAND

2016

Acknowledgements

This store of detailed recommendations comes partly from my own notes and mainly from those of a great number of kind friends. Without the generous help and cooperation of innumerable winemakers, merchants and critics, I could not attempt it. I particularly want to thank the following for help with research or in the areas of their special knowledge:

Sarah Ahmed, Helena Baker, Amanda Barnes, Nicolas Belfrage MW, Jim Budd, Poh Tiong Chng, Michael Cooper, Cole Danehower, Michael Edwards, Sarah Jane Evans MW, Rosemary George MW, Caroline Gilby MW, Anthony Gismondi, Annie Kay, Anne Krebiehl MW, James Lawther MW, Konstantinos Lazarakis MW, John Livingstone-Learmonth, Wes Marshall, Campbell Mattinson, Adam Montefiore, Jasper Morris MW, Margaret Rand, Ulrich Sautter, Eleonora Scholes, Stephen Skelton MW, Paul Strang, Marguerite Thomas, Larry Walker, Gal Zohar, Philip van Zyl

Contents

How to use this book

The top line of most entries consists of the following information:

1. Aglianico del Vulture Bas

2. r dr (s/sw sp)

3. ★★★

4. 05 06' **07** 08 09' 10 (11)

1. Aglianico del Vulture Bas

Wine name and the region the wine comes from, abbreviations of regions are listed in each section.

2. r dr (s/sw sp)

Whether it is red, rosé, or white (or brown/amber), dry, sweet, or sparkling, or several of these (and which is most important):

r	red
p	rosé
w	white
br	brown
dr	dry*
sw	sweet
s/sw	semi-sweet
sp	sparkling

( ) brackets here denote a less important wine
* assume wine is dry when dr or sw are not indicated

3. ★★★

Its general standing as to quality; a necessarily rough-and-ready guide based on its current reputation as reflected in its prices:

★	plain, everyday quality
★★	above average
★★★	well known, highly reputed
★★★★	grand, prestigious, expensive

So much is more or less objective. Additionally there is a subjective rating:

★ etc.   Stars are coloured for any wine which in my experience is usually especially good within its price range. There are good everyday wines as well as good luxury wines. This system helps you find them.

4. 05 06' 07 08 09' 10 (11)

Vintage information: those recent vintages that can be recommended, and of these, which are ready to drink this year, and which will probably improve with keeping. Your choice for current drinking should be one of the vintage years printed in **bold** type. Buy light-type years for further maturing.

05 etc. recommended years that may be currently available
06' etc. vintage regarded as particularly successful for the property in question
07 etc. years in bold should be ready for drinking (those not in bold will benefit from keeping)
08 etc. vintages in colour are those recommended as first choice for drinking in 2016. (*See also* Bordeaux introduction, p.97.)
(11) etc. provisional rating

The German vintages work on a different principle again: *see* p.156.

Other abbreviations & styles

DYA	Drink the youngest available.
NV	Vintage not normally shown on label; in Champagne this means a blend of several vintages for continuity.
CHABLIS	Properties, areas or terms cross-referred within the section; all grapes cross-ref to Grape Varieties chapter on pp.16–26.
Aiguilloux	Entries styled this way indicate wine (mid-2014–2015) especially enjoyed by Hugh Johnson.

Agenda 2016

Is it possible to have too much choice? Too much to fit in your pocket, certainly. Even my obsessive abbreviation can't squeeze all the possibilities between these covers. It is the unique feature of wine, among all the products of agriculture and art, that everyone who has a go wants to distinguish their efforts by a new label. Some of them are pretty odd: I don't know who will be tempted by Splattered Toad, for example. (It's on p.312.) In fact, the ingenious originality of maker after maker is a sub-theme of these pages. And they keep coming.

In last year's Agenda I wrote that we have reached the Age of Divergence. While the mainstream grape varieties in the mainstream vineyards would plough on with nothing to challenge their confidence, the signal has been given to branch out, to try varieties that no one has heard of in regions of unknown potential, to make wines in wacky ways in funny-shaped containers, to take risks by ditching the sulphur that has always been wine's number one antiseptic.

Why do today's producers feel free to buck convention? Because their market is all ears: drinkers are getting tired of scores; what poetry is there in 92/100? They want stories. Originality trumps typicity – at least in many, particularly young, customers' minds. (And sommeliers, a growing force, need the oxygen of novelty.)

I always enjoy snatches of vox pop about wine. What matters in mass-marketing terms are not readers of wine books. We're committed already. I overheard this little exchange in a Welsh farmer's kitchen recently: someone is just going shopping, "...and we'll need some white". "Sauvignon or Pinot Gris"? Wine, and varietal choice, have reached pretty deep into a culture where four or five years ago it was almost something exotic. Now it's part of the groceries.

And there's a new approach to describing it. Wine professionals and critics play with the limits of language. It's their job; they enjoy it – but they're not under oath. The first person to risk the word "minerality" to justify an elusive taste or impression thought he or she was being pretty edgy. After all, though Chablis has been characterized as "stony" or "like stones" time out of mind, no one actually thinks it tastes of stone (or knows what stones taste like).

But now the tentative has gone mainstream. Wine bars and restaurants print a string of hyperbolic half-truths beside every name. Sauvignon Blanc, as we all now know, tastes of grass, nettles, green peppers and/or gooseberries, elderflowers, sometimes peas or (when overripe) melons. There are bolder descriptions involving cats. And "minerality" is the universal clincher, supplanting even "terroir". Every wine has its clichés, like the list of ingredients that enlarges on every dish on the menu. Why is this a problem? Because it sets up unrealistic expectations. And it's not true: it's a glass of wine – tasting of wine – that you're buying, not a selection from the greengrocer's.

In general over the years I have avoided drawing attention to one region or country or chapter of this book over the others. We all buy our wines in different circumstances and with different priorities. These days most winemakers, wherever they are, proceed in parallel, sharing the same sources of technical information (and visited by similar supermarket buyers). The exceptions are the producers too small to appear on the radar, little family businesses that would panic if someone tried to order a pallet-load of wine. If anything this book gives priority to them rather than the Yellow Tails.

Showers of euro-gold
Seismic movements are rare. Expansion in the New World apart, much the fastest progress in the past generation or so has been the effects of the European Union on the Mediterranean wine countries. The countless millions of euros that were shovelled south in Europe fell on remarkably fertile ground. Spain and Portugal had been oenological basket cases. Italy had much more varied traditions, grapes, terroirs and capabilities: different regions moving at different speeds. No one will argue, though, that these "transfers" were not a good investment. The motorways and airports get northerners to the sun quicker, vegetables to the north quicker and raise everyone's standard of living. Most important in the world of wine, they forced every region to examine its USPs. Many hauled themselves up by using Cabernet, Chardonnay and the easy-sellers to get their eye in, as it were, for selling to the world.

Hence, as I wrote last year, our arrival in The Age of the Ampelographer. How come, you may well ask, so many hundreds of different grape varieties ever came into existence? Each variety is a man-made creation – or rather a selection that has to be propagated and preserved. Who on earth, in the long centuries of endless work for little if any reward, had the time and patience to sort them out? There is no real answer except a sort of agricultural evolution, at glacial speed, happening in endlessly varied natural conditions. (Italy is the prime example; the conditions between the Alps and Sicily are an environmental allsorts.) Most old vineyards inherited a haphazard mix of more and less successful vines – some not even identified. The massive job of sorting and understanding them, in archives and vine nurseries, was going slowly – until DNA arrived on the scene.

If I do suggest one country now for special consideration it is Greece – and not for its seemingly endless misfortunes. Until it received its share of the shower of euro-gold, wine in Greece was primitive. They added resin to mask the taste. It was also unintelligible to most mortals. The discovery of its potential excellence was the biggest surprise of all, and it's almost untried native varieties one of our most exciting new resources.

Arguing about alcohol

Too-strong wine has been a hobby horse of mine for almost a decade now. You could have said, up until now, that it was merely a matter of personal taste. I have a traditional palate. I drink wine for refreshment and to complement my food – almost always at table (and at most meals). If others want a more potent brew, more in keeping with cocktails, so be it. But there has been a shift in the last few years – not actually in alcohol content but in arguing about it. Only recently has it been common practice to cite it alongside the price; 15% ABV is still a strong sales point in some markets, but for how long?

This year there is a conference in California on how to get wine strength back down to where it used to be – between 12% and 13% instead of between 14% and 15% ABV. It won't be simple. Critics have been as easily fooled as their public by simple concentration: inky-dark wines that leave your palate in shock and awe. Poke is easy; harmony is hard.

The option of picking late for high sugar levels is easier than judging the precise moment when all the elements are in balance. Many producers will probably go for a technical solution: keep picking late, then use one or another of the new dodges for removing some of the alcohol in the cellar. Some, reasonably enough, will just add water.

Can there be too much choice? Some of the world's best wine-growers insist they don't make choices; their vineyards tell them what to do – which is usually to let well alone. We consumers have to feel our way through a blizzard of alternatives that can make us feel seriously in need of help. "Know what you're looking for" is easy advice, but not very helpful. "Know your own taste" is better. "Be honest about it" is better still. But all of us need to experiment to know what's out there. It is, after all, how we put this book together.

Next year will see the 40th edition. I started at the same time as *Star Wars* and Concorde. What other fields have seen as much expansion and as many improvements over those years as the world of wine?

The word most often being used by European growers about 2014 is "challenging". That means a lot of fingernails bitten to the quick, a lot of time spent looking at weather updates, and a lot of fingers very tightly crossed. Reports confirm that it is perfectly possible to cross your fingers and bite your fingernails at the same time.

Burgundy had a warm early spring and a quick start to the season, but then the Côte de Beaune was hit by hail at the end of June: for the third year running. Anne Parent in Pommard said it was like a machine-gun attack. Beaune, Volnay, Meursault and Santenay were also hit.

In **Bordeaux**, a warm September saved the day after a cool summer, with the Cabernets ripening well – Merlot is always less of a challenge. Tannins are rich and soft, and while it's clearly a good year, it's not another 2010, much though some producers would like to tell us it is.

In **Italy** poor weather produced the smallest harvest overall for 64 years, with the far north and the far south faring worst in terms of quantity. A wet July, with 73 per cent more rain than usual, was to blame. Quality-wise it's not all bad news, however, with Sicily in particular producing excellent whites.

In **Portugal** the Douro was plagued by unsettled weather; on 3 July a massive rainstorm destroyed farm roads and caused an avalanche that destroyed one winemaker's car. For several days, says Paul Symington, the Douro ran golden yellow with all the topsoil that had been washed down. After that the weather improved, and had September been warm and settled it would have been a uniformly great vintage. As it was, quality varies: there'll be some brilliant wines, but not everywhere.

German Riesling vineyards entered September some ten days ahead of normal – always good news – but then the rain came down, and in the Saar, hail. Acidity is high: in the Mosel and Saar it's not a year for dry wines.

In **Austria**, drought until April was followed by the wettest May since 1820 and a generally cool summer. Even September didn't oblige. Good viticulture and strict sorting of grapes, however, will mean lower quantities, but fresh, peppery Grüner Veltliner. Muskateller suffered from the rain, as did reds.

England, however, had nothing but good news. For once the good weather migrated northwards, and an excellent summer produced excellent fizz.

Vintage report 2014

In California, one extreme event followed another. The earthquake in south **Napa** on 24 August caused around $80 million of damage, but within two weeks 99 per cent of wineries were back in business. Then there was hail. In spite of this – and in spite of California's persistent drought – wineries in Napa are reporting good quality.

On the other side of the country, **Finger Lakes** had the opposite weather: a late spring and a late vintage, with rain in between. But September came up trumps and lovely wines are the result: Rieslings in particular are showing well.

A closer look at 2013

After **Burgundy**'s tiny 2012 vintage, and a summer of 2013 in which hailstones the size of golf balls sliced through the vineyards, it's reassuring to see that the 2013 wines, as they appear on the shelves, are pretty good, even though it was another small vintage. Chablis found it hard to recover from its heavy September rain, true, and quality here is mixed – you need to hunt for anything outstanding. But whites on the Côte d'Or are looking splendid: concentrated, intensely flavoured, with fine balance and raciness: they're terrifically moreish and full of salty minerality. Reds are pretty: mid-weight and for mid-term drinking. Some have the power to last many years, but most will appeal to those who don't want to have to stash wine away for decades.

It's a heterogenous vintage, with quality varying a lot, and while some reds are supple and silky, others are, in youth, a bit on the lean and mean side. But they may well have picked up more charm by the time they're bottled. All have lovely perfumes. The differences in style come from the nature of the weather at vintage: did you pick early, because of disease pressure in a coolish and humid September, and risk high acidity and lean tannins, or did you wait, and risk rot and further storms – both of which duly arrived? Either way, it was a white-knuckle ride. Some started picking in the third week of September; some didn't finish until the end of October.

Taste reds before you buy if you can, and go for good growers. Prices are being kept to around the same level as the 2012s: the Burgundians have watched Bordeaux lose credibility because of pricing, and they don't want to follow it.

Bordeaux, on the other hand, still declined to accept that it had a problem, and even though 2013 produced a tiny crop, and even though there were some good wines even after a grim summer, and even though some prices fell (never enough of them, and never by enough: it's hard to slash your prices because it makes older vintages look overpriced), the wines didn't sell very well. Yes, most of the big-name châteaux shifted their wines, but the bulk of the vintage, at the time of writing, was still owned by the châteaux. The 2011 and 2012 vintages were mostly in the hands of the Bordeaux négociants, that inner circle of merchants who in turn sell to your local wine merchant. This might be a good year to time a trip to France to coincide with the French supermarkets' Foires aux Vins, which is where the négoce unload their surplus stocks. The keynote of the reds is a certain fresh leanness, with richness hard to find, though there are certainly some good wines, perfumed and generous; the dry whites, fresh and expressive, are rather better; and there are some lovely Sauternes.

Blends in Bordeaux are sometimes atypical: no Merlot at all, or more Merlot than usual (Châteaux Margaux and Palmer respectively); in the Southern **Rhône** there's often less Grenache than normal in the blends, and more Syrah, and the wines are mostly easy, forward and appealing. Yields were low but the wines are not overly tannic and have good freshness. Reds from the north are poised and elegant, probably more serious than those of the south. Whites, in both cases, are very good.

If you want really successful 2013s, however, go to **Austria**. Grüner Veltliner and Riesling from Kamptal, Kremstal and the Wachau are startlingly good. As elsewhere it was an uneven year. Flowering took three weeks, which means uneven ripening, and according to Fred Loimer you could have bunches with three or four normal-sized berries and the rest tiny. It was also a small vintage: as well as poor flowering, there was late frost, and hail. The wines are concentrated, ripe, juicy and racy. Either drink them young or do as the Austrians don't do but should, and lay them down.

Germany also produced little, but what there was looks good. It's not really a Kabinett year: those who picked early were generally less successful than those who waited, so wines with higher sugar levels (though it wasn't a botrytis year) are the picks of the year. Go for Spätlesen and Auslesen, if you like that style; there are also very good racy *Grosses Gewächs* for those who favour dry Rieslings.

On the other side of the equator, the year was coolish in **Chile**: Sauvignon Blanc looks a bit unripe, but late-ripening Carmenère is fresh and good. In **Argentina** a cool spring slowed ripening and boosted quality in the reds. In **Australia** the situation was the opposite: a hot to very hot summer that has produced rich wines. Sometimes their freshness might owe more to the cellar than the vineyard, but that's show business.

This book is not just about discovering new wines; sometimes old wines get forgotten and need to be rediscovered. That's when it's fun to find new connections, new resemblances, that put them into a different context. Perspective changes everything.

If you like Frascati, try Aligoté

Frascati is an old favourite in Rome, sometimes maligned, but with lovely fresh sour-cream flavours and a refreshing lightness. Those same sour-cream notes crop up again in Aligoté, which is Burgundy's second white grape and has its own ACs in Bourgogne Aligoté and Bouzeron. Expect more weight than in Frascati and more bite.

If you like light Chardonnay, try Orvieto

Chardonnay has changed in recent years: oak is out, delicacy is in. If you're a fan of the new lightly nutty, fresh Chardonnays with a touch of cream and subtle, elegant fruit – and many places in the world are making these, from Australia to the south of France – then you might want to revisit Orvieto. Top Orvieto can have the bracing quality of Vouvray, but simpler dry ones and modern unoaked Chardonnay share a sparky freshness and a reviving minerality.

If you like dry Muscat, try Malagousia

Dry Muscat can be highly aromatic, with a delicate structure, and a flavour of roses, perhaps basil, perhaps citrus. Malagousia, a Greek grape that is increasingly being seen as one of Greece's great specialities, has a silky texture and a certain savouriness to add to its aromas of roses, basil and citrus. It can be good in blends, usually with something more acidic. If you see it, grab it.

If you like Aussie Riesling, try Godello

Australian Riesling from Clare or Eden Valleys is distinguished by its intense lime-cordial flavours, allied in the best examples to a salty minerality. Godello is a high-quality grape of northwest Spain, which was rescued from near-extinction in the 1970s and gives racy wines, rounder than Albariño, with a silky texture more like that of Viognier, and concentrated ripe lime and peach flavours.

If you like this, try this

If you like Northern Rhône, try Bairrada

Northern Rhône Syrah is notable for its acidity, its pungent herbal flavours combined with black olives and a certain stoniness of taste – like licking rock. Those herbs, and often the stoniness too, are also found in Portuguese Bairrada, a wine that has enjoyed a resurgence in recent years. Better winemaking and more sensitive viticulture are producing beautifully complex and unexpected reds from the high-acid, high-tannin Baga grape. The stars are the Pato family.

If you like young Syrah, try Lambrusco

The Syrah we're thinking of here is not the complex, deep wine of the Northern Rhône, but lighter versions, made to be drunk young, perhaps from Chile or New Zealand. They're bright, bouncy, acidic, and full of hedgerow perfumes. And they lead straight back to Lambrusco, that stalwart of retro parties, now being reassessed. And it's delicious: fizzy black-red wine with magenta froth, lowish in alcohol, high in acidity and with some fruity sweetness to balance – and full of those same hedgerow flavours. Classic with prosciutto.

If you like Languedoc-Roussillon reds, try Chilean Carignan

Languedoc-Roussillon reds based on traditional varieties (as opposed to the likes of Cab Sauv) often have some Carignan in them. It never used to be rated very highly, but now it is, especially from old bush vines that give deep, rich flavours of damsons and earth and herbs. Chile has some very old Carignan vineyards and nowadays sometimes makes it as a varietal, with deep curranty fruit and that same herby earthiness.

If you like Merlot, try Zinfandel

Zinfandel has got a reputation for being fantastically heavy and jammy, and some is like that. But not all. There is plenty of lighter Zin, which has ripe, sweet fruit, flavours of blueberry and blackberry, and a dash of pepper. That sounds like a lot of reds, true, but lovers of Merlot will recognize Zinfandel's silky texture and toffee notes, combined with relatively low acidity. Both grapes are extremely varied, and flavours can vary from place to place; Merlot aficionados might well enjoy a bit of exploring.

Grape varieties

In the past two decades a radical change has come about in all except the most long-established wine countries: the names of a handful of grape varieties have become the ready-reference to wine. In senior wine countries, above all France and Italy, more complex traditions prevail. All wine of old prestige is known by its origin, more or less narrowly defined – not just by the particular fruit juice that fermented. For the present the two notions are in rivalry. Eventually the primacy of place over fruit will become obvious, at least for wines of quality. But for now, for most people, grape tastes are the easy reference point – despite the fact that they are often confused by the added taste of oak. If grape flavours were really all that mattered, this would be a very short book. But of course they *do* matter, and a knowledge of them both guides you to flavours you enjoy and helps comparisons between regions. Hence the originally Californian term "varietal wine", meaning, in principle, made from one grape variety. At least seven varieties – Cabernet Sauvignon, Pinot Noir, Riesling, Sauvignon Blanc, Chardonnay, Gewurztraminer and Muscat – taste and smell distinct and memorable enough to form international wine categories. To these add Merlot, Malbec, Syrah, Sémillon, Chenin Blanc, Pinots Blanc and Gris, Sylvaner, Viognier, Nebbiolo, Sangiovese, Tempranillo. The following are the best and/or most popular wine grapes.

All grapes and synonyms are cross-referenced in small capitals throughout every section of this book.

Grapes for red wine

Aghiorgitiko (Agiorgitiko) Greek; grape of Nemea, now planted almost everywhere. Versatile, delicious, from soft and charming to dense and age-worthy. Must-try.

Aglianico S Italian, the grape of Taurasi; dark, deep and fashionable.

Aragonez See TEMPRANILLO.

Auxerrois See MALBEC, if red. White Auxerrois has its own entry in White Grapes.

Băbească Neagră Traditional "black grandmother grape" of Moldova; light body and ruby-red colour.

Babić Dark grape from Dalmatia, grown in stony seaside v'yds round Šibenik. Exceptional quality potential.

Baga Portugal. Bairrada grape. Dark and tannic. Great potential but hard to grow.

Barbera Widely grown in Italy, best in Piedmont: high acidity, low tannin, cherry fruit. Ranges from barriqued and serious to semi-sweet and frothy. Fashionable in California and Australia; promising in Argentina.

Blauburger Austrian cross between BLAUER PORTUGIESER/BLAUFRÄNKISCH. Simple wines.

Blauburgunder See PINOT N.

Blauer Portugieser Central European, esp Germany (Rheinhessen, Pfalz, mostly for rosé), Austria, Hungary. Light, fruity reds to drink slightly chilled when young. Not for laying down.

Blaufränkisch (Kékfrankos, Lemberger, Modra Frankinja) Widely planted in Austria's Mittelburgenland: medium-bodied, peppery acidity, a characteristic salty note, berry aromas and eucalyptus. Often blended with CAB SAUV or ZWEIGELT. Lemberger in Germany (speciality of Württemberg), Kékfrankos in Hungary, Modra Frankinja in Slovenia.

Boğazkere Tannic and Turkish. Produces full-bodied wines.

Bonarda Ambiguous name. In Oltrepò Pavese, an alias for Croatina, soft, fresh *frizzante* and still red. In Lombardy and Emilia-Romagna an alias for Uva Rara. Different in Piedmont. Argentina's Bonarda can be any of these, or something else. None are great.

Bouchet St-Émilion alias for CAB FR.

Brunello SANGIOVESE, splendid at Montalcino.

Cabernet Franc [Cab Fr] The lesser of two sorts of Cab grown in Bordeaux, but dominant in St-Émilion. Outperforms CAB SAUV in Loire (Chinon, Saumur-Champigny, rosé), in Hungary (depth and complexity in Villány and Szekszárd) and often in Italy. Much of ne Italy's Cab Fr turned out to be CARMENÈRE. Used in Bordeaux blends of Cab Sauv/MERLOT across the world.

Cabernet Sauvignon [Cab Sauv] Grape of great character: slow-ripening, spicy, herby, tannic, with blackcurrant aroma. Main grape of the Médoc; also makes some of the best California, South American, East European reds. Vies with SHIRAZ in Australia. Grown almost everywhere, and led vinous renaissance in eg. Italy. Top wines need ageing; usually benefits from blending with eg. MERLOT, CAB FR, SYRAH, TEMPRANILLO, SANGIOVESE etc. Makes aromatic rosé.

Cannonau GRENACHE in its Sardinian manifestation; can be v. fine, potent.

Carignan (Carignane, Carignano, Cariñena) Low-yielding old vines are now v. fashionable everywhere from s of France to Chile; best: Corbières. Lots of depth and vibrancy. Overcropped Carignan is wine-lake fodder. Common in North Africa, Spain (as Cariñena) and California.

Carignano See CARIGNAN.

Cariñena See CARIGNAN.

Carmenère An old Bordeaux variety now a star, rich and deep, in Chile (where it's pronounced *carmeneary*). Bordeaux is looking at it again.

Castelão See PERIQUITA.

Cencibel See TEMPRANILLO.

Chiavennasca *See* NEBBIOLO.

Cinsault (Cinsaut) A staple of s France, v.gd if low-yielding, wine-lake stuff if not. Makes gd rosé. One of parents of PINOTAGE.

Cornalin du Valais Swiss speciality with high potential, esp in Valais.

Corvina Dark and spicy; one of best grapes in Valpolicella blend. Corvinone, even darker, is a separate variety.

Côt *See* MALBEC.

Dolcetto Source of soft, seductive dry red in Piedmont. Now high fashion.

Dornfelder Gives deliciously light reds, straightforward and often rustic, and well-coloured, in Germany, parts of the USA, England. German plantings have doubled since 2000.

Fer Servadou Exclusive to Southwest France, particularly important in Marcillac, Gaillac and St-Mont. Redolent of soft fruits and spice.

Fetească Neagră Romania: "black maiden grape" with potential as showpiece variety; can give deep, full-bodied wines with character. Acreage increasing.

Frühburgunder An ancient German mutation of PINOT N, mostly in Ahr but also in Franken and Württemberg, where it is confusingly known as Clevner. Lower acidity than Pinot N.

Gamay The Beaujolais grape: v. light, fragrant wines, best young, except in Beaujolais *crus* (*see* France) where quality can be high, wines for 2–10 yrs. Grown in the Loire Valley, in central France, in Switzerland and Savoie. California's Napa Gamay is Valdiguié.

Gamza *See* KADARKA.

Garnacha (Cannonau, Garnatxa, Grenache) Widespread pale potent grape now fashionable with *terroiristes*, who admire the way it expresses its site. Also gd for rosé, Vin Doux Naturel – esp in the s of France, Spain and California – but also the mainstay of beefy Priorat. Old-vine versions are prized in South Australia. Usually blended with other varieties. Cannonau in Sardinia, Grenache in France.

Garnatxa *See* GARNACHA.

Graciano Spanish; part of Rioja blend. Aroma of violets, tannic, lean structure, a bit like PETIT VERDOT. Difficult to grow but increasingly fashionable.

Grenache *See* GARNACHA.

Grignolino Italy: gd everyday table wine in Piedmont.

Kadarka (Gamza) Makes spicy, light reds in East Europe. In Hungary revived esp for Bikavér.

Kékfrankos Hungarian BLAUFRÄNKISCH.

Lagrein N Italian, deep colour, bitter finish, rich, plummy fruit. DOC in Alto Adige (*see* Italy).

Lambrusco Productive grape of the lower Po Valley; quintessentially Italian, cheerful, sweet and fizzy red.

Lefkada Rediscovered Cypriot variety, higher quality than Mavro. Usually blended as tannins can be aggressive.

Lemberger *See* BLAUFRÄNKISCH.

Malbec (Auxerrois, Côt) Minor in Bordeaux, major in Cahors (alias Auxerrois) and the star in Argentina. Dark, dense, tannic but fleshy wine capable of real quality. High-altitude versions in Argentina are the bee's knees. Bringing Cahors back into fashion.

Maratheftiko Deep-coloured Cypriot grape with quality potential.

Mataro *See* MOURVÈDRE.

Mavro Most planted black grape of Cyprus but only moderate quality. Best for rosé.

Mavrodaphne Greek; the name means "black laurel". Used for sweet fortifieds; speciality of Patras, but also found in Cephalonia. Dry versions on the increase, show great promise.

Mavrotragano Greek, almost extinct but now revived; found on Santorini. Top quality.

Mavrud Probably Bulgaria's best. Spicy, dark, plummy late-ripener native to Thrace. Ages well.

Melnik Bulgarian grape from the region of the same name. Dark colour and a nice dense, tart cherry character. Ages well.

Mencía Making waves in Bierzo, Spain. Aromatic, with steely tannins, lots of acidity.

Merlot The grape behind the great fragrant and plummy wines of Pomerol and (with CAB FR) St-Émilion, a vital element in the Médoc, soft and strong (and à la mode) in California, Washington, Chile, Australia. Lighter, often gd in n Italy (can be world-class in Tuscany), Italian Switzerland, Slovenia, Argentina, South Africa, NZ, etc. Perhaps too adaptable for own gd: can be v. dull; less than ripe it tastes green. Much planted in Eastern Europe, esp Romania.

Modra Frankinja See BLAUFRÄNKISCH.

Modri Pinot See PINOT N.

Monastrell See MOURVÈDRE.

Mondeuse Found in Savoie; deep coloured, gd acidity. Related to SYRAH.

Montepulciano Deep-coloured grape dominant in Italy's Abruzzo, important along Adriatic coast from Marches to s Puglia. Also name of a Tuscan town, unrelated.

Morellino SANGIOVESE in Maremma, s Tuscany. Esp Scansano.

Mourvèdre (Mataro, Monastrell) A star of s France (eg. Bandol), Australia (aka Mataro) and Spain (aka Monastrell). Excellent dark, aromatic, tannic grape, gd for blending. Enjoying new interest in eg. South Australia and California.

Napa Gamay Identical to Valdiguié (s of France). Nothing to get excited about.

Nebbiolo (Chiavennasca, Spanna) One of Italy's best red grapes; makes Barolo, Barbaresco, Gattinara and Valtellina. Intense, nobly fruity, perfumed wine with steely tannin: improves for yrs.

Negroamaro Puglian "black bitter" red grape with potential for either high quality or high volume.

Nerello Mascalese Characterful Sicilian red grape; potential for elegance.

Nero d'Avola Dark-red grape of Sicily, quality levels from sublime to industrial.

Nielluccio Corsican; plenty of acidity and tannin. Gd for rosé.

Öküzgözü Soft, fruity Turkish grape, usually blended with BOĞASKERE, rather as MERLOT in Bordeaux is blended with CAB SAUV.

País Pioneer Spanish grape in Americas. Rustic; some producers now trying harder.

Pamid Bulgarian: light, soft, everyday red.

Periquita (Castelão) Common in Portugal, esp round Setúbal. Originally nicknamed Periquita after Fonseca's popular (trademarked) brand. Firm-flavoured, raspberryish reds develop a figgish, tar-like quality.

Petite Sirah Nothing to do with SYRAH; gives rustic, tannic, dark wine. Brilliant blended with ZIN in California; also found in South America, Mexico, Australia.

Petit Verdot Excellent but awkward Médoc grape, now increasingly planted in CAB areas worldwide for extra fragrance. Mostly blended but some gd varietals, esp in Virginia.

Pinotage Singular South African cross (PINOT N X CINSAULT). Has had a rocky ride, getting better from top producers. Gd rosé too. "Coffee Pinotage" is espresso-flavoured, sweetish, aimed at youth.

Pinot Crni See PINOT N.

Pinot Meunier (Schwarzriesling) Third grape of Champagne, scorned by some, used by most. Less acid than PINOT N; invaluable for blending. Found in many places, either vinified as a white for fizz, or occasionally (eg. Germany's Württemberg, as Schwarzriesling) as still red. Samtrot is a local variant in Württemberg.

Pinot Noir (Blauburgunder, Modri Pinot, Pinot Crni, Spätburgunder) [Pinot N] The glory of Burgundy's Côte d'Or, with scent, flavour and texture unmatched anywhere. Recent German efforts have been excellent. V.gd in Austria, esp in Kamptal, Burgenland, Thermenregion. Light wines in Hungary; mainstream, light to weightier in Switzerland (aka Clevner). Splendid results in Sonoma, Carneros, Central Coast, as well as Oregon, Ontario, Yarra Valley, Adelaide Hills, Tasmania, NZ's South Island (Central Otago) and South Africa's Walker Bay. Some v. pretty Chileans. New French clones promise improvement in Romania. Modri Pinot in Slovenia; probably country's best red. In Italy, best in ne and gets worse as you go s. PINOTS BL and GR are mutations of Pinot N.

Plavac Mali (Crljenak) Croatian, and related to ZIN, like so much round there. Lots of quality potential, can age well, though can also be alcoholic and dull.

Primitivo S Italian grape, originally from Croatia, making big, dark, rustic wines, now fashionable because genetically identical to ZIN. Early ripening, hence the name. The original name for both seems to be Tribidrag.

Refosco (Refošk) Various DOCs in Italy, esp Colli Orientali. Deep, flavoursome and age-worthy wines, particularly in warmer climates. Dark, high acidity. Refošk in Slovenia and points e, genetically different, tastes similar.

Refošk See REFOSCO.

Rubin Bulgarian cross, NEBBIOLO X SYRAH. Peppery, full-bodied.

Sagrantino Italian grape grown in Umbria for powerful, cherry-flavoured wines.

St-Laurent Dark, smooth, full-flavoured Austrian speciality. Can be light and juicy or deep and structured. Also in Pfalz.

Sangiovese (Brunello, Morellino, Sangioveto) Principal red grape of Tuscany and central Italy. Hard to get right, but sublime and long-lasting when it is. Dominant in Chianti, Vino Nobile, Brunello di Montalcino, Morellino di Scansano and various fine IGT offerings. Also in Umbria (eg. Montefalco and Torgiano) and across the Apennines in Romagna and Marches. Not so clever in the warmer, lower-altitude v'yds of the Tuscan coast, nor in other parts of Italy despite its nr-ubiquity. Interesting in Australia.

Sangioveto See SANGIOVESE.

Saperavi The main red of Georgia, Ukraine, etc. Blends well with CAB SAUV (eg. in Moldova). Huge potential, seldom gd winemaking.

Schiava See TROLLINGER.

Schwarzriesling PINOT MEUNIER in Württemberg.

Sciacarello Corsican, herby and peppery. Not v. tannic.

Shiraz See SYRAH.

Spanna See NEBBIOLO.

Spätburgunder German for PINOT N.

Syrah (Shiraz) The great Rhône red grape: tannic, purple, peppery wine that matures superbly. Important as Shiraz in Australia, increasingly gd under either name in Chile, South Africa, terrific in NZ (esp Hawke's Bay). Widely grown.

Tannat Raspberry-perfumed, highly tannic force behind Madiran, Tursan and other firm reds from Southwest France. Also rosé. Now the star of Uruguay.

Tempranillo (Aragonez, Cecibel, Tinto Fino, Tinta del País, Tinta Roriz, Ull de Llebre) Aromatic, fine Rioja grape, called Ull de Llebre in Catalonia, Cencibel in La Mancha, Tinto Fino in Ribera del Duero, Tinta Roriz in Douro, Tinta del País in Castile, Aragonez in s Portugal. Now Australia too. V. fashionable; elegant in cool climates, beefy in warm. Early ripening, long maturing.

Teran (Terrano) A close cousin of REFOSCO, esp on limestone (karst) in Slovenia and thereabouts.

Teroldego Rotaliano Trentino's best indigenous variety; serious, full-flavoured wine, esp on the flat Campo Rotaliano.

Tinta Amarela See TRINCADEIRA.

Tinta del País See TEMPRANILLO.

Tinta Negra (Negramoll) Until recently called Tinta Negra Mole. Easily Madeira's most planted grape and the mainstay of cheaper Madeira. Now coming into its own in Colheita wines (*see* Port, Sherry & Madeira chapter).

Tinta Roriz *See* TEMPRANILLO.

Tinto Fino *See* TEMPRANILLO.

Touriga Nacional [Touriga N] The top Port grape, now widely used in the Douro for floral, stylish table wines. Australian Touriga is usually this; California's Touriga can be either this or Touriga Franca.

Trincadeira (Tinta Amarela) Portuguese; v.gd in Alentejo for spicy wines. Tinta Amarela in the Douro.

Trollinger (Schiava, Vernatsch) Popular pale red in Germany's Württemberg; aka Vernatsch and Schiava. Covers a group of vines, not necessarily related. In Italy, snappy and brisk.

Vernatsch *See* TROLLINGER.

Xinomavro Greece's answer to NEBBIOLO. "Sharp-black"; the basis for Naoussa, Rapsani, Goumenissa, Amindeo. Some rosé, still or sparkling. Top quality, can age for decades. Being tried in China.

Zinfandel [Zin] Fruity, adaptable grape of California with blackberry-like, and sometimes metallic, flavour. Can be structured and gloriously lush, aging for decades, but also makes "blush" pink, usually sweet, jammy. Genetically the same as s Italian PRIMITIVO.

Zweigelt (Blauer Zweigelt) BLAUFRÄNKISCH x ST-LAURENT, popular in Austria for aromatic, dark, supple, velvety wines. Also found in Hungary, Germany.

Grapes for white wine

Airén Bland workhorse of La Mancha, Spain: fresh if made well.

Albariño (Alvarinho) Fashionable, expensive in Spain: apricot scented, with gd acidity. Superb in Rías Baixas; shaping up elsewhere, but sadly not all live up to the hype. Alvarinho in Portugal just as gd: aromatic Vinho Verde, esp in Monção, Melgaço.

Aligoté Burgundy's 2nd-rank white grape. Sharp wine for young drinking, perfect for mixing with cassis (blackcurrant liqueur) to make Kir. Widely planted in East Europe, esp Russia.

Alvarinho *See* ALBARIÑO.

Amigne One of Switzerland's speciality grapes, traditional in Valais, esp Vétroz. Total planted: 43 ha. Full-bodied, tasty, often sweet but also bone-dry.

Ansonica *See* INSOLIA.

Arinto Portuguese; the mainstay of aromatic, citrus wines in Bucelas; also adds welcome zip to blends, esp in Alentejo.

Arneis Nw Italian. Fine, aromatic, appley-peachy, high-priced grape, DOCG in Roero, DOC in Langhe, Piedmont.

Arvine Rare but excellent Swiss *spécialité*, from Valais. Also Petite Arvine. Dry or sweet, fresh, long-lasting wines with salty finish.

Assyrtiko From Santorini; one of the best grapes of the Mediterranean, balancing power, minerality, extract and high acid. Built to age. Could conquer the world....

Auxerrois Red Auxerrois is a synonym for MALBEC, but white Auxerrois is like a fatter, spicier version of PINOT BL. Found in Alsace and much used in Crémant; also Germany.

Beli Pinot *See* PINOT BL.

Blanc Fumé *See* SAUV BL.

Boal *See* BUAL.

Bourboulenc This and the rare Rolle make some of the Midi's best wines.

Bouvier Indigenous aromatic Austrian grape, esp gd for Beerenauslese and Trockenbeerenauslese, rarely for dry wines.

Bual (Boal) Makes top-quality sweet Madeira wines, not quite so rich as MALMSEY.

Carricante Italian. Principal grape of Etna Bianco, regaining ground.

Catarratto Prolific white grape found all over Sicily, esp in w in DOC Alcamo.

Cerceal See SERCIAL.

Chardonnay (Morillon) [Chard] The white grape of Burgundy and Champagne, now ubiquitous worldwide, partly because it is one of the easiest to grow and vinify. Also the name of a Mâcon-Villages commune. The fashion for overoaked butterscotch versions now thankfully over. Morillon in Styria, Austria.

Chasselas (Fendant, Gutedel) Swiss (originated in Vaud). Neutral flavour, takes on local character: elegant (Geneva); refined, full (Vaud); exotic, racy (Valais). Fendant in Valais. Makes almost 3rd of Swiss wines but giving way, esp to red. Gutedel in Germany; grown esp in s Baden. Elsewhere usually a table grape.

Chenin Blanc [Chenin Bl] Wonderful white grape of the middle Loire (Vouvray, Layon, etc). Wine can be dry or sweet (or v. sweet), but with plenty of acidity. Formerly called Steen in South Africa; many ordinary but best noble. California can do it well but doesn't bother.

Cirfandl See ZIERFANDLER.

Clairette Important Midi grape, low-acid, part of many blends. Improved winemaking helps.

Colombard Slightly fruity, nicely sharp grape, makes everyday wine in South Africa, California and Southwest France. Often blended.

Dimiat Perfumed Bulgarian grape, made dry or off-dry, or distilled. Far more synonyms than any grape needs.

Ermitage Swiss for MARSANNE.

Ezerjó Hungarian, with sharp acidity. Name means "thousand blessings".

Falanghina Italian: ancient grape of Campanian hills. Gd dense, aromatic dry whites.

Fendant See CHASSELAS.

Fernão Pires See MARIA GOMES.

Fetească Albă / Regală Romania has two Fetească grapes, both with slight MUSCAT aroma. F. Regală is a cross of F. Albă and GRASĂ; more finesse, gd for late-harvest wines. F. NEAGRĂ is dark-skinned.

Fiano High-quality grape giving peachy, spicy wine in Campania, s Italy.

Folle Blanche (Gros Plant) High acid/little flavour make this ideal for brandy. Gros Plant in Brittany, Picpoul in Armagnac, but unrelated to true PICPOUL. Also respectable in California.

Friulano (Sauvignonasse, Sauvignon Vert) N Italian: fresh, pungent, subtly floral. Used to be called Tocai Friulano. Best in Collio, Isonzo, Colli Orientali. Found in nearby Slovenia as Sauvignonasse; also in Chile, where it was long confused with SAUV BL. Ex-Tocai in Veneto now known as Tai.

Fumé Blanc See SAUV BL.

Furmint (Šipon) Superb, characterful. The trademark of Hungary, both as the principal grape in Tokaji and as vivid, vigorous table wine, sometimes mineral, sometimes apricot-flavoured, sometimes both. Šipon in Slovenia. Some grown in Rust, Austria for sweet and dry.

Garganega Best grape in Soave blend; also in Gambellara. Top, esp sweet, age well.

Garnacha Blanca (Grenache Blanc) The white version of GARNACHA/Grenache, much used in Spain and s France. Low acidity. Can be innocuous, or surprisingly gd.

Gewurztraminer (Traminac, Traminec, Traminer, Tramini) [Gewurz] One of the most pungent grapes, spicy with aromas of rose petals, face-cream, lychees, grapefruit. Wines are often rich and soft, even when fully dry. Best in Alsace; also gd in Germany (Baden, Pfalz, Sachsen), Eastern Europe, Australia, California,

Pacific Northwest and NZ. Can be relatively unaromatic if just labelled Traminer (or variants). Italy uses the name Traminer Aromatico for its (dry) "Gewürz" versions. (The name takes an Umlaut in German.) Identical to SAVAGNIN.

Glera Uncharismatic new name for the Prosecco vine: Prosecco is now only a wine, no longer a grape.

Godello Top quality (intense, mineral) in nw Spain. Called Verdelho in Dão, Portugal, but unrelated to true VERDELHO.

Grasă (Kövérszölö) Romanian; name means "fat". Prone to botrytis; important in Cotnari, potentially superb sweet wines. Kövérszölö in Hungary's Tokaj region.

Graševina See WELSCHRIESLING.

Grauburgunder See PINOT GR.

Grechetto Ancient grape of central and s Italy noted for the vitality and stylishness of its wine. Blended, or used solo in Orvieto.

Greco S Italian: there are various Grecos, probably unrelated, perhaps of Greek origin. Brisk, peachy flavour, most famous as Greco di Tufo. Greco di Bianco is from semi-dried grapes. Greco Nero is a black version.

Grenache Blanc See GARNACHA BLANCA.

Grignolino Italy: gd everyday table wine in Piedmont.

Gros Plant See FOLLE BLANCHE.

Grüner Veltliner [Grüner V] Austria's fashionable flagship white grape. Remarkably diverse; from simple, peppery everyday wines to others of great complexity and ageing potential. A little elsewhere in Central Europe, now showing potential in NZ.

Gutedel See CHASSELAS.

Hárslevelű Other main grape of Tokaji, but softer, peachier than FURMINT. Name means "linden-leaved". Gd in Somló, Eger as well.

Heida Swiss for SAVAGNIN.

Humagne Swiss speciality, older than CHASSELAS. Fresh, plump, not v. aromatic. Humagne Rouge, also common in Valais, is not related but increasingly popular. Humagne Rouge is the same as Cornalin du Aosta; Cornalin du Valais is different. (Keep up at the back, there.)

Insolia (Ansonica, Inzolia) Sicilian; Ansonica on Tuscan coast. Fresh, racy wine at best. May be semi-dried for sweet wine.

Irsai Olivér Hungarian cross of two table varieties, makes aromatic, MUSCAT-like wine for drinking young.

Johannisberg Swiss for SILVANER.

Kéknyelű Low-yielding, flavourful grape giving one of Hungary's best whites. Has the potential for fieriness and spice. To be watched.

Kerner A quite successful German cross. Early ripening and flowery (but often too blatant) wine with gd acidity.

Királyleanyka Hungarian; gentle, fresh wines (eg. in Eger).

Kövérszölö See GRASĂ.

Laski Rizling See WELSCHRIESLING.

Leányka Hungarian. Soft, floral wines.

Listán See PALOMINO.

Loureiro Best Vinho Verde grape variety after ALVARINHO: delicate floral whites. Also found in Spain.

Macabeo See VIURA.

Malagousia Rediscovered Greek grape for gloriously perfumed wines.

Malmsey See MALVASIA. The sweetest style of Madeira.

Malvasia (Malmsey, Malvazia, Malvoisie, Marastina) Italy, France and Iberia. Not a single variety but a whole stable, not necessarily related or even alike. Can be white or red, sparkling or still, strong or mild, sweet or dry, aromatic or neutral.

Slovenia's and Croatia's version is Malvazija Istarka, crisp and light, or rich, oak-aged. Sometimes called Marastina in Croatia. "Malmsey" (as in the sweetest style of Madeira) is a corruption of Malvasia.

Malvoisie *See* MALVASIA. A name used for several varieties in France, incl BOURBOULENC, Torbato, VERMENTINO. Also PINOT GR in Switzerland's Valais.

Manseng, Gros / Petit Gloriously spicy, floral whites from Southwest France.The key to Jurançon. Superb late-harvest and sweet wines too.

Maria Gomes (Fernão Pires) Portuguese; aromatic, ripe-flavoured, slightly spicy whites in Barraida and Tejo.

Marsanne (Ermitage) Principal white grape (with ROUSSANNE) of the Northern Rhône (Hermitage, St-Joseph, St-Péray). Also gd in Australia, California and (as Ermitage Blanc) the Valais. Soft, full wines that age v. well.

Melon de Bourgogne *See* MUSCADET.

Misket Bulgarian. Mildly aromatic; the basis of most country whites.

Morillon CHARD in parts of Austria.

Moscatel *See* MUSCAT.

Moscato *See* MUSCAT.

Moschofilero Pink-skinned, rose-scented, high-quality, high-acid, low-alcohol Greek grape. Makes white, some pink, some sparkling.

Müller-Thurgau [Müller-T] Aromatic wines to drink young. Makes gd sweet wines but usually dull, often coarse, dry ones. In Germany, most common in Pfalz, Rheinhessen, Nahe, Baden, Franken. Has some merit in Italy's Trentino-Alto Adige, Friuli. Sometimes called Ries x Sylvaner (incorrectly) in Switzerland.

Muscadelle Adds aroma to white Bordeaux, esp Sauternes. In Victoria used (with MUSCAT, to which it is unrelated) for Rutherglen Muscat.

Muscadet (Melon de Bourgogne) Makes light, refreshing, v, dry wines with a seaside tang around Nantes in Brittany. Also found (as Melon) in parts of Burgundy.

Muscat (Moscatel, Moscato, Muskateller) Many varieties; the best is Muscat Blanc à Petits Grains (alias Gelber Muskateller, Rumeni Muškat, Sarga Muskotály, Yellow Muscat). Widely grown, easily recognized, pungent grapes, mostly made into perfumed sweet wines, often fortified, as in France's *vin doux naturel*. Superb, dark and sweet in Australia. Sweet, sometimes v.gd in Spain. Most Hungarian Muskotály is Muscat Ottonel, except in Tokaj, where Sarga Muskotály rules, adding perfume (in small amounts) to blends. Occasionally (eg. Alsace, Austria, parts of south Germany) made dry. Sweet Cap Corse Muscats often superb. Light Moscato fizz in n Italy.

Muskateller *See* MUSCAT.

Narince Turkish; fresh and fruity wines.

Neuburger Austrian, rather neglected; mainly in the Wachau (elegant, flowery), Thermenregion (mellow, ample-bodied) and n Burgenland (strong, full).

Olaszriesling *See* WELSCHRIESLING.

Païen *See* SAVAGNIN.

Palomino (Listán) The great grape of Sherry; with little intrinsic character, it gains all from production method. As Listán, makes dry white in Canaries.

Pansa Blanca *See* XAREL-LO.

Pecorino Italian: not a cheese but alluring dry white from a recently nr-extinct variety. IGT in Colli Pescaresi.

Pedro Ximénez [PX] Makes sweet brown Sherry under its own name, and used in Montilla and Málaga. Also grown in Argentina, the Canaries, Australia, California and South Africa.

Picpoul (Piquepoul) Southern French, best known in Picpoul de Pinet. Should have high acidity. Picpoul Noir is black-skinned.

Pinela Local to Slovenia. Subtle, lowish acidity; drink young.

Pinot Bianco *See* PINOT BL.

Pinot Blanc (Beli Pinot, Pinot Bianco, Weißburgunder) [Pinot Bl] A cousin of PINOT N, similar to but milder than CHARD. Light, fresh, fruity, not aromatic, to drink young. Gd for Italian *spumante*, potentially excellent in ne, esp high sites in Alto Adige. Widely grown. Weissburgunder in Germany, best in s: often racier than Chard.

Pinot Gris (Pinot Grigio, Grauburgunder, Ruländer, Sivi Pinot, Szürkebarát) [Pinot Gr] Ultra-popular as Pinot Grigio in n Italy, even for rosé, but top, characterful versions can be excellent (from Alto Adige, Friuli). Cheap versions are just that. Terrific in Alsace for full-bodied, spicy whites. Once important in Champagne. In Germany can be alias Ruländer (sw) or Grauburgunder (dr): best in Baden (esp Kaiserstuhl) and s Pfalz. Szürkebarát in Hungary, Sivi P in Slovenia (characterful, aromatic).

Pošip Croatian; mostly on island of Korčula. Quite characterful, citrus; high yielding.

Prosecco Old name for the grape that makes Prosecco. Now you have to call it GLERA.

Renski Rizling Rhine RIES.

Rèze Super-rare ancestral Valais grape used for *vin de glacier*.

Ribolla Gialla / Rebula Acidic but characterful. In Italy, best in Collio. In Slovenia, traditional in Brda. Can be v.gd, even made in eccentric ways.

Rieslaner German cross (SILVANER X RIES); low yields, difficult ripening, now v. rare (less than 50 ha). Makes fine Auslesen in Franken and Pfalz.

Riesling Italico *See* WELSCHRIESLING.

Riesling (Renski Rizling, Rhine Riesling) [Ries] The greatest, most versatile white grape, diametrically opposite in style to CHARD. Offers a range from steely to voluptuous, always positively perfumed; far more ageing potential than Chard. Great in all styles in Germany; forceful and steely in Austria; lime cordial and toast fruit in South Australia; rich and spicy in Alsace; Germanic and promising in NZ, NY State, Pacific Northwest; has potential in Ontario, South Africa.

Rkatsiteli Found widely in Eastern Europe, Russia, Georgia. Can stand cold winters and has high acidity, which protects it to some degree from poor winemaking. Also grown in ne States

Robola In Greece (Cephalonia) a top-quality, floral grape, unrelated to Ribolla Gialla.

Roditis Pink grape grown all over Greece, usually makes whites. Gd when yields low.

Roter Veltliner Austrian; unrelated to GRÜNER V. There is also a Frühroter and an (unrelated) Brauner Veltliner.

Rotgipfler Austrian; indigenous to Thermenregion. With ZIERFANDLER, makes lively, lush, aromatic blend.

Roussanne Rhône grape of real finesse, now popping up in California, Australia. Can age many yrs.

Ruländer *See* PINOT GR.

Sauvignonasse *See* FRIULANO.

Sauvignon Blanc [Sauv Bl] Makes distinctive aromatic, grassy-to-tropical wines, pungent in NZ, often minerally in Sancerre, riper in Australia. V.gd in Rueda, Austria, n Italy (Isonzo, Piedmont, Alto Adige), Chile's Casablanca Valley and South Africa. Blended with SÉM in Bordeaux. Can be austere or buxom (or indeed nauseating). Sauv Gris is a pink-skinned, less aromatic version of Sauv Bl with untapped potential.

Sauvignon Vert *See* FRIULANO.

Savagnin (Heida, Païen) Grape of Vin Jaune from Savoie: aromatic form is GEWURZ. In Switzerland known as Heida, Païen or Traminer. Full-bodied, high acidity.

Scheurebe (Sämling) Grapefruit-scented German RIES X SILVANER (possibly), v. successful in Pfalz, esp for Auslese and upwards. Can be weedy: must be v. ripe to be gd.

Sémillon [Sém] Contributes lusciousness to Sauternes; decreasingly important for Graves and other dry white Bordeaux. Grassy if not fully ripe, but can make soft dry wine of great ageing potential. Superb in Australia; NZ, South Africa promising.

Sercial (Cerceal) Portuguese: makes the driest Madeira. Cerceal, also Portuguese, seems to be this plus any of several others.

Seyval Blanc [Seyval Bl] A French-made hybrid of French and American vines. V. hardy and attractively fruity. Popular and reasonably successful in e US states and England but dogmatically banned by EU from "quality" wines.

Silvaner (Johannisberg, Sylvaner) Can be excellent in Germany's Rheinhessen, Pfalz, esp Franken, with plant/earth flavours and mineral notes. V.gd (and powerful) as Johannisberg in the Valais, Switzerland. The lightest of the Alsace grapes.

Šipon See FURMINT.

Sivi Pinot See PINOT GR.

Spätrot See ZIERFANDLER.

Sylvaner See SILVANER.

Tămâioasă Românească Romanian: "frankincense" grape, with exotic aroma and taste. Belongs to MUSCAT family.

Torrontés Name given to a number of grapes, mostly with an aromatic, floral character, sometimes soapy. A speciality of Argentina; also in Spain. DYA.

Traminac Or Traminec. See GEWURZ.

Traminer Or Tramini (Hungary). See GEWURZ.

Trebbiano (Ugni Blanc) Principal white grape of Tuscany, found all over Italy in many different guises. Rarely rises above the plebeian except in Tuscany's Vin Santo. Some gd dry whites under DOCs Romagna or Abruzzo. Trebbiano di Soave or di Lugana, aka VERDICCHIO, is only distantly related. Grown in southern France as Ugni Blanc, and Cognac as St-Émilion. Mostly thin, bland wine; needs blending (and more careful growing).

Ugni Blanc [Ugni Bl] See TREBBIANO.

Ull de Llebre See TEMPRANILLO.

Verdejo The grape of Rueda in Castile, potentially fine and long-lived.

Verdelho Great quality in Australia (pungent and full-bodied); rare but gd (and medium-sweet) in Madeira.

Verdicchio Potentially gd, muscular dry wine in central-e Italy. Makes wine of the same name.

Vermentino Italian, sprightly with satisfying texture, ageing capacity. Potential here.

Vernaccia Name given to many unrelated grapes in Italy. Vernaccia di San Gimignano is crisp, lively; Vernaccia di Oristano is Sherry-like.

Vidal French hybrid much grown in Canada for Icewine.

Viognier Ultra-fashionable Rhône grape, finest in Condrieu, less fine but still aromatic in the Midi. Gd examples from California, Virginia, Uruguay, Australia.

Viura (Macabeo, Maccabéo, Maccabeu) The workhorse white grape of n Spain, widespread in Rioja and Catalan Cava country. Also found over border in Southwest France. Gd quality potential.

Weißburgunder PINOT BL in Germany.

Welschriesling (Graševina, Laski Rizling, Olaszriesling, Riesling Italico) Not related to RIES. Light and fresh to sweet and rich in Austria; ubiquitous in Central Europe, where it can be remarkably gd for dry and sweet wines.

Xarel-lo (Pansa Blanca) Traditional Catalan grape, used for Cava, along with Parellada and MACABEO. Neutral but clean. More character (lime cordial) in Alella, as Pansa Blanca.

Xynisteri Cyprus's most planted white grape. Can be simple and is usually DYA, but when grown at altitude makes appealing, minerally whites.

Zéta Hungarian; BOUVIER X FURMINT used by some in Tokaji Aszú production.

Zierfandler (Spätrot, Cirfandl) Found in Austria's Thermenregion; often blended with ROTGIPFLER for aromatic, orange-peel-scented, weighty wines.

Wine & food

Which comes first, food or wine? The usual answer is food, which is why this chapter is a list of dishes and wines we have liked with them. On page 38 is a wine-first list for very special bottles. Are there rules? Make up your own if you like, but don't choose either food or wine you don't know you'll enjoy. If you like both separately, whatever they are, you'll probably like them together. You quickly find out what to avoid: oily fish doesn't go with tannic wine, but most things do, in these days of silky tannins. Vinegary salad dressing ruins everything – even the salad. And go from light to dark, dry to sweet. Now for the suggestions....

Before the meal – apéritifs

Conventional apéritif wines are either sparkling (epitomized by Champagne) or fortified (epitomized by Sherry in the UK, Holland, Scandinavia..., Port in France, Vermouth in Italy, etc.). A glass of a light table wine before eating is the easy choice.
Warning Avoid peanuts; they destroy wine flavours. Olives are too piquant for many wines, esp. Champagne; they need Sherry or a Martini. With Champagne eat almonds, pistachios, cashews, plain crisps, or cheese straws instead.

First courses

Aïoli A thirst-quencher is needed for its garlic heat. Young Rhône white, Provence rosé, VERDICCHIO, Loire SAUV BL. And marc or grappa too, for courage.

Antipasti With the classic ham, olives and pickled bits: dry or medium white: Italian (ARNEIS, Soave, PINOT GRIGIO, VERMENTINO, GRECHETTO); light but gutsy red, eg. Valpolicella. Or Fino Sherry.

Artichoke vinaigrette Not great for wine. An incisive dry white: NZ SAUV BL; Côtes de Gascogne or a modern Greek (precisely, 4-yr-old MALAGOUSIA, but easy on the vinaigrette); young red: Bordeaux, Côtes du Rhône.
  with hollandaise Full-bodied, crisp dry white: Pouilly-Fuissé, German *Erstes Gewächs*.

Asparagus Green or white are both difficult for wine, being slightly bitter (white is worse), so the wine needs plenty of its own. Rheingau RIES is a classic, but Ries generally gd to try. SAUV BL echoes the flavour. SÉM beats CHARD, esp Australian, but Chard works well with melted butter or hollandaise. Alsace PINOT GR, even dry MUSCAT is gd or Jurançon Sec.

Aubergine purée (Melitzanosalata) Crisp New World SAUV BL, eg. from South Africa or NZ; or modern Greek or Sicilian dry white. Baked aubergine dishes need sturdy reds: SHIRAZ, ZIN, Sicilian. Or indeed Turkish.

Avocado and tiger prawns Dry to medium slightly white with gd acidity: Rheingau or Pfalz Kabinett, GRÜNER V, Wachau RIES, Sancerre, PINOT GR; Australian CHARD (unoaked) or a dry rosé. Or *premier cru* Chablis.
  with mozzarella and tomato Crisp but ripe white: Soave, Sancerre, Greek white.

Carpaccio, beef Works well with most wines, incl reds. Tuscan is appropriate, but fine CHARDS are gd. So are vintage and pink Champagnes.
  salmon Chard or Champagne.
  tuna VIOGNIER, California Chard or NZ SAUV BL.

Caviar Iced vodka (and) full-bodied Champagne (eg. Bollinger, Krug). Cuvée Anna-Maria Clementi from Ca' del Bosco. Don't add raw onion.

Ceviche Australian RIES or VERDELHO, Chilean SAUV BL, TORRONTÉS.

Charcuterie / salami Young Beaujolais-Villages, Loire reds (ie. Saumur), NZ or Oregon PINOT N. LAMBRUSCO or young ZIN. Young Argentine or Italian reds. Bordeaux Blanc and light CHARD (eg. Côte Chalonnaise) can work well too.

Chorizo Fino is best; or Austrian RIES, GRÜNER V, but not a wine-friendly taste – either on its own or in sauces.

Crostini Dry Italian white ie. VERDICCHIO or Orvieto. or standard-grade (not Riserva) Morellino di Scansano, MONTEPULCIANO d'Abruzzo, Valpolicella, Manzanilla.

Crudités Light red or rosé: Côtes du Rhône, Minervois, Chianti, PINOT N; or Fino Sherry. Alsace SYLVANER or PINOT BL.

Dim sum Classically, China tea. For fun: PINOT GR or RIES; light PINOT N. For reds, soft tannins are key; mature reds go surprisingly well. Bardolino, Rioja or light Southern Rhône are also contenders. Also NV Champagne or gd New World fizz.

Eggs See also SOUFFLÉS. Not easy: they clash with most wines and can ruin gd ones. VIOGNIER, esp Australian, is remarkably gd. As a last resort I can bring myself to drink Champagne with scrambled eggs – easily at weekends.

    quail's eggs Blanc de blancs Champagne; Viognier.

    seagull's (or gull's) eggs Mature white burgundy or vintage Champagne.

    oeufs en meurette Burgundian genius: eggs in red wine with glass of the same.

Escargots (or frogs legs) A comfort dish calling for Rhône reds (Gigondas, Vacqueyras). In Burgundy white: St-Véran or Rully. In the Midi *petits-gris* go with local white, rosé or red. In Alsace, PINOT BL or dry MUSCAT. On the Loire, frogs' legs and semi-dry CHENIN BL.

Fish terrine or fish salad (incl crab) Calls for something fine. Pfalz RIES Spätlese Trocken, GRÜNER V, *premier cru* Chablis, Clare Valley RIES, Sonoma CHARD; or Manzanilla.

Foie gras Sweet white. In Bordeaux, Sauternes. Others prefer a late-harvest PINOT GR or RIES, Vouvray, Montlouis, Jurançon *moelleux* or GEWURZ. Tokaji Aszú 5 Puttonyos is a Lucullan choice. Old dry Amontillado can be sublime. With hot foie gras, mature vintage Champagne. But not on any account CHARD or SAUV BL. Or any red.

Goats cheese, cooked (eg. in a salad) The classic: Sancerre, Pouilly-Fumé or New World SAUV BL.

    chilled Chinon, Saumur-Champigny or Provence rosé. Or strong red: Château Musar, Greek, Turkish, Australian sparkling SHIRAZ.

Guacamole Mexican beer. Or California CHARD, NZ SAUV BL, dry MUSCAT or Sherry.

Haddock, smoked, mousse, soufflé or brandade Wonderful for showing off any stylish, full-bodied white, incl *grand cru* Chablis or Sonoma, South African or NZ CHARD.

Ham, raw or cured *See also* PROSCIUTTO. Alsace Grand Cru PINOT GR or gd, crisp Italian Collio white. With Spanish *pata negra* or *jamón*, Fino Sherry or Tawny Port. *See also* HAM, COOKED (MEAT, POULTRY, GAME).

Herrings, raw or pickled Dutch gin (young, not aged) or Scandinavian akvavit, and cold beer. If wine essential, try MUSCADET.

Mackerel, smoked An oily wine-destroyer. Manzanilla, proper dry Vinho Verde or Schnapps, peppered or bison-grass vodka. Or lager. Or black tea.

Mayonnaise Adds richness that calls for a contrasting bite in the wine. Côte Chalonnaise whites (eg. Rully) are gd. Try NZ SAUV BL, VERDICCHIO or a Spätlese Trocken. Or Provence rosé.

    with lobster: Pfalz RIES *Erstes Gewächs*, Chablis Premier Cru.

Mezze A selection of hot and cold vegetable dishes. Fino Sherry is in its element.

Mozzarella with tomatoes, basil Fresh Italian white, eg. Soave, Alto Adige. VERMENTINO from Liguria or Rolle from the Midi. *See also* AVOCADO.

Oysters, raw NV Champagne, Chablis, MUSCADET, white Graves, Sancerre or Guinness. Manzanilla is excellent.

    cooked Puligny-Montrachet or gd New World CHARD. Champagne gd with either.

Pasta Red or white according to the sauce:

cream sauce (eg. carbonara) Orvieto, Frascati, GRECO di Tufo. Young SANGIOVESE.

meat sauce MONTEPULCIANO d'Abruzzo, Salice Salentino, MALBEC.

pesto (basil) sauce BARBERA, Ligurian VERMENTINO, NZ SAUV BL, Hungarian FURMINT.

seafood sauce (eg. vongole) VERDICCHIO, Soave, white Rioja, Cirò, unoaked CHARD.

tomato sauce Chianti, Barbera, Sicilian red, ZIN, South Australian GRENACHE.

Pastrami Alsace RIES, young SANGIOVESE or St-Émilion.

Pâté, chicken liver Calls for pungent white (Alsace PINOT GR or MARSANNE), a smooth red eg. light Pomerol, Volnay or NZ PINOT N, even Amontillado Sherry. More strongly flavoured pâté (duck, etc.) needs Châteauneuf-du-Pape, Cornas, Chianti Classico or gd white Graves.

Pipérade Navarra rosado, Provence or Midi rosé. Or dry Australian RIES. For red: in Corbières.

Prawns, shrimps or langoustines MUSCADET is okay, but better a fine dry white: burgundy, Graves, NZ CHARD, Washington RIES, Pfalz Ries, Australian Ries – even fine mature Champagne. ("Cocktail sauce" kills wine and, in time, people.)

Prosciutto (also with melon, pears or figs) Full, dry or medium white: Orvieto, GRECHETTO, GRÜNER V, Tokaji FURMINT, Australian SEM or Jurançon Sec.

Risotto Follow the flavour: **with vegetables** (eg. Primavera) PINOT GR from Friuli, Gavi, youngish SÉM, DOLCETTO or BARBERA d'Alba.

with fungi porcini Finest mature Barolo or Barbaresco.

nero A rich dry white: VIOGNIER or even Corton-Charlemagne.

Salads Any dry and appetizing white or rosé wine.

NB Vinegar in salad dressings *destroys* the flavour of wine. Why don't the French know this? If you want salad at a meal with fine wine, dress it with wine or lemon juice instead of vinegar.

Salmon, smoked Dry but pungent white: Fino (esp Manzanilla) Sherry, Condrieu, Alsace PINOT GR, *grand cru* Chablis, Pouilly-Fumé, Pfalz RIES Spätlese, vintage Champagne. Vodka, schnapps or akvavit.

Soufflés As show dishes these deserve ★★★ wines.

cheese Mature red burgundy or Bordeaux, CAB SAUV (not Chilean or Australian), etc. Or fine white burgundy.

fish Dry white: ★★★ Burgundy, Bordeaux, Alsace, CHARD, etc.

spinach (tougher on wine) Mâcon-Villages, St-Véran or Valpolicella. Champagne (esp vintage) can also be gd with the texture of a soufflé.

Tapas Perfect with cold fresh Fino Sherry, which can cope with the wide range of flavours in both hot and cold dishes. Or sake.

Tapenade Manzanilla or Fino Sherry or any sharpish dry white or rosé.

Taramasalata A rustic s white with personality; even possibly retsina. Fino Sherry works well. Try a Rhône MARSANNE. A bland supermarket tarama submits to fine, delicate whites or Champagne.

Tempura The Japanese favour oaked CHARD with acidity. I prefer Champagne.

Tortilla Rioja Crianza, Fino Sherry or white Mâcon-Villages.

Trout, smoked Sancerre; California or South African SAUV BL. Rully or Bourgogne ALIGOTÉ, Chablis or Champagne. German RIES Kabinett.

Vegetable terrine Not a great help to fine wine, but Chilean CHARD makes a fashionable marriage, CHENIN BL such as Vouvray a lasting one.

Whitebait Crisp dry whites, eg. FURMINT, Greek, Touraine SAUV BL, VERDICCHIO or Fino Sherry.

Fish

Abalone Dry or medium white: SAUV BL, Meursault, PINOT GR, GRÜNER V. Chinese-style: vintage Champagne (at least) or Alsace RIES.

Anchovies, marinated Skip the marinade; it will clash with pretty well everything. In, eg. salade Niçoise; Provence rosé.

Bass, sea Weißburgunder from Baden or Pfalz. V.gd for any fine/delicate white, eg. Clare dry RIES, Chablis, white Châteauneuf-du-Pape. But rev the wine up for more seasoning, eg. ginger, spring onions; more powerful Ries, not necessarily dry.

Beurre blanc, fish with A top-notch Muscadet Sur Lie, a SAUV BL/SÉM blend, *premier cru* Chablis, Vouvray, ALBARIÑO or Rheingau RIES.

Brandade *Premier cru* Chablis, Sancerre Rouge or NZ PINOT N.

Brill V. delicate: hence a top fish for fine old Puligny and the like.

Cod, roast Gd neutral background for fine dry/medium whites: Chablis, Meursault, Corton-Charlemagne, *cru classé* Graves, GRÜNER V, German Kabinett or *Grosses Gewächs* or gd lightish PINOT N.

    black cod with miso sauce NZ or Oregon Pinot N, Meursault Premier Cru or Rheingau RIES Spätlese.

Crab Crab and RIES together are part of the Creator's plan.

    Chinese, with ginger and onion German Ries Kabinett or Spätlese Halbtrocken. Tokaji FURMINT, GEWURZ.

    cioppino SAUV BL; but West Coast friends say ZIN. Also California sparkling.

    cold, dressed Top Mosel Ries, dry Alsace or Australian Ries or Condrieu.

    softshell Unoaked CHARD, ALBARIÑO or top-quality German Ries Spätlese.

    Thai crab cakes Pungent Sauv Bl (Loire, South Africa, Australia, NZ) or Ries (German Spätlese or Australian).

    with black bean sauce A big Barossa SHIRAZ or SYRAH. Even Cognac.

    with chilli and garlic Quite powerful Ries, perhaps German *Grosses Gewächs* or Wachau Austrian.

Curry A generic term for a multitude of flavours. Chilli emphasizes tannin, so reds need supple, evolved tannins. Any fruity, non-arid rosé can be gd bet. Hot-and-sour flavours (with tamarind, tomato, eg.) need acidity (perhaps SAUV BL); mild, creamy dishes need richness of texture (dry Alsace RIES). But best of all is Sherry: Fino with fish, Palo Cortado or dry Amontillado with meat. And a glass of water. It's revelatory.

Eel, smoked RIES, Alsace or Austrian or dry Tokaji FURMINT. Vintage Champagne or Fino Sherry. Schnapps.

Fish and chips, *fritto misto*, tempura Chablis, white Bordeaux, SAUV BL, PINOT BL, Gavi, Fino, Montilla, Koshu, sake, tea; or NV Champagne or Cava.

Fish pie (with creamy sauce) ALBARIÑO, Soave Classico, RIES *Erstes Gewächs* or Spanish GODELLO.

Gravadlax SERCIAL Madeira (eg. 10-yr-old Henriques), Amontillado, Tokaji FURMINT.

Haddock Rich, dry whites: Meursault, California CHARD, MARSANNE or GRÜNER V.

Hake SAUV BL or any fresh fruity white: Pacherenc, Tursan, white Navarra. Cold with mayonnaise: fine CHARD.

Halibut As for TURBOT.

Herrings, fried / grilled Need a sharp white to cut their richness. Rully, Chablis, MUSCADET, Bourgogne ALIGOTÉ, Greek, dry SAUV BL. Or cider.

Kedgeree Full white, still or sparkling: Mâcon-Villages, South African CHARD, GRÜNER V, German *Grosses Gewächs* or (at breakfast) Champagne.

Kippers A gd cup of tea, preferably Ceylon (milk, no sugar). Scotch? Dry Oloroso Sherry is surprisingly gd.

Lamproie à la Bordelaise Glorious with 5-yr-old St-Émilion or Fronsac. Or Douro reds with Portuguese lampreys.

Lobster, richly sauced Vintage Champagne, fine white burgundy, *cru classé* Graves, even Sauternes, *Grosses Gewächs*, Pfalz Spätlese.

    cold with mayonnaise NV Champagne, Alsace RIES, *premier cru* Chablis, Condrieu, Mosel Spätlese or a local fizz.

Mackerel, grilled Hard or sharp white to cut the oil: SAUV BL from Touraine, Gaillac, Vinho Verde, white Rioja or English white. Or Guinness.

Monkfish A succulent but neutral dish; depends on the sauce. Full-flavoured white or red, depending.

Mullet, grey VERDICCHIO, Rully or unoaked CHARD.

Mullet, red A chameleon, adaptable to gd white or red, esp PINOT N.

Mussels marinières Muscadet Sur Lie, *premier cru* Chablis, unoaked CHARD.

    curried something s/sw; Alsace RIES.

    with garlic/parsley *see* ESCARGOTS.

Paella, shellfish Full-bodied white or rosé, unoaked CHARD. Or the local Spanish red.

Perch, sandre Exquisite fish for finest wines: top white burgundy, *grand cru* Alsace RIES or noble Mosels. Or try top Swiss CHASSELAS (eg. Dézaley, St-Saphorin).

Prawns with mayonnaise Menetou-Salon.

    with garlic keep the wine light, white or rosé, and dry.

    with spices up to and incl chilli, go for a bit more body, but not oak: dry RIES gd.

Salmon, seared or grilled PINOT N is fashionable option, but CHARD is better. MERLOT or light claret not bad. Best is fine white burgundy: Puligny- or Chassagne-Montrachet, Meursault, Corton-Charlemagne, *grand cru* Chablis; GRÜNER V, Condrieu, California, Idaho or NZ CHARD, Rheingau Kabinett/Spätlese, Australian RIES.

    fish cakes Call for similar, but less grand, wines.

Sardines, fresh grilled V. dry white: Vinho Verde, MUSCADET or modern Greek.

Sashimi The Japanese preference is for white wine with body (Chablis Premier Cru, Alsace RIES) with white fish, PINOT N with red. Both need acidity: low-acidity wines don't work. Simple Chablis can be a bit thin. If soy is involved, low-tannin red (again, Pinot). Remember sake (or Fino). As though you'd forget Champagne.

Scallops An inherently slightly sweet dish, best with medium-dry whites.

    in cream sauces German Spätlese, -Montrachets or top Australian CHARD.

    grilled or seared Hermitage Blanc, GRÜNER V, Pessac-Léognan Blanc, vintage Champagne or PINOT N.

    with Asian seasoning NZ Chard, CHENIN BL, VERDELHO, GODELLO, GEWURZ.

Scandi food Scandinavian dishes often have flavours of dill, caraway, cardamom and combine sweet and sharp flavours. Go for acidity and some weight: GODELLO, VERDELHO, Australian, Alsace or Austrian RIES. Pickled/fermented/raw fish is more challenging: beer or acquavit. *See also* entries for smoked fish, etc.

Shellfish Dry white with plain boiled shellfish, richer wines with richer sauces. RIES is the grape.

    with *plateaux de fruits de mer* Chablis, MUSCADET, PICPOUL de Pinet, Alto Adige PINOT BL.

Skate / raie with brown butter White with some pungency (eg. PINOT GR d'Alsace or ROUSSANNE) or a clean, straightforward wine, ie. MUSCADET or VERDICCHIO.

Snapper SAUV BL if cooked with oriental flavours; white Rhône or Provence rosé with Mediterranean flavours.

Sole, plaice, etc., plain, grilled or fried Perfect with fine wines: white burgundy or its equivalent.

    with sauce According to the ingredients: sharp, dry wine for tomato sauce, fairly rich for creamy preparations.

Sushi Hot wasabi is usually hidden in every piece. German QbA Trocken wines, simple Chablis or NV Brut Champagne. Obvious fruit doesn't work. Or, of course, sake or beer.

Swordfish Full-bodied, dry white (or why not red?) of the country. Nothing grand.

Tagine, with couscous North African flavours need substantial whites to balance – Austrian, Rhône – or crisp, neutral whites that won't compete. Go easy on the oak. VIOGNIER or ALBARIÑO can work well.

Trout, grilled, fried Delicate white: Mosel (esp Saar, Ruwer), Alsace PINOT BL, FENDANT.

Tuna, grilled or seared Best served rare (or raw) with light red wine: Loire CAB FR or PINOT N. Young Rioja is a possibility.

Turbot The king of fishes. Serve with your best rich, dry white: Meursault or Chassagne-Montrachet, Corton-Charlemagne, mature Chablis or its California, Australian or NZ equivalent. Condrieu. Mature Rheingau, Mosel or Nahe Spätlese or Auslese (not Trocken).

Meat, poultry, game

Barbecues The local wine: Australian, South African, Chilean, Argentina are right in spirit. Reds need tannin and vigour.

   Asian flavours (lime, coriander, etc.) Rosé, PINOT GR, RIES.

   chilli SHIRAZ, ZIN, PINOTAGE, MALBEC, Chilean SYRAH.

   Middle Eastern (cumin, mint) Crisp dry whites, rosé.

   fish with oil, lemon, herbs SAUV BL.

   tomato sauces Zin, SANGIOVESE.

Beef Boiled Red: Bordeaux (Bourgogne or Fronsac), Roussillon, Gevrey-Chambertin, Côte-Rôtie. Medium-ranking white burgundy is gd: Auxey-Duresses. Mustard softens tannic reds, horseradish kills your taste – but can be worth the sacrifice.

   roast Ideal for fine red wine of any kind. Amarone perhaps? *See* above (mustard).

   stew, daube Sturdy red: Pomerol or St-Émilion, Hermitage, Cornas, BARBERA, SHIRAZ, Napa CAB SAUV, Ribera del Duero or Douro red.

Beef stroganoff Dramatic red: Barolo, Valpolicella Amarone, Priorat, Hermitage, late-harvest ZIN – even Georgian SAPERAVI or Moldovan Negru de Purkar.

Boudin blanc (white pork sausage) Loire CHENIN BL, esp when served with apples: dry Vouvray, Saumur, Savennières; mature red Côte de Beaune if without.

Boudin noir **(blood sausage)** Local SAUV BL or CHENIN BL – esp in the Loire. Or Beaujolais cru, esp Morgon. Or light TEMPRANILLO. Or Fino.

Cabbage, stuffed Hungarian CAB FR/KADARKA; village Rhône; Salice Salentino, PRIMITIVO and other spicy s Italian reds. Or Argentine MALBEC.

Cajun food Fleurie, Brouilly or New World SAUV BL. **With gumbo** Amontillado.

Cassoulet Red from Southwest France (Gaillac, Minervois, Corbières, St-Chinian or Fitou) or SHIRAZ. But best of all Fronton, Beaujolais cru or young TEMPRANILLO.

Chicken Kiev Alsace RIES, Collio, CHARD, Bergerac rouge.

Chicken / turkey / guinea fowl, roast Virtually any wine, incl v. best bottles of dry to medium white and finest old reds (esp burgundy). The meat of fowl can be adapted with sauces to match almost any fine wine (eg. coq au vin with red or white burgundy).

Chilli con carne Young red: Beaujolais, TEMPRANILLO, ZIN, Argentine MALBEC or Chilean CARMENÈRE.

Chinese food Cantonese Rosé or dry to dryish white – Mosel RIES Kabinett or Spätlese Trocken – can be gd throughout a Chinese banquet. Ries should not be too dry; GEWURZ is often suggested but rarely works; Cantonese food needs acidity in wine. Dry sparkling (esp Cava) works with the textures. Reds can work, but you need the complexity of maturity, and a silky richness. Young tannins are disastrous, as are overoaked, overextracted monsters. PINOT N is first choice; try also St-Émilion ★★ or Châteauneuf-du-Pape. I often serve both whites and reds concurrently during Chinese meals; Peking duck is pretty forgiving. Champagne becomes a thirst quencher.

Shanghai Richer and oilier than Cantonese, not great for wine. Shanghai tends to be low on chilli but high on vinegar of various sorts. German and Alsace whites can be a bit sweeter than for Cantonese. For reds, mature Pinot N is again best.

Szechuan style VERDICCHIO, Alsace PINOT BL or v. cold beer. Mature Pinot N can also work; but make sure the tannins are silky.

Choucroute garni Alsace PINOT BL, PINOT GR, RIES or lager.

Cold roast meat Generally better with full-flavoured white than red. Mosel Spätlese or Hochheimer and Côte Chalonnaise are v.gd, as is Beaujolais. Leftover cold beef with leftover vintage Champagne is bliss.

Confit d'oie / de canard Young, tannic red Bordeaux, California CAB SAUV and MERLOT, Priorat cut richness. Alsace PINOT GR or GEWURZ match it.

Coq au vin Red burgundy. Ideal: one bottle of Chambertin in the dish, two on the table.

Duck or goose Rather rich white: Pfalz Spätlese or off-dry *grand cru* Alsace. Or mature, gamey red: Morey-St-Denis, Côte-Rôtie, Pauillac. With oranges or peaches, the Sauternais propose drinking Sauternes, others Monbazillac or RIES Auslese. Mature, weighty vintage Champagne is gd too, and handles red cabbage surprisingly well.

Peking *See* CHINESE FOOD.

wild duck Big-scale red: Hermitage, Bandol, California or South African CAB SAUV, Australian SHIRAZ – Grange if you can afford it.

with olives Top-notch Chianti or other Tuscans.

roast breast & confit leg with Puy lentils Madiran, St-Émilion, Fronsac.

Frankfurters German or NY RIES, Beaujolais, light PINOT N. Or Budweiser (Budvar).

Game birds, young, plain-roasted The best red wine you can afford, but not too heavy.

older birds in casseroles Red (Gevrey-Chambertin, Pommard, Châteauneuf-du-Pape or *grand cru classé* St-Émilion, Rhône).

well-hung game Vega Sicilia, great red Rhône, Château Musar.

cold game Mature vintage Champagne.

Game pie, hot Red: Oregon PINOT N.

cold Gd-quality white burgundy, cru Beaujolais or Champagne.

Goulash Flavoursome young red: Hungarian Kékoportó, ZIN, Uruguayan TANNAT, MORELLINO di Scansano, MENCÍA, young Australian SHIRAZ. Or dry white from Tokaj.

Grouse *See* GAME BIRDS – but push the boat right out.

Haggis Fruity red, eg. young claret, young Portuguese red, New World CAB SAUV or MALBEC or Châteauneuf-du-Pape. Or, of course, malt whisky.

Ham, cooked Softer red burgundies: Volnay, Savigny, Beaune; Loire Chinon or Bourgueil; sweetish German white (RIES Spätlese); Tokàji FURMINT or Czech Frankovka; lightish CAB SAUV (eg. Chilean) or New World PINOT N. And don't forget the heaven-made match of ham and Sherry. See HAM, RAW OR CURED.

Hamburger Young red: Australian CAB SAUV, Chianti, ZIN, Argentine MALBEC, Chilean CARMENÈRE or SYRAH, TEMPRANILLO. Or full-strength cola (not diet).

Hare Jugged hare calls for flavourful red: not-too-old burgundy or Bordeaux, Rhône (eg. Gigondas), Bandol, Barbaresco, Ribera del Duero, Rioja Res. The same for saddle or for hare sauce with pappardelle.

Indian dishes Various options, though a new discovery has been how well dry Sherry goes with Indian food. Choose a fairly weighty Fino with fish, and Palo Cortado, Amontillado or Oloroso with meat, according to the weight of the dish; heat's not a problem. The texture works too. Otherwise, medium-sweet white, v. cold: Orvieto *abboccato*, South African CHENIN BL, Alsace PINOT BL, TORRONTÉS, Indian sparkling, Cava or NV Champagne. Rosé can be a safe all-rounder. Tannin – Barolo or Barbaresco or deep-flavoured reds ie. Châteauneuf-du-Pape, Cornas, Australian GRENACHE or MOURVÈDRE or Valpolicella Amarone – will emphasize the heat. Hot-and-sour flavours need acidity.

Japanese dishes Texture and balance are key; flavours are subtle. Gd mature fizz works well, as does mature dry RIES; you need acidity, a bit of body, and complexity. Umami-filled meat dishes favour light, supple, bright reds: Beaujolais perhaps or mature PINOT N. Full-flavoured *yakitori* needs lively, fruity, younger versions of the same reds. *See also* SUSHI, SASHIMI.

Kebabs Vigorous red: modern Greek, Corbières, Chilean CAB SAUV, ZIN or Barossa SHIRAZ. SAUV BL, if lots of garlic.

Kidneys Red: St-Émilion or Fronsac, Castillon, Nuits-St-Georges, Cornas, Barbaresco, Rioja, Spanish or Australian CAB SAUV, Douro red.

Korean dishes Fruit-forward wines seem to work best with strong, pungent Korean flavours. PINOT N, Beaujolais, Valpolicella can all work: acidity is needed. Non-aromatic whites: GRÜNER V, SILVANER, VERNACCIA. But I drink beer.

Lamb, roast One of the traditional and best partners for v.gd red Bordeaux or its CAB SAUV equivalents from the New World. In Spain, finest old Rioja and Ribera del Duero Res or Priorat, in Italy ditto SANGIOVESE.

    cutlets or chops As for roast lamb, but a little less grand.

    slow-cooked roast Flatters top reds, but needs less tannin than pink lamb.

    shanks Young red burgundy: Santenay. Crozes-Hermitage. Montefalco SAGRANTINO.

Liver Young red: Beaujolais-Villages, St-Joseph, Médoc, Italian MERLOT, Breganze CAB SAUV, ZIN, Priorat, Bairrada.

    calf's Red Rioja Crianza, Fleurie. Or a big Pfalz RIES Spätlese.

Meatballs Tangy, medium-bodied red: Mercurey, Crozes-Hermitage, Madiran, MORELLINO di Scansano, Langhe NEBBIOLO, ZIN, CAB SAUV.

    Keftedes or spicy Middle-Eastern style Simple, rustic red.

Moussaka Red or rosé: Naoussa, SANGIOVESE, Corbières, Côtes de Provence, Ajaccio, young ZIN, TEMPRANILLO.

Mutton A stronger flavour than lamb, and not served pink. Robust red; top-notch, mature CAB SAUV, SYRAH. Some sweetness of fruit (eg. Barossa) suits it.

Osso bucco Low-tannin, supple red such as DOLCETTO d'Alba or PINOT N. Or dry Italian white such as Soave.

Ox cheek, braised Superbly tender and flavoursome, this flatters the best reds: Vega Sicilia, St-Émilion. Best with substantial wines.

Oxtail Rather rich red: St-Émilion, Pomerol, Pommard, Nuits-St-Georges, Barolo or Rioja Res, Priorat or Ribera del Duero, California or Coonawarra CAB SAUV, Châteauneuf-du-Pape, mid-weight SHIRAZ, Amarone.

Paella Young Spanish: red, dry white, rosé: Penedès, Somontano, Navarra or Rioja.

Pigeon PINOT N is perfect; young Rhône, Argentine MALBEC, young SANGIOVESE. Or try Franken SILVANER Spätlese.

Pork, roast A gd, rich, neutral background to a fairly light red or rich white. It deserves ★★ treatment: Médoc is fine. Portugal's suckling pig is eaten with Bairrada Garrafeira; Chinese is gd with PINOT N.

    pork belly Slow cooked and meltingly tender, this needs a red with some tannin or acidity. Italian would be gd: Barolo, DOLCETTO or BARBERA. Or Loire red or lightish Argentine MALBEC.

Pot au feu, bollito misto, cocido Rustic reds from region of origin; SANGIOVESE di Romagna, Chusclan, Lirac, Rasteau, Portuguese Alentejo; Yecla, Jumilla (Spain).

Quail Carmignano, Rioja Res, mature claret, PINOT N. Or a mellow white: Vouvray or St-Péray.

Rabbit Lively, medium-bodied young Italian red, eg. AGLIANICO del Vulture; Chiroubles, Chinon, Saumur-Champigny or Rhône rosé.

    with prunes Bigger, richer, fruitier red.

    with mustard Cahors.

    as ragu Medium-bodied red with acidity.

Satay McLaren Vale SHIRAZ, Alsace or NZ GEWURZ. Peanut sauce: problem with wine.

Sauerkraut (German) Franken SILVANER, lager or Pils. (But *see also* CHOUCROUTE GARNI.)

Sausages *See also* CHARCUTERIE, FRANKFURTERS. The British banger requires a young MALBEC from Argentina (a red wine, anyway) or London Pride (ale).

Singaporean dishes Part Indian, part Malay and part Chinese, Singaporean food has big, bold flavours that don't match easily with wine. Off-dry RIES is as gd as anything. With meat dishes, ripe, supple reds: Valpolicella, PINOT N, DORNFELDER, unoaked MERLOT or CARMENÈRE.

Steak *au poivre* A fairly young Rhône red or CAB SAUV.

    filet, ribeye or tournedos Any gd red, esp burgundy (but not old wines with Béarnaise sauce: top New World PINOT N is better).

    Fiorentina (bistecca) Chianti Classico Riserva or BRUNELLO. The rarer the meat, the more classic the wine; the more well-done, the more you need New World, sweet/strong wines. Argentine MALBEC is the perfect partner for steak Argentine style ie. cooked to death.

    Korean *yuk whe* (world's best steak tartare) Sake.

    tartare Vodka or light young red: Beaujolais, Bergerac, Valpolicella.

    T-bone Reds of similar bone structure: Barolo, Hermitage, Australian CAB SAUV or SHIRAZ, Chilean SYRAH.

Steak-and-kidney pie or pudding Red Rioja Res or mature Bordeaux.

Stews and casseroles Burgundy such as Nuits-St-Georges or Pommard if fairly simple; otherwise lusty, full-flavoured red: young Côtes du Rhône, Toro, Corbières, BARBERA, SHIRAZ, ZIN, etc.

Sweetbreads A rich dish, so grand white wine: Rheingau RIES or Franken SILVANER Spätlese, *grand cru* Alsace PINOT GR or Condrieu, depending on sauce.

Tafelspitz Best-known of a series of typical Viennese boiled beef and veal dishes. A glass of GRÜNER V is mandatory.

Tagines These vary enormously, but fruity young reds are a gd bet: Beaujolais, TEMPRANILLO, SANGIOVESE, MERLOT, SHIRAZ. Amontillado is the discovery of the yr. **chicken with preserved lemon, olives** VIOGNIER.

Tandoori chicken RIES or SAUV BL, young red Bordeaux or light n Italian red served cool. Also Cava and NV Champagne, dry Palo Cortado or Amontillado Sherry.

Thai dishes Ginger and lemon grass call for pungent SAUV BL (Loire, Australia, NZ, South Africa) or RIES (Spätlese or Australian). Most curries suit aromatic whites with a touch of sweetness: GEWURZ is also gd.

Tongue Gd for any red or white of abundant character, esp Italian. Also Beaujolais, Loire reds, TEMPRANILLO and full, dry rosés.

Veal, roast Gd for any fine old red that may have faded with age (eg. a Rioja Res) or a German or Austrian RIES, Vouvray, Alsace PINOT GR.

Venison Big-scale reds, incl MOURVÈDRE, solo as in Bandol or in blends. Rhône, Bordeaux, NZ Gimblett Gravels or California CAB SAUV of a mature vintage; or rather rich white (Pfalz Spätlese or Alsace PINOT GR). With a sweet and sharp berry sauce, try a German *Grosses Gewächs* RIES or a Chilean CARMENÈRE or SYRAH.

Vitello tonnato Full-bodied whites: CHARD; light reds (eg. Valpolicella) served cool.

Wild boar Serious red: top Tuscan or Priorat. NZ SYRAH.

Vegetarian dishes

(*See also* FIRST COURSES)

Baked pasta dishes *Pasticcio*, lasagne and cannelloni with elaborate vegetarian fillings and sauces: an occasion to show off a grand wine, esp finest Tuscan red, but also claret and burgundy.

Beetroot Mimics a flavour found in red burgundy. You could return the compliment. **and goat's cheese gratin** Sancerre, Bordeaux SAUV BL.

Cauliflower Increasingly fashionable.

   roasted, etc go by the other (usually bold) flavours. Try Austrian GRÜNER V, Valpolicella, NZ PINOT N.

   cauliflower cheese Crisp, aromatic white: Sancerre, RIES Spätlese, MUSCAT, ALBARIÑO, GODELLO. Beaujolais-Villages.

Couscous with vegetables Young red with a bite: SHIRAZ, Corbières, Minervois; or well-chilled rosé from Navarra or Somontano; or a robust Moroccan red.

Fennel-based dishes SAUV BL: Pouilly-Fumé or NZ; SYLVANER or English SEYVAL BL; or young TEMPRANILLO.

Fermented foods *See also* SAUERKRAUT, CHOUCROUTE, KOREAN. Kimchi and miso are being worked into many dishes. Fruit and acidity are generally needed. If in sweetish veg dishes, try Alsace.

Grilled Mediterranean vegetables Brouilly, BARBERA, TEMPRANILLO or SHIRAZ.

Kale, cavalo nero, cabbage Usually part of a more complex dish, so go by the overall flavours. Fruity young red works well: MERLOT, MALBEC, SHIRAZ.

Lentil dishes Sturdy reds such as Corbières, ZIN or SHIRAZ.

   dhal, with spinach Tricky. Soft light red or rosé is best, and not top-flight.

Macaroni cheese As for CAULIFLOWER CHEESE.

Mushrooms (in most contexts) A boon to many reds. Pomerol, California MERLOT, Rioja Res, top burgundy or Vega Sicilia. On toast, best claret. Ceps/porcini, Ribera del Duero, Barolo, Chianti Rufina, Pauillac or St-Estèphe, NZ Gimblett Gravels.

Onion / leek tart Fruity, off-dry or dry white: Alsace PINOT GR or GEWURZ; Canadian, Australian or NZ RIES; Jurançon. Or Loire CAB FR.

Peppers or aubergines (eggplant), stuffed Vigorous red wine: Nemea, Chianti, DOLCETTO, ZIN, Bandol, Vacqueyras.

Pumpkin / squash ravioli or risotto Full-bodied, fruity dry or off-dry white: VIOGNIER or MARSANNE, demi-sec Vouvray, Gavi or South African CHENIN.

Ratatouille Vigorous young red: Chianti, NZ CAB SAUV, MERLOT, MALBEC, TEMPRANILLO; young red Bordeaux, Gigondas or Coteaux du Languedoc.

Root vegetables Sweet potatoes, carrots etc, often mixed with eg. beetroot, garlic, onions and others have plenty of sweetness. Rosé is a winner, esp one with some weight: Spanish, Italian, South American.

Seaweed Depends on context. *See* Sushi. Iodine notes go with Austrian GRÜNER V, RIES.

Spanacopitta **(spinach and feta pie)** Young Greek or Italian red or white.

Spiced vegetarian dishes *See* INDIAN DISHES, THAI DISHES (MEAT, POULTRY, GAME).

Watercress, raw Makes every wine on earth taste revolting. Soup is slightly easier, but doesn't need wine.

Wild garlic leaves, wilted Tricky: a fairly neutral white with acidity will cope best.

Desserts

Apple pie, strudel or tarts Sweet German, Austrian or Loire white, Tokaji Aszú or Canadian Icewine.

Apples, Cox's Orange Pippins Vintage Port (and sweetmeal biscuits) is the Saintsbury [wine] Club plan.

Bread-and-butter pudding Fine 10-yr-old Barsac, Tokaji Aszú or Australian botrytized SEM.

Cakes and gâteaux *See also* CHOCOLATE, COFFEE, GINGER, RUM. BUAL or MALMSEY Madeira, Oloroso or Cream Sherry.

Cheesecake Sweet white: Vouvray, Anjou or Vin Santo – nothing too special.

Chocolate A talking point. Generally only powerful flavours can compete. Texture matters. BUAL, California Orange MUSCAT, Tokaji Aszú, Australian Liqueur Muscat, 10-yr-old Tawny or even young Vintage Port; Asti for light, fluffy mousses. Experiment with rich, ripe reds: SYRAH, ZIN, even sparkling SHIRAZ.

Banyuls for a weightier partnership. Médoc can match bitter black chocolate, though Amarone is more fun. Armagnac or a tot of gd rum.

and olive oil mousse 10-yr-old Tawny Port or as for black chocolate, above.

Christmas pudding, mince pies Tawny Port, Cream Sherry or liquid Christmas pudding itself, PEDRO XIMÉNEZ Sherry. Tokaji Aszú. Asti or Banyuls.

Coffee desserts Sweet MUSCAT, Australia Liqueur Muscats or Tokaji Aszú.

Creams, custards, fools, syllabubs See also CHOCOLATE, COFFEE, RUM. Sauternes, Loupiac, Ste-Croix-du-Mont or Monbazillac.

Crème brûlée Sauternes or Rhine Beerenauslese, best Madeira or Tokaji Aszú. (With concealed fruit, a more modest sweet wine.)

Crêpes Suzette Sweet Champagne orange MUSCAT or Asti.

Ice cream and sorbets Fortified wine (Australian Liqueur MUSCAT or Banyuls). PEDRO XIMÉNEZ.

Lemon flavours For dishes like tarte au citron, try sweet RIES from Germany or Austria or Tokaji Aszú; v. sweet if lemon is v. tart.

Meringues Recioto di Soave, Asti or top vintage Champagne, well-aged.

Mille-feuille Delicate sweet sparkling white, ie. MOSCATO d'Asti, demi-sec Champagne.

Nuts (incl praliné) Finest Oloroso Sherry, Madeira, Vintage or Tawny Port (nature's match for walnuts), Tokaji Aszú, Vin Santo or Setúbal MOSCATEL.

salted nut parfait Tokaji Aszú, Vin Santo.

Orange flavours Experiment: old Sauternes, Tokaji Aszú or California Orange MUSCAT.

Panettone Jurançon *moelleux*, late-harvest RIES, Barsac, Tokaji Aszú.

Pears in red wine A pause before the Port. Try Rivesaltes, Banyuls, RIES Beerenauslese.

Pecan pie Orange MUSCAT or Liqueur Muscat.

Raspberries (no cream, little sugar) Excellent with fine reds which themselves taste of raspberries: young Juliénas, Regnié.

Rum flavours (baba, mousses, ice cream) MUSCAT – from Asti to Australian Liqueur, according to weight of dish.

Salted caramel mousse / parfait Late-harvest RIES, Tokaji Aszú.

Strawberries, wild (no cream) Serve with red Bordeaux (most exquisitely Margaux) poured over.

Strawberries and cream Sauternes or similar sweet Bordeaux, Vouvray *moelleux* or *vendange tardive* Jurançon.

Summer pudding Fairly young Sauternes of a gd vintage.

Sweet soufflés Sauternes or Vouvray *moelleux*. Sweet (or rich) Champagne.

Tiramisú Vin Santo, young Tawny Port, MUSCAT de Beaumes-de-Venise, Sauternes or Australian Liqueur Muscat.

Trifle Should be sufficiently vibrant with its internal Sherry.

Zabaglione Light-gold Marsala or Australian botrytized SEM or Asti.

WINE & CHEESE

The notion that wine and cheese were married in heaven is not borne out by experience. Fine red wines are slaughtered by strong cheeses; only sharp or sweet white wines survive. Principles to remember (despite exceptions): first, the harder the cheese, the more tannin the wine can have; second, the creamier the cheese, the more acidity is needed in the wine – and don't be shy of sweetness. Cheese is classified by its texture and the nature of its rind, so its appearance is a guide to the type of wine to match it. Below are examples. I always try to keep a glass of white wine for my cheese.

Bloomy rind soft cheeses, pure-white rind if pasteurized or dotted with red: Brie, Camembert, Chaource, Bougon (goats milk "Camembert") Full, dry white burgundy or Rhône if the cheese is white and immature; powerful, fruity St-Émilion, young Australian (or Rhône) SHIRAZ/SYRAH or GRENACHE if it's mature.

Blue cheeses It is the sweetness of Sauternes (or Tokaji), especially old, that complements the extreme saltiness of Roquefort. Stilton and Port, (youngish) Vintage or Tawny, is a classic. Intensely flavoured old Oloroso, Amontillado, Madeira, Marsala and other fortifieds go with most blues.

Fresh, no rind – cream cheese, crème fraîche, mozzarella Light crisp white: Chablis, Bergerac, Entre-Deux-Mers; rosé: Anjou, Rhône; v. light, young, fresh red: Bordeaux, Bardolino, Beaujolais.

Hard cheeses, waxed or oiled, often showing marks from cheesecloth – Gruyère family, Manchego and other Spanish cheeses, Parmesan, Cantal, Comté, old Gouda, Cheddar and most "traditional" English cheeses Hard to generalize; Gouda, Gruyère, some Spanish, and a few English cheeses complement fine claret or CAB SAUV and great SHIRAZ/SYRAH. But strong cheeses need less refined wines, preferably local ones. Sugary, granular old Dutch red Mimolette or Beaufort are gd for finest mature Bordeaux. Also for Tokaji Aszú. But try whites too.

Natural rind (mostly goats cheese) with bluish-grey mould (the rind becomes wrinkled when mature), sometimes dusted with ash – St-Marcellin Sancerre, Valençay, light SAUV BL, Jurançon, Savoie, Soave, Italian CHARD.

Semi-soft cheeses, thickish grey-pink rind – Livarot, Pont l'Evêque, Reblochon, Tomme de Savoie, St-Nectaire Powerful white Bordeaux, CHARD, Alsace PINOT GR, dryish RIES, S Italian and Sicilian whites, aged white Rioja, dry Oloroso Sherry. The strongest of these cheeses kill almost any wines. Try marc or Calvados.

Washed-rind soft cheeses, with rather sticky orange-red rind – Langres, mature Époisses, Maroilles, Carré de l'Est, Milleens, Munster Local reds, esp for Burgundy cheeses; vigorous Languedoc, Cahors, Côtes du Frontonnais, Corsican, S Italian, Sicilian, Bairrada. Also powerful whites, esp Alsace GEWURZ, MUSCAT.

FOOD AND FINEST WINES

With very special bottles, the wine guides the choice of food rather than vice versa. The following is based largely on gastronomic conventions and newer experiments, plus much diligent research. They should help bring out the best in your best wines.

Red wines

Amarone Classically, in Verona, *risotto all'Amarone* or *pastissada*. But if your butcher doesn't run to horse, then shin of beef, slow-cooked in more Amarone.

Barolo, Barbaresco Risotto with white truffles; pasta with game sauce (eg. *pappardelle alla lepre*); porcini mushrooms; Parmesan.

Great Syrahs: Hermitage, Côte-Rôtie, Grange; also Vega Sicilia Beef (such as the super-rich, super-tender, super-slow-cooked ox cheek I had at Vega Sicilia), venison, well-hung game; bone marrow on toast; English cheese (esp best farm Cheddar) but also hard goat's or ewe's milk cheeses eg. UK's Berkswell or Ticklemore.

Great vintage port or Madeira Walnuts or pecans. A Cox's Orange Pippin and a digestive biscuit is a classic English accompaniment.

Red Bordeaux V. old, light, delicate wines, (eg. pre-59) Leg or rack of young lamb, roast with a hint of herbs (not garlic); *entrecôte*; simply roasted partridge or grouse; sweetbreads.

   fully mature great vintages (eg. 59 61 82 85) Shoulder or saddle of lamb, roast with a touch of garlic; roast ribs or grilled rump of beef.

mature but still vigorous (eg. 89 90) Shoulder or saddle of lamb (incl kidneys) with rich sauce. Fillet of beef *marchand de vin* (with wine and bone marrow). Avoid beef Wellington: pastry dulls the palate.

Merlot-based Beef as above (fillet is richest) or well-hung venison. In St-Émilion, lampreys.

Red burgundy Consider the weight and texture, which grow lighter/more velvety with age. Also the character of the wine: Nuits is earthy, Musigny flowery, great Romanées can be exotic, Pommard renowned for its four-squareness. Roast chicken or capon is a safe standard with red burgundy; guineafowl for slightly stronger wines, then partridge, grouse or woodcock for those progressively more rich and pungent. Hare and venison (*chevreuil*) are alternatives.

great old burgundy The Burgundian formula is cheese: Époisses (unfermented); a fine cheese but a terrible waste of fine old wines.

vigorous younger burgundy Duck or goose roasted to minimize fat. Or *faisinjan* (pheasant cooked in pomegranate juice). Or lightly smoked gammon.

Rioja Gran Reserva, Pesquera... Richly flavoured roasts: wild boar, mutton, saddle of hare, whole suckling pig.

White wines

Beerenauslese / Trockenbeerenauslese Biscuits, peaches and greengages. Desserts made from rhubarb, gooseberries, quince, apples.

Condrieu, Château-Grillet, Hermitage Blanc V. light pasta scented with herbs and tiny peas or broad beans. Or v. mild tender ham.

Grand cru Alsace: Riesling *Truite au bleu*, smoked salmon or *choucroute garni*.

Pinot Gr Roast or grilled veal. Or truffle sandwich (slice a whole truffle, make a sandwich with salted butter and gd country bread – not sourdough or rye – wrap and refrigerate overnight. Then toast it in the oven).

Gewurztraminer Cheese soufflé (Münster cheese).

vendange tardive Foie gras or tarte tatin.

Old vintage Champagne (not Blanc de Blancs) As an apéritif or with cold partridge, grouse, woodcock. The evolved flavours of old Champagne make it far easier to match with food than the tightness of young wine. Hot foie gras can be sensational. Don't be afraid of garlic or even Indian spices, but omit the chilli.

late-disgorged old wines have extra freshness plus tertiary flavours. Try with truffles, lobster, scallops, crab, sweetbreads, pork belly, roast veal, chicken.

Sauternes Simple crisp buttery biscuits (eg. *langues de chat*), white peaches, nectarines, strawberries (without cream). Not tropical fruit. Pan-seared foie gras. Lobster or chicken with Sauternes sauce. Château d'Yquem recommends oysters (and indeed lobster). Experiment with blue cheeses. Rocquefort is classic, but needs a powerful wine.

Tokaji Aszú (5–6 puttonyos) Foie gras recommended. Fruit desserts, cream desserts, even chocolate can be wonderful. It even works with some Chinese, though not with chilli – the spice has to be adjusted to meet the sweetness. Szechuan pepper is gd. Havana cigars are splendid. So is the naked sip.

Very good Chablis, white burgundy, other top-quality Chards White fish simply grilled or *meunière*. Dover sole, turbot, halibut are best; brill, drenched in butter, can be top. (Sea bass too delicate; salmon passes but does little for finest wine.)

Vouvray moelleux, etc. Buttery biscuits, apples, apple tart.

White burgundy (ie. Montrachet, Corton-Charlemagne) or equivalent Graves Roast veal, farm chicken stuffed with truffles or herbs under the skin or sweetbreads; richly sauced white fish (turbot for choice) or scallops as above. Or lobster or poached wild salmon.

France

**More heavily shaded areas are
the wine-growing regions.**

Abbreviations used in the text:

Al	Alsace
Beauj	Beaujolais
Burg	Burgundy
B'x	Bordeaux
Champ	Champagne
Chab	Chablis
Cors	Corsica
C d'O	Côte d'Or
L'doc	Languedoc
Lo	Loire
Mass C	Massif Central
Prov	Provence
Pyr	Pyrénées
N/S Rh	Northern/Southern Rhône
Rouss	Roussillon
Sav	Savoie
SW	Southwest
AC	appellation contrôlée
ch, chx	château(x)
dom, doms	domaine(s)

France's greatest vinous strength is its diversity. People might tire of ever-higher prices for classed-growth Bordeaux and look instead to the Rhône; they might become increasingly intrigued by the detail of Burgundy, and then become nervous of prices there as well; they might look to the south, and the wealth of innovation in Provence and Languedoc. They are still in France, moving around from one style to another, exploring regions that produce such different styles that you could drink nothing but French wine for a year without getting bored.

We choose wine increasingly by the name of the grower, not the appellation. Does this make France look dated? Not a bit: more and more French growers think exactly the same way. They work within

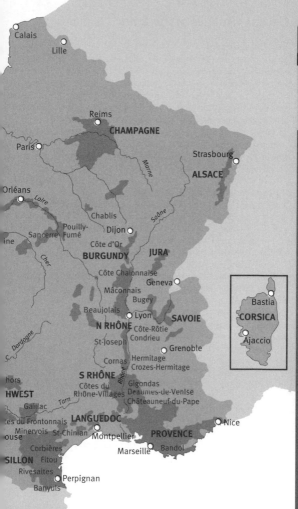

the appellation system when it suits them, outside it when it doesn't. Especially in the south, it's normal for a grower to make some wines within the system, some outside it; and before anyone knocks the appellation system for being too restrictive, they should think that, without it, the 80s and 90s would have seen the wholesale uprooting of traditional local grapes and the wholesale planting of Cabernet and Chardonnay. That heritage of indigenous grapes is now seen as a blessing – and something for the New World to draw on as it searches for new things to plant and new flavours to seek. If you want novelty, France got there first.

France entries also cross-reference to Châteaux of Bordeaux

Recent vintages of the French classics

Red Bordeaux

Médoc / Red Graves For some wines, bottle age is optional: for these it is indispensable. Minor châteaux from light vintages need only 2 or 3 years, but even modest wines of great years can improve for 15 or so, and the great châteaux of these years can profit from double that time.

2014 Saved by an Indian summer. Cab Sauv bright and resonant. Good to very good in terms of quality and quantity. Classic in style.

2013 Worst vintage since 1992. Disastrous spring, rain and rot. Patchy success at classed growth level; some good wines have emerged.

2012 Erratic weather. Small crop. Difficulties ripening Cab Sauv. Be choosy.

2011 Complicated year: spring drought, cool July, rain, heat, rot. Indian summer saved the day. Mixed quality but better than its reputation. Classic freshness with moderate alcohol. Modest crus ready to drink.

2010 Outstanding. Magnificent Cab Sauv, deep coloured, concentrated, firmly structured. At a price. To keep for years.

2009 Outstanding year, touted as "The Greatest". Structured wines with an exuberance of fruit. Don't miss this. Accessible or to keep.

2008 Much better than expected; fresh, classic flavours. Cab Sauv ripened in late-season sun. Ageing potential.

2007 Miserable summer, a difficult year. Not many will age. Be selective.

2006 Cab Sauv difficulty ripening; best fine, tasty, nervous, long-ageing. Good colour, acidity. Starting to drink.

2005 Rich, balanced, long-ageing; outstanding vintage. Keep all major wines.

2004 Mixed bag; top wines good in a classic mould. Drinking now.

2003 Hottest summer on record. Cab Sauv can be great (St-Estèphe, Pauillac). Powerful at best (keep), unbalanced at worst (drink up). Soon, for most.

2002 Some good wines if selective. Drink now–2018.

Older fine vintages: 00 98 96 95 90 89 88 86 85 82 75 70 66 62 61 59 55 53 49 48 47 45 29 28.

St-Émilion / Pomerol

2014 More rain than Médoc, Merlot variable. Very good Cab Fr. Satisfactory.

2013 Difficult flowering (so tiny crop) and rot in Merlot. Modest to poor year.

2012 Conditions as Médoc. Earlier picked Merlot marginally more successful.

2011 Complicated, as Médoc. Good Cab Fr. Pomerol best overall? Don't shun it.

2010 Outstanding. Powerful, high alcohol. Small berries so concentration.

2009 Again, outstanding. Powerful wines (high alcohol) but seemingly balanced. Hail in St-Émilion cut production at certain estates.

2008 Similar conditions to the Médoc. Tiny yields helped quality, which is surprisingly good. Starting to drink but best will age.

2007 Same pattern as the Médoc. Huge disparity in picking dates (up to five weeks). Extremely variable, but nothing to keep for long.

2006 Rain and rot at harvest. Earlier ripening Pomerol a success but St-Émilion and satellites variable.

2005 Same conditions as the Médoc. An overall success. Start to drink.

2004 Merlot often better than 2003 (Pomerol). Good Cab Fr.

2003 Merlot suffered in the heat, but exceptional Cab Fr. Very mixed. Top St-Émilion on the plateau good. Most need drinking.

2002 Problems with rot and ripeness. Modest to good. Drink.

Older fine vintages: 01 00 98 95 90 89 88 85 82 71 70 67 66 64 61 59 53 52 49 47 45.

Red burgundy

Côte d'Or Côte de Beaune reds generally mature sooner than grander wines of Côte de Nuits. Earliest drinking dates are for lighter commune wines – eg. Volnay, Beaune; latest for *grands crus*, eg. Chambertin, Musigny. Even the best burgundies are more attractive young than equivalent red Bordeaux.

2014 Relief for most after decent sized crop, but Beaune, Volnay, Pommard hailed again. Should make attractive, healthy wines of medium density.

2013 Another hailstorm horror for red Côte de Beaune: looks tricky for Volnay, Pommard, Beaune, Savigny. Small crop for Nuits, delicious perfumed wines for those who waited.

2012 Very small crop of fine wines in Côte de Nuits, disastrous flowering. Côte de Beaune even worse after multiple hailstorms. Exuberant yet classy.

2011 Some parallels with 2007, an early harvest but indifferent summer. But thicker skins in 2011 mean more structured wine. Small crop again. Starting to be accessible.

2010 Much better than expected. Fresh and classic red, gaining in reputation all the time. Fine-boned classics. Now to 2030?

2009 Beautiful, ripe, plump reds will be accessible before the 2005s. Slightly clumsy adolescents now. Beware overripe examples. Now to 2030?

2008 Fine, fresh, structured wines from those who avoided fungal diseases; choose carefully. Best wines show Pinot purity. Now to early 2020s.

2007 Small crop of attractive, perfumed wines. Don't expect real density. Rather good in Côte de Beaune. Now to 2020.

2006 An attractive year in Côte de Nuits (less rain) with power to develop in medium term. Côte de Beaune reds good now. Best to 2025.

2005 Best for more than a generation, outstanding everywhere. Top wines must be kept. Enjoy generics, lesser villages now. Otherwise 2018–2040.

2004 Light. Some pretty, others spoiled by herbaceous flavours. Mostly drink up.

2003 Reds coped with the heat better than the whites. Muscular, rich. Best outstanding, others short and hot. No hurry for top wines.

2002 Mid-weight wines of great class with an attractive point of freshness. Now showing their paces. No hurry. Now to 2027.

Older fine vintages: 99 96 (keep) 95 93 90 88 85 78 71 69 66 64 62 61 59 (mature).

White burgundy

Côte de Beaune White wines are now rarely made for ageing as long as they did 20 years ago. Top wines should still improve for up to 10 years.

2014 A decent-sized crop, great early enthusiasm all round. Certain to be attractive, best will be classy and concentrated.

2013 The July hail mostly spared white vineyards. Those who picked early made concentrated, lively wines. Late-picked examples to be avoided.

2012 Tiny production after calamitous flowering and subsequent hail. Decent weather later; very intense, sometimes fine but some are clumsy.

2011 Large harvest; fine potential for conscientious producers; some flesh, good balance, but it was easy to overcrop. Attractive early and drinking well.

2010 Exciting wines with good fruit-acid balance, some damaged by September storms. Meursault and Corton-Charlemagne are first class. Now to 2020.

2009 Full crop, healthy grapes, definite charm, but enough acidity to age? Yes, if picked early, otherwise drink up.

2008 Small crop, ripe flavours, high acidity. Most reaching apogee, top to 2020.

2007 Attractive crisp wines, best if not picked too early. Most fully accessible.

2006 Plentiful crop of charming, aromatic wines. Drink up.

2005 Small, outstanding crop of dense, concentrated wines. Some currently lack charm so allow time. Some showing at least superficial oxidation. Mâconnais (Pouilly-Fuissé, St-Véran, Mâcon-Villages) follow a similar pattern, but do not last as long: appreciated more for their freshness than their richness.

Chablis *Grand cru* Chablis of vintages with strength and acidity can age superbly for 10 years plus; *premiers crus* proportionately less, but give them 3 years at least.
2014 Potentially excellent; early crop, happy vignerons.
2013 Small crop, late harvest, rot issues. Mixed bag, some wonderful wines.
2012 Crop not quite as tiny as Côte d'Or; too small nonetheless. Early pickers ultra-concentrated, classically austere; late pickers soft, low acid after rain.
2011 Early season, large crop of attractive wines. Similar to 2002. Now to 2022.
2010 Harvested at same time as Côte d'Or; excellent results. Fine vintage: body, powerful mineral acidity. A great year for classical Chablis. Now to 2030.
2009 Rich, accessible wines. Best will keep, otherwise drink now.
2008 Excellent; small crop of powerful, juicy wines; *grands crus* still improving, otherwise drink up.

Beaujolais 14 Fine crop, excellent potential. 13 Late vintage with mixed results. 12 Tiny crop, economic misery, vineyards abandoned. 11 The 3rd smasher in a row! Refined, classy wines, drinking well. 10 Compact and concentrated, maturing now. 09 Wonderful rich vintage which helped many rediscover Beaujolais. 05 Concentrated wines, best still worth keeping.

Southwest France
2014 Cool winter, stop-start summer with glorious sun at end. Great expectations.
2013 Good harvest made some decent wines after otherwise appalling season.
2012 Hail, frost, cold until mid-June reduced crop, but what was made is good.
2011 Good, but some blowsy Cahors and Madiran. Excellent whites.
2010 Indian summer ensured good crop. Good year for current drinking.
2009 Reliable. For current drinking.
2008 Moderate. Late sunshine just about saved the day.

The Midi
2014 Tricky year: some hail in La Clape and Minervois, and torrential rain in September. Picking before the rain was key.
2013 Some lovely wines, developing nicely; some areas better than others.
2012 Quantity down, but quality good; wines beginning to drink well.
2011 Coolish summer, so fresher wines, nicely balanced. Quality, quantity good.
2010 Fine quality; yields low after summer drought. Wines drinking deliciously.
2009 Cool spring; hot, dry summer. Excellent quality, drinking beautifully.

Northern Rhône
2014 Fruit fly attacks reduced yields, reds with free fruit emphasis, can gain depth over time. Very good whites, plenty of content and freshness.
2013 Very good reds: body, freshness. 15–20 years. Exceptional whites, especially Hermitage, St-Joseph, St-Péray.
2012 Very good Hermitage, Côte-Rôtie. Fresh reds come together well, will last 15 years+. Whites have style, freshness (Condrieu).
2011 Mid-weight year. Sound Crozes-Hermitage, gd Hermitage, Cornas. Côte-Rôtie needs more time. Better than 08. Whites fresh, satisfactory.
2010 Wonderful. Reds: marvellous fruit, balance, freshness, flair. Long-lived. Côte-Rôtie as good as 78. Very good Condrieu, rich whites elsewhere.

2009 Excellent, sun-packed wines. Some deep, rich Hermitage, very full Côte-Rôtie. Best Crozes, St-Joseph ageing well. Rather big whites: can live.
2008 Rain. Top names best. Good, clear whites. Reds: 8–12 yrs.
2007 Shapely, attractive depth, ageing well. Best for 18 yrs+. Good whites.
2006 Rich, satisfying wines, especially Côte-Rôtie. Heady Condrieu.
2005 Mostly excellent, be patient with tannins. Full whites drinking well now.
2004 Mid-weight, supple but fine wines, especially Côte-Rôtie. Superb whites; Hermitages will live very well.

Southern Rhône

These big wines used to need years to become agreeable. This is changing; you can enjoy even last year's Châteauneuf these days – if you like it really gutsy.
2014 Damp summer brought rot. Rely on best names, who threw away most of crop. Wines will give quiet pleasure, but will take time. Good whites.
2013 Easy, fun, fresh reds, little Grenache. Châteauneuf can be deep, best from old vines. Gd-value Côtes du Rhône. Very good whites.
2012 Full, dark reds, plenty of fruit, good tannins. Food-friendly whites.
2011 Supple, mild, drink quite early. Value Côtes du Rhône reds.
2010 Outstanding. Excellent, full-bodied, balanced reds. Top Châteauneuf. Clear-fruited, well-packed tannins. Whites deep, long.
2009 Full, sunswept, dense reds. Drought: some baked features, grainy tannins. Ripe Châteauneuf reds will age on concentration. Sound whites.
2008 Dodgy; life 12–15 years. Choose top names. Very good, lively whites.
2007 Very good: Grenache-only wines are big, intense, but drink with gusto. Exceptional Châteauneuf from top names.
2006 Underrated; fruity, flavourful Châteauneuf, Gigondas: more open than 2005, less sweet, potent than 07. Good full whites, ideal for food.
2005 Slow to evolve. Tight-knit, serious, concentrated. Will age well: 20 yrs+ for top Châteauneufs. Whites developed well, real body.
2004 Good, but variable. Intricate flavours in Châteauneuf. Gigondas best: grainy, profound. Drinking well now. Gd complex whites near drink-up.

Champagne

2014 Fine June flowering, but very wet August before dry hot September. Fine wines in northern Montagne, Côte des Blancs, Aube. Elsewhere variable quality, frail Meunier, picking date key to success.
2013 Reverse of 2012, Chard year of vintage promise: Pinot N more mixed, Aÿ glorious exception. Aube hit by hail, rain.
2012 Small crop of top Pinot N, Meunier, best since 1952? Chards less brilliant.
2011 Not a vintage year for big houses; attractive Chards from top growers (JL Vergnon, Fourny, Lancelot-Pienne, Armand Margaine).
2010 Drought, rain, rot. Some Chard okay; Pinot N not.
2009 Ripeness, elegance, perfect balance. In shadow of 2008, can be fine.
2008 One of three best vintages since 2000. Classic balance of powerful, poised fruit, great ripe acidity. At least rivals 2002.
2007 Underrated at first, now showing classic purity, elegance. Exceptional Roederer; grower Rodolphe Péters single-vineyard Chétillons (Le Mesnil).
Older fine vintages: 04 02 00 98 96 95 92 90 89 88 82 76.

The Loire

2014 After wet, cool summer, lovely September and largely good October saved vintage. Well-balanced dry whites and ripe reds but another small crop apart from Central Loire – Sancerre, etc. Outstanding Muscadet.

2013 Very difficult, challenging vintage. Low sugar levels, high acidity. Some attractive wines for early drinking. A little sweet wine in Anjou.

2012 Very difficult and small vintage: frost, widespread mildew. Melon de Bourgogne, Sauv Bl high quality, but little sweet wine made.

2011 Topsy-turvy. Rot in Muscadet. Quality variable. Some fine sweet Anjou.

2010 Beautifully balanced dry whites, great Anjou sweet. Reds quite often better than 2009. Long ageing potential.

2009 Generally very good. High alcohol a problem in some Sauv Bl.

2008 Very healthy grapes, high acidity. Good age-worthy reds, excellent dry whites (Chenin Bl), sweets hit by wet November.

Alsace

2014 Challenging; wet August. Warm September assured some fine dry wines.

2013 Fine, crisp and mineral wines with elegant acidity. Ries year.

2012 Small crop of concentrated wines, in dry style of 2010.

2011 Round, fruity wines of charm and aroma for early drinking.

2010 Very small crop, excellent wines for long keeping, most naturally dry.

2009 Great Pinot Gr, Gewurz; some fine late-harvest wines.

2008 Dry, crisp wines: Ries a great delight, especially Weinbach, Trimbach.

2007 Hot spring; cold, wet summer; sunny autumn: ripe grapes. Drink up.

Abymes Sav w ★ DYA. Hilly area nr Chambéry; light, mild Vin de SAV AC from Jacquère grape has Alpine charm. Savoie has many such crus.

Ackerman Lo r p w (dr) (sw) (sp) ★→★★ Major pan-Lo expansionist négociant. First SAUMUR sparkling wine house; eight co-ops involved. Ackerman group incl Rémy-Pannier, Donatien-Bahuaud, Monmousseau.

Agenais SW Fr r p w ★ DYA IGP of Lot-et-Garonne. Its prunes (Agen Provocateurs) more famous than its wines, but DOMS such as Boiron, Lou Gaillot and Campet better than boring co-ops.

Alain Chabanon, Dom L'doc ★★★ Leading MONTPEYROUX producer. Esp Campredon, Esprit de Font Caude, MERLOT-based Merle aux Alouettes. White Trélans is VERMENTINO/CHENIN BL.

Allemand, Thiérry N Rh r ★★★ 90' 91' 93 94' 95' 98' 99' 00' 01' 02 03 04 05' 06' 07' 08 09' 10' 11' 12' 13' 14 CORNAS 5-ha DOM, low sulphur, organic. Characterful wines, deep, smoky. Top Reynards (complex; 20 yrs+), Chaillot drinks earlier.

Alliet, Philippe Lo r w ★★★→★★★★ 02 04 05' 06 08 09' 10' 11 12 13 (14) Top CHINON, B'x-lover; reds 100% CAB FR. Cuvées: Tradition VIEILLES VIGNES 50-yr-old+ vines on gravel. Two steep v'yds just e of Chinon: L'Huisserie and Coteau Noire.

Aloxe-Corton Burg r w ★★→★★★ 99' 02' 03 05' 06 08 09' 10' 11 12' 14 The n end of CÔTE DE BEAUNE, famous for GRANDS CRUS CORTON, CORTON-CHARLEMAGNE, but less interesting at village or PREMIER CRU level. Reds attractive if not overextracted. Best DOMS: Follin-Arbelet, Senard, Terregelesses, TOLLOT-BEAUT.

Alquier, Jean-Michel L'doc r w Stellar FAUGÈRES producer. White MARSANNE/ROUSSANNE/GRENACHE Vignes du Puits. Also SAUV Pierres Blanches; red CUVÉES Les Premières (younger vines), Maison Jaune; noble old-vine SYRAH; GRENACHE-based Les Bastides. Don't confuse with brother Frédéric.

AOP and IGP: what's happening in France

The Europe-wide introduction of AOP (*Appellation d'Origine Protegée*) and IGP (*Indication Géographique Protegée*) means that these terms may now appear on labels. AC/AOC will continue to be used, but for simplicity and brevity this book now uses IGP for all former VDP.

Alsace (r) w (sw) (sp) ★★→★★★★ 04 05 06 08' 09 10' 11 12 13 14 Sheltered e slope of Vosges mts makes France's Rhine wines: aromatic, fruity, full-strength, mostly dry and expressive of variety. Sugar levels vary widely: dry wines now mainstream again. Much sold by variety (PINOT BL, RIES, GEWURZ). Matures well (except Pinot Bl, MUSCAT) 5–10 yrs; GRAND CRU even longer. Gd-quality and -value CRÉMANT. Formerly fragile *Pinot N improving fast* (esp 10). *See* VENDANGE TARDIVE, SÉLECTION DES GRAINS NOBLES.

Alsace Grand Cru Al w ★★★→★★★★ 00 05 06 07 08' 09 10 11 12 13' 14 AC. Restricted to 51 of the best-named v'yds (approx 1,600 ha, 800 in production) and four noble grapes (RIES, PINOT GR, GEWURZ, MUSCAT). Production rules require higher min ripeness, no *chaptalization*. New concept of local management allows extra rules specific to each cru.

Exotic Alsace match: *grand cru* Pinot Gris, Cornish lobster Goan-style – spicy fusion.

Amiel, Mas ROUSS r w sw ★★★ Large MAURY DOM continues to innovate; others follow. Serious CÔTES DU ROUSS *Carérades* (r), Altaïr (w), *vin de liqueur* Plénitude from MACCABEU. Vintage wines and cask-aged VDN. Prestige 15 yrs the star. STÉPHANE DERENONCOURT (B'X) consults.

Amirault, Yannick Lo r ★★→★★★ 03 05' 06 08' 09' 10' 11 12 13 14 Modest Yannick and son Benoît are top producers in BOURGUEIL (20 ha) and ST-NICOLAS-DE-BOURGUEIL (10 ha). Top CUVÉES: La Petite Cave, Les Quartiers (BOURGUEIL); La Mine (St-Nicolas).

Ampeau, Robert C d'O w MEURSAULT DOM; unique record for selling mature vintages.

Angerville, Marquis d' C d'O r w ★★★★ Bio superstar in VOLNAY, esp legendary CLOS des Ducs (MONOPOLE), but Champans, Taillepieds also first rate. New interests in Jura (Dom du PÉLICAN) to watch for.

Anglès, Ch d' L'doc ★★★ Traditional old LA CLAPE estate transformed by Eric Fabre, ex-technical director of CH LAFITE, captivated by MOURVÈDRE. B'x-style with Classique (r p w) and oak-aged *grand vin* (r w).

Anjou Lo r p w (dr) (sw) (sp) ★→★★★★ Both region and umbrella AC covering ANJOU, SAUMUR. Often better than its reputation. CHENIN BL dry whites range from light quaffers to fine and age-worthy; juicy reds, incl GAMAY; fruity CAB FR-based Anjou Rouge; age-worthy but tannic ANJOU-VILLAGES, incl CAB SAUV. Also mainly dry SAVENNIÈRES; lightly sweet to luscious COTEAUX DU LAYON Chenin Bl; rosé (dr s/sw), sparkling. AC Anjou v. variable, but can be v.gd value. Sweets: buy 2010 or 11, wait for 14.

Anjou-Coteaux de la Loire Lo w sw s/sw ★★→★★★ 02 05' 07' 09 10' 11' (14) Small (30 ha) w-most ANJOU AC for sweet CHENIN BL; less rich but nervier than COTEAUX DU LAYON. Esp Delaunay, Fresche, Musset-Roullier, CH de Putille. Little made in 2012 or 13.

Anjou-Villages Lo r ★→★★★ 05' 06 08 09' 10' 11 12 13 (14) Superior and improving ANJOU AC for reds (CAB FR/CAB SAUV, a few pure Cab Sauv). Tannins can be fierce but top wines are gd value, esp Bergerie, Branchereau, Brizé, CADY, CLOS de Coulaine, Delesvaux, Ogereau, CH Pierre-Bise, Sauveroy, Soucherie. Sub-AC Anjou-Villages-Brissac same zone as COTEAUX DE L'AUBANCE; look for Bablut, DOM de Haute Perche, Montigilet, Princé, Richou, Rochelles, Ch de Varière.

Appellation Contrôlée (AC or AOC) / AOP Government control of origin and production (but not quality) of most top French wines; around 45 per cent of total. Now being converted to AOP (*Appellation d'Origine Protegée* – which is much nearer the truth than *Contrôlée*).

Aprémont Sav w ★★ DYA One of best villages of SAV for fresh mtn whites from Jacquère grape and gd CHARD too. Fine producer: Pierre Boniface.

Arbin Sav r ★★ Deep-coloured, lively red from MONDEUSE grapes, rather like a LO CAB SAUV. Ideal après-ski. Drink at 1–2 yrs.

Arbois Jura r p w (sp) ★★→★★★ Various gd original wines, real sense of terroir; speciality VIN JAUNE. Best producers: Stephane Tissot, Jacques Puffeney (retiring; buy up his stock). Gd CRÉMANT sparkling from local co-op Fruitière d'Arbois. Delicious PINOT-like red Poulsard grape/wine.

Ariège SW Fr r p w ★ 11 12 (14) ★★ Ancient region s of Toulouse looking for a renaissance. Many grapes, interesting quality. DOM des Coteaux d'Engravies heads short list of growers.

Arjolle, Dom de l' L'doc ★★★ Important CÔTES DE THONGUE estate. Z for ZIN and K for CARMENÈRE plus original blends and more conventional L'DOC varieties.

Arlaud C d'O r ★★★ Leading MOREY-ST-DENIS estate revitalized by new generation. Class throughout from BOURGOGNE Roncevie to *grands crus* CHARMES-CHAMBERTIN, CLOS DE LA ROCHE. Energized by new generation, now ploughing by horse. Fine Bourgogne Roncevie.

Arlay, Ch d' Jura r w sw ★→★★ Major Jura estate in skilful hands. Wines incl: v.gd VIN JAUNE, VIN DE PAILLE, PINOT N, MACVIN.

Arlot, Dom de l' C d'O r w ★★→★★★ Formerly famous exponent of whole-bunch fermentation (to 2010); style modified under new management. AXA taking closer control. NUITS-ST-GEORGES CLOS des Forêts St-Georges offers haunting fragrance, also VOSNE-ROMANÉE Suchots, ROMANÉE-ST-VIVANT. Rare whites v.gd too.

Armand, Comte C d'O r ★★★ Sole owner of exceptional CLOS des Epeneaux in POMMARD and other v'yds in AUXEY, VOLNAY. On top form since 1999. Bio. New manager from 2013 promises continuity.

Aube Champ S v'yds of CHAMP, aka Côte de Bar. V.gd PINOT N 09 10 14.

Aupilhac, Dom d' L'doc Early leader in MONTPEYROUX, now followed by others. Sylvain Fadat favours CARIGNAN and CINSAULT, as well as L'DOC classics.

Auxey-Duresses C d'O r w ★★ 99' 02' 03 05' 06 07 08 09' 10' 11 12 14 CÔTE DE BEAUNE village in valley behind MEURSAULT. Reds more fragrant, structured but not too rustic now; attractive mineral whites are value. Best: (r) COMTE ARMAND, COCHE-DURY, Gras, MAISON LEROY (Les Boutonniers), Prunier; (w) Lafouge Leroux, ROULOT.

Aveyron SW Fr r r p w ★ IGP DYA. Wild country, wild wines; home of Roquefort MARCILLAC. ★★ Nicolas Carmarans and Patrick Rols make ★★ "natural" wines. Rare local grapes incl Négret de Banyars. More orthodox ★ DOMS Bertau, Pleyjean.

Avize Champ Fine Côte des Blancs CHARD village. Excellent growers' wines, Selosse Agrapart and great co-op Union Champagne.

Aÿ Champ Revered PINOT N village, home of BOLLINGER. Mix of merchants and growers' wines, some made in barrel: eg. Claude Giraud, master of Argonne oak. Gosset-Brabant Noirs d'Aÿ (no wood) epitome of purity.

Price of vineyard land in Champagne? Around €2 million/ha.

Ayala Champ Revitalized, AŸ-based, owned by BOLLINGER. Fine Brut Zéro, ideal with oysters. Ace Prestige Perle d'Ayala 08' 09 12 13 14. Precise, racy, linear flavours.

Bachelet Burg r w ★★→★★★ Widespread family name in Burg. Excellent whites from B-Monnot (MARANGES), Jean-Claude B (ST-AUBIN), B-Ramonet (CHASSAGNE) while at other end of C D'O Denis Bachelet makes heady GEVREY-CHAMBERTIN.

Bandol Prov r p (w) ★★★ 96 97 98 99 00 01 02 03 04 05 06 07 08 09 10 11 12 13 Compact coastal AC; PROV's best. Superb barrel-aged reds; ageing potential enormous. MOURVÈDRE the key, with GRENACHE, CINSAULT; stylish rosé from young vines, and a drop of white from CLAIRETTE, UGNI BLANC, occasionally SAUV BL. Stars incl: DOMS de la Laidière, Lafran Veyrolles, La Suffrène, TEMPIER, Pibarnon, Mas de la Rouvière, La Bégude, La Bastide Blanche, Terrebrune, Vannières, Gros'Noré, Pradeaux.

Banyuls Rouss br sw ★★→★★★ Characterful and delicious VDN, based on old

GRENACHE (GRAND CRU, aged 2 yrs+ fairly irrelevant). Newer vintage style resembles Ruby Port; more satisfying are traditional RANCIOS, aged for yrs. Think fine old Tawny Port or even Madeira. Best: DOMS du Mas Blanc (★★★), la Rectorie (★★★), Vial Magnères, Coume del Mas (★★), la Tour Vieille (★★★). Clos de Paulilles, Madeloc. *See also* MAURY.

Baronne, Ch la L'doc ★★★ Family estate in CORBIÈRES, by Montagne d'Alaric. IGP Hauterive (w); Corbières les Lanes, les Chemins, Alaric and CARIGNAN planted 1892: Pièce de Roche.

Barrique The B'X (and Cognac) term for an oak barrel holding 225 litres. Used globally, but the global mania for excessive new oak is now mercifully fading. Oak dominating fruit now looks dated.

Barsac Saut w SW ★★ →★★★★ 88' 89' 90' 95 96 97' 98 99' 01' 02 03' 05' 07' 09' 10' 11' 12 13 (14) Neighbour of SAUT with similar botrytized wines from lower-lying limestone soil; fresher, less powerful. Better than Saut in difficult 2012. Top: CAILLOU, CLIMENS, COUTET, DOISY-DAËNE, DOISY-VÉDRINES, NAIRAC.

Barthod, Ghislaine C d'O r ★★★ →★★★★ Wines of perfume, delicacy, yet depth, concentration. Impressive range of nine PREMIER CRUS in CHAMBOLLE-MUSIGNY incl Les Baudes, Charmes, Cras, Fuées.

Bâtard-Montrachet C d'O w ★★★★ 99' 00 02' 04' 05' 06 07' 08' 09' 10 11 12 13 14' 12-ha GRAND CRU downslope from LE MONTRACHET itself. Grand, hefty whites that should need time, more power than neighbours BIENVENUES-B-M and CRIOTS B-M. Seek out: BACHELET-Monnot, BOILLOT, CARILLON, GAGNARD, FAIVELEY, LATOUR, DOM LEFLAIVE, Leroux, MOREY, Pernot, Ramonet, SAUZET, VOUGERAIE.

Baudry, Dom Bernard Lo r p w ★★ →★★★ 05 06 08 09' 10' 11 12 13 (14) 30 ha DOM on gravel, limestone. Top CHINON across the range, from CHENIN BL whites to CAB FR (r p); early-drinking Les Granges to structured Les Grézeaux, CLOS Guillot, Croix Boissée. Organic; hand-harvested. Bernard retiring, son Matthieu in charge.

Baudry-Dutour Lo r p w (sp) ★★ →★★★ 03 05' 06 08 09' 10' 11 13 (14) CHINON'S largest producer, incl CHX de St Louans and La Grille (new visitor centre 2013). Reliable quality: light, early-drinking to age-worthy reds. New pink fizz in 2014. Hit by hail Sept 2014, so lots of ROSÉ MADC.

Baumard, Dom des Lo r p w sw sp ★★ →★★★ 03 05' 06 07' (sw) 08 09 10 11 13 (14) Controversial producer of ANJOU, esp CHENIN BL whites, incl SAVENNIÈRES (CLOS St Yves, Clos du Papillon), QUARTS DE CHAUME, Clos Ste Catherine. Proponent of cryoextraction (freezing grapes to concentrate sugars). Humiliating defeat in 2014 for its legal challenge to Quarts de Chaume GRAND CRU.

Baux-en-Provence, Les Prov r p w ★★ →★★★ 07 08 09 10 11 12 13 14 V'yds on dramatic bauxite outcrop of the Alpilles round tourist village of Les Baux: tourism can breed complacency. White from CLAIRETTE, GRENACHE, Rolle, ROUSSANNE. Reds CAB SAUV, SYRAH, Grenache. Most v'yds organic. Best estate is TRÉVALLON: Cab/Syrah blend. Also Estoublon, Mas de la Dame, DOM Hauvette, Ste Berthe, CH Romanin, Terres Blanches. Valdition.

Béarn SW Fr r p w ★ →★★ (r) 12 (14) DYA. Rural province n of Basque country. AOP that pioneered rosés. ★ DOMS de la Callabère, Lapeyre/Guilhémas gd reds. Also rare whites from Ruffiat de Moncade grape. Gd co-op at ★ Bellocq.

Beaucastel, Ch de S Rh r w ★★★★ 78' 81' 83 85 88 89' 90' 94' 95' 96' 97 98' 99' 00' 01' 03' 04 05' 06' 07' 08 09' 10' 11' 12' 13' 14 Major organic CHÂTEAUNEUF estate: old MOURVÈDRE, 100-yr-old ROUSSANNE. Smoky, darkly fruited, complex, sometimes rustic wines, drink at 2 yrs or from 7–8 yrs. Recent vintages more swell. Dense, top-level 60% Mourvèdre Hommage à Jacques Perrin (r). *Wonderful old-vine Roussanne*: enjoy over 5–25 yrs. Excellent Famille Perrin S Rh (some owned, others managed). Genuine, polished own-vines CÔTES DU RH Coudoulet de Beaucastel (r), lives 8 yrs+. Famille Perrin CAIRANNE (gd value) GIGONDAS, RASTEAU,

VINSOBRES all v.gd, authentic. Gd organic Perrin Nature Côtes du Rh (r w). Gd N Rh merchant venture, Nicolas Perrin. (*See also* Tablas Creek, California.)

Beaujolais r (p) (w) ★ DYA. Basic appellation of the huge Beauj region. Light wines; dire straits. Can now be sold as COTEAUX BOURGUIGNONS. Beauj from hills around Bois d'Oingt can be excellent.

Beaujolais Primeur / Nouveau Beauj More of an event than a drink.The BEAUJ of the new vintage, hurriedly made for release at midnight on the 3rd Wednesday in Nov. Should be headily fruity and tempting; may be sharp, alcoholic, or both.

Beaujolais-Villages Beauj r ★★ 12 13 14 The middle category between straight BEAUJ and the ten named crus, ie. MOULIN-À-VENT. Often too simple but best sites around Beaujeu, Lantigné worth waiting for.

Feel like bathing in Beaujolais Nouveau? Go to Japan: www.yunessun.com.

Beaumes-de-Venise S Rh r (p) (w) br ★★ (r) 07' 09' 10' 11 12' 13 (MUSCAT) DYA. CÔTES DU RH village s of GIGONDAS, famous for VDN Muscat apéritif/dessert. Serve v. cold: grapey, honeyed, can be fine eg. DOMS Beaumalric, Bernardins (musky, traditional), Durban (rich), Fenouillet (brisk), JABOULET, Pigeade (fresh, v.gd), VIDAL-FLEURY, co-op. Also punchy, grainy reds, best in sunny yrs. (CH Redortier, Doms Cassan, de Fenouillet, Durban, St-Amant, Ferme St Martin.) Leave for 2–3 yrs. Simple whites (some dry MUSCAT, VIOGNIER), lively rosés are Côtes du Rh.

Beaumont des Crayères Champ sp Côte d'Epernay co-op making model PINOT MEUNIER-based Grande Rés NV. Vintage Fleur de Prestige top value 04 06 08' 09 12'. Great CHARD-led CUVÉE Nostalgie 02' 06 08. New Fleur de Meunier BRUT Nature 08.

Beaune C d'O r (w) ★★★ 02' 03 05' 07 08 09'10' 11 12 14 Historic walled wine capital of Burg, home of HOSPICES DE BEAUNE and classic merchants: BOUCHARD, CHAMPY, CHANSON, DROUHIN, JADOT, LATOUR, Remoissenet as well as young pretenders Gambal, Lemoine, Leroux, Roche de Bellène. No GRANDS CRUS v'yds but some graceful, perfumed reds from PREMIER CRU eg. Bressandes, Cras, Teurons, Vignes Franches; more power from Grèves, and an increasing amount of white: Drouhin's CLOS DES MOUCHES best.

Becker, Caves J Al r w ★→★★ Organic estate, now certified bio. Stylish wines, incl poised, mineral GRAND CRU Froehn in GEWURZ, RIES 06 08 10' 13 14'.

Bellet Prov r p w ★★ Minuscule AC; 48 ha within Nice, scarcely seen there. Rolle white surprisingly age-worthy and delicious. Braquet, Folle Noire for light red (DYA). A handful of valiant producers: CH de Bellet is oldest; also Les Coteaux de Bellet, CLOS St Vincent, DOM de la Source, Collet de Bovis, Toasc.

Bellivière, Dom de Lo r w sw ★★→★★★ 05' 07 08 09' 10' 11' 13 (14) 13-ha bio DOM of Christine and Eric Nicolas: lovely precise CHENIN BL in top JASNIÈRES and COTEAUX DU LOIR, peppery red Pineau d'Aunis.

Bergerac SW Fr r p w dr sw ★→★★★ 09' 10 11 12 (14) AOP adjoining B'x. Same grapes, much cheaper. Whites (dr sw) mostly from SÉM, reds mostly MERLOT. ★★★ CLOS des Verdots, *Tour des Gendres*, ★★ CH TOUR DE GRANGEMONT, DOMS du Cantonnet, Fleur de Thénac, Jaubertie, Jonc Blanc. *See also* growers in sub-AOPS MONBAZILLAC, MONTRAVEL, PÉCHARMANT, ROSETTE, SAUSSIGNAC.

Berlioz, Giles Sav Leading DOM in CHIGNIN. Brilliant whites, pristine Chez l'Odette (Jacquère), fuller ROUSSETTE DE SAVOIE El Hem ("miracle man") named after friend.

Berthet-Bondet, Jean Jura Former mayor of CH-CHALON making classic VIN JAUNE. Fine exponent of CHARD and Trousseau grapes.

Bertrand, Gérard L'doc r p w ★★ Ambitious grower now one of biggest in MIDI; Villemajou (CORBIÈRES cru Boutenac), Laville-Bertou (MINERVOIS-La Livinière), l'Aigle (LIMOUX), IGP Hauterive Cigalus, la Sauvageonne (Terrasses du Larzac). Flagship: l'Hospitalet (LA CLAPE), new aspirational Clos d'Ora (Minervois-La Livinière).

Besserat de Bellefon Champ Épernay house specializing in gently sparkling CHAMPAGNES (old CRÉMANT style). Part of LANSON-BCC group. Respectable quality and decent value.

Beyer, Léon Al r w ★★→★★★ Intense, dry wines often needing 10 yrs+ bottle age. Superb RIES Comtes d'Eguisheim 08' 10 13 14', actually GRAND CRU PFERSIGBERG (not mentioned on label). Ideal gastronomic wines found in many Michelin-starred restaurants. Serious PINOT N 10' 12.

Bichot, Maison Albert Burg r w ★★→★★★ Major BEAUNE merchant/grower. Steadily more impressive wines in a powerful rather oaky style. Best wines from own DOMS, LONG-DEPAQUIT (CHAB), CLOS Frantin (NUITS), du Pavillon (Beaune).

Bienvenues-Bâtard-Montrachet C d'O ★★★→★★★★ 02' 04 05 06 07 08 09 10 11 12 13 14' Fractionally lighter, earlier-maturing version of BÂTARD, with tempting creamy texture. Best: CARILLON, FAIVELEY, LEFLAIVE, Pernot, Ramonet.

Billecart-Salmon Champ Family-run house with new horsepower from financial partner, exquisite vintage CUVÉES fermented in wood. Superb CLOS St-Hilaire BLANC DE NOIRS 96 98 99 00 02', NF Billecart 99 00 02' 04 06 08' 12', top BLANC DE BLANCS 08', BRUT 04 great value Extra Brut ★★ NV. Oaked Cuvée Sous Bois. Exquisite ★★★★ *Elizabeth Salmon Rosé* 02.

Bize, Simon C d'O r w ★★★ The late Patrick Bize produced an exemplary range from BOURGOGNE (r w) to LATRICIÈRES-CHAMBERTIN by way of multiple bottlings of fine SAVIGNY-LÈS-BEAUNE. Quality has been maintained.

Blagny C d'O r ★★→★★★ 99' 02' 03' 05' 08 09' 10' 11 12 13 14 Hamlet on hillside above MEURSAULT, PULIGNY. Austere reds out of fashion as growers replant with CHARD, sold as Meursault-Blagny PREMIER CRU. Best red v'yds: Pièce sous le Bois, Sous le Dos d'Ane, La Jeunelotte. Best growers (r): Matrot, Martelet de Cherisey.

Blanc de Blancs Any white wine made from white grapes only, esp CHAMP. Indication of style, not of quality.

Blanc de Noirs White (or slightly pink or "blush") wine from red grapes, esp CHAMP. Generally rich, even blunt, in style.

Blanck, Paul & Fils Al r w ★★→★★★ Grower at Kientzheim with huge range. Finest from 6 ha GRAND CRU Furstentum (RIES, GEWURZ, PINOT GR) grand cru SCHLOSSBERG (great Ries 06 08' 10 12 13), Also gd PINOT BL.

Blanquette de Limoux L'doc w sp ★★ Great-value bubbles from cool hills sw of Carcassonne; older history than CHAMP. 90% Mauzac with a little CHARD, CHENIN BL. AC CRÉMANT de Limoux is more elegant. Large co-op with Sieur d'Arques label. Also RIVES-BLANQUES, Antech, Laurens, Robert, Delmas.

Blaye B'x r →★★★ 05' 06 08 09' 10' 11 12 (14) Designation for better reds (lower yields, higher v'yd density, longer maturation) from AC BLAYE-CÔTES DE B'X.

Blaye-Côtes de Bordeaux B'x r w ★→★★ 08 09' 10' 12 (14) Mainly red AC on right bank of Gironde. A little dry white. Formerly Premières Côtes de Blaye. Generally gd value. Best CHX: Bel Air la Royère, Cantinot, Gigault (CUVÉE Viva), Haut-Bertinerie, Haut-Colombier, Haut-Grelot, Jonqueyres, Monconseil-Gazin, Mondésir-Gazin, Montfollet, Roland la Garde, Segonzac, des Tourtes. Also Charron and CAVE des Hauts de Gironde co-op for whites.

Boillot C d'O r w Interconnected Burg growers. Look for Jean-Marc (POMMARD) ★★★, fine oaky reds and whites; Henri (DOM and merchant in MEURSAULT) ★★→★★★★, potent whites and modern reds; Louis (Chambolle, married to GHISLAINE BARTHOD) ★★★ and his brother Pierre (GEVREY) ★★→★★★.

Boisset, Jean-Claude Burg r w Ultra-successful group created over last 50 yrs. Boisset label and own v'yds DOM DE LA VOUGERAIE excellent. Recent additions to empire are VINCENT GIRARDIN brand and HENRI MAIRE in JURA. Also projects in Canada, California (Gallo connection), Chile, Uruguay.

Boizel Champ Exceptional aged BLANC DE BLANCS NV and prestige Joyau de France

02' 04 06 08 12', Joyau Rosé 02' 04 06 09 12. Also Grand Vintage BRUT 02 04 06 08' 09, CUVÉE Sous Bois. Fine quality, great value.

Bollinger Champ Great classic house, sings in recent vintages (Grande Année 09 08' 05 04 02' 00 97 96). Great attention to PINOT N; fine GA Rosé 05 04 02. Also v.gd NV Rosé. De luxe: RD 00 02 to keep, VIEILLES VIGNES Françaises 02, La Côte aux Enfants AŸ 09' 12'. New winemaker. *See also* LANGLOIS-CH.

Bonneau du Martray, Dom C d'O r w (r) ★★★ (w) ★★★★ Reference producer for CORTON-CHARLEMAGNE, glorious mineral wines once again designed for long ageing. Small amount of fine red CORTON.

Bonnes-Mares C d'O r ★★★→★★★★ 90' 91 93 95 96' 98 99' 00 02' 03 05' 06 07 08 09' 10' 11 12' 13 14 GRAND CRU between CHAMBOLLE-MUSIGNY and MOREY-ST-DENIS with some of latter's wilder character. Sturdy, long-lived wines, less fragrant than MUSIGNY. Best: BOUCHARD PÈRE, BRUNO CLAIR, Drouhin-Laroze, DUJAC, Groffier, JADOT, MUGNIER, ROUMIER, DE VOGÜÉ, VOUGERAIE.

Bonnezeaux Lo w sw ★★★→★★★★ 89' 90' 95' 96' 97' 03' 05' 07' 09 10' 11' (14) Wonderfully rich, almost everlasting CHENIN BL from s-facing site in COTEAUX DU LAYON. Rules less tight than QUARTS DE CHAUME. Esp: CHX de Fesles, de Varière, Grandes Vignes, du Petit Val. Avoid any 2012s; 13 difficult so wait for 14.

Around €2 million/ha Burgundy has twice as many ACs as Bordeaux: 100.

Bordeaux r (p) w ★→★★ 09' 10' 12 (14) Catch-all AC for generic B'x (represents nearly half region's production). Mixed quality, but usually recognizable. Most brands (DOURTHE, MOUTON CADET, SICHEL) are in this category. *See also* CHX Bauduc, BONNET, Reignac, Tire Pé, Tour de Mirambeau.

Bordeaux Supérieur r ★→★★ 08 09' 10' 12 (14) A superior denomination to the above. Higher min alcohol, lower yield and longer ageing. Mainly bottled at the property. Consistent CHX: Camarsac, de Courteillac, La France, Grand Village, Grée-Laroque, Landereau, Parenchère, Penin, PEY LA TOUR (Rés), Pierrail, Reignac, THIEULEY.

Borie-Manoux B'x Admirable B'x shipper, CH-owner. Chx incl BATAILLEY, BEAU-SITE, DOM DE L'EGLISE, HAUT-BAGES-MONPELOU, TROTTEVIEILLE. Now owns MÄHLER-BESSE.

Bouchard Père & Fils Burg r w ★★→★★★★ Largest v'yd owner in C D'O, based in CH de Beaune. Whites esp strong in MEURSAULT and GRANDS CRUS, esp CHEVALIER-MONTRACHET. Flagship reds are BEAUNE Grèves, Vigne de L'Enfant Jésus, VOLNAY Caillerets Ancienne CUVÉE Carnot. Basic wines okay. Part of HENRIOT Burg interests with WILLIAM FÈVRE (CHAB), Villa Ponciago (BEAUJ).

Bouches-du-Rhône Prov r p w ★ IGP from Marseille environs. Simple, hopefully fruity, reds from s varieties, plus CAB SAUV, SYRAH, MERLOT.

Bourgeois, Henri Lo r w ★★→★★★ 05 06 07 08 10 11 12 13 (14) V. impressive SANCERRE grower/merchant. Excellent range incl POUILLY-FUMÉ, MENETOU-SALON, QUINCY, COTEAUX DU GIENNOIS, CHÂTEAUMEILLANT, IGP Petit Bourgeois. Top wines: MD de Bourgeois, La Bourgeoise (r w), Jadis, Sancerre d'Antan can age beautifully. Also CLOS Henri (r w) in Marlborough, NZ.

Bourgogne Burg r (p) w ★★ (r) 05' 09' 10' 11 12' 13 14 (w) 10' 11 12 13 14' Ground-floor AC for Burg, ranging from mass-produced to bargain beauties from fringes of C D'O villages, top tip for value. Sometimes comes with subregion attached, eg. CÔTE CHALONNAISE, HAUTES CÔTES or local would-be appellation, Chitry, Tonnerre, VÉZELAY etc. From PINOT N (r) or CHARD (w) but can be declassified BEAUJ crus (sold as Bourgogne GAMAY).

Bourgogne Passe-Tout-Grains Burg r (p) ★ Age 1–2 yrs. Not just any old grape but a Burg mix of PINOT N (more than 30%) and GAMAY. Can be fun from C D'O DOMS, eg. CHEVILLON, Clavelier, LAFARGE, ROUGET.

Bourgueil Lo r (p) ★★→★★★ 96' 03 05' 06 08 09' 10' 11 13 (14) Dynamic AC,

1,400 ha, full-flavoured TOURAINE reds and big, fragrant rosés based on CAB FR. Gd vintages can age 40 yrs+. Esp AMIRAULT, Audebert, DOMS de la Butte, la Chevalerie, Courant, Gambier, Herlin, Lamé Delisle Boucard, Minière, Nau Frères, Omasson. *See* ST-NICOLAS-DE-BOURGUEIL.

Bouscassé, Dom SW Fr r w ★★★ 05′ 06 08 09 10 11 12 (14) BRUMONT'S MADIRAN base. Wines can be even more austere than his Montus. Petit Courbu-based dry PACHERENC gorgeous.

Bouvet-Ladubay Lo w sp ★→★★★ Major sparkling SAUMUR house owned by Indian United Breweries, run by dynamic Patrice Monmousseau and daughter Juliette. CUVÉE Trésor (p w) best. Still wines mainly from ANJOU-Saumur. Hosts art events.

Bouzereau C d'O r w ★★→★★★ Shake a bush in MEURSAULT and a Bouzereau will fall out. Jean-Baptiste (DOM Michel B), Vincent B or B-Gruère & Filles are all gd sources for whites.

Bouzeron Burg w ★★ CÔTE CHALONNAISE village with unique AC for ALIGOTÉ, with stricter rules and greater potential than straight BOURGOGNE ALIGOTÉ. Briday, FAIVELEY, Jacqueson gd; A & P de Villaine best.

Bouzy Rouge Champ r ★★★ 95 97 99 02 09 12 Still red of famous PINOT N village. Formerly like v. light burg, now with more intensity (climate change?). CLOS Colin ★★★.

Brocard, J-M Chab w ★★→★★★ Father Jean-Marc created dynamic business with ACS in and around CHAB. Son Julien has introduced bio principles. Successful alliance of commerce, quality. Try DOM Ste Claire.

Brouilly Beauj r ★★ 09′ 11′ 12 13′ 14′ Largest of the ten BEAUJ crus: solid, rounded wines with some depth of fruit, approachable early but can age 3–5 yrs. Top growers: CH de la Chaize, Chermette, Dubost, Lapalu, Michaud, Piron.

Brumont, Alain SW Fr r w ★★★ Commands MADIRAN market, with his slow-maturing Le Tyre, MONTUS and BOUSCASSÉ, despite local trend to easier drinking wines. ★ Torus softer and fruitier. ★ IGPs from local grapes gd value. ★★★ PACHERENCS (dry and sw) outstanding.

Brut Champ Term for the dry classic wines of CHAMP. Most houses have reduced *dosage* (adjustment of sweetness) in recent yrs.

Brut Ultra / Zéro Term for bone-dry wines (no *dosage*) in CHAMP (also known as Brut Nature) back in fashion, mixed success. Needs ripeness, old vines, max care.

Bugey Sav r p w sp ★→★★ DYA Sub-Alpine VDQS for light sparkling, still, or half-sparkling wines from Roussette (or Altesse), CHARD (gd). Best from Montagnieu; also Rosé de Cerdon, mainly GAMAY.

Burguet, Alain C d'O r ★★→★★★ Sons Eric and Jean-Luc make tasty GEVREY, esp Mes Favorites. Some négociant wines, eg. CHAMBERTIN CLOS DE BÈZE.

Buxy, Caves de Burg r (p) w ★→★★ Leading co-op for decent CHARD, PINOT N; easily largest supplier of AC MONTAGNY.

Buzet SW Fr r (p) (w) ★★ 12 (14) B'X with the Gascon touch. Power-seeking ★ co-op dominates this AOP, but quirky bio ★★★ DOM du Pech leads more traditional independents eg. ★★ CHX du Frandat, de Salles, DOM Salisquet.

Cabernet d'Anjou Lo p s/sw ★→★★ Delicate, sweet rosé strong in home market. Age-worthy old vintages (★★★) v. rare but remarkable. Now DYA. CH PIERRE-BISE, Bablut, CADY, Chauvin, Clau de Nell, Grandes Vignes, Montgilet, Ogereau, de Sauveroy, Varière.

Cadillac-Côtes de Bordeaux B'x r ★→★★ 05′ 08 09′ 10′ 12 (14) Long, narrow, hilly zone on right bank of Garonne opposite GRAV. Formerly Premières Côtes de B'X. Medium-bodied, fresh reds. Dry whites labelled AC B'X Blanc. Quality extremely varied. Best: Alios de Ste-Marie, Biac, Carignan, *Carsin*, CLOS Chaumont, Clos Ste-Anne, Le Doyenné, Grand-Mouëys, Lezongars, Mont-Pérat, Plaisance, Puy Bardens, REYNON, de Ricaud, Suau.

Cady, Dom Lo r p sw sp ★★→★★★ 03 04 05' 07' (sw) 09 10' 11' 13 (14) V.gd ANJOU family in St Aubin de Luigné. Dry whites, off-dry rosés, lusciously sweet COTEAUX DU LAYON, Chaume. Sweet is best.

Cahors SW Fr r ★★→★★★★ 01' 05' 06 08 09' 10 11 12' (14) Once famous for blackness. Despite efforts to develop typicity, style is now all over the place. All red; 70% MALBEC. Lighter, fruitier from ★★ CHX Paillas, Les Ifs, CLOS Coutale. Bigger from ★★★ Ch Chambert, ★★ Chx Armandière, La Coustarelle, Croze de Pys, Gaudou, Nozières, Vincens, Clos Troteligotte, DOM de la Bérengeraie. Traditional, age-worthy: ★★★ *Clos de Gamot* (Vignes Centenaires, ★★★★ Clos St Jean), Clos Triguedina. Modern: ★★★ CH DU CÈDRE, Clos d'Un Jour, La Périé, Lamartine, La Reyne, DOM du Prince, ★★ La Caminade, Les Croisille, Eugénie. Cult ★★★★ Dom Cosse-Maisonneuve straddles the range.

Old-style "black wine" from Cahors now thankfully a memory: Clos Triguedina makes a New Black Wine, gd with chocolate.

Cailloux, Les S Rh r (w) ★★★ 78' 79' 81' 85' 89' 90' 95' 96' 98' 99 00' 01 03' 04' 05' 06' 07' 09' 10' 11' 12' 13 18 ha CHÂTEAUNEUF DOM; elegant, profound, floral GRENACHE, top-value, joyous handmade reds. Special wine Centenaire, oldest Grenache 1889 noble, costly. Also Dom André Brunel (esp CÔTES DU RH red Est-Ouest), sound Féraud-Brunel CÔTES DU RH merchant range.

Cairanne S Rh r p w ★★→★★★ 05' 06' 07' 09' 10' 11 12' 13 14 Red and white finally made cru rank (above Villages category). Wide range of gd-quality DOMS, wines of character, dark fruit, herbs, smoky tannins, esp Doms Alary (stylish), Ameillaud (fruit), Armand, Brusset (deep), Escaravailles (flair), Féraud-Brunel, Grosset, Hautes Cances (traditional), Oratoire St Martin (classy), Présidente, Rabàsse-Charavin (punchy), Richaud (great fruit), Famille Perrin. Food-friendly whites.

Cal Demoura, Dom L'doc r p w ★★★ New estate to watch in TERRASSES DU LARZAC. Careful winemaking: try L'Etincelle (w), L'Infidèle, Combariolles, Feu Sacré.

Canard-Duchêne Champ House owned by ALAIN THIÉNOT. BRUT Vintage 07 08' 09 12 13. Charles VII Prestige multi-vintage. Cuvée Léonie ★★. Improved Authentique CUVÉE (organic). Vintages best value.

Canon-Fronsac B'x r ★★→★★★ 01 03 05' 06 08 09' 10' 11 12 (14) Small enclave within FRONSAC, otherwise same wines. Best are rich, full, finely structured, usually gd value. Try CHX Barrabaque, Canon Pécresse, Cassagne Haut-Canon la Truffière, la Fleur Cailleau, DU GABY, Grand-Renouil, Haut-Mazeris, MOULIN PEY-LÀBRIE, Pavillon, Vrai Canon Bouché.

Carillon, Louis C d'O w ★★★ Classic PULIGNY producer, separated between brothers. Jacques carries on old tradition; more ambitious François added new v'yds. Top sources for PREMIERS CRUS, eg. Combettes, Perrières, Referts. Reds less interesting.

Cassis Prov (r) (p) w ★★ DYA. Fashionable pleasure port e of Marseille best-known for savoury dry whites based on CLAIRETTE, MARSANNE, eg. DOM de la Ferme Blanche, Fontcreuse, CLOS Ste Magdeleine, Paternel, Fontcreuse. Growers fight with property developers, so prices high.

Castillon-Côtes de Bordeaux B'x r ★★→★★★ 03 04 05' 08 09' 10' 12 (14) Previously Côtes de Castillon, renamed 2008. Appealing e neighbour of ST-ÉM; similar wines, usually less plump. Much recent investment from newcomers. Top: DE L'A, D'AIGUILHE, Alcée, Ampélia, Cap de FAUGÈRES, La Clarière-Laithwaite, CLOS l'Église, Clos Les Lunelles, Clos Puy Arnaud, Côte Montpezat, Joanin Bécot, Montlandrie, Poupille, Robin, Verniotte, Veyry, Vieux CH Champs de Mars.

Cathiard C d'O r ★★★ Sylvain Cathiard produced brilliant, perfumed VOSNE-ROMANÉE, esp Malconsorts, and NUITS-ST-GEORGES, esp Murgers, from 90s. Since 2011 son Sébastien continues, maybe more precision, less overt seduction.

Cave Cellar, or any wine establishment.

Cave coopérative Wine-growers' co-op winery; over half of all French production. Often well-run, well-equipped, and wines gd value for money, but many disappearing in economic crisis.

Cazes, Dom Rouss r p w sw ★★ →★★★ Largest organic producer in ROUSS, combines tradition and innovation. IGP pioneer with MERLOT, CAB SAUV. Le Canon du Maréchal now incl SYRAH, and Crédo now CÔTES DU ROUSS-VILLAGES with Ego, Alter. COLLIOURE and sublime aged RIVESALTES CUVÉE Aimé Cazes. CLOS de Paulilles in BANYULS. Now part of Advini, but still family run. Great value.

Cèdre, Ch du SW Fr r w ★★ →★★★ 06 08 09' 10 11 12 (14) One of most admired modern CAHORS. ★★ Le Prestige is quicker-maturing than oaky top growths. The Verhaeghe Brothers also make a delicious VIOGNIER IGP.

Cépage Grape variety. *See* pp.16–26 for all.

Cérons B'x w sw ★★ 05' 07 09' 10' 11 13 (14) Little-known sweet AC next to SAUT. Less intense wines, eg. CHX de Cérons, CHANTEGRIVE, Grand Enclos.

Chablis w ★★ →★★★ 08' 10' 11 12' 13 14' Lean but lovely n Burg CHARD (except where overcropped or overoaked). My default white when properly made.

Chablis Grand Cru w ★★★ →★★★★ 00' 02' 05' 06 07' 08' 09 10' 11 12' 13 14' Small block of v'yds on steep slope n of river Serein. Richest CHAB as age-worthy as fine CÔTE DE BEAUNE whites. Wait for minerality and individual style to develop. V'yds: Blanchots (floral), Bougros (incl Côte Bouguerots), CLOS (usually best), Grenouilles (spicy), Preuses (richness), Valmur, Vaudésir (plus brand La Moutonne).

Chablis Premier Cru w ★★★ 00' 02' 05' 07' 08' 09 10' 11 12' 13 14' Well worth premium over straight CHAB: better sites on rolling hillsides; more white-flower character on s bank of river Serein (Vaillons, Montmains, Côte de Léchet), yellow fruit on n bank (Fourchaume, Mont de Milieu, Montée de Tonnerre).

Chablisienne, La Chab r w ★★ →★★★ Major player; many own-label CHAB by this dynamic co-op. Sound wines across whole range; top GRAND CRU Grenouilles.

Chaize, Ch de la Beauj r ★★★ Showplace of BEAUJ, magnificent CH, 7th-generation ownership, also fine gardens, with 99 ha of BROUILLY all in one block.

Chambertin C d'O r ★★★★ 90' 93 95 96' 98 99' 01 02' 03 05' 06 07 08 09' 10 11 12' 13 14 13 ha (or 28 ha incl CHAMBERTIN-CLOS DE BÈZE) of Burg's most imperious wine; amazingly dense, sumptuous, long-lived, expensive. Not everybody up to standard, but try from BOUCHARD PÈRE & FILS, Charlopin, Damoy, DUGAT-Py, DROUHIN, DOM LEROY, MORTET, PRIEUR, Rémy, ROSSIGNOL-TRAPET, ROUSSEAU, TRAPET.

Chambertin-Clos de Bèze C d'O r ★★★★ 88 89 90' 93 95 96' 98 99' 01 02' 03 05' 06 07 08 09' 10' 11 12' 13 14 May be sold under name of neighbouring CHAMBERTIN. Similarly splendid wines, velvet texture, possibly more accessible in youth. Best CLAIR, Damoy, DROUHIN, Drouhin-Laroze, FAIVELEY (incl super-CUVÉE Les Ouvrées Rodin), Groffier, JADOT, Prieuré-Roch, ROUSSEAU.

Chablis

There is no better expression of the all-conquering CHARD than the full but tense, limpid but stony wines it makes on the heavy limestone soils of CHABLIS. Best makers use little or no new oak to mask the precise definition of variety and terroir: Barat, Bessin ★, Samuel Billaud ★, Billaud-Simon ★, Boudin ★, J-M BROCARD, J Collet ★, D Dampt, V DAUVISSAT ★, B Defaix, Droin ★, DROUHIN ★, Duplessis, JEAN DURUP, FÈVRE ★, Geoffroy, J-P Grossot ★, LAROCHE, LONG-DEPAQUIT, DOM des Malandes, L Michel ★, Christian MOREAU ★, Picq ★, Pinson ★, Piuze, RAVENEAU ★, G Robin ★, Servin, Temps Perdu, Tribut, Vocoret. Simple, unqualified "Chablis" may be thin; best is PREMIER CRU or GRAND CRU. The co-op, LA CHABLISIENNE, has high standards (esp Grenouille ★) and many different labels. (★ = outstanding)

Chambolle-Musigny C d'O r ★★★→★★★★ 90' 93 95' 96' 98 99' 02' 03 05' 07 08 09' 10' 11 12' 13 14 The epitome of elegance in the CÔTE DE NUITS: look for fragrance and silky texture from PREMIERS CRUS Amoureuses, Charmes, Cras, Fuées and majesty from GRANDS CRUS BONNES MARES, MUSIGNY. BARTHOD, Groffier, MUGNIER, ROUMIER, DE VOGÜÉ the superstars but try also Amiot-Servelle, Bertheau, Digioia-Royer, DROUHIN, Felletig, HUDELOT-Baillet, RION.

Champagne Sparkling wines of PINOTS N and MEUNIER and/or CHARD, and region (33,000 ha, 150 km e of Paris); made by *méthode traditionnelle*. Bubbles from elsewhere, however gd, cannot be Champ.

Champagne le Mesnil Champ Top-flight co-op in greatest GRAND CRU CHARD village. Exceptional CUVÉE Sublime 04 08' 11' 12 13' from finest sites. Impressive Cuvée Prestige 05. Real value.

Champs-Fleuris, Dom des Lo r p w sw ★★→★★★ 05' 08 09' 10 11 12 13 (14) Fine, gd-value DOM for SAUMUR Blanc. SAUMUR-CHAMPIGNY, incl juicy, screwcapped Audace; fine CRÉMANT, incl Prestige Zéro. Succulent COTEAUX DE SAUMUR CUVÉE Sarah.

Champy Père & Cie Burg r w ★★→★★★ Ancient négociant house (1720) under new ownership since 2013. Strengths are BEAUNE and around CORTON, incl former DOM Laleure-Piot.

Chandon de Briailles, Dom C d'O r w ★★→★★★ DOM known for fine, lighter style yet perfumed reds, esp PERNAND-VERGELESSES, Île de Vergelesses, CORTON Bressandes. Bio, lots of stems and no new oak define the style. Some sulphur-free wines.

Chanson Père & Fils Burg r w ★→★★★ An old name in BEAUNE, now one to watch for quality, fair pricing. Try any of its Beaunes (r w), esp CLOS des Fèves (r), CLOS DES MOUCHES (w). Great CORTON-Vergennes (w).

Chapelle-Chambertin C d'O r ★★★ 90' 93 95 96' 98 99' 01 02' 03 05' 07 08 09 10' 11 12' 13 14 A 5.2-ha neighbour of CHAMBERTIN. Fine-boned, less meaty. V.gd in cooler yrs. Top: Damoy, Drouhin-Laroze, JADOT, ROSSIGNOL-TRAPET, TRAPET, Tremblay

Chapoutier N Rh ★★→★★★★ Vocal, bio grower/merchant from base at HERMITAGE. Stylish wines, focus on low-yield, small plot-specific CUVÉES: thick GRENACHE CHÂTEAUNEUF: Barbe Rac, Croix de Bois (r); CÔTE-RÔTIE La Mordorée; Hermitage L'Ermite (outstanding), Le Pavillon (deep, crunchy) (r), Cuvée de l'Orée, Le Méal (w). Also ST-JOSEPH Les Granits (r w). Complex, 100% MARSANNE N Rh whites. Gd-value ***Meysonniers Crozes***. V'yds in COTEAUX D'AIX-EN-PROV, CÔTES DU ROUSS-VILLAGES (gd DOM Bila-Haut), RIVESALTES. Michel Chapoutier has AL v'yds and Australian joint ventures, esp Doms Tournon and Terlato & Chapoutier (fragrant, fine) and Portuguese: Estremadura.

Charbonnière, Dom de la S Rh r (w) ★★★ 95' 98 99' 00 01' 03 04 05' 06' 07' 09 10' 11' 12' 13' Progressive 17-ha CHÂTEAUNEUF estate run by sisters. Sound Tradition wine, distinguished, authentic Mourre des Perdrix, also Hautes Brusquières new L'Envol, VIEILLES VIGNES. Tasty, fresh white. Also genuine VACQUEYRAS red.

Chardonnay As well as a white wine grape, also the name of a MÂCON-VILLAGES commune, hence Mâcon-Chardonnay.

Charmes-Chambertin C d'O r ★★★ 90' 93 95 96' 98 99' 01 02' 03 05' 06 07 08 09 10' 11 12' 13 14 31 ha, incl neighbour MAZOYÈRES-CHAMBERTIN, middle-rank GRAND CRU, at best with explosive deep, dark-cherry fruit, sumptuous texture, fragrant finish. Try ARLAUD, BACHELET, DUGAT, DUJAC, Duroché, Jouan, LEROY, Perrot-Minot Roty, ROUSSEAU, VOUGERAIE.

Chassagne-Montrachet C d'O r w ★★→★★★★ (w) 02' 04 05' 06' 07 08' 09' 10 11 12 13 14' Large village at s end of CÔTE DE BEAUNE. Great whites from eg. Caillerets La Romanée, Blanchots, GRANDS CRUS. Best reds from CLOS St Jean, Morgeot others more rustic. Try from Coffinet, COLIN, GAGNARD, MOREY, Pillot families plus top DOMS MOREAU, Niellon, Ramonet (reds too), CH de Maltroye. But too much indifferent village white grown on land better suited to red.

Champagne growers to watch in 2016

Armand (Arnaud) Margaine Leading grower-winemaker in Villers-Marmery, best-known for some of best CHARD of Montagne de Reims, robust but with enduring finesse. Ace Club BLANC DE BLANCS 08 09 10 11 12'. Great value.

Fleury Pére et Fils Father of bio farming in Aube (1989), still best. Lovely 09 Sonate, PINOT N 09, superb vintage rosé 09'. No slouch at Blanc de Blancs , incl extant PINOT BL.

J-L Vergnon Fine restored Le Mesnil estate making exquisite all-Chard Extra BRUT CUVÉES, esp Confidence 06 08' 09 11'.

Jacques Selosse Avize's best-known grower in top form with two exquisite releases: Le Mesnil, Les Carelles 99 04 and Ambonnay Le Bout du CLOS 02.

Jean-Luc Lallement Exceptional Verzenay grower making muscular yet exquisitely refined BLANC DE NOIRS. Top 12' from 2020. Great rosé too.

Lancelot-Pienne Discreet top Cramant producer, exceptional unoaked Chard cuvées. Exquis Marie Lancelot 08, Perceval.

Lilbert et Fils Scion of blue-chip Cramant DOM takes his GRAND CRU Chard CHAMP to higher level: great purity of flavours, great energy. Textbook 04 06 08 13 Cramant Grand Cru.

Michel Loriot Top grower on the great hill of Festigny, Marne Valley. Subtle, poised PINOT MEUNIER, expansive Chard.

Nicolas Maillart Innovation with respect for tradition marks this exceptional Ecueil (Montagne) producer. Stunning ungrafted Pinot N in Les Francs de Pied 05 08'.

Veuve Fourny Rising Côte des Blancs star at Vertus: Extra Brut 02' 08' and superb single-v'yd Clos du Faubourg Notre Dame 00 02 04' 08'.

Vilmart Rilly la Montagne. One of first growers in 90s to return to barrel fermentation. Since then, Laurent Champs' mastery of wood goes from strength to strength, eg. rich but subtle Coeur de Cuvée 06 08 09. Brilliant rosé too.

Château (Ch) Means an estate, big or small, gd or indifferent, particularly in B'X (*see* pp.97–121). Means, literally, castle or great house. In Burg, DOM is usual term.

Château-Chalon Jura w ★★★ Not a CH but AC and village. Unique dry, yellow, Sherry-like wine (SAVAGNIN grape). Develops *flor* (*see* Sherry) while ageing in barrels for min 6 yrs. Madly expensive compared to often better Sherry. Ready to drink when bottled, but ages almost forever. A curiosity, but great from top growers: Berthet-Bondet, Macle, Mossu.

Château-Grillet N Rh w ★★ 91' 95' 98' 00' 01' 04' 05 06' 07' 08 09' 10' 11 12' 13 France's smallest AC. 3.6-ha amphitheatre v'yd at CONDRIEU, loose, sandy granite. Since purchase by F Pinault of CH LATOUR (*see* p.112) in 2011, prices up, wine modernized. Smooth, less pungent, less muscular, more restrained take on VIOGNIER now: subtle, big, drink at cellar temp, decanted, with new-wave food (in a smart restaurant, of course).

Châteaumeillant Lo r p ★→★★ DYA. 86-ha AC promoted 2010, sw of Bourges in Georges Sand country. GAMAY, PINOT N for v. light reds (75%), gris and rosés (25%). Foolishly 100% Pinot N no longer allowed. Look for: BOURGEOIS, Chaillot, Geoffrenet-Morval, Rouzé, Siret-Courtaud.

Châteauneuf-du-Pape S Rh r (w) ★★★ 78' 81' 83 85 88 89' 90' 95' 96 98' 99' 00' 01' 03' 04' 05' 06' 07' 08 09' 10' 11 12' 13 Nr Avignon, about 45 gd DOMS for best wines (remaining 85 inconsistent to poor). Up to 13 grapes (r w), headed by GRENACHE, plus SYRAH, MOURVÈDRE, Counoise. Warm, aromatic, textured, long-lived; should be fine, round, pure, but too many sweet, heavy, sip-only wines (Parker taste). Small, traditional names can be gd value (great in 2010), while prestige old-vine wines (worst are late-harvest, new oak, 16%) are often too pricey. Whites fresh, fruity, or sturdy, best can age 15 yrs. Top names: CHX DE BEAUCASTEL, Fortia, Gardine (lovely modern, also w), Mont-Redon, LA NERTHE, RAYAS (unique, marvellous), Sixtine, Vaudieu; DOMS de Barroche, Beaurenard, Bois de Boursan (value), Bosquet des Papes (value), LES CAILLOUX, Chante Cigale, Chante Perdrix, CHARBONNIÈRE, Charvin (terroir), Cristia, Font-de-Michelle, Grand Veneur (oak), Marcoux (fantastic VIEILLES VIGNES), Pegaü, Roger Sabon, Sénéchaux (modern), VIEUX TÉLÉGRAPHE, Henri Bonneau, CLOS du Caillou, Clos du Mont-Olivet, CLOS DES PAPES, Clos St-Jean (sip), P Usseglio, Vieux Donjon.

Chave, Dom Jean-Louis N Rh r w ★★★★ 85' 88' 89' 90' 91' 94 95' 96 97 98' 99' 00 01' 03' 04 05' 06' 07' 08 09' 10' 11' 12' 13' 14 Excellent family DOM at heart of HERMITAGE. Clever, detailed blending from best, mainly w-central hillside sites. Classy, fruit-laden, supple, long-lived reds (more plush recently), incl expensive, occasional Cathelin. V.gd white (mainly MARSANNE); marvellous, occasional VIN DE PAILLE. Deep, copious ST-JOSEPH red (incl Dom Florentin 2009 and new v'yds), fruity J-L Chave brand St-Joseph Offerus, sound merchant Hermitage (r w).

Chavignol Lo Picturesque SANCERRE village with famous steep v'yds Les Monts Damnés and Cul de Beaujeu. Clay-limestone soil gives full-bodied, mineral whites and reds that age 10 yrs+; esp from Boulay, BOURGEOIS, Cotat, DAGUENEAU, Thomas Laballe, Yves & Pierre Martin, ALPHONSE MELLOT, Paul Thomas. Whites perfect with *crottin de Chavignol*.

Chénas Beauj r ★★★ 09' 11' 12 13 14' Smallest BEAUJ cru, between MOULIN-À-VENT and JULIÉNAS, less well-known so gd value for meaty wine. Try: Aufranc, DUBOEUF, LAPIERRE, Pacalet, Piron, Thillardon (rising star), Trichard, CO-OP.

Chevalier-Montrachet C d'O w ★★★★ 99' 00' 02' 04 05' 06' 07' 08 09' 10 11 12 13 14' Just above MONTRACHET geographically, just below in quality, though still capable of brilliant crystalline wines. Long-lived but often enjoyable early. Special CUVÉES Les Demoiselles from JADOT and LOUIS LATOUR and La Cabotte from BOUCHARD, but top example is LEFLAIVE. Try also Dancer, Niellon, SAUZET.

Cheverny Lo r p w ★→★★ 08 09' 10 11 13 14 LO AC nr Chambord. Pungent dry white from SAUV BL, CHARD. Light reds mainly GAMAY, PINOT N (also CAB FR, CÔT). Richer, age-worthy, fascinating *Cour-Cheverny*, local Romorantin grape only. Esp Cazin, CLOS Tue-Boeuf, Gendrier, Huards, de Montcy, Philippe Tessier; DOMS de la Desoucherie, du Moulin, Veilloux, Villemade.

Chevillon, R C d'O r ★★★ Top NUITS-ST-GEORGES address; fairly priced. Supple, sensual style; more structure from top v'yds eg. Les St-Georges, Cailles, Vaucrains.

Chidaine, François Lo (r) w dr sw sp ★★★ 08' 09 10' 11 13 (14) Maker of v. precise MONTLOUIS, VOUVRAY. Owns historic CLOS Baudoin (Vouvray). Focus on dry, DEMI-SEC. AC TOURAINE at Chissay (Cher Valley). Bio champion. Big new winery but frosted (2012), hailed (2013 in Vouvray). La Cave Insolite (retail) in Montlouis.

Chignin Sav w ★ DYA. Light, soft white from Jacquère grapes for Alpine summers. Chignin-Bergeron (with ROUSSANNE grapes) is best and liveliest.

Chinon Lo r p (w) ★★→★★★ 96' 97 03 05' 06 08 09' 10' 11 12 13 14' 2,300 ha. Rabelais the patron saint. Light to rich TOURAINE CAB FR, ten per cent rosé. Top wines age 20 yrs+. A little dry CHENIN BL, some wood-fermented. Try ALLIET, BAUDRY, BAUDRY-DUTOUR, Couly-Dutheil, Couly (Pierre & Bertrand), Grosbois, L'R, Pain, JM Raffault; CHX de la Bonnelière, de Coulaine, DOM de la Noblaie. 2014 excellent but small crop. Seven communes w of Chinon to join AC in 2017.

Chiroubles Beauj r 11' 12 13' 14 Rarely seen BEAUJ cru in the hills above FLEURIE: fresh, fruity, silky wine for early drinking (1–3 yrs). Growers: Cheysson, Coquelet, DUBOEUF, Fourneau, Métrat, Passot, Raousset, Trenel.

FRANCE

Chorey-lès-Beaune C d'O r (w) ★★ 05′ 08 09′ 10′ 11 12 14 Pleasurable, affordable burg adjoining BEAUNE. Tollot-Beaut is famous. Try Arnoux, DROUHIN, JADOT, Loichet.

Chusclan S Rh r p w ★→★★ 09′ 10′ 11′ 12′ 13 CÔTES DU RH-VILLAGES with above-average Laudun-Chusclan co-op, incl gd clean-cut whites. Easy reds, direct rosés. Best co-op labels (r) Chusclan DOM de l'Olivette, CÔTES DU RH Femme de Gicon, LIRAC. Also full CH Signac (best Chusclan, can age), Dom La Romance, special CUVÉES from *André Roux*. Drink most young.

Clair, Bruno C d'O r p w ★★★→★★★★ Top class CÔTE DE NUITS estate for supple, subtle, savoury wines. Gd-value MARSANNAY, old-vine SAVIGNY La Dominode, GEVREY-CHAMBERTIN (CLOS ST-JACQUES, Cazetiers) and standout CHAMBERTIN-CLOS DE BÈZE. Best whites from MOREY-ST-DENIS, CORTON-CHARLEMAGNE.

Clairet B'x Between rosé/red. B'x Clairet is AC. Try CHX Fontenille, Penin, Turcaud.

Clairette de Die N Rh w dr s/sw sp ★★ NV Alpine bubbles: flinty or (better) semi-sweet MUSCAT sparkling wine from low Alps. Underrated, muskily fruited; or dry CLAIRETTE, can age 3–4 yrs. NB: Achard-Vincent, Carod, Jaillance (value), Poulet et Fils (terroir), J-C Raspail.

Clape, Auguste, Pierre, Olivier N Rh r (w) ★★★→★★★★ 89′ 90′ 95′ 97 98′ 99′ 00 01′ 02 03′ 04′ 05′ 06′ 07′ 08 09′ 10′ 11′ 12′ 13′ 14 *The kings of Cornas*. Network of supreme SYRAH central v'yds at CORNAS, many old vines. Profound, consistent reds, great body, lingering tannins, need 6 yrs+, live 25. Well-fruited youngish-vines Renaissance. Gd CÔTES DU RH, VIN DE FRANCE (r), ST-PÉRAY.

Clape, La L'doc r p w ★★→★★★ Compact area of limestone hills on coast nr Narbonne, once an island. Warming, spicy reds. Original *tangy, salty whites* age surprisingly well. Appellation status imminent; future Cru du L'doc; *see* COTEAUX DU L'DOC. Gd: CHX *l'Hospitalet*, Moyau, La Négly, Pech-Céléyran, Pech-Redon, *Rouquette-sur-Mer*, Ricardelle, Anglès, Mas du Soleila, Camplazens, Mire l'Etang.

Climat Burg Individually named v'yd in Burg, eg. MEURSAULT Tesson, BEAUNE Grèves.

Clos A term carrying some prestige, reserved for distinct (walled) v'yds, often in one ownership (esp Burg, CHAMP, AL).

Clos Rougeard Lo r w (sw) ★★★★ 03 04 05′ 06 07 08 09′ 10′ 11 12 13 (14) Legendary DOM run by Charly and Nady Foucault. Age-worthy wines with great finesse: SAUMUR-CHAMPIGNY, SAUMUR *Blanc*, COTEAUX DE SAUMUR.

Clos St-Denis C d'O r ★★★ 90′ 93′ 95 96′ 98 99′ 01 02′ 03 05′ 06 07 08 09′ 10′ 11 12′ 13 14 GRAND CRU at MOREY-ST-DENIS. Sumptuous wine in youth, growing silky with age. Try from ARLAUD, Bertagna, Castagnier, DUJAC, Jouan, Leroux, PONSOT.

Clos St-Jacques C d'O r ★★★ 90′ 93 95 96′ 98 99′ 01 02′ 03 05′ 06 07 08 09′ 10′ 11 12′ 13 14 Hillside PREMIER CRU in GEVREY-CHAMBERTIN with perfect se exposure. Excellent producers: CLAIR, ESMONIN, FOURRIER, JADOT, ROUSSEAU; powerful, velvety reds often ranked above many GRANDS CRUS.

Clos Ste-Hune Al w ★★★★ Top TRIMBACH bottling from GRAND CRU ROSACKER. Greatest RIES in ALSACE? (06 08′ 10′ 12 13′ 14.) Initially austere, needing 5–10 yrs+ ageing (magnificent 89); complex mineral contrast to volcanic-rich CLOS St-Urbain from ZIND-HUMBRECHT – the other contender to the Ries throne.

Clos de Gamot SW Fr r ★★★ 00 01′ 02′ 04 05′ 06 08 09′ 10′ 11 (12) Quintessential CAHORS from Jouffreau family's 19th-century MALBEC vines. ★★★ CUVÉE Vignes Centenaires (best yrs only) and hilltop ★★★★ CLOS St Jean miraculously survive modern Cahors fashions, deer and wild boar.

Clos de Tart C d'O r ★★★★ 99′ 01′ 02′ 03 05′ 06 07 08′ 09 10 11 12′ 13 14 MOREY-ST-DENIS GRAND CRU, upgraded substantially in quality and price on the watch of director Sylvain Pitiot (1996–2014). Often most exciting in less ripe yrs.

Clos de Vougeot C d'O r ★★★→★★★★ 90′ 93′ 96′ 98 99′ 01 02′ 03′ 05′ 06 07 08 09′ 10′ 11 12′ 13′ 14 Celebrated CÔTE DE NUITS GRAND CRU with many owners. Occasionally sublime, esp with age. Style and quality depend on grower's means, philosophy, technique, position. Top growers: CH de la Tour, DROUHIN, EUGÉNIE, FAIVELEY, GRIVOT, GROS, HUDELOT-Noëllat, JADOT, LEROY, LIGER-BELAIR, MÉO-CAMUZET, MONTILLE, MUGNERET, *Vougeraie*.

Clos de la Roche C d'O r ★★★ 90' 93' 95 96' 98 99' 01 02' 03 05' 06 07 08 09' 10' 11 12' 13 14 Maybe the finest GRAND CRU of MOREY-ST-DENIS, with as much grace as power, more savoury than sumptuous. Needs time. PONSOT, DUJAC are references but try Amiot, ARLAUD, Castagnier, LEROY, LIGNIER, ROUSSEAU.

Clos des Lambrays C d'O r ★★★ 99' 02 03 05' 06 09' 10' 11 12' 13 14 GRAND CRU v'yd at MOREY-ST-DENIS. A virtual monopoly of the DOM du CLOS des Lambrays, invigorating wine in early-picked, spicy, stemmy style, total contrast to neighbour CLOS DE TART. New owner LVMH from 2014 may mean new prices.

Clos des Mouches C d'O r w ★★★ 02 05' 09' 10' 11 14' Splendid PREMIER CRU BEAUNE v'yd, made famous by DROUHIN. Whites and reds spicy, memorable and consistent. BICHOT, CHANSON gd too. Little-known v'yds of the same name also found in SANTENAY (Clair, Moreau, Muzard), MEURSAULT (Germain).

Clos des Papes S Rh r w ★★★★ 89' 90' 95 98' 99' 00 01' 02' 03' 04' 05' 06' 07' 08 09' 10' 11 12' 13' Always classy CHÂTEAUNEUF DOM of Avril family, deliberately tiny yields. Rich, complex red, more showy and succulent recently (mainly GRENACHE, MOURVÈDRE, drink at 2–3 yrs or from 8 yrs); *great white* (six varieties, complex, allow time, deserves fine cuisine; 5–18 yrs).

Clos du Mesnil CHAMP KRUG'S famous walled v'yd in GRAND CRU Le Mesnil. Esp long-lived, pure CHARD vintage, great yrs like 92 95 perfect now and to 2020+; 00 v.gd; 03 a fresh miracle.

Clos du Roi C d'O r ★★→★★★ Best v'yd in GRAND CRU CORTON, top PREMIER CRU v'yd in MERCUREY, less so in BEAUNE, special site in MARSANNAY. The king usually chose well.

Clovallon, Dom de L'doc ★★★ Haute Vallée de l'Orb for PINOT N Pomarèdes and white blend Aurièges, also Mas d'Alezon, FAUGÈRES for ★★★ Presbytère, Montfalette.

Coche-Dury C d'O r w ★★★★ Superb MEURSAULT DOM led by Jean-François Coche and son Raphaël. Exceptional whites from ALIGOTÉ to CORTON-CHARLEMAGNE and v. pretty reds too. Hard to find.

Colin C d'O r w ★★★ Leading CHASSAGNE-MONTRACHET and ST-AUBIN family; new generation making waves, esp Pierre-Yves C-Morey (outstanding whites) and DOM Marc C. Try also Bruno or Philippe C (sons of Michel C-Deleger).

Collines Rhodaniennes N Rh r w ★★ Character and quality. N Rh IGP, clear-fruited hillside reds v.gd value. Can contain young-vine CÔTE-RÔTIE, also recent schist v'yds at Seyssuel (deep, flinty, expensive). Mostly SYRAH (best), plus MERLOT, GAMAY, mini-CONDRIEU VIOGNIER (best), CHARD. Reds: Bonnefond, L Cheze, J-M Gérin, Jamet, Jasmin, Monier-Pérreol, M&S Ogier, S Pichat. Whites: Alexandrins, Barou, Y Cuilleron, F Merlin, Perret (v.gd), *G Vernay (v.gd)*.

Collioure Rouss r p w ★★ Table-wine twin of BANYULS. Most producers make both. Gutsy reds, mainly GRENACHE, from dramatic terraces above picturesque town. Also rosé, white based on GRENACHE BLANC and Gris since 2002. Top: Les CLOS de Paulilles, DOMS du Mas Blanc, de la Rectorie, La Tour Vieille, Vial-Magnères, Madeloc, Coume del Mas. Co-ops Cellier des Templiers, l'Étoile.

Comté Tolosan SW Fr r p w ★→★★ Mostly DYA IGP dotted all over the sw. ★★★ CH de Cabidos (luscious dessert PETIT MANSENG), ★★ DOM de Moncaut (JURANÇON in all but name) and pioneering ★★ Dom de Ribonnet (all colours) stand out from a mediocre crowd.

Condrieu N Rh w ★★★ 08' 09 10' 11' 12' 13 14 Floral, mineral/musky aromas of apricot/pear bounce out from granite hills; home of VIOGNIER. Best: cool, pure, precise; danger of excess oak, sweetness and alcohol. Rare white to accompany asparagus. 75 growers, so quality varies (v.gd 08, lovely 10). Best:

Benetière (character), CHAPOUTIER, Y Cuilleron, DELAS, Faury (esp La Berne), Gangloff (great style), GUIGAL (big), F Merlin, Niéro, A Perret, C Pichon, ROSTAING, G Vernay, F Villard.

Corbières L'doc r (p) (w) ★★→★★★ 07 08 09 10 11 12 13 14 Largest AC of the L'DOC, with lone cru of Boutenac; others may follow. Wines as varied, wild as the scenery: from coastal lagoons to sun-baked, rugged hills. Try: CHX Aiguilloux, Aussières, de Cabriac, LA BARONNE, Borde-Rouge, Les CLOS Perdus, Lastours, Ollieux Romanis, Les Palais, Pech-Latt, la Voulte Gasparets, DOMS du Grand Crès, de Fontsainte, Trillol, du Vieux Parc, de Villemajou, Villerouge, Clos de l'Anhel, Grand Arc, Serres-Mazard. Co-ops: Camplong, Castelmaure.

Cornas N Rh r ★★★ 78' 83' 85' 88' 89' 90' 91' 94' 95' 96 97' 98' 99' 00' 01' 02 03' 04 05' 06' 07' 08 09' 10' 11' 12' 13' 14 Top quality N Rh SYRAH. Deep, abundantly fruited, mineral-tinted. Can drink some on vibrant early fruit, mostly needs age 5 yrs+. Stunning 2010. Top: ALLEMAND (top 2), Balthazar (traditional), M Barret (organic), *Clape* (benchmark), Colombo (new oak), Courbis (modern), *Delas*, J & E Durand (racy fruit), G Gilles, JABOULET (St-Pierre CUVÉE), Lemenicier, V Paris, Tardieu-Laurent (oak), DOM *du Tunnel*, Voge (oak).

Corsica / Corse r p w ★→★★ From France's wild island. ACS Ajaccio, PATRIMONIO; better crus Coteaux du Cap Corse, Sartène, Calvi. IGP: Île de Beauté. Light, spicy reds from SCIACARELLO, more structured wines from NIELLUCCIO; gd rosés; *tangy, herbal Vermentino whites.* Also sweet MUSCATS. Top growers: Abbatucci, Antoine Arena, CLOS d'Alzeto, Clos Capitoro, Gentile, Yves Leccia, Montemagni, *Peraldi,* Vaccelli, Saperale, Fiumicicoli, *Torraccia,* Canarelli, Pieretti, Nicrosi, Alzipratu, Clos Poggiale. Original wines that rarely travel, but well worth seeking out.

Côte d'Or vineyards: France's next candidate for Unesco World Heritage site status.

Corton C d'O r (w) ★★★ 90' 95 96' 98 99' 01 02' 03' 05' 06 07 08 09' 10' 11 12' 13 14 The 160 ha classified as GRAND CRU is much too much: only top v'yds CLOS DU ROI, Bressandes, Le Rognet really deserve it; others make fair, softer reds. Look for d'Ardhuy, BONNEAU DU MARTRAY, BOUCHARD, CHANDON DE BRIAILLES, DOM des Croix, DRC (since 2009), Dubreuil-Fontaine, FAIVELEY, Camille Giroud, MÉO-CAMUZET, Senard, TOLLOT-BEAUT. Occasional whites, eg. HOSPICES DE BEAUNE, less interesting than CORTON-CHARLEMAGNE.

Corton-Charlemagne C d'O w ★★★→★★★★ 99' 00' 02' 03 04 05' 06 07' 08 09' 10' 11 12' 13 Potentially scintillating GRAND CRU white burg, in style between MONTRACHET and CHAB Grand Cru. Sw- and w-facing limestone slopes, plus e band round the top. Intense minerality, great ageing potential often unused. Top growers: BONNEAU DU MARTRAY, BOUCHARD, COCHE-DURY, FAIVELEY, HOSPICES DE BEAUNE, JADOT, P Javillier, LATOUR, Rapet, Rollin, VOUGERAIE.

Costières de Nîmes S Rh r p w ★→★★ 07' 09' 10' 11 12' 13 Region sw of CHÂTEAUNEUF, similar stony soils, strong quality. Red (GRENACHE, SYRAH) ages well, gd value. Best: CHX de Grande Cassagne, Mas des Bressades (gd fruit), Mas Carlot, Mas Neuf, Mourgues-du-Grès, Nages, d'Or et des Gueules, Roubaud; DOMS M KREYDENWEISS, Petit Romain, Tardieu-Laurent, du Vieux Relais. Gd, lively rosés, stylish whites (ROUSSANNE). 2012, 13 both gd to drink young.

Côte Chalonnaise Burg r w sp ★★ Region immediately s of C D'O; lghter wines, lower prices. BOUZERON for ALIGOTÉ *Mercurey* and GIVRY for structured reds and interesting whites; *Rully* for lighter wines in both colours; MONTAGNY for its leaner CHARD. Region lacks a real champion, though.

Côte Roannaise Lo r p ★★ 11 12 13 14 Quality dynamic AC, lower slopes of high granite hills w of Roanne. Fine juicy GAMAY – some serious. Producers: Désormière, Fontenay, Giraudon, Paroisse, Plasse, Pothiers, Sérol, Vial. White IGP Urfé from CHARD and increasingly VIOGNIER.

Côte-Rôtie N Rh r ★★★→★★★★★ 78' 85' 88' 89' 90' 91' 95' 98' 99' 00 01' 03' 04 05' 06' 07' 08 09' 10' 11 12' 13' 14 Finest Rh red, mainly SYRAH, drop of VIOGNIER, style ties to Burg. Violet airs, pure, complex, v. fine with age (5–10 yrs+). Exceptional, v. long-lived 2010. Top: *Barge* (traditional), Bernard, Bonnefond (oak), Bonserine (GUIGAL-owned), Burgaud, CHAPOUTIER, Clusel-Roch (organic), DELAS, Duclaux, Gaillard (oak), Garon, J-M Gérin (oak), Guigal (long oaking), *Jamet* (wonderful), Jasmin, Levet (traditional), M&S Ogier (oak), DOM de Rosiers, ROSTAING (fine), J-M Stéphan (organic), VIDAL-FLEURY (La Chatillonne).

Côte d'Or Burg *Département* name applied to the central and principal Burg v'yd slopes: CÔTE DE BEAUNE and CÔTE DE NUITS. Not used on labels except for proposed BOURGOGNE C D'O AC, expected imminently.

Côte de Beaune C d'O r w ★★→★★★★ The s half of the C D'O. Also a little seen AC in its own right applying to top of the hill above BEAUNE itself. Try from DROUHIN.

Côte de Beaune-Villages C d'O r ★★ 09' 10' 11 12 14 Red wines from the lesser villages of the s half of the C D'O. Rarely exciting, now rarely seen.

Côte de Brouilly Beauj r ★★ 09' 11' 12 13' 14 Flanks of the hillside above BROUILLY provide one of the richest BEAUJ crus. Deserves a premium over BROUILLY, but not normally applied. Try J-P Brun, L Martray, CH Thivin.

Little-known Loire ACs like St-Pourçain, Côte Roannaise, Côtes du Forez worth exploring these days.

Côte de Nuits C d'O r (w) ★★→★★★★ The n half of C D'O. Mostly red wine from MARSANNAY, FIXIN, GEVREY-CHAMBERTIN, MOREY-ST DENIS, CHAMBOLLE-MUSIGNY, VOUGEOT, VOSNE-ROMANÉE, NUITS-ST GEORGES.

Côte de Nuits-Villages C d'O r (w) ★★ 05' 09' 10' 11 12' 13 14 Junior AC for extreme n/s ends of CÔTE DE NUITS; investigate for bargains. Single-v'yd versions beginning to appear. Try Ardhuy, BACHELET, Chopin, Gachot-Monot, Jourdan, Loichet.

Coteaux Bourguignons Burg ★ DYA. New AC from 2011 replacing BOURGOGNE GRAND ORDINAIRE. Mostly reds, GAMAY, PINOT N. Main take-up is hard-to-sell basic BEAUJ (which is neither from Coteaux, nor Bourguignon) reclassified under this sexier name. Rare whites ALIGOTÉ, CHARD, MELON, PINOTS BL and GR.

Coteaux Champenois Champ r (p) w ★★★ (w) DYA. AC for still wines of CHAMP eg. BOUZY. Vintages as for Champ. Better reds with climate change and better viticulture (esp 09 12').

Coteaux d'Aix-en-Provence Prov r p w ★★ Sprawling AC from hills around Aix and nearby plain n of Etang de Berre. No real identity. Fruit-salad of varieties, both B'X and MIDI. Reds are best, esp CHX Beaupré, Calissanne, Revelette, les Bastides la Realtière, les Béates, Bas. Vignelaure. *See also* LES BAUX-EN-PROV.

Coteaux d'Ancenis Lo r p w (sw) ★★★ 13 14 Generally DYA. AOP (between Nantais and ANJOU). Dry, DEMI-SEC, sweet CHENIN BL whites, plus age-worthy *Malvoisie* also light reds and rosés mainly GAMAY, plus CABS FR, SAUV. Esp Athimon et ses Enfants, Guindon, Pléiade, Quarteron.

Coteaux de Chalosse SW Fr r p w ★ DYA. Modest IGP from Les Landes, made from local grape varieties, popular in local restaurants. Co-op (now merged with TURSAN) dominates.

Coteaux de Glanes SW Fr r p ★★ DYA. Segalin grape gives extra pep to the MERLOT and GAMAY from the co-op here.

Coteaux de l'Ardèche S Rh r p w ★→★★ Rocky hills w of Rh, a wide selection generally gd value. New DOMS; fresh reds, some oaked (boo!); VIOGNIER (eg. Mas de Libian, CHAPOUTIER), MARSANNE. Best from SYRAH, also GAMAY (often old vines) CAB SAUV (Serret). Restrained, Burg-style Ardèche CHARD by LOUIS LATOUR. DOMS du Colombier, Favette, Flacher, Grangeon, Mazel, Vigier, CH de la Selve.

Coteaux de l'Aubance Lo w SW ★★→★★★★ 89' 90' 95' 96' 97' 02 03 05' 07'

09 10' 11' **13** (14) Small AC for sweet whites from CHENIN BL. Nervier, less rich
than COTEAUX DU LAYON except SÉLECTION DES GRAINS NOBLES. S of Lo nr Angers,
gentler slopes than Layon. Often gd value. Esp Bablut, Haute-Perche, Montgilet,
CH Princé, Richou, Rochelles, Ch la Varière. Promising 2014.

Coteaux de Saumur Lo w sw ★★–★★★ 03, 05, 07' 09 10' 11 (14) Sweet, hand-picked
CHENIN BL. Like COTEAUX DU LAYON but less rich, more delicate, citric. Esp CHAMPS
FLEURIS, CLOS ROUGEARD, Régis Neau, St Just, Targé, Vatan. Potential in 2014.

Coteaux des Baronnies S Rh r p w ★ DYA. Late-ripening Rh IGP in high pastures
e of VINSOBRES. SYRAH (best), CAB SAUV, MERLOT, CHARD (for once gd, cheap), plus
GRENACHE, CINSAULT, etc. Improving simple reds, also fresh VIOGNIER. NB: DOMS du
Rieu-Frais, Rosière, Le Mas Sylvia.

Coteaux du Giennois Lo r p w ★–★★★ DYA. Small AC (196 ha) n of POUILLY. Scattered
v'yds from Cosne to Gien. Citric SAUV BL (103 ha) like junior SANCERRE or POUILLY-
FUMÉ can be v.gd. Light reds hampered by statutory blend of GAMAY/PINOT N.
Best: Émile Balland, Jean Marie Berthier (esp L'Inédit), BOURGEOIS, Catherine &
Michel Langlois, Paulat, Treuillet, Villargeau.

Coteaux du Languedoc L'DOC is a vast area and not all ACS have much specific
identity: go by grower. Subregions incl Quatourze, Pézenas, Grès de Montpellier,
Cabrières, St Saturnin: usual L'doc grapes. Tiny Cabardès and Malepère are
where B'X meets MIDI. Clairette du Languedoc tiny, traditional white.

Coteaux du Layon Lo w sw ★★–★★★★ 89 90 95 96 97 02 03 05' 07' 09 10' 11 13
(14) Heart of ANJOU: sweet CHENIN BL varying sweetness with admirable acidity,
best nearly immortal. Seven villages can add name to AC with Chaume as
a PREMIER CRU. Top ACs: BONNEZEAUX, QUARTS DE CHAUME. Growers: Baudouin,
BAUMARD, Pierre Chauvin, Delesvaux, des Forges, Guegniard, Juchepie, Ogereau,
CH PIERRE-BISE, Pithon-Paillé. Avoid 2012 (downpour in Oct), potential in 2014.

Coteaux du Loir Lo r p w dr sw ★–★★★ 05' 07 08 09' 10' 11 13 (14) The n tributary
of the river Loire, Le Loir is marginal but dynamic region with Coteaux du
Loir, JASNIÈRES. Steely, fine, precise CHENIN BL. GAMAY, peppery Pineau d'Aunis
occasionally sparkling, plus Grolleau (rosé), CAB, CÔT. Top growers: Ange Vin,
DOM DE BELLIVIERE, Breton, Le Briseau, Fresneau, Gigou, Janvier, Les Maisons
Rouges, de Rycke. 2013 small, but gd and promising 2014.

Coteaux du Lyonnais Beauj r p (w) ★ DYA Junior BEAUJ. Best *en primeur*.

Coteaux du Quercy SW Fr r p ★ 09' 10 11 12 (14) AOP based on CAB FR. Gd everyday
winter wines (can be kept) from worthy co-op, only marginally outshone by ★★
DOM du Merchien (IGP), ★ Doms d'Ariès, de Guillau, Mystère d'Éléna (Dom de
Revel). Gd with stews and game.

Coteaux du Vendômois Lo r p w ★–★★ DYA. AC, 28 communes around 150 ha:
Vendôme, Montoire in Le Loir Valley. Mostly typical VIN GRIS from Pineau d'Aunis
grape, which also gives peppery notes to red blends alongside CAB FR, PINOT N,
GAMAY. Whites are CHENIN BL, CHARD. Producers: Brazilier, Patrice Colin, Four à
Chaux, J Martellière, Montrieux (Émile Hérédia), CAVE du Vendôme-Villiers.

Coteaux et Terrasses de Montauban SW Fr r p w ★–★★ DYA IGP, created almost
single-handed by DOM de Montels with huge range of gd-value wines. Not quite
a monopoly; try ★ Dom Biarnès, Mas des Anges.

Coteaux Varois-en-Provence Prov r p w ★–★★ 08 09 10 11 12 13 14 Overlooked
AC sandwiched between bigger COTEAUX D'AIX and CÔTES DE PROV. Warming reds,
fresh rosés from usual s varieties. Potential being realized, esp Syrah. Try CHX
la Calisse, Miraval (Brangelina's), DOM les Alysses, *des Aspras*, du Deffends, du
Loou, des Chaberts, *Routas*, Trians.

Côtes Catalanes Rouss r p w ★★–★★★ A mere IGP, covering much of ROUSS, but
quality far exceeds ACS. Exciting source of innovation. Old vines galore, mainly
GRENACHE, CARIGNAN, provide rewarding drinking. Best: DOMS GÉRARD GAUBY,

Matassa, La Préceptorie Centernach, Casenove, *Dom of the Bee*, Olivier Pithon Padié, Soulanes, le Soula, Vaquer, Treloar, *Jones*, L'Horizon.

Côtes d'Auvergne Mass C r p (w) ★→★★ Generally DYA. Small AC (400 ha, was 50,000 ha in 19th century). GAMAY, with some PINOT N (100% banned!), CHARD Best reds improve 2–3 yrs. Top villages: Boudes, Chanturgue, Châteaugay Madargues (r), Corent (p). Producers: CAVE St-Verny, Maupertuis, Sauvat.

Côtes de Bordeaux B'x ★ Superfluous AC launched in 2008 for reds. Embraces and permits cross-blending between CASTILLON, FRANCS, BLAYE, CADILLAC (formerly Premières Côtes de B'x). Growers who want to maintain the identity of a single terroir have stiffer controls but can put Castillon, Cadillac, etc. before Côtes de B'x. BLAYE-CÔTES DE B'X, FRANCS-CÔTES DE B'X also produce a little dry white. CÔTES DI BOURG is not part of new system. Try CH Réaut.

Côtes de Bourg B'x r w ★→★★ 04 05' 08 09' 10' 12 (14) Solid, savoury reds, a little white from e bank of Gironde. Independent of CÔTES DE B'X AC. Usually gd value Top CHX: Brûlescaille, Bujan, Civrac, *Falfas*, Fougas-Maldoror, Grand-Maison Grave (Nectar VIEILLES VIGNES), Haut-Guiraud, Haut-Macô, Haut Mondésir Macay, Martinat, Mercier, Nodoz, *Roc de Cambes*, Rousset, Sociondo.

Côtes de Duras SW Fr r p w ★→★★★ 11' 12 (14) AOP between B'x and Bergerac. Dul co-op firmly outclassed by organically led ★★★ DOMS Mouthes-les-Bihan, Peti Malromé, Dom Mont Ramé and Nadine Lussau, then ★★ La Tuilerie la Brille Les Hauts de Riquet, Les Cours, Mauro-Guicheney. CH Condom Perceval's ★★★ sw still outstanding. Older gd growers incl ★★ Doms Chater, de Laulan, Grand Mayne, Les Allegrets.

Côtes de Gascogne SW Fr (r) (p) w ★★ DYA IGP. ★★ PRODUCTEURS PLAIMONT, and esp 900-ha DOM Tariquet, dominate the market for these easy-quaffing wine-ba whites. Smaller estates incl ★★ Doms d'Arton, Chiroulet, Haut-Campagnau Ménard, Millet, Pellehaut, de San Guilhem. Or★ CH des Cassagnoles, de Jöy, de Laballe, de Lauroux, de Magnaut, Papolle, St Lannes. Reds less successful bu note★ Sédouprat red CUVÉE Sanglier. Best product: Armagnac.

Côtes de Millau SW Fr r p w IGP ★ DYA. Tarn Valley wines, dominated by gd co-op and Foster's viaduct. Try gd independents eg. ★ DOM du Vieux Noyer.

Côtes de Montravel SW Fr w sw ★★ 09 10 11' 12 (13) Sub-AOP of BERGERAC; not dry bu not sticky either. Attractive unfashionable apéritif-style wines mostly from SÉM Perfect with local foie gras.

Côtes de Provence r p w ★→★★★ 07 08 09 10 11 12 13 14(p w) DYA. Large AC Mainly rosé, research improving quality (nowhere else takes rosé quite so seriously). Satisfying reds, CAB plus MIDI varieties. Herbal whites. STE-VICTOIRE Fréjus, La Londe and most recently Pierrefeu are subzones. Leaders incl: Caste Roubine, de Peyrassol, DOMS Bernarde, de la Courtade, Léoube *Gavoty* (superb), CHX d'Esclans, de Selle and CLOS Mireille, des Planes, Rabiéga *Richeaume*, Rimauresq, Ste Rosaline. *See* COTEAUX D'AIX, BANDOL, COTEAUX VAROIS.

Top Côtes du Rhône producers
La Borie, La Courançonne, Fonsalette (beauty), Grand Moulas, Hugues, Montfaucon (w also), St-Estève, Trignon (incl VIOGNIER); co-ops CAIRANNE, RASTEAU; CAVE Estézargues, DOMS Bramadou, André Brunel (stylish), Charvin (terroir, v.gd), Chaume-Arnaud, CLOS des Cîmes, Combebelle, Coudoulet de BEAUCASTEL (classy r), Cros de la Mûre (great-value), M Dumarcher (organic), Espigouette, Ferrand (full), Gourget, Gramenon (organic), Haut-Musiel, Janasse (old GRENACHE), Jaume, Famille Perrin, Manarine, Réméjeanne (w also), Romarins, Rouge-Bleu (organic, clear), Soumade, Vieille Julienne (classy); Mas Poupéras; DUBOEUF, DELAS, GUIGAL (great value).

Côtes de Thongue L'doc r p w ★★ (p w) DYA. Most dynamic IGP of HÉRAULT, in Thongue Valley. Experimental blends and single varietals. Best reds age. DOMS ARJOLLE, les Chemins de Bassac, LA CROIX BELLE, Monplézy, des Henrys.

Côtes de Toul Al r p w ★ DYA. V. light wines from Lorraine; mainly VIN GRIS.

Côtes du Brulhois SW Fr r p (w) ★→★★ 11 12 (14) Lively AOP nr Agen; reds (better than p and w) "black" like CAHORS. Some TANNAT compulsory. Gd co-op works with independents ★★ DOM des Thermes, du Pountet, Bois de Simon, ★ CH la Bastide, Coujétou-Peyret.

Côtes du Forez Lo r p (sp) ★→★★ DYA. Promising s-most LO AC in Massif Central. GAMAY (r p). Les Vignerons Foréziens, Bonnefoy, CLOS de Chozieux, Guillot, Mondon & Demeure, Real, Verdier/Logel. IGP: CHARD, PINOT GR, ROUSSANNE, VIOGNIER, plus future CHENIN BL.

Côtes du Jura Jura r p w (sp) ★★→★★★ 99' 00 03' 05' 06 09 10 11 12 14 Revitalized region for CHARD, SAVAGNIN, styles from fresh and fruity to deliberately oxidative, incl VIN JAUNE. Light, bright reds from PINOT N, Poulsard, Trousseau. Look for BERTHET-BONDET, Bourdy, CH D'ARLAY, PIGNIER, DOM LABET, RATA-POIL. Growing markets in Scandinavia, USA.

Côtes du Rhône S Rh r p w ★→★★ 09' 10' 11' 12' 13 Broad base of S Rh, across 170 communes. Split between enjoyable, handmade quality (numbers rising) and mass-produced. Lively fruit more accentuated. 2013 drink early. Mainly GRENACHE, also SYRAH, CARIGNAN. Best drunk young. Vaucluse top, then GARD (Syrah).

Côtes du Rhône-Villages S Rh r p w ★→★★★ 07' 09' 10' 11' 12' 13 Full-bodied, forthright reds from 7,700 ha, incl 18 named S Rh villages. Best hold generous, spiced dark fruit, gd value. Red core is GRENACHE, plus SYRAH, MOURVÈDRE. Improving whites, often incl VIOGNIER, ROUSSANNE added to rich base CLAIRETTE, GRENACHE BLANC – gd with food. See CHUSCLAN, LAUDUN, ST-GERVAIS, SABLET, SÉGURET (quality), VISAN (improving). New villages from 2005: MASSIF D'UCHAUX (gd), PLAN DE DIEU (robust), PUYMÉRAS, SIGNARGUES, Gadagne. NB: CHX Fontségune, Signac, DOMS Aphillantes (character), Aure, Cabotte (bio), Coulange, Coste Chaude, Grand Moulas, Grand Veneur, Gravennes, Jérome, Montbayon, Mourchon, Pique-Basse, Rabasse-Charavin, Réméjeanne, Renjarde, Romarins, Ste-Anne, St-Siffrein, Saladin, Valériane, Viret (cosmopolitan), Mas de Libian, CAVE Estézargues, Cave RASTEAU.

Côtes du Roussillon-Villages Rouss r ★★ 07 08 09 10 11 12 13 14 28 Villages in best part of ROUSS. Dominated by co-ops and VIGNERONS Catalans; plus independent estates: des Chênes, CAZES, *la Cazenove*, GAUBY, Piquemal, CH de Jau, Mas Crémat, CLOS des Fées, Clot de l'Oum, Bila Haut, Roc des Anges, Thunevin-Calvet, Modat, Rancy. Plain Côtes du Rouss closer to Perpignan and even more dominated by co-ops. Simple, warming reds. See also CÔTES CATALANES.

Côtes du Tarn SW Fr r p w ★ DYA. IGP roughly co-extensive with GAILLAC. Often useful for wines not conforming with AOP rules. Try off-dry SAUV BL from ★★ DOM d'en Segur and the Lou Bio range from VIGNES de Garbasses.

Côtes du Vivarais S Rh r p w ★ 12 13 Mostly DYA. Across hilly Ardèche country w of Montélimar. Definite improvement: quaffable wines based on GRENACHE, SYRAH; some more sturdy, oak-aged reds. NB: Gallety (best), Mas de Bagnols, VIGNERONS de Ruoms (many wines, value).

Coulée de Serrant Lo w dr sw ★★★ 95 96 97 98 99 02 03 04 05 07 08 10' 11 12 13 (14) Historic, steep CHENIN BL monopole 7-ha v'yd in heart of AC SAVENNIÈRES. Wines have been below par, better now daughter Virginie Joly in charge. Don't chill; decant well in advance. Old vintages can be v. fine.

Courcel, Dom de C d'O r ★★★ Leading POMMARD estate, fine floral wines with whole-bunch vinification. Top PREMIERS CRUS Rugiens and Epenots, plus interesting Croix Noires. Wines age well.

Crémant In CHAMP, meant "creaming" (half-sparkling): now called *demi-mousse/*

perle. Since 1975, AC for quality classic-method sparkling from AL, B'X, BOURGOGNE, Die, Jura, LIMOUX, Lo and Luxembourg.

Crépy Sav w ★★ DYA. Light, soft, Swiss-style white from s shore of Lake Geneva. *Crépitant* has been coined for its faint fizz.

Criots-Bâtard-Montrachet C d'O ★★★ 02' 04 05 06 07 08 09 10 11 12 13 14' Tiniest of the MONTRACHET family, just 1.57 ha. Not quite the concentration of full-blown BÂTARD, but pure, sensual at best: try Belland, Blain-GAGNARD, Fontaine G.

Crozes-Hermitage N Rh r w ★★→★★★ 05' 07 09' 10' 11' 12' 13' 14 SYRAH from (mainly) flat v'yds nr river Isère, also granite hills beside HERMITAGE; lively, dark-berry fruit, liquorice, tar; mostly early-drinking (2–5 yrs). Best (simple CUVÉES) ideal for grills, parties. Some oaked, older-vine wines cost more. Top: Belle, Y Chave, CH Curson, Darnaud, DOMS Les Bruyères (big fruit), du Colombier, Combier (organic), Dumaine (organic), des Entrefaux (oak), Fayolle Fils & Fille (stylish), *A Graillot*, Hauts-Chassis, Lises (fine), Mucyn, de Thalabert of JABOULET, *Chapoutier, Delas* (Tour d'Albon, Le CLOS v.gd). Drink white (MARSANNE) early, v.gd vintages recently. Value.

Cuve close Short-cut method of making sparkling wine in a tank. Sparkle dies away in glass much quicker than with *méthode traditionnelle* wine.

Cuvée Wine contained in a *cuve* or vat. A word of many uses, incl synonym for "blend" and first-press wines (as in CHAMP). Often just refers to a "lot" of wine.

Dagueneau, Didier Lo w ★★★→★★★★ 02 03 04 05' 07 08' 09' 10 11 12 13 (14) Best producer of POUILLY-FUMÉ, reference for brilliantly precise SAUV BL. Meticulous son Louis-Benjamin and daughter Charlotte succeeded Didier. Cleanliness paramount in stunning winery. Top CUVÉES: Pur Sang, Silex. Also SANCERRE – Les Monts Damnés (CHAVIGNOL) – and JURANÇON.

Dauvissat, Vincent Chab w ★★★★ Imperturbable bio producer of great classic CHAB from old barrels, esp local 132-litre *feuillettes*. Age-worthy wines similar to his RAVENEAU cousins. Best: Les Forêts, Séchet, Preuses, Les CLOS. Try also Fabien D.

Degré alcoolique Degrees of alcohol, ie. % by volume (%ABV).

Deiss, Dom Marcel Al r w ★★★ Bio grower at Bergheim. Favours blended wines from individual v'yds, often different varieties co-planted, mixed success. Best wine RIES Schoenenbourg 08 10 12 14'.

Delamotte Champ BRUT; *Blanc de Blancs* 02 04 06 08; CUVÉE Nicholas Delamotte. Fine small CHARD-dominated CHAMP house at LE MESNIL. V.gd *saignée* rosé. Managed with SALON by LAURENT-PERRIER. Called "the poor man's Salon" but sometimes surpasses it, as in 85 02 04.

Delas Frères N Rh r p w ★→★★★ Swiss watch consistency from N Rh v'yd owner/merchant, with CONDRIEU, CROZES-HERMITAGE, CÔTE-RÔTIE, HERMITAGE v'yds. Best: Condrieu (CLOS Boucher), *Côte-Rôtie Landonne*, Hermitage DOM des Tourettes (r), M de la Tourette (w), Les Bessards (r, terroir, v. fine, smoky, long life). S Rh: esp VACQUEYRAS Dom des Genêts (r), C D RH St-Esprit (r). Whites lighter recently. Owned by ROEDERER.

Demi-sec Half-dry: in practice more like half-sweet (eg. of CHAMP).

Derenoncourt, Stéphane B'x Leading international consultant; self-taught, focused on terroir, fruit, balance. Own property, *Dom de l'A* in Castillon.

Deutz Champ BRUT Classic and Rosé NV; Brut 04 06 07. Top-flight CHARD CUVÉE Amour de Deutz 04 06 08; new Amour de Deutz Rosé 06. One of top small CHAMP houses, ROEDERER-owned. V. dry, classic wines. *Superb Cuvée William Deutz* 02. Careful buyer in top GRAND CRU sites.

Dirler-Cadé, Dom Al Excellent estate in Bergholtz. Exceptional old-vines MUSCAT GRAND CRU Saering, depth and sculpted elegance 08 12 14.

Domaine (Dom) Property, particularly in Burg and rural France. *See* under name, eg. TEMPIER, DOM.

FRANCE

Dom Pérignon Champ Superb 02', gd 03 (a surprise), 04 06 08'; Rosé 02 04 06 08' 12'. Luxury CUVÉE of MOËT & CHANDON. Ultra-*consistent quality*, creamy character, esp with 10–15 yrs bottle age; v. tight in youth. Oenotèque (long bottle-age, recent disgorgement) now renamed Plenitude; 7, 16, 30 yrs+ (P1, 2, 3 respectively): superb P2 98, P3 70.

Dopff au Moulin Al w ★★★ Ancient, top-class family producer. Poised class in GEWURZ GRANDS CRUS Brand, Sporen 10' 11 12 13 14; lovely RIES SCHOENENBOURG 10' 12 13' 14; *Sylvaner de Riquewihr*. Pioneers of Alsace CRÉMANT; gd CUVÉES: Bartholdi, Julien. Specialist in classic dry wines, now again in fashion.

Dourthe, Vins & Vignobles B'x Sizeable merchant and grower; wide range and quality emphasis: gd, notably CHX BELGRAVE, LE BOSCQ, LA GARDE. Grand Barrail Lamarzelle Figeac improving ST-ÉM. PEY LA TOUR, *Dourthe No 1* (esp white) are well-made generic B'x, reliable quality.

Drappier, André Champ Great family-run AUBE CHAMP house. *Pinot-led NV*, BRUT ZÉRO, Brut *sans souffre* (no sulphur) ★★, Millésime d'Exception 04 06 08 09, superb Prestige CUVÉE Grande Sendrée 06 09'. Cuvée Quatuor (four *cépages*). Superb older vintages 95 85 82 (magnums).

DRC C d'O The wine geek's shorthand for DOM DE LA ROMANÉE-CONTI.

Drouhin, Joseph & Cie Burg r w ★★★→★★★★ Deservedly prestigious BEAUNE grower/ merchant; v'yds (all bio) incl (w) Beaune *Clos des Mouches*, LAGUICHE MONTRACHET. Notably fragrant reds from pretty CHOREY-LÈS-BEAUNE to majestic *Musigny*, GRANDS-ÉCHÉZEAUX, etc. Also DDO (Dom Drouhin Oregon), *see* United States.

Duboeuf, Georges Beauj r w ★★→★★★ Most famous name of BEAUJ, architect of worldwide Nouveau craze. Huge range of CUVÉES and crus, plus MÂCON whites.

Dugat C d'O r ★★★ Cousins Claude and Bernard (Dugat-Py) make excellent, deep-coloured GEVREY-CHAMBERTIN, respective labels. Tiny volumes, esp GRANDS CRUS, huge prices, esp Dugat-Py.

Dujac, Dom C d'O r w ★★★→★★★★ MORFY-ST-DENIS grower; exceptional range of seven GRANDS CRUS, esp CLOS ST DENIS, CLOS DE LA ROCHE, ÉCHÉZEAUX. Lighter colours but intense fruit, smoky, strawberry character from use of stems. Slightly deeper, denser wines in recent years. Also DOM Triennes in COTEAUX VAROIS.

Dureuil-Janthial Burg r w ★★ Top DOM in RULLY in capable hands of Vincent D-J, with *fresh, punchy whites* and cheerful, juicy reds. Try Maizières (r w) or PREMIER CRU Meix Cadot (w).

Durup, Jean Chab w ★★ Volume CHAB producer as DOM de l'Eglantière and CH de Maligny, now allied by marriage to Dom Colinot in IRANCY.

Duval-Leroy Champ Dynamic Côte des Blancs CHAMP house. Family-owned v'yds; source of gd, crowd-pleasing Fleur de Champagne NV, fine Blanc de CHARD 04 06 08, excellent Prestige *Femme* 96' 04. New single-village/-v'yd bottlings, esp Authentis Cumières 04 06 09 11 12'.

Échézeaux C d'O r ★★★ 90' 93 96' 99' 02' 03 05' 06 07 08 09' 10' 11 12' 13 14 GRAND CRU next to CLOS DE VOUGEOT. Middling weight, but can have exceptionally intricate flavours and startling persistence. Best from Arnoux, DRC, DUJAC, EUGÉNIE, GRIVOT, GROS, Lamarche, LIGER-BELAIR, Mongeard-MUGNERET, MUGNERET-Gibourg, ROUGET, Tremblay.

Ecu, Dom de l' Lo (r) w dr (sp) ★★★ 09' 10' 11 12 13 14' Fine bio MUSCADET-SÈVRE-ET-MAINE (esp CUVÉE Granite), GROS PLANT. Dynamic Niger Van Herck with Guy Bossard semi-retired. Gd CAB FR, PINOT N. Park of amphorae.

Edelzwicker Al w ★ DYA. Blended light white. CH d'Ittenwiller, HUGEL Gentil are gd.

Eguisheim, Cave Vinicole d' Al r w ★★ Impeccable AL co-op. Excellent value: fine GRANDS CRUS Hatschbourg, HENGST, Ollwiller, Spiegel. Owns Willm. Top label: WOLFBERGER. Best: Grande Rés 09 10 11 12, Sigillé, Armorié. Gd CRÉMANT, PINOT N (esp 10' 11).

Émile Boeckel, Dom Al Long-est estate in picture-postcard Mittelbergheim, with exemplary mineral wines. Great RIES esp Clos Eugénie 05 10', also GRAND CRU Zotzenberg SYLVANER 12, zesty complexity and class.

Entraygues et du Fel and Estaing SW Fr r p w ★→★★ DYA. Tiny twin AOPS in wildest Aveyron. Ice-cool tingling CHENIN whites mostly best. ★★ DOM Méjanassère, richer from ★★ Nicolas Carmarans now making AOP incl reds from FER SERVADOU. Laurent Mousset for reds esp ★★ La Pauca and excellent rosé.

Entre-Deux-Mers (E-2-M) B'x w ★→★★ DYA. Often gd-value, dry white B'x from between the rivers Garonne and Dordogne. Best CHX BONNET, Castenet Greffier, Fontenille, Haut-Rion, Landereau, Lestrille, Marjosse, La Mothe du Barry French Kiss, Nardique-la-Gravière, Ste-Marie, *Tour de Mirambeau*, Turcaud.

Esmonin, Dom Sylvie C d'O r ★★★ Rich, dark wines from fully ripe grapes, esp since 2000. Lots of oak and lots of stems. Notable GEVREY-CHAMBERTIN VIEILLES VIGNES, CLOS ST-JACQUES. Cousin Frédéric has Estournelles St-Jacques.

Eugénie, Dom C d'O r (w) ★★★→★★★★ Formerly DOM Engel, bought by François Pinault of CH LATOUR in 2006. Now impressive wines at ditto prices. CLOS VOUGEOT, GRANDS-ÉCHÉZEAUX best.

Faiveley, J Burg r w ★★→★★★★ More grower than merchant, making succulent and richly fruity wines since sea-change in 2007. Gd value from CÔTE CHALONNAISE, but save up for top wines from CHAMBERTIN-CLOS DE BÈZE, CHAMBOLLE-MUSIGNY, CORTON, NUITS. Ambitious recent acquisitions throughout C D'O and now DOM Billaud-Simon in CHAB.

Old vineyard tracks in Alsace usually follow geological fault lines.

Faller, Théo / Weinbach, Dom Al w ★★★→★★★★ Founded by Capuchin monks in 1612. Laurence Faller, who died young in 2014, made wines of great complexity: often drier, esp GRANDS CRUS SCHLOSSBERG (RIES, esp 08 10'). Wines of great *character and elegance*. Esp CUVÉE Ste Catherine SÉLECTION DES GRAINS NOBLE Gewurz 05 09 10. Sister Catherine and her son now at helm.

Faugères L'doc r (p) (w) ★→★★★ 08 09' 10 11 12 13 14 Leading L'DOC AC and cru. Driven by individuality of schist soil. Spicy reds from SYRAH, GRENACHE, CARIGNAN, plus MOURVÈDRE, CINSAULT, grown only on schist hillsides; whites from Grenache, MARSANNE, ROUSSANNE, Rolle. Energetic AC with much outside investment. Drink DOMS JEAN-MICHEL ALQUIER, Léon Barral, des Trinités, St Antonin, OLLIER-TAILLEFER, Cébène, Mas d'Alezon, Chenaie, Chaberts, Sarabande.

Fèvre, William Chab w ★★★ Biggest owner of CHAB GRANDS CRUS; Bougros and Les CLOS outstanding. Small yields, no expense spared, priced accordingly, a top source for concentrated, age-worthy wines.

Fiefs Vendéens Lo r p w ★→★★★ 09 10 13 (14) Mainly DYA AC. Wines from the Vendée nr Sables d'Olonne, from tourist wines to serious and age-worthy. CHARD, CHENIN BL, SAUV BL, MELON (whites), Grolleau Gris, CAB FR, CAB SAUV, GAMAY, Negrette, PINOT N (r p). Producers: Coirier, Mourat (122 ha), Prieure-la-Chaume, DOM St-Nicolas (bio). Promising 2014.

Fitou L'doc r ★★ 08 09 10 11 12 13 14 Powerful, rugged red from hills s of Narbonne as well as tamer coastal v'yds. The MIDI's oldest AC for table wine, created in 1948. 11 mths' barrel-ageing, benefits from bottle-age. Seek out CH de Nouvelles, DOM Bergé-Bertrand, Jones, Lérys, Maria Fita, Rolland.

Fixin C d'O r (w) ★★★ 99' 02' 03 05' 06 07 08 09' 10' 11 12' 13 14 Worthy and undervalued n neighbour of GEVREY-CHAMBERTIN. Sometimes splendid reds. Best v'yds: CLOS de la Perrière, Clos du Chapitre, Clos Napoléon. Growers: Bart, CLAIR, FAIVELEY, Gelin, Guyard, MORTET and revitalized Manoir de la Perrière.

Fleurie Beauj r ★★★ 11' 12 13' 14 Top BEAUJ cru for perfumed, strawberry fruit, silky texture. Racier from La Madone hillside, richer below. Look for Balagny,

Chapelle des Bois, Chignard, CLOS de la Roilette, Depardon, Desprès, DUBOEUF, CH de Fleurie, Métrat, Sunier, Villa Ponciago, co-op.

Fourrier, Jean-Claude C d'O r ★★★★ In the hands of Jean-Marie Fourrier this GEVREY-CHAMBERTIN DOM has reached cult status, prices to match. Profound yet succulent reds, esp Combe aux Moines, CLOS ST-JACQUES, GRIOTTE-CHAMBERTIN.

Francs-Côtes de Bordeaux B'x r w ★★ 05' 08 09' 10' 12 (14) Tiny B'X AC next to CASTILLON. Previously Côtes de Francs. Fief of the Thienpont (PAVIE-MACQUIN) family. Mainly red but some gd white: can be tasty. Reds can age a little. Top CHX: Charmes-Godard, Francs, Laclaverie, Marsau, Pelan, La Prade, *Puygueraud*.

Fronsac B'x r ★★→★★★ 03 05' 06 08 09' 10' 11 12 (14) Underrated hilly AC w of ST-ÉM; great-value MERLOT-dominated reds. Top CH: DALEM, *la Dauphine*, Fontenil, la Grave, Haut-Ballet, Haut-Carles, Mayne-Vieil, *Moulin-Haut-Laroque*, Richelieu, la Rivière, la Rousselle, Tour du Moulin, LES TROIS CROIX, LA VIEILLE CURE, Villars. *See also* CANON-FRONSAC.

Fronton SW Fr r p ★★ 12' 14 AOP, "the Beaujolais of Toulouse". Nr-exclusivity for Négrette grape (sometimes 100%) suggesting violets, cherries, liquorice. Try ★★ CHX Baudare, *Bellevue-la-Forêt*, *Bouissel*, Boujac, Caze, du Roc, Plaisance (esp Alabets), DOMS des Pradelles, Viguerie de Belaygues. IGP whites not (yet) AOP.

Fuissé, Ch Burg w ★★→★★★ A leader in POUILLY-FUISSÉ with some grand terroirs (Le CLOS, Combettes) and some more commercial bottlings.

Gagnard C d'O r w ★★★→★★★★ A well-known clan in CHASSAGNE-MONTRACHET. Long-lasting, esp Caillerets, BÂTARD from Jean-Noël G; while Blain-G, Fontaine G have full range incl rare CRIOTS-BÂTARD and MONTRACHET. Gd value offered by all Gagnards.

Gaillac SW Fr r p w dr sw sp ★→★★★ (r) 11 12 14 (w sw) 09 10 11' 12 (p w dr sp) DYA. AOP w of Albi. Where else do you find grapes like Duras, Braucol, Len de l'El, Mauzac? Large eclectic range of wines from ★★★ *Plageoles*, Causse-Marines, de la Ramaye, Peyres-Roses, Stéphane Lucas (all bio), ★★ L'Enclos des Roses, DOMS Brin, d'Escausses, de la Valière, du Moullin, Laubarel, Mayragues (bio), Rotier, Sarrabelle, CHX Bourguet (w sw), Larroque, Palvié (r). Bargains from ★★ Mas Pignou, Doms La Chanade, Duffau, Lamothe.

Gauby, Dom Gérard Rouss r w ★★★ Leading innovative ROUSS producer to watch; bio. While IGP CÔTES CATALANES, eg. Les Calcinaires; red CÔTES DU ROUSS-VILLAGES Muntada; Les Calcinaires VIEILLES VIGNES. Associated with DOM Le Soula. Dessert wine Le Pain du Sucre. Inspiration to other newcomers.

Gers SW Fr r p w ★ DYA IGP usually sold as CÔTES DE GASCOGNE; indistinguishable.

Gevrey-Chambertin C d'O r ★★★ 90' 96' 99' 02' 03 05' 06 07 08 09' 10' 11 12' 13 14 Village containing the great CHAMBERTIN, its GRAND CRU cousins and many other noble v'yds eg. PREMIERS CRUS Cazetiers, Combe aux Moines, Combettes, CLOS ST-JACQUES. Succulent fruit with a savoury edge, these days more consistent. Top growers: BACHELET, L BOILLOT, BURGUET, Damoy, DROUHIN, Drouhin-Laroze, DUGAT, Dugat-Py, Duroché, ESMONIN, FAIVELEY, FOURRIER, Géantet-Pansiot, Harmand-Geoffroy, JADOT, LEROY, MORTET, ROSSIGNOL-TRAPET, Roty, ROUSSEAU, SÉRAFIN, TRAPET.

Gigondas S Rh r p ★★→★★★ 78' 89' 90' 95' 98' 99' 00' 01' 03' 04' 05' 06' 07 08 09' 10' 11 12' 13' Top S Rh red. V'yds on stony clay-sand plain rise to Alpine, limestone hills e of Avignon; GRENACHE, plus SYRAH, MOURVÈDRE. Robust, smoky, often cool wines, best offer fine, clear, dark-red fruit. Ace 2010s. More oak recently, esp for US market, higher prices, but genuine local feel in many. Top: CH de Montmirail, St-Cosme (swish), CLOS du Joncuas (organic, traditional), P Amadieu, DOM Boissan, Bouïssière (punchy), Brusset, Cayron, Espiers (fruit), Goubert, Gour de Chaulé (fine), Grapillon d'Or, Moulin de la Gardette, *les Pallières*, Pesquier, *Raspail-Ay*, Roubine, St Gayan (long-lived), Santa Duc, *Famille Perrin*. Heady rosés.

Girardin, Vincent C d'O r w ★★→★★★ Top Meursault DOM. Vincent has left, but business continues as before under BOISSET ownership; same winemaking. Sound, polished whites; competent reds.

Givry Burg r (w) ★★ 09' 10' 11 12 13 14 Top tip in CÔTE CHALONNAISE for tasty reds that can age. Better value than MERCUREY. Rare whites nutty in style. Best (r): JOBLOT, CLOS Salomon, *Faiveley*, F Lumpp, Masse, THÉNARD.

Gosset Champ Old AŸ house founded in 16th century, for complex CHAMP in vinous style. Now moved to Épernay. V.gd CUVÉE Elegance NV more racy. Traditional Grand Millésime 02 04 08 12'. Gosset Celebris 08 09 is finest cuvée. Remarkable Celebris Rosé 09.

Gouges, Henri C d'O r w ★★★ Grégory Gouges continues family success with rich, meaty, long-lasting NUITS-ST-GEORGES from several PREMIER CRU v'yds. Try Vaucrains, Les St-Georges or Chaignots. Interesting white too.

Grand Cru Official term neaning different things in different areas. One of top Burg v'yds with its own AC. In ALSACE, one of 51 top v'yds, each now with its own rules. In ST-ÉM, 60 per cent of production is St-Ém Grand Cru, often run-of-the-mill. In MÉD there are five tiers of *grands crus classés*. In CHAMP top 17 villages are *grand cru*. Now a new designation in Lo for QUARTS DE CHAUME, and an emerging system in L'DOC. Take with pinch of salt in PROV.

Grande Champagne SW Fr AC of the best area of Cognac. Nothing fizzy about it.

Grande Rue, La C d'O r ★★★ 90' 95 96' 98 02' 03 05' 06 07 08 09' 10' 11 12' 13 14 We are starting to see the best of this narrow strip of GRAND CRU between LA TÂCHE and ROMANÉE-CONTI. Not quite in same league, certainly not same price. MONOPOLE of DOM Lamarche.

Grands-Échézeaux C d'O r ★★★★ 90' 93 95 96' 99' 00 02' 03 05' 06 07 08 09' 10' 11 12' 13 14 Superlative GRAND CRU next to CLOS DE VOUGEOT, may be more akin to MUSIGNY. Wines not weighty but aromatic. Viz BICHOT (CLOS Frantin), DRC, DROUHIN, EUGÉNIE, GROS, Lamarche, Mongeard-MUGNERET.

Grange des Pères, Dom de la L'doc r w ★★★ IGP Pays l'Hérault. Cult estate neighbouring MAS DE DAUMAS GASSAC, created by Laurent Vaillé for first vintage (1992). Red from SYRAH, MOURVÈDRE, CAB SAUV; white 80% ROUSSANNE, plus MARSANNE, CHARD. Stylish wines with ageing potential; well worth seeking out.

Salmanazar of Champagne (9 litres/12 bottles) weighs 20 kg: 10 kg glass, 10 kg wine.

Gratien, Alfred and Gratien & Meyer Champ ★★→★★★ BRUT 83' 97 02 04 07 08'; BRUT NV. Superb Prestige CUVÉE Paradis Brut, Rosé (multi-vintage). Excellent quirky CHAMP and Lo house, now German-owned. Fine, v.-dry, lasting, oak-fermented wines, incl *The Wine Society's house Champagne*. Careful buyer of top crus from favourite growers for many yrs. Gratien & Meyer is counterpart at SAUMUR.

Graves B'x r w ★→★★ 04 05' 06 08 09' 10' 11 12 (14) Region s of B'x city. Juicy, appetizing reds and fresh SAUV/SÉM dry whites. Gd value. Top CHX: ARCHAMBEAU, Auney l'Hermitage, Brondelle, CHANTEGRIVE, *Clos Floridène*, CRABITEY, Ferrande, Fougères, Haura, Léhoul, Magneau, Rahoul, Respide, *Respide-Médeville*, St-Robert CUVÉE Poncet Deville, Toumilon, Venus, Vieux Ch Gaubert, Villa Bel Air. Best zone is now PE-LÉ.

Graves de Vayres B'x r w ► DYA. Tiny AC in E-2-M zone. Mainly red, drunk locally.

Grignan-les-Adhémar S Rh r (p) w ★→★★ 10' 12' Mid-Rh AC; limited quality spread; best reds hearty, tangy, herbal. Leaders: DOMS de Bonetto-Fabrol, Grangeneuve best (esp VIEILLES VIGNES), de Montine (stylish red, gd white), St-Luc, CH La Décelle (incl white CÔTES DU RH).

Griotte-Chambertin C d'O r ★★★★ 90' 95 96' 99' 02' 03 05' 06 07 08 09' 10' 11 12' 13 14 Small GRAND CRU next to CHAMBERTIN. Less weight but brisk red fruit and ageing potential, at least from DUGAT, DROUHIN, FOURRIER, R Leclerc, *Ponsot*.

FRANCE

Grivot, Jean C d'O r w ★★★→★★★★ Huge improvements at this VOSNE-ROMANÉE DOM in past decade, reflected in higher prices. Superb range topped by GRANDS CRUS CLOS DE VOUGEOT, ÉCHÉZEAUX, RICHEBOURG.

Gros, Doms C d'O r w ★★★→★★★★ Fine family of VIGNERONS in VOSNE-ROMANÉE with stylish wines from Anne (sumptuous RICHEBOURG), succulent reds from Michel (CLOS de Réas), much improved Anne-Françoise (now in BEAUNE) and Gros Frère & Soeur (CLOS VOUGEOT En Musigni). Most offer value HAUTES-CÔTES DE NUITS. Anne has a stake in CORBIÈRES.

Gros Plant du Pays Nantais Lo w (sp) ★→★★ DYA. Improved AC from GROS PLANT (FOLLE BLANCHE), best crisply citric: gd with oysters, shellfish. Try: Basse Ville, Ecu, Luneau-Papin, Preuille, Poiron-Dabin. Also sparkling: either pure or blended.

Guigal, Ets E N Rh r w ★★→★★★★ Famous grower-merchant: CÔTE-RÔTIE at heart, plus CONDRIEU, CROZES-HERMITAGE, HERMITAGE, ST-JOSEPH v'yds. Merchant: CONDRIEU, Côte-Rôtie, Crozes-Hermitage, Hermitage, S Rh. Owns DOM de Bonserine, VIDAL-FLEURY (fruit, quality rising). Top, v. expensive Côte-Rôties La Mouline, La Landonne, La Turque (deep, rich, new oak for 42 mths, so atypical); all reds dense. Standard wines: gd top-value CÔTES DU RH (r p w). Best whites: Condrieu, Condrieu La Doriane (oaky), Hermitage.

Hautes-Côtes de Beaune / Nuits C d'O r w ★★ (r) 09' 10' 12 13 14 (w) 12' 13 14' ACS for the villages in the hills behind the CÔTE DE BEAUNE/NUITS. Attractive lighter reds, whites for early drinking. Best whites: Devevey, Montchovet, MÉO-CAMUZET, Thevenot-le-Brun. Top reds: Carré, Cornu, Duband, Féry, GROS, Jacob, Jouan, Magnien, Mazilly, Naudin-Ferrand, Verdet. Also useful large co-op nr BEAUNE.

Haut-Médoc B'x r ★★→★★★★ 01 02 03 04 05' 06 08 09' 10' 11 12 (14) Prime source of minerally, digestible CAB/MERLOT reds. Some variation in soils and wines: sand and gravel in s; heavier clay and gravel in n; sturdier wines. All need age. Five classed growths (BELGRAVE, CAMENSAC, CANTEMERLE, LA LAGUNE, LA TOUR-CARNET). Other top CHX: D'AGASSAC, BELLE-VUE, CAMBON LA PELOUSE, Charmail, CISSAC, CITRAN, Clément-Pichon, COUFRAN, Gironville, LANESSAN, Larose Perganson, Paloumey, SÉNÉJAC, SOCIANDO-MALLET.

Haut-Montravel SW Fr w sw ★★ 09 10 11' 12 (14) Sweet end of Montravel. Fine stickies from ★★★ CH Puy-Servain-Terrement, ★★ DOMS Moulin Caresse and bargain Libarde rank alongside best from better-known MONBAZILLAC, SAUSSIGNAC.

Haut-Poitou Lo r p w sp ★→★★ Top age 3–4 yrs. AC n of Poitiers from CAB SAUV, CAB FR, GAMAY, CHARD, PINOT N, SAUV BL. CAVE du Haut-Poitou was largest producer, now bust, run by *dynamic Ampelidae* (Frédéric Brochet). IGP wines from 107 ha.

Heidsieck, Charles Legendary CHAMP house, smaller than before, but wines as fine as ever in spite of early death of ace cellarmaster; BRUT Rés all toasty elegance, Peerless *Blanc des Millénaires* 95' still perfect. Fine 05 08 12'. *See* PIPER-HEIDSIECK.

Heidsieck Monopole Once great CHAMP house. Fair quality, gd price. Gold Top 07 09. Part of VRANKEN group.

Hengst AL GRAND CRU. Gives powerful wines. Excels with top GEWURZ from ZIND-HUMBRECHT, JOSMEYER; AUXERROIS, CHASSELAS, PINOT N (latter not yet *grand cru*).

Henriot Champ BRUT Souverain NV much improved; ace BLANC DE BLANCS de CHARD NV; Brut 04 06 08'; Brut Rosé 06 09. Fine family CHAMP house. New long-aged Cuve 38, a solera (*see* Sherry) of GRAND CRU Chard since 1990. Outstanding long-lived Prestige CUVÉE Les Enchanteleurs 88' 95' 02 04 08'. Also owns BOUCHARD PÈRE & FILS, FÈVRE, Villa Ponciago (BEAUJ).

Hermitage N Rh r w ★★★→★★★★ 61' 66' 78' 83' 85' 88 89' 90' 91' 95' 96 97' 98' 99' 00 01' 03' 04 05' 06' 07' 09' 10' 11' 12' 13' 14 Robust, "manly" SYRAH from striking granite hill on e bank of river Rhône. Red, white both develop well over 20 yrs+. 2010, 12 both v.gd. Complex, nutty/white-fruited, fascinating white (MARSANNE, some ROUSSANNE) best left for 6–7 yrs+. Best: Belle, *Chapoutier, J-L Chave* (rich, elegant), Colombier, DELAS, Faurie (pure wines), GUIGAL, Habrard (w), *Jaboulet*, M Sorrel, Tardieu-Laurent (oak). TAIN co-op gd (esp Epsilon, Gambert de Loche).

Hortus, Dom de l' L'doc r w ★★★ Leading PIC ST-LOUP producer. Stylish white IGP Val de Montferrand; elegant reds Bergerie and oak-aged Grande Rés. Also red CLOS du Prieur in TERRASSES DU LARZAC.

Hospices de Beaune C d'O Spectacular medieval foundation with grand charity auction 3rd Sunday in Nov, run since 2005 by Christie's. Individuals can buy as well as trade. Standards more consistent under Roland Masse; Ludivine Griveau takes over in 2015. Look for BEAUNE CUVÉES, VOLNAYS or expensive GRANDS CRUS, eg. (r) CORTON, ÉCHÉZEAUX (new in 2013), (w) BÂTARD-MONTRACHET.

Hudelot C d'O r w ★★★ VIGNERON family in CÔTE DE NUITS. New life breathed into H-Noëllat (VOUGEOT), while H-Baillet (CHAMBOLLE) challenging hard. Former more stylish, latter more punchy.

Huet Lo w ★★★★ 89' 90' 95' 96' 97' 02' 03' 05' 06 07 08' 09' 10' 11 13 (14) VOUVRAY bio estate. Anthony Hwang (owner) plus Királyudvar in Tokaji (*see* Central & SE Europe). Three single v'yds: Le Haut Lieu, Le Mont, CLOS du Bourg. Great agers: look for vintages such as 1919, 21, 24, 47, 59, 89, 90. Also *pétillant*. CHENIN BL benchmark. Disappointing 2012; on track 13.

Growers' entries in this book are multiplying as their wines get better and better.

Hugel & Fils Al r w sw ★★→★★★ Top AL house at Riquewihr famed for late-harvest wines: **09** both RIES VENDANGE TARDIVE and SÉLECTION DE GRAINS NOBLES. Fine GEWURZ Vendange Tardive **07**. Classy dry Ries **10**. Always elegant acidity.

Indication Géographique Protegée / IGP The successor to VDQS. No difference in status, only in unhelpful name.

Irancy Burg r (p) ★★ 05' 09' 10 12 14' Light red, made nr CHAB from PINOT N and local César. Best v'yds: Palotte, Mazelots. Best growers: *Colinot*, DAUVISSAT, Renaud, Richoux, Goisot.

Irouléguy SW Fr r p (w) ★→★★★ 10 11' 12 (14) Basque AOP. Reds from TANNAT/CAB FR and full-bodied whites from Petit Courbu join large production of rosés, which help cash-flow of growers like ★★★ Arretxea, Mourguy, Ameztia, ★★ Brana, Etchegaraya, Ilarria, ★ Abotia, Bordathio, Gutizia. Excellent co-op (esp ★★★ Xuri d'Ansa white).

Jaboulet Aîné, Paul N Rh r w Owner-merchant founded 1834 at Tain, sold to Swiss investor 2006, prices rose, wines now polished, international. Once-leading producer of HERMITAGE (esp La Chapelle ★★★★, quality varied from 90s on, some revival 2010 on), CORNAS St-Pierre, CROZES Thalabert, Roure (sound); owns DOM de Terre Ferme CHÂTEAUNEUF, merchant of other Rh, notably CÔTES DU RH *Parallèle 45*, CONDRIEU, VENTOUX (r, quality/value), VACQUEYRAS. Whites lack proper Rh body, drink most young, range incl new v. expensive La Chapelle white.

Jacquart Champ Simplified range from co-op-turned-brand, concentrating on what it does best: PREMIERS CRUS Côte des Blancs CHARD from member growers. Fine range of Vintage BLANC DE BLANCS **10 08 07 06 05 02** targeted at restaurants. V.gd Vintage Rosé **02 04 06**. Globetrotting new winemaker.

Jacquesson Champ Bijou Dizy house for precise, v. dry wines. Outstanding single-v'yd Avize Champ Caïn **02 04 05 08**'; *saignée* Rosé Terre Rouge **09** – buy now, to be discontinued. Corne Bautray, Dizy **04 08**', excellent *numbered NV cuvées* 728 730' 731 732 733 734 735 736 737.

Jadot, Louis Burg r p w ★★→★★★★ High-performance merchant house across board with significant v'yd holdings in C D'O, MÂCON, BEAUJ; esp POUILLY-FUISSÉ (DOM Ferret), MOULIN-À-VENT (CH des Jacques, *Clos du Grand Carquelin*). New winemaker maintaining same style but some refinement, incl fresher whites.

Jasnières Lo w dr (sw) ★★→★★★ 03 05' 07 08' 09' 10' 11 13 (14) CHENIN BL (dry and off-dry) dynamic AC (65 ha), s-facing slopes in Loir Valley. Growers: L'Ange Vin (also Vin de France), Aubert la Chapelle, DE BELLIVIÈRE, Breton, le Briseau, Gigou, Janvier, les Maisons Rouges, Ryke. 2013 better but small, 14 promising quality.

Jeanjean L'doc ★★ Family company, a big player in L'DOC. Also runs Advini group. Incl Mas Neuf, MUSCAT de Mireval; DOM de Fenouillet, FAUGÈRES; Le Devois des Agneaux and Mas de Lunès, COTEAUX DU L'DOC and now Causse d'Arboras, TERRASSES DU LARZAC.

Jobard C d'O r w ★★★ VIGNERON family in MEURSAULT. Top DOMS are Antoine J, esp long-lived Poruzots, Genevrières, Charmes; and Rémi Jobard for immediately classy Meursaults plus reds from MONTHÉLIE, VOLNAY.

Joblot Burg r w ★★★ Outstanding GIVRY DOM with v. high viticultural standards. Try PREMIER CRU La Servoisine in both colours.

Joseph Perrier Champ Fine family-run CHAMP house with fine PINOTS N, MEUNIER v'yds. Supple, fruity style. Top Prestige CUVÉE Joséphine 02 04 08' 12; now drier, finer Cuvée Royale BRUT NV; distinctive BLANC DE BLANCS 02 04 06 08 13'.

Josmeyer Al w ★★→★★★ Fine, elegant, long-lived, organic dry wines. Superb RIES *grand cru* Hengst 08' 10 12 13' 14. Also v.gd lesser varieties, esp 10 AUXERROIS. Smart bio, rigorous but realistic.

Juliénas Beauj r ★★★ 09' 11' 12 13 14 Rich, hearty BEAUJ, both juicy and structured from surprisingly unfashionable cru. Discover Aufranc, Burrier, Santé, Michel Tête and Trenel.

Jurançon SW Fr w dr sw ★→★★★ (sw) 05' 07' 10 11' 12 (dr) 09 10 11' 12 Separate AOPS for underestimated sw and dr w, characterized by racy balance of acidity and sugar. Dagueneau's tiny ★★★★ Jardins de Babylon respected by larger ★★★ DOMS *Cauhapé*, Lapeyre, Larrédya, de Souch, Thou, ★★ CHX Jolys, Lapuyade, Doms Bellauc, Bellegarde, Bordenave, Capdevielle, Castéra, Guirardel, Nigri, Uroulat, CLOS Benguères. ★ Gd-value Gan co-op produces range of dry whites and single-dom range.

Kaefferkopf Al w dr (sw) ★★★ The 51st GRAND CRU of AL at Ammerschwihr. Permitted to make blends as well as varietal wines, possibly not top-drawer.

Kientzler, André Al w sw ★★ ★★★ Small, v. fine grower at Ribeauvillé. V.gd RIES from GRANDS CRUS Osterberg, Geisberg 06 08 09 10 11 12 13', lush GEWURZ from *grand cru* Kirchberg 05 09 12. Rich, classic sweet wines.

Kreydenweiss, Marc Al w sw ★★→★★★ Fine bio grower, esp for PINOT GR (v.gd GRAND CRU Moenchberg), PINOT BL, RIES. Top wine: *grand cru* Kastelberg, ages 20 yrs+ 89 06 08' 10' 12 13; gd VENDANGE TARDIVE. Use of oak now more subtle. Gd Ries/Pinot Gr blend CLOS du Val d'Eléon. Also in Rh Valley (bio GRENACHE, SYRAH, MOURVÈDRE).

Krug Champ Grande CUVÉE, esp mature Grande Cuvée (*Equilibre*, 2002 base) ★★★★; Vintage 95' 98' 00 03; Rosé; CLOS DU MESNIL 00' 03; Krug Collection 69' 76' 81 85. Supremely prestigious house. Rich, nutty wines, oak-fermented; highest quality, ditto price. ££££ Clos d'Ambonnay 95 96 98. Vintage 03 a fine surprise. No straight vintage in 2012.

Kuentz-Bas Al w sw ★→★★★ Grower-merchant at Husseren-les CHX, esp PINOT GR, GEWURZ. Gd VENDANGES TARDIVES, esp successful in 05 09. Fine classic drier RIES 08 10 11 12 13.

Labet, Dom Jura Welcoming family estate. Expressive wines, esp superb CHARD (Les Varrons, La Bardettes 11). Classic VIN JAUNE and Paille Perdu, sw from straw-dried grapes. New generation in charge.

La Croix Belle, Dom L'doc ★★★ Leading estate of CÔTES DE THONGUE. Stars incl GRENACHE-based Cascaillou; No 7 (7 grape varieties), sw Soulenque.

Ladoix C d'O r w ★★ 02' 03 05' 07 08 09' 10' 11 12 13 14 Village at n end of CÔTE DE BEAUNE, incl some CORTON, CORTON-CHARLEMAGNE. Juicy reds and whites both exuberant and mineral, esp les Joyeuses (r), Gréchons (w). DOMS Chevalier, Loichet, Mallard, Ravaut leading revival.

Ladoucette, de Lo (r) (p) w ★★★ 08 09 10 12 13 (14) Largest individual producer of POUILLY-FUMÉ at CH du Nozet. Expensive deluxe brand Baron de L. SANCERRE Comte Lafond, La Poussie (serious erosion in potentially fine Bué site now under repair); VOUVRAY Marc Brédif, CHAB Albert Pic.

Lafarge, Michel C d'O r ★★★★ Classic VOLNAY bio estate run by Frédéric L, son of ever-present Michel. Outstanding, long-lived PREMIERS CRUS *Clos des Chênes*, Caillerets, CLOS du CH des Ducs. Also fine BEAUNE, esp Grèves and some whites. New FLEURIE project from 2014.

Lafon, Dom des Comtes Burg r w ★★★→★★★★ Iconic DOM for great MEURSAULT, MONTRACHET, with red VOLNAY (esp *Santenots*) equally outstanding. Try separate Mâconnais dom for value, while Dominique L also has own label in MEURSAULT.

Laguiche, Marquis de C d'O r w ★★★★ Largest owner of Le MONTRACHET and a fine PREMIER CRU CHASSAGNE, both excellently made by DROUHIN.

Lalande de Pomerol B'x r ★★ 01' 04 05' 06 08 09' 10' 11 12 (14) Variable satellite neighbour of POM. Similar style but less density. Follow the top growers. Top CHX: Ame de Musset, Belles-Graves, BERTINEAU ST-VINCENT, Chambrun, Les Cruzelles, La Fleur de Boüard, Garraud, Grand Ormeau, Jean de Gué, Haut-Chaigneau, *Les Hauts Conseillants*, Laborderie-Mondésir, Perron (La Fleur), Sabines, La Sergue, Siaurac, TOURNEFEUILLE.

Landron, Doms Lo w dr sp ★★→★★★ 09 10 11 12 13 (14) Mustachioed producer (46 ha) of bio MUSCADET-SÈVRE-ET-MAINE: Amphibolite, age-worthy Fief du Breil. Gd sparkling GROS PLANT/PINOT N.

Langlois-Château Lo (r w) sp ★★→★★★ Fine CRÉMANT de Lo, BOLLINGER-owned, SAUMUR based. Still wines, esp v.gd age-worthy Saumur Blanc VIEILLES VIGNES 05 08.

Languedoc r p w General term for MIDI, often linked with ROUSS. Now AC enlarging COTEAUX DU L'DOC to incl MINERVOIS, CORBIÈRES and also Rouss. Rules same as for Coteaux du L'doc, with period for name-changing extended to May 2017. Bottom of pyramid of Midi ACs. Hierarchy of superior crus is work in progress.

Lanson Champ Black Label NV; Rosé NV; ace BRUT 02' 04 06 08' 12 13. Improving CHAMP house, part of LANSON-BCC group. Long-lived luxury Noble CUVÉE BLANC DE BLANCS, rosé and vintage; Brut vintage real value. Single-vyd CLOS Lanson 08 09. Extra Age multi-vintage, Blanc de B esp gd. Change of cellar guard as J-P Gandron retires.

Lapierre, Marcel Beauj r ★★★ Mathieu runs cult DOM making sulphur-free MORGON, as pioneered by the late Marcel L. Try also fresh, juicy Raisins Gaulois.

Laroche Chab w ★★ Large-scale CHAB grower and merchant with interests in s of France, Chile, South Africa. Majority owner now Groupe JEANJEAN. GRAND CRU *Réserve de l'Obédiencerie* is ★★★+.

Latour, Louis Burg r w ★★→★★★ Famous traditional family merchant making full-bodied whites from C d'O v'yds (esp CORTON-CHARLEMAGNE), Mâconnais, Ardèche (all CHARD) and less exciting reds (all PINOT) from C d'Or, Coteaux du Verdon. Also owns Henry Fessy in BEAUJ.

Latricières-Chambertin C d'O r ★★★ 90' 93 95 96' 99' 02' 03 05' 06 07 08 09' 10' 11 12' 13 14 GRAND CRU next to CHAMBERTIN, rich if not quite as intense. Best from BIZE, Drouhin-Laroze, Duband, FAIVELEY, LEROY, Remy, ROSSIGNOL-TRAPET, TRAPET.

Laudun S Rh r p w ★→★★ 10' 11' 12' 13 Front rank CÔTES DU RH-VILLAGE, w bank. Excellent, dashing whites. Early, red fruit/peppery reds (lots of SYRAH), lively rosés. Immediate flavours from CHUSCLAN-Laudun co-op. *Dom Pelaquié* best, esp stylish white. Also CHX de Bord, Courac, Juliette, Marjolet, St-Maurice, DOM Duseigneur (bio), Prieuré St-Pierre.

Laurent-Perrier Champ Important CHAMP house; family presence less obvious now. BRUT NV (CHARD-led) is perfect apéritif. Distinctive skin-contact Rosé. Fine vintages: 02 04 06 08. Grand Siècle CUVÉE multi-vintage (02 99 07) on form, peerless Grand Siècle Alexandra Rosé 06. Ultra-Brut so-so.

Leflaive, Dom Burg r w ★★★★ Reference bio white burg producer at PULIGNY-MONTRACHET with GRANDS CRUS, incl LE MONTRACHET, CHEVALIER. *Fabulous premiers crus*: Pucelles, Combettes, Folatières etc. Try MÂCON Verzé for value.

Leflaive, Olivier C d'O r w ★★→★★★ Négociant at PULIGNY-MONTRACHET, cousin of above. Reliable wines, mostly white, but drink young. Olivier's share from family DOM now incorporated as Récolte du Dom. Also La Maison d'Olivier, hotel, restaurant and tasting room.

Leroy, Dom C d'O r w ★★★★ Lalou Bize Leroy, bio pioneer, delivers exceptional quality from tiny yields. Also separate Dom d'Auvenay. Also treasure house of mature wines from family négociant, Maison Leroy.

L'Etoile Jura w dr (sw) sp ★★ Subregion of Jura known for stylish whites, incl VIN JAUNE, similar to CH-CHALON; gd sparkling. Top grower Philippe Vandelle.

Liger-Belair C d'O r ★★★→★★★★ Two recently re-est DOMS of high quality. Comte Louis-Michel L-B makes brilliantly ethereal wines in VOSNE-ROMANÉE, while cousin Thibault makes plump reds in NUITS-ST-GEORGES. Former now also in Chile, latter in MOULIN-À-VENT.

Lignier C d'O r w ★★→★★★ Family in MOREY-ST-DENIS. Best is Hubert (eg. CLOS DE LA ROCHE), now managed by son Laurent. Class also from Virgile Lignier-Michelot, but still awaiting return to form at DOM Georges L.

Limoux Rouss r w ★★ Still wine AC to complement sparkling BLANQUETTE, CRÉMANT de Limoux. Obligatory oak-ageing for white, from CHARD, CHENIN, Mauzac. White may become a Cru du L'DOC. Red AC based on MERLOT, plus SYRAH, GRENACHE, CABS, CARIGNAN. PINOT N illogically for a cool climate, only in CRÉMANT and for IGP. Growers: DOMS de Fourn, Martinolles, Mouscaillo, RIVES-BLANQUES, Baron d'Arques, *Jean-Louis Denois*.

Lirac S Rh r p w ★★ 09' 10' 11 12' 13 Four villages nr TAVEL, stony soils. Medium depth, spicy red (can age 5 yrs+), recent momentum from new CHÂTEAUNEUF owners achieving clearer fruit, more flair. Reds best, esp DOMS Beaumont, Famille Brechet, Duseigneur (bio), Giraud, Joncier, Lafond Roc-Epine, Lorentine (stylish), Maby (Fermade), André Méjan, *de la Mordorée* (best), Rocalière, Rocca Maura, R Sabon, CHX Bouchassy, Manissy, Mont-Redon, St-Roch, Ségriès, Mas Isabelle (handmade). Whites capture freshness, body (5 yrs).

Listrac-Médoc H-Méd r ★★→★★★ 03 05' 06 08 09' 10' 11 12 (14) Neighbour of MOULIS in s MÉD. Much improved AC for Méd-lovers with shallow(er) pockets; now more fruit, depth and Merlot. A little dry white AC B'X. Best CHX: Cap Léon Veyrin, CLARKE, Ducluzeau, l'Ermitage, FONRÉAUD, Fourcas-Borie, FOURCAS-DUPRÉ, FOURCAS-HOSTEN, Mayne-Lalande, Reverdi, SARANSOT-DUPRÉ.

Long-Depaquit Chab w ★★★ BICHOT-owned CHAB DOM, incl flagship GRAND CRU brand La Moutonne.

Lorentz, Gustave Al w ★★→★★★ Grower and merchant at Bergheim. Esp GEWURZ, RIES from GRANDS CRUS Altenberg de Bergheim, Kanzlerberg 06 09. As fine for aged as young, volume wines.

Alsace evolves

For intelligent, flexible evolution, AL can teach CHAMP and Burg a thing or two about classifying top v'yds. Each of the 51 crus can now apply its own extra rules. What's more, PINOT N is about to join the group of *grand cru* noble varieties, and SYLVANER, the Cinderella of white grapes, may soon follow.

Lot SW Fr ★→★★ DYA. Increasingly important IGP of Lot *département* for wines that stray beyond AOP rules (eg. whites from CAHORS growers). ★★ DOMS Belmont, Sully, Tour de Belfort, do not eclipse ★ CLOS d'Auxonne.

Loupiac B'x w sw ★★ 03' 05' 07 09' 10' 11 13 (14) Facing SAUT across river Garonne. Lighter, fresher in style. Top CHX: CLOS-Jean, Dauphiné-Rondillon, Loupiac-Gaudiet, Noble, de Ricaud, Les Roques.

Lubéron S Rh r p w ★→★★ 10' 12' Modish hilly annex to S Rh; terroir is okay, not more. Too many technical wines, low on soul. SYRAH lead role; many wannabes. Bright star: CH de la Canorgue. Also gd: DOM de la Citadelle, Chx Clapier, Edem, Fontvert, O Ravoire, St-Estève de Neri (improving), Tardieu-Laurent (rich, oak), Cellier de Marrenon, Val-Joanis, *La Vieille Ferme*.

Lussac-St-Émilion B'x r ★★ 03 05' 08 09' 10' 12 (14) Lightest of ST-ÉM satellites; co-op main producer. Top CHX: Barbe Blanche, Bel Air, Bellevue, Courlat, la Grenière, DE LUSSAC, DU LYONNAT, Mayne-Blanc, Le Rival, La Rose-Perrière.

Macération carbonique Traditional fermentation technique: whole bunches of unbroken grapes in a closed vat. Fermentation inside each grape eventually bursts it, giving vivid, fruity, mild wine, not for ageing. Esp in BEAUJ, though not for best wines; now much used in the MIDI and elsewhere, even CHÂTEAUNEUF.

Macle, Dom Jura Revered Ch-Chinon VIN JAUNE needs 10 yrs; 83 is still magnificent. Serious, gd-value CÔTES DE JURA CHARD 12.

Mâcon Burg r (p) w DYA. Simple, juicy GAMAY reds and most basic rendition of Mâconnais whites from CHARD.

Mâcon-Villages Burg w ★★→★★★ 12' 13 14' Chief appellation for Mâconnais whites. Individual villages may also use their own names eg. Mâcon-Lugny. Look to Lugny, Viré, Terres Secretes co-ops for best prices, or growers for individual quality: Guffens-Heynen, Guillot, Guillot-Broux, LAFON, LEFLAIVE, Maillet, Merlin.

Macvin Jura w sw ★★ AC for "traditional" MARC and grape-juice apéritif. Popular in Jura.

Madiran SW Fr r ★★→★★★ 05' 06 07 08 09' 10' 11 12 (14) Gascon AOP. Tannat grapes = tannic wine, but macho toughies needing 10 yrs are yielding to more upfront wines. ★★★ DOMS Berthoumieu, Capmartin, CLOS Basté, Damiens, des Maouries, Labranche-Laffont, Laffitte-Teston, *Laplace* giving CHX **Montus**, BOUSCASSÉ gd run for their money. Also gd: ★★ Barréjat, Crampilh, Dou Bernés, Pichard.

Madura, Dom de L'doc ★★★ Ex-*régisseur* of B'x CH FIEUZAL created own estate in ST-CHINIAN. Stylish Classique and Grand Vin.

Mähler-Besse B'x First-class négociant in B'x. Now owned by BORIE-MANOUX. Loads of old vintages. Mähler-Besse family retains a share in CH PALMER.

Mailly-Champagne Champ ★★★ Top CHAMP co-op, all GRAND CRU grapes. Prestige CUVÉE des *Echansons* 02' 04 08' 12' great wine for long ageing. V. refined L'Intemporelle 99 02 04.

Maire, Henri Jura r w sw ★→★★ Largest Jura grower/merchant, with half of entire AC. Some top wines, but many cheerfully commercial. Fun to visit, though.

Mann, Albert Al r w ★→★★★ Top grower at Wettolsheim: rich, elegant wines. V.gd PINOT BL, AUXERROIS, PINOT N; gd range of GRAND CRU wines from SCHLOSSBERG, HENGST, Furstentum, Steingrubler. Esp fine 08 10. Immaculate bio v'yds.

Maranges C d'O r (w) ★★ 05' 08 09' 10' 11 12 13 14 The s-most AC of CÔTE DE BEAUNE with relatively tannic reds. Gd value from PREMIER CRU. Best growers: BACHELET-Monnot, Chevrot, Contat-Grangé, Moreau.

Marc Grape skins after pressing; the strong-smelling brandy made from them.

Marcillac SW Fr r p ★★ Thirst-quenching like-or-hate AOP from Aveyron: Mansois grape (aka FER SERVADOU) needs 2–3 yrs. Redcurrants, raspberries, cassis. Great with charcuterie or strawberries. ★★ co-op (eg. single DOM de Ladrecht), ★★ DOMS du Cros, Costes, Vieux Porche, ★ de l'Albinie, Carles-Gervas, la Carolie.

Margaux H-Méd r ★★→★★★★ 98 00′ 01 02 04 05′ 06 08 09′ 10′ 11 12 (14) Large communal AC in S MÉD famous for elegant, fragrant wines. Reality is diversity of style. Top CHX: BOYD-CANTENAC, BRANE-CANTENAC, DAUZAC, FERRIÈRE, GISCOURS, ISSAN, KIRWAN, LASCOMBES, MALESCOT-ST-EXUPÉRY, MARGAUX, PALMER, RAUZAN-SÉGLA, SIRAN, DU TERTRE. Gd-value CHX: D'ANGLUDET, LABÉGORCE, Paveil de Luze.

Marionnet, Henry Lo r w ★★→★★★ 12 13 (14) An e TOURAINE DOM, owners fascinated by local varieties, esp ungrafted. SAUV BL (top CUVÉE Touraine SAUV L'Origine), GAMAY (esp Cépages Oubliés), Provignage (Romorantin vines from 1850); also La Pucelle de Romorantin: new planting using stock from 1850 v'yd.

Marmande SW Fr r p (w) ★→★★★ (r) 11′ 12 (14) Ambitious AOP on threshold of Gascony. Rare Abouriou grape featured by ★★★ cult grower Elian da Ros. ★★ CH de Beaulieu likes SYRAH while B'X grapes feature with ★★ DOMS Beyssac, Bonnet, Cavenac and Ch Lassolle. Co-ops still dull.

Marque déposée Trademark.

Marsannay C d'O r p (w) ★★→★★★ (r) 09′ 10′ 11 12′ 13 14 Far n of CÔTE DE NUITS. Easy-to-drink, if not the ripest. Reds best from eg. Audoin, Bart, Bouvier, Charlopin, CLAIR, Fournier, *Pataille*, TRAPET. No PREMIERS CRUS yet, but plans afoot. Top v'yds CLOS du Roy, Longeroies; rosé needs 1–2 yrs age, whites often dull.

Mas, Doms Paul L'doc r p w ★★ Ambitious big player; 452 ha of own estates, controls 1,285 ha nr PÉZENAS as well as LIMOUX. Mainly IGP. Innovative marketing. Known for Arrogant Frog IGP range; La Forge, les Tannes, Les Vignes de Nicole. Also DOM Ferrandière, Crès Ricards in TERRASSES DU LARZAC, Martinolles in Limoux, Côté Mas Pézenas a new project.

c.€100 million: said to be what LVMH paid for 8.66 ha of *grand cru* Clos des Lambrays in 2014.

Mas Bruguière L'doc ★★★ A pioneering PIC ST-LOUP estate; Xavier is talented 7th generation. L'Arbouse, la Grenadière and Le Septième.

Mas de Daumas Gassac L'doc r p w ★★★(★) 04 05 06 07 08 09 10 11 12 13 Once unique pioneering estate, set new standards in MIDI with CAB-based reds from apparently unique soil. Quality now surpassed by eg. neighbour GRANGE DES PÈRES. Also *perfumed white* from CHARD, PETIT MANSENG, VIOGNIER; super-*cuvée Émile Peynaud* (r); rosé Frizant. Delicious sweet wine Vin de Laurence (MUSCAT, SERCIAL).

Mas Jullien L'doc ★★★ Early TERRASSES DU LARZAC leader. Grapes incl Carignan Blanc, Terret Bl, CHENIN BL. Range simplified to COTEAUX DU L'DOC (r w) Etats d'Ame and Carlan, from L'doc varieties.

Massif d'Uchaux S Rh r ★★10′ 11 12′ 13 Gd Rh village, coolly textured, clearly fruited reds, not easy to sell; best deliver quality. NB: CH St Estève, DOMS La Cabotte (bio), Chapoton, *Cros de la Mûre* (v.gd, value), de la Guicharde, Renjarde (polished fruit).

Maury Rouss r sw ★★→★★★ NV VDN from ROUSS. GRENACHE Noir, Blanc, Gris grown on island of schist in midst of limestone hills. Much recent improvement, esp at *Mas Amiel*. Several new estates, eg. *Dom of the Bee*; sound CO-OP. RANCIOS age beautifully (1928 still in play). Huge red table wines now also AC Maury, but SEC to distingush from *doux*.

Mazis- (or Mazy-) **Chambertin** C d'O r ★★★ 90′ 93 95 96′ 99′ 02′ 03 05′ 06 07 08 09′ 10′ 11 12′ 13 14 The n-most GRAND CRU of GEVREY-CHAMBERTIN, top-class in upper part; *heavenly wines*. Best: Bernstein, DUGAT-PY, FAIVELEY, HOSPICES DE BEAUNE, LEROY, Maume, ROUSSEAU.

Mazoyères-Chambertin C d'O *See* CHARMES-CHAMBERTIN.

Médoc B'x r ★★→★★★ 03 04 05′ 06 08 09′ 10′ 11 (14) AC for reds in the nr-flat n part of the Méd peninsula. Often more guts than grace. Many growers, so be selective. Top CHX: CLOS Manou, Fontis, *Goulée*, Les Grands Chênes, GREYSAC, LOUDENNE, Lousteauneuf, LES ORMES-SORBET, PATACHE D'AUX, POITEVIN, *Potensac*,

New on the Beaujolais block

The BEAUJ is one of greater Burg's most dynamic regions, where prices remain relatively affordable: so much so that many C D'O producers are investing in land down s: JADOT and Thibault LIGER-BELAIR in MOULIN-À-VENT, BOUCHARD, DROUHIN and LAFARGE in FLEURIE, and Louis BOILLOT in BROUILLY. Others are sniffing around…. Alternatively look to hungry "new kid in town" producers such as Julie Balagny or Julien Sunier in FLEURIE, P-H Thillardon in CHÉNAS, Richard Rottiers in Moulin-à-Vent.

PREUILLAC, Ramafort, Rollan-de-By (HAUT-CONDISSAS), *La Tour-de-By*, TOUR HAUT-CAUSSAN, TOUR ST-BONNET, Vieux Robin.

Meffre, Gabriel S Rh r w ★★ Reliable large merchant, owns gd GIGONDAS DOM Longue-Toque. Recently better fruit, less oak. Also bottles, sells small CHÂTEAUNEUF doms. Reliable N Rh Laurus (new oak) range, esp CROZES-HERMITAGE, ST-JOSEPH.

Mellot, Alphonse Lo r p w ★★ →★★★★ 05 06 08' 09' 10' 11 12' 13 (14) V.gd SANCERRE (w, esp r), bio, La Moussière (r w), CUVÉE Edmond, Génération XIX (r w); several gd single v'yds: incl *Satellite* (w – Les Monts Damnés). Les Pénitents (Côtes de La Charité IGP) CHARD, PINOT N. Alphonse Jnr in charge.

Menetou-Salon Lo r p w ★★ →★★★ 05 08 10 11 12 13 (14) AOP 535 ha (349 w, 186 r) Nr-SANCERRE; fresh, gentle SAUV BL from v'yds on gentler hills running e to w. Also some gd reds (PINOT N). Best: BOURGEOIS, *Clement* (Chatenoy), Gilbert (bio), Jacolin, *Henry Pellé*, Jean-Max Roger, Teiller, Tour St-Martin.

Méo-Camuzet C d'O r w ★★★★ V. fine DOM in VOSNE-ROMANÉE (NB: Brûlées, Cros Parantoux), plus GRANDS CRUS CORTON, CLOS DE VOUGEOT, RICHEBOURG. Rich, oaky style but with class. Also less expensive négociant CUVÉES.

Merande, Ch de Sav Top producer delivers lasting MONDEUSE red (12) – violets, spices, black fruits, saline finish of a great v'yd. Value.

Mercier & Cie BRUT NV, Brut Rosé NV, DEMI-SEC Brut. One of biggest CHAMP houses, at Épernay. Controlled by MOËT & CHANDON. Sold mainly in France. Quality not remarkable. Demi-Sec gd. Full-bodied, PINOT N-led CUVÉE Eugene Mercier.

Mercurey Burg r (w) ★★ →★★★ 05' 09' 10' 11 12 13 14 Leading village of CÔTE CHALONNAISE, mostly muscular reds, improving whites, value. Try CH de Chamirey, FAIVELEY, M Juillot, Juillot-Theulot, Lorenzon, Raquillet, de Suremain.

Mesnil-sur-Oger, Le Champ ★★★★ One of top Côte des Blancs villages. Structured mineral CHARD for long life.

Méthode champenoise Champ Traditional method of putting bubbles into CHAMP by refermenting wine in its bottle. Outside Champ region, makers must use terms "classic method" or *méthode traditionnelle*.

Meursault C d'O (r) w ★★★ →★★★★★ 02' 04 05' 06' 07' 08 09' 10' 11 12 13 14 Source of some of BURG's best whites, rounded and rich from PREMIERS CRUS: Charmes, Genevrières, Perrières, more nervy from hillside v'yds Narvaux, Tesson, Tillets. Producers: Ampeau, Boisson-Vadot, M BOUZEREAU, *V Bouzereau*, Boyer-Martenot, CH DE MEURSAULT, COCHE-DURY, Ente, Fichet, *Javillier*, JOBARD, *Lafon*, Latour-Labille, Martelet de Cherisey, Matrot, Mikulski, *P Morey*, PRIEUR, *Roulot*. See also BLAGNY.

Meursault, Ch de C d'O r w ★★ 61-ha estate making BEAUNE, MEURSAULT, POMMARD, VOLNAY. CH itself is impressive, cellars open to public. Refocusing under new owner Olivier Halley (from 2012).

Midi The s of France. Broad term covering L'DOC, ROUSS, even PROV. Extremes of quality, improvements every vintage. Great promise, but of course no guarantee.

Minervois L'doc r (p) (w) ★★ 07' 08 09 10 11 12 13 14 Hilly AC region, one of L'DOC's best. CRU La Livinière has stricter selection, longer ageing; more surely on the way. Lively, characterful, savoury reds, esp CHX Bonhomme, Coupe-Roses, la Grave, Oupia, St Jacques d'Albas, La Tour Boisée, Villerembert-Julien, CLOS Centeilles, Borie-de-Maurel, **Ste Eulalie**, Faiteau; Abbaye de Tholomies, Borie de Maurel, Combe Blanche, **Ch de Gourgazaud**, Clos Centeilles, Laville-Bertrou, **Ste-Eulalie**, DOM l'Ostal Cazes. Co-ops Peyriac, Pouzols. *New wines from Gros and Tollot* (Burg) raising the bar.

Miquel, Laurent L'doc ★★★ V'yds in CORBIÈRES (Les Auxines) and ST-CHINIAN (Cazal Viel). IGP VIOGNIER, now adventurous ALBARIÑO too. Négociant labels incl Vendanges Nocturnes, Nord Sud.

Mis en bouteille au château / domaine Bottled at CH, property, or estate. NB: *dans nos caves* (in our cellars) or *dans la région de production* (in the area of production) often used but mean little.

Moët & Chandon By far largest CHAMP house, impressive quality of wines for such a giant. Now owns 1,500 ha, in best sites. Greatly improved BRUT NV, fresher, less sweet. Recent fine run of matured Grand Vintages 76 90 92 93. Elegant 06, great 08. Branches across Europe and New World. *See* also DOM PÉRIGNON.

Monbazillac SW Fr w ★★★★ 05' 07' 09 10 11' 12 (14) BERGERAC sub-AOP: ★★★★ **Tirecul-la-Gravière** challenges the best stickies in the world, supported by ★★★ L'Ancienne Cure, CLOS des Verdots and Les Hauts de Caillavel, ★★ CHX de Belingard-Chayne, Haut-Theulet, Ladesvignes, la Robertie, Pécoula, Theulet and co-op's **Ch de Monbazillac**.

Mondeuse Sav r ★★ DYA. SAVOIE red grape and wine. V.gd Gilles Berlioz La Deuse.

Monopole A v'yd that is under single ownership.

Montagne-St-Emilion B'x r ★★ 03 05' 08 09' 10' 12 (14) Largest, quality-orientated satellite of ST-ÉM. Top CHX: Beauséjour, Calon, La Couronne, Croix Beauséjour, Faizeau, La Fleur-Carrère, Haut Bonneau, Maison Blanche, Roudier, Teyssier, **Vieux Ch St-André**.

Montagny Burg w ★★ 12 13 14 CÔTE CHALONNAISE village with crisp whites, mostly in hands of CAVE DE BUXY and négociants. More growers needed; Aladame is best.

Montcalmès, Dom L'doc ★★★ Brother and sister team in TERRASSES DU LARZAC. IGP GHARD and VIOGNIER; stylish L'DOC from SYRAH, GRENACHE, MOURVÈDRE.

Monthélie C d'Or (w) ★★→★★★ 02' 03' 05' 08 09' 10' 11 12 13 14 Uphill from VOLNAY but a touch more rustic. Best v'yds: Champs Fulliot, Duresses. Best producers: BOUCHARD PÈRE & FILS, **Coche-Dury**, Darviot-Perrin, Florent Garaudet, LAFON, **Ch de Monthélie** (Suremain).

Montille, de C d'O r w ★★★ Etienne de M has expanded classic VOLNAY DOM with v'yds in BEAUNE, NUITS-ST-GEORGES and outstanding VOSNE-ROMANÉE Malconsorts. Top whites incl PULIGNY-MONTRACHET Caillerets. Also mini-negociant Deux Montille (white wines) with sister Alix, part of Puligny.

Montlouis Lo w dr sw sp ★★→★★★ 89' 95' 96' 97 02' 03' 05' 07 08' 09 10' 11 13 (14) Sister AC to VOUVRAY on S side of Lo, CHENIN BL; 55% sparkling. Excitement from newcomers. Small vintages in 2012, 13, 14. Top growers: Berger, CHANSON, CHIDAINE, Delecheneau, Flamand-Délétang, Jousset, Les Loges de la Folie, Moyer, Saumon, TAILLE-AUX-LOUPS, Weisskopf.

Montpeyroux L'doc ★★→★★★ Lively village within TERRASSES DU LARZAC with a growing number of talented growers. Aspring to cru status. Try Aupilhac, Chabanon, Villa Dondona, Several other newcomers. Gd co-op.

Montrachet C d'O w ★★★★ 92' 93 95 96' 99 00' 01 02' 04 05' 06 07 08 09' 10 11 12 13 14' GRAND CRU v'yd in PULIGNY- and CHASSAGNE-MONTRACHET. Potentially greatest white burg: monumental, perfumed, intense, dry yet luscious. Top wines: LAFON, LAGUICHE (DROUHIN), LEFLAIVE, Ramonet, ROMANÉE-CONTI. DOM THÉNARD improving?

Montravel SW Fr p w dr ★★ (r) 08 09 10 11 12 (14) (p w) DYA. Sub-AOP of BERGERAC. Oak-ageing compulsory for MERLOT-based hefty reds (★★ DOMS de Bloy, de Krevel, CHX Jonc Blanc, Laulerie, Masburel, Masmontet, Moulin-Caresse). Traditional dry whites and rosés ★★ from same and other growers. *See* CÔTES DE MONTRAVEL, and HAUT-MONTRAVEL, for sweeter styles.

Montus, Ch SW Fr r w ★★★ 00 01' 02 04 05' 06 08 09' 10 11 (12) Hard to choose between ALAIN BRUMONT's classy sweet PACHERENCS DU VIC-BILH (drink at 4 yrs) and the monumental age-worthy all-TANNAT generously-oaked MADIRAN.

Moreau Burg r w ★★→★★★ Widespread family in CHAB esp *Dom Christian M* (try CLOS des Hospices) and DOM M-Naudet. Other Moreau families in CÔTE DE BEAUNE, esp Bernard M for vigorous CHASSAGNE and David M in SANTENAY.

Morey, Doms C d'O r w ★★★ VIGNERON family in CHASSAGNE-MONTRACHET, esp Jean-Marc (Chenevottes), Marc (Virondot), Thomas (fine, mineral Baudines), Vincent (Embrazées, plumper style), Michel M-Coffinet (La Romanée). Also Pierre M in MEURSAULT for M Perrières and BÂTARD-MONTRACHET.

Morey-St-Denis C d'O r (w) ★★★ 90' 93 96' 99' 02' 03 05' 06 07 08 09' 10' 11 12' 13 14 Small village with four GRANDS CRUS between GEVREY-CHAMBERTIN and CHAMBOLLE-MUSIGNY. Glorious wine often overlooked. Amiot, ARLAUD, Castagnier, CLOS DE TART, *Clos des Lambrays*, Dujac, Jeanniard, H LIGNIER, LIGNIER-Michelot, Perrot-Minot, PONSOT, Remy, ROUMIER, Taupenot-Merme.

20 ha of vineyard in the Île de France – only 1 ha in Suresnes is commercial.

Morgon Beauj r ★★★ 09' 10' 11' 12 13 14 Firm, tannic BEAUJ cru, esp from Côte du Py. Becomes meaty with age. Les Charmes is softer for earlier drinking. Try Burgaud, Desvignes, Foillard, Gaget, Lafont, LAPIERRE, *Ch des Lumières* (JADOT), Piron, CH de Pizay.

Mortet, Denis C d'O r ★★★→★★★★ Arnaud Mortet has refined late father's dark, powerful wines, from BOURGOGNE Rouge to CHAMBERTIN. Key wines GEVREY-CHAMBERTIN En Champs, PREMIERS CRUS Lavaut St-Jacques and Champeaux.

Moueix, J-P et Cie B'x Libourne-based négociant and proprietor named after legendary founder. Son Christian runs company, his son Edouard increasingly prominent. CHX incl: LA FLEUR-PÉTRUS, HOSANNA, LATOUR-À-POMEROL, TROTANOY, BELAIR-MONANGE (since 2012 incorporating MAGDELAINE). Distributes PETRUS. Also in California (see Dominus Estate).

Moulin-à-Vent Beauj r ★★★ 99 03 05' 09' 10' 11' 12 13 14 Potentially finest BEAUJ cru, transcending the GAMAY grape. Weight, richness of Rh but can mature towards gamey PINOT flavours. Increasing interest in single-v'yd bottlings from eg. CH du Moulin-à-Vent, JADOT's Ch *des Jacques*, Janin (CLOS Tremblay), Janodet, LIGER-BELAIR (Les Rouchaux), Merlin (La Rochelle), Prieur.

Moulis H-Méd r ★★→★★★ 02 03 04 05' 06 08 09' 10' 11 12 (14) Tiny inland AC adjacent to LIST-MÉD; some honest, gd-value, often tannic wines. Top CHX: Anthonic, Biston-Brillette, BRANAS GRAND POUJEAUX, BRILLETTE, CHASSE-SPLEEN, Duplessis, Dutruch Grand Poujeaux, Gressier Grand Poujeaux, MAUCAILLOU, POUJEAUX.

Moutard Champ Quirky Aubois CHAMP house attached to old local grapes incl PINOT BL and esp boudoirish Arban(n)e. Quality greatly improved by the current Moutard, François. Fine CUVÉE des Six CÉPAGES 00 02 04 06 09.

Mouton Cadet B'x Biggest-selling B'x brand – 12 million bottles (80 per cent red). Same owner as MOUTON ROTHSCHILD. Also white (some screwcap), rosé and Rés GRAV, MÉD, ST-ÉM, SAUT.

Mugneret C d'O r w ★★★ VIGNERON family in VOSNE-ROMANÉE. Dr. Georges M-Gibourg best (esp ÉCHÉZEAUX), also Gérard M, Dominique M and, returning to form, DOM Mongeard-M.

Mugnier, J-F C d'O r w ★★★→★★★★ Outstanding grower of CHAMBOLLE-MUSIGNY *les Amoureuses* and *Musigny* at CH de Chambolle. Expect finesse not blockbusters. Style works well with NUITS-ST-GEORGES CLOS de la Maréchale (reclaimed 2004).

Mumm, G H & Cie Champ Cordon Rouge NV; fine new BRUT Sélection ★★ (base

08); Mumm de Cramant reborn as BLANC DE BLANCS NV (just as gd); Cordon Rouge **02 04 06'**; Rosé NV. Major house of Pernod-Ricard. Ongoing rise in quality, esp CUVÉE R Lalou **99**, BLANC DE NOIRS (pure GRAND CRU Verzenay) **02**.

Muré, Clos St-Landelin Al r w ★★ ···★★★ One of AL's great names; esp fine, full-bodied GRAND CRU *Vorbourg Ries* and PINOT GR. *Pinot N Cuvée "V"* **05 09** 10 11 12 13, ripe and vinous, is region's best. Exceptional 09s across range.

Muscadet Lo w ★···★★★ 79, 89, **10, 12, 13** (14) Popular, often delicious bone-dry wine from nr Nantes. Should be refreshing, never acidic. Perfect with fish, seafood. Choose a SUR LIE. Best from zonal ACS (*see* next entries). Can be v.gd value but many growers struggling financially, made worse by small crops in 2012, 13, 14.

Muscadet-Coteaux de la Loire Lo w ···★★★ **10 12 13** (14) Small (200 ha), least-known MUSCADET zone e of Nantes (best SUR LIE). Esp Guindon, La Pléiade, CH du Ponceau, Quarteron, Les VIGNERONS de la Noëlle.

Muscadet Côtes de Grand Lieu Lo ···★★★ **10 12 13 14'** MUSCADET's zonal AOP (300 ha) nr Atlantic. Best SUR LIE from eg. Eric Chevalier, Choblet (des Herbauges – 112 ha), Malidain. Three small crops 2012–14.

Muscadet-Sèvre-et-Maine Lo ★···★★★ **02 05'** 06 **09'** 10 12 13 **14'** Largest and best MUSCADET zone. Top: Bonnet-Huteau, Caillé, *Chéreau Carré*, Cormerais, Delhommeau, Douillard, DOM DE L'ECU), *Gadais*, Gunther-Chereau, Dom de la Haute Fevrie, Huchet, Landron, Luneau-Papin, Métaireau, Olivier, *Sauvion*. V.gd value, can age decades. **NB**: New *Crus Communaux*: longer lees ageing adds extra dimension. Three so far, more to come.

Muscat de Frontignan L'doc sw ★★ NV Small AC outside Sète for MUSCAT VDN. Also late-harvest, unfortified, oak-aged IGP wines. Quality improving. Leaders: CHX la Peyrade, de Stony, DOM du Mas Rouge. Delicious with blue cheese. Nearby Muscat de Lunel and Muscat de Mireval v. similar.

Muscat de Rivesaltes Rouss w sw ★★ NV Luscious sweet, fortified MUSCAT VDN AC wine nr Perpignan. Muscat SEC IGP increasingly popular, best worth seeking out: DOM CAZES, CH de Jau, Corneilla, Treloar, Baixas co-op.

Muscat de St Jean de Minervois L'doc w sw ★★ Fresh, honeyed VDN MUSCAT. Much recent improvement, esp from DOM de Barroubio, Michel Sigé, CLOS du Cravillas, Clos Bagatelle, village co-op.

Musigny C d'O r (w) ★★★★(★) 85' 88' 89' 90' 91 93 95 96' 98 99' 01 02' 03 05' 06 07 08 09' 10' 11 12' 13 14 GRAND CRU in CHAMBOLLE-MUSIGNY. Can be most beautiful, if not most powerful, of all red burg. Best growers: DROUHIN, JADOT, LEROY, MUGNIER, PRIEUR, ROUMIER, DE VOGÜÉ, VOUGERAIE.

Nature Unsweetened, esp for CHAMP (no *dosage*). Fine if v. ripe grapes, raw otherwise.

Négociant-éleveur Merchant who "brings up" (ie. matures) the wine.

Nerthe, Ch la S Rh r w ★★★ 78' 81' 89' 90' 95' 96' 98' 99' 00 01 03 04' 05' 06' 07' 09' 10' 11 12 13 CHÂTEAUNEUF estate. Sleek, oaked, polished wines, sadly more mainstream lately. Special CUVÉES delicious, deeply fruited Cadettes (r), oaked, rich, food-friendly Beauvenir (w). Also runs v. fine TAVEL Prieuré Montézargues, gd-value DOM de la Renjarde CÔTES DU RH, gd CH Signac CHUSCLAN.

Nuits-St-Georges C d'O r ★★···★★★★ 90' 93 96' 99' 02' 03 05' 06' 07 08 09' 10' 11 12' 13 14 Important wine town: underrated wines, typically sturdy, tannic, need time. Best v'yds: Cailles, Vaucrains, Les St-Georges in centre; Boudots, Cras, Murgers nearer VOSNE; various CLOS – des Corvées, des Forêts, de la Maréchale, St-Marc in Prémeaux. Many merchants and growers: Ambroise, L'ARLOT, J Chauvenet, R CHEVILLON, Confuron, *Faiveley*, Gavignet, GOUGES, GRIVOT, Lechéneaut, LEROY, *Liger-Belair*, Machard de Gramont, Michelot, *Mugnier*, Rion.

Ollier-Taillefer, Dom L'doc ★★★ Dynamic FAUGÈRES family estate. Allegro (w); Collines (r p); Grand Rés (r) from old vines and oak-aged Castel Fossibus (r).

Orléans Lo r p w ★ DYA. Famous for vinegar, but AC for white (chiefly CHARD – locally

Auvergnat Blanc), VIN GRIS, rosé, reds (PINOT N, esp MEUNIER) around Orléans (13 communes – 83 ha). Top: Deneufbourg, CLOS St Fiacre.

Orléans-Clery Lo r ★ DYA. Separate tiny AOP (28 ha) for simple CAB FR (difficult to ripen in poor yrs) reds from same zone as AC ORLÉANS. Producers incl Deneufbourg, CLOS St Fiacre.

Ostertag, Dom Al Bio DOM run with talent and originality in prime RIES country. GRAND CRU RIES Muenchberg 12 exquisite, subtle. Fine PINOT N Franholtz.

Pacherenc du Vic-Bilh SW Fr w dr sw ★★→★★★ AOP for whites of MADIRAN based on GROS and PETIT MANSENG grapes. Same growers (qv.) but note too ★★ CHX Mascaaras, DOMS Crampilh, Poujo. Dry wines are DYA, but sweets, esp if oaked, should be kept.

Paillard, Bruno Champ BRUT Première CUVÉE NV; Rosé Première Cuvée; CHARD Rés Privée, Brut 02 04 06 08. New vintage BLANC DE BLANCS 95 02 04. Superb Prestige Cuvée Nec-Plus-Ultra 95' 02. Youngest major CHAMP house. Refined, v. dry style esp in long-aged Blanc de Blancs *Rés Privée*, Nec-Plus-Ultra. Bruno P heads LANSON-BCC and owns CH de Sarrin, PROV.

Palette Prov r p w ★★★ Tiny AC nr Aix-en-PROV. Characterful reds, fragrant rosés, intriguing whites. Traditional *Ch Simone*; more innovative CH Henri Bonnaud.

Patriarche Burg r w sp ★→★★ One of larger BEAUNE-based Burg merchants, bought by Castel in 2011. Main brand is sparkling Kriter.

Patrimonio Cors r p w ★★→★★★ AC. Some of island's finest, from dramatic limestone hills in n CORS. Individual reds from NIELLUCCIO, intriguing whites, even *late-harvest*, from *Vermentino*. Top growers: Antoine Arena, CLOS de Bernardi, Gentile, Yves Leccia at E Croce, Pastricciola, Montemagni.

Pauillac H-Méd r ★★★→★★★★★ 90' 94 95' 96' 98 00' 01 02 03' 04' 05' 06 08' 09' 10' 11 12 (14) Communal AC in MÉD with three First Growths (LAFITE, LATOUR, MOUTON). Famous for pungent, long-lived wines, the acme of CAB SAUV. Other top CHX: D'ARMAILHAC, CLERC MILON, DUHART-MILON, GRAND-PUY-LACOSTE, HAUT-BATAILLEY, LYNCH-BAGES, PICHON-BARON, PICHON-LALANDE, PONTET-CANET.

Pays d'Oc, IGP L'doc r p w ★→★★ Largest IGP, formerly VDP d'Oc, covering the whole of L'DOC-ROUSS. Focus on varietal wines; 56 different grapes. Technical advances continue apace. Main producers: JEANJEAN, VAL D'ORBIEU, DOMS PAUL MAS, GÉRARD BERTRAND, village co-ops, plus many individual growers. Extremes of quality; the best innovative, exciting.

Pécharmant SW Fr r ★★ 08 09' 10 11' (12) Inner BERGERAC AOP. Iron, manganese underlie its terroir. Big wines, best kept. ★★★ *Ch de Tiregand*, Les Chemins d'Orient, CLOS des Côtes, DOM du Haut-Pécharmant, ★★ La Métairie, CHX de Biran, Champarel, Corbiac, du Rooy, Hugo, Terre Vieille, Doms des Bertranoux.

Pélican, Dom du Jura New property started by Burg's MARQUIS D'ANGERVILLE: 2012 first vintage. Wants to be tops in Jura.

Pernand-Vergelesses C d'O r w ★★★ (r) 99' 02' 03' 05' 06 08 09' 10' 11 12 13 14 Village next to ALOXE-CORTON, incl part of CORTON-CHARLEMAGNE, CORTON. Île des Vergelesses v'yd also first rate for reds. Growers: CHANDON DE BRIAILLES, CHANSON, Delarche, Dubreuil-Fontaine, JADOT, LATOUR, Rapet, Rollin.

Perrier-Jouët Champ BRUT NV; Blason de France NV; Blason de France Rosé NV; Brut 02 04 06 08. Fine new BLANC DE BLANCS (09 base). First to make dry CHAMP for English market; strong in GRAND CRU CHARD and best for gd vintage wines and de luxe Belle Epoque 95 02' 04 06 08' (Rosé 04 06) in a painted bottle.

Pessac-Léognan B'x r w ★★★→★★★★ 96 98 00' 01 02 04 05' 06 08 09' 10' 11 12 (14) AC created in 1987 for best part of n GRAV, incl all GRANDS CRUS: HAUT-BAILLY, HAUT-BRION, LA MISSION-HAUT-BRION, PAPE-CLÉMENT, etc. Plump, minerally MERLOT-inclined reds; B'x's finest dry whites. Value from Cantelys, Haut-Vigneau, Lafont-Menaut, DE ROCHEMORIN, Seguin.

Petit Chablis Chab w ★ DYA. Fresh and easy would-be CHAB from outlying v'yds not on kimmeridgian clay. LA CHABLISIENNE co-op is gd.

Pfaffenheim Al ★→★★★ Respectable AL co-op. Ripe, balanced wines from warm sites. Dopff & Irion, a once-famous house, now a brand of Pfaffenheim.

Pfersigberg Al GRAND CRU in two parcels; v. aromatic wines. GEWURZ does v. well (09). RIES, esp Paul Ginglinger 08 10, BRUNO SORG, LÉON BEYER Comtes d'Eguisheim

Philipponnat Champ Small house known for winey CHAMP, now owned by LANSON-BCC group. NV, Rosé NV, BRUT 99 02, CUVÉE 1522 02, remarkable single-v'yd *Clos des Goisses* 85' 92 95 96 02 04 08 12', late-disgorged vintage 99.

Picpoul de Pinet L'doc w ★→★★ DYA. MUSCADET of the MIDI. New AC, and Grand Vin du L'DOC, from old variety PICPOUL. Best growers: Félines-Jourdan, Mas Autanel, co-ops Pomérols, Pinet. Fresh and salty, so perfect *with an oyster* but sadly can be a victim of fashion, losing its lemony tang.

Pic St-Loup L'doc r (p) ★★→★★★ 07 08 09 10 11 12 13 14 One of n-most and coolest L'DOC v'yds, based on SYRAH. Potential AC and possibly Cru du L'doc. Growers: Cazeneuve, CLOS Marie, de Lancyre, Lascaux, Mas Bruguière, *Dom de l'Hortus*, Valflaunès and many new. Great potential, some of Midi's best: stylish, age-worthy. Whites are IGP, COTEAUX DU L'DOC or L'doc.

Pierre-Bise, Ch Lo r p w ★★→★★★★ 02 03 04 05' 06 07' (sw) 08 09 10' 11 13 14' Benchmark family DOM in COTEAUX DU LAYON, incl Chaume, QUARTS DE CHAUME, SAVENNIÈRES (CLOS de Grand Beaupréau, ROCHE-AUX-MOINES). V.gd, rich ANJOU-GAMAY, ANJOU-VILLAGES (both CUVÉE Schist, Spilite), Anjou Blanc Haut de la Garde. New generation (Réné and Christophe) taking over.

Average price of 1 ha in Pauillac in 2014: €2 million. *Grand cru* Burgundy: €4 million. Both rising.

Pignier Jura r w sw sp ★★★ Two bio brothers. Eclectic range: Poulsard, Trousseau, PINOT N, SAVAGNIN. Excellent CRÉMANT de Jura, great VIN JAUNE 99' 07, etc.

Pineau des Charentes SW Fr Off-dry apéritif made with unfermented white grape juice and Cognac

Pinon, François Lo w sw sp ★★★ 89 90 95 96 97 02 03 04 05 08 09 10' 11 14 V.gd organic producer of v. pure wine in Vernou, VOUVRAY. Sadly hit by frost (2012), hail (13). Gd small crop in 14.

Piper-Heidsieck CHAMP house on up again with new owner. Much-improved BRUT NV and fruit-driven Brut Rosé Sauvage 04; Brut 02 04 06 09. V.gd CUVÉE Sublime DEMI-SEC, rich yet balanced. *Piper-Heidsieck Rare* (esp 02 88') is one of Champ's best-kept secrets.

Plageoles, Robert & Bernard SW Fr r w sp GAILLAC retro-rebel stars, guardians of traditional varieties (eg. Ondenc for their justly famous sw ★★★★ Vin d'Autan). Also ★★★ Prunelard, deep fruity red; Verdanel (rare dry white, oak-aged); a big spicy red from Duras, and brilliant dry sparkling from Mauzac.

Plan de Dieu S Rh r ★→★★ 10' 11 12' 13 A Rh village nr CAIRANNE with stony, windswept plain. Heady, robust, authentic, mainly GRENACHE wines; drink with game. Best: CH la Courançonne, DOMS Aphillantes, Arnesque, Bastide St Vincent, Durieu, Espigouette, Martin, Pasquiers, St-Pierre (gd traditional).

Pol Roger Champ Family-owned Épernay house with vines in AVIZE joining family v'yds. BRUT Rés NV excels, slightly lower dosage; Brut 98' 02' 04 06 08'; Rosé 04 06; Blanc de CHARD 04 06 08'. Fine *Pure Brut* (*zéro dosage*) a great choice for seafood. Sumptuous CUVÉE Sir Winston Churchill 96' 02' 04 08'. Always blue-chip choice.

Pomerol B'x r ★★★→★★★★ 95 96 98' 00' 01 04 05' 06' 08 09' 10' 11 12 (14) Tiny AC bordering ST-ÉM; clay, gravel and sandy soils. MERLOT-led, rich, supple style but long life. Top estates: CLINET, LA CONSEILLANTE, L'ÉGLISE-CLINET, L'ÉVANGILE, LA FLEUR-

PÉTRUS, HOSANNA, LAFLEUR, PETRUS, LE PIN, TROTANOY, VIEUX-CH-CERTAN. Prices generally high; some value (CLOS du Clocher, CLOS RENÉ, LA POINTE).

Pommard C d'O r ★★★ 90' 96' 98 99' 02' 03 05' 06 07 08 09' 10' 11 12 14 V. different neighbour of VOLNAY; potent, tannic wines to age 10 yrs+. Best v'yds: Rugiens for power, Epenots for grace. Talk of promotion to GRAND CRU for these two. Growers: COMTE ARMAND, J-M BOILLOT, COURCEL, HOSPICES DE BEAUNE, Huber-Vedereau, Lejeune, DE MONTILLE, Parent, CH de Pommard, Pothier, Rieusset, Rebourgeon.

Pommery Champ Historic house; brand now owned by VRANKEN. BRUT NV sure bet. Rosé NV; Brut 04 08 09 12'. Outstanding *Cuvée Louise* 02 04 08' 12 13, supple Wintertime BLANC DE NOIRS.

Ponsot C d'O r w ★★→★★★★ Idiosyncratic, top-quality MOREY-ST-DENIS DOM now with 12 GRANDS CRUS, from CORTON to CHAMBERTIN, but esp *Clos de la Roche*, CLOS ST-DENIS. Laurent P also at forefront of fight against fraud.

Potel, Nicolas C d'O r w ★★→★★★ Brand owned by Cottin Frères; without founder Nicolas, who now owns DOM de Bellene and Maison Roche de Bellene in BEAUNE.

Pouilly-Fuissé Burg w ★★→★★★ 05' 06 07 08 09' 10' 11 12 13 14' Top AC of MÂCON, potent, rounded but mineral, whites; classification of terroirs pending, maybe for 2017. Wines from Fuissé most powerful, Vergisson for minerality. Top names: Barraud, de Beauregard, Cornin, Ferret, Forest, CH de FUISSÉ, Guerrin, Merlin, Ch des Rontets, Saumaize, VERGET.

Pouilly-Fumé Lo w ★→★★★ 05' 08 09' 10 12 13 14' Across-river neighbour of SANCERRE. Best are round, full-flavoured, can improve 7–8yrs+. 2014 gd in quality and quantity. Growers: Bain, BOURGEOIS, Cailbourdin, Chatelain, DIDIER DAGUENEAU, Serge Daguenau & Filles, CH de Favray, Edmond and André Figeat, LADOUCETTE, Masson-Blondelet, Jean Pabiot, Jonathan Pabiot, Redde, Tabordet, Ch de Tracy, Treuillet.

Pouilly-Loché Burg w ★★ 12 13 14 Less-well-known neighbour of POUILLY-VINZELLES. CLOS des Rocs, Tripoz, Bret Bros gd, co-op dominant for volume.

Pouilly-sur-Loire Lo w ★→★★ DYA. Historic but now marginal CHASSELAS wine from same v'yds as POUILLY-FUMÉ. Only 30 ha. Keeping flag flying: Serge Daguenau & Filles, Gitton, Landrat-Guyollot, Masson-Blondelet, Jonathan Pabiot, Redde.

Pouilly-Vinzelles Burg w ★★ 12 13 14' Between POUILLY-LOCHÉ and POUILLY-FUISSÉ geographically and in quality. Best v'yd: Les Quarts. Best producers: Bret Bros, Valette. Volume from CAVE des GRANDS CRUS Blancs.

Premier Cru First growth in B'X; 2nd rank of v'yds (after GRAND CRU) in Burg; 2nd rank in Lo: one so far, COTEAUX DU LAYON Chaume: BAUMARD legal challenge rejected by Conseil d'État (2014).

Premières Côtes de Bordeaux B'x w sw ★→★★ 07 09' 10' 11 13 (14) Same zone as CADILLAC-CÔTES DE B'X but for sweet white wines only. Gently sweet rather than full-blown, noble-rotted *liquoreux*. Quality varies. Best CHX: Crabitan-Bellevue, Fayau, du Juge, Suau.

Prieur, Dom Jacques C d'O ★★★ Old MEURSAULT estate with extraordinary range of GRANDS CRUS from MONTRACHET to MUSIGNY. Style aims at weight from late picking and oak more than finesse, but now signs of livelier approach. Labruyère MOULIN À-VENT and CH Rouget POM under same ownership.

Prieuré St Jean de Bébian L'doc ★★★ Pioneering Pézenas estate with all 13 grape varieties of CHÂTEAUNEUF. Owned by Russians with talented Aussie winemaker.

Primeur "Early" wine for refreshment, uplift; esp BEAUJ; VDP too. Wine sold *en primeur* still in barrel, for delivery when bottled. Caution: fingers can get burned.

Producteurs Plaimont SW Fr Most successful co-op in sw? Authentic Gascon grapes, three appellations: MADIRAN, ST MONT, CÔTES DE GASCOGNE. Huge range, all colours and styles, mostly ★★, all tastes, purses.

FRANCE

ropriétaire récoltant Champ Owner-operator, literally owner-harvester.

rovence *See* CÔTES DE PROV, CASSIS, BANDOL, PALETTE, LES BAUX-EN-PROV, BOUCHES-DU-RH, COTEAUX D'AIX-EN-PROV, COTEAUX VAROIS-EN-PROV. Also Pierrevert AC.

uisseguin St-Émilion B'x r ★★ 03 05' 08 09' 10' 12 (14) One of the four ST-ÉM satellites; wines firm, solid. Top CHX: Bel Air, Le Bernat, Branda, Clarisse, Durand-Laplagne, Fongaban, Guibot la Fourvieille, Haut-Bernat, DES LAURETS, La Mauriane, Soleil. Also Roc de Puisseguin from co-op.

uligny-Montrachet C d'O (r) w ★★★→★★★★ 02' 04 05' 06 07 08 09' 10' 11 12 13 14 Smaller neighbour of CHASSAGNE-MONTRACHET: potentially even finer, more vital, floral, complex wine (though apparent finesse can signal overproduction). Top v'yds: Caillerets, Champ Canet, Combettes, Folatières, Pucelles and MONTRACHET GRANDS CRUS. Producers: *J-M Boillot*, *Bouchard Père & Fils*, CARILLON, Chartron, CH de Puligny, DROUHIN, JADOT, *Dom Leflaive*, O LEFLAIVE, Pernot, *Sauzet*.

uyméras S Rh r w ★ 12' Respectable, low-profile S Rh village, high, breezy v'yds, straightforward, supple plum-fruited reds based on GRENACHE, fair whites, decent co-op. Try CAVE la Comtadine, DOM du Faucon Doré (bio), Puy du Maupas.

ook for fresh but savoury whites from N & S Rhône with enough weight for food.

yrénées-Atlantiques SW Fr DYA. IGP for wines not qualifying for local AOPS in far SW. Esp ★★★ CH Cabidos (superb PETIT MANSENG w SW), ★★ DOM Moncaut (nr Pau), ★ BRUMONT varietals. Otherwise pot luck.

uarts de Chaume Lo w sw ★★★→★★★★ 89' 90' 95' 96' 97' 02 03 05' 07' 10' 11' 14' Tiny, exposed slopes close to Layon, CHENIN BL. Lo's first AC GRAND CRU: strict rules may be further tightened. Best richly textured. Esp Baudouin, BAUMARD, Bellerive, Branchereau, FL, Guegniard, CH PIERRE-BISE, Pithon-Paillé, Suronde. Avoid 2012.

uincy Lo w ★→★★ 13, 14' Small AOP (224 ha) on gravel w of Bourges in Cher Valley. Citric, quite SANCERRE-style SAUV BL. Hail-prone. 2014 gd quality and quantity. Growers: Mardon, Portier, Rouzé, Siret-Courtaud, Tatin-Wilk (DOMS Ballandors, Tremblay), Villalin.

ancio Rouss The most original, lingering, delicious style of VDN, reminiscent of Tawny Port, or old Oloroso Sherry in BANYULS, MAURY, RIVESALTES, RASTEAU, wood-aged and exposed to oxygen and heat. Same flavour (pungent, tangy) is a fault in table wine.

angen Al Most s GRAND CRU of AL at Thann. Extremely steep (average 90 per cent) slopes, volcanic soils. Top wines: majestic RIES from ZIND-HUMBRECHT (CLOS St Urbain 00' 10) and SCHOFFIT (St Theobald 08 10). With mercurial climate change, Rangen 10 has extra finesse.

asteau S Rh r (p) (w) br (dr) sw ★★ 09' 10' 11 12' 13 Robust reds from clay soils, carry local stamp, mainly GRENACHE. Best in hot yrs. NB: Beaurenard (serious, age well), *Cave Ortas* (gd), CH du Trignon, DOMS Beau Mistral, Didier Charavin, Collière, Coteaux des Travers, Escaravailles, Girasols, Gourt de Mautens (talented, IGP wines from 2010), Grand Nicolet (character), Rabasse-Charavin, Soumade, St Gayan, Famille Perrin. Grenache dessert VDN quality on the up (Doms Banquettes, Coteaux des Travers, Escaravailles, Trapadis).

atafia de Champagne Champ Sweet apéritif made in CHAMP of 67 per cent grape juice and 33 per cent brandy. Not unlike PINEAU DES CHARENTES.

ata-Poil Jura New bio ARBOIS estate. Pure SAVAGNIN La Pierre, 40-yr-old Poulsard.

avanès, Dom De L'doc IGP Coteaux de Murviel ★★★ Guy and Marc Benin grow B'x varieties in L'DOC. Le Prime Verd is PETIT VERDOT; also experimental white Le Renard Blanc (GRENACHE Gris/MACABEO).

aveneau Chab w ★★★★ Great CHAB producer using old methods for *extraordinary long-lived wines*. Cousin of DAUVISSAT. Look for Vaillons, Blanchots, Les CLOS.

Rayas, Ch S Rh r w ★★★→★★★★ 78' 79 81' 85 86 88' 89 90' 93 94 95' 96' 98
99 00 01 03 04' 05' 06' 07' 08 09' 10' 11' 12' 13' Out of the loop, wonderful,
highly traditional CHÂTEAUNEUF estate. Pale, subtle, aromatic, complex red
(100% GRENACHE) whisper their quality, age superbly. White Rayas (GRENACHE
BLANC, CLAIRETTE) v.gd over 18 yrs+. Gd-value second label: *Pignan*. Supreme C1
Fonsalette CÔTES DU RH, incl SYRAH. Decant them all; each is an occasion. Also g
Ch des Tours VACQUEYRAS, VIN DE PAYS.

Regnié Beauj r ★★ 11' 12 13 14 Usually lightest of BEAUJ crus. Sandy soil gives easy
fruity wines. But try Burgaud, Dupré, de la Plaigne, Rochette, Sunier.

Reuilly Lo r p w ★→★★★ 05' 08 09' 10 11 13 14' Small AC (186 ha) w of Bourge
for SAUV BL whites, plus rosés and *Vin Gris* made from PINOT N and/or PINOT GR
Improving reds from Pinot N. Best: Jamain, Claude Lafond, Mardon, Rouze
Sorbe. 2014 gd quality and quantity.

Riceys, Rosé des Champ p ★★★ DYA. Key AC in AUBE for a notable PINOT N rosé. Principal
producers: *A Bonnet*, Jacques Defrance, Morize. Great 09; v. promising 14 afte
lean period 11 12 13.

Richebourg C d'O r ★★★★ 90' 93' 95 96' 98 99' 00 02' 03 05' 06 07 08 09' 10
11 12' 13 14 VOSNE-ROMANÉE GRAND CRU. Magical burg with great depth of flavou
vastly expensive. Growers: DRC, GRIVOT, GROS, HUDELOT-Noëllat, LEROY, LIGER-BELAIR
MÉO-CAMUZET.

Rimage Rouss A growing mode: vintage VDN, super-fruity for drinking young
Think gd Ruby Port.

Rion, Patrice C d'O r ★★★ Excellent NUITS-ST-GEORGES DOM, esp CLOS des Argillière
Clos St-Marc, plus CHAMBOLLE-M. NB: also Dom Daniel R in Prémeaux, B &
Rion in VOSNE-ROMANÉE.

Rivesaltes Rouss r w br dr sw ★★ Often NV or solera. Fortified wine, nr Perpignan
A struggling but worthwhile tradition. Top: DOM CAZES, CH de Jau, Sarda-Malet
des Schistes, Vaquer. Rancy, des Chênes. Best are delicious, original, es
immortal old RANCIOS. *See* MUSCAT DE RIVESALTES.

Rives-Blanques, Ch L'doc sp w ★★★ LIMOUX. Irish-Dutch couple make BLANQUET
and more recently CRÉMANT. Still wines, incl blend Trilogie and age-worthy CHEN
BL Dédicace. Dessert Lagremas d'Aur.

Roche-aux-Moines, La Lo w sw ★★→★★★ 89' 90' 96' 99 02 03 05' 06 07 08'
10' 11 12 13 14' Cru of SAVENNIÈRES, ANJOU. Strict rules on chemicals and yield
(30 hl/ha). Complex age-worthy wine. Growers: Le CLOS de la Bergerie (Joly), DO
des Forges, FL, Laroche, Laureau, *Ch Pierre-Bise*.

Roederer, Louis Champ Top-drawer family-owned house with enviable estate of to
v'yds, many now part bio. Flavoury BRUT Premier NV, Brut 04 06 07, BLANC
BLANCS 08' 09 13, Brut Saignée Rosé 09. Magnificent *Cristal* (can be greatest
all prestige CUVÉES, viz 88' 04 06) and Cristal Rosé 96' 02'. New late-release
Cristal 95 due 2015. V.gd new Brut NATURE (pure Cumières 2006). Also own
DEUTZ, DELAS, CHX DE PEZ, PICHON-LALANDE. *See also* California.

Rolland, Michel B'x Ubiquitous, fashionable consultant winemaker and MERLO
specialist working in B'x and worldwide. Family properties (BERTINEAU ST-VINCEN
BON PASTEUR) sold to a Chinese concern but he still handles the winemaking.

Rolly Gassmann Al w sw ★★★ Revered grower at Rorschwihr, esp fro
Moenchreben. Off-dry style culminates in great rich GEWURZ CUVÉE Yves 05 07
09 11. New generation and bio methods bring more finesse.

Romanée, La C d'O r ★★★★ 02' 03 05' 06 07 08 09' 10' 11 12' 13 14 Tiniest GRAND CR
in VOSNE-ROMANÉE, MONOPOLE of Comte LIGER-BELAIR. Exceptionally fine, perfume
intense and understandably expensive.

Romanée-Conti, Dom de la / DRC C d'O r w ★★★★ Grandest estate in Bur
MONOPOLES ROMANÉE-CONTI and LA TÂCHE, major parts of ÉCHÉZEAUX, GRAND

ÉCHÉZEAUX, RICHEBOURG, ROMANÉE-ST-VIVANT and a tiny part of MONTRACHET. Also
CORTON from 2009. Crown-jewel prices. Keep top vintages for decades.

Romanée-Conti, La C d'O r ★★★★ 78′ 85′ 88′ 89′ 90′ 93′ 95 96′ 97 98 99′ 00 01
02′ 03 05′ 06 07 09′ 10′ 11 12′ 13 14 MONOPOLE GRAND CRU in VOSNE-ROMANÉE; 450
cases/annum. Most celebrated and expensive red wine in world, at best with
reserves of flavour beyond imagination. Cellar 15 yrs+.

Romanée-St-Vivant C d'O r ★★★★ 90′ 93 95 96′ 99′ 02′ 03 05′ 06 07 08 09′
10′ 11 12′ 13 14 GRAND CRU in VOSNE-ROMANÉE. Downslope from LA ROMANÉE-CONTI,
haunting perfume, delicate but intense. Ready a little earlier than its famous
neighbours. Growers: if you can't afford DRC or LEROY, try ARLOT, CATHIARD,
JJ Confuron, Follin-Arbelet, HUDELOT-Nöellat, LATOUR.

Rosacker Al GRAND CRU at Hunawihr. Limestone/clay makes some of longest-lived
RIES in AL (CLOS STE-HUNE).

Rosé d'Anjou Lo p ★→★★ DYA. Rosé – off-dry to sweet (mainly Grolleau). Avoid
cheap versions. Some gd, esp: Mark Angeli, Clau de Nell, DOMS de la Bergerie,
les Grandes Vignes, des Sablonnettes.

Rosé de Loire Lo p ★→★★ DYA. Driest of ANJOU's rosés: six grapes, esp GAMAY,
Grolleau. Large AC technically incl SAUMUR, TOURAINE. Best incl: Bablut,
Branchereau, Cady, Cave de Saumur, Ogereau, Passavant, CH PIERRE-BISE, Richou,
Soucherie.

Rosette SW Fr w s/sw ★★ DYA. BERGERAC's birthplace, today a tiny sub-AOP for off-
dry apéritif wines. Try ★★ CLOS Romain, CHX Combrillac, Monplaisir, Puypezat-
Rosette, Spingulèbre, DOMS de la Cardinolle, de Coutancie, du Grand-Jaure; with
foie gras or mushrooms.

Rossignol-Trapet Burg r ★★★ Equally bio cousins of DOM TRAPET, with healthy holdings
of GRAND CRU v'yds esp CHAMBERTIN. Gd value across range from GEVREY VIEILLES
VIGNES up. Also some BEAUNE v'yds from Rossignol side.

Rostaing, René N Rh r w ★★★ 95′ 99′ 01′ 05′ 06′ 07′ 09′ 10′ 11 12′ 13′ 14
CÔTE-RÔTIE DOM: old, central v'yds; three tightly bound wines, all v. fine, pure
fruit, careful oak, wait 6 yrs, then decant. Enticing, top-class Côte Blonde (5%
VIOGNIER), also La Landonne (dark fruits, 15–20 yrs). Intricate, unshowy **Condrieu**,
also L'DOC Dom Puech Noble (r w).

Rouget, Emmanuel C d'O r ★★★★ Inheritor of legendary Henri Jayer estate in
ÉCHÉZEAUX, NUITS-ST-GEORGES, VOSNE-ROMANÉE. Top wine Vosne-Romanée Cros
Parantoux (alarming price).

Roulot, Dom C d'O w ★★★→★★★★ Outstanding MEURSAULT DOM; great PREMIERS CRUS
eg. CLOS des Bouchères (from 2011), Charmes, Perrières, but try also top village
sites Luchets, esp Tesson Clos de Mon Plaisir.

Roumier, Georges C d'O r ★★★★ Reference DOM for BONNES-MARES and other **brilliant
Chambolle** wines in capable hands of Christophe R. Long-lived wines but still
attractive early. Has become expensive in secondary market.

Rousseau, Dom Armand C d'O r ★★★★ Unmatchable GEVREY-CHAMBERTIN DOM with
thrilling CLOS ST-JACQUES and GRANDS CRUS. Fragrance, balance, persistence
throughout range, now increased with CH de Gevrey-Chambertin v'yds.

Roussette de Savoie Sav w ★★ DYA. Tastiest fresh white from s of Lake Geneva.

Roussillon Leading MIDI region for traditional VDN (eg. MAURY, RIVESALTES, BANYULS).
Younger vintage RIMAGE now competing with aged RANCIO. Also fine table wines.
See CÔTES DU ROUSS-VILLAGES, COLLIOURE, new AC MAURY and IGP CÔTES CATALANES.
Region incl under AC L'DOC.

Ruchottes-Chambertin C d'O r ★★★★ 90′ 93′ 95 96′ 99′ 00 02′ 03 05′ 06 07 08
09′ 10′ 11 12′ 13 14 Tiny GRAND CRU neighbour of CHAMBERTIN. Less weighty but
ethereal, intricate, lasting wine of great finesse. Top growers: MUGNERET-Gibourg,
ROUMIER, ROUSSEAU.

> **Languedoc rising stars**
> All founded since 2000, and looking gd:
> **Cabrières** Les Deux Rocs
> **Cabardès** Cazaban
> **Corbières** CLOS Perdus
> **Faugères** Trinités; Cebène
> **La Clape** Mas Soleilla
> **Limoux** J Laurens
> **Montpeyroux** Mas d'Amile, Joncas
> **Muscat de Mireval** La Rencontre
> **Pézenas** Le Conte de Floris, Monplézy, Mas Gabriel, Turner-Pageot
> **Terrasses du Larzac** Pas de l'Escalette, Clos du Serres, La Traversée,
> Les Vignes Oubliées
> **IGP** Mas des Dames (also COTEAUX DU L'DOC), Senti-Kreyden

Ruinart Champ Oldest house, owned by Moët-Hennessy. Already high standard going higher still. Rich, elegant wines. "R" de Ruinart BRUT NV; Ruinart Rosé NV "R" de Ruinart Brut 02' 04 06 08. Prestige CUVÉE *Dom Ruinart* is one of two best vintage BLANC DE BLANCS in CHAMP (viz 88' 95' 02' 04). DR Rosé also v. special 88 96 02'. NV Blanc de Blancs much improved – needed to be.

Rully Burg r w ★★ (r) 10' 12 13 14' (w) 12 13 14' CÔTE CHALONNAISE village. *Whites ar light, fresh, tasty,* gd value. Reds also fruit-forward. Try Devevey, DROUHIN, DUREUIL JANTHIAL, FAIVELEY, Jacqueson, Claudie Jobard, Ninot, Rodet.

Sablet S Rh r (p) w ★★ 12' 13 Fun but also serious wines from improving CÔTES DU RH-VILLAGE. Sandy soils, red-berry reds, esp CAVE co-op Gravillas, DOMS de Boissar (full), Espiers (fruit), Les Goubert, Pasquiers (full), Piaugier. *Gd full whites* fo apéritifs, food.

Saint Mont SW Fr r p w ★★ (r) 11 12 (14) (p w) DYA. AOP in s Gers. J-L Garoussia (★ DOM de Turet) plays sax. He, CH de Bergalasse and Dom des Maouries preven PRODUCTEURS PLAIMONT having a *monopole* of the appellation.

St-Amour Beauj r ★★ 12 13 14 N-most cru of BEAUJ: light, fruity, rather anonymous Tediously recommended on 14 Feb. Growers to try: Janin, *Patissier*, Revillon.

St-Aubin C d'O r w ★★★ (r) 05' 09' 10' 11 12 13 14 (w) 08 09' 10' 11 12 13 14 Fine source for *lively, refreshing whites,* adjacent to PULIGNY and CHASSAGNE, als pretty reds. Best v'yds: En Remilly, Murgers Dents de Chien. Best growers: J(Bachelet, COLIN, COLIN-MOREY, Lamy, Prudhon.

St-Bris Burg w ★ DYA. Neighbour to CHAB. AC for only SAUV BL in Burg. Fresh, lively worth keeping from J-H Goisot. Try also Bersan, de Moor, Simonnet-Febvre.

St-Chinian L'doc r ★→★★★ 07' 08 09' 10 11 12 13 Hilly area of growing reputation AC for red (since 1982) and white (since 2005). Incl CRUS of Berlou, Roquebrun Warm, spicy s reds, based on SYRAH, GRENACHE, CARIGNAN. Gd co-op Roquebrun CH de Viranel, Coujan. DOMS MADURA, Rimbaud, Navarre, Borie la Vitarèle, l Dournie, des Jougla, CLOS Bagatelle, Mas Champart and many others, new an old. Well worth the detour.

St-Émilion B'x r ★★→★★★★ 98' 00' 00' 01 03 04 05' 08 09' 10' 11 12 (14) Larg MERLOT-led district on B'x's Right Bank. ACS St-Ém and St-Ém GRAND CRU. To designation St-Ém PREMIER GRAND CRU CLASSÉ. Warm, full, rounded style; bes firm, v. long-lived. Also modern and traditional styles. Quality varies. Top CHX ANGÉLUS, AUSONE, CANON, CHEVAL BLANC, CLOS FOURTET, FIGEAC, PAVIE.

St-Estèphe H-Méd r ★★→★★★★ 95' 96' 98 00' 01 02 03 04 05' 06 08 09' 10 11 12 (14) Most n communal AC in the MÉD. Solid, structured wines for ageing consistent quality; big price range. Top CHX: COS D'ESTOURNEL, MONTROSE, CALON SÉGUR have had enormous investment. Also many top unclassified estates eg

CLAUZET, LE CROCK, HAUT-MARBUZET, MEYNEY, ORMES-DE-PEZ, DE PEZ, PHÉLAN-SÉGUR.

t-Gall Champ Brand used by Union-CHAMP, top growers' co-op at AVIZE. BRUT NV; Extra Brut NV; Brut BLANC DE BLANCS NV; Brut Rosé NV; Brut Blanc de Blancs **04 06 08'**; CUVÉE Orpale Blanc de Blancs **95 02' 04 08' 09** 13. Fine-value PINOT-led *Pierre Vaudon* NV.

t-Georges d'Orques L'doc r p ★★→★★★ More individual part of sprawling Grès de Montpellier, aspires to individual CRU status; CH l'Engarran, DOMS la Prose, Henry.

t-Georges-St-Émilion B'x r ★★ **03 05' 08 09' 10' 12** (14) Miniscule ST-ÉM satellite. Usually gd quality. Best CHX: Calon, MACQUIN-ST-GEORGES, ST-GEORGES, TOUR DU PAS-ST-GEORGES, Vieux Montaiguillon.

t-Gervais S Rh r (p) (w) ★ **12' 13** W-bank Rh village; gd soils but limited choice. Co-op trying to improve, but clear best is top-grade, long-lived (10 yrs+) DOM Ste-Anne red (firm, strong MOURVÈDRE liquorice flavours); gd VIOGNIER.

t-Jacques d'Albas, Ch L'doc Dynamic MINERVOIS estate since 2001. ★★★ Le Petit St-Jacques and CH St-Jacques (p); DOM (r), Ch (r), and SYRAH-dominant Chapelle (r).

t-Joseph N Rh r w ★★★ **99' 05' 06' 07' 09' 10' 11' 12' 13'** 14 65 km of granite v'yds along w bank of N Rh. SYRAH reds. Best, oldest zone nr Tournon: stylish, soft, red-fruited wines; further n darker, peppery wines, more obvious oak. More complete wines than CROZES-HERMITAGE, esp CHAPOUTIER (Les Granits), J-L CHAVE, Gonon (top class), *B Gripa*, GUIGAL (*lieu-dit* St-Joseph); also Chèze, Courbis (modern), Coursodon (racy, modern), Cuilleron, E Darnaud, *Delas*, J & E Durand (fruit), Faury, Gaillard, P Marthouret, Monier-Perréol (organic), A Perret, Nicolas Perrin, Vallet, P-J Villa, F Villard. Gd food-friendly *white (mainly Marsanne)*, esp Barge, CHAPOUTIER (Les Granits), Cuilleron, Gonon (fabulous), Gouye (traditional), B Gripa, Faury, A Perret, J Pilon.

t-Julien H-Méd r ★★★→★★★★ **96' 98 00' 01 02 03 04 05' 06 08 09' 10' 11 12** (14) Small mid-MÉD communal AC. 11 classified (1855) estates own 80 per cent of the v'yds. Incl three LÉOVILLES, BEYCHEVELLE, DUCRU-BEAUCAILLOU, GRUAUD-LAROSE, LAGRANGE. Epitome of harmonious, fragrant, savoury red wine.

t-Nicolas-de-Bourgueil Lo r p ★→★★★ **96' 05' 06 08 09' 10' 11 12 13 14'** AC (1,050 ha) W of BOURGUEIL; similar but pricier wines from CAB FR. Mostly sand/gravel light wines; age-worthy on limestone slopes. Try: Amirault (DOM), *Yannick Amirault*, Cognard, David, Delanoue, Lorieux, Frédéric Mabileau, Laurent Mabileau, Mabileau-Rezé, Taluau-Foltzenlogel, Vallée.

t-Péray N Rh w sp ★★ **10' 11' 12' 13'** 14 Underrated white Rh (MARSANNE plus ROUSSANNE) from hilly granite and lime v'yds opposite Valence. *Méthode Champenoise esp worth trying* (J-L Thiers, R Nodin). Still white should have grip, be smoky. Avoid fat wines from v. ripe fruit plus oak. Best: S Chaboud, CHAPOUTIER, *Clape* (pure), Colombo (stylish), Cuilleron, B Gripa (v.gd), R Nodin, J-L Thiers, TAIN co-op, *du Tunnel*, Voge (oak).

:-Pierre de Soucy Sav From steep schist hillsides; cru makes assertive fresh mix of Jacquère, CHARD and Mondeuse Blanche. Top producer: DOM des Ardoisière.

:-Pourçain Mass C r p w ★→★★ DYA. AC (600 ha – 19 communes. Light red, rosé from GAMAY, PINOT N (AOP rules stupidly forbid pure PINOT N), white from local Tressalier and/or CHARD or SAUV BL. Growers: Berioles, DOM de Bellevue, Grosbot-Barbara, Laurent, Nebout, Pétillat, Ray, gd co-op (VIGNERONS de St-Pourçain). Hail in 2014.

-Romain C d'O r w ★★ (w) **10' 11 12 13** 14 *Crisp, mineral whites* and clean-cut reds from vines tucked away in back of CÔTE DE BEAUNE. Try Bellene, Buisson, De Chassorney, Gras, HOSPICES.

-Véran Burg w ★★ **12 13 14'** AC outside POUILLY-FUISSÉ with variable soils, DOMS and results. Best are quality (Chagnoleau, Corsin, Merlin) and value (DUBOEUF, Deux Roches, Poncetys).

Ste-Croix-du-Mont B'x w sw ★★ 03' 05' 07 09' 10' 11 13 (14) Sweet white AC facing SAUTERNES across the river Garonne. Worth trying the best, ie. CHX Crabitan Bellevue, *Loubens*, du Mont, Pavillon, la Rame.

Ste-Victoire Prov r p ★★ Subzone of CÔTES DE PROV from s slopes of Montagne Ste Victoire. Dramatic scenery goes with gd wine. Try Mas de Cadenet, Mauvan.

Salon Champ ★★★(★) Original BLANC DE BLANCS, from LE MESNIL in Côte des Blancs. Tiny quantities. Awesome reputation for long-lived luxury-priced wines: in truth sometimes inconsistent. On song recently, viz 88' 90 97', but 99 disappoints and where is 02 going? Experts differ.

Sancerre Lo (r) (p) w ★→★★★ 05' 08' 10 12 13 14' Benchmark SAUV BL. Increasing emphasis on single v'yds. Best wines age 10 yrs+. Now many fine reds (PINOT N). Rosé rarely worth money. Best: Boulay, BOURGEOIS, Cotat (variable), François Crochet, Lucien Crochet, Dezat, Dionysia, Fouassier, Thomas Laballe, ALPHONSE MELLOT, Joseph Mellot, Pierre Martin, Mollet, Pinard, P & N Reverdy, Raimbault, Claude Riffault, Jean-Max Roger, Roblin, Thomas, Vacheron, Vatan, Vattan. Both quality and quantity in 2014.

Santenay C d'O r (w) ★★★ 99' 02' 03 05' 06 08 09' 11 12 13 14' Sturdy reds from spa village s of CHASSAGNE-MONTRACHET. Best v'yds more succulent: La Comme, Le Gravières, CLOS Rousseau, Clos de Tavannes. More interest in whites. Gd growers: Belland, GIRARDIN, Lequin-Colin, Jessiaume, MOREAU, V MOREY, Muzard, Vincent.

Sancerre and Central Loire ACs want to ban nearby IGT Sauvignon Blanc and Pinot Noir plantings. Green-eyed monster?

Saumur Lo r p w sp ★→★★★ 05' 08 09' 10' 12 13 14' Umbrella AC: whites from light to v. serious, mainly easy reds except SAUMUR-CHAMPIGNY, pleasant rosés, centre of Lo fizz production: CRÉMANT, Saumur Mousseux. Saumur-Le-Puy-Notre-Dame AOP for CAB FR reds covering 17 communes: misleadingly wide. Producers: BOUVET LADUBAY, CHAMPS FLEURIS, Antoine Foucault, René-Hugues Gay, Guiberteau, CLOS Mélaric, Paleine, St-Just, Clos ROUGEARD, CHX DE VILLENEUVE, Parnay, Rocheville, Yvonne; CAVE des VIGNERONS de Saumur. Difficult 2012, 13, better 14.

Saumur-Champigny Lo r ★★→★★★ 96' 03 05' 08' 09' 10 12 13 14' Nine-commune popular AC for CAB FR, aromatic, should be nervy; ages 15 yrs in gd vintages. Look for Bruno Dubois, CHX de Targé, DE VILLENEUVE; CLOS Cristal, CLOS ROUGEARD, CHAMPS FLEURIS, de la Cune, Filliatreau, Hureau, Legrand, Nerleux, Roches Neuves, Rocheville, St-Just, Antoine Sanzay, Saumur Co-op, Vadé, Val Brun, Yvonne.

Saussignac SW Fr w sw ★★→★★★ 09' 10 11 12' (14) BERGERAC sub-AOP, cousin and neighbour to MONBAZILLAC, but with a touch more acidity. Best: ★★★ DOMS de Richard, La Maurigne, Les Miaudoux, *Clos d'Yvigne*, Lestevénie, ★★ CHX Le Chabrier, Le Payral, Le Tap.

Sauternes B'x w sw ★★→★★★★ 89' 90' 95 96 97' 98 99' 01' 02 03' 05' 07' 09' 10' 11' 13 (14) AC of five villages (incl BAR) that make France's best sweet wine from "noble rotted" grapes. Strong, luscious, golden, lives for many yrs. Some great yrs recently (except 2012). Top CHX: D'YQUEM, CLOS HAUT-PEYRAGUEY, GUIRAUD, LAFAURIE-PEYRAGUEY, RIEUSSEC, SIGALAS-RABAUD, SUDUIRAUT, LA TOUR BLANCHE. Dry wines are labelled AC B'X Blanc.

Sauzet, Étienne C d'O w ★★★ Leading PULIGNY DOM with superb PREMIERS CRUS (Combettes, Folatières) and GRANDS CRUS (BÂTARD, etc). Fresh, lively wines, once again capable of ageing.

Savennières Lo w dr (sw) ★★→★★★ 89' 96' 97' 99 02' 03 05' 07 08' 09 10' 12 13 14' Small ANJOU AC varied in style and quality; long-lived acidic whites (CHENIN BL). Baudouin, BAUMARD, Boudignon, Closel, CH d'Epiré, FL, Guignian, Laureau, Mahé, Mathieu-Tijou, Morgat, Ogereau, CH PIERRE-BISE, Pithon-Paillé, Ch Soucherie. Top sites: COULÉE DE SERRANT, ROCHE-AUX-MOINES, CLOS du Papillon.

Savigny-lès-Beaune C d'O r (w) ★★★ 99' 02' 03 05' 08 09' 10' 11 12 14 Important village next to BEAUNE; similar mid-weight wines, shd be fresh and lively; can be rustic. Top v'yds: Dominode, Guettes, Lavières, Marconnets, Vergelesses. Growers: *Bize*, Camus, *Chandon de Briailles*, CLAIR, DROUHIN, Ecard, Girard, Guyon, LEROY, Pavelot, TOLLOT-BEAUT.

Savoie r w sp ★★ DYA. Alpine area with light, dry wines like some Swiss or minor Lo. APRÉMONT, CRÉPY, SEYSSEL best-known whites; Roussette more interesting. *Also gd Mondeuse red.*

Schlossberg Al GRAND CRU at Kientzheim famed since 15th century. Glorious compelling RIES from FALLER: Outstanding class in 10, sumptuous in 11.

Schlumberger, Doms Al w sw ★→★★★ Vast, top-quality AL DOM at Guebwiller owning approx one per cent of all Al v'yds. Holdings in GRANDS CRUS Kitterlé, Kessler and racy Saering 08' 09 10' 12 13, Spiegel. Rich wines. Rare RIES, signature CUVÉE Ernest and now PINOT GR Grand Cru Kessler 09' 10' 12 13 14.

Schoenenbourg Al V. rich, successful Riquewihr GRAND CRU: PINOT GR, RIES and v. fine VENDANGE TARDIVE and SÉLECTION DES GRAINS NOBLES, esp DOPFF AU MOULIN. Also v.gd MUSCAT.

Schoenheitz Al Rising estate in Munster Valley. Esp gd dry entry-level RIES 09 10' 11 12 13 14. Lovely floral Ries Linnenberg 08 10 12.

Schoffit, Dom Al w ★★★ Exceptional Colmar grower Bernard S makes superb late-harvest GEWURZ and PINOT GR VENDANGE TARDIVE GRAND CRU RANGEN CLOS St Theobald 07' 09' 10' 12 14 on volcanic soil. Contrast with RIES Grand Cru Sonnenberg 08 10' on limestone. Delicious CHASSELAS.

Sec Literally means dry, though CHAMP so called is medium-sweet (and better at breakfast, teatime, weddings than BRUT).

Séguret S Rh r p w ★★ 10' 11 12' 13 14 Classic postcard PROV hillside village nr GIGONDAS. V'yds mix plain and heights. One of top 18 Rh villages. Mainly GRENACHE, peppery, quite deep reds, some full-on; clear-fruited whites. Esp CH la Courançonne (gd w), DOMS *de l'Amauve* (fine), de Cabasse (elegant), J David (bold, organic), Garancière, *Mourchon* (robust), Pourra (big), Soleil Romain.

Sélection des Grains Nobles Al Term coined by HUGEL for AL equivalent to German Beerenauslese, subject to ever-stricter rules. *Grains nobles* are grapes with "noble rot" for v. sweet wines.

Sérafin C d'O r ★★★ Christian Sérafin offers intense GEVREY-CHAMBERTIN VIEILLES VIGNES, CHARMES-CHAMBERTIN. Plenty of new wood; new-generation refinement.

Seyssel Sav w sp ★★ NV Delicate white, pleasant sparkling. eg. Corbonod.

Sichel & Co B'x r w One of B'x's most respected merchants (Sirius a top brand). Family-run; interests in CHX D'ANGLUDET, PALMER and in CORBIÈRES. New €10 million storage facility.

Signargues S Rh ★→★★ 12' 13 Modest CÔTES DU RH village between Avignon and Nîmes. Fruity, slightly spiced reds to drink inside 4 yrs. NB: CAVE Estézargues (punchy), la Font du Vent (best, deepest), Haut-Musiel, DOM Valériane.

Simone, Ch Prov r p w ★★→★★★ Historic estate just outside Aix-en-PROV, where Winston Churchill painted Mont STE-VICTOIRE. Run by the same family for over two centuries. Virtually synonymous with AC PALETTE. Age-worthy whites worth seeking out; characterful rosé and warming reds. Rare red grape varieties: Castet, Manosquin.

Sipp, Louis Al w sw ★★→★★★ Grower/négociant in Ribeauvillé. V.gd RIES GRAND CRU Kirchberg, superb grand cru Osterberg GEWURZ VENDANGE TARDIVE, esp 07 09'. Fine in classic drier yrs 08 10 12 13 14.

Sipp-Mack Al w sw ★★→★★★ Excellent DOM at Hunawihr. Great RIES from GRANDS CRUS ROSACKER 08 10 – esp fine acidity, Osterberg; v.gd PINOT GR.

Sorg, Bruno Al w ★★→★★★ A 1st-class small grower at Eguisheim for GRANDS CRUS

Florimont (RIES **08 09 10' 11** 12 13 14) and PFERSIGBERG (MUSCAT). Immaculate eco-friendly v'yds.

Sur lie "On the lees". MUSCADET is often bottled straight from the vat, for max zest body and character.

Tâche, La C d'O r ★★★★ **90' 93' 95 96' 98 99' 00 01 02' 03** 05' 06 07 09' 10' 1 12' 13 14 GRAND CRU of VOSNE-ROMANÉE, MONOPOLE of DRC. One of best v'yds on earth full, perfumed, luxurious wine, tight in youth.

Taille-aux-Loups, Dom de la Lo w sw sp ★★★ 02' 03' 05' 07' 08' 09 10' 11 12 1 14' Jacky Blot, purveyor of the Lo's most dynamic, meticulous producers: barrel fermented MONTLOUIS, VOUVRAY, majority dry, esp single v'yds – CLOS Mosny and Michet (Montlouis); Venise (Montlouis) Triple Zéro Montlouis *pétillant* (p w) and v.gd reds from DOM de la Butte BOURGUEIL. Small crops 2012, 13, 14.

Tain, Cave de N Rh ★★→★★★ Top N Rh co-op, 290 members, often mature v'yds incl 25 per cent of HERMITAGE. Sound to v.gd red Hermitage, esp Epsilon, Gamber de Loche, full white Hermitage Au Coeur des Siècles. Gd ST-JOSEPH (r w), other wines modern, mainstream. Two gd new CROZES reds from hill and plain v'yds "GN" and "BM". MARSANNE whites gd value, distinguished VIN DE PAILLE.

Taittinger Champ BRUT NV, Rosé NV, Brut **04 06 08**, Collection Brut **89 90 95** are jewels of this again family-run Reims house. Epitome of classic apéritif style Excellent luxury *Comtes de Champagne* 95' 99 02' 04 05 08; Comtes Rosé shine in **06**. Excellent single-v'yd La Marquetterie. (*See also* DOM Carneros, California.

Cost price of making basic NV Champagne, 15 months on lees: €7.50/bottle.

Tavel S Rh p ★★ DYA. GRENACHE rosé, once red-hued, potent, for strong Mediterranean dishes. Now many slighter PROV-style wines, often for apéritif; a pity. Top: DOM Corne-Loup, GUIGAL (gd), Lafond Roc-Epine, Maby, Dom de la Mordorée (full) Prieuré de Montézargues (fine), Moulin-la-Viguerie (organic), Rocalière (fine), CF Correnson (stylish), de Manissy, *Trinquevedel* (fine), VIDAL-FLEURY.

Tempier, Dom Prov r p w ★★★★ Pioneering estate, est MOURVÈDRE in AC BANDOL Wines of great elegance, longevity. Excellent quality rivalled by several others.

Terrasses du Larzac L'doc r p w ★★→★★★ The n-most part of AC L'DOC. Wild, hilly region from Lac du Salagou to Aniane, incl MONTPEYROUX, St-Saturnin. Cru du L'doc since 2014. Cool temperatures, fresh wines, scarcely homogeneous Several est and many rising stars, incl: Mas de l'Ecriture, CLOS des Serres, CA DEMOURA, MONTCALMÈS, Pas de l'Escalette, *Mas Jullien*. Definitely to watch.

Thénard, Dom Burg r w Major grower, GIVRY AC: excellent reds. Whites improving incl large holding of Le MONTRACHET, mostly sold on to merchants eg. JADOT.

Thévenet, Jean Burg r w sw ★★★ MÂCONNAIS purveyor of rich, some semi-botrytized CHARD, eg. CUVÉE Levroutée at DOM de la Bongran. Also Dom Emilian Gillet.

Thézac-Perricard SW Fr r p w ★★ **12'** (14) IGP adjoining CAHORS (reds from MALBE and MERLOT), where Sandrine Annibal's ★★ DOM de Lancement keeps well ahead of a worthy ★ co-op.

Thiénot, Alain Champ New generation takes this house forward. Ever-improving quality; impressive, fairly priced BRUT NV, Rosé NV Brut, vintage Stanislas **02 0**. **06** 08' 09 12, voluminous Vigne aux Gamins (single-v'yd Avize **02 04**). CUVÉ Garance Epernay **07** sings. Owns CHAMP CANARD-DUCHÊNE, CH Ricaud in LOUPIAC.

Thomas, André & fils Al w ★★★ V. fine grower at Ammerschwihr, rigorously organic, artist-craftsman in the cellar. V.gd RIES Kaefferkopf **08** 10', magnificent GEWURZ VIEILLES VIGNES **05 09' 10'** 12.

Tollot-Beaut C d'O r ★★★ Consistent CÔTE DE BEAUNE grower with 20 ha in BEAUN (Grèves, CLOS du Roi), CORTON (Bressandes), SAVIGNY and at CHOREY-LÈS-BEAUNE base (NB: Pièce du Chapitre). Oaky style but it works.

Touraine Lo r p w d or sw sp ★→★★★★ **09' 10 12 13 14'** Huge region with man

ACS (eg. VOUVRAY, CHINON, BOURGUEIL) as well as umbrella AC of variable quality: zesty reds (CAB FR, CÔT, GAMAY, PINOT N), whites (SAUV BL), rosés, sparkling. Often value. Producers: Bois-Vaudons, Corbillières, La Chapinière, Joël Delaunay, de la Garrelière, Gosseaume, CLOS Roche Blanche, Mandard, Jacky Marteau, *Marionnet*, Morantin, Presle, Puzelat, Petit Thouars, Ricard, Roussely, Tue-Boeuf, Villebois. Large village ACs Touraine-Oisly and Touraine-Chenonceaux (27 communes). Overconcentration on Sauv Bl and weedkillers.

Touraine-Amboise Lo r p w ★→★★ TOURAINE sub-AC (220 ha), 60 per cent red. François 1er basic blend (GAMAY/CÔT/CAB FR), top reds: Côt/Cab Fr. White: CHENIN BL. Best: Closerie de Chanteloup, Bessons, Dutertre, Frissant, de la Gabillière, Grange Tiphaine. Wants to be a cru.

Touraine-Azay-le-Rideau Lo p w ★→★★ Tiny TOURAINE sub-AC: rosé (60 per cent of AC; Grolleau 60% min), CHENIN BL-based dry, off-dry white. Best: de l'Aulée, Grosbois, Nicolas Paget, Pibaleau, de la Roche.

Touraine-Mesland Lo r p w ★→★★ 10 13 14 Small TOURAINE sub-AC (105 ha) w of Blois, on n bank of Lo. No better than straight Touraine.

Touraine-Noble Joué Lo p ★→★★ DYA. Great name for a minor rosé from three PINOTS (N, GR, MEUNIER). AC (2001), 28 ha just s of Tours.

Trapet C d'O r ★★★ Long-est GEVREY-CHAMBERTIN DOM enjoying new life; sensual bio wines. CHAMBERTIN is flagship, PREMIER CRUS also v.gd. Cousins ROSSIGNOL-TRAPET.

Trévallon, Dom de Prov r w ★★★ 97 98 99 00′ 01 03 04 05 06 07 08 09 10 11 12 13 Pioneer estate in LES BAUX, but IGP BOUCHES-DU-RH as no GRENACHE grapes. Deserves huge reputation. Intense CAB SAUV/SYRAH to age. *Barrique-aged white* from MARSANNE, ROUSSANNE, a drop of CHARD and now GRENACHE BL. Seek it out.

Trimbach, F E Al w ★★★→★★★★ Matchless grower of AL RIES on limestone soils at Ribeauvillé, esp CLOS STE-HUNE 06 08 09 10′ 12; almost-as-gd (and much cheaper) *Frédéric Émile* 06 08 10 12. Dry, elegant wines for great cuisine.

Tursan SW Fr r p w ★★ (Mostly DYA.) AOP in the Landes. Worthy ★ co-op can't keep up with famous chef Michel Guérard's modern atypical wines from his CH de Bachen. ★★ DOM de Perchade is more authentic.

Vacqueyras S Rh r (p) w ★★ 05′ 06′ 07′ 09′ 10′ 11 12′ 13 Hearty, peppery, GRENACHE-centred neighbour of GIGONDAS with earlier, hotter v'yds; so wine for game, big flavours. Lives 10 yrs+. NB: Arnoux Vieux Clocher, JABOULET, CHX de Montmirail, *des Tours* (v. fine); CLOS des Cazaux (gd value), DOMS Amouriers, Archimbaud-Vache, Charbonnière, Couroulu (v.gd, traditional), Font de Papier (organic), Fourmone (gd form), Garrigue (traditional), Grapillon d'Or, Monardière (v.gd), Montirius (bio), Montvac (fruity), Famille Perrin, Roucas Toumba (organic), Sang des Cailloux (v.gd). Full whites (Clos des Cazaux, Sang des Cailloux).

Val de Loire Lo r p w DYA. One of France's four regional IGPS, was Jardin de la France.

Val d'Orbieu, Vignerons du L'doc ★ Once-pioneering co-op of co-ops. Sound range of AC and IGP wines. Red CUVÉE Mythique is flagship.

Valençay Lo r p w ★→★★ AOP (165 ha) in e TOURAINE; esp SAUV BL, (CHARD); reds CÔT, GAMAY, PINOT N. CLOS Delorme, Lafond, Jacky Preys, Sinson, Sébastien Vaillant, VIGNERONS de Valençay.

Valréas S Rh r (p) (w) ★★ 10′ 11′ 12′ 13 Previously ordinary, late-ripening CÔTES DU RH-VILLAGE in n Vaucluse truffle country is getting better; large co-op. Grainy, peppery, sometimes heady, red (mainly GRENACHE), improving white. Esp Emmanuel Bouchard (organic, character), CLOS Bellane (gd white), DOM des Grands Devers, du Séminaire, CH la Décelle, du Mas de Ste-Croix.

VDQS *Vins délimité de qualité supérieure.* Now phased out.

Vendange Harvest. **Vendange tardive:** late-harvest; AL equivalent to German Auslese but usually higher alcohol.

Venoge, de Champ Venerable house revitalized under LANSON-BCC ownership.

> **Bio and organic growers in the Southwest**
>
> **Nicolas Carmarans (Entraygues et le Fel)** Former wine-bar owner from Paris has returned to his native AVEYRON: classy results.
>
> **Dom du Cros (Marcillac)** Philippe Teulier expands to make white VINS DE FRANCE, SW (SÉM/PETIT MANSENG) and dr (SÉM/MUSCAT). Excellent value.
>
> **Dom Peyres-Roses (Gaillac)** Astrid Bonnafont and her sons are strict biodynamicists. Authentic, well-made, characterful wines.
>
> **Luc de Conti (Bergerac)** Nearly all organic.
>
> **Ch Richard (Saussignac)** Organic; by former geologist Richard Doughty.
>
> **Dom Mouthes-le-Bihan (Côtes de Duras)** Organic wines here from 1999 onwards. Possibly best in appellation.
>
> **Dom du Pech (Buzet)** Magali Tissot, working with partner Ludovic Bonnelle; "natural" wines so quirky they're often refused the appellation.
>
> **Clos Lapeyre (Jurançon)** Jean-Bernard Larrieu works his soil by hand, partly because of terracing of land, partly because of his bio philosophy.
>
> **Dom de Souch (Jurançon).** Mondovino star Yvonne Hégoburu, now in her 80s and bio since the beginning, is still top of the pops in JURANÇON.

Gd niche blends: Cordon Bleu Extra-Brut, Vintage BLANC DE BLANCS **00 04 06 08**, CUVÉE 20 Ans, Prestige CUVÉE Louis XV 10-yr-old BLANC DE NOIRS.

Ventoux S Rh r p w ★★ 10′ 11′ 12′ 13 14 Rambling AC all around Mont Ventoux between Rh and PROV. A few front-running DOMS are gd value. Juicy, tangy red (GRENACHE/SYRAH, café-style to deeper, improving quality), rosé, gd white (more oak). Best: CLOS des Patris, Ferme St-Pierre (p w), Gonnet, **La Vieille Ferme** (r) owned by BEAUCASTEL, CHX Unang (gd w), Valcombe, co-op Bédoin, Goult, St-Didier, Doms Anges, Berane, Brusset, Cascavel, Champ-Long, Croix de Pins, Fondrèche (v.gd), Grand Jacquet, JABOULET (v.gd), Martinelle, Murmurium, **Pesquié** (excellent), Pigeade, St-Jean du Barroux, Terres de Solence, Verrière, VIDAL-FLEURY.

Verget Burg w ★★ →★★★ Jean-Marie Guffens' MÂCONNAIS-based white wine merchant venture, nearly as idiosyncratic as his own DOM. Also varietal wines from s now.

Vernay, Dom Georges N Rh r w ★★→★★★ 12′ 13′ 14′ Top CONDRIEU name; three wines, all stylish; Terrasses de l'Empire *apéritif de luxe*; Chaillées d'Enfer, depth, richness; Coteau de Vernon, supreme style, lives 15 yrs+. CÔTE-RÔTIE, ST-JOSEPH reds emphasize elegance, purity of fruit. Also gd VIN DE PAYS (r w).

Veuve Clicquot Champ Historic house of highest standing. Full-bodied, rich, fine: one of CHAMP's sure things. Yellow Label NV, White Label DEMI-SEC NV, Vintage Rés **02 04 06 08** 12′, Rosé Rés **08** 12′. Luxury La Grande Dame **98 04**, fine **06** from 2015, Rich Rés **02 06**, La Grande Dame Rosé **95 04 06**. Part-oak-fermented vintages from 08. New CAVE Privée re-release of older vintages in fine condition esp **90 82** (in mags). New project for serious rosé from lower yields.

Veuve Devaux Champ Premium brand of powerful Union Auboise co-op. Excellent aged Grande Rés NV, Œil de Perdrix Rosé, Prestige CUVÉE D **02′ 04**, BRUT Vintage **04 06 09′**.

Vézelay Burg r w ★→★★ Age 1–2 yrs. Up-and-coming n subdistrict of generic BOURGOGNE for reds. Tasty whites from CHARD or the resurrected MELON sold as COTEAUX BOURGUIGNONS. Try DOM de la Cadette, La Croix Montjoie, des Faverelles, Elise Villiers.

Vidal-Fleury, J N Rh r w sw ★★→★★★ GUIGAL-owned Rh merchant and grower of CÔTE-RÔTIE. Top-notch, v. elegant **La Chatillonne** (12% VIOGNIER, much oak, wait min 5 yrs). Range wide and improving. Gd CAIRANNE, CÔTES DU RH (r p w), TAVEL, VENTOUX, MUSCAT DE BEAUMES-DE-VENISE.

Vieille Ferme, La S Rh r w ★→★★ Reliable gd-value brand; VENTOUX (r) and LUBÉRON (w) from Famille Perrin of CH DE BEAUCASTEL. Lighter in last 3 yrs.

FRANCE

Vieilles Vignes Old vines, which should make the best wine. Eg. DE VOGÜÉ, MUSIGNY, Vieilles Vignes. But no rules about age and can be a tourist trap.

Vieux Télégraphe, Dom du S Rh r w ★★★ 78' 81' 85 88 89' 90 94' 95' 96' 97 98' 99' 00 01' 03' 04' 05' 06' 07' 09' 10' 12' 13 14 Big highest-quality estate, maker of smoky, intricate, slow-to-develop red CHÂTEAUNEUF, top two wines La Crau and since 2011 Pied Long. Also rich whites La Crau, CLOS La Roquète (great with food, gd in lesser yrs eg. 02 08 11 13). Owns fine, slow-to-evolve, quietly complex **Gigondas Dom Les Pallières** with US importer Kermit Lynch.

Vigne or vignoble Vineyard (v'yd), vineyards (v'yds).

Vigneron Vine-grower.

Villeneuve, Ch de Lo r w ★★→★★★★ 96 99 03 05 06 07 08' 09' 10' 11 12 13 (14) Benchmark estate. Wonderful SAUMUR Blanc (esp Les Cormiers) and SAUMUR-CHAMPIGNY (esp VIEILLES VIGNES, Grand CLOS but only in gd vintages). Converting to organic. High-quality but small 2014.

Vin de France Replaces VDT. Allows mention of grape variety and vintage. Often blends of regions with brand name. Can be source of unexpected delights if talented winemaker uses this category to avoid bureaucractic hassle. Eg. Yves Cuilleron VIOGNIER (N Rh).

Vin de paille Wine from grapes dried on straw mats, so v. sweet, like Italian passito. Esp in the Jura. See also CHAVE, VIN PAILLÉ DE CORRÈZE.

Vin de Pays (VDP) Potentially most dynamic category in France (with over 150 regions), allowing scope for experimentation. Renamed IGP (*Indication Géographique Protegée*) from 2009 vintage, but position unchanged and new terminology still not accepted by every area. The zonal names are most individual: eg. CÔTES DE GASCOGNE, CÔTES DE THONGUE, Haute Vallée de l'Orb, Duché d'Uzès, among others. Enormous variety in taste and quality but never ceases to surprise.

Vin de table (VDT) Standard everyday table wine category, replaced by VIN DE FRANCE.

Vin doux naturel (VDN) Rouss Sweet wine fortified with wine alcohol: sweetness is natural, strength is not. Speciality of ROUSS based on GRENACHE, Noir, Blanc or Gris, or MUSCAT. Top wines, esp aged RANCIOS, can provide fabulous drinking.

Vin gris "Grey" wine is v. pale pink, made of red grapes pressed before fermentation begins – unlike rosé, which ferments briefly before pressing. Or from eg. PINOT GR, not-quite-white grapes. "Œil de Perdrix" and "blush" mean much the same.

Vin jaune Jura w ★★★ Speciality of ARBOIS: inimitable yellow wine of France, like Fino Sherry but far more expensive. Normally ready when bottled (after at least 6 yrs). Best: CH-CHALON. A halfway-house oxidized white sold locally as *vin typé*.

Vin paillé de Corrèze SW Fr r w 25 small growers and a tiny co-op have revived the old tradition of laying out grapes on straw to make a pungent wine with an acquired taste, once recommended to breast-feeding mothers. The wines will keep as long as you. Try ★ Christian Tronche.

Vinsobres S Rh r (p) (w) ★★ 10' 11 12' 13 14 AC notable for SYRAH, older hill v'yds, younger windy plateau v'yds. Best reds: clear red fruit, punchy content ideal with red meats. Top: CAVE la Vinsobraise, DOMS les Aussellons, Bicarelle, Chaume-Arnaud, Constant-Duquesnoy, Coriançon, Deurre (traditional), Jaume (modern), Moulin (traditional), Famille Perrin (value), Péquélette (bio), CH Rouanne.

Viré-Clessé Burg w ★★ 09' 10' 11 12 13 14' AC based around two of best white villages of MÂCON. Known for exuberant rich style, sometimes late-harvest. Try Bonhomme, Bret Bros, Chaland, Gondard-Perrin, LAFON, J-P Michel, THÉVENET, DOM de la Verpaille.

Visan S Rh r (p) (w) ★★ 10' 11' 12' 13 Improving. Later-ripening Rh village: reds with fair depth, clear fruit, pepper; some more suave. Whites okay. Best: DOMS Coste Chaude (gd fruit), Florane, Fourmente (bio, esp Nature), des Grands Devers, Montmartel, Philippe Plantevin, Roche-Audran (organic), Vignoble Art Mas.

Vogüé, Comte Georges de C d'O r w ★★★★ Iconic CHAMBOLLE estate, incl lion's share of MUSIGNY. Heralded vintages from 1990s taking time to come round.

Volnay C d'O r ★★★→★★★★ 90' 95 96' 98 99' 02' 03 05' 06 07 09' 10' 11 12 14 Best source for CÔTE DE BEAUNE reds except when it hails. Can be structured should be silky. Best v'yds: Caillerets, Champans, CLOS des Chênes, Clos des Ducs, Santenots, Taillepieds, etc. Best growers: D'ANGERVILLE, H BOILLOT, HOSPICES DE BEAUNE, LAFARGE, LAFON, DE MONTILLE, Pousse d'Or, N Rossignol.

Vosne-Romanée C d'O r ★★★→★★★★ 90' 93' 95 96' 98 99' 02' 03 05' 06 07 08 09' 10' 11 12 13 14 Village with Burg's grandest crus (eg. ROMANÉE-CONTI, LA TÂCHE and outstanding PREMIERS CRUS Malconsorts, Suchots, Brûlées, etc. There are (or should be) no common wines in Vosne. Many gd if increasingly pricey growers. Try Arnoux-Lachaux, CATHIARD, Clavelier, DRC, EUGÉNIE, GRIVOT, GROS, Lamarche LEROY, LIGER-BELAIR, MÉO-CAMUZET, MUGNERET, ROUGET, Tardy, Vigot.

Vougeot C d'O r w ★★★ 90' 96' 99' 02' 03 05' 06 07 08 09' 10' 11 12' 13 14 Mostly GRAND CRU as CLOS DE VOUGEOT but also village and PREMIER CRU, incl outstanding white MONOPOLE, *Clos Blanc de V.* HUDELOT-Noëllat, VOUGERAIE best.

Vougeraie, Dom de la C d'O r w ★★★→★★★★ DOM uniting all BOISSET's v'yd holdings (since 1999). BOURGOGNE Rouge up to fine GRANDS CRUS eg. CHARMES-CHAMBERTIN BONNES-MARES, MUSIGNY and unique white CLOS Blanc de VOUGEOT. Various top whites being added, esp BÂTARD-MONTRACHET.

Vouvray Lo w dr sw sp ★★→★★★★ (dr) 89 90 96' 02' 03 05' 07 08' 09 10 11 12 13 14 (sw) 89' 90' 95' 96' 97' 03' 05' 08 09' AC e of Tours, on n bank of Lo. Best v'yds overlook river: still wines from top producers gd and reliable. DEMI-SEC is classic style, but in gd yrs *moelleux* can be intensely sweet, virtually everlasting Fizz variable (60 per cent of production): look for *pétillant*. Producers: Autran Bonneau, Brunet, Carême, *Champalou*, CLOS Baudoin, Cosme, Dhoye-Deruet, Foreau, Fouquet (DOM des Aubuisières), CH Gaudrelle, *Huet*, de la Meslerie F PINON, *Dom de la Taille-aux-Loups*, Vigneau-Chevreau. Old vintages, ie. 21 24 47 59 70 71 a must-try. 2014 promising but small crop.

Vranken Champ Powerful CHAMP group. Sound quality. Leading brand: Demoiselle. Owns HEIDSIECK MONOPOLE, POMMERY. Extensive vyds in PROV, Camargue, Douro.

Wolfberger Al ★★ Principal label of EGUISHEIM co-op. V.gd quality for such a large-scale producer. Leading sparkling CRÉMANT producer; high tech for high quality.

"Y" B'x (pronounced "ygrec") 88 94 96 00 02 04 05 06 07 08 09 10 11 12 13 (14) Intense dry white wine produced at CH D'YQUEM, now every vintage. Enticing young but interesting with age. Dry style in 2004, otherwise in classic off-dry mould. Vintages since 05 purer, fresher than in past.

Zind Humbrecht, Dom Al w sw r ★★★★ Leading bio DOM sensitively run by Olivier Humbrecht, great winemaker, president of GRAND CRU Al consortium: rich, balanced wines, drier, elegant, v. low yields. Top wines from single v'yds *Clos St-Urbain Grand Cru Rangen* ACE RIES 00' 08' 09 10' 12 14; Jebsal, superb PINOT GR 08 09 10 12 14; GRANDS CRUS Hengst and Brand (Ries 10' 12 14), Goldert (MUSCAT 12).

Châteaux of Bordeaux

Abbreviations used in the text:

B'x	Bordeaux
Bar	Barsac
E-2-M	Entre-Deux-Mers
Grav	Graves
H-Méd	Haut-Médoc
L de P	Lalande de Pomerol
List	Listrac
Mar	Margaux
Méd	Médoc
Mou	Moulis
Pau	Pauillac
Pe-Lé	Pessac-Léognan
Pom	Pomerol
St-Ém	St-Émilion
St-Est	St-Estèphe
St-Jul	St-Julien
Saut	Sauternes
AC	appellation contrôlée
ch(x)	château(x)
dom(s)	domaine(s)

The first thing a self-respecting grower shows you at a Bordeaux property these days is how he sorts his grapes. *Triage*, which means chucking out substandard ones, is what distinguishes the fiercely competitive from the merely keen. There are electronic, hydraulic, pneumatic, percussive... heaven knows what systems; all good theatre for visitors. The result: better wines, with no taints of rot, green stems or other off-flavours coming from the vineyard.

Châteaux of Bordeaux entries also cross-reference to France

For example, 20 years ago 2011, 2012 and 2013 (particularly the latter) would have been pitiable, but greater care in the vineyard and meticulous sorting helped produce acceptable, often attractive wines. 2014 was yet another testing year and after a cool, humid July and Augus was ultimately saved by a glorious Indian summer. Quality and quantity surpass the three previous years but by how much will be revealed in time (1996 and 2006 could be the references). In the meantime there is a reserve of good red vintages for drinking. The luscious 2009s are tempting at whatever level and in appellations like Castillon, Fronsac, Haut-Médoc and Graves the 2008s are drinking well. The lighter-weight 2012s also offer some early-drinking charm at *petit château* level.

For all sorts of reasons St-Émilion is on a roll just now as the place to look for substantial, satisfying, modern-tasting wines at fair prices and drinkable within two or three years. They may not be classic claret, with the freshness and "cut" of the Médoc, but they suit our cross-over cooking, and people who drink red wine without food.

Among the *grands crus* the mature vintages to look for are 2000, 2001 (particularly Right Bank), 2002 (top-end Médoc) and 2004, with the very best 2007s also worthy of consideration. Dry white Bordeaux remains consistent in quality and value, with another cracking vintage in 2014, so don't hesitate here. And Sauternes continues its winning run (apart from 2012) with a tiny quantity of a fresher-styled 2014. The problem is one of being spoilt for choice: 2011, 2010, 2009, 2007, 2005, 2003 and 2001 are as good as it gets in this sweet wine appellation.

A, Dom de L' r ★★ 02 03 04 05' 06 07 08 09' 10' 11 12 Owned by winemaking consultant STÉPHANE DERENONCOURT and his wife. One of best in CASTILLON. Bio Punches above its weight.

Agassac, D' H-Méd r ★★ 04 05 06 07 08 09' 10' 11 12 Renaissance CH in s H-MÉD. Modern, accessible wine. STÉPHANE DERENONCOURT consults (since 2014).

Aiguilhe, D' C de B'x r ★★ 05 06 07 08 09 10 11 12 Leading player in CASTILLON-CÔTES DE BORDEAUX on high plateau. Same owner as CANON LA GAFFELIÈRE and LA MONDOTTE. Wine with *power and finesse.* Can age.

Andron-Blanquet St-Est r ★★ 98 00' 01 03 04 05' 06 08 09' 10' 11 Sister CH to COS-LABORY. CAB SAUV, MERLOT and 10% CAB FR. Usually gd value.

Angélus St-Ém r ★★★★ 90' 95 96 98' 99 00' 01 02 03' 04 05 06 07 08 09' 10 11 12 13 Owner Hubert de Boüard made his 30th vintage in 2014. Promoted to PREMIER GRAND CRU CLASSÉ (A) in 2012 so prices up. Same vintage bottled in black bottle with label embossed in 21.7 carat gold to celebrate. Also theatrical new bell-tower. Pioneer of modern ST-ÉM; dark, rich, sumptuous. Second label: Le Carillon de L'Angélus.

Angludet, D' Marg r ★★★ 98' 00 02 04 05 06 08 09' 10' 11 12 Owned and run by négociant SICHEL. Lively, fragrant, stylish, consistent wines. Always gd value. Also CH Argadens (B'X SUPÉRIEUR, r and *w*).

Archambeau Grav r w dr (sw) ★★ (r) 05 06 08 09 10 11 (w) 07 08 09 10 11 12 13 Consistent property located at Illats. Gd *fruity dry white*; fragrant barrel-aged reds; Eté d'Archambeau rosé. Improving BAR classed-growth CH Suau same stable.

Arche, D' Saut w sw ★★ 96 97' 98 99 00 01' 02 03' 05 07 09' 10' 11' 13 Consistent, gd-value Second Growth on edge of SAUT. Arche Lafaurie is a special selection. B&B in 17th-century chapter house.

Armailhac, D' Pau r ★★★ 96' 98 99 00 01 02 03 04 05' 06 07 08 09' 10' 11 12 13 Substantial Fifth Growth. (MOUTON) ROTHSCHILD owned since 1934. Top-quality; more finesse than sister CLERC MILON; 15–20% CAB FR. On top form, well priced.

St-Émilion classification – current version
The latest classification (2012) incl a total of 82 CHX: 18 PREMIERS GRANDS CRUS CLASSÉS and 64 GRANDS CRUS CLASSÉS. The new classification, now legally considered an exam rather than a competition, was conducted by a commission of seven wine professionals nominated by INAO, none from B'x. Chx ANGÉLUS and PAVIE were upgraded to PREMIER GRAND CRU CLASSÉ (A) while added to the rank of PREMIER GRAND CRU CLASSÉ (B) were CANON LA GAFFELIÈRE, LARCIS DUCASSE, LA MONDOTTE and VALANDRAUD. New to the status of *grand cru classé* were Chx BARDE-HAUT, Le Chatelet, CLOS de Sarpe, La Commanderie, Côte de Baleau, FAUGÈRES, DE FERRAND, La Fleur Morange, FOMBRAUGE, JEAN FAURE, Clos la Madeleine, Péby Faugères, DE PRESSAC, QUINAULT L'ENCLOS, Rochebelle and SANSONNET. Although a motivating force for the producers, the classification (which is reviewed every ten yrs) remains an unwieldy guide for consumers. Three disappointed candidates are challenging the classification in court; if successful it could be the end of the ranking system that was originally introduced in 1955.

Arrosée, L' St-Ém r ★★★ 00 01 02 03 04 05' 06' 07 08 09' 10' 11 12 RIP from 2013, now sold and integrated into neighbouring QUINTUS. Until then on top form since 2003. Mellow, harmonious wines with plenty of CAB FR and CAB SAUV (40%).

Aurelius St-Ém r ★★ 05 06 08 09 10 11 12 Top CUVÉE from the go-ahead ST-ÉM co-op. Low yields. Modern, concentrated, oaky style.

Ausone St-Ém r ★★★★ 88 89' 90 95 96' 97 98' 99 00' 01' 02 03' 04 05' 06' 07 08 09' 10' 11 12 13 Tiny but illustrious ST-ÉM First Growth (c.1,500 cases); best position on the côtes. Lots of CAB FR (55%). Long-lived wines with volume, texture, finesse. Second label: Chapelle d'Ausone (500 cases) also excellent MOULIN-ST-GEORGES, FONBEL in same Vauthier family ownership. CH LA CLOTTE added in 2014.

Balestard la Tonnelle St-Ém r ★★ 00' 01 03 04 05 06 08 09 10 11 12 Historic DOM, 15th-century watchtower. Now rich, modern style. CAP DE MOURLIN same stable.

Barde-Haut St-Ém r ★★ 98 00 01 02 03 05' 06 07 08 09 10 11 12 Elevated to GRAND CRU CLASSÉ in 2012. Sister property of CLOS L'ÉGLISE, HAUT-BERGEY and ST-ÉM GRAND CRU Haut-Villet (2014). Rich, modern, opulent.

Bastor-Lamontagne Saut w sw ★★ 96' 97' 98 99 01' 02 03' 05 07 09' 10 11 13 Large unclassified Preignac sister to BEAUREGARD. Part owned and managed by SMITH-HAUT-LAFITTE team since 2014. Gd value; pure, harmonious. Second label: Les Remparts de Bastor. New, fruity "So" for early drinking.

Batailley Pau r ★★★ 96 00' 02 03 04 05' 06 08 09' 10' 11 12 13 Classified PAU estate owned by BORIE-MANOUX connections. *On steady form* in last decade. At this level gd value.

Beaumont H-Méd r ★★ 00' 05' 06 08 09 10' Large estate (around 42,000 cases) owned by Castel and Suntory; early-maturing, *easily enjoyable wines*. Second label: Les Tours de Beaumont.

Beauregard Pom r ★★★ 00' 01 02 03 04 05' 06 08 09' 10' 12 Consistent mid-weight POM, converting to organics. Managed by SMITH-HAUT-LAFITTE team since 2014. Pavillon Beauregard (LALANDE DE POMEROL) and BASTOR-LAMONTAGNE sister estates. Second label: Benjamin de Beauregard.

Beau-Séjour-Bécot St-Ém r ★★★ 90' 95 96 98' 99 00' 01 02 03 04 05' 06 07 08 09' 10' 11 12 Distinguished PREMIER GRAND CRU CLASSÉ on the limestone plateau. Combines elegance with depth of fruit. Gérard Bécot stepped down as general manager 2013. Brother Dominique and daughter Juliette remain.

Beauséjour-Duffau St-Ém r ★★★ 98 99 00 01 02 03 04 05' 06 08 09' 10' 11 12 Tiny

PREMIER GRAND CRU CLASSÉ estate on the côtes owned by Duffau-Lagarrosse family. Has had critics purring since 09: STÉPHANE DERENONCOURT consults.

Beau-Site St-Est r ★★ 00 03 04 05 06 08 09 10 11 CRU BOURGEOIS (2012) property owned by BORIE-MANOUX connections. 70% CAB SAUV. Supple, fresh and accessible.

Bélair-Monange St-Ém r ★★★ 90' 95' 96 98 99 00' 01 02 03 04 05' 06 08 09 10' 11 12 13 Classed-growth neighbour of AUSONE owned by négociant J-P MOUEIX. Absorbed MAGDELAINE in 2012 so now double the size but only half in production. Fine, fragrant, elegant style; riper, broader since 2008.

Belgrave H-Méd r ★★ 00' 02' 03 04' 05' 06 07 08 09' 10' 11 12 13 Sizeable Fifth Growth managed by CVBG-DOURTHE (*see* LA GARDE, REYSSON) since 1979. Modern-classic in style. Now consistent quality. Second label: Diane de Belgrave.

Bellefont-Belcier St-Ém r ★★ 00 01 02 03 04 05' 06 07 08' 09' 10' 11 12 ST-ÉM GRAND CRU CLASSÉ now owned by Chinese businessman (2012). Neighbour of LARCIS DUCASSE in St-Laurent-des-Combes. 19th-century circular cellar. Suave and fresh.

Belle-Vue H-Méd r ★★ 04 05 06 07 08 09 10 11 12 Consistent, gd-value southern H-MÉD. Lots of PETIT VERDOT (21%). Dark and dense but firm, fresh, refined. CH Gironville same stable.

Berliquet St-Ém r ★★ 00' 01 02 04 05' 06 08 09 10 12 Tiny GRAND CRU CLASSÉ on côtes next to CANON and BÉLAIR-MONANGE. Managed by the Thienpont-DERENONCOURT team. Fresh, elegant, gd value at this level.

Bernadotte H-Méd r ★★→★★★ 00' 01 02 03 04 05' 06 07 08 09' 10' 11 Northern CRU BOURGEOIS (2012). Owned by a Hong Kong-based group since 2012. Savoury H-MÉD style. Recent vintages have more finesse.

Bertineau St-Vincent B'x r ★★ 00' 01 04 05 06 00 08 09 10 12 Tiny LALANDE-DE-POMEROL estate now owned (2013) by Chinese businessman. Wine vinified at BON PASTEUR. MICHEL ROLLAND manages the property. Fairly consistent quality.

Beychevelle St-Jul r ★★★ 99 00' 01 02 03 04 05' 06 07 08 09' 10' 11 12 13 Fourth Growth with "dragon-boat" label. Castel (since 2011) and Suntory (LAGRANGE) owners. Wines of consistent elegance rather than power. On gd form. New glass-walled winery for 2016 vintage. Second label: Amiral de Beychevelle.

Biston-Brillette Mou r ★★ 01 02 03 04 05' 06 08 09 10' 11 12 Family-owned MOU estate. 50% each Cab Sauv and Merlot. Attractive, fruit-bound wines. Gd value.

Bonalgue Pom r ★★ 00 01 04 05 06 08 09 10 11 12 Dark, rich, meaty. As gd value as it gets. Owned by Bourotte family since 1926. Sister estate CLOS du Clocher. CH Les Hauts Conseillants in L DE P same stable.

Bonnet r w ★★ (r) 09 10 11 12 (w) DYA. Owned by 90-yr-old veteran André Lurton. Big producer of some of the best E-2-M and red (Rés) B'X. LA LOUVIÈRE, COUHINS-LURTON, ROCHEMORIN same stable. Reshuffle of winemaking team in 2014.

Bon Pasteur, Le Pom r ★★★ 98' 99 00 01 02 03 04 05' 06 08 09' 10' 11 12 13 Tiny property on ST-ÉM border now owned (2013) by Chinese concern. Former owner, MICHEL ROLLAND, manages. Ripe, opulent, seductive wines guaranteed.

Boscq, Le St-Est r ★★★ 03 04 05' 06 08 09' 10 11 12 Quality-driven CRU BOURGEOIS (2012) owned by CVBG-DOURTHE. Consistently gd value.

Bourgneuf Pom r ★★ 00 01' 03 04 05' 06 08 09 10 11 12 Owned by the Vayron family. Frédérique the winemaker. Subtle, savoury wines. More depth and precision since 2009. Gd value for POM.

Bouscaut Pe-Lé r w ★★ (r) 00 01 02 04 05' 06 07 08 09 10' 11 12 (w) 02 03 04 05' 06 07 08 09 10' 11 12 13 Classed growth owned by Sophie Lurton. MERLOT-based reds. Sappy, age-worthy whites. Second label: Les Chênes de Bouscaut.

Boyd-Cantenac Marg r ★★★ 00 02 03 04 05' 06 07 08 09' 10' 11 12 Cantenac-based Third Growth on top form these days. CAB SAUV-dominated with a little peppery PETIT VERDOT. Second label: Jacques Boyd. *See also* POUGET.

Branaire-Ducru St-Jul r ★★★ 96 98 00' 01 02 03 04 05' 06 08 09' 10' 11 12 13 Fourth

Growth across road from BEYCHEVELLE. V'yd scattered around AC. Consistent since the mid-90s and gd value. Ageing potential. Second label: *Duluc*.

Branas Grand Poujeaux r ★★ 05 06 08 09 10 11 12 Tiny neighbour of CHASSE-SPLEEN and POUJEAUX. Plenty of investment since 2005. Ripe and fine with supple tannins. DERENONCOURT consults. Owner has PRIEURÉ-LICHINE interest and owns Villemaurine (GRAND CRU CLASSÉ) in ST-ÉM.

Brane-Cantenac Marg r ★★★ 96 98 99 00' 01 02 03 04 05' 06 07 08 09' 10' 11 12 13 Important Second Growth on the Cantenac plateau. Owner Henri Lurton manages with aplomb. Dense, fragrant MARG. Trials with organic cultivation. Second label: Baron de Brane.

Brillette Mou r ★★ 02 03 04 05 06 08 09 10 11 12 CRU BOURGEOIS (2012) with v'yd on gravelly soils. Wines of gd depth and fruit. Second label: Les Hauts de Brillette.

Cabanne, La Pom r ★★ 00 04 05 06' 09 10 11 12 V'yd w of POM plateau. Completely renovated since fire in 2010 (2008 vintage destroyed). Signs of improvement. Second label: DOM de Compostelle.

Caillou Saut w sw ★★ 95 96 97 98 99 01' 02 03' 05' 07 09' 10' 11' 13 Discreet but well-run Second Growth BAR for firm, fruity wine. CUVÉE Reine is top selection, Cuvée du Centenaire another. Dry white Caillou Sec.

Calon-Ségur St-Est r ★★★★ 90' 95 96' 98 99 00' 01 02 03' 04 05' 06 07 08' 09' 10' 11 12 13 Third Growth with great historic reputation. Sold to a French insurance company in 2012; €20 million renovation underway. More CAB SAUV now (80%). Estate really flying since 2008. Second label: Marquis de Calon.

Cambon la Pelouse H-Méd r ★★ 04 05' 06 07 08 09 10' 11 12 Big, supple, s H-MÉD CRU BOURGEOIS (2012). L'Aura, a micro-cuvée from MARG.

Camensac H-Méd r ★★ 98 01 02 03 05 06 08 09 10' 11 12 Fifth Growth in n H-MÉD. Owned by Merlaut family. CHASSE-SPLEEN team handle winemaking; change for better (2006); riper CAB SAUV expression. Second label: La Closerie de Camensac.

Merlot is most planted red grape variety in Bordeaux: 65 per cent of the red vineyard.

Canon St-Ém r ★★★ 98' 99 00 01 02 03 04 05' 06 07 08' 09' 10' 11 12 13 Esteemed PREMIER GRAND CRU CLASSÉ with walled v'yd on plateau, currently being restored. Wertheimer-owned, like RAUZAN-SÉGLA. Now flying; elegant, long-lived wines. Former Cheval des Andes (Argentina) winemaker is new MD (2015). Rebuilt Chapelle de Mazerat new cellar for second label: Croix Canon (until 2011 CLOS Canon).

Canon la Gaffelière St-Ém r ★★★ 96 98' 99 00' 01 02 03 04 05' 06 08 09' 10' 11 12 13 Merited promotion to PREMIER GRAND CRU CLASSÉ in 2012. Same ownership as CLOS DE L'ORATOIRE, LA MONDOTTE and AIGUILHE in Castillon. Stylish, upfront, impressive wines with 40% CAB FR and 5% CAB SAUV.

Cantemerle H-Méd r ★★★ 01 02 03 04 05' 06' 07 08 09' 10' 11 12 13 Large property in s H-MÉD with beautiful wooded park. Merits its Fifth Growth status – fine, now consistent style. Second label: Les Allées de Cantemerle.

Cantenac-Brown Marg r ★★→★★★ 98 99 00 01 02 03 04 05' 06 08 09' 10' 11 12 Third Growth wines with mock-Tudor CH. Owned by Simon Halabi since 2005. Previously robust style; now more voluptuous and refined. Dry white Alto (90% Sauv Bl) from 2012. Second label: Brio de Cantenac-Brown.

Capbern-Gasqueton St-Est r ★★ 00 02 03 04 05 06 08' 09' 10' 11 12 13 Benefits from same new investor and management as sister CALON-SÉGUR. New cellars in 2010. Raised its game since 2008 – solid but polished wines.

Cap de Mourlin St-Ém r ★★→★★★ 00 01 03 04 05 06 08 09 10 11 12 16th-century property owned by Capdemourlin family. As with stablemate CH BALESTARD LA TONNELLE more power and concentration than in the past.

Carbonnieux Pe-Lé r w ★★★ 98 99 00 02 04 05' 06 07 08 09' 10 11 12 Historic

13th-century CH at Léognan for sterling red and white; large volumes of both. *The whites*, 65% SAUV BL, eg. 02 03 04 05 06 07 08 09 10 11 12 13, can age 10 yrs or more. Red can age as well. CHX Haut-Vigneau, Lafont Menaut, Le Sartre also in family.

Carles, De B'x r ★★★ 03 04 05' 06' 07 08 09 10 11 12 13 FRONSAC property with 15th-century CH. Haut Carles (★★★) is principal selection with its own modern, gravity-fed cellars. Can rival top ST-ÉM.

Carmes Haut-Brion, Les Pe-Lé r ★★★ 00 01 02 03 04 05' 06 07 08 09' 10' 11 12' 13 Tiny walled-in neighbour of HAUT-BRION; much investment under new (2010) ownership. New Philippe Starck-designed winery (2015). Second label: Le CLOS des Carmes from 2012, with vines purchased in Martillac.

Carruades de Ch Lafite Pau Second label of CH LAFITE. Refined, savoury. Accessible earlier (40% MERLOT) but can age. Prices down on 2011 peak (less Chinese demand).

Carteau Côtes-Daugay St-Ém r ★★ 03 04 05 08 09 10 11 Gd-value ST-ÉM GRAND CRU; full-flavoured, supple wines with freshness too. Mainly MERLOT (70%).

Certan-de-May Pom r ★★★ 96 98 00' 01' 04 05' 06 08 09' 10' 11 12 Tiny property on POM plateau. In same family since 1925. Solid wines with ageing potential.

Bordeaux dries up?

With annual sales of B'X running at around 5.5 million hl and the 2013 crop estimated at 3.9 million hl, there could be a dearth of B'x. The gd news for some growers is that the bulk price has risen to €1,200/ *tonneau* (900 litres). Buyers might look elsewhere, but look in vain for the style they want.

Chantegrive Grav r w ★★→★★★ 03 04 05' 06 07 08 09' 10' 11 12 Largest estate in GRAV; modern and v.gd quality and value. Reds rich and finely oaked. CUVÉE Caroline is top, *fragrant white* 04 05' 06 07 08 09 10 11 12 13.

Chasse-Spleen Mou r (w) ★★★ 01 02 03 04 05' 06 07 08 09' 10' 11 Big (100 ha) MOU estate producing gd, often outstanding, long-maturing wine; classical structure, fragrance. Second label: L'Heritage de Chasse-Spleen. Makes a little white. *See also* CAMENSAC and GRESSIER-GRAND-POUJEAUX.

Chauvin St-Ém r ★★ 03 04 05 06 08 09 10' 11 12 GRAND CRU CLASSÉ bought by Sylvie Cazes of LYNCH-BAGES in 2014. Watch out for change. Recently a steady performer

Cheval Blanc St-Ém r ★★★★ 89 90' 93 94 95 96' 97 98' 99 00' 01' 02 03 04 05' 06 07 08 09' 10' 11 12 13 PREMIER GRAND CRU CLASSÉ (A) superstar of ST-ÉM easy to love. High percentage of CAB FR (60%). Firm, fragrant wines verging on POM. Delicious young; lasts a generation, or two. Same owners, management as YQUEM, LA TOUR DU PIN, QUINAULT L'ENCLOS. New € multi-million winery. Second label: Le Petit Cheval.

Chevalier, Dom de Pe-Lé r w ★★★★ 96' 98' 99' 00' 01' 02 03 04' 05' 06 07 08 09 10' 11 12 13 Very special estate in Léognan pine woods owned for over 30 yrs by the Bernard family. Pure, dense, finely textured red. Impressive, complex long-ageing white has remarkable consistency; wait for rich flavours 95 96' 97 98' 99 00 01 02 03 04 05' 06 07' 08' 09' 10' 11 12 13. Second label: Esprit de Chevalier. New dry white B'x, CLOS des Lunes, launched by same owners in 2012

Cissac H-Méd r ★★ 98 00 02 03 04 05 08 09 10 11 CRU BOURGEOIS (2012) w of PAU Firm, CAB SAUV-dominated wines that need time. Recent vintages less austere Second label: Reflets du CH Cissac.

Citran H-Méd r ★★ 00 02 03 04 05' 06 08 09 10' Sizeable S H-MÉD estate with CHASSE-SPLEEN, CAMENSAC connections. Modern, ripe, oaky through the 2000s Recent vintages less convincing. Second label: Moulins de Citran.

Clarence de Haut-Brion, Le Pe-Lé r ★★★ 89' 90 95 96' 98 99 00 01 02 03 04 05' 06 07 08 09' 10' 11 12 Second label of CH HAUT-BRION, until 2007 known as Bahans Haut-Brion. Blend changes considerably with each vintage (generally 50%+ Merlot) but same suave texture and elegance as *grand vin*.

Clarke List r (p) (w) ★★ 01 02 03 04 05' 06 08 09' 10' 11 12. Owned and restored since 1973 by Edmond de Rothschild. Now v.gd MERLOT-based red. Dark fruit, fine tannins. Also a dry white: Le Merle Blanc du CH Clarke; and rosé. Ch Malmaison in MOU same connection. Foreign ventures too, incl gd new Rimapere, NZ.

Clauzet St-Est r ★★ 05 06 08 09 10 11 12 CRU BOURGEOIS (2012) estate owned by Baron Velge since 1997. Steady investment and improvement. Now consistent quality and value. Also sister CH de Côme (CRU BOURGEOIS 2012).

Clerc Milon Pau r ★★★ 95' 96' 98' 99 00 01 02 03 04 05' 06 07 08 09' 10' 11 12 13 V'yd tripled in size since (MOUTON) Rothschilds purchased in 1970 (now 40 ha). Broader and weightier than sister D'ARMAILHAC; consistent quality. New winemaking team in 2009 and eco-friendly cellar in 2011.

Climens Saut w sw ★★★★ 88' 89 90' 95 96 97' 98 99' 00 01' 02 03' 04 05' 06 07 09' 10' 11' 12' 13' BAR classed growth making *some of the world's most stylish wine*. Concentrated with vibrant acidity giving balance; ageing potential guaranteed. Bio run by owner Bérénice Lurton. Second label: Les Cyprès (gd value).

Clinet Pom r ★★★★ 96 98' 99 00 01 02 03 05' 06 07 08' 09' 10 11 12 Family-owned and -run (Ronan Laborde) estate on POM plateau. Now back on same form and consistency as 1980s; sumptuous but with more finesse. Fleur de Clinet introduced as second label in 1997, but now a négociant brand.

Clos Floridène Grav r w ★★ (r) 08 09' 10' 11 12 (w) 01' 04' 05' 07 08' 09 11' 12 13 **A sure thing** from one of B'x's best white winemakers, Denis Dubourdieu. SAUV BL/SÉM from limestone provides minerally freshness; much-improved red. CHX Cantegril, DOISY-DAËNE and REYNON same owner.

Clos Fourtet St-Ém r ★★★ 98 99 00 01 02 03 04 05' 06 07 08 09' 10' 11 12 13 First Growth on limestone plateau on edge of town. Classic, stylish ST-ÉM. Consistently gd form. POUJEAUX in MOU same owner, as are ST-ÉMS Côte de Baleau and Les Grandes Murailles (2013). Second label: DOM de Martialis.

Clos Haut-Peyraguey Saut w sw ★★★ 90' 95' 96 97' 98 99 00 01' 02 03' 04 05' 06 07 09' 10' 11' 12 13 Magnate Bernard Magrez made this, his fourth Classed Growth, in 2012 (*see* PAPE-CLÉMENT, LA TOUR-CARNET, FOMBRAUGE). Elegant, harmonious wines with ageing potential. Second label: Symphonie. Haut-Bommes same stable.

Clos Puy Arnaud B'x r ★★ 02 03 04 05' 06 08 09' 10 11 12 Bio estate. A leading light in CASTILLON. Wines of depth and distinction. Jazz-musician owner (jazz) formerly connected to PAVIE.

Clos René Pom r ★★ 98' 00' 01 04 05' 06 08 09 10 11 12 MERLOT-led wine with a little spicy MALBEC from sand and clay soils. Less sensuous and celebrated than top POM but gd value and can age.

Clos de l'Oratoire St-Ém r ★★ 00' 01 03 04 05' 06 07 08 09 10' 11 12 GRAND CRU CLASSÉ on the ne slopes of ST-ÉM. Same stable as CANON-LA-GAFFELIÈRE and LA MONDOTTE; polished and fair value.

Clos des Jacobins St-Ém r ★★→★★★ 98 00 01 02 03 04 05' 06 07 08 09' 10' 11 12 Côtes classed growth at top of its game. Huge progress in the last 10 yrs; powerful, modern style. ANGÉLUS owner consults. Same family owns GRAND CRU CLASSÉ (2012) CH La Commanderie.

Clos du Marquis St-Jul r ★★→★★★ 00 01 02 03 04 05' 06 07 08 09' 10' 11 12 13 More typically ST-JUL than stablemate LÉOVILLE-LAS-CASES; CAB SAUV dominates. Matures faster. Until 2007 considered the latter's second label but always a separate v'yd.

Clos l'Église Pom r ★★★ 00' 01 02 03 04 05' 06 07 08 09' 10 11 12 13 Well-sited plateau v'yd. Opulent, elegant wine that will age. Same family owns HAUT-BERGEY Haut-Villet, Branon and BARDE-HAUT. Second label: Esprit de l'Église.

Clotte, La St-Ém r ★★ 00' 01 02 03 04 05 06 08 09' 10' 11 12 Tiny côtes GRAND CRU CLASSÉ now in the same stable as AUSONE (2014). Fine, perfumed, supple wines.

Conseillante, La Pom r ★★★★ 89 90' 95' 96' 98' 99 00' 01 02 03 04 05' 06' 07 08 09' 10' 11 12 13 POM neighbour of L'EVANGILE. Same family ownership for 145 yrs Some of the noblest, most fragrant Pom; almost Médocain in style; long-ageing 80% MERLOT on clay and gravel soils. Second label: Duo de Conseillante.

Corbin St-Ém r ★★ 00' 01 02 04 05 07 08 09' 10' 11 12 Much-improved GRAND CRU CLASSÉ nr POM. Power, finesse. Consistent, gd value. Second label: Divin de Corbin

Cos d'Estournel St-Est r ★★★★ 90' 94 95 96' 98' 00 01 02 03 04 05' 06 07 08 09' 10' 11 12 13 Large and fashionable Second Growth with eccentric pagoda *chai*. Refined and suave ST-EST. State-of-the-art cellars with lift system for gravity-fed winemaking. Pricey SAUV BL-dominated white from 2005. Second label: Les Pagodes de Cos (and CH MARBUZET for some markets). Super-modern Goulée (MÉD) same stable. Also CHAMP producer Pressoirs de France (2013) and Tokaji Hetszolo.

Cos-Labory St-Est r ★★ 95 96' 98' 99 00 02 03 04 05' 06 07 08 09' 10' 11 12 Fifth Growth neighbour of COS D'ESTOURNEL and LAFON-ROCHET. More depth and structure recently. Gd value. ANDRON-BLANQUET is sister CH.

Coufran H-Méd r ★★ 00 01 02 03 04 05 06 08 09 10' 11 12 Coufran and Verdignan in extreme n of H-MÉD, are co-owned. Coufran is mainly MERLOT (85%) for supple wine; but can age. Soudars is another, smaller sister.

First mention of Haut-Brion probably 1521: "wine from the place known as Aubrion"

Couhins-Lurton Pe-Lé r w ★★→★★★ (r) 03 04 05 06 08' 09 10' 11 12 (w) 00 01 02 0 04 05 06 07 08' 09 10' 11 12 13 *Fine*, minerally, long-lived, classed-growth *whit* from SAUV BL. Supple, MERLOT-based red. André Lurton-owned (LA LOUVIÈRE, BONNET)

Couspaude, La St-Ém r ★★★ 00' 01 02 03 04 05 06 07 08 09' 10' 11 12 *Grand cr classé* on plateau close to town of ST-ÉM. Modern style; rich, creamy with lashing of spicy oak. MICHEL ROLLAND consults.

Coutet Saut w sw ★★★ 89' 90' 95 96 97' 98' 99 01' 02 03' 04 05 07 09' 10' 11' 12 13 Traditional rival to CLIMENS, but zestier style. Consistently v. fine. Long ageing CUVÉE Madame is a v. rich selection 89 90 95 97 01. Second label: Chartreuse de Coutet. V.gd dry white, barrel-fermented Opalie.

Couvent des Jacobins St-Ém r ★★ 98' 00' 01 03 04 05 06 08 09' 10' 11 12 GRAND CRU CLASSÉ vinified within walls of town. Same family ownership for over 100 yrs Lighter style. Denis Dubourdieu consults. Second label: Le Menut des Jacobins

Crabitey Grav rw ★★ (r) 05 06 08 09 10 11 12 (w) 09 10 11 12 13 Former orphanage run by religious order. V'yd replanted in the 80s and 90s. Owner Arnaud de Butler now making harmonious, classic red and small volume of livel SÉM/SAUV BL white.

Crock, Le St-Est r ★★ 00' 01 02 03 04 05 06 07 08 09' 10 11 12 Gd-value CRU BOURGEOIS (2012); same family (Cuvelier) as LÉOVILLE-POYFERRÉ. Solid, fruit-packed

Croix, La Pom r ★★ 00 01 04 05 06 07 08 09 10 11 12 Owned by négociant Janoueix. Organically run. 40% CAB FR and CAB SAUV. La Croix-St-Georges and HAUT-SARPE same stable.

Croix-de-Gay, La Pom r ★★★ 98 00' 01' 02 04 05 06 09' 10' 11 12 On POM plateau Round, elegant style; consistent over the yrs. LA FLEUR-DE-GAY is special CUVÉE from selected parcels. Same ownership as Faizeau (MONTAGNE ST-ÉM).

Croix du Casse, La Pom r ★★ 00' 01' 04 05 06 08 09 10 11 12 On sandy/gravel soil in s of POM. Sister of DOM DE L'EGLISE; same values. Progress since 2008. Medium bodied; value for the AC.

Croizet-Bages Pau r ★★→★★★ 96' 98 00' 02 03 04 05 06 07 08 09 10' 11 12 Improving Fifth Growth; still work to be done. Lately, more depth, power, consistency. Same owners as RAUZAN-GASSIES.

Cru Bourgeois Now annually awarded certificate. 267 CH'x in 2012. Quality variable.

Cruzelles, Les B'x r ★★ 05 06 08 09 10 11 12 Rich, generous wine from L DE P. Ageing potential in top yrs. Denis Durantou of L'ÉGLISE-CLINET owner and winemaker.

Dalem B'x r ★★ 04 05' 06 08 09' 10' 11 12 18th-century FRONSAC property. MERLOT-dominated. Brigitte Rullier has added more finesse since taking helm in 2002.

Dassault St-Ém r ★★ 00 01 02 03 04 05' 06 08 09' 10 11 12 Consistent, modern, juicy GRAND CRU CLASSÉ. Owning family of Dassault aviation (since 1955). La Fleur and GRAND CRU CLASSÉ Faurie-de-Souchard (since 2014) same stable.

Dauphine, De la B'x r ★★→★★★ 00 01 03 04 05 06' 08 09' 10' 11 12' Substantial FRONSAC estate. Wholesale change in last 15 yrs. Renovation of CH and v'yds plus new winery. Stablemate Canon-de-Brem integrated in 2006, more land acquired in 2012. Organic certification in 2015. Now more substance and finesse. Second label: Delphis.

Dauzac Marg r ★★→★★★ 95 96 98' 99 00' 01 02 04 05 06 08' 09' 10' 11 12 Fifth Growth at Labarde; now dense, rich, dark wines. Owned by an insurance company; André Lurton no longer involved (sold shares in 2014). Second label: La Bastide Dauzac.

Desmirail Marg r ★★→★★★ 02 03 04 05 06 07 08 09' 10' 11 12 Third Growth at Cantenac owned by Denis Lurton. Fine and delicate style. Second label: Initial de Desmirail.

Destieux St-Ém r ★★ 98 99 00' 01 03' 04 05' 06 07 08 09' 10' 11 12 Compact GRAND CRU CLASSÉ located on second-highest spot in ST-ÉM at St-Hippolyte. Bold, powerful style; consistent. CH La Clémence in POM same stable.

Doisy-Daëne Bar (r) w dr sw ★★★ 89' 90' 95 96 97' 98' 99 01' 02 03 04 05' 06 07 09 10' 11' 12 13 Family-owned (Dubourdieu) estate producing age-worthy, dry white and *fine, sweet Barsac*. Former Doisy-Dubroca v'yd integrated in 2014. L'Extravagant 96 97 01 02 03 04 05 06 07 09 10 11 12 13 is an intensely rich and expensive cuvée.

Doisy-Védrines Saut w sw ★★★ 89' 90 95 96 97' 98 99 01' 03' 04 05 07 09 10' 11' 12 13 BAR Second Growth owned by Castéja family (Joanne négociant). Delicious, sturdy, rich: ages well. Gd value as well.

Dôme, Le St-Ém r ★★★ 04 05 06 08 09 10' 11 12 13 Microwine; rich, modern with a little more freshness than in the past. Two-thirds old-vine CAB FR. Belongs to Jonathan Maltus, with string of other ST-ÉMs (eg. CH Teyssier (gd value), Le Carré, Les Astéries, Vieux-Ch-Mazerat) and a Napa winery, World's End.

Dominique, La St-Ém r ★★★ 95 96 98 99 00' 01 02 05' 06 08 09' 10' 11 12 Classed growth next to CHEVAL BLANC. Solid value until 1996, then went off the boil. Now rich, powerful and juicy. New €11 million winery in 2013 with restaurant on roof. Second label: St Paul de Dominique.

Ducru-Beaucaillou St-Jul r ★★★★ 95' 96' 98 99 00' 01 02 03 04 05' 06 07 08 09' 10' 11 12 13 Outstanding Second Growth, excellent form except for a patch in the late 80s. Added impetus from owner Bruno Borie from 2003. Talented winemaker Virginie Sallette. Classic cedar-scented claret, suited to long ageing. Croix de Beaucaillou and LALANDE-BORIE sister estates.

Duhart-Milon Rothschild Pau r ★★★ 95 96' 98 00' 01 02 03 04' 05' 06 07 08 09' 10' 11 12 13 Fourth Growth stablemate of LAFITE. V. fine quality, esp in last 10 yrs. Relatively gd value (certainly compared to CARRUADES). Second label: Moulin de Duhart.

Durfort-Vivens Marg r ★★★ 95 96 98 99 00 02 03 04 05' 06 08 09' 10' 11 12 13 This is a much-improved MARG Second Growth owned by Gonzague Lurton.

Bio, CAB SAUV-dominated. Wife Claire Villars runs FERRIÈRE and LA GURGUE. Second label: Vivens.

Eglise, Dom de l' Pom r ★★ 98 00 01 02 03 04 05' 06 07 08 09 10' 11 12 Small property to note on clay/gravel plateau. Consistent, fleshy wines of late. Same stable as TROTTEVIEILLE, CROIX DU CASSE.

Église-Clinet, L' Pom r ★★★→★★★★ 89' 90' 93' 94 95 96 98' 99 00' 01' 02 03 04 05' 06 07 08 09' 10' 11' 12 13 Tiny but top-flight estate with great consistency; full, concentrated, fleshy wine. Expensive and limited quantity. Second label: La Petite Eglise.

Évangile, L' Pom r ★★★★ 88' 89' 90 95 96 98' 99 00' 01 02 03 04 05' 06 07 08 09 10' 11 12 13 Rothschild (LAFITE)-owned property on POM plateau. Neighbour of CH LA CONSEILLANTE. Investment has greatly improved quality. Now consistently rich and opulent in style. Second label: Blason de L'Evangile.

Fargues, De Saut w sw ★★★ 90 95 96 97 98 99' 01 02 03' 04 05' 06 07 09' 10' 11' 1 V'yd attached to ruined castle owned by Lur-Saluces, ex-owners of YQUEM. Rich, unctuous wines, but balanced. Quality of SAUT First Growth.

Faugères St-Ém r ★★→★★★ 98 00' 02 03 04 05 06 07 08 09' 10' 11 12 Powerful, rich, modern GRAND CRU CLASSÉ in St-Etienne-de-Lisse. Sister CH Péby Faugère (100% MERLOT) also classified. Swiss-owned. In-your-face state-of-the-art winery. Cap de Faugères, Chambrun and LAFAURIE-PEYRAGUEY same stable.

Ferrand, De St-Ém r ★★→★★★ 00 01 03 04 05 06 08 09' 10' 12 Big St-Hippolyt GRAND CRU CLASSÉ owned by Pauline Bich (Bic pens) and husband Philippe Chandon-Moët. Fresh, firm, expressive.

Ferrande Grav (w) ★★ 05 06 08 09 10 11 12 Substantial estate owned by négociar Castel. Gravel soils. Investment and improvement; enjoyable red; fresh white.

Ferrière Marg r ★★→★★★ 96' 98 99 00' 02 03 04 05 06 08 09' 10' 12 Tiny Third Growth with a CH in MARG village. Moving towards bio. LA GURGUE same stable. Dark, firm, perfumed wines need time.

Feytit-Clinet Pom r ★★→★★★ 98 99 00 01 03 04 05' 06 07 08 09' 10' 11 12 1 Tiny family-owned and -run property. 90% MERLOT on clay-gravel soils. On great form over last 15 yrs. Rich, full POM with ageing potential. Highly prized a a fair (for Pom) price.

By 2018, all Pomerol will have to be vinified within the boundary of the AC.

Fieuzal Pe-Lé r (w) ★★★ (r) 00 01 06 07 08 09' 10' 11 12 (w) 05 06 07 08 09' 1 11 12 13 Classified PE-LÉ estate with Irish owner. White consistent; red best from 2006. New gravity-fed winery (2011). ANGÉLUS owner consults for reds. Second label: L'Abeille de Fieuzal (r w).

Figeac St-Ém r ★★★★ 95' 96 98' 99 00' 01' 02 03 04 05' 06 07 08 09' 10' 1 12 13 First Growth; gravelly v'yd with unusual 70% CAB FR, CAB SAUV. Rich bu always elegant wines; deceptively long ageing. Management upheaval in 201 new business manager, winemaker, general manager; MICHEL ROLLAND consult Second label: Petit-Figeac (from 2012). Previously Grange Neuve de Figeac.

Filhot Saut w dr sw ★★ 96' 97' 98 99 01' 02 03' 04 05 07 09' 10' 11' 13 Historic SAUT estate with splendid 19th-century CH, extensive v'yd. Difficult young, mor complex with age. Richer, purer from 2009.

Fleur Cardinale St-Ém r ★★ 00 01 02 03 04 05' 06 07 08 09' 10' 11 12 GRAND CR CLASSÉ in St-Etienne-de-Lisse. In overdrive for last 15 yrs. Always one of last harvest. Ripe, unctuous, modern style.

Fleur de Boüard, La B'x r ★★→★★★ 04 05 06 07 08 09 10 11 12 13 Leading esta in L DE P. New high-tech winery 2011. Rich, dark, dense, modern. Same owne as ANGÉLUS in ST-ÉM. Special CUVÉE, Le Plus, is more extreme: 100% MERLOT age 3 yrs in new oak barrels.

BORDEAUX

Fleur-de-Gay, La Pom r ★★★ Tiny super-CUVÉE of CH LA CROIX-DE-GAY. 100% MERLOT.

Fleur-Pétrus, La Pom r ★★★★ 90' 95 96 98' 99 00' 01 02 03 04 05' 06 08 09' 10' 11 12 13 J-P MOUEIX property; expanded v'yd with parcels from purchased CH Guillot added (2012) and Providence v'yd incorporated (2014). Finer style than PETRUS or TROTANOY. Needs time.

Fombrauge St-Ém r ★★→★★★ 98 99 00' 01 02 03 04 05 06 08 09' 10' 11 12 Big GRAND CRU CLASSÉ owned by Bernard Magrez (see PAPE-CLÉMENT, LA TOUR-CARNET, CLOS HAUT-PEYRAGUEY). Rich, dark, chocolatey, modern. Magrez-Fombrauge is special red CUVÉE; also name for a little dry, white B'X.

Fonbadet Pau r ★★ 00' 01 02 03 04 05' 06 08 09' 10' 12 Family-owned CRU BOURGEOIS (2012). Majority CAB SAUV (60%). Reliable, gd value, typically PAU.

Fonbel, De St-Ém r ★★ 05 06 07 08 09 10 11 12 Regular source of juicy, fresh, gd-value ST-ÉM. Same owner as AUSONE and MOULIN-ST-GEORGES.

Fonplégade St-Ém r ★★ 98 00' 01 03 04 05 06' 07 08 09' 10 12 GRAND CRU CLASSÉ owned by American Stephen Adams. Investment and progression, with concentrated, modern style. Organic certification from 2013. Visitor-friendly seven days a week.

Fonréaud List r ★★ 98 00' 02 03 04 05 06 08 09' 10' 11 12 One of bigger, better LISTRACS for satisfying, savoury wines. Small volume of v.gd dry white: Le Cygne, barrel-fermented. See LESTAGE. Gd value.

Fonroque St-Ém r ★★★ 96 98 01 03 04 05 06 08 09' 10' 11 12 GRAND CRU CLASSÉ on plateau n of ST-ÉM. Bio paying off; more character, elegance. Always freshness. Managed by Alain Moueix (see MAZEYRES). MOULIN DU CADET sister estate.

Fontenil B'x r ★★ 03 04 05 06 08 09' 10' 11 12 Leading FRONSAC, owned by MICHEL ROLLAND. Ripe, opulent, balanced. Always some experimentation going on.

Forts de Latour, Les Pau r ★★★→★★★★ 89' 90' 95' 96' 98 99 00' 01 02 03 04' 05' 06 07 08 09' 10' 11 12 13 The (worthy) second label of CH LATOUR; authentic flavour in slightly lighter format at Second Growth price. No more en primeur sales; only released when deemed ready to drink – the 2006 in 2014 (barely ready in fact).

Fourcas-Dupré List r ★★ 98' 00' 01 02 03 04 05 06 08 09 10' 11 12 Well-run property making fairly consistent wine in light LIST style. Gravelly soils. Austere when young; needs 4–8 yrs. Second label: CH Bellevue-Laffont.

Fourcas-Hosten List r ★★→★★★ 01 02 03 05 06 08 09 10' 11 12 Large LIST estate. Considerable investment and steady improvement over last 10 yrs. More precision, finesse. New dry, white B'X (SAUV BL/SÉM) from 2013.

France, De Pe-Lé r w ★★ (r) 00 02 03 04 05 06 08 09 10' 11 12 (w) 03 04 05 06 07 08 09 10 11 12 13 Neighbour of FIEUZAL; consistent wines in a ripe, modern style. New cuvier unveiled in 2014 (the old one burnt down). Arnaud Thomassin runs the show.

Franc-Mayne St-Ém r ★★ 98' 00' 01 03 04 05 06 08 09 10' 12 Small classified growth on the côtes. Same owners as CH DE LUSSAC and Vieux Maillet in POM. Investment, renovation. Luxury hotel. Fresh, fruity, round but structured style.

Gaby, Du B'x r ★★ 00' 01' 03 04 05 06 07 08 09 10 12 Splendid s-facing slopes in CANON-FRONSAC. MERLOT-dominated wines age well. Sister CH Moya in CASTILLON-CÔTES DE BORDEAUX same Canadian ownership.

Gaffelière, La St-Ém r ★★★ 89' 90' 95 96 98' 99 00' 01 02 03 04 05' 06 07 08 09' 10' 11 12 13 First Growth at foot of the côtes. Investment, improvement since 2004; part of v'yd replanted; new cuvier in 2013. Elegant, long-ageing wines. Three new properties acquired in 2014: CHX Mauvezin, Haut Badon, Peyrelongue.

Garde, La Pe-Lé r w ★★ (r) 01' 02 04 05 06 07 08 09' 10' 11 12 (w) 04 05 06 07 08 09 10' 11 12 13 Substantial property owned by négociant CVBG-DOURTHE; supple, CAB SAUV/MERLOT reds. Tiny production of SAUV BL/Sauvignon Gris white.

Gay, Le Pom r ★★★ 00 01 03 04 05' 06 07 08 09' 10' 11 12 Fine v'yd on n edge of

POM. Major investment, MICHEL ROLLAND consults. Now v. ripe, plummy in style Henri Parent succeeds mother, Catherine Péré-Vergé, at helm. CH Montviel La Violette same stable plus v'yds in Argentina.

Gazin Pom r ★★★ 95 96 98' 99 00' 01 02 03 04 05' 06 07 08 09' 10' 11 12 13 Large (for POM), family-owned neighbour of PETRUS. On v.gd form since mid-1990s generous, long ageing. Second label: L'Hospitalet de Gazin.

Gilette Saut w sw ★★★ 53 55 59 61 67 70 71 75 76 78 79 81 82 83 85 86 88 89 9(Extraordinary small Preignac CH stores its sumptuous wines in concrete vat for 16–20 yrs. Only around 5,000 bottles of each. Can age further in bottle. CH Les Justices is its sister 01 02 03' 05 07 09 10' 11 13.

Giscours Marg r ★★★ 96' 98 99 00' 01 02 03 04 05' 06 07 08' 09' 10' 11 1. Substantial Third Growth s of Cantenac. Full-bodied, long-ageing MARG capable of greatness (eg. 70). The 80s were wobbly; steady improvement over last 20 yr with new owner. Second label: La Sirène de Giscours. Little B'x rosé. CH DU TERTR stablemate, as are Ch Duthil, Le HAUT-MÉDOC de Giscours.

Les Carmes Haut-Brion's new winery: boat-shaped, in middle of ornamental lake Of course.

Glana, Du St-Jul r ★★ 00 02 03 04 05 06 08 09 10' 12 Big estate, expanded on ex-cr LAGRANGE land. Undemanding; robust; value. Same owner as Bellegrave in PAU Second label: Pavillon du Glana.

Gloria St-Jul r ★★→★★★ 98 99 00' 0102 03 04 05' 06 07 08 09' 10' 11 12 A widel dispersed estate with v'yds among the classed growths. Same ownership a ST-PIERRE. Superb form recently. Second label: Peymartin.

Grand-Corbin-Despagne St-Ém r ★★→★★★ 95 96 98 99 00' 01 03 04 05 06 08 09 10' 11 12 13 Gd-value GRAND CRU CLASSÉ on POM border. Family-owned (Despagne since 1812. Aromatic wines now with riper, fuller edge. On top form. Organi cultivation. Also CH Maison Blanche, MONTAGNE ST-ÉMI and Ch Ampélia, CASTILLON Second label: Petit Corbin-Despagne.

Grand Cru Classé *See* ST-ÉM classification box, p.99.

Grand-Mayne St-Ém r ★★★ 90' 94 95 96 98 99 00' 01' 02 03 04 05' 06 07 0 09' 10' 11 12 Impressive family-owned (Nony since 1934) GRAND CRU CLASSÉ on v côtes. Consistent, full-bodied, structured wines.

Grand-Puy-Ducasse Pau r ★★★ 95 96' 98' 99 00 01 02 03 04 05' 06 07 08 09' 1c 11 12 Fifth Growth owned by a bank (RAYNE VIGNEAU, MEYNEY, same bank). Stead improvement since 2005. New winemaker 2010. ANGÉLUS owner consult Second label: Prélude à Grand-Puy-Ducasse.

Grand-Puy-Lacoste Pau r ★★★ 89' 90' 94 95' 96' 98 99 00' 01 02 03 04 05' 06 0 08' 09' 10' 11 12 13 Fifth Growth famous for gd-value CAB SAUV-driven PAU to la down. Same owner as HAUT-BATAILLEY. *Cuvier* recently renovated, pretty garden Second label: Lacoste-Borie.

Grave à Pomerol, La Pom r ★★★ 98' 00 01 02 04 05 06 08 09' 10 11 12 Sma property on w slope of POM plateau owned by Christian MOUEIX since 197 Accessible, medium richness. Formerly known as La Grave Trigant de Boisset

Greysac Méd r ★★ 03 04 05' 06 08 09 10' 11 12 Same owners as CH Rollan-de-B and HAUT-CONDISSAS since 2012. MERLOT-led, fine, consistent quality.

Gruaud-Larose St-Jul r ★★★★ 89' 90' 95' 96' 98 99 00' 01 02 03 04 05' 06 07 0 09' 10' 11 12 One of biggest, best-loved Second Growths. Smooth, rich, vigorou claret. More finesse since 2007. Second label: Sarget de Gruaud-Larose. Als Osoyoos Larose in Canada..

Guadet St-Ém r ★★ 01 04 05 06 08 09 10 11 12 Tiny GRAND CRU CLASSÉ with quarrie cellars in the rue Guadet, ST-ÉM. Better form in last 10 yrs. DERENONCOURT consult Organically certified.

Guiraud Saut (r) w (dr) sw ★★★ 95 96' 97' 98 99 01' 02 03 04 05' 06 07 09' 10' 11'
13 Big organically certified First Growth. Owners incl long-time manager, Xavier
Planty, Peugeot (cars) family and DOM DE CHEVALIER, LA MONDOTTE connections.
Top quality – more SAUV BL than most. Dry white G de Guiraud. Second label:
Petit Guiraud.

Gurgue, La Marg r ★★ 02 03 04 05' 06 08 09' 10 11 12 Neighbour of CH MARGAUX.
The same management as FERRIÈRE and HAUT-BAGES-LIBÉRAL. Organic tendencies.
Fine. Gd value.

Hanteillan H-Méd r ★★ 00' 02 03 04 05' 06 09' 10 12 Large H-MÉD Cissac estate.
Round, balanced and early-drinking style. DERENONCOURT consults. Second label:
CH Laborde.

Haut-Bages-Libéral Pau r ★★★ 96' 98 99 00 01 02 03 04 05' 06 08 09' 10' 11 12
Lesser-known Fifth Growth (next to LATOUR) in same stable as FERRIÈRE and LA
GURGUE. 50 per cent of v'yd is bio. Results are excellent. Usually gd value.

Haut-Bailly Pe-Lé r ★★★★ 89' 90' 95 96' 98' 99 00' 01 02 03 04 05' 06 07 08'
09' 10' 11' 12 Top-rank PE-LÉ classed growth owned by American banker. Run by
Véronique Sanders, granddaughter of former owner. Only red wine – refined,
elegant style (parcel of v. old vines). CH Le Pape (Léognan) new acquisition in
2012. Second label: La Parde de Haut-Bailly.

Haut-Batailley Pau r ★★★ 98 99 00 02 03 04 05' 06 07 08 09' 10' 11 12 13 Smaller
part of divided Fifth Growth BATAILLEY. Gentler than sister GRAND-PUY-LACOSTE.
Cellars renovated; progression in last 10 yrs. Second label: La Tour-l'Aspic.

Haut-Beauséjour St-Est r ★★ 03 04 05 08 09 10 11 Property created and enhanced
by owner Champagne ROEDERER. Round but structured. Sister of DE PEZ.

Haut-Bergeron Saut w sw ★★ 01 02 03 04 05 06 07 09 10 11 13 A 5th-generation
family estate. One of the most consistent non-classified SAUT. 60 parcels of
old vines. Mainly SÉM (90%). Rich, opulent, gd value.

Haut-Bergey Pe-Lé r (w) ★★→★★★ (r) 00 01 02 04 05 06 07 08 09 10 11 12 (w) 06
07 08 09 10 11 12 13 Non-classified property with means of a classed growth.
Completely renovated in the 1990s. Rich, modern GRAV. Also a little dry white.
BARDE-HAUT, CLOS L'ÉGLISE, Haut-Villet, CH Branon in same stable

Haut-Brion Pe-Lé r ★★★★ (r) 85' 86' 88' 89' 90' 93 94 95' 96' 97 98' 99 00' 01 02
03 04 05' 06 08 09' 10' 11' 12 13 The first First Growth and only non-MÉD in the
list of 1855, owned by American Dillon family since 1935. Deeply harmonious,
wonderful texture. Consistently great since 1975. Can be tasted at the new
Clarence Dillon tasting room/restaurant in Paris. A little *sumptuous dry white*:
96 98 99 00' 01 02 03 04' 05' 06 07 08' 09 10' 11' 12 13. *See* LE CLARENCE DE HAUT-
BRION, LA MISSION-HAUT-BRION, LAVILLE-HAUT-BRION, QUINTUS.

Haut Condissas Méd r ★★★ 04 05 06 07 08 09' 10' 11 12 Garage-style MÉD with
international flavour. Sister to CH Rollan-de-By and GREYSAC. Rich, concentrated,
oaky. MERLOT (60%), PETIT VERDOT (20%) essential components.

Haut-Marbuzet St-Est r ★★→★★★ 98 99 00' 01 02 03 04 05' 06 07 08 09' 10' 11 12
Started in 1952 with 7 ha; now 70 ha. Fourth-Growth quality, but unclassified.
Two-thirds of the production sold directly by the CH. Rich, unctuous wines

---

Second labels – best buys

Reliable second labels from Classed Growth CH incl: Dame de
MONTROSE, Fiefs de LAGRANGE, Tourelles de Longueville (PICHON BARON),
Rés de LÉOVILLE (-BARTON), SEGLA (RAUZAN-), Alter Ego (PALMER), Allées de
CANTEMERLE. But bear in mind that you're paying a premium for the
pedigree, and that a CRU BOURGEOIS of the same price and same yr may
well be the better wine.

matured in 100% new oak BARRIQUES. Chambert-Marbuzet, Tour de Marbuze and Layauga-Duboscq same stable. Second label: MacCarthy.

Haut-Sarpe St-Ém r ★★ 98 00' 01 04 05 06 08 09 10 11 12 Classified estate wit elegant CH and park, 70% MERLOT. Same owner (Janoueix) as CH La Confessio and LA CROIX. Rich, dark, modern style.

Hosanna Pom r ★★★★ 99 00 01 03 04 05' 06 07 08 09' 10' 11' 12 Former Certan-Guiraud until bought and renamed by J-P MOUEIX in 1999. Only best par retained. Wines have power, complexity and class. No Hosanna made in 201 Stablemate of FLEUR-PÉTRUS and TROTANOY.

Issan, D' Marg r ★★★ 98 00' 01 02 03 04' 05' 06 07 08 09' 10' 11 12 13 Third Growt v'yd; moated CH. Fragrant wines; now at top of its game. 50 per cent owned b owner of LILIAN LADOUYS, PÉDESCLAUX (2013). Second label: Blason d'Issan.

Jean Faure St-Ém r ★★ 05 06 08 09 10 11 12 GRAND CRU CLASSÉ neighbour of L DOMINIQUE on clay, sand, gravel soils. Organic cultivation. 50% CAB FR gives fresh elegant style. Dynamic owner (2004) also proprietor of Mas Amiel in MAURY.

Kirwan Marg r ★★★ 95 96 98 99 00' 01 02 03 04 05' 06 07 08 09 10' 11 12 Thir Growth on Cantenac plateau. Property of the Schÿler family. Dense, fleshy i 90s; now more finesse. Former PALMER winemaker at the helm. Second labe Les Charmes de Kirwan.

Labégorce Marg r ★★ -★★★ 02 03 04 05' 07 08 09 10' 11 12 Substantial unclassifie MARG owned by Perrodo family. Considerable investment since 2006. Absorbe next-door Labégorce-Zédé in 2009. Fine, modern style. CH MARQUIS-D'ALESM same stable.

Lafaurie-Peyraguey Saut w sw ★★★ 83' 85 86' 88' 89' 90' 95 96' 97 98 99 01' 0 03' 04 05' 06 07 09' 10' 11' 13 Leading classed growth at Bommes purchase by Lalique crystal owner Silvio Denz (CHX FAUGÈRES, Chambrun) in 2014. Deni Dubourdieu consulting. Expect investment, and new focus on dry white (firs vintage 2014) plus rich, harmonious sweet 90% SÉM. Second label: La Chapell de Lafaurie.

Lafite-Rothschild Pau r ★★★★ 85 86' 88' 89' 90' 93 94 95 96' 97 98' 99 00' 01' 0: 02 03' 04' 05' 06 07 08' 09' 10' 11' 12 13 First Growth of famous elusive perfum and style, but never great weight, although more dense and sleek these days Great vintages need keeping for decades. Recent investment and expansion i the cellars. Joint ventures in Chile (1988), California (1989), Portugal (1992 Argentina (1999), now the MIDI, Italy, even China. Second label: CARRUADES D LAFITE. Also owns CHX DUHART-MILON, L'EVANGILE, RIEUSSEC.

Lafleur Pom r ★★★★ 86 88' 89' 90' 93 94 95 96 98' 99' 00' 01' 02 03 04' 05' 06 07 08 09' 10' 11' 12 13 Superb but tiny family-owned and -managed propert cultivated like a garden. Sits opposite PETRUS. Elegant, intense wine for maturing 50% CAB FR. Expensive. Second label: *Pensées de Lafleur*.

Lafleur-Gazin Pom r ★★ 00 01 04 05 06 08 09 10 11 12 Small J-P MOUEIX estat located between LAFLEUR and GAZIN. Lighter, supple style.

Dry white secrets

Only nine per cent of B'X's production is dry white and most of that is from E-2-M. Fine dry white is associated with PE-LÉ and GRAV but there are also hidden pockets elsewhere. In the MÉD certain classified estates (MARGAUX, MOUTON, TALBOT) produce dry white, as do a number of CHX in LISTRAC (FONRÉAUD, SARANSOT-DUPRÉ, CLARKE). ST-ÉM has a secret source (FOMBRAUGE, MONBOUSQUET, VALANDRAUD) and the volume in SAUT is increasing (DOISY-DAËNE, GUIRAUD, CLOS des Lunes). The problem with recognition is they all carry the less prestigious AC B'x Blanc label.

Lafon-Rochet St-Est r ★★★ 95 96' 98 99 00' 01 02 03' 04 05' 06 08 09' 10' 11 12 13 Fourth Growth neighbour of COS D'ESTOURNEL run by nephew of Alfred Tesseron of PONTET-CANET. High percentage of MERLOT (40%) adds opulence, texture but CAB SAUV provides structure to age. Former PETRUS winemaker (J-C Berrouet) consults. Second label: Les Pèlerins de Lafon-Rochet.

Lagrange St-Jul r ★★★ 89' 90' 94 95 96 98 99 00' 01 02 03 04 05' 06 08 09' 10' 11 12 13 Substantial (115 ha) Third Growth owned since 1983 by Suntory. In tip-top condition. Much investment in v'yd and cellars. Dry white Les Arums de Lagrange. Second label: Les Fiefs de Lagrange (gd value). Third label: Haut-Médoc de Lagrange.

Lagrange Pom r ★★ 98 00 01 04 05 06 09 10 Tiny POM v'yd owned by the Libourne-based négociant J-P MOUEIX since 1953. 95% MERLOT. Gd value but not in same league as HOSANNA, LA FLEUR-PÉTRUS, etc.

Lagune, La H-Méd r ★★★ 95 96' 98 00' 02 03 04 05' 07 08 09' 10' 11 12 Third Growth sandy/gravel soil in v. s of MÉD. Dipped in 90s; now on form. Fine-edged with added structure and depth. Owned by J-J Frey, owner of JABOULET AÎNÉ and CH Corton-André in Burgundy. Daughter Caroline is winemaker. Also CUVÉE Mademoiselle L from v'yd in Cussac-Fort-Méd.

Lalande-Borie St-Jul r ★★ 01 02 03 04 05 06 07 08 09' 10' 11 12 Baby brother of the great DUCRU-BEAUCAILLOU with v'yd on the w plateau of ST-JUL. Supple and relatively early drinking.

Lamarque, De H-Méd r ★★ 00' 02 03 04 05' 06 08 09' 10' 11 12 H-MÉD v'yd with splendid medieval fortress by ferry across river Gironde. Competent, mid-term wines. Gd value. Second label: D de Lamarque. Also some rosé.

Lanessan H-Méd r ★★ 00' 02 03 04 05 08 09 10' 11 Distinguished property just s of ST-JUL. Former Calvet and Cordier-Mestrezat winemaker, Paz Espejo, steadily improving the wines and estate. Second label: Les Calèches de Lanessan.

Langoa-Barton St-Jul r ★★★ 95' 96' 98 99 00' 01 02 03 04' 05' 06 07 08 09' 10' 11 12 13 Third Growth sister CH to LÉOVILLE-BARTON. 18th-century mansion of Barton family Anthony Barton. Consistent value. Second label: Rés de Léoville-Barton.

Larcis Ducasse St-Ém r ★★★ 89' 90' 95 96 98 00 02 03 04 05' 06 07 08 09' 10' 11 12 13 Well-sited, family-owned, PREMIER GRAND CRU CLASSÉ on the côtes at St-Laurent. Great in the 50s and 60s. Spectacular form since 2004. Top vintages can age 40 yrs+. Second label: Murmure de L D (from 2010).

Larmande St-Ém r ★★ 00' 01 03 04 05 06 07 07 08 09' 10 12 Big GRAND CRU CLASSÉ owned by Le Mondiale insurance (as is SOUTARD). Replanted, re-equipped; now solid if vapid wines. Second label: le Cadet de Larmande.

Laroque St-Ém r ★★-★★★ 98 99 00' 01 03 04 05 06 08 09' 10' 11 12 Large GRAND CRU CLASSÉ at St-Christophe-des-Bardes. 17th-century CH. Fresh, terroir-driven wines.

Larose-Trintaudon H-Méd r ★★ 04 05 06 07 08 09' 10 11 12 Largest v'yd in the MÉD (190 ha). Sustainable viticulture. Previously light and easy-drinking; now smooth, modern, polished. Second label: Larose St-Laurent. Special CUVÉE, Larose Perganson, from separate parcels, denser, more refined.

Laroze St-Ém r ★★ 98' 99 00 01 05 06 07 08 09' 10' 12 Family-owned (since 1610) GRAND CRU CLASSÉ. Lighter-framed wines from sandy soils; more depth in last 15 yrs. Earlier drinking; gd value. Second label: La Fleur Laroze.

Larrivet-Haut-Brion Pe-Lé r w ★★★ (r) 00 01 02 03 04 05' 06 07 08 09 10' 11 12 Unclassified PE-LÉ property owned by Bonne Maman jam. Rich, modern red. Voluptuous, aromatic, SAUV BL/SÉM barrel-fermented white 05 06 07 08 09 10' 11 12 13. Former MONTROSE manager in charge. MICHEL ROLLAND consults. Second label: Les Demoiselles de Larrivet-Haut-Brion.

Lascombes Marg r (p) ★★★ 98' 99 00 01 02 03 04 05' 06 07 08 09' 10' 11 12 Second Growth owned by insurance group. Wines were wobbly; now rich, dark, concentrated, modern, but MARG perfume can be found. Worth some bottle age. MICHEL ROLLAND consults. Second label: Chevalier de Lascombes.

Latour Pau r ★★★★(★) 85 86 88' 89 90' 91 94 95' 96' 97 98 99 00' 01 02 03' 04 05' 06 07 08 09' 10' 11' 12 13 First Growth considered the grandest statement of B'x. Profound, intense, almost immortal wines in great yrs; even weaker vintages have the unique taste and run for many yrs. *Grand vin* from historical "Enclos" vy'd. Part of estate bio cultivated (horses do ploughing). Ceased *en primeur* sales in 2012; wines now only released when considered ready to drink (the 2004 in 2014). New cellars for greater storage capacity. Second label: LE FORTS DE LATOUR; *third label: Pauillac*; even this can age 12 yrs.

Latour-à-Pomerol Pom r ★★★ 89' 90' 95 96 98' 99 00' 01 02 04 05' 06 07 08 09' 10' 11 12 J-P MOUEIX property located on plateau nr POM church. Extremely consistent, fleshy, well-structured wines that age.

Latour-Martillac Pe-Lé r w ★★ (r) 98 00 01 02 03 04 05' 06 08 09' 10' 11 12 GRAV *cru classé* owned by Kressmann family since 1929. Regular quality; gd value at this level (r w) 03 04 05 06 07 08 09 10' 11 12 13. Second label: Lagrave Martillac (r w).

Laurets, Des St-Ém r ★★ 05 06 08 09 10 12 Major property in PUISSEGUIN-ST-ÉM and MONTAGNE-ST-ÉM, with vy'd evenly split (40,000 cases). Les Laurets is a special CUVÉE. Owned by Benjamin de Rothschild of CH CLARKE (2003).

Laville Saut w sw ★★ 01 03 04 06 07 09 10 11 13 Family-owned Preignac estate nr BASTOR-LAMONTAGNE. Winemaker lectures at B'x's Faculty of Oenology. SÉM-dominated (85%), rich, lush, botrytized wine. Gd-value, non-classified SAUT.

Laville-Haut-Brion Pe-Lé w ★★★★ 94 95' 96' 98 00' 01 02 03 04' 05' 06 07 08 Former name for LA MISSION HAUT-BRION BLANC (renamed in 2009). Only 8,000 bottles/yr of v. best white GRAV for long, succulent maturing. Great consistency. Mainly SÉM. Second label: La Clarté de Haut-Brion (formerly Les Plantiers); also incl wine from HAUT-BRION.

Léoville-Barton St-Jul r ★★★★ 88' 89' 90' 94' 95' 96' 98 99 00' 01 02 03' 04 05' 06 07 08' 09' 10' 11 12 13 Second Growth with longest-standing family ownership in Anglo-Irish hands of Bartons for over 180 yrs (Anthony Barton is present incumbent, assisted by daughter Lilian and granddaughter Mélanie). Smallest of three Léovilles; harmonious, classic claret. Generally traditional approach. Shares cellars with LANGOA-BARTON.

Léoville-las-Cases St-Jul r ★★★★ 86' 88 89' 90' 93 94 95' 96' 97 98 99 00' 01 02 03' 04' 05' 06 07 08 09' 10' 11' 12 13 Largest Léoville; original "Super Second". *Grand vin* from Grand Enclos vy'd (neighbouring LATOUR). Elegant, complex, powerful wines, for immortality. Sometimes more PAU than ST JUL. Second label: Le Petit Lion; was CLOS DU MARQUIS but latter now separate wine.

Léoville-Poyferré St-Jul r ★★★★ 86' 88 89' 90' 94 95 96' 98 99 00' 01 02 03 04 05' 06 07 08 09' 10' 11' 12 13 The 3rd part of great Léoville estate. Now at "Super Second" level with dark, rich, spicy, long-ageing wines. *Ch Moulin-Riche* is a separate 21-ha parcel. Pavillon de Léoville-Poyferré is second label made from young vines from both properties.

Lestage List r ★★ 00 02 03 04 05 06 08 09 10 11 12 In same hands as CH FONRÉAUD but more MERLOT (56%). Firm, slightly austere claret. Impressive 19th-century ch. Also Ch Caroline from MOU.

Back to where we came from

Are we seeing a return to elegance in B'x, and a move away from overextraction? It's all about specificity now – the typicity of a vy'd, of a place. As opposed to the typicity of a reverse-osmosis machine.

lian Ladouys St-Est r ★★ 98 00 02 03 04 05 06 07 08 09' 10' 11 12 Created in the 80s, v'yd has 100 separate parcels of vines. Firm, sometimes robust wines; recent vintages more finesse. Same owner as PÉDESCLAUX, 50 per cent of D'ISSAN.

versan H-Méd r ★★ 98 00 02 03 04 05 07 08 09 10 12 CRU BOURGEOIS (2012) in n H-MÉD. Same owner as PATACHE D'AUX. Round but structured. Second label: Les Charmes de Liversan.

udenne Méd r ★★ 00' 01 02 03 04 05 06 09' 10' 11 12 Large CRU BOURGEOIS (2012) formerly Gilbeys, owned by Chinese since 2013. Landmark 18th-century pink-washed *chartreuse* by the river. Ripe, round reds. Also an oak-scented SAUV BL 06 07 08 09 10 11 12 13 . And, of course, a rosé, Pink de Loudenne.

uvière, La Pe-Lé r w★★★ (r) 00' 01 02 04 05' 06 07 08 09' 10' 11 12 (w) 01 02 03 04' 05' 06 07 08 09' 10' 11 12 13 André Lurton's pride and joy. Cellars recently modernized. Excellent *white* and red of classed-growth standard. *See also* BONNET, COUHINS-LURTON, DE ROCHEMORIN.

ıssac, De St-Ém r ★★ 00 03 04 05 06 07 08 09 10 11 12 Top estate in LUSSAC-ST-ÉM. Plenty of investment. Same stable as FRANC-MAYNE and Vieux Maillet in POM. Second label: Le Libertin de Lussac.

st of a top-quality new French barrique: €600–700.

nch-Bages Pau r (w) ★★★★ 88'89' 90' 94 95' 96' 98 99 00' 01 02 03 04' 05' 06 07 08 09' 10' 11 12 13 Always popular, now a star, far higher than its Fifth Growth rank. Rich, dense CAB SAUV-led wine. Second label: Echo de Lynch-Bages. Gd white, *Blanc de Lynch-Bages*, now fresher style. Same owners (Cazes family: Jean-Charles manages; aunt Sylvie owns CHAUVIN) as LES ORMES-DE-PEZ, Villa Bel-Air and L'Ostal Cazes in MINERVOIS-LA LIVINIÈRE.

nch-Moussas Pau r★★ 00' 01 02 03 04 05' 07 08 09 10' 11 12 Fifth Growth owned by BORIE-MANOUX. Improving wines for relatively early drinking. A PAU second-stringer but gd value.

onnat St-Ém r ★★ 01 03 04 05 06 07 08 09 10 12 Property in LUSSAC-ST-ÉM. More precision of late. ANGÉLUS owner consults.

acquin-St-Georges St-Ém r ★★ 00 01 03 04 05 06 08 09 10 11 Producer of delicious, not weighty, satellite ST-ÉM at ST-GEORGES. Consistent, gd value.

agdelaine St-Ém r ★★★ 89' 90' 95 96 98' 99 00 01 03 04 05 06 07 08 09' 10' 11 RIP from 2012, now integrated into BELAIR-MONANGE. Delicate, fine, deceptively long-lived. Denser weight from 2008.

alartic-Lagravière Pe-Lé r (w) ★★★ (r) 98 99 00' 01 02 03 04' 05' 06 08 09' 10' 11 12 (w) 00 01' 02 03 04' 05' 06 07 08 09' 10' 11 12 13 Léognan classed growth. Rich, modern red; a little lush SAUV BL. Belgian owner has revolutionized property and tripled the size. CH Gazin Rocquencourt (PE-LÉ) same stable. V'yd in Argentina also.

alescasse H-Méd r★★ 01 02 03 04 05 06 08 09 10 11 12 CRU BOURGEOIS (2012) nr MOULIS. Supple, value wines. No Malescasse 2013 made. Second label: La Closerie de Malescasse.

alescot-St-Exupéry Marg r★★★ 96 98 99 00' 01 02 03 04 05' 06 07 08' 09' 10' 11 12 In form MARG Third Growth. Wines ripe, fragrant, finely structured. MICHEL ROLLAND consults. Second label: La Dame de Malescot.

alle, De Saut r w dr sw★★★ (w sw) 89' 90' 95 96'97' 98 99 01' 02 03' 05 06 07 09 10' 11' 13 Preignac CH owned by de Bournazel family making v. fine, medium-bodied SAUT; also M de Malle dry white GRAV.

argaux, Ch Marg r (w)★★★★ 85' 86'88' 89'90' 93 94 95' 96' 97 98' 99 00' 01' 02 03'04' 05' 06' 07 08 09' 10' 11' 12 13 First Growth; most seductive, fabulously perfumed and consistent wines. Owned and run by Corinne Mentzelopoulos. New Norman Foster-designed cellar extension (2014). Pavillon Rouge 00' 01 02

BORDEAUX

03 04' 05' 06 08 09' 10' 11 12 is second label; third label M de Margaux; fir
vintage 2009. *Pavillon Blanc* (100% SAUV BL) is best white of MÉD, recent vintage
fresher 04' 05 06 07 08 09' 10 11' 12' 13'.

Marojallia Marg r ★★★ 99 00' 01 02 03 04 05' 06 07 08 09' 10 11 12 Micro-c
looking for big prices for big, rich, un-MARG-like wines. Less full throttle from
2011. 70% CAB SAUV. Second label: CLOS Margalaine.

Marquis-d'Alesme Marg r ★★ 98 00 01 04 05 07 08 09' 10' 11 12 Third Grow
bought by LABÉGORCE in 2006. New high-tech cellars, Chinese-inspired (2015
Disappointing in recent yrs but steady progress from 2009.

Marquis-de-Terme Marg r ★★→★★★90' 95 96 98 99 00' 01 02 03 04 05' 06 07 0
09' 10' 11 12 Fourth Growth with v'yd dispersed around MARG. On the up-and-u
since 2009. Previously solid, now more seductive. Second label: La Couronn
de Marquis de Terme.

Maucaillou Mou r ★★ 01 02 03 04 05 06 08 09 10 11 12 Family-owned (DOURTHE
visitor-friendly (museum, shop, film, tasting). Clean, fresh, value wines.

Mayne Lalande List r ★★ 05 08 09 10 11 12 Launched by Bernard Lartigue in 198
now a leader in the commune. Full and finely textured. ANGÉLUS owner consult

Mazeyres Pom r ★★ 98' 99 00 01 04 05' 06 08 09 10 12 Lighter but consistent POM
Supple, earlier-drinking style. Substantial v'yd for AC. Bio from 2012. FONROQU
owner manages.

Meyney St-Est r ★★→★★★ 00 01 02 03 04 05' 06 08 09' 10' 11' 12 Big river-slop
v'yd, superb site next to next to MONTROSE. Always robust, structured wine
ageing guaranteed, but oddly overlooked. Recent investment. Same stable
GRAND-PUY-DUCASSE and RAYNE VIGNEAU (CA Grands Crus). ANGÉLUS owner consult
Second label: Prieur de Meyney.

Mission Haut-Brion, La Pe-Lé r ★★★★85' 86 88 89' 90' 93 94 95 96' 98' 99 00' 0
02 03 04 05' 06 07 07 08 09' 10' 11' 12 13 Bought by the Dillon family of HAU
BRION and replanted from 1983. Consistently grand-scale, full-blooded, lon
maturing wine; more flamboyant than HAUT-BRION. Second label: La Chapel
de la Mission. Magnificent SÉM-dominated white: previously LAVILLE-HAUT-BRIO
renamed (2009) La Mission-Haut-Brion Blanc 09' 10' 11' 12' 13.

Monbousquet St-Ém r (w) ★★★ 00' 01 02 03 04 05' 06 07 08 09' 10' 11 12 Substanti
GRAND CRU CLASSÉ on sand/gravel plain revolutionized by owner Gerard Pérs
Concentrated, oaky, voluptuous wines. Rare *v.gd Sauv Bl/Sauv Gris* (AC B'X) fro
1998. Same ownership as PAVIE, PAVIE-DECESSE.

Monbrison Marg r ★★→★★★90 95 96' 98 99 00 01 02 04 05' 06 08 09' 10' 1
Small, family-owned property at Arsac (6,500 cases). Delicate, fragrant MARG.

Mondotte, La St-Ém r (★★★) ★ 96' 97 98' 99 00' 01 02 03 04 05' 06 07 08 09' 1
11 12 13 Tiny estate on the limestone-clay plateau. Merited promotion to PREMI
GRAND CRU CLASSÉ in 2012. Intense, firm, virile wines. Consistent quality. Sam
owner as CANON-LA-GAFFELIÈRE, CLOS DE L'ORATOIRE.

Montrose St-Est r ★★★★88 89'90 93 94 95 96'98 99 00' 01 02 03' 04 05' 06 0
08 09' 10' 11 12 13 Second Growth with riverside v'yd. Famed for deep-coloure
forceful, long-ageing claret. Vintages 1979–85 (except 82) were lighter. Bouyg
brothers owners from 2006. Huge investment since; new cellar for 800 barre
Second label: La Dame de Montrose.

Drone zone
Mind your head. Drones could soon be over flying the B'X v'yds: Bernard
Magrez has bought one for use at his classified CHX (PAPE-CLÉMENT, LA
TOUR-CARNET, FOMBRAUGE, CLOS HAUT-PEYRAGUEY). The idea is to help detect
vine diseases, measure the grape maturity, identify zones in need of
treatment or fertilizer and assist with decisions on drainage.

Moulin du Cadet St-Ém r p ★★ 96 98 00 01 03 05 08 09 10' 11 12 Tiny GRAND CRU CLASSÉ on the limestone plateau. Sister to FONROQUE. Certified bio. Formerly robust, now more finesse, fragrance.

Moulinet Pom r ★★ 00 01 04 05 06 08 09 10 11 12 One of POM's bigger CH'X. DERENONCOURT consults. Lighter style but gd value.

Moulin-Haut-Laroque B'x r ★★ 04 05' 06 08 09' 10' 11 12 Leading FRONSAC property (19th century origins). Consistent quality. Structured wines that can age from MERLOT, CAB FR, 80-yr-old MALBEC. Value.

Moulin Pey-Labrie B'x r ★★ 00' 01 02 03 04 05' 06 08 09' 10' 11 12 Leading CH in CANON-FRONSAC. Sturdy wines, MERLOT-dominated, with elegance and structure.

Moulin-St-Georges St-Ém r ★★★ 00' 01 02 03 04 05' 06 08 09' 10' 11 12 13 Same ownership as AUSONE nearby. Dense, stylish wines. Relative value.

Mouton Rothschild Pau r (w) ★★★★ 82' 83' 85' 86' 88' 89' 90' 93' 94 95' 96 97 98' 99 00' 01' 02 03 04' 05' 06' 07 08' 09' 10' 11' 12 13 RIP (2014) Philippine de Rothschild. Eldest son Philippe Sereys de Rothschild now at the helm. The most exotic and voluptuous of the PAU first growths. Attains new heights from 2004. New cellar and artists' labels museum (2012). White Aile d'Argent (SAUV BL/SÉM). Second label: Le Petit Mouton. *See also* Opus One (California) and Almaviva (Chile).

Nairac Saut w sw ★★★ 95' 96 97' 98 99 01' 02 03' 04 05' 06 07 09' 10 11 13 Classified BAR; richer style but top form. Second label: Esquisse de Nairac, equally rich but fresher in style.

Nénin Pom r ★★★ 95 96 98 99 00' 01 02 03 04 05 06 07 08 09' 10' 11 12 13 LÉOVILLE-LAS-CASES ownership since 1997. Massive investment. New cellars. V'yd expanded. Restrained in style but generous, precise and built to age. Recent vintages show the work has paid off. Gd-value second label: Fugue de Nénin.

Olivier Pe-Lé r w ★★★ (r) 95 96 00 01 02 04' 05' 06 08 09' 10' 11 12 13 (w) 01 02 03 04' 05' 06 07' 08 09 10' 11 12 13 Beautiful classified property with moated castle. Investment and application have brought a sea change in recent yrs. *One to follow.* Second label (r): Le Dauphin d'Olivier.

Ormes-de-Pez, Les St-Est r ★★★★ 96 98 99 00' 01 02 03 04 05 06' 07 08 09' 10' 11 12 Wonderfully steady ST-EST owned by LYNCH-BAGES. Dense, fleshy wines to age.

Ormes-Sorbet, Les Méd r ★★ 00' 01 02 03' 04 05 06 08 09' 10' 11 12 Reliably consistent CRU BOURGEOIS (2012) in AC MÉD. Elegant, gently oaked wines that age. CH Fontis same stable. Second label: Ch de Conques.

Palmer Marg r ★★★★ 83' 85 86' 88' 89 90 93 94 95 96' 98' 99 00 01' 02 03 04 05' 06' 07 08' 09' 10' 11' 12 13 Third Growth on a par with "Super Seconds" (occasionally Firsts). Wine of power, delicacy and much MERLOT (40%). Dutch (MÄHLER-BESSE) and British (SICHEL family) owners. 100 per cent bio from 2014. Recent investment in new cellars, buildings and an English garden. Second label: *Alter Ego de Palmer.*

Pape-Clément Pe-Lé r (w) ★★★★ (r) 90' 94 95 96 98' 99 00' 01 02 03 04 05 06 07 08 09' 10' 11 12 13 (w) 02 03 04 05' 07 08 09 10' 11 12 13 Historic estate now in suburban sprawl of Pessac. Owned by Bernard Magrez since 1985 (*see* FOMBRAUGE, La TOUR-CARNET); potent, oak-scented, long-ageing if not typical reds. Tiny production of rich, exotic white. Fastidious winemaking.

Patache d'Aux Méd r ★★ 03 04 05' 06 07 09 10 11 12 MÉD CRU BOURGEOIS (2012) located at Bégadan. Reliable largely CAB SAUV wine. Value. *See also* LIVERSAN.

Pavie St-Ém r ★★★★ 90' 94 95 96 98 99 00' 01 02 03 04 05' 06 07 08 09' 10' 11 12 13 Promoted to PREMIER GRAND CRU CLASSÉ (A) in 2012. Splendidly sited on the plateau and southern côtes. Same owner as MONBOUSQUET and adjacent Pavie-Decesse. New-wave ST-ÉM: intense, oaky, strong. Impressive €14 million winery unveiled in 2013. Second label: Arômes de Pavie.

If you want to get ahead, get a vat
A vat is a vat is a vat? No. They're tulip-shaped and concrete at CH PRIEURÉ-LICHINE's new cellar in MARG, curvaceous and concrete at CHEVAL BLANC. LA GAFFELIÈRE uses violet and B'x-coloured, truncated cone-shaped stainless-steel tanks. In PAU, PONTET-CANET ages a percentage of the wine in amphorae.

Pavie-Decesse St-Ém r ★★ 98' 99 00' 01' 02 03 04 05' 06 07 08 09' 10' 11 12 Tiny classed growth (only 1,000 cases). As powerful and muscular as sister PAVIE.

Pavie-Macquin St-Ém r ★★★ 89' 90' 94 95 96' 98' 99 00' 01 02 03 04 05' 06 07 08 09' 10' 11 12 13 PREMIER GRAND CRU CLASSÉ with v'yd on limestone plateau next to TROPLONG-MONDOT. Astute management and winemaking by Nicolas Thienpont of PUYGUERAUD; DERENONCOURT consults. Sturdy, full-bodied wines that need time.

Pédesclaux Pau r ★★ 98' 99 00 02 03 04 05 06 09 10' 11 12 Underachieving Fifth Growth being revived and reorganized. New owner in 2009 (see LILIAN LADOUYS) has extended v'yd, built new cellars. Recent vintages gd value. To watch.

Petit-Village Pom r ★★★ 98' 99 00' 01 03 04 05 06 07 08 09' 10' 11 12 13 Much-improved POM opposite VIEUX-CH-CERTAN. DERENONCOURT consults. Investment evident. Same owner (AXA Insurance) as PICHON-BARON. Suave, dense, increasingly finer tannins. Second label: Le Jardin de Petit-Village.

Petrus Pom r ★★★★ 78 79' 81 82' 83 85' 86 88' 89' 90 93' 94 95' 96 97 98' 99 00' 01 02 03 04' 05' 06 07 08 09' 10' 11' 12 13 The (unofficial) First Growth of POM: MERLOT solo in excelsis. V'yd on blue clay (with traces of crasse de fer) gives 2,500 cases of massively rich, concentrated wine. Olivier Berrouet took over the winemaking from father, Jean-Claude (45 vintages), in 2007. Jean-François MOUEIX owner. New cellar complex in 2012.

Pey La Tour B'x r ★★ 08 09 10 11 12 Value, quality-driven generic BORDEAUX SUPÉRIEUR produced on a vast scale (200 ha). Owned by DOURTHE. Rés du CH is top selection.

Peyrabon H-Méd r ★★ 01 02 03 04 05 06 09' 10 11 12 Consistent CRU BOURGEOIS (2012) owned by négociant (Millésima). Also La Fleur-Peyrabon in PAU.

Pez, De St-Est r ★★★ 98' 00 01 02 03 04 05' 06 07 08 09' 10' 11 12 13 Ancient ST-EST estate revamped by owner ROEDERER. Same winemaking team as PICHON-LALANDE. Dense, reliable style.

Phélan-Ségur St-Est r ★★★ 96' 98 99 00' 0 1 02 03 04 05' 06 07 08 09' 10' 11 12 A top ST-EST; reputation solid since 1988 but unclassified; long, supple style. Further investment since 2011. MICHEL ROLLAND consults.

Pibran Pau r ★★ 96 99 00 01 03 04 05' 06 07 08 09' 10' 11 12 13 Small property allied to PICHON-BARON. Classy wine with PAU drive.

Pichon-Baron Pau r ★★★★ 88' 89' 90' 93 94' 95 96 98 99 00' 01 02 03' 04 05' 06 07 08 09' 10' 11' 12 13 Recently renamed (2012); formerly CH Pichon-Longueville. Revitalized Second Growth with powerful, consistent PAU for long ageing. Second labels: Les Tourelles de Longueville (approachable: more MERLOT); Les Griffons de Pichon Baron (from 2012, more CAB SAUV).

Pichon-Longueville Comtesse de Lalande (Pichon Lalande) Pau r ★★★★ 85' 86' 88' 89' 90' 94 95 96 98 99 00 00 01 02 03' 04 05' 06 07 08 09' 10' 11 12 13 ROEDERER-owned (2007) Second Growth, beside LATOUR. Always among top performers; long-lived, MERLOT-marked wine of fabulous breed. More CAB SAUV in recent yrs as v'yd is replanted. New winemaker/manager (2012) and high-tech, gravity-fed winery in 2013. Second label: Rés de la Comtesse. DE PEZ, HAUT-BEAUSÉJOUR same stable.

Pin, Le Pom r ★★★★ 85 86' 88 89 90' 94 95 96 97 98' 99 00 01' 02 04 05' 06' 07 08 09' 10' 11 12 The original of the B'x cult mini-crus (first vintage: 1979) made in a cellar the size of a garage. Now a new (2011) winery. 100% MERLOT; almost as rich as its drinkers, but prices are scary. No Le Pin made in 2013. L'If is new (2011) ST-ÉM stablemate.

lince Pom r ★★ 00' 01 04 05 06 08 09 10 11 12 V'yd nr NÉNIN and LA POINTE. Machine harvested. Supple, fruit-driven style.

ointe, La Pom r ★★ 98' 99 00' 01 04 05 06 07 08 09' 10' 11 12 Large (for POM), well-managed estate. Gd-value (since 2009), quality wine. ANGÉLUS owner consults.

oitevin Méd r ★★ 08 09 10 11 12 Supple, elegant CRU BOURGEOIS (2012) from the northern MÉD. Consistent quality in recent yrs.

ontac-Monplaisir Pe-Lé r (w) ★★ 00 02 04 05' 06 07 08 09 10 12 Mainly red PE-LÉ estate. Attractive white; supple, decent red. Value.

ontet-Canet Pau r ★★★★ 88 89' 90 94' 95 96' 98 99 00' 01 02' 03 04' 05' 06' 07 08 09' 10' 11 12 13 Fashionable, bio certified, family-owned Fifth Growth. Radical improvement has seen prices soar. Second label: Les Hauts de Pontet-Canet (2012 labelled VIN DE FRANCE, not PAU).

otensac Méd r ★★ 98 00' 01 02 03 04' 05' 07 08 09' 10' 11 12 13 Well-known property of n MÉD. Delon family of LÉOVILLE-LAS-CASES; class shows. Firm, vigorous wines for long ageing. Second label: Chapelle de Potensac.

ouget Marg r ★★ 00' 01 02 03 04 05' 06 07 08 09' 10' 11 12 Obscure Fourth Growth attached to BOYD-CANTENAC. Old vines. Sturdy; needs time.

oujeaux Mou r ★★ 90' 95' 96' 98 00' 01 03 04 05 06 08 09' 10' 11 12 Same owner as CLOS FOURTET and Côte de Baleau in ST-ÉM. Leading MOU. DERENONCOURT consults. Full, robust wines that age. Second label: La Salle de Poujeaux.

remier Grand Cru Classé St-Ém *See* ST-ÉM classification box, p.99.

ressac, De St-Ém r ★★ 05 06 08 09 10 11 12 Restored estate in St-Etienne-de-Lisse rewarded classification in 2012. Quality, consistency now assured. Gd value.

reuillac Méd r ★★ 05 06 08 09 10 11 12 Savoury, structured wine from AC MÉD. Acquired by Chinese investor in 2014. Crop decimated by hail in 2014.

rieuré-Lichine Marg r ★★★ 89' 90' 95 96 98' 99 00' 01 02 03 04 05 06 07 08 09' 10' 11 12 13 Fourth Growth owned by a négociant; put on the map by Alexis Lichine. DERENONCOURT consults. Fragrant MARG currently on gd form. New cuvier with cement vats since 2013. Second label: Confidences du Prieuré-Lichine. Gd white B'x too.

uygueraud B'x r ★★ 01' 02 03' 05' 06 08 09 10 11 12 Leading CH of this tiny FRANCS-CÔTES DE BORDEAUX AC. Owned by Thienpont family (see PAVIE-MACQUIN). Mainly MERLOT. Oak-aged wines of surprising class. Value Les Charmes-Godard white, same owner. Special CUVÉE George with MALBEC (35%+) in blend.

uinault L'Enclos St-Ém r ★★→★★★ 09 10 11 12 GRAND CRU CLASSÉ located in Libourne. New owner (2008) CHEVAL BLANC; change of style (more freshness and finesse). No Quinault L'Enclos in 2013 (hail).

uintus St-Ém r ★★★ 11 12 13 Formerly well-respected Tertre Daugay. Now owned by Dillons of HAUT-BRION; consequent upgrade. To watch. Neighbouring L'ARROSÉE acquired and merged in 2013 making this a 28-ha estate. Price has soared. Second label: Le Dragon de Quintus.

abaud-Promis Saut w sw ★★→★★★ 96 97' 98 99 01' 02 03' 04 05' 06 07 09' 10 11 12 13 A family-owned First Growth at Bommes. Organic tendencies. Quality and gd value.

ahoul Grav r w ★★ (r) 02 04 05 08 09' 10 11 12 Balanced red; fleshy, SÉM-dominated white 05 07 08 09 10 11 12 13. Constant progress since 2007. Gd value.

amage-la-Batisse H-Méd r ★★ 04 05' 07 08 09 10 11 12 Reasonably consistent, widely distributed, CRU BOURGEOIS (2012). Owned by insurance company. Second label: L'Enclos de Ramage.

auzan-Gassies Marg r ★★★ 98 00 01' 02 03 04 05' 06 07 08 09' 10' 11 12 Second

Growth neighbour of RAUZAN-SÉGLA that has long lagged behind it; now catchin up. New generation making strides. Second label: Gassies.

Rauzan-Ségla Marg r ★★★★ 88′ 89′ 90′ 94′ 95 96 98 99 00′ 01 02 03 04′ 05 0◄ 07 08 09′ 10′ 11 12 13 MARG Second Growth long famous for its fragrance; owne by Wertheimers of Chanel (*see* CANON). Former Cheval des Andes (Argentina winemaker now on board. On fine form. Second label: Ségla (value).

Raymond-Lafon Saut w sw ★★★ 88 89′ 90′ 95 96′ 97 98 99′ 01′ 02 03′ 04 0◄ 06 07′ 09′ 10′ 11′ 13 Unclassified but top SAUT estate acquired by former YQUE◄ manager in 1972; now run by his children. Rich, complex wines that age.

Rayne Vigneau Saut w sw ★★★ 90′ 95 96 97 98 99 01′ 02 03 05′ 07 09′ 10′ 1◄ 13 Big First Growth owned by a bank (*see* GRAND-PUY-DUCASSE). Much improve◄ Second label: Madame de Rayne. Dry, white B′x Le Sec de Rayne Vigneau.

Respide Médeville Grav r w ★★ (r) 04 05′ 06 08 09 10 11 12 (w) 04′ 05′ 07 08 09 10 ◄ 12 13 Top GRAV property for elegant red and complex *white*. CH GILETTE, CHAMPAG◄ Gonet-Medeville same stable.

Reynon B′x r w ★★ Leading CADILLAC-CÔTES DE BORDEAUX estate. Serious red 05′ o 07 09′ 10 11 12. Fragrant B′x white from SAUV BL 09 10′ 11′ 12 13. *See also* CLO FLORIDÈNE. Owned by Dubourdieu family.

Reysson H-Méd r ★★ 05 06 08 09′ 10′ 11 12 Renovated CRU BOURGEOIS (201◄ managed by négociant CVBG-DOURTHE (*see* BELGRAVE, LA GARDE). Rich, modern sty◄

Rieussec Saut w sw ★★★★ 83′ 85 86′ 88′ 89′ 90′ 95 96′ 97′ 98 99 01′ 02 o 04 05′ 06 07 09′ 10′ 11′ 13 Worthy neighbour of YQUEM with v′yd in Fargue owned by the (LAFITE) Rothschilds. Fabulously powerful, opulent wine. Averag production 6,000 cases/yr. No Rieussec produced in 1977, 1993, 2012. Secon◄ label: Carmes de Rieussec. Dry wine is "R".

Rivière, De la B′x r ★★ 00′ 01 02 03 04 05′ 06 08 09′ 10 12 The biggest (60 ha) an◄ most impressive FRONSAC property, with Wagnerian castle and cellars. Former big, tannic wines; now more refined. Special CUVÉE, Aria, produced from the be◄ parcels. Uncertainty after tragic death of owner in 2014; hotel-spa future proje◄

Roc de Cambes B′x r ★★★ 04 05 06 07 08 09 10 11 12 13 Undisputed leader in CÔT DE BOURG; wines as gd as top ST-ÉM. Savoury, opulent but pricey. Same metho◄ as sister TERTRE-RÔTEBOEUF.

Rochemorin, De Pe-Lé r w ★★→★★★ (r) 01 02 04 05 06 08 09′ 10′ 11 12 (w) 06 ◄ 08 09 10 11 12 13 An important restoration at Martillac by André Lurton of ◄ LOUVIÈRE: vast estate (75 per cent red). SAUV BL-dominated white. Modern wine◄ Fairly consistent quality. CH Coucheroy (r w) also produced.

Rol Valentin St-Ém r ★★★ 00′ 01′ 02 03 04 05′ 06 07 08 09′ 10′ 11 12 13 On◄ garage-sized; now new owner (2010) and bigger v′yd. Wines rich, modern b◄ balanced. DERENONCOURT consults.

Rouget Pom r ★★ 98′ 00′ 01′ 03 04 05′ 06 07 08 09′ 10′ 11 12 13 Go-ahead estate ◄ n edge of POM. Same owner as DOM JACQUES PRIEUR and Dom Labruyère in MOUL◄ À-VENT. Rich, unctuous wines. Gd value.

Bordeaux's new wine museum opens

BORDEAUX's new wine museum, the *Cité des Civilisations du Vin*, opens its doors in May 2016. The €81 million wine cultural centre is on the riverside in downtown B′x and expects over 400,000 visitors/yr. Something of a cross between a museum and theme park, the CCV uses digital technology to explore wine culture and civilization: it's interactive, and you can also interact at workshops, tastings, in wine bars and in a viewing tower atop the building, which takes the form of a swirling decanter.

t-Georges St-Ém r ★★ 00' 01 03 04 05' 06 08 09 10 11 Same family ownership since 1891 (Hortense Desbois present incumbent). V'yd represents 25 per cent of ST-GEORGES AC. Gd wine sold direct to the public. Second label: Puy St-Georges.

St-Pierre St-Jul r ★★★ 89 90' 95' 96' 98 99 00' 01' 02 03 04 05' 06 07 08 09' 10' 11 12 13 Once understated Fourth Growth owned by Jean-Louis Triaud. Stylish, consistent, classic ST-JUL. Only 17 ha. See GLORIA.

ales, De Pom r ★★ 00' 01' 04 05 06 08 09 10 12 Biggest v'yd of POM (10,000 cases). Same family ownership for five centuries. Lightish wine; never quite poetry. Try top vintages. Second label: CH Chantalouette.

ansonnet St-Ém r ★★ 00' 01 02 03 04 05' 06 08 09' 10' 11 12 13 GRAND CRU CLASSÉ on limestone-clay plateau. Ambitiously run in modern style (rich, dark, concentrated). On the up since 2009.

aransot-Dupré List r (w) ★★ 00' 01 02 03 04 05 06 09' 10' 11 12 Small property with firm, fleshy wines. Lots of MERLOT but PETIT VERDOT significant. Also one of LIST's growing band of whites (50-yr-old SÉM).

énéjac H-Méd r (w) ★★ 00 01 02 03 04 05' 06 08 09' 10' 11 12. In s 11-MÉD (Pian). Consistent, well-balanced wines that age. Same ownership as CH TALBOT. Gd value.

erre, La St-Ém r ★★ 98' 00' 01 02 03 04 05 06 08 09' 10 11 12 Small classed growth on the limestone plateau. Fresh, stylish wines with plenty of fruit.

igalas-Rabaud Saut w sw ★★★ 88 89' 90' 95' 96' 97' 98 99 01' 02 03 04 05' 07' 09' 10' 11 12 13 Tiny First Growth; family owned; Eric Boissenot consults. V. fragrant and lovely. Top-ranking now. Second label: Le Lieutenant de Sigalas.

iran Marg r ★★ →★★★ 96 98 00' 01 02 03 04 05 06 07 08 09' 10' 11 12 Owned by the Miailhe family (1859); Edouard runs the show today. Denis Dubourdieu consults. Wines have substance, classic MARG fragrance. Second label: S de Siran.

mith-Haut-Lafitte Pe-Lé r (p) (w) ★★★★ (r) 96 98 99 00 01 02 03 04 05' 06 07 08 09' 10' 11 12 13 (w) 03 04 05 06 07' 08' 09 10' 11 12 13 Celebrated classed growth with spa hotel (Caudalie), regularly one of the stars of PE-LÉ. White is full, ripe, sappy; red oaky/generous. New carbon-neutral cellar for second label: Les Hauts de Smith. Also CAB SAUV-based Le Petit Haut Lafitte. Minor share and management of BEAUREGARD and BASTOR LAMONTAGNE from 2014.

ociando-Mallet H-Méd r ★★★ 89 90' 94 95 96' 98' 99 00' 01' 02 03 04 05' 06 07 08 09' 10' 11 12 Splendid estate just n of ST-EST built from scratch by independent-minded owner since 1969; now 85 ha. Classed growth quality. Conservative, big-boned wines to lay down for yrs. Second label: La Demoiselle de Sociando-Mallet. Also special CUVÉE Jean Gautreau.

ours, De B'x r p w ★★ Valid reputation for B'x rosé (DYA). 300,000 bottles annually. Gd white; improving B'x red. CLOS Cantenac in ST-ÉM same owner.

outard St-Ém r ★★★ 95 96 98' 99 00' 01 05 06 07 08 09 10 11 12 Potentially excellent GRAND CRU CLASSÉ on limestone plateau owned by same insurance group as LARMANDE. Cadet-Piola integrated in 2012. Massive investment, still room for improvement. Finer style since 2010. Second label: Les Jardins de Soutard.

iduiraut Saut w sw ★★★★ 86 88' 89' 90' 95 96 97' 98 99 01' 02 03' 04 05' 06 07' 09' 10' 11' 13 One of the v. best SAUT. Owner AXA has achieved greater consistency and luscious quality. Second labels: Castelnau de Suduiraut; Les Lions de Suduiraut (fresher, fruitier). Dry wine "S" v. promising. No CH Suduiraut produced in 2012.

illefer Pom r ★★ 98' 00' 01' 02 03 04 05' 06 08 09' 10 11 12 Family property managed by Catherine Moueix and daughter. Denis Dubourdieu consults. Lighter weight but polished and refined.

lbot St-Jul r (w) ★★★ 90 94 95 96' 98' 99 00' 01 02 03 04 05' 08' 09' 10' 11 12 Substantial (107 ha) Fourth Growth in the heart of AC ST-JUL owned by Cordier family since 1917. Wine rich, consummately charming, reliable (though wobbly in 2006–7). DERENONCOURT consults. Second label: Connétable de Talbot. Excellent white: Caillou Blanc. New barrel cellar 2012.

Tertre, Du Marg r ★★★ 96' 98' 99 00' 01 03 04' 05' 06 08 09' 10' 11 12 Fifth Growth isolated s of MARG. Fragrant (20% CAB FR) fresh, fruity wines. Since 1997 same Dutch owner as CH GISCOURS. Former LATOUR winemaker. New techniques, massive investment. Now a concentrated, structured wine. On top form in new millennium. Remains gd value.

Tertre Daugay St-Ém See QUINTUS.

Tertre-Rôteboeuf St-Ém r ★★★★ 89' 90' 93 94 95 96 97 98' 99 00' 01 02 03' 04 05' 06' 07 08 09' 10' 11 12 13 Tiny cult star making concentrated, dramatic wine since 1979. Hugely consistent. Frightening prices. Also CÔTES DE BOURG property ROC DE CAMBES of ST-ÉM classed growth quality.

Thieuley B'x r p w ★★ E-2-M supplier of consistent quality AC B'x (r w); fruity CLAIRET. oak-aged CUVÉE Francis Courselle (r w). Also owns CLOS Ste-Anne in CADILLAC CÔTES DE BORDEAUX.

Tour-Blanche, La Saut (r) w sw ★★★ 86 88' 89' 90' 95 96 97' 98 99 01' 02 03 04 05' 06 07 09' 10' 11' 12 13 Excellent First Growth SAUT in Bommes. Also winemaking school. Rich, full, powerful wines on sweeter end of scale. Second label: Les Charmilles de Tour-Blanche.

Tour-Carnet, La H-Méd r ★★ 98 00' 01 02 03 04 05' 06 08 09' 10' 11 12 A n H-MÉD Classed Growth owned by Bernard Magrez (see FOMBRAUGE, PAPE-CLÉMENT). Rich concentrated modern wines. MICHEL ROLLAND consults. Second label: Les Douves de CH La Tour Carnet. Also special CUVÉE Servitude Volontaire du Tour Carnet.

Tour Figeac, La St-Ém r ★★ 98' 00' 01' 02 04 05' 06 07 08 09' 10' 11 12 GRAND CRU CLASSÉ in FIGEAC, CHEVAL BLANC sector. Bio methods (DERENONCOURT and his wife consult). Full, fleshy, harmonious.

Tour Haut-Brion, La Pe-Lé See LA MISSION-HAUT-BRION.

Tour Haut-Caussan Méd r ★★ 02 03 04 05' 06 08 09' 10' 11 12 Consistent CRU BOURGEOIS (2012) at Blaignan. Value. Interests in CORBIÈRES too.

Tour-de-By, La Méd r ★★ 00 01 02 03 04 05' 06 08 09 10 11 12 Big (109 ha) family run estate in n MÉD. Sturdy, reliable wines with a fruity note. Eric Boissenot consults. Also rosé and special CUVÉE Héritage Marc Pagès.

Tour de Mons, La Marg r ★★ 98' 00 01 02 04 05' 06 08 09' 10 11 12 MARG CRU BOURGEOIS (2012). Management by CA Grands Crus (see MEYNEY). Improvement in the new millennium.

Tour-du-Haut-Moulin H-Méd r ★★ 98 00' 02 03 04 05' 06 08 09 10 11 12 In H-MÉD. Same family since 1870. Intense, consistent, wines to mature.

Tour-du-Pas-St-Georges St-Ém r ★★ 00' 01 03 04 05' 06 08 09' 10 11 12 ST-GEORGES ST-ÉM estate owned by Pascal Delbeck (ex-BELAIR-MONANGE). Classic style.

Tour-St-Bonnet Méd r ★★ 02 03 04 05 06 08 09' 10 11 12 CRU BOURGEOIS (2012) in the n MÉD at St-Christoly. Reliable. Value.

Tournefeuille B'x r ★★ 00' 01' 02 03 04 05' 06 07 08 09 10' 11 12 Reliable L DE P on edge of Barbanne stream. 30% CAB FR adds spice. CHX Lécouyer (POM) same stable.

Trois Croix, Les B'x r ★★ 05 06 07 08 09 10 11 12 13 Fine, balanced wines from consistent producer in FRONSAC. Gd value. Owned by former MOUTON-ROTHSCHILD winemaker. Son and daughter manage estate.

Why Bordeaux?
People ask whether B'x still justifies its own separate section of this international guide. The answer: it remains the motor of the fine wine world, by far its biggest producer, stimulating debate, investment and collectors worldwide. Besides, there are few better drinks.

Where to stay? Where to eat?
Tourism is booming in B'X, and with it, new projects. There's the Philippe Starck-decorated Mama Shelter hotel (2013); 270-seater brasserie Le Grand Comptoir at the St-Jean railway station (2013); Coup 2 Foudres accommodation in two Seguin Moreau-built *foudres* (2013); Bernard Magrez boutique hotel and restaurant in partnership with multi-Michelin-starred chef Joël Robuchon (2014); and the €81 million wine cultural centre, the *Cité des Civilisations du Vin*, opens 2016.

ronquoy-Lalande St-Est r ★★ 00' 02 03 04 05 06 07 08 09' 10' 11 12 Same owners as MONTROSE (2006); replanting and new *cuvier* since. Progress: wines dark, fresh, satisfying. Second label: Tronquoy de Ste-Anne.

roplong-Mondot St-Ém r ★★★ 89' 90' 95 96' 98' 99 00' 01' 02 03 04 05' 06 07 08 09' 10 11 12 13 RIP Christine Valette, owner who propelled Troplong to the top. First Growth on a high point of the limestone plateau. *Wines of power and depth* with increasing elegance. Second label: Mondot.

rotanoy Pom r ★★★★ 89' 90' 93 94 95 96 98' 00' 01 02 03 04' 05' 06 07 08 09' 10' 11 12 13 Owned by J-P MOUEIX. Top site on plateau with clay/gravel soils. On flying form since 1989; power and elegance combined. Second label: L'Espérance de Trotanoy (from 2009; not every yr).

rottevieille St-Ém r ★★★ 89' 90 94 95 96 98 99 00' 01 03' 04 05' 06 07 08' 09' 10' 11 12 First Growth on limestone plateau. BORIE-MANOUX-owned. Much improved in new millennium. Lots of CAB FR (40–50%). Denis Dubourdieu consults. Former GRAND CRU CLASSÉ CH Bergat integrated in 2012. Second label: La Vieille Dame de Trottevieille.

alandraud St-Ém r ★★★★ 93 94 95' 96 98 99 00' 01' 02 03 04 05' 06 07 08 09' 10' 11 12 13 Wine that launched garage movement (1991). Now a PREMIER GRAND CRU CLASSÉ; 8 ha at St-Etienne-de-Lisse. Originally super-concentrated; since 1998 greater complexity. Virginie de Valandraud another selection. Valandraud Blanc as well.

ieille Cure, La B'x r ★★ 00' 01' 02 03 04 05' 06 08 09' 10' 11 12 13 Leading FRONSAC estate; US-owned. VALANDRAUD owner consults since 2013. Value.

ieux-Ch-Certan Pom r ★★★★ 83' 85 86' 88' 89 90' 94 95' 96' 98' 99 00' 01 02 04 05' 06 07 08 09' 10' 11' 12 13 Traditionally rated close to PETRUS in quality; totally different in style (30% CAB FR and 10% CAB SAUV); *elegance, harmony, fragrance*. Old vines (average 40–50 yrs). Second label: La Gravette de Certan.

ieux Ch St-André St-Ém r ★★ 05 06 08 09' 10 11 12 Small MERLOT-based v'yd in MONTAGNE-ST-ÉM owned by former PETRUS winemaker. Consistent value.

illegeorge, De H-Méd r ★★ 00' 02 04 05 06 08 09' 10 12 Tiny H-MÉD close to MARG. Owned by Marie-Laure Lurton. Classic MÉD style. CHX Duplessis (MOU) and La Tour de Bessan (Marg) same stable.

ray Croix de Gay Pom r ★★ 98' 00' 04 05' 06 08 09' 10' 11 12 Tiny v'yd in the best part of POM. Greater consistency since 2005. Sister CHX Siaurac in L DE P and Le Prieuré in ST-ÉM. Ch LATOUR owner now shareholder in all.

quem Saut w sw (dr) ★★★★ 83' 85 86' 88' 89' 90' 93 94 95' 96 97' 98 99' 00 01' 02 03' 04 05' 06' 07' 08 09' 10' 11' 12' King of sweet wines. Strong, intense, luscious; kept 3 yrs in barrel. Most vintages improve for 15 yrs+, some live 100 yrs+ in transcendent splendour. Subtle changes since 2000 under LVMH ownership: more freshness, less time in barrel. Denis Dubourdieu consults. No Yquem made in 52, 72, 92, 2012. Same owner and manager as CHEVAL BLANC. Also makes dry "Y" (pronounced "ygrec").

Italy

More heavily shaded areas are the wine-growing regions.

Abbreviations used in the text:

Ab	Abruzzo	Mar	Molise
Bas	Basilicata	Pie	Piedmont
Cal	Calabria	Pu	Puglia
Cam	Campania	Sar	Sardinia
E-R	Emilia-Romagna	Si	Sicily
F-VG	Friuli-Venezia Giulia	T-AA	Trentino-Alto Adige
Lat	Latium	Tus	Tuscany
Lig	Liguria	Umb	Umbria
Lom	Lombardy	VdA	Valle d'Aosta
Mar	Marches	Ven	Veneto

It has been a long haul; but Italy is at last ready to take on the great wines of the world on equal terms. Until the 50s Italian fine wine was in a depressed state; production volume ruled. The 60s was the decade in which Italian wines were introduced to legal descriptions and restrictions in the form of the DOC regulations – still often overprizing volume but it was a start. The 70s saw the blossoming of upmarket "crus" unofficially dubbed (at least the ones from Tuscany) "Super Tuscans", often in defiance of the law. In the 80s Italian winemakers began what would become a mass movement to improve conditions in their wineries until then subject to widespread neglect and disadvantaged by primitive or faulty equipment. The 90s was when Italians, now believing in but rarely achieving great wine, began in earnest to analyze and revise their vineyard practices in recognition of the time-honoured truism that "great wine can only be made from great grapes".

Which brings us to the 21st century, a decade-plus in which words like "terroir" and "zoning" have risen to the fore. As Burgundy boasts its *grands crus* and *premiers crus*, and Bordeaux its *crus classés*, so do the likes

f Barolo and Barbaresco, Brunello and Vino Nobile and Chianti Classico, and more than a few others aspire to official recognition hat their particular sites are uniquely qualified to produce, at least otentially, great wine. In fact efforts to divide the classic Piemontese ommunes into subzones have been going on for a number of years, nd recently, convincing Bordeaux-style classifications of Brunello have een advanced. There is still much work to do and many problems, not east political, to resolve. But zoning is the future and we will be hearing nuch more about it.

Recent vintages

Amarone, Veneto & Friuli

2014 Disastrously cool, wet summer followed by good September (whites), October (reds). November more rain. Not memorable for Amarone.

2013 Good whites. Reds, especially passito, suffered from sporadic rain and hail in October/November.

2012 Prolonged heat, drought hit quantity, quality. Amarone should be good.

2011 "Best year ever" for Amarone. Whites balanced and concentrated. Some reds very tannic, with high alcohol.

2010 Cool year, good for lighter wines. Start drinking soon.

2009 Ideal drying conditions for passito: classic wines. Good for Prosecco, Pinot Gr, etc. Drink Amarone from 2015.

2008 Classic wines of high quality. Drink from 2016.

2007 Some excellent wines; selection needed.

Campania & Basilicata

2014 Production 25 per cent down on 2013. Low temperatures and summer rains: spotty quality (reds and white). Choose carefully.

2013 Whites balanced, perfumed; reds less so, especially late-picked Aglianico.

2012 September rain saved whites. Indian summer: outstanding Aglianicos.

2011 Wines concentrated; high alcohol, tannin in reds. Whites better balanced.

2010 Whites lightish with good aromas; reds good to average.

2009 Ripe, healthy, aromatic whites; reds with substance and concentration. Drink Aglianico/Taurasi from 2014.

2008 Classic year for Aglianico; good too for whites. Drinking well.

2007 Good to excellent quality. Drinking well.

Marches & Abruzzo

2014 Challenging July; late August, September much better. Marches: good red white. In Abruzzo interesting wines at higher levels, mainly late-picked.

2013 Hailstorms, rot. Fine September saved whites; reds better than was feared

2012 Warm days and cool nights at vintage time. Later-picked varieties best.

2011 Some overconcentrated, alcoholic and tannic reds. Best should age well.

2010 A difficult year but some good results. Drinking now.

2009 Good to very good quality, especially whites. Reds drink now.

2008 Some excellent wines. Drink from now for 3 years.

Piedmont

2014 Coolish rainy summer. September, early October better; there's hope for later varieties, especially Nebbiolo.

2003 Bright, crisp whites and reds good but not great.

2012 Quality good to very good, volume very low.

2011 High alcohol; danger of overconcentration. Good average quality.

2010 Quality seemed patchy, but patient growers made very good wines. Now seen as potentially top vintage.

2009 Good to very good, especially Nebbiolo. Drink Barolo/Barbaresco from 2014 for 10 years+.

2008 Some great Barberas; Nebbiolo good, not spectacular. Drink for 10 years.

2007 Good to excellent Barolo, Barbaresco, Barbera. Some classic wines. Drink now–10 years+.

Older fine vintages: 06 04 01 00 99 98 97 96 95 90 89 88. Vintages to keep: 01 99 96. Vintages to drink up: 03 00 97 90 88.

Tuscany

2014 Very mild winter, cool, wet summer, fine late season. Quantity up but quality patchy, buyer beware.

2013 Uneven ripening. Not a great year, but some peaks.

2012 Drought and protracted heat, but classic wines saved by early September rain; turning out very well.

2011 Some charmingly fruity if alcoholic classic reds. Whites a bit unbalanced.

2010 Patchy. Brunello very successful.

2009 Quality very good at least. Drink Chianti/Brunello now for 2–3 yrs.

2008 Mixed results, points of excellence. Drink from now for 5 years.

2007 High-quality crop. Drink from now for 10 years.

Older fine vintages: 06 04 01 99 97 95 90. Vintages to keep: 01 99. Vintages to drink up: 03 00 97 95 90.

What do the initials mean?

Denominazione di Origine Controllata (DOC)
Controlled Denomination of Origin, cf. AC in France.

Denominazione di Origine Controllata e Garantita (DOCG)
"G" = "Guaranteed". Italy's highest quality designation.

Indicazione Geografica Tipica (IGT)
"Geographic Indication of Type". Broader and more vague than DOC, cf. Vin de Pays in France.

Denominazione di Origine Protetta / Indicazione Geografica Protetta (DOP / IGP)
"P" = "Protected". *See* Italy's introduction.

Aglianico del Vulture Bas DOC(G) r dr ★→★★★ 06 07 08 10 11 12 DOC after 1 yr, SUPERIORE after 2 yrs, RISERVA after 5. A noble red, best from slopes of extinct volcano Monte Vulture. Top producers incl Alovini, Basilisco, CANTINA di Venosa, Cantine del Notaio, Donato d'Angelo, Dragone, Elena Fucci, Grifalco, Madonna delle Grazie, Mastrodomenico, Parco dei Monaci PATERNOSTER, Serra dei Prete, Terre degli Svevi.

Alba Pie Major wine city of PIE, se of Turin in LANGHE hills; truffles, hazelnuts and Pie's, if not Italy's, most prestigious wines: BAROLO, BARBARESCO, NEBBIOLO D'ALBA, Langhe, ROERO, BARBERA d'Alba, DOGLIANI (DOLCETTO).

Albana di Romagna E-R DOCG w dr sw s/sw (sp) ★→★★★ DYA. Italy's first white DOCG, justified only by sweet PASSITO; dry and sp unremarkable. Bertinoro is commune with best producers: Raffaella Alessandra Bissoni, Celli, Madonia Giovanna, *Fattoria Paradiso*. ZERBINA's Scacco Matto is perhaps best sweet version.

Alberello Bush- or head-trained vines, the traditional method of pruning in the s, now increasingly in the centre, notably TUS. Most of best and oldest v'yds of trendy ETNA, eg, are *alberelli*.

Allegrini Ven ★★★ Grower world-famous for VALPOLICELLA; top wines incl *La Grola*, Palazzo della Torre, La Poja, AMARONE, RECIOTO. Also owns POGGIO al Tesoro in BOLGHERI and Poggio San Polo in MONTALCINO, TUS.

Altare, Elio Pie ★★★ Leading exponent of modern NEBBIOLO (BAROLO) and BARBERA: brief maceration in roto-fermentors, ageing in barriques. Look for Barolo VIGNA Bricco Cerretta from Serralunga and La Morra cru Barolo Arborina; also Arborina (Nebbiolo), Larigi (Barbera), Langhe Rosso La Villa (Barbera/Nebbiolo).

Alto Adige T-AA DOC r p w dr sw sp ★★→★★★ Largely German-speaking province of Bolzano, alias SÜDTIROL. Phenomenal success with mtn-fresh whites; PINOT B can be a world-beater. Remarkably gd PINOT N; less so other reds, except for the odd *Lagrein*. Excellent co-ops; many quality growers.

Ama, Castello di Tus ★★★ Top CHIANTI CLASSICO estate of Gaiole. The plain *Chianti Classico is one of best*, and most expensive, of its type. Different and worth seeking is TUS-Bordeaux blend Haiku; also MERLOT L'Apparita despite the high price. Latest is Chianti Classico GRAN SELEZIONE San Lorenzo.

Amarone della Valpolicella Ven DOCG r ★★→★★★★ 04 06' 07 08 09 10 11' 12 (13) Intense strong red from winery-raisined VALPOLICELLA grapes, a relatively dry version of the ancient RECIOTO DELLA VALPOLICELLA; one of Italy's true classics. CLASSICO if from historic zone. (For producers *see* box, p.151 and also *see* box, p.152.) Older vintages are rare; beyond 20 yrs they tend to dry out.

Angelini, Tenimenti Tus *See* BERTANI DOMAINS (TOSCANA).

Antinori, Marchesi L & P Tus ★★→★★★★★ V. influential Florentine house of the Antinori family, led by Piero, one of Italian wine's heroes, from the futuristic new winery at Bargino, s of Florence. Famous for CHIANTI CLASSICO (TENUTA Marchese Antinori and *Badia a Passignano*, the latter now elevated to the status of Gran Selezione). Umb (*Castello della Sala*), PIE (PRUNOTTO) wines. Pioneer TIGNANELLO and SOLAIA are among the few successful SUPER TUSCANS remaining. Also estates in TUS MAREMMA (Fattoria Aldobrandesca), MONTEPULCIANO (La Braccesca), MONTALCINO (Pian delle Vigne), BOLGHERI (Guado al Tasso), FRANCIACORTA (*Montenisa*), PUG (Tormaresca). Latest is a RIES-based white from the estate of Monteloro n of Florence.

Argiano, Castello di Tus Aka **Sesti**. Astronomer Giuseppe Maria Sesti makes classy bio BRUNELLO and Brunello RISERVA Phenomena. Not to be confused with neighbour called simply Argiano.

Argiolas, Antonio Sar ★★→★★★ Top producer; native island grapes. Outstanding crus incl *Turriga* (★★★), Antonio Argiolas, Korem, Iselis Bianco, VERMENTINO di Sardegna Meri.

Ar.Pe.Pe. Lom ★★→★★★ Historic VALTELLINA estate first est 1860, re-est in 1984 by the Pelizzati Perego family. From their 13 ha in this breathtaking mtn country they produce around 70,000 bottles of Chiavennasca (NEBBIOLO)-based wine of various styles in traditional mode. Top wines are Grumello Buon Consiglio Riserva, Sassella VIGNA Regina Riserva and Inferno Fiamme Antiche.

Ascheri ★★→★★★ In cellars in the town of Bra, from v'yds in Serralunga and Verduno, larger-than-life Matteo Ascheri makes fine BAROLOS, mixing new and old methods. Also exceptional MOSCATO D'ASTI.

Asti Pie DOCG sw sp ★→★★★ NV PIE sparkler from MOSCATO Bianco grapes; known in past as Asti SPUMANTE. Now too cheap for its own gd; DOCG status questionable. *See* MOSCATO D'ASTI, BARBERA. Rare top producers: BERA, Cascina Fonda, Caudrina, Vignaioli di Santo Stefano.

Azienda agricola / agraria An estate (large or small) making wine from own grapes.

Badia a Coltibuono Tus ★★→★★★ Historic CHIANTI CLASSICO. Star wine is 100% SANGIOVESE barrique-aged Sangioveto. Chianti Classico Cultus Boni back-to-basics blend of Sangiovese and indigenous Foglia Tonda, MALVASIA Nera, Ciliegiolo.

Banfi (Castello or Villa) Tus ★→★★★ MONTALCINO CANTINA of major US importer. Huge plantings on lower-lying s slopes of Montalcino, incl in-house-developed

---

Ten top Barberas

Most of best BARBERAS are from the PIE DOCS of Barbera d'Asti and Barbera d'ALBA, but there are occasional examples of excellence from elsewhere.
Barbera d'Alba: BOGLIETTI (VIGNA dei Romani); CLERICO (Trevigne); PRUNOTTO (Pian Romualdo); Voerzio, Gianni (Ciabot della Luna); VOERZIO, ROBERTO (Pozzo dell'Annunziata).
Barbera d'Asti: BRAIDA (Bricco dell'Uccellone); COPPO (Pomorosso); Perrone (Mongovone); CS Vinchio Vaglio (Vigne Vecchie).
Langhe: Altare (Larigi).

Barbaresco subzones

BARBARESCO may be queen to BAROLO's king, but it has also often been looked down upon as Barolo's poor cousin. While there are similarities (100% NEBBIOLO, soils and exposure, comparable climate and sub-climate) there is sufficient difference between them to justify the division into two separate wines. Within these parameters there are further delimitations based, as in Barolo, on villages and "geographic mentions" unofficially known as crus or subzones. Barbaresco derives from only 3–4 villages: Barbaresco, Neive and Treiso (plus a sliver of ALBA called San Rocco Seno d'Elvio), and 66 geographic mentions. If a Barbaresco does not display a subzone name it is probably a blend. Some of the best subzones to look out for are (by commune):

Barbaresco: Asili, Faset, Martinenga, Montefico, Montestefano, Ovello, Pora, Rabaja, Rio Sordo, Roncaglie, Ronchi, Trestelle;

Neive: Albesani, Basarin, Bricco di Neive, Currá, Gallina, Rivetti, Serraboella, Starderi;

Treiso: Bricco di Treiso, Marcarini, Nervo, Pajoré, Rizzi;

San Rocco Seno d'Elvio: Montersino, Rocche Massalupo.

---

clones of SANGIOVESE; also CAB SAUV, MERLOT, SYRAH, PINOT N, CHARD, SAUV BL, PINOT GR. SUPER TUSCAN blends Cum Laude and *Summus* tend to work better than somewhat overextracted BRUNELLOS.

Barbaresco Pie DOCG r ★★→★★★★ 01 04 06' 07 08 09 10 11 (12) Like its twin, BAROLO, 100% NEBBIOLO. Similar complex aromas and flavour; less power, more elegance. Min 26 mths ageing, 9 mths in wood; at 4 yrs becomes RISERVA. Like Barolo, most Barbaresco these days is sold under a cru name or *menzione geografica* (geographic mention), as it's currently unpoetically called. (*See* box above for best producers.)

Barbera Grape and wine found all over Italy but the principal red in terms of volume in PIE and Lombardy's OLTREPO PAVESE, therefore the default red of Milan, DOCS incl B. d'Auti, B. d'ALBA, B. del Monferrato & Oltrepò Pavese, etc. (*See* box left for best producers.)

Bardolino Ven DOC(G) r p ★→★★ DYA Light summery red from Lake Garda. Bardolino SUPERIORE DOCG much lower yield than Bardolino DOC. Pale-pink CHIARETTO one of Italy's best rosés. Gd: Albino Piona, Cavalchina, Corte Gardoni, Costadoro, *Guerrieri Rizzardi*, Le Fraghe, Le VIGNE di San Pietro, ZENATO, Zeni.

Barolo Pie DOCG r ★★★→★★★★ 96' 99' 01' 04' 06' 07' 08 09' 10 (11) (12) Italy's greatest red, 100% NEBBIOLO, from any of 11 communes incl Barolo itself. Traditionally sold simply as "Barolo", and could be a blend of v'yds or communes, but these days most is single-v'yd (like Burgundian *crus*), here called *menzione geografica*. The best combine power and elegance, plentiful, sometimes rasping tannins and alluring floral scent with a long, sweet finish. Must age 38 mths before release (5 yrs for RISERVA), of which 18 mths in wood. Divided between traditionalists (long maceration, large oak barrels) and modernists (shorter maceration, often barriques). (*See* box p.128 for best producers.)

Bartoli, Marco de Si ★★★ Famous estate for MARSALA Vergine-like (dry) VECCHIO SAMPERI. Best sweet Marsala is barrel-aged Ventennale, blend of young and v. old vintages. Sons of lamented founder Marco de B. also make a top sticky from PANTELLERIA under the name Bukkuram. Also excellent dry whites *Grillo* and Zibibbo.

Beato Bartolomeo da Breganze Ven ★★ Well-run co-op in hills of Ven with one of the largest plantings of genuine PINOT GRIGIO. Also still, sparkling, sweet (TORCOLATO) wines from native Vespaiolo grape.

> **Ten top Barolos**
>
> "Italy's greatest wine" is too tough for some. Here are a few top crus with which to test both parts of that statement:
> BURLOTTO (Monvigliero); Cavallotto (Bricco Boschis VIGNA San Giuseppe); CONTERNO FANTINO SORÍ GINESTRA); CONTERNO GIACOMO (Monprivato); MASCARELLO Giuseppe (Monprivato); Rinaldi Giuseppe (Brunate-Le Coste); SANDRONE (Cannubi Boschis); SCAVINO PAOLO (Bric del Fiasc); VIETTI (Lazzarito); VOERZIO, ROBERTO (La Serra).

Bellavista Lom ★★★ FRANCIACORTA estate; convincing, Gran Cuvée Franciacorta top.

Bera, Walter Pie ★★→★★★ Small estate for top-quality MOSCATO (Moscato d'ASTI, Asti), also fine reds (BARBERA d'Asti, BARBARESCO, LANGHE NEBBIOLO).

Berlucchi, Guido Lom ★★ Italy's largest producer of sparkling METODO CLASSICO with five million+ bottle production.

Bertani Ven ★★→★★★ Long-est producer; VALPOLICELLA and SOAVE, v'yds in various parts of Verona province. Basic Veronese/Valpantena lines plus restoration of abandoned techniques, eg. white using traditional skin maceration, red (Secco Bertani Original Vintage Edition). *See also* BERTANI DOMAINS (TOSCANA).

Bertani Domains (Toscana) Tus ★★→★★★ Previously Tenimenti Angelini, the Angelini group having taken over BERTANI of VALPOLICELLA and renamed the TUS operation. Three major wineries: Val di Suga in MONTALCINO, Trerose in MONTEPULCIANO and San Leonino in CHIANTI CLASSICO.

Bianco di Custoza or Custoza Ven DOC w (sp) ★→★★ DYA Fresh, uncomplicated white from Lake Garda, made from GARGANEGA, Cortese. Gd: Cavalchina, Le Tende, Le VIGNE di San Pietro, Montresor, Zeni.

Biferno Mol DOC r p w ★→★★ (r) 10 11 12 Gd to interesting wines from easily forgotten region of Molise, sandwiched between Ab and PUG. Red based on MONTEPULCIANO, white on TREBBIANO. *Di Majo Norante* (Ramitello), Borgo di Colloredo (Gironia) worthwhile.

Biondi-Santi Tus ★★★★ The late Franco Biondi-Santi maintained the classic traditions of his famous MONTALCINO estate to the end, making BRUNELLOs and esp RISERVAS so uncompromising that, from top vintages, they couldn't be drunk for decades. Son Jacopo is tipped to make them more user-friendly, possibly at the expense of elegance and/or complexity. No 2014 Brunello.

Bisol Ven Top brand of PROSECCO.

Boca Pie *See* GATTINARA.

Boglietti, Enzo Pie ★★★ Dynamic modern-leaning producer at La Morra in BAROLO. Top Barolos (VIGNA Arione, Case Nere); outstanding BARBERA d'ALBA (Vigna dei Romani, Roscaleto).

Bolgheri Tus DOC r p w (sw) ★★→★★★★ Arty walled village on TUS's w coast giving its name to a stylish and expensive group of SUPER TUSCANS mainly based on French varieties. Big names: SASSICAIA (original inspirer of the cult), ANTINORI (at Guado al Tasso), FRESCOBALDI (at ORNELLAIA), GAJA (at CÀ MARCANDA), ALLEGRINI (at Poggio al Tesoro), FOLONARI (at Campo al Mare), plus the odd local in LE MACCHIOLE and MICHELE SATTA. Many of the best producers are following SASSICAIA's lead and dumping IGT status for BOLGHERI DOC.

Bolla Ven ★★ Historic Verona firm for SOAVE, VALPOLICELLA, AMARONE, RECIOTO DELLA VALPOLICELLA, RECIOTO DI SOAVE. Today owned by powerful GRUPPO ITALIANO VINI.

Borgo del Tiglio F-VG ★★★→★★★★ Nicola Manferrari is one of Italy's top white winemakers. Impressive COLLIO FRIULANO RONCO della Chiesa, Studio di Bianco.

Boscarelli, Poderi Tus ★★★ Small estate of Genovese de Ferrari family with reliably high-standard VINO NOBILE DI MONTEPULCIANO, cru Nocio dei Boscarelli and RISERVA.

Botte Big barrel, anything from 6–250 hl, usually between 20–50, traditionally of

Slavonian but increasingly of French oak. To traditionalists, the ideal vessel for ageing wines in which an excess of oak aromas is undesirable.

Brachetto d'Acqui / Acqui Pie DOCG r sw (sp) ★★ DYA. Sweet sparkling red with enticing MUSCAT scent. Elevated DOCG status disputed by some.

Braida Pie ★★★ Late Giacomo Bologna's estate, well run by his children Giuseppe, Raffaella. Top BARBERA D'ASTI (Bricco dell'Uccellone, Bricco della Bigotta, Ai Suma).

Bramaterra Pie *See* GATTINARA.

Breganze Ven DOC r w sp ★→★★★ (w) DYA (r) 06 07 08 09 10 11 13 Major production area for PINOT GR, also gd Vespaiolo (white, still and sp, and sticky TORCOLATO); PINOT N, CAB. Main producers MACULAN, BEATO BARTOLOMEO.

Brezza Pie ★★★ Ultra-trad BAROLO-maker Enzo B. makes classic, virtually organic wines from crus Cannubi, Castellero and Sarmassa. In top vintages he bottles Bricco Sarmassa from highest Sarmassa v'yd.

Brigaldara Ven ★★★ Elegant but powerful AMARONES, benchmarks of the genre, from estate of Stefano Cesari.

Brindisi Pug DOC r p ★★ (r) 08 09 10 11 12 (13) (p) DYA. Smooth NEGROAMARO-based red with MONTEPULCIANO, esp from VALLONE, Due Palme, Rubino. ROSATO can be among Italy's best.

Brolio, Castello di Tus ★★→★★★ Historic estate, CHIANTI CLASSICO's largest, now thriving again under RICASOLI family after foreign-managed decline. *V.gd* Chianti Classico and IGT Casalferro.

Brunelli, Gianni Tus ★★★ Small-scale producer of elegant, refined BRUNELLO DI MONTALCINO. Don't confuse with other Brunellis. Run by Gianni's widow, Laura.

Barolo subzones

The concept of "cru" is becoming ever more important in Italy, although unfortunately the word itself, being jealously guarded by the French, is not allowed on the label, and is replaced (in BAROLO and BARBARESCO at least) by the prosaic term "geographic mentions", known unofficially to most producers as subzones (if not "crus"). Currently Barolo has 11 village mentions and 179 geographic mentions. For a full list consult Alessandro Masnaghetti's Barolo subzones map in the *Enogea* series, or Kerin O'Keefe's excellent book *Barolo and Barbaresco* (2014). Some of the best incl (by commune):

Barolo: Bricco delle Viole, Brunate, Bussia, Cannubi, Cannubi Boschis, Cannubi Muscatel, Cannubi Sann Lorenzo, Cannubi Valletta, Cerequio, La Volta, Le Coste, Ravera, Sarmassa, Zonchetta;

Castiglione Falletto: Bricco Boschhis, Bricco Rocche, Codana, Fiasco, Mariondino, Monprivato, Pira, Rocche di Castiglione, Vignolo, Villero;

Cherasco: Mantoetto;

Diano d'Alba: La VIGNA;

Grinzane Cavour: Canova, Castello;

La Morra: Annunziata, Arborina, Bricco Manzoni, Bricco San Biagio, Brunate, Case Nere, Cerequio, Fossati, La Serra, Rocche dell'Annunziata, Rocchettevino, Roggeri, Roncaglie;

Monforte d'Alba: Bussia, Ginestra, Gramolere, Mosconi, Perno, Rocche di Castiglione, San Giovanni;

Novello: Panerole, Ravera;

Roddi: Bricco Ambrogio;

Serralunga d'Alba: Arione, Baudana, Boscareto, Bricco Voghera, Cerretta, Falletto, Fontanafredda, Francia, Gabutti, Lazzarito, Marenca, Ornato, Parafada, Prapò, San Rocco, Serra, Sorano, Vignarionda;

Verduno: Massara, Monvigliero.

> **The best of Brunello – top ten and the rest**
>
> Any of the below provide a satisfying BRUNELLO DI MONTALCINO, but we have
> put a star next to the ten we think best:
>
> Pieri Agostina, Altesino, ARGIANO (CASTELLO DI), Baricci, BIONDI-SANTI ★,
> Gianni BRUNELLI ★, Camigliano, La Campana, Campogiovanni,
> Canalicchio di Sopra, Canalicchio di Sotto, Caparzo, CASANOVA DI NERI,
> CASE BASSE ★, CASTELGIOCONDO, Ciacci Piccolomini, COL D'ORCIA,
> Collemattoni, Corte Pavone, Costanti, Eredi FULIGNI, Il Colle, Il Paradiso
> di Manfredi, La Fuga, La Gerla, Lambardi, LISINI ★, La Magia, La
> Mannella, Le Potazzine, Marroneto, Mastrojanni ★, Oliveto, Salvioni ★,
> Siro Pacenti, Palazzo, Pertimali, Pieve di Santa Restituta, La Poderina,
> Pian dell'Orino ★, Il POGGIONE ★, POGGIO ANTICO, Poggio di Sotto ★,
> Salvioni-Cerbaiola ★, Uccelliera, Val di Suga, Valdicava.

Brunello di Montalcino Tus DOCG r ★★★→★★★★ 90' 95 97 99' 00 01' 04' 05
06' 07 09 (10') (11) (12) (13) The top wine of TUS, dense but elegant with scent
and structure, potentially v. long-lived. Min 4 yrs ageing, 5 for RISERVA. There
are moves to allow small quantities of eg. CAB in this supposedly 100% varietal
(SANGIOVESE), which have been fought off, but continual vigilance is needed.
See also ROSSO DI MONTALCINO. (*See* box above for best producers.)

Bucci Mar ★★★ Quasi-Burgundian VERDICCHIOS, slow to mature but complex with
age. Compared with most Verdicchio RISERVA Villa Bucci is on another planet.
Red Pongelli is less exciting.

Burlotto, Commendatore G B Pie ★★★ Beautifully crafted and defined wines, esp
BAROLO Cannubi and Monvigliero, the latter's grapes being crushed by foot.

Bussola, Tommaso Ven ★★★★ Leading producer of AMARONE, RECIOTO and RIPASSO in
VALPOLICELLA. Excellent Amarone VIGNETO Alto and Recioto TB.

Ca' dei Frati Lom ★★★ Foremost quality estate of revitalized DOC LUGANA, I Frati a
fine example at entry level; Brolettino a superior cru. Tre Filer, from indigenous
Turbiana with SAUV BL and CHARD, is a particularly well-made PASSITO sticky.

Ca' del Bosco Lom ★★★★ No 1 FRANCIACORTA estate owned by giant PINOT GR producer
Santa Margherita; run by founder Maurizio Zanella. *Outstanding Classico-method*
fizz, esp Annamaria Clementi (Italy's Dom Pérignon), Dosage Zero. Excellent
Bordeaux-style red Maurizio Zanella, burgundy-style PINOT N Pinero and CHARD.

Caiarossa Tus ★★★ Dutch owner Eric Jelgersma (Château Giscours; *see* Bordeaux)
and Oz-trained French oenologist run this international estate, n of BOLGHERI.
Excellent Caiarossa Bianco and Rosso plus reds Pergolaia and Aria.

Caluso / Erbaluce di Caluso Pie DOCG w ★★ DYA. Bright, mineral white from
Erbaluce grape in n PIE. Best: Orsolani, esp La Rustia.

Ca' Marcanda Tus ★★★★ The BOLGHERI estate of Angelo GAJA (founded 1996). Three
wines in order of price (high, higher and highest): Promis, Magari and Ca'
Marcanda. Grapes mainly international.

Campania Country playground of Romans has turned out, in modern as in ancient
times, to be one of most fascinating wine regions. Viticulture is divided between
coast, incl islands like ISCHIA and Capri, and inland mtn areas, almost invariably
better. Characterful white grapes incl FALANGHINA, FIANO, GRECO, while AGLIANICO
rules among reds. Classic DOCS incl FIANO d'Avellino, GRECO DI TUFO, TAURASI, with
newer areas emerging, eg. Sannio and Benevento. Gd producers: Caggiano,
CANTINA del Taburno, Caputo, Colli di Lapio, D'Ambra, De Angelis, Benito
Ferrara, *Feudi di San Gregorio*, GALARDI, LA GUARDIENSE, *Mastroberardino*, Molettieri,
MONTEVETRANO, Mustilli, Luigi Tecce, Terredora di Paolo, Trabucco, VILLA MATILDE.

Canalicchio di Sopra Tus ★★★ Dynamic terroir-conscious Ripaccioli family
produce, from a blend of two v'yds, one on Montosoli slopes, beautifully

balanced, complex yet drinkable BRUNELLO (and RISERVA) and ROSSO DI MONTALCINO.

Cantina A cellar, winery or even a wine bar.

Caparra & Siciliani Cal ★→★★ Co-op in Cal's best-known zone, CIRÒ. 200 ha+ of Classico v'yds, 50 yrs experience.

Capezzana, Tenuta di Tus ★★★ Noble TUS family estate of late wine legend Count Ugo Contini Bonacossi, w of Florence, now run by his children. Gd Barco Reale DOC, excellent CARMIGNANO (*Villa di Capezzana*, Villa di Trefiano). Also v.gd Bordeaux-style red, Ghiaie della Furba, exceptional VIN SANTO.

Capichera Sar ★★★ V.gd if pricey producer of VERMENTINO DI GALLURA, esp Vendemmia *tardiva*. Excellent red Mantèghja from CARIGNANO. Also: Assaje' (r) and VT (w).

Cappellano Pie ★★★ The late Teobaldo Cappellano, a BAROLO hero, devoted part of his cru Gabutti to ungrafted NEBBIOLO (Pie Franco). Son Augusto continues in highly traditional style; also "tonic" Barolo Chinato, invented by an ancestor.

Caprai Umb ★★★→★★★★ Enterprising, enigmatic, experimental Marco Caprai runs large, top-quality MONTEFALCO estate. Superb DOCG *Montefalco Sagrantino*, esp 25 Anni, v.gd DOC ROSSO DI MONTEFALCO.

Carema Pie DOC r ★★→★★★ 06' 07 08 09 10 11 (13) Little-known, light, intense NEBBIOLO from steep lower Alpine slopes nr Aosta. Best: Luigi Ferrando (esp Etichetta Nera), Produttori Nebbiolo di Carema.

Carignano del Sulcis Sar DOC r p ★★→★★★ 08 09 10 12 (13) (14) Mellow but intense red from SAR's sw. Best: *Terre Brune*, Rocca Rubia from CS di SANTADI.

Carmignano Tus DOCG r ★★★ 02 04 06 07 08 09 10 11 (12) (13) Fine SANGIOVESE/ Bordeaux-grape blend invented in 20th century by late Count Bonacossi of CAPEZZANA. Best: Ambra, CAPEZZANA, Farnete, Piaggia, Le Poggiarelle, Pratesi.

Carnasciale, Il Tus ★★★ Exceptional Bordeaux-style red from spontaneous CABERNET X MERLOT cross jealously guarded by Bettina Rogosky and family. "*Caberlot*" was discovered decades ago by their consultant agronomist Remigio Bordini. Carnasciale is second label.

Carpenè-Malvolti Ven ★★ Historic and still important brand of PROSECCO and other sparkling wines at CONEGLIANO.

Cartizze Ven ★★ Famous, frequently too expensive and too sweet, DOC PROSECCO of supposedly best subzone of Valdobbiadene.

Casanova di Neri Tus ★★★ Modern BRUNELLO DI MONTALCINO, highly prized Cerretalto and TENUTA Nuova, plus Petradonice CAB SAUV and v.gd ROSSO DI MONTALCINO.

Case Basse Tus ★★★★ Eco-geek/ego-freak Gianfranco Soldera defies everybody, was seriously vandalized, quit the Consorzio and carries on making mostly bio, long-oak-aged, definitive-quality BRUNELLO-style (if not DOCG) wines as before. Remaining bottles are more rare and precious than ever.

Castel del Monte Pug DOC r p w ★→★★ (r) 08 09 10 11 (13) (p w) DYA. Dry, fresh, increasingly serious wines of mid-PUG DOC. Gd Pietrabianca and excellent *Bocca di Lupo* from Tormaresca (ANTINORI). V.gd Le More from Santa Lucia. Interesting reds from Cocevola, Giancarlo Ceci. *See also* RIVERA: Il Falcone RISERVA is iconic.

Castellare Tus ★★★ Classy Castellina-in-CHIANTI producer of long standing. First-rate SANGIOVESE-MALVASIA Nera I Sodi di San Niccoló and updated CHIANTI CLASSICO, esp RISERVA Il Poggiale. Also POGGIO ai Merli (MERLOT), Coniale (CAB SAUV).

Castell' in Villa Tus ★★★ Individual, traditionalistn CHIANTI CLASSICO estate in extreme sw of zone. Wines of class, excellence by self-taught Princess Coralia Pignatelli.

Castelluccio E-R ★★→★★★ Quality SANGIOVESE from E-R estate of famous oenologoist Vittorio Fiore, run by son Claudio. IGT RONCO dei Ciliegi and Ronco delle Ginestre are the stars. Le More is his tasty and relatively inexpensive Romagna DOC.

Cavallotto Pie ★★★ Leading BAROLO traditionalist of Castiglione Falletto, v'yds in heart of zone. Outstanding Barolo RISERVA Bricco Boschis Vigna San Giuseppe, Riserva Vignolo, v.gd LANGHE NEBBIOLO.

> **Who makes really good Chianti Classico?**
>
> CHIANTI CLASSICO is a seriously large zone with hundreds of producers, so picking out the best is tricky. The top get a ★: AMA ★, ANTINORI, BADIA A COLTIBUONO ★, Bibbiano, Le Boncie, Il Borghetto, Bossi, BROLIO, Cacchiano, CAFAGGIO, Capannelle, Capraia, Carobbio, Casaloste, Casa Sola, CASTELLARE, CASTELL' IN VILLA, Le Cinciole, Collelungo, Le Corti, Mannucci Droandi, FELSINA ★, Le Filigare, FONTERUTOLI, FONTODI ★, ISOLE E OLENA ★, Lilliano, Il Molino di Grace, MONSANTO ★, Monte Bernardi, Monteraponi ★, NITTARDI, NOZZOLE, Palazzino, Paneretta, Petroio-Lenzi, Poggerino, Poggiolino, Poggiopiano, POGGIO al Sole, QUERCIABELLA ★, RAMPOLLA, Riecine, Rocca di Castagnoli, Rocca di Montegrossi ★, RUFFINO, San Fabiano Calcinaia, SAN FELICE, SAN GIUSTO A RENTENNANO ★, Savignola Paolina, Selvole, Vecchie Terre di Montefili, Verrazzano, Vicchiomaggio, VIGNAMAGGIO, Villa La Rosa ★, Viticcio, VOLPAIA ★.

Cerasuolo d'Abruzzo Ab DOC p ★ DYA ROSATO version of MONTEPULCIANO D'ABRUZZO don't confuse with red CERASUOLO DI VITTORIA from SI. Can be brilliant; try Contesa

Cerasuolo di Vittoria Si DOCG r ★★ 10 11 13 Medium-bodied red from Frappato NERO D'AVOLA in se of island. Try COS, Nicosia, PLANETA, Valle dell'Acate.

Ceretto Pie ★★→★★★★ Leading producer of BARBARESCO (Bricco Asili), BAROLO (Bricco Rocche, Brunate, Prapò), plus LANGHE Rosso Monsoro (French-variety blend), Langhe Bianco Blange (ARNEIS).

Cerro, Fattoria del Tus ★★★ Estate owned by insurance giant SAI, making v.g. DOCG VINO NOBILE DI MONTEPULCIANO (esp cru Antica Chiusina). SAI also own La Poderina (BRUNELLO DI MONTALCINO), Colpetrone (MONTEFALCO SAGRANTINO) and 1,000-ha n MAREMMA estate of Monterufoli.

Cesanese del Piglio or Piglio Lat DOCG r ★→★★ Medium-bodied red, gd for moderate ageing. Best: Petrucca e Vela, Terre del Cesanese. Cesanese di Olevano Romano, Cesanese di Affile are similar.

Chianti Tus DOCG r ★→★★★ Since forever the glugging wine of central TUS, fresh, fruity, astringent, easy to drink, once with a percentage of white grapes. The creation of subzones, unwarranted elevation to DOCG and the banishing of the whites introduced unnecessary complication. There is a case for fundamental change. (*See* box p.149.)

Chianti Classico Tus DOCG r ★★→★★★★ 04 06 07 08 09 10 11 12 (13) The historic CHIANTI zone became "Classico" when the Chianti area was extended to most of central TUS in early 20th century. Covering all or part of nine communes, the land is hilly (altitude 250–500m) and rocky. The "Black Rooster" wine is traditionally blended: the debate continues over whether the support grapes should be French or native. (*See also* box above and on p.149.)

Chiaretto Ven Pale, light-blush-hued rosé (the word means "claret"), produced esp around Lake Garda. *See* BARDOLINO.

Ciabot Berton Pie ★★★ Small La Morra grower; classy BAROLOS at modest prices Crus incl Roggeri and new Rochettevino.

Ciliegiolo Tus Varietal red of MAREMMA, from eponymous grape of which SANGIOVESE is an offspring. Try Rascioni e Cecconello, Sassotondo.

Cinque Terre Lig DOC w dr sw ★★ Dry VERMENTINO-based whites from steepest Riviera coast of LIG. Sweet version is called SCIACCHETRÀ. Seek out Arrigoni, Bisson, Buranco.

Cirò Cal DOC r (p) (w) ★→★★★ Brisk strong red from Cal's main grape, Gaglioppo, or light, fruity white from GRECO (DYA). Best: Barone di Bolaro, Caparra & Siciliani, Ippolito, *Librandi* (Duca San Felice ★★★), San Francesco (Donna Madda, Ronco dei Quattroventi), Santa Venere.

lassico Term for wines from a restricted, usually historic and superior-quality area within limits of a commercially expanded DOC. *See* CHIANTI CLASSICO, VALPOLICELLA, SOAVE, numerous others.

lerico, Domenico Pie ★★★ Modernist BAROLO producer of Monforte d'ALBA, esp crus Percristina, Ciabot Mentin Ginestra, Pajana. Also gd, modern-style BARBERA Trevigne, DOLCETTO Visadi.

offele Ven ★★★ Grower with some of the finest v'yds in SOAVE CLASSICO, making steely, minerally wines of classic style. Try cru Cà Visco.

ol d'Orcia Tus ★★★ Top-quality MONTALCINO estate (the 3rd-largest) owned by Francesco Marone Cinzano. Best wine: BRUNELLO RISERVA POGGIO al Vento.

olli = hills; singular: Colle. **Colline** (singular Collina) = smaller hills. *See also* COLLIO and POGGIO.

olli di Catone Lat ★→★★★ Top FRASCATI, IGT producer in Roman hills of Monteporzio Catone. Antonio Pulcini makes outstanding aged whites from MALVASIA del Lazio (aka Malvasia Puntinata), GRECHETTO. Look for Colle Gaio or Casal Pilozzo labels.

olli Euganei Ven DOC r w dr s/sw (sp) ★→★★ DYA. DOC sw of Padua. Pleasant r w sp, rarely better. Best producers incl Ca' Lustra, La Montecchia, Vignalta.

ollio F-VG DOC r w ★★→★★★★ Hilly zone on border with Slovenia. Esp known for complex, sometimes deliberately oxidized whites, some vinified on skins in earthenware vessels/amphorae in ground. Some excellent, some shocking blends from various French, German, Slavic grapes. Numerous gd-to-excellent producers: BORGO DEL TIGLIO, La Castellada, Castello di Spessa, MARCO FELLUGA, Fiegl, GRAVNER, Renato Keber, Livon, Aldo Polencic, Primosic, Princic, Russiz SUPERIORE, *Schiopetto*, Tercic, Terpin, Venica & Venica, VILLA RUSSIZ, Zuani.

olli Piacentini E-R DOC r p w ★→★★ DYA Light gulping wines, often fizzy – red or white – from various grapes incl BARBERA, BONARDA (r), MALVASIA, Pignoletto (w), plus various PINOT varieties. Similar to OLTREPO' PAVESE. Gd producers incl Montesissa, Mossi, Romagnoli, Solenghi, La Stoppa, Torre Fornello, La Tosa. *See also* GUTTURNIO.

olognole Tus ★★ Ex-Conti Spalletti estate making increasingly classy CHIANTI RÚFINA, RISERVA del Don from steep s-facing slopes of Monte Giovi.

olterenzio CS / Schreckbichl T-AA ★★→★★★ Cornaiano-based main player among ALTO ADIGE co-ops. Whites (SAUV Lafoa, CHARD Altkirch, PINOT BIANCO Weisshaus Praedium) tend to be better than reds, despite renown of CAB SAUV Lafoa.

onegliano Valdobbiadene Ven DOCG w sp ★→★★ DYA. Name for top PROSECCO, daunting to pronounce: may be used separately or together.

onterno, Aldo Pie ★★★→★★★★ Deceased top grower of Monforte d'ALBA, was considered a traditionalist, esp concerning top BAROLOS Granbussia, Cicala, Colonello. His sons moving winery in more modernist direction.

onterno, Giacomo Pie ★★★★ Iconic grower of super-trad BAROLO with cellar at Monforte d'ALBA; grandson Roberto now carrying on the gd work. Two Barolos from Cascina Francia v'yd in Serralunga: Cascina Francia and **Monfortino**, long-macerated to age for yrs. Stellar prices.

onterno Fantino Pie ★★★ Two families joined; excellent modern-style BAROLO Sorì Ginestra, VIGNA del Gris at Monforte d'ALBA. Also NEBBIOLO/BARBERA blend Monprà.

onterno Paolo Pie ★★→★★★ A family of NEBBIOLO and BARBERA growers since 1886, current *titolare* Giorgio continues with textbook cru BAROLOS Ginestra and Riva del Bric, plus particularly fine LANGHE **Nebbiolo Bric Ginestra**.

ontesa Ab ★★→★★★ Collecorvino v'yd (province of Pescara) of oenologist Rocco Pasetti, who makes excellent red MONTEPULCIANO D'ABRUZZO, rosé CERASUOLO and white PECORINO under Contesa label. Top range has Persian names like Sorab.

ontini, Attilio Sar ★→★★★ Famous SAR producer of Sherry-like, *flor*-affected VERNACCIA DI ORISTANO. Best is vintage blend Antico Gregori.

Conti Zecca Pug ★★→★★★ SALENTO estate with 320-ha v'yd producing almost tw
million bottles. Donna Marzia line of Salento IGT wines is gd value, as is SALIO
SALENTINO Cantalupi. Many wines; NEGROAMARO/CAB SAUV blend Nero best-known

Contucci Tus ★★→★★★ Millennial producer of traditional-style VINO NOBILE. A
ancient cellar at MONTEPULCIANO *vaut le detour*.

Copertino Pug DOC r (p) ★★★ 08 10 11 (12) Smooth, savoury red of NEGROAMAF
from heel of Italy. Gd producers: MONACI, CS Copertino.

Coppo Pie ★★→★★★ Top producers of BARBERA d'Asti (Pomorosso), RISERVA del
Famiglia). Also excellent CHARD Monteriolo, sparkling Riserva del Fondatore.

Cortona TUS DOC contiguous to MONTEPULCIANO VINO NOBILE. Various indigenous ar
international grapes, red and white. Gd wines incl Avignonesi's Desideri
MERLOT/CAB, first-rate SYRAH from Luigi d'Alessandro, Il Castagno, *La Braccesca*.

CS (Cantina Sociale) Cooperative winery.

Cubi Ven ★★→★★★ Valentina Cubi's fine small estate, making AMARONE
individuality and breeding and VALPOLICELLA CLASSICO of charm and complexity.

Cusumano Si ★★→★★★ Recent major player with 500 ha in various parts of SI. Re
from NERO D'AVOLA, CAB SAUV, SYRAH; whites from CHARD, INSOLIA. Gd quality, valu

Dal Forno, Romano Ven ★★★ V. high-quality VALPOLICELLA, AMARONE, RECIOTO grow
whose perfectionism is the more remarkable for the fact that his v'yds a
outside the CLASSICO zone.

Dei Pie ★★→★★★ Pianist Caterina Dei runs this aristocratic estate in MONTEPULCIAN
making VINO NOBILES with artistry and passion. Her *chef d'oeuvre* is Bossona.

Di Majo Norante Mol ★★→★★★ Rare quality producer of Mol with v.gd Biferno Ros
Ramitello, Don Luigi Molise Rosso RISERVA, Mol AGLIANICO Contado, white bler
FALANGHINA/GRECO Biblos, MOSCATO PASSITO Apianae.

DOC / DOCG Quality wine designation: *see* box, p.125.

Dogliani Pie DOCG r ★→★★★ 08 09 10 11 12 DOCG DOLCETTO from PIE, though th
have dropped the grape from the label to confuse you. Some to drink your
some for moderate ageing. Gd producers: Marziano Abbona, Osvaldo Barbar
Francesco Boschis, Chionetti, Clavesana, Einaudi, Pecchenino.

Donnafugata Si r w ★★→★★★ Classy range of SI wines incl reds Mille e Una Not
Sherazade, Tancredi; whites Chiaranda, Ligheia. Also v. fine MOSCATO PASSITO
PANTELLERIA Ben Ryé.

Dorigo ★★→★★★ Prestige winery in FRIULI COLLI ORIENTALI (as it must now be calle
long known chiefly for Bordeaux-style Montsclapade. Now Alessio Dorigo
growing more local grapes: REFOSCO, Pignolo and Schioppettino (reds) and RIBOL
GIALLA, VERDUZZO and PICOLIT (whites). The Picolit PASSITO is particularly deliciou

Duca di Salaparuta Si ★★ Once on the list of every trattoria in Christendom with
Corvo brand, now owned by American liqueur co Ilva of Saronno. More upsca
wines incl Kados (w) from Grillo grapes and NERO D'AVOLA wines Passo de
Mule, Triskele (Nero d'Avola/MERLOT). Plus old favourite Duca Enrico.

Elba Tus r w (sp) ★→★★ DYA. The island's white, based on Ansonica and TREBBIAN
can be v. drinkable with fish. Dry reds are based on SANGIOVESE. Gd sweet wh
(MOSCATO) and red (*Aleatico Passito DOCG*). Gd producers: Acquabona, Sapere

Enoteca Wine library; also shop or restaurant with ambitious wine list. There i
national enoteca at the *fortezza* in Siena.

Esino Mar DOC r w ★→★★★ (r) 06 07 08 09 10 11 (12) (13) Alternative DOC
VERDICCHIO country permits 50% other grapes with Verdicchio for Bian
40% with SANGIOVESE/MONTEPULCIANO for Rosso. Best reds from Monte Schia
(Adeodato), Belisario (Colferraio).

Est! Est!! Est!!! Lat DOC w dr s/sw ★ DYA. An unextraordinary white from n
Rome in Montefiascone. Trades on improbable origin of name. FALESCO best.

Etna Si DOC r p w ★★→★★★ (r) 06 07 08 09 10 11 12 (13) (14). Wine from volca slopes, often high on n side of mtn. V'yds declined in 20th century, but new money has brought a flurry of planting and some excellent if expensive wines, rather in style of burgundy, though based on NERELLO MASCALESE (r) and CARRICANTE (w). Gd producers: Benanti, Calcagno, Il Cantante, Cottanera, Terre Nere, Nicosia (a bargain version), *Passopisciaro*, Girolamo Russo, *Barone di Villagrande*.

alanghina Useful fresh citrus white of Benevento area inland from Naples, esp SANNIO DOC. The SOAVE of the s. Biggest producer: La GUARDIENSE.

alchini Tus ★★→★★★ Producer of gd DOCG VERNACCIA DI SAN GIMIGNANO (VIGNA a Solatio and oaked Ab Vinea Doni), plus top Bordeaux blend *Campora*, SANGIOVESE-based Paretaio. Riccardo Falchini was a champion of fine SAN GIMIGNANO, ably succeeded by his half-American children.

alerno del Massico Cam ★★→★★★ DOC r w ★★ (r) 07 08 09 10 11 (12) (13) Falernum was Yquem of ancient Rome. Today elegant red from AGLIANICO, fruity dry white FALANGHINA. Best: VILLA MATILDE, Amore Perrotta, Felicia, Moio, Trabucco.

ara Pie *See* GATTINARA.

aro Si DOC r ★★★ 06' 07 08 09 10 11 12 (13) (14) Intense, harmonious red from NERELLO MASCALESE and Nerello Cappuccio in hills behind Messina. Salvatore Geraci of Palari, the major producer, administered the kiss of life when extinction seemed likely. Also Bonavita.

elluga, Livio F-VG ★★★ Consistently fine FRIULI COLLI ORIENTALI wines, esp blends Terre Alte, Illivio. *Pinot Gr*, SAUV BL, FRIULANO, PICOLIT, MERLOT/REFOSCO blend Sossó.

elluga, Marco F-VG *See* RUSSIZ SUPERIORE.

elsina Tus ★★★ Giuseppe Mazzocolin has run this CHIANTI CLASSICO estate for over 30 yrs: classic RISERVA Rancia and IGT Fontalloro, both 100% SANGIOVESE. Also gd CHARD, I Sistri. Castello di Farnetella, gd CHIANTI COLLI Senesi, in same family.

enocchio Giacomo ★★★ Small Monforte d'ALBA-based cellar. Trad style, min intervention, ageing in large Slavonian oak *botti*. Crus: Bussia, Villero, Cannubi.

errari T-AA sp ★★→★★★ Trento maker of the best METODO CLASSICO wines outside FRANCIACORTA. Giulio Ferrari is top cru; also gd are CHARD-based Brut RISERVA Lunelli, PINOT N-based Extra Brut Perle' Nero.

eudi di San Gregorio Cam ★★ →★★★ Hyped CAM producer. DOCGS TAURASI Piano di Montevergine, FIANO di Avellino Pietracalda, GRECO DI TUFO Cutizzi. IGT (r) Serpico (AGLIANICO), Patrimo (MERLOT), (w) FALANGHINA, *Campanaro* (Fiano/Greco).

lorio Si Historic quality maker of MARSALA. Specialist in Marsala Vergine Secco. For some reason Terre Arse (= burnt lands), its best wine, doesn't do well in the UK.

olonari Tus ★★→★★★ Ambrogio Folonari and son Giovanni, having split from the giant RUFFINO, have quite a quiver-full of their own. NB *Cabreo* (CHARD and SANGIOVESE/CAB SAUV), wines of NOZZOLE (incl top Cab Sauv Pareto), BRUNELLO DI MONTALCINO La Fuga, VINO NOBILE DI MONTEPULCIANO Gracciano Svetoni, plus wines from BOLGHERI, MONTECUCCO, FRIULI COLLI ORIENTALI.

ontana Candida Lat ★★ Biggest producer of once-fashionable FRASCATI. Single-v'yd Santa Teresa stands out. Part of huge GRUPPO ITALIANO VINI.

ontanafredda Pie ★★ →★★★ Much-improved large producer of PIE wines on former royal estates, incl BAROLO Serralunga and Barolo crus Lazzarito Mirafiore, VIGNA La Rosa. Excellent LANGHE NEBBIOLO *Mirafiore*. Plus ALBA DOCS, sparklers dry (Contessa Rosa Pas Dosè) and sweet (ASTI).

onterutoli Tus ★★★ Historic CHIANTI CLASSICO estate of Mazzei family at Castellina with castle and space-age CANTINA in wild heart of TUS hills. Notable: Castello di Fonterutoli (dark, oaky CHIANTI), IGT Siepi (SANGIOVESE/MERLOT). The Mazzei also own TENUTA di Belguardo in MAREMMA, gd MORELLINO DI SCANSANO and IGT wines. Also Philip (SI): beautiful Effe Emme PETIT VERDOT.

ontodi Tus ★★★→★★★★ Outstanding Manetti family estate at Panzano making one of the absolute best CHIANTI CLASSICOS, also VIGNA del Sorbo (was RISERVA, now Gran

---

Balsamina, anyone?
Italy fairly bristles with strange and wonderful grape varieties, and
the large region of E-R, which claims most of the Po Valley plus hills/
mts to n and s, boasts the following obscure indigenous varieties,
some of which even we had never heard of before a recent visit to the
region: Balsamina, Cagnina, Centesimino, Famoso, Fantini, Longanesi,
Pagadebit, Pignoletto, Rebola, Ruggine, Spargola, Tarmarina. To say
nothing of the various LAMBRUSCO sub-varieties such as L di Sorbara,
L Salamino (little sausage), L Grasparossa, L Marani. And the deep-
coloured Ancellotta and its associates.... The list could go on.

Selezione) and outstanding all-SANGIOVESE Flaccianello, an IGT, which could and
ought to be Chianti Classico. Proper IGTs PINOT N, SYRAH Case Via among best
of these varieties in TUS.

Foradori T-AA ★★★ Elizabetta Foradori has been one of the pioneers of Italian
viniculture for 30 yrs, mainly via the great red grape of Trentino, *Teroldego*. Now
she ferments in *anfora* with reds like Morei, Sgarzon and whites like Nosiol
Fontanabianca. Top wine remains Teroldego-based Granato.

Franciacorta Lom DOCG w (p) sp ★★→★★★★ Italy's major zone for top-quality
METODO CLASSICO sparkling. Best producers: Barone Pizzini, BELLAVISTA, CA' DEL
BOSCO, Castellino, Cavalleri, Gatti, Uberti, Villa. Also v.gd: Contadi Gastaldi
Monte Rossa, Ricci Curbastri.

Frascati Lat DOC w dr sw s/sw (sp) ★→★★ DYA. Best-known wine of Roman hills
under constant threat from urban expansion. From MALVASIA di Candia and/or
TREBBIANO, most is disappointingly neutral. The gd stuff is made from Malvasia
del Lazio (aka M Puntinata), whose low crop makes it uncompetitive. Look
for Castel de Paolis, Conte Zandotti, Villa Simone, Santa Teresa from FONTANA
CANDIDA or Colle Gaio from COLLI DI CATONE, 100% Malvasia del Lazio though IGT

Frascole ★★→★★★ The n-most winery of the n-most CHIANTI zone, tucked up in
the foothills of the Apennines, a small estate run organically by Enrico Lippi
with an eye for authenticity and typicity. CHIANTI RUFINA is the main driver but
the *Riserva really is special* and the Bianco di Toscana is one of the best TREBBIANO
you'll taste. VIN SANTO is quite simply to die for.

Freisa d'Asti Pie DOC r dr sw s/sw (sp) ★→★★★ Two styles: frivolous, may be
FRIZZANTE, may be sweetish; or serious, dry and tannic for ageing (so follow
BAROLO vintages). Best: Brezza, Cigliuti, CLERICO, ALDO CONTERNO, COPPO, Franco
Martinetti, GIUSEPPE MASCARELLO, Parusso, Pecchenino, Pelissero, Sebaste
Trinchero, VAJRA, VOERZIO.

Frescobaldi Tus★★→★★★★ Ancient noble family, leading CHIANTI RÙFINA pioneer at
NIPOZZANO estate (look for *Montesodi* ★★★), also BRUNELLO from Castelgiocondo
estate in MONTALCINO. Sole owners of LUCE estate (MONTALCINO), ORNELLAIA (BOLGHERI)
V'yds also in MAREMMA, Montespertoli, COLLIO.

Friulano F-VG ★→★★ EU forced new name of what used to be called Tocai FRIULANO
due to pressure from Hungary. Fresh, pungent, subtly floral whites, best
from COLLIO, ISONZO, COLLI ORIENTALI. Many gd producers: BORGO DEL TIGLIO, LIVIO
FELLUGA, LIS NERIS, Pierpaolo Pecorari, RONCO del Gelso, Ronco del Gnemiz, Russiz
SUPERIORE, SCHIOPETTO, LE VIGNE DI ZAMÒ, VILLA RUSSIZ. The new name for ex-Tocai
from Ven, by the way, is "TAI".

Friuli Colli Orientali F-VG DOC r w dr sw ★★→★★★★ (Was Colli Orientali del
Friuli.) Eastern hills of F-VG, on the Slovenian border. Zone similar to COLLIO
but less experimental, making more reds and stickies. Top producers: Meroi
Miani, Moschioni, LIVIO FELLUGA, Rosa Bosco, RONCO del Gnemiz. Sweet wines

from VERDUZZO grapes (called Ramandolo if from around Nimis: Anna Berra, Giovanni Drì) or PICOLIT grapes (Ronchi di Cialla) can be amazing.

'riuli-Venezia Giulia The ne region of Italy. Best part wine-wise is the hills on the Slovenian border rather than on the wide alluvial plains to the w. Quality DOCS are ISONZO, COLLIO, COLLI ORIENTALI. Some gd reds, but considered the home of Italy's most adventurous and accomplished whites.

'rizzante Semi-sparkling, up to 2.5 atmospheres, eg. MOSCATO D'ASTI, much PROSECCO, LAMBRUSCO and the like. Nw of Italy is home to large numbers of lightly fizzing wines that never seem to make it out into the wide world. It's the world's loss.

'uligni Tus ★★★→★★★★ Outstanding producer of BRUNELLO, ROSSO DI MONTALCINO.

aja Pie ★★★★ Old family firm at BARBARESCO led by Angelo Gaja, highly audible apostle of Italian wine; daughter Gaia G following. High quality, even higher prices. BARBARESCO is only PIE DOCG Gaja makes, he declassified crus Sorì Tildìn, Sorì San Lorenzo, Costa Russi as well as BAROLO Sperss to LANGHE DOC (so he can blend BARBERA with NEBBIOLO). Splendid CHARD (Gaia e Rey), CAB SAUV Darmagi. Also owns of Pieve di Santa Restituta in MONTALCINO, Ca' Marcanda in BOLGHERI.

alardi Cam ★★★ Producer of Terra di Lavoro, a highly touted blend of AGLIANICO and Piedirosso, in n CAM.

arda Ven DOC r p w ★→★★ (r) 10 11 12 13 (p w) DYA. Catch-all DOC for early-drinking wines of various colours from provinces of Verona in Ven, Brescia and Mantua in Lom. Gd producers: Cavalchina, Zeni.

arofoli Mar ★★→★★★ Quality leader in the Marches, specialist in VERDICCHIO (Podium, Macrina, Serra Fiorese), ROSSO CONERO (Piancarda, Grosso Agontano).

attinara Pie DOCG r ★★→★★★ 04' 06 07 08 09 10 11 12 (13) Best-known of a cluster of n PIE DOC(G)s based on NEBBIOLO, here called Spanna. Best producers: Travaglini, Antoniolo, Bianchi, Nervi, Torraccia del Piantavigna. Similar DOC(G)s of zone: Ghemme, Boca, Bramaterra, Colline Novaresi, Costa della Sesia, Fara, Lessona, Sizzano. None of them, sadly, measure up to BAROLO/BARBARESCO at best.

avi / Cortese di Gavi Pie DOCG w ★→★★★ DYA. At best, subtle dry white of Cortese, though much is monolinear. Best comes from commune of Gavi, hence Gavi di Gavi, more prosaically known as Gavi del Comune di Gavi. Best: Castellari Bergaglio, Franco Martinetti, Toledana, Villa Sparina, Broglia, Cascina degli Ulivi, Castello di Tassarolo, Chiarlo, La Giustiniana, Podere Saulino.

Ghemme Pie DOCG. *See* GATTINARA.

Giacosa, Bruno Pie ★★★→★★★★ Considered by some Italy's greatest winemaker, this brooding genius suffered a stroke in 2006, but goes on crafting splendid trad-style BARBARESCOS (Asili, Santo Stefano), BAROLOS (Falletto, Rocche del Falletto). Top wines (ie. RISERVAS) get famous red label. Also makes a range of fine reds (DOLCETTO, NEBBIOLO, BARBERA), whites (ARNEIS), amazing METODO CLASSICO Brut.

Grappa Pungent spirit made from grape pomace (skins, etc., after pressing), can be anything from disgusting to inspirational. What the French call "marc".

Grasso, Elio Pie ★★★→★★★★ Top BAROLO producer (crus Gavarini VIGNA Chiniera, Ginestra Casa Maté); v.gd BARBERA D'ALBA VIGNA Martina, DOLCETTO d'Alba, CHARD Educato. Son Gianluca has now effectively taken over from dad Elio.

Grave del Friuli F-VG DOC r w ★→★★ (r) 10 11 12 (13) Largest DOC of F-VG, mostly on plains. Important volumes of underwhelming wines. Exceptions from Borgo Magredo, Di Lenardo, RONCO Cliona, Villa Chiopris, San Simone.

Gravner, Josko F-VG ★★★→★★★★ Controversial COLLIO producer, macerates reds and whites on skins in buried amphorae, followed by long ageing and bottling without filtration. Wines either loved for complexity or loathed for oxidation and phenolic components. Wines incl Rosso, white blend Breg, varietal RIBOLLA GIALLA. His 06s have at last emerged on the market.

Greco di Tufo Cam DOCG w (sp) ★★→★★★ DYA One of best whites of s, citrus with hints of orange peel, at best age-worthy. V.gd examples from Caggiano, Caputo, Benito Ferrara, FEUDI DI SAN GREGORIO, Macchialupa, *Mastroberardino* (Nova Serra Vignadelangelo), Vesevo, Villa Raiano.

Grignolino Pie DOC r ★★ DYA lively light red of ASTI zone. Best: BRAIDA, Marchesi Incisa della Rocchetta. Also G del Monferrato Casalese DOC (Accornero, Bricco Mondalino, La Tenaglia).

Gruppo Italiano Vini (GIV) Complex of co-ops and wineries, biggest v'yd holders in Italy. Estates incl: Bigi, BOLLA, Ca'Bianca, Conti Serristori, FONTANA CANDIDA, Lamberti, Macchiavelli, MELINI, Negri, Santi, Vignaioli di San Floriano. Also expanded into s: SI, Bas.

Italy has nearly 400 vine varieties. That's just the ones that are officially recognized

Guardiense, La Cam ★★ Dynamic co-op, 1,000+ grower-members, 2,000 ha v'yd for better-than-average whites and reds at lower-than-average prices under technical direction of Riccardo Cotarella. World's largest producer of FALANGHINA.

Guerrieri Rizzardi ★★→★★★ Long-est aristocratic producers of Verona wines, esp o: Veronese GARDA. Gd BARDOLINO CLASSICO Tacchetto, elegant AMARONE Villa Rizzardi and cru Calcarole, and ROSATO Rosa Rosae. V.gd SOAVE Classico Costeggiola.

Gutturnio dei Colli Piacentini E-R DOC r dr ★→★★ DYA. BARBERA/BONARDA blend from the COLLI PIACENTINI; sometimes frothing. Producers: Castelli del Duca, La Pergola, La Stoppa, La Tosa.

Haas, Franz T-AA ★★★ ALTO ADIGE producer; v.gd PINOT N, LAGREIN (Schweizer) and IGT blends, esp the white Manna.

Hofstätter T-AA ★★★ Tramin-based top-quality private producer of ALTO ADIGE wines; producing outstanding *Pinot N*, possibly the best in Italy. Look for Barthenau VIGNA Sant'Urbano. Also a range of typical South Tyrol whites mainly, of course, GEWURZ.

Indicazione Geografica Tipica (IGT) Increasingly known as Indicazione Geografica Protetta (IGP). (*See* box, p.125.)

Ischia DOC (r) w ★→★★ DYA. Island off Naples, own grape varieties (eg. Forastera, Biancolella), wines mainly drunk by tourists. Top producer: D'Ambra (Biancolella Frassitelli, Forastera Euposia). Also gd: Il Giardino Mediterraneo, Pietratorcia.

Isole e Olena Tus ★★★→★★★★ Top CHIANTI CLASSICO estate run by astute Paolo de Marchi, with superb red IGT Cepparello. V.gd VIN SANTO, CAB SAUV, CHARD, SYRAH. Also owns Sperino in Lessona (*see* GATTINARA).

Isonzo F-VG DOC r w ★★★ Gravelly, well-aired plain of Friuli Isonzo, a multi-DOC area with many varietals and blends. The stars are mostly white, scented and structured, such as VIE DI ROMANS' Flors di Uis, LIS NERIS' Fiore di Campo. Also gd: Borgo Conventi, Pierpaolo Pecorari, RONCO del Gelso.

Jermann, Silvio F-VG ★★→★★★ Famous estate with v'yds in COLLIO and ISONZO: top white blend Vintage Tunina, oak-aged blend Capo Martino, CHARD ex-Dreams.

Lacrima di Morro d'Alba Mar DYA. Curiously named rose-scented MUSCATTY light red from a small commune in the Mar, no connection with ALBA or La Morra (PIE). Gd producers: Mancinelli, MONTE SCHIAVO.

Lacryma (or Lacrima) Christi del Vesuvio Cam r p w dr (sw) (sp) ★→★★ DOC Vesuvio wines based on Coda di Volpe (w), Piedirosso (r). Despite romantic name Vesuvius comes nowhere nr ETNA in quality stakes. Caputo, De Angelis, MASTROBERARDINO make uninspired versions.

Lageder, Alois T-AA ★★→★★★★ Top ALTO ADIGE producer. Most exciting wines are single-v'yd varietals: *Sauv Bl Lehenhof*, PINOT GR Benefizium Porer, CHARD Löwengang, GEWURZ Am Sand, PINOT N Krafuss, LAGREIN Lindenberg, CAB SAUV Cor Römigberg. Also owns Cason Hirschprunn for v.gd IGT blends.

ago di Corbara Umb r ★★ 08 09 10 11 12 Relatively recent DOC for quality reds of ORVIETO area. Best from Barberani (Villa Monticelli), Decugnano dei Barbi (Il).

Lagrein Alto Adige T-AA DOC r p ★★→★★★ 06 07 08 09 11 12 *Plummy reds with bitter finish* from LAGREIN grape. Best growing zone: Gries, suburb of Bolzano. Best producers: Colterenzio co-op, Gojer, Gries co-op, HAAS, HOFSTÄTTER, LAGEDER, Laimburg, Josephus Mayr, Thomas Mayr, MURI GRIES, NALS MARGREID, Niedermayr, Niedrist, St-Magdalena, TERLANO CO-OP, TIEFENBRUNNER.

Lambrusco E-R DOC (or not) r p w dr s/sw ★→★★ DYA. Once v. popular fizzy red from nr Modena, mainly in industrial, semi-sweet, non-DOC version. The real thing is dry, acidic, fresh, lively and *combines magically with rich* E-R fare. DOCs: L Grasparossa di Castelvetro, L Salamino di Santa Croce, L di Sorbara. Best: Albinea Canali, Bellei, Caprari, Casali, Cavicchioli, Graziano, Lini Oreste, Medici Ermete (esp Concerto), Rinaldo Rinaldini, Venturini Baldini.

Langhe Pie Hills of central PIE, home of BAROLO, BARBARESCO, etc. DOC name for several Pie varietals plus blends Bianco and Rosso. Those wishing to blend other grapes with their NEBBIOLO, such as GAJA, can do so at up to 15% as "Langhe Nebbiolo".

Lessona Pie See GATTINARA. See also ISOLE E OLENA.

Librandi Cal ★★★ Top producer pioneering research into Cal varieties. V.gd red CIRÒ (*Riserva Duca San Felice* is ★★★), IGT Gravello (CAB SAUV/Gaglioppo blend), Magno Megonio (r) from Magliocco grape, IGT Efeso (w) from Mantonico. Other local varieties in experimental phase. To follow.

Liguria Lig ★→★★ Steep, rocky Italian riviera: most wines sell to sun-struck tourists at fat profits, so don't travel much. Main grapes: VERMENTINO (w) – best producer is Lambruschi – and DOLCETTO (r), but don't miss CINQUE TERRE'S SCIACCHETRÀ or red Ormeasco di Pornassio.

Lisini Tus ★★★→★★★★ Historic estate for some of the finest and longest-lasting BRUNELLO, esp RISERVA Ugolaia.

Lis Neris F-VG ★★★ Top ISONZO estate for whites, esp PINOT GR (Gris), CHARD (Jurosa), SAUV BL (Picol), FRIULANO (Fiore di Campo), plus blends Confini and Lis. Also v.gd Lis Neris Rosso (MERLOT/CAB FR), sweet white Tal Luc (VERDUZZO/RIES).

Locorotondo Pug DOC w (sp) ★ DYA Thirst-quencher dry white from Verdeca and Bianco d'Alessano grapes.

Luce Tus ★★★ FRESCOBALDI is sole owner of this exercise in hyperbole and high price, having bought out original partner Mondavi. A SANGIOVESE/MERLOT blend for oligarchs.

Lugana DOC w (sp) ★★→★★★ DYA. Much-improved white of s Lake GARDA, main grape TREBBIANO di Lugana (= VERDICCHIO). Best: CA' DEI FRATI, ZENATO. Particularly fine crus (Lugana SUPERIORE): Ottella (Le Creete; Molceo), Selva Capuzza (Selva; Menasasso RISERVA).

Lungarotti Umb ★★★ Leading producer of TORGIANO; cellars, hotel, museum nr Perugia. Star wines DOC Rubesco, DOCG RISERVA *Villa Monticchio*. Gd IGT Sangiorgio (SANGIOVESE/CAB SAUV), Aurente (CHARD), Giubilante. Gd MONTEFALCO SAGRANTINO.

Lew in Florence: a Chianti Classico wine bar, in the Mercato Centrale. 2,000+ wines.

Macchiole, Le Tus ★★★ One of the few native-owned wineries of BOLGHERI. Cinzia Merli, with oenologist Luca d'Attoma, continues late husband's fine work with CAB FR (Paleo Rosso), MERLOT (Messorio), also SYRAH (Scrio).

Maculan Ven ★★★ Quality pioneer of Ven, Fausto Maculan continues to make excellent CAB SAUV (Fratta, Palazzotto). Perhaps best-known for sweet TORCOLATO (esp RISERVA Acininobili).

Malenchini Tus ★★ Estate of old Florentine family (from their balcony you can see the Duomo) making *honest simple Chianti* and more complex CHIANTI COLLI Fiorentini, plus CAB SAUV/SANGIOVESE blend Bruzzico.

Malvasia delle Lipari Si DOC w sw ★★★ Luscious sweet wine, made with one o several grape varieties in Italy going by name of MALVASIA. Lipari is a fascinatin island off si coast; vaut le voyage.

Mamete Prevostini Lom ★★→★★★ Relatively new producer of VALTELLINA. Pur varietal (NEBBIOLO) DOCG wines of class mainly from Sassella SUPERIORE but als Inferno, Grumello Superiore. Two *fine Sforzatos.*

Manduria (Primitivo di) Pug DOC r s/sw ★★→★★★ Manduria is the spiritual hom of PRIMITIVO, alias ZIN, so expect wines that are gutsy, alcoholic, sometimes por to go with full-flavoured fare. Gd producers, located in Manduria or not: Cantel de Castris, Gianfranco Fino, Polvanera, Racemi, CS Manduria.

Marchesi di Barolo Pie ★★ Historic, perhaps original, BAROLO producer, in commur of Barolo, making crus Cannubi and Sarmassa, plus other ALBA wines.

Maremma Tus Fashionable coastal area of s TUS, largely recovered from malari marshland in the early 20th century. DOC(G)s: MONTEREGIO, MORELLINO DI SCANSAN PARRINA, Pitigliano, SOVANA (Grosseto). Maremma Toscana IGT now DOC.

Marsala Si DOC w sw si's once famous fortified wine (★→★★★), invented b Woodhouse Bros from Liverpool in 1773. Deteriorated in the 20th century t cooking wine, which no longer qualifies for DOC status. Several versions fror dry to v. sweet; best is bone-dry Marsala Vergine, potentially a useful, if hard fashionable, aperitif. *See also* DE BARTOLI.

Marzemino Trentino T-AA DOC r ★→★★ 10 11 12 Pleasant everyday red, fruity an slightly bitter. Esp from Bossi Fedrigotti, CA' VIT, De Tarczal, Gaierhof, Letran Longariva, Simoncelli, E Spagnolli, Vallarom.

Mascarello Pie Name of two top producers of BAROLO: the late Bartolo M, of Barol whose daughter Maria Teresa continues highly traditional path; and Giusepp M, of Monchiero, whose son Mauro makes v. fine, traditional-style Barolo fror great *Monprivato* v'yd in Castiglione Falletto. Beware other Mascarellos.

Masi Ven ★★→★★★ Archetypal yet innovative producer of the wines of Verona, le by inspirational Sandro Boscaini. VALPOLICELLA, AMARONE, RECIOTO, SOAVE, etc., in fine Rosso Veronese *Campo Fiorin.* Made also Amarone-style wines from F-v and Argentina. V.gd barrel-aged red IGT Toar, from CORVINA and Oseleta grape also Osar (Oseleta). Top Amarones Costasera, Campolongo di Torbe.

Traditional bush vines on Pantelleria (*Alberello pantesco*) now have UNESC World Heritage status.

Massa, La Tus ★★★ Giampaolo Motta is a Bordeaux lover making claret-like 10 wines with a TUS accent (La Massa, Giorgio Primo), from CAB SAUV, MERLOT an decreasingly, SANGIOVESE, at his fine estate in Panzano (CHIANTI CLASSICO), whic denomination he has abandoned.

Massolino Vigna Rionda Pie ★★★ One of finest estates of BAROLO commur Serralunga, reputed for typically tannic wines. Excellent B Parafada and Margheria have firm structure, but fruity drinkability too. Top cru is RISER VIGNA Rionda, capable of v. long ageing.

Mastroberardino Cam ★★★ Historic producer of mountainous Avellino provinc in CAM, quality torch-bearer for Italy's s during dark yrs of mid-20th centu Top *Taurasi* (look for Historia Naturalis, Radici), also FIANO di Avellino Mo Maiorum, GRECO DI TUFO Nova Serra.

Matura, Gruppo Group of agronomists and oenologists headed by Alberto Antoni and Attilio Pagli, helping producers not only throughout TUS but elsewhere i country and indeed world.

Melini Tus★★ Major CHIANTI CLASSICO producer at Poggibonsi, part of GIV. Gd qualit price, esp Chianti Classico Selvanella, RISERVAS La Selvanella and Masovecchio.

Metodo classico or tradizionale Italian for "Champagne method".

Mezzacorona T-AA ★→★★ Massive TRENTINO co-op in the commune of Mezzocorona (sic) with wide range of gd technical wines, esp TEROLDEGO ROTALIANO Nos and METODO CLASSICO Rotari.

Monaci Pug r p ★★→★★★ Estate owned by family of Severino Garofano, leading oenologist in SALENTO. Characterful NEGROAMARO red (Eloquenzia, I Censi, late-picked Le Braci), ROSATO (Girofle); Uva di Troia (Sine Pari), AGLIANICO (Sine Die).

Monferrato Pie DOC r p w sw ★→★★ Hills between river Po and Apennines; mostly wines for everyday drinking rather than of serious intent.

Monica di Sardegna Sar DOC r ★→★★ DYA. Lightish quaffing-wine red grape widely grown in SAR.

Monsanto Tus ★★★ Esteemed CHIANTI CLASSICO estate, esp for Il POGGIO RISERVA (first single-v'yd Chianti Classico), Chianti Classico Riserva, IGTs Fabrizio Bianchi (CHARD) and Nemo (CAB SAUV).

Montalcino Tus Small but exquisite hilltop town in province of Siena, famous for concentrated, expensive BRUNELLO and more approachable, better-value ROSSO DI MONTALCINO.

Montecarlo Tus DOC r w ★★ (w) DYA. White, and increasingly red, wine area nr Lucca. Try: Buonamico, Carmignani, La Torre, Montechiari, Fattoria del Teso.

Montecucco Tus SANGIOVESE-based TUS DOC between Monte Amiata and Grosseto, increasingly trendy as MONTALCINO land prices ineluctably rise. As Montecucco Sangiovese it is DOCG. Try CASTELLO DI POTENTINO (Sacromonte, Piropo); Begnardi, Ciacci Piccolomini, Colli Massari, Fattoria di Montecucco, Villa Patrizia.

Montefalco Sagrantino Umb DOCG r dr (sw) ★★★→★★★★ Super-tannic, powerful, long-lasting wines, until recently thought potentially great. Now doubts; difficult to tame the phenolics without denaturing the wine. Traditional bittersweet PASSITO version may be better suited to the grape, though harder to sell. Gd: Adanti, Antonelli, Paolo Bea, Benincasa, CAPRAI, Colpetrone, LUNGAROTTI, Scacciadiavoli, Tabarrini, Terre de' Trinci.

Montepulciano d'Abruzzo Ab DOC r p ★★→★★★ (r) 09 10 11 12 13 Gd-value, full-flavoured red and zesty, savoury pink (CERASUOLO) from grapes of this name. Region, e of Rome, dominated by co-ops. Citra, Migliaricci Rosati, Tullu Excellent privato: Cornacchia, CONTESA, Illuminati, Marramiero, Masciarelli, Contucci Ponno, Pepe, La Valentina, VALENTINI, Zaccagnini. Not to be confused with TUS town where SANGIOVESE-based VINO NOBILE DI MONTEPULCIANO comes from.

Monteregio Tus DOC nr Massa Marittima in MAREMMA, gd SANGIOVESE, CAB SAUV (r) and VERMENTINO (w) wines from eg. MORIS FARMS, TENUTA del Fontino. Big-name investors attracted by relatively low land prices, but DOC remains obscure.

Monte Schiavo Mar ★★→★★★ Switched-on, medium-size producer of VERDICCHIO, MONTEPULCIANO-based wines of various qualities, gd to excellent. Owned by world's largest manufacturer of olive-oil processing equipment, Pieralisi.

Montescudaio Tus DOC r w ★★ Modest DOC between Pisa and Livorno; best are SANGIOVESE or Sangiovese/CAB SAUV blends. Try Merlini, POGGIO Gagliardo, La Regola, Sorbaiano.

Montevertine Tus ★★★★ Radda estate. Non-DOCG but classic CHIANTI-style wines. IGT *Le Pergole Torte* a fine, sometimes great example of pure, long-ageing SANGIOVESE.

Montevetrano Cam ★★★ Iconic CAMPANIA *azienda*, wine supervised by consultant Riccardo Cotarella. Superb IGT Montevetrano (CAB SAUV, MERLOT, AGLIANICO).

Morellino di Scansano Tus DOCG r ★→★★★ 09 10 11 13 SANGIOVESE red from the MAREMMA. Used to be relatively light and simple, now, sometimes regrettably, gaining weight and substance, perhaps to justify its lofty DOCG status. Best: Belguardo, Mantellasi, MORIS FARMS, Podere 414, POGGIO Argentiera, LE PUPILLE, Terre di Talamo, *Vignaioli del Morellino di Scansano* (co-op).

Moris Farms Tus ★★★ One of first new-age producers of TUS'S MAREMMA, with

MONTEREGIO and *Morellino di Scansano* DOCS, plus VERMENTINO IGT. Top cru: iconi IGT Avvoltore, a rich SANGIOVESE/CAB SAUV/SYRAH blend. But *try the basic Morellin*

Moscato d'Asti Pie DOCG w sw sp ★★→★★★ DYA Similar to DOCG ASTI; usually better grapes; lower alcohol and pressure, sweeter, fruitier, often from small producers Best DOCG MOSCATO: L'Armangia, BERA, *Braida*, Ca'd'Gal, Cascina Fonda, Cascin Pian d'Oro, Caudrina, Il Falchetto, Forteto della Luja, Marchesi di Grésy, Icard Isolabella, Manfredi/Patrizi, Marino, La Morandina, Marco Negri, Elio Perrone Rivetti, Saracco, Scagliola, *Vajra*, Vietti, Vignaioli di Sante Stefano.

Muri Gries T-AA ★★→★★★ This monastery, in Bolzano suburb of Gries, is traditional and still top producer of LAGREIN ALTO ADIGE DOC. Esp cru Abtei-Muri.

Nals Margreid T-AA ★★→★★★ Small quality co-op making mtn-fresh whites (es PINOT BIANCO Sirmian), from two separate communes of ALTO ADIGE.

Nebbiolo d'Alba Pie DOC r dr ★★→★★★ 09 10 11 12 13 (14) Sometimes a worth replacement for BAROLO/BARBARESCO, gd examples: PIO CESARE, GIACOSA, SANDRONE VAJRA. Sometimes fresh and unoaked, more of a quaffing wine, eg. Bogliett The poor 2014 crop may paradoxically offer some gd and gd-value bottles downgraded from BAROLO/BARBARESCO.

Nebbiolo delle Langhe Pie ★★ Like the above but from a wider area, the LANGHE hills G Vajra makes a cracking example; a light, crisp baby BAROLO.

Negrar, Cantina Ven ★★→★★★ Aka CS VALPOLICELLA. Major producer of high-qualit Valpolicella, RIPASSO, AMARONE; grapes from various parts of the CLASSICO zone Look for brand name Domini Veneti.

Nicolucci E-R ★★→★★★ Winery since 1885 at Predappio in heart of SANGIOVESE D ROMAGNA country. Pino N and son make gd to excellent wine, mainly SANGIOVESE based, like RISERVA VIGNA del Generale Predappio di Predappio, lighter I Mandorl and Tre Rocche and Nero di Predappio (Sangiovese blended with REFOSCO, here called Terrano).

Nino Franco Ven ★★★→★★★★ The winery of Primo Franco, named after hi grandfather. Among the v. finest PROSECCOS are Rive di San Floriano Brut, Prim Franco Dry. Excellent CARTIZZE, *delicious basic Prosecco di Valdobbiadene Brut.*

Nipozzano, Castello di Tus ★★★ FRESCOBALDI estate in RÚFINA, e of Florence, making excellent CHIANTI Rúfina RISERVAS Nipozzano and esp *Montesodi.*

Nittardi Tus ★★→★★★ Reliable source of quality modern CHIANTI CLASSICO. German proprietor Peter Femfert; oenologist Carlo Ferrini.

Nozzole Tus ★★→★★★ Famous estate in heart of CHIANTI CLASSICO, n of Greve owned by Ambrogio and Giovanni FOLONARI. V.gd Chianti Classico Nozzole and excellent CAB SAUV Pareto.

Nuragus di Cagliari Sar DOC w ★★ DYA. Lively, uncomplicated SAR wine from Nuragus grape.

Occhio di Pernice Tus "Partridge's eye". A type of VIN SANTO made predominantly from black grapes, mainly SANGIOVESE. *Avignonesi's is definitive.* Also an obscure black variety found in RÚFINA and elsewhere.

Oddero Pie ★★→★★★ Traditionalist La Morra estate for gd to excellent BAROLO (Brunate, Villero) and BARBARESCO (Gallina) crus, plus other serious PIE wines.

Oltrepò Pavese Lom DOC r w dr sw sp ★→★★★ Multi-DOC, incl numerous varietal and blended wines from Pavia province, mostly drunk in Milan. Sometimes v.gd PINOT N and SPUMANTE. Gd growers: Anteo, Barbacarlo, Casa Re, Castello di Cigognola, CS Casteggio, Le Fracce, Frecciarossa, Monsupello, Mazzolino, Ruiz de Cardenas, Travaglino, La Versa co-op.

Ornellaia Tus ★★→★★★★ 04' 06' 08 10 11 12 Fashionable estate nr BOLGHERI founded by Lodovico ANTINORI, who sold to FRESCOBALDI/Mondavi consortium, now owned solely by Frescobaldi. Top wines, Bordeaux grapes, method: Bolgheri DOC Ornellaia, IGT Masseto (MERLOT). Gd Bolgheri DOC Le Serre Nuove, IGT Le Volte.

Orsi Vigneto San Vito E-R ★★ Property in Colli Bolognesi run by dynamic young producer, Federico Orsi. Speciality is sparkling Pignoletto *sui lieviti* (on the yeasts): second fermentation in the bottle, no disgorgement. Also experimenting with Georgian *quevri* (amphorae).

Orvieto Umb DOC w dr sw s/sw ★→★★★ DYA The classic Umbrian white, a blend of several varieties, mainly Procanico (TREBBIANO) and GRECHETTO. Wines can be comparable to Vouvray from tufa soil. *Secco* version most popular today, *amabile* is more traditional. Sweet versions from noble rot (*muffa nobile*) grapes can be superb, eg. Barberani's Calcaia. Other gd producers: Bigi, Cardeto, **Castello della Sala**, Decugnano dei Barbi, La Carraia, Palazzone.

Pacenti, Siro Tus ★★★ Modern-style BRUNELLO and ROSSO DI MONTALCINO from a small, caring producer.

Paltrinieri ★★ Specialist in LAMBRUSCO di Sorbara, Alberto Paltrinieri runs this 15-ha family estate (following mother and grandfather) as if the end product were vintage Champagne. Various bottlings are all pale in colour with lively acidity and sparkle and ripe fruit, *v. much the real thing* and a million miles from the sweet industrial gloop of yore.

Pantelleria Si Windswept, black-earth (volcanic) SI island off Tunisian coast, famous for superb MOSCATO d'Alessandria stickies. PASSITO versions are particularly dense/intense. Look for: Abraxas, Colosi, DE BARTOLI, DONNAFUGATA, Murana.

Passito Tus, Ven One of Italy's most ancient and most characteristic wine styles, from grapes hung up, or spread on trays to dry, briefly under the harvest sun (in the s) or over a period of weeks or months in the airy attics of the winery – a process called *appassimento*. Best-known versions: VIN SANTO (TUS); VALPOLICELLA/SOAVE, AMARONE/RECIOTO (Ven). *See also* MONTEFALCO, ORVIETO, TORCOLATO, VALLONE.

Pecorino Ab ★★→★★★ Not cheese. Complex, highly drinkable (and age-worthy) dry white from a just-rescued old variety native to Ab. Gd producers: CONTESA, **Farnese**, Franco Pasetti, Illuminati, San Lorenzo, Terre d'Aligi, Tiberio.

Pian dell'Orino ★★★ Caroline Pobitzer and spouse from ALTO ADIGE run this small MONTALCINO estate as committed biodynamicists. BRUNELLO is both seductive and technically perfect, Rosso nearly as gd.

Plave Ven DOC r w ★→★★ (r) 10 11 12 (w) DYA. Volume DOC on plains of e Ven for budget varietals. CAB SAUV, MERLOT, Raboso reds can all age moderately. Above-average examples from Loredan Gasparini, Molon, Villa Sandi.

Picolit F-VG DOCG w sw s/sw ★★→★★★ 08 09 10 12 13. Quasi-mythical sweet white from FRIULI COLLI ORIENTALI, might disappoint those who can a) find it and b) afford it. Gd from DORIGO, LIVIO FELLUGA, Meroi, Perusini, Specogna, VILLA RUSSIZ, Vinae dell'Abbazia.

Piedmont / Piemonte Pie Alpine foothill region; with TUS, Italy's most important for top quality. Turin is the capital, ASTI and ALBA the wine centres. No IGTS allowed; Piemonte DOC is lowest denomination, covering basic reds, whites, SPUMANTE, FRIZZANTE. Grapes incl: NEBBIOLO, BARBERA, BONARDA, Brachetto, Cortese, DOLCETTO, GRIGNOLINO, CHARD, MOSCATO. *See also* BARBARESCO, BAROLO, GATTINARA, ROERO.

Pieropan Ven ★★★ Nino Pieropan is the veteran quality leader of SOAVE, the man who brought a noble wine back to credibility. Cru *La Rocca* is still the ultimate Soave, and Calvarino, indeed the screwcapped CLASSICO, are not far behind.

Pio Cesare Pie ★★→★★★ Veteran ALBA producer, BAROLO, BARBARESCO in both modern (barrique) and traditional (large-cask-aged) versions. Also the Alba range, incl whites (eg. GAVI). Particularly gd NEBBIOLO D'ALBA, *a little Barolo at half the price*.

Planeta Si ★★→★★★ Leading SI estate; six v'yd holdings in various parts of the island incl Vittoria (CERASUOLO), Noto (NERO D'AVOLA Santa Cecilia) and most recently on ETNA. Wines from native and imported varieties. La Segreta is brand of gd-value white (Grecanico, CHARD, VIOGNIER, FIANO) and red (Nero d'Avola, MERLOT, SYRAH).

ITALY

Prosecco by numbers
The UK drank over 38 million bottles of PROSECCO SPUMANTE in 2014, with a value of €93 million; a 63% increase. The USA drank €82 million's worth. Of the top three Prosecco-loving countries, only Germany drank slightly less, but there can hardly be anyone in those three countries that didn't have at least one glass.

Podere Tus Small TUS farm, once part of a big estate.

Poggio Tus Means "hill" in TUS dialect. "**Poggione**" means "big hill".

Poggio Antico Tus ★★★ Admirably consistent, sometimes inspired producer of MONTALCINO. Basic BRUNELLO is aged in traditional BOTTE. Altero is Brunello aged in barriques. RISERVA blends the two.

Poggio di Sotto ★★★★ Small MONTALCINO estate but a quality giant of the illustrious denomination. Outstanding BRUNELLO and Rosso; traditional character with an idiosyncratic twist. New owner Claudio Tipa pursues existing lines.

Poggione, Tenuta Il Tus ★★★ Marker for fine BRUNELLO, esp considering large volume; also v.gd ROSSO DI MONTALCINO.

Poggiopiano Tus ★★→★★★ Smooth-drinking yet serious CHIANTI CLASSICO from Bartoli family of San Casciano. Blend of old and new techniques. Polished Chianti Classico and RISERVA La Tradizione. Chiantis are pure SANGIOVESE, but SUPER TUSCAN Rosso di Sera incl up to 15% of Colorino grape.

Poggio Scalette Tus ★★★ Oenologist Vittorio Fiore's family estate. Above-average CHIANTI CLASSICO and Bordeaux-blend Capogatto. Pride of place goes to 100% SANGIOVESE Il Carbonaione; needs several yrs bottle age.

Poliziano Tus ★★★ MONTEPULCIANO estate of Federico Carletti. Superior VINO NOBILE (esp cru Asinone) and gd IGT Le Stanze (CAB SAUV/MERLOT).

Pomino Tus DOC r w ★★★ (r) 09 10 11 12 (13) An appendage of RÙFINA, with fine red and white blends (esp Il Benefizio). Virtually a FRESCOBALDI exclusivity.

Potazzine, Le Tus ★★★ BRUNELLO and ROSSO DI MONTALCINO of Giuseppe and Gigliola Gorelli; high-altitude site just s of MONTALCINO. Wines keep improving; now much admired. Drink them at the family's restaurant in centre of Montalcino.

Potentino, Castello di Tus ★★ English eccentric Charlotte Horton takes on the might of what she calls "Mort-alcino" at this medieval redoubt on Monte Amiata. V.gd SANGIOVESE *Sacromonte*; better PINOT N Piropo, Lyncurio (blush).

Prà Ven ★★★ Leading SOAVE CLASSICO producer, esp crus Monte Grande, Staforte, the latter 6 mths in steel tanks on lees with mechanical *bâtonnage*. Now also excellent VALPOLICELLAS under the names Morandina, La Formica.

Produttori del Barbaresco Pie ★★★→★★★★ One of Italy's earliest co-ops, considered by some the best, if not indeed best in the world. Aldo Vacca and his team make excellent traditional straight BARBARESCO as well as crus Asili, Montefico, Montestefano, Ovello, Pora, Rio Sordo.

Prosecco Ven DOC(G) w sp ★→★★ DYA. Italy's favourite fizz. Current laws, designed to protect the name, mean "Prosecco" is no longer a grape but only a wine derived from the GLERA grape grown in specified DOC/DOCG zones (IGT no longer permitted) of Ven, F-VG. May be still, SPUMANTE, FRIZZANTE.

Prunotto, Alfredo Pie ★★★→★★★★ Traditional ALBA company modernized by ANTINORI in the 90s, run by Piero's daughter Albiera. V.gd BARBARESCO (Bric Turot), BAROLO (Bussia), NEBBIOLO (Occhetti), BARBERA D'ALBA (Pian Romualdo), Barbera d'ASTI (Costamiole), MONFERRATO Rosso (Mompertone, Barbera/SYRAH blend).

Puglia / Apulia The 360-km heel of the Italian boot, now in wine context generally known as Puglia rather than Latin Apulia. Generally gd-value, easy-drinking wines (mainly red) from various grapes like NEGROAMARO, PRIMITIVO and Uva di

Troia. The most interesting wines are from SALENTO peninsula incl DOCS BRINDISI, COPERTINO, SALICE SALENTINO.

Querciabella Tus ★★★★ Top CHIANTI CLASSICO estate with IGT crus Camartina (CAB SAUV/SANGIOVESE) and barrel-fermented CHARD/PINOT BL Batàr. Purchases in Radda and MAREMMA provide more grapes for Chianti Classico and recent, as yet unconvincing, Turpino (CAB FR, SYRAH, MERLOT) respectively.

Quintarelli, Giuseppe Ven ★★★★ Arch-traditionalist, artisanal producer of sublime VALPOLICELLA, RECIOTO, AMARONE; fine Bianco Secco, a blend of various grapes. Bepi died 2012; daughter Fiorenza and her sons have taken over, altering nothing.

Rampolla, Castello dei Tus ★★★ CAB SAUV-loving estate in Panzano, CHIANTI CLASSICO, top wines being IGTS Sammarco and d'Alceo. International-style Chianti Classico.

Ratti, Renato ★★→★★★ Iconic BAROLO estate. Renato's son Pietro now in charge. Modern-style wines; short maceration but plenty of substance, esp Barolos Rocche dell'Annunziata and Conca.

Recioto della Valpolicella Ven DOCG r sw (sp) ★★★→★★★★ This most historic of all Italian wines, made from PASSITO grapes along lines est before the 6th century, is unique and potentially stunning. Sumptuous cherry-chocolate sweet fruitiness.

Recioto di Soave Ven DOCG w sw (sp) ★★★→★★★★ SOAVE from half-dried grapes: sweet, fruity, slightly almondy; sweetness is cut by high acidity. Drink with cheese. Outstanding from Anselmi, COFFELE, Gini, PIEROPAN, Tamellini, often v.gd from Ca' Rugate, PASQUA, PRÀ, Suavia, Trabuchi. As with RECIOTO DELLA VALPOLICELLA the vintage is less important than the process.

Refosco (dal Peduncolo Rosso) F-VG ★★ 10 11 12 13 Gutsy red of rustic style. Best from: FRIULI COLLI ORIENTALI DOC, Moschioni, Le Vigne di Zamo, *Volpi Pasini*; gd from LIVIO FELLUGA, Miani and from Dorigo, Ronchi di Manzano, Venica, Ca' Bolani, Denis Montanara in Aquileia DOC.

Ribolla F-VG DOC (Friuli Colli Orientali and Collio) w ★→★★ DYA. Characterful acidic white, the best from COLLIO. Top estates: Il Carpino, La Castellada, Damijan, Fliegl, GRAVNER, Primosic, Radikon, Tercic.

Ricasoli Tus Historic Tuscan family. 19th-century Prime Minister Bettino R devised the classic CHIANTI blend. The main branch in Cupion the medieval Castello di WIIII, Related Rirnsole own Castello di Cacchiano, Rocca di Montegrossi.

Riecine ★★→★★★★ Smallish, high-quality estate at Gaiole-in-CHIANTI. SANGIOVESE specialist; CHIANTI CLASSICO among finest as is IGT Toscana La Gioia. Brit Sean O'Callaghan is seasoned winemaker, American Gary Baumann owner, John Dunkley legendary founder.

Rinaldi, Giuseppe Pie ★★★ Beppe R is an arch-traditionalist BAROLO personality whose CANTINA on the outskirts of Barolo is not always a model of hygiene. Characterful Barolos incl crus Brunate (Le Coste, Cannubi San Lorenzo) – Ravera.

Ripasso Ven *See* VALPOLICELLA RIPASSO.

Riserva Wine aged for a statutory period, usually in casks or barrels.

Rivera Pug ★★ Reliable winemakers at Andria in CASTEL DEL MONTE DOC, best example being RISERVA Il Falcone. V.gd Nero di Troia-based Puer Apuliae.

The best of Prosecco

PROSECCO continues to boom in the market, helped no doubt by a massive planting programme, recently altered laws categorizing Prosecco as a wine from a specific area and no longer a grape (thus eliminating, or at least reducing, copycat wines from emerging v'yds of the world) and a consequent noticeable rise in the general quality level. Gd producers: Adami, Biancavigna, BISOL, Bortolin, Canevel, CARPENÈ-MALVOLTI, Case Bianche, Col Salice, Le Colture, Col Vetoraz, Nino Franco, Gregoletto, La Riva dei Frati, Ruggeri, Vignarosa, Zardetto.

Rivetti, Giorgio (La Spinetta) Pie ★★★ Fine MOSCATO D'ASTI, excellent BARBERA interesting IGT Pin, series of super-concentrated, oaky BARBARESCOS. Owner of v'yd in BAROLO, CHIANTI COLLI Pisane DOCGS and traditional SPUMANTE house Contratto.

Rizzi Pie ★★→★★★ Sub-area of Treiso, commune of BARBARESCO, where th Dellapiana family look after 35 ha of v'yd. Top cru is Barbaresco Pajore. Fondett and Boito also gd, seem light but go deep.

Rocca, Bruno Pie ★★★ Admirable modern-style BARBARESCO (Rabajà) and other ALB wines, also v. fine BARBERA D'ASTI.

Rocca Albino ★★★ A foremost producer of elegant, sophisticated BARBARESCO: to crus VIGNETO Loreto and Brich Ronchi.

Roero Pie DOCG r ★★→★★★ 06 07 08 09 10 11 (13) Serious, occasionally BAROLO level NEBBIOLOS from the LANGHE hills across river Tanaro from ALBA. Best Almondo, Buganza, Ca' Rossa, Cascina Chicco, Correggia, Funtanin, Malvirà Monchiero-Carbone, Morra, Pace, Pioiero, Taliano, Val di Prete. *See also* ARNEIS.

Romagna Sangiovese Mar DOC r ★★→★★★ Often well-made even classy varietà red from what may be the birthplace of SANGIOVESE. Gd producers incl Cesari Drei Donà, NICOLUCCI, Papiano, Paradiso, San Patrignano, Tre Monti, Trere (E-I DOC), Villa Venti (Primo Segno), ZERBINA. Seek also IGT RONCO delle Ginestre Ronco dei Ciliegi from CASTELLUCCIO.

Metodo Ancestrale: traditional Lambrusco, can be cloudy – no disgorgement.

Ronco Term for a hillside v'yd in ne Italy, esp F-VG.

Rosato The general Italian name for rosé. Other rosé wine names incl CHIARETTO from Lake Garda; CERASUOLO from Abruzzo; Kretzer from ALTO ADIGE.

Rosso Conero Mar DOCG r ★★→★★★ 09 11 12 13 Aka plain "Conero". Smal zone growing some of Italy's most powerful MONTEPULCIANO (the grape, tha is). Recommended: Marchetti's Villa Bonomi, GAROFOLI's Grosso Agontano Moroder's Dorico, MONTE SCHIAVO's Adeodato, TERRE CORTESI MONCARO's Nerone and Vigneti del Parco, Le Terrazze's Sassi Neri and Visions of J.

Rosso di Montalcino Tus DOC r ★★→★★★ 10 11 12 13 DOC for earlier-maturing wines from BRUNELLO grapes, usually from younger or lesser v'yd sites. Could be go in 2014 as downgraded Brunello. Recently an attempt by a few big producers to allow "international" grapes into the blend was defeated. They'll try again.

Rosso di Montefalco Umb DOC r ★★→★★★ 09 10 11 12 13 SANGIOVESE/SAGRANTINO blend, often with splash of softening MERLOT. *See also* MONTEFALCO SAGRANTINO.

Rosso di Montepulciano Tus DOC r ★ 12 13 Junior version of VINO NOBILE D MONTEPULCIANO, growers similar. Seen much less than ROSSO DI MONTALCINO, probably because of confusion with MONTEPULCIANO D'ABRUZZO, with which it has nothing in common.

Rosso Piceno Mar DOC r ★ 08 09 10 11 13 Gluggable MONTEPULCIANO/SANGIOVESE blend from s half of Marches; SUPERIORE from classic zone nr Ascoli, much improved in recent yrs and v.gd value. Best: Aurora, Boccadigabbia, BUCCI, Fonte della Luna, Montecappone, MONTE SCHIAVO, Saladini Pilastri, TERRE CORTESI MONCARO, Velenosi Ercole, Villamagna.

Ruchè di Castagnole Monferrato Pie DOCG r ★★ DYA. Intense pale red of quintessentially PIE style: sour-berry fruit, sharp acid, firm tannins. Calls for a bit of practice. Gd: Pierfrancesco Gatto.

Ruffino Tus ★→★★★ The venerable CHIANTI firm of Ruffino, in hands of FOLONARI family for 100 yrs, split apart a few yrs ago. Both branches are busy acquiring new TUS estates. At last count this branch – the one that kept the name Ruffino – was up to seven, of which three are in CHIANTI CLASSICO, incl Santedame (top wine Romitorio), one in MONTALCINO (Greppone Mazzi), one in MONTEPULCIANO (Lodola Nuova). Also owns Borgo Conventi in F-VG.

Rúfina Tus ★★★ Small but important n subregion of CHIANTI, e of Florence, hilly and cool. Best wines: Basciano, CASTELLO DI NIPOZZANO (FRESCOBALDI), Castello del Trebbio, Colognole, Frascole, Grati/Villa di Vetrice, I Veroni, Lavacchio, *Selvapiana*, Tenuta Bossi, Travignoli.

Sala, Castello della Umb ★★→★★★ ANTINORI estate at ORVIETO. Top wine is splendid *Cervaro della Sala*, oak-aged CHARD/GRECHETTO. Bramito del Cervo is lesser but still v.gd, same grapes. Muffato della Sala was pioneer example of an Italian botrytis dessert wine.

Salento Pug Flat s peninsula at the tip of Italy's heel; seems unlikely for quality grapes, but deep soils, old ALBERELLO vines and constant sea breezes combine to produce remarkable red and rosé wines from NEGROAMARO and PRIMITIVO, with a bit of help from MONTEPULCIANO, MALVASIA Nera, local Sussumaniello. *See also* PUG, SALICE SALENTINO.

Salice Salentino Pug DOC r ★★→★★★ 07 08 10 11 (13) Best-known of SALENTO's many (too many) NEGROAMARO-based DOCs, made famous by veteran firms like Leone de Castris, Candido, TAURINO, Apollonio, VALLONE. RISERVA after 2 yrs.

Salvioni Tus ★★★→★★★★ Aka La Cerbaiola, this small, high-quality operation belongs to the irrepressible Giulio Salvioni. BRUNELLO, ROSSO DI MONTALCINO among v. best available, worth not-inconsiderable price.

Sandrone, Luciano Pie ★★★ Exponent of modern-style ALBA wines with deep, concentrated BAROLO Cannubi Boschis and Le Vigne. Also gd DOLCETTO, BARBERA d'Alba, NEBBIOLO d'Alba.

San Felice Tus ★★→★★★ Important historic TUS grower, owned by Gruppo Allianz and run by Leonardo Bellaccini. Fine CHIANTI CLASSICO and RISERVA POGGIO Rosso from estate in Castelnuovo Berardenga. Vitiarium is an experimental v'yd for obscure varieties, the excellent Pugnitello (IGT from that grape) is a first result. Gd too: IGT Vigorello (the first SUPER TUSCAN, from 1968) and BRUNELLO DI MONTALCINO Campogiovanni.

San Gimignano Tus Tourist-overrun TUS town famous for its towers and dry white VERNACCIA DI SAN GIMIGNANO DOCG, often overpriced, occasionally convincing as a wine if not as a *vin de terroir*. Some gd sumptuous-based reds under DOC San Gimignano. Producers incl: Bulichini, Cesani, Guicciardini Strozza, Montenidoli, Mormoraia, Il Palagione, Panizzi, Podera del Paradiso, Pietrafitta, Pietrasereno, La Rampa di Fugnano.

San Giusto a Rentennano Tus ★★★→★★★★ Top CHIANTI CLASSICO estate owned by cousins of RICASOLI. Outstanding SANGIOVESE IGT Percarlo and sublime VIN SANTO (Vin San Giusto).

San Guido, Tenuta Tus *See* SASSICAIA.

San Leonardo T-AA ★★★ Top TRENTINO estate of Marchesi Guerrieri Gonzaga, consultant Carlo Ferrini. Main wine is Bordeaux blend *San Leonardo*, "the SASSICAIA of the north". Also v. promising MERLOT Villa Gresti.

San Michele Appiano T-AA Top ALTO ADIGE CO-OP, esp for whites. Look for PINOT BIANCO Schulthauser and Sanct Valentin (★★★) selections: CHARD, PINOT GR, SAUV BL, CAB SAUV, PINOT N, GEWURZ.

Sannio Cam DOC r p w sp ★→★★★ (w) DYA. Wines of the Samnites of inland, upland CAM. Home of FALANGHINA. V.gd varietals (r w) eg. FIANO, GRECO, AGLIANICO.

San Patrignano E-R ★★ Drug rehab colony with 100 ha v'yd. Winemaking overseen by Riccardo Cotarella, tendency to international style with Bordeaux-inspired Montepirolo and Noi. Excellent SANGIOVESEs too (Avi and more modest Aulente).

Santadi Sar ★★★ SAR's, and one of Italy's best co-ops, esp for CARIGNANO-based reds Terre Brune, Grotta Rossa, Rocca Rubia RISERVA (all DOC CARIGNANO DEL SULCIS). Also whites *Vermentino Villa Solais*, Villa di Chiesa (VERMENTINO/CHARD).

Santa Maddalena / St-Magdalener T-AA DOC r ★→★★ DYA. A teutonic-style red from SCHIAVA grapes from v. steep slopes behind ALTO ADIGE capital Bolzano. Gd reputation, but could (ought to be?) better. Notable producers: CS St-Magdalena (Huck am Bach), Gojer, Josephus Mayr, Hans Rottensteiner (Premsttalerhof), Heinrich Rottensteiner.

Sant'Antimo Tus DOC r w sw ★★→★★★ Lovely little Romanesque abbey gives its name to this catch-all DOC for (almost) everything in MONTALCINO zone that isn't BRUNELLO DOCG or Rosso DOC.

Sardinia / Sardegna The Med's 2nd-largest island produces much decent and some v.gd wine, eg. Turriga from ARGIOLAS, VERMENTINO of CAPICHERA, CANNONAU RISERVAS of Jerzu and Loi, Vermentino and Cannonau from Dettori and amazing sherryish VERNACCIA from CONTINI. Best DOCS: Vermentino di Gallura (eg. Canayli from Cantina Gallura), CARIGNANO DEL SULCIS (Terre Brune, Rocca Rubia from SANTADI).

Sassicaia Tus DOC r ★★★★ 85' 88' 90' 95' 97 98' 99 01' 04' 05 06 07' 08 09 10 11 (12) (13) Italy's sole single-v'yd DOC (BOLGHERI), a CAB (SAUV and FR) made on First Growth lines by Marchese Incisa della Rocchetta at TENUTA San Guido. More elegant than lush, made for age – and often bought for investment, but hugely influential in giving Italy a top-quality image.

Satta, Michele Tus ★★★ Virtually the only BOLGHERI grower to succeed with 100% SANGIOVESE (Cavaliere). Bolgheri DOC red blends Piastraia, SUPERIORE I Castagni.

Scavino, Paolo Pie ★★★ Modernist BAROLO producer of Castiglione Falletto, esp crus Rocche dell'Annunziata, Bric del Fiasc, Cannubi, Carobric. Gd BARBERA LANGHE Corale.

Schiava Alto Adige T-AA DOC r ★ DYA. Traditional light red, popular in Teutonic markets, from what is still the most-grown red grape of ALTO ADIGE, locally called VERNATSCH. Other Schiava DOCS incl Lago di Caldaro, SANTA MADDALENA and COLLI di Bolzano.

Schiopetto, Mario F-VG ★★★→★★★★ Legendary late COLLIO pioneer with spacious modern winery. Mario's children do gd job of following his footsteps, incl since selling to Volpe Pasini's Rotolo family. V.gd DOC SAUV BL, *Pinot Bl*, FRIULANO, IGT blend Blanc des Rosis, etc.

Sciacchetrà Lig *See* CINQUE TERRE.

Sella & Mosca Sar ★★ Major SAR grower and merchant with v. pleasant white Torbato (esp Terre Bianche) and light, fruity VERMENTINO Cala Viola (DYA). Gd Alghero DOC Marchese di Villamarina (CAB SAUV) and Tanca Farrà (CANNONAU/Cab Sauv). Also interesting Port-like Anghelu Ruju.

Selvapiana Tus ★★★ With possible exception of more famous NIPOZZANO, the no. 1 CHIANTI RÙFINA estate. Best wines: RISERVA Bucerchiale, IGT Fornace; but even *basic Chianti Rùfina is a treat.* Also fine red POMINO, Petrognano.

Settesoli, CS Si ★→★★ Co-op with c.6,000 ha, giving SI a gd name with reliable, gd-value native and international varietals (*Nero d'Avola*, SYRAH, MERLOT, CAB SAUV, CHARD, Grecanico, Grillo, VIOGNIER, blends) under various labels incl Mandrarossa.

Sforzato / Sfursat Lom ★★★ AMARONE-like dried-grape NEBBIOLO from VALTELLINA in extreme n of Lom on Swiss border. Ages beautifully.

Sicily The Med's largest island, modern source of *exciting original wines and value.* Native grapes (r: NERO D'AVOLA, NERELLO MASCALESE, Frappato; w: INZOLIA, Catarratto, Grecanico, Grillo) as well as internationals. V'yds on flatlands in w, hills in centre and volcanic altitudes on Mt ETNA. Gd wineries too numerous to list. One of the few Italian regions to prosper in 2014

Sizzano Pie *See* GATTINARA.

Soave Ven DOC w (sw) ★→★★★ DYA. The famous, still underrated Veronese white. Wines from the volcanic soils of the CLASSICO zone can be intense, mineral, v. fine and quite long-lived. When labelled SUPERIORE is DOCG, but best Classico producers

---

Chianti Classico Gran Selezione – the French stay on
In 2014 a new super CHIANTI CLASSICO was introduced in the hopes of
reviving, under a more official title, the ever-unofficial and somewhat
superannuated concept of SUPER TUSCAN. The new category is for specific
wines (after chemical and organoleptic analysis), and is conceived as
sitting at the top of the Chianti Classico quality pyramid, immediately
above RISERVA and two places above Chianti Classico. Alas, it was a
classic case of missed opportunity. It could have rid Chianti Classico of
French grapes: these may improve quality (although that's debatable),
but they certainly detract from the authenticity and individuality without
which no wine can ever be considered truly great.

---

shun the "honour", stick to DOC. Sweet RECIOTO can be superb. Best: CANTINA del
Castello, La Cappuccina, Ca' Rugate, COFFELE, Fattori, Gini, GUERRIERI RIZZARDI,
Inama, Montetondo, PIEROPAN, Portinari, PRÀ, Suavia, Tamellini, TEDESCHI.

olaia Tus r ★★★★ 85′ 90′ 95′ 97′ 99′ 01 04 06 07 08 09 10 11 (12) Potentially
magnificent if somewhat massive CAB SAUV/SANGIOVESE blend by ANTINORI, made
to the highest Bordeaux specs; needs yrs of laying down.

ovana Tus MAREMMA DOC, inland nr Etruscan town of Pitigliano. Look for CILIEGIOLO
from TENUTA Roccaccia, Pitigliano, Ripa, Sassotondo, MALBEC from ANTINORI.

peri Ven ★★★ Quality VALPOLICELLA family estate with sites such as outstanding
Monte Sant'Urbano. Unpretentious, traditional-style CLASSICO SUPERIORE,
AMARONE, RECIOTO. No frills, just gd wine.

pumante Sparkling. What used to be called ASTI Spumante is now just Asti.

üdtirol T-AA The local name of German-speaking South Tyrol ALTO ADIGE.

uperiore Wine with more ageing than normal DOC and 0.5–1% more alcohol. May
indicate a restricted production zone, eg. ROSSO PICENO Superiore.

uper Tuscan Tus Wines of high quality and price developed in the 70s/80s to get
round the silly laws then prevailing. Now increasingly irrelevant. Never was an
official designation.

inca d'Almerita Si ★★★★ New generation of Tasca d'Almeritas runs the historic, still
prestigious estate, which kept the flag flying for SI in the dark yrs. High-altitude
v'yds; balanced IGT wines under its old Regaleali label, CHARD and CAB SAUV gd, but
star, as ever, is NERO D'AVOLA-based *Rosso del Conte*.

aurasi Cam DOCG r ★★★ 04 06 07 08 09 10 11 (12) The s's answer to the n's
BAROLO and the centre's BRUNELLO, needs careful handling and long ageing. There
are friendlier versions of AGLIANICO but none so potentially *complex, demanding,
ultimately rewarding*. Made famous by MASTROBERARDINO, other outstanding
producers are Caggiano, Caputo, FEUDI DI SAN GREGORIO, Molettieri, Luigi Tecce,
Terredora di Paulo.

edeschi, Fratelli Ven ★★→★★★ One of the original quality growers of VALPOLICELLA
when the zone was still ruled by mediocrities. "Capitel" tends to figure in the
names of octogenarian Renzo Tedeschi's best wines: AMARONE Capitel Monte
Olmi, RECIOTO Capitel Fontana, RIPASSO Capitel San Rocco.

enuta An agricultural holding (*see* under name – eg. SAN GUIDO, TENUTA).

erlano T-AA w ★★→★★★ DYA. ALTO ADIGE Terlano DOC applies to one white blend
and eight white varietals, esp PINOT BL, SAUV BL. Can be v. fresh, zesty. Best: CS
Terlano (Pinot Bl Vorberg ages remarkably), LAGEDER, Niedermayr, Niedrist.

eroldego Rotaliano T-AA DOC r p ★★→★★★ TRENTINO's best local variety makes
seriously tasty wine on the flat Campo Rotaliano. *Foradori* is tops, also gd:
Dorigati, Endrizzi, MEZZACORONA's RISERVA Nos, Zeni.

erre Cortesi Moncaro Mar ★★→★★★ Marches co-op; competes with the best of the

---

Stars of the Tuscan coast
Recent yrs have seen a rush to plant in an area not historically noted for its fine (or indeed any) wines – the coast of TUS, ie. the provinces of Pisa, Livorno, Grosseto. First it was French grapes such as the CAB brothers, MERLOT, SYRAH, PETIT VERDOT; now Italians like SANGIOVESE, CILIEGIOLO, Alicante are in fashion. Best producers: Argentiera, Belguardo (Mazzei), CAIAROSSA, CA' MARCANDA (GAJA), CASTELLO DEL TERRICCIO, COLLE Massari, Guado al Tasso (ANTINORI), Gualdo del Re, LE MACCHIOLE, LE PUPILLE, Michele SATTA, Montepeloso, MORIS FARMS, ORNELLAIA (FRESCOBALDI), POGGIO al Tesoro (ALLEGRINI), Tenuta San Guido (SASSICAIA), TUA RITA.

---

region at v. modest prices: gd VERDICCHIO DEI CASTELLI DI JESI (Le Vele), ROSSO CONERO RISERVA (Nerone), ROSSO PICENO SUPERIORE (Campo delle Mura).

Terriccio, Castello del Tus ★★★ Large estate s of Livorno: excellent, v. expensive Bordeaux-style IGT Lupicaia, v.gd IGT Tassinaia. Impressive IGT Terriccio, a unusual blend of mainly Rhône grapes.

Tiefenbrunner T-AA ★★→★★★ Grower-merchant in Teutonic castle (Turmhof) in ALTO ADIGE. Christof T succeeds father (winemaker since 1943), making wide range of mtn-fresh white and well-defined red varietals: French, Germanic and local, esp 1,000m-high MÜLLER-T *Feldmarschall*, Linticlarus range CHARD/LAGREIN, PINOT N.

Tignanello Tus r ★★★★ 04' 06' 07' 08 09 10 11 (12) (13) SANGIOVESE/CAB SAUV blend barrique-aged, the wine that put SUPER TUSCANS on map, created by ANTINORI great oenologist, Giacomo Tachis, in the early 70s. Today one of greatest cash cows of world wine.

Torcolato Ven Sweet wine from BREGANZE in Ven; Vespaiolo grapes laid on mat or hung up to dry for mths, as nearby RECIOTO DI SOAVE. Best: MACULAN, CS BEATO BARTOLOMEO DA BREGANZE.

Torgiano Umb DOC r p w (sp) ★★ and **Torgiano, Rosso Riserva** DOCG r ★★→★★★ 01' 04 06 07 08 09 10 (11) (12) Gd to excellent red from Umb, virtually a exclusivity of LUNGAROTTI. *Vigna Monticchio* Rubesco RISERVA is outstanding i vintages such as 75 79 85 97; keeps many yrs.

Travaglini Pie Leads the somewhat underwhelming world of n PIE NEBBIOLO, with v.gd GATTINARA RISERVA, Gattinara Tre Vigne, pretty gd Nebbiolo Coste della Sesia.

Trebbiano d'Abruzzo Ab DOC w ★→★★★★ DYA. Generally crisp and low-flavou wine. VALENTINI's exceptional version is widely considered to be one of Italy greatest whites.

Trentino T-AA DOC r w dr sw ★→★★★ DOC for 20-odd wines, mostly varietally named. Best: CHARD, PINOT BL, MARZEMINO, TEROLDEGO. Provincial capital is Trento which is DOC name for potentially high quality METODO CLASSICO wines.

Trinoro, Tenuta di Tus ★★★ Individualist TUS red wine estate, pioneer in DOC Val d'Orcia between MONTEPULCIANO and MONTALCINO. Heavy accent on Bordeaux grapes in flagship TENUTA di Trinoro, also in Palazzi, Le Cupole and Magnacosta. Andrea Franchetti also has v'yds on Mt ETNA.

Tua Rita Tus ★★→★★★★ First producer to est Suvereto, some 20 km down coast as new BOLGHERI in the 90s. Producer of possibly Italy's greatest MERLOT i Redigaffi, also outstanding Bordeaux blend *Giusto di Notri*. *See* VAL DI CORNIA.

Tuscany / Toscana The focal point of Italian wine's late-20th century renaissance with experimental SUPER TUSCANS and modernized classics, CHIANTI, VINO NOBILE BRUNELLO. The development of coastal zones like BOLGHERI and MAREMMA, from almost nowhere, has been a major feature of Tus viniculture over last half century. But classics still come from inland.

Umani Ronchi Mar ★★→★★★ Leading Mar producer, esp for VERDICCHIO (Casal di Serra, Plenio), ROSSO CONERO Cumaro, IGTS Le Busche (w), Pelago (r).

Vajra, G D Pie ★★★ The Vajra family produce immaculate BAROLO, BARBERA, DOLCETTO, FREISA, also surprisingly gd RIES, in Barolo *frazione* of Vergne. Also now own Luigi Baudana estate in Serralunga.

Valcalepio Lom DOC r w sw ★→★★ (w) DYA. Wines of the zone of Bergamo, where Po Valley meets last foothills of the Alps. Grapes largely international (CAB, MERLOT, PINOT BIANCO, CHARD), but mainly drunk locally.

Valdadige T-AA DOC r w dr s/sw ★ Name (in German: *Etschtaler*) for simple wines of valley of Adige, from ALTO ADIGE through TRENTINO to n Ven.

Val di Cornia Tus DOC r p w ★★→★★★ 06'07 08 09 10 11 12 DOC s of BOLGHERI. SANGIOVESE, CAB SAUV, MERLOT, SYRAH, MONTEPULCIANO. Look for: Ambrosini, Jacopo Banti, Bulichella, Gualdo del Re, Incontri, Montepeloso, Petra, Russo, San Michele, TENUTA Casa Dei, Terricciola, TUA RITA.

Valentini, Edoardo Ab ★★★→★★★★ Son Francesco continues tradition of long-macerated, non-filtered, unfined, hand-bottled MONTEPULCIANO, CERASUOLO, TREBBIANO D'ABRUZZO. Quality, availability unpredictable; potentially outstanding. *See* MONTEPULCIANO D'ABRUZZO, Trebbiano d'Abruzzo.

Valle d'Aosta VdA DOC r p w ★★ Regional DOC for some 25 Alpine wines, geographically or varietally named, incl Premetta, Fumin, Blanc de Morgex, Chambave, Nus MALVOISIE, Arnad Montjovet, Torrette, Donnas, Enfer d'Arvier. Tiny production, wines rarely seen abroad but potentially worth seeking out.

Valle Isarco T-AA DOC w ★★ DYA. ALTO ADIGE DOC for seven Germanic varietal whites made along the Isarco (Eisack) River ne of Bolzano. Gd GEWURZ, MÜLLER-T, RIES, SILVANER. Top producers: Abbazia di Novacella, Eisacktaler, Kuenhof.

Vallone, Agricole Pug ★★→★★★ Large-scale grower on SALENTO peninsula. Excellent, gd-value BRINDISI VIGNA Flaminio (r p) and SALICE SALENTINO Vereto, both having RISERVAS. Best-known for AMARONE-like, semi-dried-grape wine Graticciaia. Vigna Castello is a classy addition to range.

Valpolicella Ven DOC(G) r ★→★★★★ Complex denomination, incl everything from light quaffers with a certain fruity warmth (though stronger styles could (which may or may not be RIPASSO) to AMARONES and RECIOTOS of ancient lineage. Bitter cherry is the common flavour characteristic of constituent CORVINA and Corvinone (plus other) grapes. Today straight Valpol is getting hard to source, all best grapes going into trendy, profitable Amarone. (*See* box below)

Valpolicella Ripasso Ven DOC r ★★→★★★ 09 10 11 12 VALPOLICELLA refermented on RECIOTO or AMARONE grape skins to make a more age-worthy wine. Gd to excellent: BUSSOLA, CANTINA NEGRAR, Castellani, DAL FORNO, QUINTARELLI, ZENATO.

Valtellina Lom DOC/DOCG r ★→★★★ Long e to w valley (most Alpine valleys run

---

Valpolicella: the best

VALPOLICELLA started with the Romans on the first foothills of the Alps above the Po Valley at Verona. It has never been better than today. AMARONE DELLA VALPOLICELLA and RECIOTO DELLA VALPOLICELLA have now been elevated to DOCG status, while Valpolicella RIPASSO has at last been recognized as a historic wine in its own right. The following producers make gd to great wine: Accordini Stefano ★, Serego Alighieri, ALLEGRINI ★, Begali, BERTANI, BOLLA, Boscaini, Brigaldara, BRUNELLI, BUSSOLA ★, Ca' la Bianca, Campagnola, Ca' Rugate, Castellani, Corteforte, Corte Sant'Alda, CS Valpantena, CANTINA Valpolicella, Valentina Cubi, DAL FORNO ★, GUERRIERI-RIZZARDI ★, MASI, Mazzi, Nicolis, QUINTARELLI ★, Roccolo Grassi ★, Le Ragose, Le Salette, Speri ★, TEDESCHI ★, Tommasi, Venturini, VIVIANI ★, ZENATO, Zeni.

> **Drying tonight**
> The barriers between straightforward VALPOLICELLA and expensive AMARONE,
> made from dried grapes, are breaking down – or perhaps shrivelling.
> *Appassimento*, the process of drying grapes for Amarone, brings complex bio-
> chemical changes to grapes; but if you dry grapes for less time you just get,
> well, semi-dried grapes. And they can give a nice dose of extra concentration
> to basic Valpol. Wines appearing now sort of halfway house between straight
> Valpol and Amarone: try Tommasi's Arele. IGT – for moment.

n to s) on Swiss border. Steep terraces have for millennia grown NEBBIOLO (here called CHIAVENNASCA) and related grapes. DOCG Valtellina SUPERIORE divides into five zones: Sassella, Grumello, Inferno, Valgella, Maroggia. Wines and scenery both worth the detour. Best today are: Fay, Mamete Prevostini, Nera, Nino Negri, Plozza, Rainoldi, Triacca. DOC Valtellina has less stringent requirements *Sforzato* is its AMARONE.

Vecchio Samperi Si *See* DE BARTOLI.

Venegazzu Ven ★★★ Once iconic Bordeaux blend from e Ven producer Loredan Gasparini. Prestige line is cru Capo di Stato (created for Italy's head of state).

Verdicchio dei Castelli di Jesi Mar DOC w (sp) ★★→★★★ DYA. Versatile white from nr Ancona, can be light and quaffable, or sparkling, or structured, complex long-lived (esp RISERVA DOCG, min 2 yrs old). Also CLASSICO. Best from: Accadia Bonci-Vallerosa, Brunori, BUCCI, Casalfarneto, Cimarelli, Colonnara, Coroncino Fazi-Battaglia, Fonte della Luna, GAROFOLI, Laila, Lucangeli Aymerich di Laconi Mancinelli, Montecappone, MONTE SCHIAVO, Santa Barbara, SARTARELLI, TERRI CORTESI Moncaro, UMANI RONCHI.

Verdicchio di Matelica Mar DOC w (sp) ★★→★★★ DYA. Similar to above, smaller more inland, higher, therefore more acidic, therefore longer lasting though less easy-drinking in youth. RISERVA is likewise DOCG. Esp Barone Pizzini, Belisario Bisci, La Monacesca, Pagliano Tre, San Biagio.

Verduno Pie DOC r ★★ DYA. Pale red similar to GRIGNOLINO, from Pelaverga grape grown only in BAROLO-zone commune of Verduno. Gd: Bel Colle, BURLOTTO Alessandria, CASTELLO DI VERDUNO.

Verduno, Castello di Pie ★★★ Husband/wife team Franco Bianco with v'yds in Neive, and Gabriella Burlotto, v'yds in VERDUNO, make v.gd BARBARESCO Rabaja and BAROLO Monvigliero.

Verduzzo F-VG DOC (Friuli Colli Orientali) w dr sw s/sw ★★→★★★ Full-bodied white from local variety. Ramandolo (DOCG) is well-regarded subzone for sweet wine. Top: Dario Coos, Dorigo, Giovanni Drì, Meroi.

Vermentino di Gallura Sar DOCG w ★★→★★★ DYA. *Best dry white of Sar*, from ne o island, stronger and more intensely flavoured than VERMENTINO DI SARDEGNA. Es from Capichera, CS di Gallura, CS del Vermentino, Depperu.

Vermentino di Sardegna Lig DOC w ★★ DYA. More widespread but less intense than VERMENTINO DI GALLURA. Vermentino is one of Italy's best white grapes, grows well also in LIG and on TUS coast. Gd producers: *Santadi, Sella & Mosca*.

Vernaccia di Oristano Sar DOC w dr ★→★★★ Vintage less important than process SAR *flor*-affected wine, similar to light Sherry, a touch bitter, full-bodied. SUPERIOR 15.5% ABV, 3 yrs of age. Vintage less important than process. Delicious wit *bottarga* (compressed fish roe). Kill to try it. Top: CONTINI.

Vernaccia di San Gimignano Tus *See* SAN GIMIGNANO.

Vesuvio *See* LACRYMA CHRISTI.

Vie di Romans F-VG ★★★→★★★★ Gianfranco Gallo has built up his father's ISONZ estate to top F-VG status. Excellent ISONZO CHARD, PINOT GR Dessimis, SAUV BL Pier and Vieris (oaked), MALVASIA/RIES/FRIULANO blend called Flors di Uis.

ietti Pie ★★★ Veteran grower of characterful PIE wines at Castiglione Falletto, incl BARBARESCO Masseria, BARBERA D'ALBA Scarrone, Barbera d'Asti la Crena. *Textbook Barolos:* Lazzarito, Rocche, Brunate, Villero.

ignalta Ven ★★ Top producer in COLLI EUGANEI, nr Padua (Ven); v.gd COLLI Euganei CAB SAUV RISERVA, MERLOT/Cab Sauv blend Gemola.

ignamaggio Tus ★★→★★★ Historic, beautiful, v.gd CHIANTI CLASSICO estate, nr Greve. Leonardo da Vinci painted Mona Lisa here. RISERVA's name – you guessed it.

igna (or vigneto) A single v'yd, generally indicating superior quality.

illa Matilde Cam ★★★ Top CAM producer of FALERNO Rosso (VIGNA Camarato), Bianco (Caracci), PASSITO Eleusi.

illa Papiano E-R ★★→★★★ 10-ha estate of Francesco Bordini, who consults for several passionate experimentists of Romagna. Le Papesse and I Probi are conceived of as showing respectively the feminine and masculine, while Terra is a dry ALBANA vinified on skins in Georgian *quevri* (amphorae).

illa Russiz F-VG ★★★ Historic estate for DOC COLLIO. V.gd SAUV BL and MERLOT (esp "de la Tour" selections), PINOT BL, PINOT GR, FRIULANO, CHARD.

ino Nobile di Montepulciano Tus DOCG r ★★→★★★ 04 06' 07 08 09 10 11 (12) Historic Prugnole Gentile aka SANGIOVESE-based wine from TUS town (as distinct from the Ab grape) MONTEPULCIANO, often tough with drying tannins, but complex and long-lasting from best producers: AVIGNONESI, Bindella, BOSCARELLI, La Braccesca, La Calonica, Canneto, Le Casalte, CONTUCCI, DEI, Fattoria del Cerro, Gracciano della Seta, Gracciano Svetoni, Icario, Nottola, Palazzo Vecchio, POLIZIANO, Romeo, Salcheto, Trerose, Valdipiatta, Villa Sant'Anna. RISERVA after 3 yrs.

in Santo / Vinsanto / Vin(o) Santo T-AA, Tus DOC w sw s/sw ★★→★★★★ Sweet wine made from PASSITO grapes, usually TREBBIANO, MALVASIA and/or SANGIOVESE in TUS ("Vin Santo"), Nosiola in TRENTINO ("Vino Santo"). Tus versions extremely variable, anything from off-dry and Sherry-like to sweet and v. rich. May spend 3–10 unracked yrs in small barrels called *caratelli*. *Avignonesi's is legendary*; plus CAPEZZANA, Corzano & Paterno, Fattoria del Cerro, FELSINA, Frascole, ISOLE E OLENA, Rocca di Montegrossi, San Gervasio, ░░░ ░░░░░░░ ░ ░░░░░░░░░░░, ░░░░░░░░░░░, Villa Sant'Anna, Villa di Vetrice. *See also* OCCHIO DI PERNICE.

ivaldi-Arunda T-AA ★★→★★★ Top ALTO ADIGE sparkling wines. Best: Extra Brut RISERVA, Cuvée Marianna.

iviani Ven ★★★ Claudio Viviani shows how modern a wine VALPOLICELLA and AMARONE can be. V.gd CLASSICO SUPERIORE Campo Morar, better RECIOTO La Mandrella, outstanding Amarone Casa dei Bepi, Tulipano Nero.

erzio, Roberto Pie ★★★→★★★★ BAROLO modernist. Top, v. expensive, single-v'yd Barolos: Brunate, Cerequio, Rocche dell'Annunziata-Torriglione, Sarmassa, Serra; impressive BARBERA D'ALBA.

olpaia, Castello di Tus ★★→★★★ V.gd CHIANTI CLASSICO estate at Radda. SUPER TUSCANS Coltassala (SANGIOVESE/Mammolo), Balifico (Sangiovese/CAB SAUV).

enato Ven ★★ V. reliable, sometimes inspired for GARDA wines, also VALPOLICELLA, SOAVE, AMARONE, LUGANA.

erbina, Fattoria E-R ★★★ Leader in Romagna; best sweet ALBANA DOCG (Scacco Matto), v.gd SANGIOVESE (Pietramora); barrique-aged IGT Marzieno.

ibbo Si ★★ dr sw Alluring SI table wine from the MUSCAT d'Alessandria grape, most associated with PANTELLERIA and extreme w Si. Dry version well exemplified by Ottoventi of Trapani, DE BARTOLI.

onin ★→★★ One of Italy's biggest estate owners, based at Gambellara in Ven, but also big in F-VG, TUS, PUG, SI and elsewhere in the world.

uani Lom ★★★ Small COLLIO estate of Patrizia Felluga, daughter of MARCO FELLUGA. Superior white blend Zuani RISERVA (oaked), Zuani Vigne (unoaked).

Germany

Abbreviations used in the text:

Bad   Baden
Frank   Franken
M-M   Mittelmosel
M Rh   Mittelrhein
Mos   Mosel
Na   Nahe
Pfz   Pfalz
Rhg   Rheingau
Rhh   Rheinhessen
Sa-Un   Saale-Unstrut
Sachs   Sachsen
Würt   Württemberg

More heavily shaded areas are the wine-growing regions.

What makes a "better" German vintage? In the past I've annotated the "classic" vintages that produced lots of Spätlesen and Auslesen since these were considered Germany's finest wines; certainly its most expensive. But climate change has had a more radical effect in Germany's marginal vineyards than any others. There hasn't been a real old-style lousy vintage with no ripe grapes for a generation. Conditions today are right for ripe, dry wines – which are what fashion is demanding.

Some drinkers, especially in the UK, still hanker after the old sweet standards. But they can now choose between old and new, which gives the great Rieslings infinitely more chance to shine at table.

So this year we've changed the vintage notation a little. We've kept the existing ratings for "classic" wines, and introduced, alongside these, ratings for verticals of individual dry *Grosses Gewächs* (GG) wines in certain ntries. We hope they help.

Germany is certainly changing. Not so long ago, German growers sed to say that the odd years tend to be better vintages than even ones; ok at star years like 1959, 1971, 1983. But recently... hmm. 2001 was rilliant, 03 much better than initially thought, 05, 07, 09, 11... all of ese were fine vintages. But were they really better than 02, 04, 08, 10, 2? 2006 had a lot of rain and botrytis. But if we had to choose between 3 and 14, most of us would prefer 14. And the 04s and 08s have eveloped beautifully. The conclusion is that German vintages are much ore regular today than in past decades. Climate change continues to ring German wines within their comfort zone. Which is why dry wines natter more than ever: they're riper and better balanced than ever. If you aven't tried them, now is the time.

Recent vintages

Mosel

Mosels (including Saar and Ruwer wines) are so attractive young that their eeping qualities are not often enough explored. But well-made Kabinetts gain om at least 5 years in bottle and often much more: Spätlesen from 5–20, and uslesen and Beerenauslesen anything from 10–30 years. The Mosel is still ntative about the Trocken style. As a rule, in poor years the Saar and Ruwer nake sharp, lean wines, but in good years, which are increasingly common, ey surpass the whole world for elegance and thrilling, steely "breeding".

14 Warm winter, good spring, wet summer. September sunshine saved the vintage, but some rain in October made careful selection necessary. Classical wines from Trocken to Auslese.

13 Half a crop. Top wines have freshness, elegance (but are rare). Middle Mosel better than Saar, Ruwer.

12 Classic wines mostly from QbA to Auslese. Low quantity.

11 A brilliant vintage, particularly successful in the Saar, Ruwer, with sensational TBAs.

10 High acidity is the identifying feature of this vintage, some good Spätlesen, Auslesen.

09 Magnificent Spätlesen, Auslesen, good balance. Keep.

08 Not a vintage for Auslesen, but Kabinetts, Spätlesen can be fine and elegant. Drink or keep.

07 Good quality and quantity too. Now increasingly mature.

06 Lots of botrytis, not only noble; drink.

05 Very high ripeness, but with far better acidity than, say, 2003. Exceptional, especially in Saar. Drink or keep.

04 Fine year to drink.

03 Vintage of heat; considerable variation in quality. Best wines may turn out to be as good as the 59s.

02 Succulent, lively Kabinett, Spätlese wines now ready to drink.

01 The best Mosel Ries since 90. Saar, Ruwer less exciting but still perfect balance. Lots of Spätlesen, Auslesen to drink or keep.

ne older vintages: 99 97 95 94 93 90 89 88 76 71 69 64 59 53 49 45 37 34 21.

Rheinhessen, Nahe, Pfalz, Rheingau, Ahr

Apart from Mosel, Rheingau wines tend to be longest-lived of all German regions, improving for 15 years or more, but best wines from Rheinhessen, the Nahe and Pfalz can last as long. Modern-style dry wines such as *Grosses Gewächs* are generally intended for drinking within 2 to 4 years, but the best undoubtedly have the potential to age interestingly. The same holds for Ahr Valley reds: their fruit makes them attractive young, but best wines can develop for 10 years and longer.

2014 Complicated: summer rain, and warm and wet end of September. Fruitfly *Drosophila suzukii* attacked dark berries. Ries and Spätburgunder generally okay, even good if selection was careful.

2013 Much variation; best in south Rheinhessen, Franconia and the Ahr Valley. Generally low yields.

2012 Quantities below average, but very good wines, classical at every level.

2011 The wines are fruity, with harmonious acidity.

2010 Uneven quality, dry wines should be drunk now.

2009 Excellent wines, especially dry. Some acidification was needed.

2008 Riesling of great raciness, ageing well.

2007 Dry wines are now mature. Drink.

2006 Lots of botrytis, top estates managed fair middle-weight wines. Drink now

2005 High ripeness levels with excellent acidity, extract. Superb year. Drink or keep.

2004 Ripe, healthy grapes throughout Rhine. Big crop; some dilution, though not at top estates.

2003 Rich wines; many lack acidity. Reds fared well if alcohol levels were unde control. Drink.

2002 Few challenge the best of 2001, but very good for both classic Kabinett/ Spätlese and dry. Excellent Pinot N. Drink.

2001 An exciting vintage for both dry and classic styles; excellent balance. Drink or keep.

Fine older vintages: 99 98 97 96 93 90 83 76 71 69 67 64 59 53 49 45 37 34 21.

German vintage notation

The vintage notes after entries in the German section are mostly given in a different form from those elsewhere in the book. If the vintages of a single wine are rated, the vintage notation is identical with the one used elsewhere (*see* front jacket flap). But for regions, villages or producers, two styles of vintage are indicated:

Bold type (eg. **09**) indicates classic, ripe vintages with a high proportion of SPÄTLESEN and AUSLESEN; or, in the case of red wines, gd phenolic ripeness and must weights.

Normal type (eg. 09) indicates a successful but not outstanding vintage. Generally, German white wines, esp RIES, can be drunk young for their intense fruitiness, or kept for a decade or two to develop more aromatic subtlety and finesse.

Adelmann, Weingut Graf Würt ★★→★★★ Young count Felix Adelmann now charge at idyllic Schloss Schaubeck. New winemaker too: a lot of drive, but palace revolution. V.gd 2013 RIES (GROSSE LAGE Süssmund).

Ahr ★★→★★★★ 97 05 09 11 12 13 14 Region s of Bonn. Crisp, structured but fru SPÄTBURGUNDER, FRÜHBURGUNDER from slate soils. Best: Adeneuer, Deutzerh

Heiner-Kreuzberg, Josten & Klein, KREUZBERG, MEYER-NÄKEL, Nelles, Paul Schumacher, STODDEN, co-op Mayschoss-Altenahr.

Aldinger, Gerhard Würt ★★★ Leading estate of Gerhard Aldinger and sons for dense LEMBERGER, SPÄTBURGUNDER, complex SAUV BL, TROLLINGER now available unfined, unfiltered – and without added sulphur (Sine).

Alte Reben Old vines. Increasingly common designation on German labels, and an obvious analogy to the French term *vieilles vignes*. The analogy is perfect – no min age.

Amtliche Prüfungsnummer (APNr) Official test number, on every label of a quality wine. Useful for discerning different lots of AUSLESEN a producer has made from the same v'yd.

Assmannshausen Rhg r ★★→★★★★ 97 01 02 05 08 09 10 11 12 13 Craggy RHG village known for its cassis-scented, *age-worthy Spätburgunders* from slate soils. GROSSE LAGE v'yd: Höllenberg. Growers: BISCHÖFLICHES WEINGUT, Chat Sauvage, KESSELER, König, Mumm, KRONE, HESSISCHE STAATSWEINGÜTER (53 Höllenberg NATURREIN still top form in 2014).

Oldest existing German wine: 1540 Würzburger Stein from Bürgerspital – one bottle left.

Auslese Wine from selective harvest of super-ripe bunches, in many yrs affected by noble rot (*Edelfäule*) and correspondingly unctuous in flavour. Dry Auslesen are often too alcoholic and clumsy for me.

Ayl Mos ★→★★★ All Ayl v'yds are known since 1971 by the name of its historically best site: Kupp. Such are German wine laws. Growers: BISCHÖFLICHE WEINGÜTER, *Lauer*, Vols.

Bacharach M Rh ★→★★★ 01 02 04 05 08 09 10 11 12 13 14 Small, idyllic old town on Rhine, the centre of M RH RIES. Classified GROSSE LAGE: Hahn, Posten, Wolfshöhle. Growers incl Bastian, JOST, KAUER, RATZENBERGER.

Baden r w 90 97 05 08 09 10 11 12 13 14 Huge sw region, 15,000 ha, best-known for PINOT N, GRAU- and WEISSBURGUNDER and pockets of RIES, usually dry. Many co-ops. Best areas: KAISERSTUHL, ORTENAU.

Bassermann-Jordan Pfz ★★★ MITTELHAARDT estate with 49 ha of outstanding v'yds in DEIDESHEIM, FÖRST, RUPPERTSBERG, etc. *Majestic dry Ries* and lavish sweet wines too.

Becker, Friedrich Pfz ★★→★★★ Outstanding SPÄTBURGUNDER 07' 08 09 11 12 from the s-most part of the PFZ; some v'yds actually lie across border in Alsace. Gd whites (RIES, PINOT GR) too.

Becker, J B Rhg ★★→★★★ 90 92 94 97 01 02 05 08 09 10 11 12 13 The best estate at WALLUF, now organic, known for delightfully old-fashioned, cask-aged (and long-lived) dry RIES, SPÄTBURGUNDER. Mature (great value) vintages back to the 90s.

Beerenauslese (BA) Luscious sweet wine from exceptionally ripe, individually selected berries concentrated by noble rot. Rare, expensive.

Bercher Bad ★★★ Family estate, 25 ha, at Burkheim, specialist in barrique-aged PINOT varieties from GROSSE LAGE Feuerberg. Spicy Feuerberg SPÄTBURGUNDER GG 12' should last for a decade.

Bergdolt Pfz ★★★ An organic estate at Duttweiler, traditionally known for WEISSBURGUNDER (GG Mandelberg 98' 01' 02 04' 05 07 08 09' 10 11 12' 13). Young Carolin Bergdolt focuses equally on RIES and SPÄTBURGUNDER.

Bernkastel M-M ★→★★★★ 90 94 96 97 01 02 03 05 07 08 09 10 11 12 13 Senior wine town of the M-M, known for its perfectly round and fruity style. GROSSE LAGE: Doctor, Lay. Top growers: Kerpen, LOOSEN, J J PRÜM, Studert-Prüm, THANISCH (both estates), WEGELER. Any Bernkastel (Bereich), sold under the "Kurfürstlay" GROSSLAGE name is a deception: avoid.

Bischöfliches Weingüt Rüdesheim Rhg ★★★ Famous little church domain of

> **New EU terminology**
> Germany's part in the new EU classification involves, firstly, abolishing
> the term *Tafelwein* in favour of plain *Wein* and secondly changing
> LANDWEIN to *geschützte geographische Angabe* (ggA), or Protected
> Geographical Indication. QUALITÄTSWEIN and QUALITÄTSWEIN MIT PRÄDIKAT
> will be replaced by *geschützte Ursprungsbezeichnung* (gU), or Protected
> Designation of Origin. The existing terms – SPÄTLESE, AUSLESE and so on
> (*see* box, Germany's quality levels, p.163) – will be tacked on to gU where
> appropriate; the rules for these styles won't change.

Hildegard von Bingen's historic monastery. 8 ha of best sites in RÜDESHEIM
ASSMANNSHAUSEN, JOHANNISBERG. Peter Perabo, ex-KRONE estate, is a *Pinot N
specialist*, but RIES also v.gd.

Bischöfliche Weingüter Trier Mos ★★ 130 ha of top v'yds, uniting TRIER cathedral'
v'yds with those of three other charities. Long underperforming; is it now
turning round?

Blanc de noir(s) Increasingly popular still wine – white or pale pink – from re
grapes (mostly SPÄTBURGUNDER, TROLLINGER, or SCHWARZRIESLING).

Bocksbeutel Inconvenient flask-shaped bottle used in FRANK and n BAD.

Bodensee Bad Idyllic district of s BAD, on Lake Constance. Dry MÜLLER-T with
rare elegance, and light but delicate SPÄTBURGUNDER. Top villages: Meersburg
Hagnau. Lovely holiday wines.

Boppard M Rh ★→★★★ Wine town of M RH with GROSSE LAGE Hamm, an amphitheatr
of vines. Growers incl Lorenz, M Müller, Perll and WEINGART. Unbeatable *valu
for money.

Brauneberg M-M ★★★→★★★★ 59 71 83 90 93 94 95 96 97 99 01 02 04 05 07 08
09 10 11 12 13 14 Top village nr BERNKASTEL; excellent full-flavoured RIES of grea
raciness. GROSSE LAGE v'yds Juffer, Juffer-Sonnenuhr. Growers: *F Haag, W Haag*
KESSELSTATT, Paulinshof, RICHTER, SCHLOSS LIESER, THANISCH.

Bremer Ratskeller Town hall cellar in n Germany's commercial town of Bremen
founded in 1405, a UNESCO World Heritage Site. Oldest wine is a barrel of 165
RÜDESHEIMER Apostelwein.

Breuer Rhg ★★★→★★★★ Family estate in RÜDESHEIM and RAUENTHAL, known fo
distinctly dry RIES, SEKT, SPÄTBURGUNDER. Theresa Breuer follows her father
maintaining a classical style. Gelber Orleans, from an old local vine rediscovered
in the 1990s, is a white rarity.

Buhl, Reichsrat von Pfz ★★★ Historic PFZ estate in DEIDESHEIM, FORST, RUPPERTSBERG
owned by the Niederberger family (also BASSERMANN-JORDAN, DR. DEINHARD, VON
WINNING). Since 2013 led by ex-Bollinger (*see* France) cellarmaster Mathieu
Kauffmann. Obviously, promising SEKT to come.

Bürgerspital zum Heiligen Geist Frank ★★→★★★ Ancient charitable estate
Traditionally made whites (*Silvaner*, RIES) from best sites in and around WÜRZBURG
Recently, particular emphasis on Ries, with complex GG Stein Hagemann at the
top. Monopoly Stein-Harfe.

Bürklin-Wolf, Dr. Pfz ★★→★★★★ Historic estate with one of best v'yd portfolios in
MITTELHAARDT district, 30 ha GROSSE LAGE and ERSTE LAGE sites at FORST, DEIDESHEIM
etc. Bio farming (incl the use of horses) brings about terroir-driven, age-worthy
dry and off-dry RIES.

Busch, Clemens Mos ★★→★★★ Clemens Busch and son Florian make powerful
dry and elegant sweet RIES from steep Pündericher Marienburg. Best parcels are
bottled separately: Fahrlay, Falkenlay, Rothenpfad, Raffes. Bio.

Castell'sches Fürstliches Domänenamt Frank ★→★★★ Historic princely estate. SILVANER

RIES, SPÄTBURGUNDER from superb monopoly v'yd *Casteller Schlossberg* (a GROSSE LAGE) are traditionally crafted.

ristmann Pfz ★★★ Bio estate in Gimmeldingen making rich, *dry Ries* and SPÄTBURGUNDER, notably from GROSSE LAGE Königsbacher Idig 04 05' 08' 10' 11 12' 13. Steffen Christmann is president of the VDP.

isserath, Ansgar Mos ★★★ Young Eva Clüsserath (married to Philipp WITTMANN) crafts mineral RIES from TRITTENHEIMER Apotheke. KABINETTS are delicious, crystalline. Excellent 2013 Apotheke Ries TROCKEN.

usius, Dr. Na ★★→★★★ Family estate at TRAISEN, NA. Vivid, age-worthy RIES from sun-baked Bastei and Rotenfels of Traisen and SCHLOSSBÖCKELHEIM.

idesheim Pfz ★★→★★★★ 90 97 01 02 04 05 08 09 10 11 12 13 14 Central MITTELHAARDT village. Richly flavoured, lively wines from GROSSE LAGE parcels in six v'yds: Grainhübel, Hohenmorgen, Kalkofen, Kieselberg, Langenmorgen, Paradiesgarten. Langenmorgen, Paradiesgarten and Grainhübel also contain parcels classified as ERSTE LAGE. Top growers: BASSERMANN-JORDAN, Biffar, BUHL, BÜRKLIN-WOLF, CHRISTMANN, DEINHARD, MOSBACHER, VON WINNING.

inhard, Dr. Pfz ★★★ Since 2008, a brand of the new VON WINNING estate, but continuing to produce PFZ RIES of classical style.

el, Schlossgut Na ★★★→★★★★ Caroline Diel follows her father: exquisite *v'yd-designated* Ries (Burgberg, Goldloch, Pittermännchen of Dorsheim and Schlossberg of Burg Layen). Magnificent SPÄTLESEN, serious SEKT (Cuvée Mo 6 yrs on lees).

nnhoff Na ★★★★ 90 94 96 97 99 01 02 03 04 05 07 08 09 10 11 12 13 14 NA estate of admirable consistency; one of Germany's best. Cornelius D now in charge, perhaps slightly drier style than father Helmut. Gd value are RIES Tonschiefer and Roxheim Höllenpfad (mineral, elegant). Outstanding GG from NIEDERHAUSEN (Hermannshöhle), *Norheim (Dellchen)*; SCHLOSSBÖCKELHEIM (Felsenberg). Dazzling EISWEIN from Oberhauser Brücke v'yd.

rbach Bad ★★→★★★ 09 12 13 14 ORTENAU village for full-bodied RIES, locally called Klingelberger, from granite soils in steep Plauelrain v'yd. Top growers: Graf Metternich, LAIBLE, H Männle, Schloss Staufenberg.

uerkraut was probably a Chinese invention, not German – nevertheless v.gd with Riesling.

n Müller zu Scharzhof Mos ★★★★ 59 71 76 83 85 88 89 90 93 94 95 96 97 98 99 01 02 03 04 05 06 07 08 09 10 11 12 (13) 14 Legendary SAAR estate at WILTINGEN. Its racy SCHARZHOFBERGer RIES is among the world's greatest wines: sublime, vibrant, immortal. *Kabinett* feather-light but keep 10 yrs+, SPÄTLESEN miraculously rich and slender at the same time, AUSLESEN ethereal, Goldkapsel the ultimate. Watch out for the 12s: yield a mere 16 hl/ha, 53 (superb yr) showed many similarities, according to Egon's father's diaries.

zellage Individual v'yd site. Never to be confused with GROSSLAGE.

wein Made from frozen grapes with the ice (ie. water content) discarded, thus v. concentrated – of BA ripeness or more. Alcohol content can be as low as 5.5%. Outstanding Eiswein vintages: 98, 02, 04, 08. But as global warming proceeds, Eiswein is more and more an endangered species: winter 2013/14 was almost frost-free in Germany.

wanger Würt ★★→★★★ Jürgen Ellwanger pioneered oak-aged reds in WÜRT; his sons Jörg and Felix turn out sappy but structured LEMBERGER, SPÄTBURGUNDER and ZWEIGELT.

rich-Schönleber Na ★★★ Werner Schönleber and son Frank produce precise RIES from Monzingen's classified Halenberg and Frühlingsplätzchen. Dry and sweet equally outstanding.

Erden M-M ★★★→★★★★ 90 97 01 03 05 08 09 10 11 12 13 14 Village on red sla
soils; noble AUSLESEN and TROCKEN RIES with rare balance of power, delica
GROSSE LAGE: Prälat, Treppchen. Growers: BREMER RATSKELLER, JJ Christoffel, LOOSE
Mönchhof, Schmitges, WEINS-PRÜM.

Erste Lage Classified v'yd, second-from-top level, according to the VDP. (Not a
growers belong to the VDP, though the best usually do.) At present ambiguo
for vintages before 2012: v'yd site of exceptional quality, marked with a gra
logo with a "1" next to it. Starting with 2012, most of the former *Erste Lage* v'y
are renamed GROSSE LAGE (logo: grape with "GG"), while *Erste Lage* defines
new category between the ORTSWEIN level and *Grosse Lage*, similar to Burgundy
premier cru. However, AHR, M RH, MOS, NA and RHH will completely give up th
Erste Lage designation; all classified v'yds will be named *Grosse Lage*. I'll test yo
on this later.

Erstes Gewächs Rhg "First growth". Only for RHG v'yds, but VDP-members the
changed to the GG designation after 2012.

Erzeugerabfüllung Bottled by producer. Incl the guarantee that only own grap
have been processed. May be used by co-ops also. GUTSABFÜLLUNG is strictl
applies only to estates.

Escherndorf Frank ★★★ 08 09 10 11 12 13 Village with steep GROSSE LAGE Lum
("scrap" – as in tiny inherited parcels). Marvellous *Silvaner* and RIES, dry a
sweet. Growers: Fröhlich, H SAUER, R SAUER, Schäffer.

Feinherb Imprecisely defined traditional term for wines with around 10–20 g suga
litre, not necessarily tasting sweet. Favoured by some as more flexible alternati
to HALBTROCKEN. I often choose Feinherbs.

Forst Pfz ★★→★★★★ 90 97 01 05 08 09 11 12 13 14 Outstanding MITTELHAAR
village. Ripe, richly fragrant, full-bodied but subtle wines. GROSSE LAGE V'y
Jesuitengarten, Kirchenstück, Freundstück, Pechstein, Ungeheuer. Top growe
Acham-Magin, BASSERMANN-JORDAN, VON BUHL, BÜRKLIN-WOLF, DR. DEINHARD/V
WINNING, MOSBACHER, WOLF.

Franken 01 02 04 05 07 08 09 11 12 13 14 (Franconia) Region of distinctive d
wines, esp *Silvaner*, mostly bottled in round-bellied flasks (BOCKSBEUTEL). T
centre is WÜRZBURG. Top villages: Bürgstadt, Klingenberg, RANDERSACKER, IPHOF
and ESCHERNDORF.

Franzen Mos ★★→★★★ From Europe's steepest v'yd, Bremmer Calmont, a
nearby Neefer Frauenberg, young Kilian Franzen produces dense, minera
RIES, mostly dry.

Fricke, Eva Rhg ★★→★★★ GEISENHEIM trained oenologist Eva Fricke, born nr Brem
with no family ties to viticulture, is a rising star in the RHG: expressive, mine
RIES from KIEDRICH, LORCH.

Fuder Traditional German cask with sizes from 600–1,800 litres depending on t
region, traditionally used for fermentation and (formerly long) ageing.

Fürst, Weingut Frank ★★★→★★★★ 97 99 01 02 05 08 09 10 11 12 13 14 Family esta

---

Grosse Lage / grosslage: spot the difference

Bereich means district within an *Anbaugebiet* (region). *Bereich* on a
label should be treated as a flashing red light; the wine is a blend
from arbitrary sites within that district. Do not buy. The same holds
for wines with a GROSSLAGE name, though these are more difficult to
identify. Who could guess if "Forster Mariengarten" is an EINZELLAGE or
a *Grosslage*? But now, from the 2012 vintage, it's even more tricky. Don't
confuse *Grosslage* with GROSSE LAGE: the latter refers to best single v'yds,
Germany's *grands crus* according to the classification set up by wine-
grower's association VDP.

in Bürgstadt with v'yds there and on steep terraces of Klingenberg. Delicate, long-lived *Spätburgunder (among Germany's best)*, dense FRÜHBURGUNDER, classical SILVANER, pure CHARD, dry RIES of distinction and to age. Paul F's son Sebastian brings Burgundy experience.

Gallais, Le Mos Second estate of EGON MÜLLER ZU SCHARZHOF with 4-ha-monopoly Braune Kupp of WILTINGEN. Soil is schist with more clay than in SCHARZHOFBERG; AUSLESEN can be exceptional.

Geisenheim Rhg RHG town without first class v'yds, but home of Germany's top university of oenology and viticulture.

Most popular grape variety being planted now: Grauburgunder.

Graach M-M ★★★→★★★★ Small village between BERNKASTEL and WEHLEN. GROSSE LAGE v'yds: Domprobst, Himmelreich, Josephshof. Top growers: Kees-Kieren, VON KESSELSTATT, LOOSEN, M MOLITOR, *J J Prüm*, S A PRÜM, SCHAEFER, *Selbach-Oster*, Studert-Prüm, WEGELER, Weins-Prüm. Threatened by planned new Autobahn.

Grans-Fassian Mos ★★★ Fine MOS estate, known for steely, age-worthy RIES from v'yds in TRITTENHEIM, PIESPORT, Leiwen, Drohn. EISWEIN a speciality.

Grosse Lage The top level of the VDP's new classification, but only applies to VDP members. *NB* Not on any account to be confused with GROSSLAGE. Meant to replace ERSTE LAGE for v. best v'yd sites. The dry wine from a *Grosse Lage* site is called GG (*see* below).

Grosser Ring Mos Group of top (VDP) MOS estates, whose annual Sept auction at TRIER sets world-record prices.

Grosses Gewächs (GG) "Great/top growth". The top dry wine from a VDP-classified ERSTE LAGE (until 2012), or GROSSE LAGE (since 2012). *See also* ERSTES GEWÄCHS.

Grosslage A collection of secondary v'yds with supposedly similar character – but no indication of quality. Not on any account to be confused with GROSSE LAGE.

Gunderloch Rhh ★★★→★★★★ 90 97 01 05 07 08 09 10 11 12 13 14 Nackenheim estate where Johannes Hasselbach (cellarmaster) and father Fritz (boss) make some of the finest RIES on the Rhine, esp AUSLESE and above. Elegant, fruity *Kabinett Jean Baptiste* is perfect with spicy food. Best v'yds: Rothenberg, Pettenthal.

Gut Hermannsberg Na ★★→★★★ Former state domain at NIEDERHAUSEN, privatised and reborn in 2010. Powerful RIES from GROSSE LAGE v'yds in NIEDERHAUSEN, SCHLOSSBÖCKELHEIM, TRAISEN.

Gutsabfüllung Estate-bottled, and made from own grapes.

Gutswein Wine with no v'yd or village designation, but only the producer's name: entry-level category. Ideally, Gutswein should be an ERZEUGERABFÜLLUNG (from own grapes), but is not always the case.

Haag, Fritz Mos ★★★★ 90 94 95 96 97 99 01 02 04 05 07 08 09 10 11 12 13 14 BRAUNEBERG's top estate, of impeccable reliability; Oliver Haag continues the work of father Wilhelm in a slightly more modern style. *See* also SCHLOSS LIESER.

Haag, Willi Mos ★★→★★★ BRAUNEBERG family estate, led by Marcus Haag. Old-style RIES, mainly sweet, rich but balanced, and inexpensive.

Haart, Julian Mos ★★→★★★ Talented nephew of Theo Haart (REINHOLD HAART). First vintage 2010, v'yds in Wintrich and PIESPORT. An estate to watch.

Haart, Reinhold M-M ★★★→★★★★ Best estate in PIESPORT. Aromatic, mild RIES, SPÄTLESEN, AUSLESEN and higher PRÄDIKAT wines are *racy, copybook, Mosel Ries* – with great ageing potential.

Halbtrocken Medium-dry with 9–18 g unfermented sugar/litre, inconsistently distinguished from FEINHERB (which sounds better).

Hattenheim Rhg ★★→★★★★ 97 01 05 08 09 11 12 13 14 Town famous for GROSSE LAGEN STEINBERG, Nussbrunnen, Wisselbrunnen, Mannberg, Hassel, Schützenhaus. Estates: Barth, HESSISCHE STAATSWEINGÜTER, Knyphausen, Lang,

LANGWERTH, Ress,Schönborn, SPREITZER. Classic RHG RIES. The **Brunnen** ("well") v'yds lie on a rocky basin that collects water, protection against drought.

Heger, Dr. Bad ★★→★★★★ 08 09 11 12 13 14 KAISERSTUHL family estate. Serious dry wines from steep v'yds in Achkarren and IHRINGEN, esp GROSSE LAGE parcel selections: Häusleboden (SPÄTBURGUNDER), Gras im Ofen and Rappenecker (WEISSBURGUNDER, GRAUBURGUNDER). Vorderer Berg ("v.B.") for the v. best dramatically steep Winklerberg terraces. Weinhaus Joachim Heger wines are from rented v'yds and bought-in grapes.

Hessische Bergstrasse Hess ★→★★★ 09 11 12 13 14 Germany's smallest wine region, n of Heidelberg. Pleasant RIES from HESSISCHE STAATSWEINGÜTER, Simon-Bürkle, Stadt Bensheim.

Hessische Staatsweingüter Hess, Rhg State domain at KLOSTER EBERBACH with important v'yd holdings: 220 ha in ASSMANNSHAUSEN, RÜDESHEIM, RAUENTHAL HOCHHEIM and along HESSISCHE BERGSTRASSE. Spectacular new cellar within walls of STEINBERG. Quality is sound, but selective.

Heyl zu Herrnsheim Rhh ★★→★★★ Historic NIERSTEIN estate, bio, now part of the ST-ANTONY estate. GG from monopoly site Brudersberg can be excellent, but overall quality is uneven.

Heymann-Löwenstein Mos ★★★ Family estate at WINNINGEN nr Koblenz, 14 ha of RIES in steep terraces. Spontaneously fermented Uhlen parcel selections (Blaufüsser Lay, Rothlay, Laubach) have individuality and character.

Hochgewächs Designation for a MOS RIES that obeys stricter requirements than plain QBA, today rarely used. A worthy advocate is *Kallfelz* in Zell-Merl.

Hochheim Rhg ★★→★★★★ 90 97 01 04 05 08 09 10 11 12 13 14 Town e of main RHG area. Rich, distinctly earthy RIES from GROSSE LAGE v'yds: Domdechaney, Hölle Kirchenstück, Reichestal. Growers: Domdechant Werner, Himmel, *Künstler*, HESSISCHE STAATSWEINGÜTER.

Hock Traditional English term for Rhine wine, derived from HOCHHEIM.

Hoensbroech, Weingut Reichsgraf zu Bad ★★→★★★ Top KRAICHGAU estate on v calcareous loess soils. Dry WEISSBURGUNDER Michelfelder Himmelberg is a classic.

Hövel, Weingut von Mos ★★★ Fine SAAR estate with v'yds at Oberemmel (Hütte – filigree wines – is 4.8 ha monopoly), at KANZEM (Hörecker), and in SCHARZHOFBERG. Dynamic Maximilian von Kunow is now converting the estate to bio.

Huber, Bernhard Bad ★★★ Leading estate in Breisgau, with intensely fruity SPÄTBURGUNDER (esp *Alte Reben*, Bombacher Sommerhalde) and burgundy-style CHARD (Hecklinger Schlossberg). Bernhard Huber died 2014 and son Julian is taking over.

Ihringen Bad ★→★★★ 08 09 11 12 13 14 Village in KAISERSTUHL known for fine SPÄTBURGUNDER, GRAUBURGUNDER on steep volcanic Winklerberg. Stupidly the law permits wines from the loess plateau to use the same name. Top growers: DR HEGER, Konstanzer, Michel, Stigler.

Immich-Batterieberg M-M ★★ Comeback of an old name: New owners (since 2009) produce piquant dry and off-dry RIES from Steffensberg, Ellergrub and Batterieberg v'yds in Enkirch, but no sweet wines.

Iphofen Frank ★★→★★★ 90 97 01 04 05 08 09 10 11 12 13 14 Famous STEIGERWALD village. Rich, aromatic, well-ageing SILVANER. Classified v'yds: Julius-Echter-Berg, Kronsberg. Growers: Arnold, JULIUSSPITAL, RUCK, Vetter, *Wirsching*, WELTNER.

Jahrgang Year – as in "vintage".

Johannisberg Rhg ★★→★★★★ 90 97 99 01 04 05 07 08 09 10 11 12 13 14 RHG village known for berry- and honey-scented RIES. GROSSE LAGE v'yds: Hölle, Klaus, SCHLOSS JOHANNISBERG. GROSSLAGE (avoid!): Erntebringer. Top growers: JOHANNISHOF (Eser), SCHLOSS JOHANNISBERG, PRINZ VON HESSEN.

Johannishof (Eser) Rhg ★★→★★★ Family estate with v'yds at JOHANNISBERG and

Germany's quality levels

The official range of qualities and styles in ascending order is:

1 **Wein:** formerly known as *Tafelwein*. Light wine of no specified character, mostly sweetish.

2 **ggA:** *geschützte geographische Angabe*, or Protected Geographical Indication, formerly known as Landwein. Dryish Wein with some regional style. Mostly a label to avoid, but some thoughtful estates use the *Landwein*, or ggA designation in order to bypass constraints of state authorities.

3 **gU:** *geschützte Ursprungsbezeichnung*, or protected Designation of Origin. Replacing QUALITÄTSWEIN

4 **Qualitätswein:** dry or sweetish wine with sugar added before fermentation to increase its strength, but tested for quality and with distinct local and grape character. Don't despair.

5 **Kabinett:** dry or dryish natural (unsugared) wine of distinct personality and distinguishing lightness. Can occasionally be sublime – esp with a few yrs' age.

6 **Spätlese:** stronger, often sweeter than KABINETT. Full-bodied. Today many top SPÄTLESEN are Trocken or completely dry.

7 **Auslese:** sweeter, sometimes stronger than Spätlese, often with honey-like flavours, intense and long-lived. Occasionally dry and weighty.

8 **Beerenauslese (BA):** v. sweet, sometimes strong and intense. Can be superb.

9 **Eiswein:** from naturally frozen grapes of BA or TBA quality: concentrated, sharpish and v. sweet. Some examples are extreme and unharmonious.

10 **Trockenbeerenauslese (TBA):** intensely sweet and aromatic; alcohol slight. Extraordinary and everlasting.

RÜDESHEIM. Johannes Eser produces RIES in perfect balance between ripeness and steely acidity.

Josephshöfer Mos 83 90 02 03 05 08 09 11 12 13 14 GROSSE LAGE v'yd at GRAACH, the sole property of KESSELSTATT. Harmonious, berry-flavoured RIES, both dry and sweet. Like its neighbours, under threat from new Autobahn.

Jost, Toni M Rh ★★★ Leading estate in BACHARACH with monopoly Hahn, now led by Cecilia J. Aromatic RIES with nerve, and recent trials with PINOT N. Family also run an estate at WALLUF (RHG).

Juliusspital Frank ★★★ Ancient WÜRZBURG charity with top v'yds all over FRANK. Look for *dry Silvaners* (they age well), RIES and top blend BT. House style usually emphasizes power over elegance.

Kabinett *See* "Germany's quality levels" box above. Germany's unique featherweight contribution, but with climate change ever more difficult to produce.

Kaiserstuhl Bad r w Outstanding district with notably warm climate and volcanic soil. Renowned above all for SPÄTBURGUNDER and GRAUBURGUNDER.

Kanzem Mos ★★★ 90 97 99 01 04 05 07 08 09 10 11 12 13 14 Saar village with steep GROSSE LAGE v'yd on slate and weathered Rotliegend (red rock): Altenberg. Growers: BISCHÖFLICHE WEINGÜTER, OTHEGRAVEN, *Van Volxem*.

Karlsmühle Mos ★★★ Estate with two Lorenzhöfer monopoly sites. classic RUWER RIES.

Karthäuserhof Mos ★★★★ 90 93 95 97 99 01 04 05 07 08 09 10 11 12 13 14 Outstanding RUWER estate at Eitelsbach with monopoly v'yd Karthäuserhofberg. Easily recognized by bottles with only a neck label. Christoph Tyrell has now handed over to a cousin.

Kasel Mos ★★→★★★ Flowery and well-ageing RUWER Valley RIES. GROSSE LAG v'yds: Kehrnagel, Nies'chen. Top growers: Beulwitz, BISCHÖFLICHE WEINGÜTE Karlsmühle, *Kesselstatt*.

Kauer M Rh ★★→★★★ Family estate at BACHARACH. Crystalline, aromatic RIE organically grown. Randolf Kauer is professor of organic viticulture at GEISENHEIM

Keller, Weingut Rhh ★★★→★★★★ Superlative, powerful GG RIES from Dalsheime Hubacker and pricey Ries called G-Max from an undisclosed single v'yd. Now also Ries from NIERSTEIN (Hipping and Pettenthal).

Kesseler, August Rhg ★★→★★★★ Passionate grower; fine SPÄTBURGUNDER from ASSMANNSHAUSEN, RÜDESHEIM. Also v.gd classic-style RIES (Rüdesheim, LORCH).

Kesselstatt, Reichsgraf von Mos ★★→★★★★ 35 ha of top v'yds on the MOS and both its tributaries, incl a remarkable stake in SCHARZHOFBERG, led by quality-obsesse Annegret Reh-Gartner. JOSEPHSHÖFER at GRAACH a monopoly.

Kiedrich Rhg w ★★→★★★★ Village linked inseparably to the WEIL estate; top v'y Gräfenberg. Other growers (eg. FRICKE, PRINZ VON HESSEN, Knyphausen) own onl small plots here.

Kloster Eberbach Rhg Glorious 12th-century Cistercian abbey in HATTENHEIM wit iconic STEINBERG, domicile of HESSISCHE STAATSWEINGÜTER.

Knipser, Weingut Pfz ★★★→★★★★ Northern PFZ family estate specializing i barrique-aged SPÄTBURGUNDER, straightforward RIES (GG Steinbuckel) and Cuvé X (a Bordeaux blend).

Koehler-Ruprecht, Weingut Pfz ★★→★★★ 97 99 01 02 05 07 08 09 10 11 1 Kallstadt estate, formerly known for Bernd Philippi's traditional winemaking esp RIES Saumagen. Now in new hands: Philippi has left.

Kraichgau Bad Small district se of Heidelberg. Top growers: Burg Ravensburg Heitlinger, HOENSBROECH, Hummel.

Kreuzberg Ahr ★★★ Ludwig Kreuzberg has made a name for minerally, not over alcoholic, distinctly cool-climate SPÄTBURGUNDER.

Krone, Weingut Rhg ★★→★★★ 97 99 02 05 06 07 08 09 10 11 12 Estate i ASSMANNSHAUSEN, run by WEGELER; some of best and oldest SPÄTBURGUNDER v'yds i the GROSSE LAGE Höllenberg. Sublime reds; whites less exciting.

Kühling-Gillot Rhh ★★★ Caroline Gillot and husband HO Spanier (of Battenfeld Spanier estate) produce powerful RIES from OPPENHEIM, NIERSTEIN and NACKENHEIM

Kühn, Peter Jakob Rhg ★★★ Excellent estate in OESTRICH led by P J Kühn and son Obsessive bio v'yd management and long macerations shape *nonconformist bu exciting* RIES. Sensational 13 Lenchen TBA.

Kuhn, Philipp Pfz ★★★ Reliable producer in Laumersheim. Dry RIES rich an harmonious, barrel-aged SPÄTBURGUNDER succulent, complex, potent. Rich barre fermented VIOGNIER a novelty.

Künstler Rhg ★★★ 90 97 01 05 08 09 10 11 12 13 Superb dry RIES (even in difficul yrs like 13) in GROSSE LAGE sites at HOCHHEIM, Kostheim, and now on other side o RHG at RÜDESHEIM.

Healthy vineyard soil has 25,000 kg of living matter/ha.

Laible, Alexander ★★→★★★ New DURBACH estate of ANDREAS LAIBLE's (*see* next entry younger son; aromatic dry RIES and WEISSBURGUNDER. 2012 Ries Tausend Stern is spontaneously fermented and comes close to the style of natural wine (*see A Little Learning).

Laible, Andreas Bad ★★★ Crystalline dry RIES from DURBACH's Plauelrain v'yd and g SCHEUREBE and GEWÜRZ. Andreas Sr hands over to Andreas Jr.

Landwein Now "ggA". *See* "Germany's quality levels" box on p.163.

Langwerth von Simmern Rhg ★★→★★★ Famous Eltville estate; traditional wine making. Top v'yds: Baiken, Mannberg (monopoly), MARCOBRUNN. Back on form.

ᴸauer Mos ★★★ Florian Lauer works hard to correct the errors of the 1971 wine law, with parcel selections from the huge AYLER Kupp v'yd. Best: Schonfels, Stirn and Kern.

Leitz, Josef Rhg ★★★ Growing RÜDESHEIM family estate for rich but elegant dry and sweet RIES, esp from classified v'yds in the Rüdesheimer Berg.

Liebfrauenstift-Kirchenstück Rhh A walled v'yd in city of Worms producing flowery RIES renowned for its harmony. Producers: Gutzler, Schembs. Not to be confused with Liebfrauenmilch, a cheap and tasteless imitation.

Only 22 per cent of Mosels are dry; 64 per cent are sweet, 14 per cent Halbtrocken.

Loewen, Carl Mos ★★★ Rich RIES, dry and sweet, from Leiwen (GROSSE LAGE Laurentiuslay), Thörnicher Ritsch and Longuicher Maximin Herrenberg (v'yd planted 1896). Entry-level Ries Varidor excellent value.

Loosen, Weingut Dr. M-M ★★→★★★ 90 97 01 02 04 05 08 09 10 11 12 13 14 The charismatic Ernie Loosen produces traditional RIES from old vines in BERNKASTEL, ERDEN, GRAACH, ÜRZIG, WEHLEN. Erdener Prälat AUSLESE is cultish. Reliable Dr. L Ries is from bought-in grapes. *See also* WOLF (PFZ), Chateau Ste Michelle (Washington State).

Lorch Rhg ★→★★★ Village in extreme w of the RHG. Sharply mineral wines, now re-discovered. Best: Chat Sauvage, FRICKE, Johanninger, von Kanitz, KESSELER.

Löwenstein, Fürst Frank, Rhg ★★★ Princely estate with holdings in RHG and FRANK, now led by gifted young oenologist Bastian Hamdorf. Classic Rhg RIES from HALLGARTEN and terroir-driven *Silvaner and Ries from ultra-steep v'yd Homburger Kallmuth*.

Marcobrunn Rhg Historic v'yd in Erbach; potentially one of Germany's v. best. Contemporary wines scarcely match its past fame.

Markgräflerland Bad District s of Freiburg, historically possession of the Markgraf (Margrave) von BADEN. Typical GUTEDEL a pleasant companion for local cuisine.

Maximin Grünhaus Mos ★★★★ 83 90 97 98 99 01 05 07 08 09 11 12 13 14 Supreme RUWER estate at Mertesdorf. V. traditional winemaking shapes herb-scented, *delicate, long-lived Ries*. Now WEISSBURGUNDER, PINOT N too.

Meyer Näkel Ahr ★★★→★★★★ Father-daughter team make fine AHR Valley SPÄTBURGUNDER that exemplify a modern oak-aged (nevertheless mineral) style.

Mittelhaardt Pfz The n-central and best part of the PFZ, incl DEIDESHEIM, FORST, RUPPERTSBERG, WACHENHEIM; largely planted with RIES.

Mittelmosel The central and best part of the MOS, a RIES eldorado, incl BERNKASTEL, BRAUNEBERG, GRAACH, PIESPORT, WEHLEN, etc.

Mittelrhein M Rh ★★→★★★ The n and dramatically scenic Rhine area nr tourist-magnet Loreley. Best villages: BACHARACH, BOPPARD. Delicate yet *steely Ries, underrated* and underpriced. Many gd sites lie fallow.

Molitor, Markus M-M ★★★ 60 ha of prime v'yds, esp at ZELTINGEN and throughout the M-M. Powerful dry and magisterial sweet RIES; acclaimed SPÄTBURGUNDER.

Mosbacher Pfz ★★★ Some of best GG RIES of FORST: rather refined than massive. Traditional ageing in big oak casks.

Mosel Wine-growing area, which was formerly known as Mosel-Saar-Ruwer. From 2007, all wines from Saarburg to Koblenz are labelled as Mosel, even though growing conditions on the RUWER and SAAR tributaries may be v. different from the M-M. 60% RIES.

Moselland, Winzergenossenschaft Mos Huge MOS co-op, at BERNKASTEL, after mergers with co-ops in the NA and PFZ. 3,290 members, 2,400 ha. Little is above average.

Müller-Catoir, Weingut Pfz ★★→★★★★ Aged AUSLESEN, BA, TBA 83 90 97 98 01 can be delicious; 2011 Schlössel RIESLANER TBA.

Nackenheim Rhh ★→★★★★ NIERSTEIN neighbour with GROSSE LAGE Rothenberg

> **Fair 'n Green**
>
> Perhaps only in Germany would a group of growers measure their environmental impact in such detail. The group is called Fair 'n Green, and it has a complex system of plus and minus points to find the best solution for each estate. (Questions involve, eg. balancing organics with extra diesel used if organics means more spraying.) After only 2 yrs, the list of members of Fair 'n Green is already impressive: BREUER, BUSCH, DÖNNHOFF, FRICKE, R HAART, HEYMANN-LÖWENSTEIN, KARTHÄUSERHOF, KUHN, MEYER-NÄKEL, STODDEN, SANKT-URBANSHOF.

on red shale, famous for RHH's richest RIES, superb TBA. Top growers inc *Gunderloch*, KÜHLING-GILLOT.

Nahe 01 05 07 08 09 11 12 13 14 Tributary of the Rhine and dynamic wine region. A handful of top estates, dozens of lesser-known producers, excellent value. Various soils: grey and green slate, volcanic rock, Rotliegend (red loam), gravel, limestone. Best RIES have almost MOS-like raciness.

Naturrein "Naturally pure": designation on old labels (pre-1971), indicating that wine had been vinified and aged with as little technical intervention as possible, esp without chaptalizing (enrichment with sugar before fermentation). PRÄDIKATSWEIN meant to replace *Naturrein* from 1971 – but doesn't prohibit the use of eg. selected yeasts, fining, filtration. In light of "natural wine" (*see* A Little Learning), the *Naturrein* concept seems more modern than ever.

Neipperg, Graf von Würt ★★★ A noble estate in Schwaigern: reds (LEMBERGER and SPÄTBURGUNDER) of grace and purity. A scion of the family, Count Stephan von Neipperg, makes wine at Château Canon la Gaffelière in St-Émilion and elsewhere.

Niederhausen Na ★★→★★★★ 90 97 01 02 04 05 07 08 09 11 12 13 14 Village in the middle NA Valley. Complex RIES from steep GROSSE LAGE v'yds: Felsensteyer, Hermannsberg, Hermannshöhle, Kertz. Growers: CRUSIUS, DÖNNHOFF, GUT HERMANNSBERG, Mathern, von Racknitz, Jakob Schneider.

Nierstein Rhh ★→★★★★ 90 97 01 04 05 07 08 09 11 12 13 14 Rich but balanced RIES, both dry and sweet. GROSSE LAGE v'yds: Brudersberg, Hipping, Oelberg, Orbel, Pettenthal. Growers incl Gehring, GUNDERLOCH, Guntrum, HEYL ZU HERRNSHEIM, KELLER, KÜHLING-GILLOT, Manz, Schätzel, ST-ANTONY, Strub. *Beware Grosslage Gutes Domtal*: a supermarket deception.

Ockfen Mos ★★→★★★ Village that shapes sturdy, intense SAAR RIES from GROSSE LAGE v'yd Bockstein. Growers: OTHEGRAVEN, SANKT URBANS-HOF, WAGNER, *Zilliken*.

Odinstal, Weingut Pfz ★★→★★★ The highest v'yd of PFZ, 150m above WACHENHEIM. Bio farming and low-tech vinification bring pure RIES, SILVANER, GEWURZ. Harvest often extends into Nov.

Oechsle Scale for sugar content of grape juice.

Oestrich Rhg ★★→★★★ Exemplary steely RIES and fine AUSLESEN from GROSSE LAGE v'yds: Doosberg, Lenchen, St. Nikolaus. Top growers: August Eser, KÜHN, Querbach, SPREITZER, WEGELER.

Oppenheim Rhh ★→★★★ Town s of NIERSTEIN, GROSSE LAGE Kreuz, Sackträger. Growers: Heyden, Kissinger, KÜHLING-GILLOT, Manz. Spectacular 13th-century church.

Ortenau Bad (r) w District around and s of city of Baden-Baden. Mainly Klingelberger (RIES) and SPÄTBURGUNDER from granite soils. Top villages: DURBACH, Neuweier, Waldulm.

Ortswein The 2nd rank up in the VDP's pyramid of qualities: a village wine, rather than a single v'yd.

Othegraven, Weingut von Mos ★★★ Fine KANZEM estate (superb GROSSE LAGE

Altenberg). Since TV star Günther Jauch took over in 2010 wines have gained in precision. 2012 SPÄTLESE ALTE REBEN and AUSLESE raise the bar. Also parcels in OCKFEN (Bockstein) and forgotten Herrenberg at Wawern.

alatinate English for PFZ.

falz r w 90 01 05 07 08 09 11 12 13 14 Usually balmy region bordering Alsace in s and RHH to n. Its MITTELHAARDT area is the source of full-bodied, mostly dry RIES. Southerly SÜDLICHE WEINSTRASSE is better suited to PINOT varieties.

iesport M-M ★→★★★★ 90 92 97 01 02 03 04 05 07 08 09 11 12 13 Tiny village with famous amphitheatre of GROSSE LAGE v'yds (esp Domherr, Goldtröpfchen). At best glorious, rich, aromatic RIES. Growers: GRANS-FASSIAN, Joh Haart, JULIAN HAART, R HAART, Kurt Hain, KESSELSTATT, SANKT URBANS-HOF. Avoid GROSSLAGE Michelsberg.

rädikat Legally defined special attributes or qualities. *See* QMP.

rinz von Hessen Rhg ★★★→★★★★ Glorious wines of vibrancy and precision from historic JOHANNISBERG estate, esp at SPÄTLESE and above, and mature vintages.

rüm, J J Mos ★★★★ 71 76 83 88 89 90 94 95 96 97 98 99 01 02 03 04 05 07 08 09 10 11 12 13 14 Legendary WEHLEN estate; also GRAACH and BERNKASTEL. Delicate but extremely long-lived wines with astonishing finesse and distinctive character. Dr. Manfred Prüm now joined by daughter Katharina.

rüm, S A Mos ★★→★★★ More popular and less traditional in style than WEHLEN neighbour J J PRÜM. Sound, sometimes inconsistent wines.

Qualitätswein bestimmter Anbaugebiete (QbA) Middle quality of German wine, with sugar added before fermentation (as in French *chaptalization*), but controlled as to areas, grapes, etc. New name: gU (*see* box p.158) is little improvement.

Qualitätswein mit Prädikat (QmP) Top category, for all wines ripe enough not to need sugaring (KABINETT to TBA).

andersacker Frank ★★→★★★ Village s of WÜRZBURG with GROSSE LAGE: Pfülben. Top growers: BÜRGERSPITAL, JULIUSSPITAL, STAATLICHER HOFKELLER, SCHMITT'S KINDER, Störrlein & Krenig.

atzenberger M Rh ★★→★★★ Estate making racy dry and off-dry RIES in BACHARACH; best from GROSSE LAGE v'yds: Posten and Steeger St-Jost. Gd SEKT too.

auenthal Rhg ★★→★★★★ Once the RHG's most expensive RIES. *Spicy, austere but complex* from inland slopes. GROSSE LAGE v'yds: Baiken, Rothenberg. Top growers: BREUER (with monopoly Nonnenberg), HESSISCHE STAATSWEINGÜTER, A Eser, LANGWERTH VON SIMMERN.

ebholz, Ökonomierat Pfz ★★★→★★★★ Top SÜDLICHE WEINSTRASSE estate known for bone-dry, minerally RIES, eg. GG Im Sonnenschein, Ganz Horn. Legendary Kastanienbusch GG 04 05 07' 08' 09 11' 12 from red schist soils (no 2013). Focused CHARD; tight, age-worthy SPÄTBURGUNDER.

estsüsse Unfermented grape sugar remaining in (or in cheap wines added to) wine to give it sweetness. Can range from 1 g/litre in a TROCKEN wine to 300 g in a TBA.

Rheingau (r) w 90 97 99 01 04 05 07 08 09 10 11 12 13 The only Rhine region with s-facing slopes bordering the river. Classic and substantial RIES, famous for steely acidity, and small amounts of delicate SPÄTBURGUNDER. Also the centre of SEKT production.

Rheinhessen (r) w 05 07 08 09 11 12 13 14 Germany's largest region, between Mainz and Worms. Much dross, but also top RIES from NACKENHEIM, NIERSTEIN, etc. Remarkable spurt in quality in formerly unknown areas, from growers such as KELLER, WITTMANN in s, WAGNER-STEMPEL in w.

Richter, Weingut Max Ferd M-M ★★→★★★ Reliable M-M estate, at Mülheim. Esp gd RIES KABINETT and SPÄTLESEN: full and aromatic.

Rings, Weingut Pfz ★★→★★★ Brothers Steffen and Andreas Rings are shooting stars in PFZ: remarkable dry RIES esp from Kallstadt (Steinacker, Saumagen).

Ruck, Johann Frank ★★★ Spicy SILVANER, RIES, SCHEUREBE, TRAMINER from IPHOFEN
STEIGERWALD. Recently less bone-dry than before.

Rüdesheim Rhg ★★→★★★★ 90 01 04 05 08 09 10 11 12 13 14 Rhine resort wit
outstanding GROSSE LAGE v'yds on slate: the four best (Roseneck, Rottlan
Schlossberg, Kaiserstfeinfels) are called Rüdesheimer Berg. Full-bodie
wines, floral-flavoured, often remarkable in off-yrs. Best growers incl *Breue*
Chat Sauvage, Corvers-Kauter, *Johannishof*, KESSELER, HESSISCHE STAATSWEINGÜTE
KÜNSTLER, LEITZ, Ress.

Ruppertsberg Pfz ★★→★★★ MITTELHAARDT village known for elegant RIES. Growe
incl BASSERMANN-JORDAN, Biffar, BUHL, BÜRKLIN-WOLF, CHRISTMANN, DR. DEINHARI
VON WINNING.

Ruwer Mos 90 97 99 01 02 03 04 05 07 08 09 10 11 12 13 Tributary of MOS nr TRIE
renowned for delicate long-lived sweet RIES and quaffable light dry ones. Be
growers: Beulwitz, Karlsmühle, KARTHÄUSERHOF, KESSELSTATT, MAXIMIN GRÜNHAUS.

Saale-Unstrut 09 11 12 (13) Northerly region around confluence of these two rive
nr Leipzig. Terraced v'yds have Cistercian origins. Mainly white; quality leader
Böhme, Born, Gussek, Kloster Pforta, Lützkendorf, Pawis.

Saar Mos 90 93 94 97 99 01 02 04 05 07 08 09 10 11 12 (13) 14 Hill-lined tributa
of the MOS, colder climate. The most brilliant, austere, steely RIES of all. Village
incl: AYL, KANZEM, Ockfen, SAARBURG, Serrig, WILTINGEN (SCHARZHOFBERG).

Saarburg Mos SAAR Valley small town. Growers: WAGNER, ZILLIKEN, GROSSE LAGE: Rausc
Sachsen 03 05 08 09 11 12 13 14 Region in the Elbe Valley around Dresdei
Characterful dry whites. Best growers: Aust, Richter, *Schloss Proschwitz*, Schlos
Wackerbarth, Schuh, Schwarz, ZIMMERLING.

**Sachsen produces the highest percentage of dry wines (81 per cent) of any of th
German regions.**

St-Antony Rhh ★★→★★★ NIERSTEIN estate with exceptional v'yds. Improvemen
through new owner (same as HEYL ZU HERRNSHEIM).

Salm, Prinz zu Na, Rhh Owner of Schloss Wallhausen ★★→★★★ in NA and Vill
Sachsen ★→★★ in RHH. RIES at Schloss Wallhausen (organic) has made g
progress recently.

Salwey Bad ★★★ Leading KAISERSTUHL estate at Oberrotweil. Konrad Salwey pick
early for freshness. Best: Henkenberg and Eichberg GRAUBURGUNDER, Kirchber
SPÄTBURGUNDER Rappen (fermented with stems).

Sankt Urbans-Hof Mos ★★★ Large family estate based in Leiwen, v'yds along M-
and SAAR. Limpid RIES, impeccably pure and racy. Magnificent 2013 PIESPOR
Goldtröpfchen TBA.

Sauer, Horst Frank ★★★ The finest exponent of ESCHERNDORF's top v'yd Lump. Rac
straightforward *dry Silvaner* and RIES, sensational TBA.

Sauer, Rainer Frank ★★★ Rising family estate at ESCHERNDORF. Complex dry SILVANE
from vibrant KABINETT to creamy, full-bodied SPÄTLESEN.

Schaefer, Willi Mos ★★★ The finest grower of GRAACH (but only 4 ha). MOS RIES at it
best: pure, crystalline, feather-light, rewarding at all quality levels.

Schäfer-Fröhlich Na ★★★ NA family estate known for spontaneously fermented RIE
of great intensity. Superb range of GG incl Bockenau Felseneck and Stromberg
SCHLOSSBÖCKELHEIM Kupfergrube and Felsenberg. Breathtaking EISWEIN too.

Scharzhofberg Mos ★★→★★★★ Superlative SAAR v'yd: rare coincidence of micro
climate, soil and human intelligence to bring about the perfection of RIES. To
estates: BISCHÖFLICHE WEINGÜTER, EGON MÜLLER, VON HÖVEL, KESSELSTATT, VAN VOLXEM.

Schlossböckelheim Na ★★→★★★★ 97 01 02 04 05 08 09 11 12 13 14 Village with to
NA v'yds, incl GROSSE LAGE Felsenberg, Kupfergrube. Firm, demanding RIES tha
ages well. Top growers: CRUSIUS, DÖNNHOFF, GUT HERMANNSBERG, SCHÄFER-FRÖHLICH.

Hochmoselbrücke
The 160m-high Autobahn bridge at Ürzig may never be finished. Geologists have accused the government of criminal irresponsibiity in building it on unstable ground. It was always a folly, and has already altered the ecology of some of Germany's best v'yds, such as Wehlener Sonnenuhr. Fingers crossed....

Schloss Johannisberg Rhg ★★→★★★ Historic RHG estate, 100% RIES, owned by Henkell (Oetker group). Usually v.gd SPÄTLESE Grünlack ("green sealing-wax"), AUSLESE Rosalack. V.gd 13 GG.

Schloss Lieser M-M ★★★ Thomas Haag, Wilhelm Haag's elder son (*see* FRITZ HAAG) produces pure, racy RIES from underrated Niederberg Helden v'yd, as well as from plots in BRAUNEBERG.

Schloss Proschwitz Sachs ★★ Prince Lippe's resurrected estate at Meissen, leading former East Germany in quality; esp with *dry Weissburgunder*, GRAUBURGUNDER. A great success.

Schloss Reinhartshausen Rhg ★★ Famous estate in Erbach, formerly in Prussian royal family, changed hands in 2013, lost VDP membership.

Schloss Vollrads Rhg ★★ One of the greatest historic RHG estates, now owned by a bank. RIES in rather commercial style.

Schmitt's Kinder Frank ★★→★★★ Family estate in RANDERSACKER known for classical dry SILVANER (superb 2013 Pfülben GG), barrel-aged SPÄTBURGUNDER, sweet RIESLANER.

Schnaitmann Würt ★★★ Excellent barrel-aged reds from WÜRT: SPÄTBURGUNDER, LEMBERGER from GROSSE LAGE Lämmler v'yd. In conversion to organic farming.

Schneider, Cornelia and Reinhold Bad ★★★ Family estate in Endingen, KAISERSTUHL. Age-worthy SPÄTBURGUNDERS 00 01 02 05 07 08 09 10 11 denoted by letters – R for volcanic soil, C for loess – and old-fashioned RULÄNDER.

Schneider, Markus Pfz ★★ Shooting star in Ellerstadt, PFZ. A full range of soundly produced, trendily labelled wines.

Schönberger A minor RIES in three movements: Pesto, Aldente and Piccante *ma non troppo*.

Schoppenwein Café (or bar) wine, ie. wine by the glass.

Schwarzer Adler Bad ★★→★★★ One-star-restaurant at Oberbergen, KAISERSTUHL, and wine estate for burgundy-influenced GRAU-, WEISS-, SPÄTBURGUNDER. Spectacular new cellar in 2013.

Schwegler, Albrecht Würt ★★★ Small estate known for gd, unusual red blends, such as Granat (MERLOT, ZWEIGELT, LEMBERGER and others). Worth looking for. Fancy off-dry KERNER too.

Sekt German sparkling wine, v. variable in quality. Bottle fermentation is not mandatory. Sekt specialists incl Raumland, Schembs, Schloss Vaux, Solter, S Steinmetz, Wilhelmshof.

Selbach-Oster M-M ★★★ Scrupulous ZELTINGEN estate with excellent v'yd portfolio, best-known for sweet PRÄDIKAT wines.

Sonnenuhr Mos Sundial. Name of several v'yds, esp GROSSE LAGE sites at WEHLEN and ZELTINGEN threatened by new Autobahn.

Spätlese Late-harvest. One level riper and usually also one sweeter than KABINETT. Gd examples age at least 7 yrs. Spätlese TROCKEN designation is now about to be given up by VDP members: a shame.

Spreitzer Rhg ★★★→★★★★ Andreas and Bernd Spreitzer produce deliciously racy, harmonious RIES (both dr sw), vinified with patience in FUDER casks. V'yds in HATTENHEIM, OESTRICH, Winkel.

Staatlicher Hofkeller Frank ★★ The Bavarian state domain. 120 ha of the finest

FRANK v'yds, with spectacular cellars under the great báɾuɋuø Rɐsidenz at WÜRZBURG. Quality sound but rarely exciting.

Staatsweingut / Staatliche Weinbaudomäne State wine estates or domains exist in BAD (IHRINGEN, Meersburg), WÜRT (Weinsberg), RHG (HESSISCHE STAATSWEINGÜTER), RHH (OPPENHEIM), PFZ (Neustadt) MOS (TRIER). Some have been privatized in recent yrs, eg. at Marienthal (AHR) and NIEDERHAUSEN (NA).

Steigerwald Frank (r) w District in e FRANK. V'yds at considerable altitude; powerful SILVANER, RIES. Best: Castell, Roth, RUCK, WELTNER, WIRSCHING.

Steinberg Rhg ★★★ Famous HATTENHEIM walled RIES v'yd on phyllite schist, a German Clos de Vougeot, planted by Cistercian monks 700 yrs ago. The monopoly of HESSISCHE STAATSWEINGÜTER.

Steinwein Frank Wine from WÜRZBURG's best v'yd, Stein. Goethe's favourite. In 2014 hail decimated crop few weeks before harvest.

Stodden Ahr ★★★ Gerhard Stodden died in 2013, but Alexander continues his father's work: AHR SPÄTBURGUNDER with a burgundian touch.

Südliche Weinstrasse Pfz r w District name for s PFZ. Quality has forged ahead in past 25 yrs. Best growers: BECKER, Leiner, Münzberg, REBHOLZ, Siegrist, WEHRHEIM.

Tauberfranken Bad (r) w Underrated cool-climate district of ne BAD: FRANK-style SILVANER, RIES from limestone soils. Frost a problem. Best grower: Schlör.

Thanisch, Weingut Dr. M-M ★★→★★★ BERNKASTEL estate, founded 1636, famous for its share of the Doctor v'yd. After family split-up in 1988 two homonymous estates with similar qualities: Erben (heirs) Müller-Burggraef, Erben Thanisch.

Traisen Na ★★★ Small NA village, incl GROSSE LAGE v'yds Bastei and Rotenfels.

Trier Mos Great city of Roman origin, on MOS, between RUWER and SAAR. Big charitable estates have cellars here among awesome Roman remains.

Trittenheim M-M ★★→★★★ 01 04 05 07 08 09 11 12 13 14 Racy, attractive M-M wines. GROSSE LAGE v'yd Apotheke too varied; only a few v gd plots. Growers: A CLÜSSERATH, E Clüsserath, Clüsserath-Weiler, GRANS-FASSIAN, Milz.

Trocken Dry. Used to be defined as max 9 g/l unfermented sugar. Now, under new EU regulations, an additional tolerance of +2 g/l. Generally the further s in Germany, the more Trocken wines.

Trockenbeerenauslese (TBA) Sweetest, most expensive category of German wine, extremely rare, with concentrated honey flavour. Made from selected shrivelled grapes affected by noble rot (botrytis). Half bottles a gd idea.

Ürzig M-M ★★★★ 71 83 90 93 94 95 96 97 01 02 04 05 07 08 09 10 11 12 13 14 Village on red sandstone and red slate, famous for ungrafted old vines and unique spicy RIES. GROSSE LAGE v'yd: Würzgarten. Growers: Berres, Erbes, Christoffel, LOOSEN, Mönchhof, Rebenhof, WEINS-PRÜM. Threatened by unneeded Autobahn bridge 160m high.

Van Volxem Mos ★★→★★★ Historical SAAR estate revived by brewery heir Roman Niewodniczanski. Low yields from top sites (SCHARZHOFBERG, KANZEM Altenberg, WILTINGEN Gottesfuss), mainly dry or off-dry wines. Recently lower alcohol and trials of sweet and nobly sweet styles.

Verband Deutscher Prädikatsweingüter (VDP) The pace-making association of

---

Where do *Kirschessigfliege* go in winter?

They're fruit flies to you and me. There can be clouds of them in a ripe v'yd; and in 2014 they were joined by *Drosophila suzukii*, a heavyweight species from Asia. You can't spray insecticides close to harvest time, so growers tried traps filled with vinegar and washing-up liquid, or they sprayed kaolin – a china clay that makes grape skins slippery. Luckily, *Drosophila suzukii* has a preference for dark-coloured grapes: RIES was less affected than eg. DORNFELDER.

200 premium growers. Look for its eagle insignia on wine labels, and for the GROSSE LAGE logo on wines from classified v'yds. VDP wine usually a gd bet. President: Steffen CHRISTMANN.

Vollenweider Mos ★★★ Daniel Vollenweider from Switzerland has revived the Wolfer Goldgrube v'yd nr Traben-Trarbach (since 2000). *Excellent Ries*, but only in v. small quantities.

Wachenheim Pfz ★★★ Celebrated village with, according to VDP, NO GROSSE LAGE v'yds. See what you think. Top growers incl Biffar, BÜRKLIN-WOLF, ODINSTAL, Karl Schäfer and WOLF.

Deterrent for destructive wild boar in vineyards: tigers. Worked in Sumatran rubber plantations...

Wagner, Dr. Mos ★★→★★★ Estate with v'yds in OCKFEN and Saarstein led by young GEISENHEIM graduate Christiane W. SAAR RIES with purity and freshness.

Wagner-Stempel Rhh ★★★ RHH estate nr NA border in obscure Siefersheim. Excellent RIES, both GG (Heerkretz) and nobly sweet.

Walluf Rhg ★★★ Underrated village, first with important v'yds as one leaves Wiesbaden, going w. GROSSE LAGE v'yd: Walkenberg. Growers: *J B Becker, Jost.*

Wegeler M-M, Rhg ★★→★★★ Important family estates in OESTRICH and BERNKASTEL plus a stake in the famous KRONE estate of ASSMANNSHAUSEN. Gd in quantity and quality. Geheimrat J brand was dry RIES pioneer in the 70s and maintains v. high standards.

Wehlen M-M ★★★→★★★★ 90 93 94 95 96 97 98 01 02 03 04 05 07 08 09 10 11 12 13 Wine village with legendary steep SONNENUHR v'yd expressing RIES from slate soils at its v. best. Sweet wines from SPÄTLESE upwards last for decades. Top growers: Kerpen, KESSELSTATT, LOOSEN, MOLITOR, J J PRÜM, S A PRÜM, RICHTER, SELBACH-OSTER, Studert-Prüm, WEGELER, WEINS-PRÜM. New Autobahn above v'yds will have unknown influence.

Wehrheim, Weingut Dr. Pfz ★★★ Top family estate of SÜDLICHE WEINSTRASSE. Organic; mineral, v. dry wines, eg. WEISSBURGUNDER Muschelkalk, RIES, SPÄTBURGUNDER from GROSSE LAGE Kastanienbusch.

Weil, Robert Rhg ★★★→★★★★ 17 37 49 59 75 90 97 01 02 04 05 07 08 09 10 11 12 13 14 Outstanding estate in KIEDRICH owned by Suntory of Japan. Superb EISWEIN, TBA 13', BA; entry-level wines more variable. Gräfenberg on phyllite schist is best of three classified v'yds.

Weingart M Rh ★★★ Outstanding estate at Spay, v'yds in BOPPARD (esp Hamm Feuerlay). Refined, mineral RIES, low-tech in style, superb value.

Weingut Wine estate.

Weins-Prüm, Dr. M-M ★★★ Small estate based at WEHLEN. Superb v'yds in M-M. Scrupulous winemaking from owner Bert Selbach, who favours a taut and mineral style.

Weissherbst Pale pink wine, made from a single variety, often SPÄTBURGUNDER. V. variable quality.

Weltner, Paul Frank ★★→★★★ STEIGERWALD family estate. Densely structured, age-worthy SILVANER from underrated Rödelseer Küchenmeister v'yd and neighbouring plots at IPHOFEN.

Wiltingen Mos ★★→★★★★ Heartland of the SAAR. SCHARZHOFBERG crowns a series of GROSSE LAGE v'yds (Braune Kupp, Kupp, Braunfels, Gottesfuss). Top growers: BISCHÖFLICHE WEINGÜTER, Le GALLAIS, EGON MÜLLER, KESSELSTATT, SANKT URBANS-HOF, Vols, VAN VOLXEM.

Winning, von Pfz ★★★→★★★★ DEIDESHEIM estate, incl former DR. DEINHARD. The von Winning label is used for top wines from Dr. Deinhard v'yds. *Ries of great purity* and terroir expression, slightly influenced by fermentation in new FUDER casks.

Winningen Mos ★★→★★★ Lower MOS town nr Koblenz; excellent dry RIES and TBA. GROSSE LAGE v'yds: Röttgen, Uhlen. Top growers: HEYMANN-LÖWENSTEIN, Knebel, Kröber, Richard Richter.

Wirsching, Hans Frank ★★★ Renowned estate in IPHOFEN. Sisters Andrea and Lena Wirsching continue to produce classically structured dry RIES and **Silvaner**, but spontaneously fermented Ries Sister Act sets a new tone. GROSSE LAGE v'yds: Julius-Echter-Berg, Kronsberg.

Wittmann Rhh ★★★ Philipp Wittmann has propelled this organic estate to the top ranks. Crystal-clear, mineral, dry RIES from QBA to GG (Morstein **04 05 06 07'** 08 11 12' 13).

Wöhrwag Würt ★★→★★★ Just outside Stuttgart, this estate produces succulent reds, but above all elegant dry RIES and brilliant EISWEIN.

Wolf J L Pfz ★★→★★★ WACHENHEIM estate, leased by Ernst LOOSEN of BERNKASTEL. Dry PFZ RIES (esp Forster Pechstein), sound and consistent rather than dazzling.

Württemberg r (w) 05 07 08 09 11 12 13 14 Red wine region around Stuttgart and Heilbronn, traditionally producing light TROLLINGER. But now ambitions are rising: LEMBERGER, SPÄTBURGUNDER can be v.gd. RIES needs altitude v'yds.

Würzburg Frank ★★→★★★★ Great baroque city on the Main, the centre of FRANK wine: dry RIES and esp SILVANER. Classified v'yds incl Innere Leiste, Stein, Stein-Harfe. Growers incl BÜRGERSPITAL, JULIUSSPITAL, Reiss, STAATLICHER HOFKELLER, Weingut am Stein.

Zell Mos ★→★★ Best-known lower MOS village, notorious for GROSSLAGE Schwarze Katz (Black Cat). A gd v'yd is Merler Königslay-Terrassen. Top grower: Kallfelz.

400,000 tourists visit the Middle Mosel each year; average stay is 3.5 days.

Zeltingen M-M ★★→★★★ Top but sometimes underrated MOS village nr WEHLEN. Rich though crisp RIES. GROSSE LAGE v'yd: SONNENUHR. Top growers: M MOLITOR, J J PRÜM, SELBACH-OSTER.

Ziereisen Bad ★★★ 03 04 05 07 08 09 10 11 12 13 14 Outstanding estate at Efringen-Kirchen in MARKGRÄFLERLAND, mainly GUTEDEL and PINOTS. Ex-carpenter Ziereisen is a genius; even entry-level wines show class. Best are SPÄTBURGUNDERS from small plots with dialect names: Schulen, Rhini. Jaspis is the name for old-vine selections. Newest sensation: Gutedel at €120 – and worth it.

Zilliken, Forstmeister Geltz Mos ★★★→★★★★ 93 94 95 96 97 99 01 02 04 05 07 08 09 10 11 12 13 14 Perfectionistic SAAR family estate led by Hans-Joachim Zilliken and daughter Dorothee. Produces intensely minerally **Ries from Saarburg Rausch** and OCKFEN Bockstein, incl superb AUSLESE, EISWEIN with excellent ageing potential. V.gd SEKT too.

Zimmerling, Klaus Sachs w ★★★ Small, perfectionistic estate, one of first to be est after the wall came down. Klaus works the steep Königlicher Weinberg (king's v'yd) at Pillnitz nr Dresden. RIES, sometimes off-dry, can be exquisite. Gd WEISSBURGUNDER, GRAUBURGUNDER, SCHEUREBE and TRAMINER too.

The clue is in the name
Faced with an unfamiliar bottle? If the v'yd name contains the word "Sonnenuhr" you know there's a sundial there: in other words it faces s. "Berg" usually means a steep slope: a plus. Schloss Johannisberg's "Grünlack", however, merely refers to the green sealing wax originally used on the bottle.

Luxembourg

You have to be an optimist to grow wine in Luxembourg. At least you had to be before global warming. An old chronicle describes the troubles at the beginning of the 20th century: "1900: a quarter of a normal crop. 1901: three-quarters. 1902: an eighth. 1903: three-quarters. 1904: three-quarters. 1905: not much. 1906: even less." The reason was not even phylloxera, but frost, hail, mildew, grape berry moths and rain at harvest time. Today, much has changed, and Luxembourg's growers have been on a roll of splendid vintages. 2013 was different, though: cold and wet, and a bit too much like the old days. Luckily, 2014 showed much better: very good in quantity and quality. The 1,270 ha of vines along the *Moselle luxembourgeoise* are a mix. There's more Rivaner (Müller-Thurgau, 27%), Auxerrois (14%) and Pinot Gris (14%) than Riesling (12%). Of course, Luxembourg wines are Mosel wines – but they are completely different from what we usually expect from Mosels. Here on the upper Mosel schist doesn't exist (it's mainly shell limestone). And in terms of quality, Pinot varieties rival or even surpass Riesling. Auxerrois is Luxembourg's speciality – even in 2013 it produced brilliant wines: Château Pauqué's oak-influenced Clos du Paradis is amazingly well-structured and fresh, and the co-op Vinsmoselle made two excellent 2013 Auxerrois: full-bodied Vieilles Vignes and salty Grevenmacher Rosenberg. Most whites have strong acidity and some sweetness – labels don't discern between dry and off-dry. A common term (but of little significance) is "Premier Grand Cru". More reliable are charter designations: Domaine et Tradition (seven producers) has the most credibility. Two more charters are Privat-Wenzer (Private Wine-growers) and Charta Schengen Prestige (designed to include producers in neighbouring areas of Germany and France).

Alice Hartmann ★★★ 09 10 11 12 13 Perfectionist in Wormeldange. Complex RIES from Luxembourg's best Ries v'yd Koeppchen, incl parcel selections. Delicate PINOT N, refined Crémant (Grande Cuvée, Rosé Brut). Owns v'yds in Burgundy (St-Aubin), on Middle Mosel (Trittenheim) and leases a plot in Scharzhofberg.

Aly Duhr ★★→★★★ Family estate at Ahn specializing in a somewhat sweeter style. V.gd PINOT GR from Machtum, gd off-dry RIES from Ahn and elegant Ries Vendange Tardive. Culinary barrel-aged PINOT BL.

Gales ★★→★★★ Reliable producer at Remich uniting the v'yds of Caves St Martin with family estate. Best from Gales are Crémant (Héritage Brut) and whites under the Domaine et Tradition label. Caves St Martin has a gd series called De Nos Rochers and produces Charta Schengen. It's worth seeing the old cellar labyrinth, dug into a shell-limestone *massif*.

Pauqué, Château ★★★ Well-crafted Luxembourg wines in an international style. V.gd CHARD, silky RIES Sous la Roche.

Schumacher-Knepper ★★→★★★ Lovely 2013 Lyra, a fruity PINOT N/ST LAURENT blend.

Sunnen-Hoffmann ★★★ Bio family estate at Remerschen, textbook AUXERROIS, seriously crafted RIES, tight, dry PINOT GR (Wintrange Hammelsberg). Brilliant 13s.

Vinsmoselle, Domaines ★→★★★ Union of co-ops. Premium label Art+Vin, Crémant Poll-Fabaire and active young grower's circle ("Jongwënzer").

Further producers at ★★ or ★★→★★★ incl Château de Schengen, Cep d'Or, Clos de Rochers, Duhr Frères/Clos Mon Vieux Moulin, Fränk Kayl, Paul Legill, Ruppert, Schmit-Fohl, Stronck-Pinnel.

Spain & Portugal

Abbreviations used in the text:

Alel	Alella	**P Vas**	País Vasco
Alen	Alentejo	**Pen**	Penedès
Alg	Algarve	**Pri**	Priorat
Alic	Alicante	**Rib del D**	Ribera
Ara	Aragón		del Duero
Bair	Bairrada	**Rio**	Rioja
Bei Int	Beira Interior	**R Ala**	Rioja Alavesa
Bier	Bierzo	**R Alt**	Rioja Alta
Bul	Bullas	**RB**	Rioja Baja
Các	Cádiz	**Rue**	Rueda
Can	Canaries	**Set**	Setúbal
C-La M	Castilla-	**Som**	Somontano
	La Mancha	**Tej**	Tejo
C y L	Castilla y León	**U-R**	Utiel-Requena
Cat	Catalonia	**V'cia**	Valencia
Cos del S	Costers del Segre	**Vin**	Vinho Verde
Emp	Empordà		
Gal	Galicia		
Jum	Jumilla		
La M	La Mancha		
Lis	Lisboa		
Mad	Madrid, Vinos de		
Mall	Mallorca		
Man	Manchuela		
Min	Minho		
Mont-M	Montilla-Moriles		
Mur	Murcia		
Nav	Navarra		

In the nicest possible way, Spain's winemakers are going backwards. The country relied for a long time – too long – on its top grape and best-selling red: Tempranillo and Rioja. It began to look like a one-trick pony. Not any more. Spain's winemakers are busy reviving old abandoned vineyards, and rediscovering old ways of viticulture and winemaking. For a few that means fermenting in clay amphorae, and for most it means returning to local grape varieties. Tempranillo Blanco, Maturana, Albillo and plenty more varieties are starting to make their special flavours felt: Spain is returning to its original regional diversity, making its wines well worth exploring. The classics are better than ever, but there's room for some new favourites too.

Portugal's white wines have come of age later than its reds, although the sins of over-oaking and overripeness were much less visited on whites. They are fresh, mineral and compellingly different. In Vinho Verde, leader of this white wine revolution, producers are planting more top grapes – Alvarinho, Loureiro and Avesso – to meet future demand. Reds too are being picked earlier, extracted more lightly and aged in

SPAIN

lder, larger oak barrels, allowing a much clearer focus on Portugal's
nique native grapes and terroir. Who knew the clear fruit flavours
f the great Port grapes? We do now.

Spain

Recent Rioja vintages

o14 After two small vintages, a return to form in quality and quantity.
 A long growing season with some rain during harvest.

o13 Cool, wet year, small harvest. Best wines show lively acidity.

o12 Good. One of lowest yields for two decades.

o11 Officially *excelente*; warm year, some jammy fruit, more concentrated
 than 2010.

o10 Also *excelente*. Perfect in many ways. Top wines still have many
 years ahead.

o09 Drink now, but will develop further. Some wines notably tannic.

pain & Portugal entries cross-reference each other

2008 Cool year, wines fresh and aromatic, a little lower in alcohol.
2007 Difficult vintage, not for laying down.
2006 Drinking well now. Light, fragrant vintage.
2005 A stand-out vintage on heels of 2004. Enjoy now or keep.
2004 Outstanding vintage. Drinking now, best have ten and more years ahead

Aalto Rib del D r ★★★★ Mariano Garcia, ex-VEGA SICILIA, plus ex-president of CONSEJ set out to make best TINTO FINO. Bold, dense wines, needing time. Aalto or' o 12 is dark, savoury; PS (from 200 small plots) concentrated, needs a decad Garcia's family wineries: Astrales (RIB DEL D), MAURO (C Y L), Maurodos (TORO Partner makes elegant Sei Solo, Preludio at Aalto.

Abadía Retuerta C y L r ★★→★★★ Just outside RIB DEL D; grand hotel in form monastery. Wines are modern, incl international grapes, steadily improving. C white blend DYA Le Domaine, welcome in red region. Single v'yds Valdeballó CABERNET, La Garduña SYRAH.

Agustí Torelló Mata Cat ★★→★★★ CAVA producer working with traditional varietie Kripta and GRAN RES Barrica stand out.

Alicante r w sw ★→★★ In the region, Gutierrez de la Vega leads with outstandin MOSCATEL and with Fondillón, fortified SOLERA-aged MONASTRELL. He has left th DO, disagreeing with the regulations. In dry hills, rich, spicy Monastrell thrive Top producers: ENRIQUE MENDOZA, Bernabé Navarro (natural wines pioneer, use clay *tinajas*), ARTADI, Bruno Prats, Salvador Poveda.

Angosto, El V'cia r w ★★ A promising project run by Cambra family in low-profi V'CIA DO. SAUV BL blend Almendros; Angosto is GARNACHA/SYRAH/Marselan.

Artadi Alic, Nav, R Ala r ★★→★★★★ BODEGA for outstanding modern RIO: powerf single-v'yd El Pisón needs 8–10 yrs; as does spicy, smoky PAGOS Viejos. Gd-valu VIÑAS de Gain. V.gd, equally modern El Sequé (r) ALIC, Artazuri (r, DYA p) NA (*See also* box, p.185.)

Baigorri R Ala r w ★★→★★★ Wines as glamorous as the architecture, a clear glas box; vats below. Bold modern RIO. Primary black fruits, bold tannins, upbea oak, fresh finish. Garage wins the prizes. RES more approachable. Restaura with gd views.

Rioja gets its name (perhaps) from *rialia* (many rivers), or from old Basque *arrioxa* (land of rocks).

Barón de Ley RB r p w ★→★★ Reliable, value wines from one-time Benedictin monastery. Gd range of newer varieties/blends.

Báscula, La Alic, Rib del D, Rio r w sw ★★ Young brand with gd-value wines i upcoming regions, plus classics, eg. ALIC, JUM, RIB DEL D, RIO, Terra Alta, YECL South African winemaker, British MW.

Belondrade C y L, Rue w ★★→★★★ France came to RUE with Didier Belondrade an son Jean. Belondrade is savoury, textured VERDEJO, lees-aged in oak. Second labe Quinta Apollonia. DYA Clarisa TEMPRANILLO (r).

Beronia Rio r p w ★→★★★ A transformation. Owner GONZÁLEZ BYASS has invested i oak, winemaking. Confidently revived RES; gd DYA red.

Bierzo Bier r w ★→★★★ Slate soils, a crunchy *Pinot-like red – Mencía* – and ethere GODELLO (w) have brought young winemakers buzzing. Best: Dominio de Tare DESCENDIENTES DE J PALACIOS, Gancedo, Luna Berberide, Peique, Pittacum. T watch: Castro Ventosa, Ultreia St Jacques.

Binissalem Mall r p w ★→★★ Traditional MALL DO ne of Palma. Mainly red, mainl tannic Mantonegro grape. Jaume de Puntiró, Macià Batle, Tianna Negre.

Bodega A cellar; a wine shop; a business making, blending and/or shipping wine.

Briones R Alt Small RIO hilltop town nr HARO, peppered with underground cellars

Producers incl FINCA ALLENDE, Miguel Merino. Worth a detour to the *Dinastía Vivanco wine museum.*

Calandria, La Nav r ★★ One of new wave of small producers making old-vine GARNACHA. Great-value Cientruenos; Tierga is essence of Garnacha.

Calatayud Ara r p w ★→★★★ Small DO gaining attention for its old-vine GARNACHA, which delivers flavour and value. Best: BODEGAS ATECA (*see* JUAN GIL), EL ESCOCÉS VOLANTE; Lobban (El Gordito Garnacha by Pamela Geddes), Virgén de la Sierra (Cruz de Piedra).

Campo de Borja Ara r p w ★→★★★ Spot-on source of gd-value juicy GARNACHA, eg. BODEGAS Alto Moncayo, Aragonesas, Borsao.

Campo Viejo Rio r w p ★→★★ RIO's biggest brand. Juicy TEMPRANILLO and GARNACHA, gd-value RES and GRAN RES. Part of the Pernod Ricard group (also Calatrava-designed Ysios winery).

Canary Islands Can r p w ★→★★ Canary Islands have no fewer than nine DOS; LANZAROTE DOs winning most attention. Dry white LISTÁN (aka PALOMINO) and Marmajuelo, black Listán Negro, Negramoll (TINTA NEGRA), Vijariego offers *enjoyable original flavours.* Gd dessert MOSCATELS, MALVASÍAS, esp fortified El Grifo from Lanzarote.

Cañas, Luis R Ala r w ★→★★★ Widely awarded family business; honest quality from JOVEN to garage-style wines. Offers classics eg. Selección de la Familia RES, and moderns eg. ultra-concentrated Hiru 3 Racimos and Amaren.

Capçanes, Celler de Cat r p w sw ★→★★ One of Spain's top co-ops. Great-value, expressive wines from MONTSANT. Also a kosher specialist, esp Peraj Ha'abib.

Cariñena Ara r p w ★→★★ The one DO that is also name of a grape variety. Solid, not exciting, but gd value; top pick is FINCA Aylés.

Casa Castillo Jum r ★★→★★★ A charming property, high up in JUM. Great-value MONASTRELL. Excellent El Molar GARNACHA and Valtosca SYRAH, plus superb Las Gravas single-v'yd blend and Pie Franco – a plot of Monastrell that escaped the recent phylloxera.

Castaño Mur r p w sw ★→★★ The Castaño family is YECLA. Fine MONASTRELLS, from value young wines to excellent Casa Cisca. Delicious sweet DULCE (r).

Castell d'Encus Cos del S r w ★★★ Fascinating project by former TORRES MD Raül Bobet, also of FERRER-BOBET, making *superbly fresh wines* at altitude. Ancient meets modern: grapes fermented in stone *lagares*, winery is up to date. Ekam RIES, Thalarn SYRAH, Quest Bordeaux blend. Plans for CHENIN, SAUV BL, SÉM.

Castilla y León C y L r p w ★→★★★ Spain's largest wine region. Plenty to enjoy, easy to get lost. Often great value: famous producers and unknowns; ditto grapes. Discover DOS: Arribes (esp La Setera Selección Especial – from TOURIGA grapes), BIERZO, CIGALES, Tierra de León, Tierra del Vino de Zamora, quality region Valles de Benavente. Red grapes incl MENCÍA, Juan Garcia, TINTA DEL PAÍS; whites Doña Blanca. Gd, deeply coloured rosado from Prieto Picudo grape.

Castillo Perelada Emp, Pri r p w sp ★→★★★ Glamorous estate with diverse offering. Vivacious CAVAS esp Gran Claustro; modern reds, incl coastal FINCA Garbet SYRAH. Rare 12-yr-old, solera-aged GARNATXA de l'EMPORDÀ. V. fine Casa Gran del Siurana, Gran Cruor, Syrah blend from PRI.

Catalonia r p w sp Less than 20 yrs old, this vast DO covers the whole of Catalonia – sea-shore, mtn and in-between. It contains some of Spain's top names, incl TORRES. There is no strong identity but this enables smart producers to carry out clever cross-DO blends.

Cava Spain's traditional-method sparkling is getting better and better. Made not just in PEN – in or around San Sadurní d'Anoia – but in other regions incl RIO (esp MUGA Conde de Haro). Market leaders are FREIXENET and CODORNÍU. Top names incl AGUSTÍ TORELLÓ MATA, CASTILLO PERELADA, Colet, GRAMONA and RECAREDO (bio).

CHARD and PINOT N were invading blends, but now there is much research into improving quality of local varieties. Some producers leaving Cava because of poor image; *see* CONCA DEL RIU ANOIA. The DO is introducing a highest category for single v'yds – *paraje calificada*.

Cérvoles Cos del S r w ★★→★★★ Powerful, modern wines from the border with PRI. Negre is youthful, approachable; Estrats, CABERNET/TEMPRANILLO blend with plenty of oak, needs time. Part of historic Castell del Remei group.

Chacolí / Txakoli P Vas (r) (p) w sw ★→★★ DYA The Basque wine, from the DOs Getariako Txakolina and Bizkaiko Txakolina. V'yds face chilly Atlantic winds hence sharp crunchiness of *pétillant* whites, locally poured into tumblers from a height. Top names: Ameztoi, Txomin Etxaniz. Fascinating late-harvest Urezti from Itsasmendi; luscious botrytis Arima from Gorka Izagirre.

Cigales C y L r p ★→★★ Lying between RIB DEL D and TORO, tiny Cigales fights to make itself heard. Look for DYA TEMPRANILLO (r p).

Clos Mogador Pri r w ★★★→★★★★ René Barbier is one of PRI's founders. Clos Mogador still commands respect; powerful CARIÑENA blend Manyetes. Spicy honeyed Clos Nelin white, forerunner of the trend for GARNACHA BLANCA blends. Partner in Espectacle, MONTSANT.

Codorníu Raventós Cos del S, Pen, Pri, Rib del D, Rio r p w sp ★→★★★ One of the two largest CAVA firms. Extensive research in experimental BODEGA leading to improvements to est names, eg. Jaume de Codorníu; new releases incl outstanding single v'yd Cavas, *Gran Codorníu*. Elsewhere Raimat in COS DEL improving, eg. Ànima blend (r w). Legaris in RIB DEL D also improving; Bilbainas in RIO shows promise with bestseller Viña Pomal, plus plans for GARNACHA/GRACIANO, TEMP BLANCO. *See also* SCALA DEI.

Conca de Barberà Cat r p w Small Catalan DO once purely a feeder of quality fruit to large enterprises, now some excellent wineries, incl bio Escoda-Sanahuja. Top TORRES wines Grans Muralles, Milmanda both made in this DO.

Conca del Riu Anoia Cat Traditional-method sparkling wine DO created in 2013 by RAVENTÓS I BLANC to provide tighter quality controls than CAVA. Requires organic production, minimum ageing 18 months, only local grape varieties.

Consejo Regulador Organization that controls a DO – each DO has its own. Quality as inconsistent as wines they represent: some bureaucratic, others enterprising.

Number of barrels in Rioja: c.1.3 million. Keeps the coopers busy.

Contino R Ala r p w ★★★★ Jesus Madrazo focuses on his single v'yd (RIO's 1st) with consistent success. Outstanding portfolio: RES has many yrs ahead, superb GRACIANO, single-v'yd Viña del Olivo, ripe, white GARNACHA blend and aromatic rosado. CVNE-owned.

Costers del Segre r p w sp ★→★★★ Geographically divided DO between mountainous CASTELL D'ENCUS and lower-lying Castell del Remei, CÉRVOLES, Raimat.

Crianza Guarantees the ageing of the wine, not the quality. New or unaged wine is Sin Crianza (without) or JOVEN. In general Crianzas must be at least 2 yrs old (with 6 mths–1 yr in oak) and must not be released before the 3rd yr. *See* RES.

Cusiné, Tomás Cos del S r w ★★→★★★ One of Spain's most innovative winemakers, originally behind Castell del Remei, CÉRVOLES. Individual, modern wines, incl TEMPRANILLO blend Vilosell; creative ten-variety white blend Auzells.

CVNE R Ala, R Alt r p w ★→★★★★ Pronounced *"coo-nee"*, the family-run Compañía Vinícola del Norte de España (1879) now offers some outstanding wines. RES is reliable. Real quality shows with fresh, elegant Imperial wines from RIO Alta and VIÑA Real range from RIO Alavesa. Wines can be long-ageing: seek out 62 64 70. CONTINO is a member of the group.

Denominación de Origen (DO), Denominación de Origen Protegida (DOP) Th former *Denominación de Origen* (DO) and DO *Calificada* are now grouped as DOP along with the single-estate PAGO denomination. Lesser category VCPRD is becoming VCIG, *Vinos de Calidad de Indicación Geografica*. Got that?

Dinastía Vivanco R Alt r w ★★ Large family-run BODEGA in BRIONES, with some interesting varietal wines. *Wine museum is worth the detour*.

Domaines Lupier Nav r ★★★ Young couple making old-vine GARNACHA. Two wines: floral La Dama; dense, bold El Terroir. Bio.

Dominio de Tares Bier r w ★★★ Outstanding MENCÍA: old-vine Cepas Viejas, Tares P3. Also gd GODELLO. In same group, Pazos de Lusco (RÍAS BAIXAS), Dominio dos Tares (C Y L) – its Cumal is fine example of local Prieto Picudo grape.

Dominio de Valdepusa C-La M r w ★★→★★★ Carlos Falcó, Marqués de Griñon, has been a confident rule-breaker since the 70s at family estate nr Toledo, pioneering SYRAH, PETIT VERDOT, drip irrigation, soil science, working with top consultants. Wines are savoury, concentrated. Estate is now a PAGO. Also in VINOS DE MADRID DO at El Rincón.

Dulce Sweet.

Empordà Cat r p w sw ★→★★ Small and fashionable DO nr the French border – centre of creativity. Best wineries incl CASTILLO PERELADA, Celler Marti Fabra, Pere Guardiola and Vinyes dels Aspres. Quirky, young Espelt grows 17 varieties: try GARNACHA/CARIGNAN Sauló. Sumptuous natural sweet wine from Celler Espolla: SOLERA GRAN RES.

Enrique Mendoza Alic r w sw ★★ Pepe Mendoza is key figure in resurgence of DO and of MONASTRELL grape. Wines as expressive as the man. Vibrant Tremenda 10, intense, savoury single v'yd Las Quebradas. Honeyed, sweet MOSCATEL; FONDILLÓN SOLERA est (takes min a decade).

Escocés Volante, El Ara r w ★★ Norrel Robertson, Scotsman, MW, lives in Calatayud, specializes in old-vine GARNACHA grown on slate at altitude, eg. Es Lo Que Hay, El Puño, La Multa. Also The Cup & Rings (RÍAS BAIXAS).

Espumoso Sparkling wine, but not made according the traditional method, unlike CAVA. Therefore usually cheaper.

Ferrer-Bobet Pri r ★★★ Polished, complex wines by Sergi Ferrer-Salat (also founder of Barcelona's Monvinic wine bar/shop) and Raül Bobet (CASTELL D'ENCUS). Slate soils, old vines culminate in Selecció Especial Vinyes Velles.

Finca Farm or estate (eg. FINCA ALLENDE).

Finca Allende R Alt r w ★★→★★★★ Top (in all senses) RIO BODEGA at BRIONES in ancient merchant's house with splendid tower, great view of v'yds, run by irrepressible Miguel Ángel de Gregorio. The *06' is superbly elegant, lovely now but will keep*; single-v'yd Calvario is foursquare, v. youthful; Aurus sumptuous with minerality. Two whites: powerful Rioja Blanco, v. fine, oak-influenced Martires, partner to Calvario. FINCA Nueva is recent range of less pricey wines. Also Finca Coronado in LA MANCHA.

Finca Sandoval C-La M r ★★→★★★ In wine-writer Victor de la Serna, DO MANCHUELA and SYRAH, MONASTRELL and BOBAL have an outspoken champion. Finca Sandoval is his top wine, Salia the second label.

Finca Valpiedra Rio r p w ★→★★ Beautifully sited single v'yd in bend in river Ebro; fine quality. Also FINCA Antigua in LA M. (*See also* FAMILIA MARTÍNEZ BUJANDA).

Fondillón Alic sw ★→★★★ A once-fabled unfortified sweet red from MONASTRELL, aged to survive sea voyages. Now matured in oak for min 10 yrs; some SOLERAS (*see* Sherry) of great age. Only a small production by eg. Gutiérrez de la Vega and Primitivo Quiles.

Freixenet Pen p w sp ★→★★★ Huge CAVA firm owned by Ferrer family. Best-known for frosted, black-bottled Cordón Negro, standard Carta Nevada. Elyssia is a real step up; refreshed by CHARD, PINOT N. Also controls Castellblanch,

Conde de Caralt, Segura Viudas, Bordeaux négociant Yvon Mau, Henri Abel (Champagne), Gloria Ferrer (USA), Wingara (Australia).

Galicia r w The rainy nw corner of Spain, with some of Spain's best whites (*se* RÍAS BAIXAS, MONTERREI, RIBEIRA SACRA, RIBEIRO, VALDEORRAS); and bright, crunchy red from MENCÍA.

Garnachas de España Pri, Rio, Ara r ★★ Winemaking project reflecting curren keen interest in old-vine GARNACHA. Links four small wineries in different DO along river Ebro. Makes one of rare Spanish Icewines.

Gramona Pen r w sw sp ★★→★★★★ Star CAVA cellar, one of the leaders in showin there is character in Cava; 5th generation makes impressive long-aged Cavas incl Imperial GRAN RES, *III Lustros*. Research and experimental plantings also giv rise to gd XAREL-LO-dominated *Celler Batle Gran Res*, sweet wines incl Icewine impressive CHARD/SAUV BL Gra a Gra Blanco DULCE.

Gran Reserva In RIO Gran Res spends minimum 2 yrs in cask and 3 yrs in bottle Superb Gran Res still to be found cheaply in Spain.

Hacienda Monasterio Rib del D r ★★→★★★ At his hillside winery, with famil farm next door, cult winemaker Peter Sisseck of PINGUS makes TINTO FINO/CA blends. Aims to make enough to be accessible to more consumers than Pingus Youthful Cosecha (unaged) and complex RES wines; Res Especial is richl textured and dense.

Haro R Alt Picturesque old city at heart of R ALT, with the historic names of RI clustered in the station district. Visit LÓPEZ DE HEREDIA, MUGA, LA RIOJA ALTA, as we as modern RODA.

Izquierdo, Basilio Rio r w ★★ Retired cellar master at CVNE, VIÑA REAL, CONTINO make wines under own name with great success. Burgundy-like B de Basilio GARNACH BLANCA. Red showcases all his experience with RIO.

J Chivite Family Estates Nav r p w sw ★★→★★★ Historic NAV family bodega nov divided into separate businesses. Popular DYA range Gran Feudo, esp Rosad Sobre Lías (*sur lie*). Excellent *Colección 125*, incl outstanding CHARD, late harves MOSCATEL; Finca de Villatuerta Chard, SYRAH. PAGO wines of beautiful *Señorío a Arínzano* estate, still improving; second wine *Casona*. Long-term consultar winemaker Denis Dubourdieu. In RIO, owns VIÑA Salceda (v.gd Conde de l Salceda), in RIB DEL D and RUE *Baluarte* (superb DYA VERDEJO).

Joven Young, unoaked wine. *Also see* CRIANZA.

Juan Gil Family Estates Jum r w ★★→★★★ Old family business relaunched in 200 to make the best in JUM. Gd young MONASTRELLS (eg. 4 Meses); powerful, long lived top wines Clio and El Nido. Group also incl modern wineries in rising DO incl Shaya (RUE), Can Blau (MONTSANT), Ateca (CALATAYUD).

Jumilla Mur r (p) (w) ★→★★★ Arid v'yds in mts n of Mur; old MONASTRELL vine revived by ambitious winemakers. TEMPRANILLO, MERLOT, CAB, SYRAH, PETIT VERDO also feature. Top producer: JUAN GIL. Also follow: Agapito Rico, CASA CASTILLO CASTAÑO, Carchelo, Luzón, Valle del Carche, Valtosca.

Juvé & Camps Pen w sp ★★→★★★ Consistently gd family firm for top-quality CAV RES de la Familia is the stalwart, with top-end GRAN RES, Milesimé CHARD Gra Res, Selección XAREL-LO.

La Mancha C-La M r p w ★→★★ Spain's least-impressive wine region, s of Madri Yet within there are outstanding examples: PESQUERA'S El Vínculo, MARTINE BUJANDA'S FINCA Antigua, JUAN GIL Volver.

León, Jean Pen r w ★★→★★★ Pioneer of CAB, CHARD in Spain; TORRES-owned sinc 1995, recovering quality under Mireia Torres. Gd, oaky Chards, expressive 305 *Merlot*; elegant Vinya La Scala Cab.

López de Heredia R Alt r p w ★★→★★★★ A remarkable "château", and a landmar in HARO. Delicate, old-style, long-aged wines are suddenly back in fashior

Cubillo is younger range with GARNACHA, darker Bosconia, delicate and ripe *Tondonia* 45 64 68 70 81 94 95 96 01 04. Whites have seriously extensive barrel and bottle age: fascinating Gravonia 04, Tondonia GRAN RES 81 87 91 96. Parchment-like Gran Res Rosado 00.

oxarel Pen sp ★★ An original. Cent Nou 109 Brut Nature RES is quirky treat for lovers of natural wine: traditional-method sparkling, but lees are never taken out of bottle, so it's not CAVA. Complex, cloudy, unsulphured, v. youthful after 109 mths.

Iadrid, Vinos de Mad r p w ★→★★ For many years GARNACHA provided workhorse wines. Today the old vines are part of an exciting wave of quality. Go-ahead names: Bernabeleva, with burgundian white and top Garnacha VIÑA Bonita. Also Marañones, Gosálbez-Ortí (run by former pilot), Jeromín, Divo, Viñedos de San Martín (part of Enate group), El Regajal.

Iálaga r w sw ★→★★★ Once-famous DO awakened by TELMO RODRIGUEZ who revived moribund MOSCATEL industry with subtle, sweet *Molino Real*. Exceptional No 3 Old Vines Moscatel from Jorge Ordoñez, US importer. Bentomiz, with Ariyanas wines, has an impressive portfolio of sweet and dry sweet Moscatel, also reds, incl local Romé variety.

Iallorca r w ★→★★★ Formerly tourist wines, now much improved, fashionable in domestic market, and high-priced. Inc 4 Kilos, Án Negra, Binigrau, Biniagual, Sa Vinya de Can Servera, Hereus de Ribas, Son Bordils, C'an Vidalet. Reds blend traditional varieties (Mantonegro, Callet, Fogoneu) plus CAB, SYRAH, MERLOT. Whites (esp CHARD) improving fast. Two DOS: BINISSALEM, PLÁ I LLEVANT.

Ianchuela C-La M r w sw ★→★★ Traditional region for bulk wine, now showing promise with eg. Bobal, MALBEC, PETIT VERDOT. Pioneer FINCA SANDOVAL followed by Alto Landón and Ponce, producer of *pie franco* (ungrafted vines) wine.

ibera del Duero region grew white wine only until the 17th century. Now being considered again.

Iarqués de Cáceres R Alt r p w ★→★★ Significant contribution to RIO in 70s, introducing French winemaking techniques. Faded glory at present. Gaudium is modern style; GRAN RES classic.

Iarqués de Murrieta R Alt r p w ★★★→★★★★ One of RIO's greats, famous for magnificent long-aged Castillo de Ygay GRAN RES. Latest release of Gran Res Blanco to be 86, and of Gran Res Tinto to bc 75. Best-value is dense, flavoursome Res. Dalmau is contrastingly modern, if oaky. *Capellania* is fresh, mineral, complex white, one of Rio's best.

Iarqués de Riscal R Ala r (p) w ★★→★★★ Each Marqués in turn has made an exceptional contribution to RIO, not just with Frank Gehry's titanium-roofed hotel. Reliable RES, modern, youthful FINCA Torrea, finely balanced GRAN RES. For a modern take on Rio pick powerful *Barón de Chirel Res*. A pioneer in RUE (since 72) making vibrant DYA SAUV BL, VERDEJO.

Iartínez Bujanda, Familia C-La M r p w ★→★★ Commercially astute business with a number of wineries; also makes private-label wines. Most attractive are *Finca Valpiedra*, charming single estate in RIO; FINCA Antigua in LA M.

Ias Alta Cat r ★★ Young (1999) PRI project coming to fruition with advice from Rhône specialists Tardieu and Cambie. La Creu Alta is impressive blend of CARIÑENA/GARNACHA/SYRAH.

Ias Martinet Pri r ★★★ PRI pioneer with excellent Clos Martinet, Els Escurçons. Now run by 2nd generation, ever innovating, practising fermentation in the v'yds, and in *tinajas* (clay jars).

Iauro C y L r ★★→★★★★ With Mariano Garcia of AALTO and formerly VEGA SICILIA as founder, Mauro has a great pedigree. Now run by Garcia's sons, Eduardo and

182 |

Alberto, who continue their father's work at Maurodos (TORO), Astrales (RIB DEL D
Paixar (BIERZO), focusing on old vines.

Méntrida C-La M r p ★→★★ Former co-op country s of Madrid, now being put o
the map by Arrayán, Canopy and esp Daniel Jiménez-Landi.

Monterrei Gal r w ★→★★★ Small DO in Ourense. Its jigsaw of grape varietie
and blends, and its reds, show there's much more to GAL than ALBARIÑO. Bes
QUINTA da Muradella.

Montsant Cat r (p) w ★→★★★ Tucked in around PRI, MONTSANT echoes its neighbou
at lower prices. Fine GARNACHA BLANCA, esp from Acústic. Dense, balsamic red
CAPÇANES, Can Blau, Espectacle, Joan d'Anguera, Mas Perinet, Venus la Universa

Muga R Alt r p w (sp) ★★★→★★★★ Classic family firm in HARO producing some
RIO's most aromatic, balanced reds. Gd barrel-fermented DYA VIURA reminiscen
of burgundy; textbook dry rosado; reds finely crafted, delicate. Best: wonderful
fragrant GRAN RES Prado Enea; warm, full *Torre Muga* 09; expressive, comple
Aro; dense, rich, structured Selección Especial.

Mustiguillo V'cia r w ★★★ Pioneering BODEGA has led renaissance of the unlove
local Bobal grape. Now a PAGO, El Terrerazo. Mestizaje is a juicy young red, whi
FINCA Terrerazo shows refinement. Top wine is Quincha Corral. Now developir
local white, Merseguera.

Navarra r p (w) ★★→★★★ Next door to RIO and always in its shadow. Focus o
international varieties has confused its real identity. Best: expressive, ol
vine GARNACHA eg. DOMAINES LUPIER, LA CALANDRIA. Up-and-coming incl Pago d
Larrainzar, confident Tandem. Best producers: ARTADI's Artazu, *J Chivite*, Nekea
Ochoa, Otazu, Pago de Cirsus, Señorío de Sarría with gd rosado.

Ochoa Nav r p w sw sp ★→★★ Ochoa *padre* made significant technical contributio
to growth of NAV. Daughters are working to return the family BODEGA to a ne
glory. V.gd rosado; fine, sweet MOSCATEL; fun, sweet, Asti-like sparkling.

Ordoñez, Grupo Jorge Run by MÁLAGA born, US-based importer of Spanish wine
with wineries across Spain incl CALATAYUD, JUM, ALIC. Excellent collection
Málaga MOSCATELS incl dry, mineral Botani.

**Haro Batalla de Vino, June: 10,000 people soaked in 130,000 litres of win
Wear white.**

Pago, Vinos de Pago denotes v'yd. Roughly equivalent to French *grand cru*. B
criticisms persist about lack of objective quality, differing traditions of *pag
so far. Obvious absentees incl ALVARO PALACIOS' L'Ermita, PINGUS, Calvario (FINC
ALLENDE), CONTINO's Viña del Olivo, TORRES properties.

Palacio de Fefiñanes Gal w ★★★★ Most ethereal of ALBARIÑOS. *Standard DYA wine* or
of finest. Two superior styles: barrel-fermented 1583 (yr winery was founde
making it oldest winery of DO); super-fragrant, pricey, lees-aged, mandari
scented III.

Palacios, Álvaro Pri r ★★★→★★★★ By force of personality and the quality of h
wines, Álvaro Palacios helped build a global reputation for Spanish wine.
founder of PRI. Now developing Burgundy-style approach with village wine
offering top wine *en primeur*. Camins del PRI is v.gd-value introduction. L
Terrasses is bigger, spicier; FINCA Dofí has a dark undertone of CAB SAUV, SYRA
MERLOT, CARIÑENA. Super-pricey L'Ermita is powerful and dense from low-yieldir
GARNACHA. Also in BIER, RIO.

Palacios, Descendientes de J Bier r ★★★ Ricardo Pérez Palacios, nephew of Álvar
focuses on old-vine MENCÍA grown on steep slate. Excellent expression of varie
Gd-value, floral *Pétalos*. Villa de Corullón and Las Lamas are both super
exceptional single-v'yd La Faraona in tiny quantity. Bio.

Palacios, Rafael Gal w ★★★ Rafael Palacios, ÁLVARO's younger brother, runs th estate in VALDEORRAS. Intense focus on GODELLO: textured, oak-aged Louro do Bolo; As Sortes, with citrus, white peach, bright acidity, one of Spain's top whites.

lacios Remondo RB r w ★★→★★★ At the family winery ÁLVARO PALACIOS is working to restore GARNACHA to its rightful place in RIO, as well as promoting the concept of villages or crus, as in Burgundy. Complex, oaked white Plácet originally created by brother RICARDO. Reds: organic, Garnacha-led, red-fruited La Montesa; big, mulberry-flavoured, old-vine 100% Garnacha Propriedad. Promises much.

riente, José Rue w ★★→★★★ Victoria Pariente makes VERDEJOs of shining clarity. Cuvée Especial fermented in concrete eggs gains fascinating complexity. Silky late-harvest Apasionado.

zo de Señorans Gal w ★★★ Exceptionally fragrant ALBARIÑOs from a benchmark BODEGA in RÍAS BAIXAS. V. fine Selección de Añada **05** – proof that the v. best Albariños age beautifully.

nedès Cat r w sp ★→★★★★ Demarcated region w of Barcelona, best-known for CAVA. Identity has been confused since the arrival of all-embracing CAT DO. Best: Agustí Torelló Mata, Alemany i Corrio, Can Rafols dels Caus, GRAMONA, JEAN LEÓN, Parés Baltà, TORRES.

rez Pascuas Rib del D r ★★→★★★ Family business making classic RIB DEL D wines from TINTO FINO. Gd-value RES.

squera, Grupo Rib del D r ★★→★★★ Farmer and tractor-businessman Alejandro Fernández was the making of the reputation of RIB DEL D with his simply named Tinto Pesquera. Wines less exciting than they once were. Daughters have joined business but father is still hands-on. Also at Condado de Haza, Dehesa La Granja (C y L), El Vínculo (LA MANCHA). Visit original stone *lagar* in winery.

gus, Dominio de Rib del D r ★★★★ Consistent excellence from the tiny bio winery of Pingus (Dane Peter Sisseck's childhood name), made with old-vine TINTO FINO. Pingus reveals refinement of the variety. *Flor de Pingus* from younger vines; Amelia is a single barrel named after his wife. PSI is a growing business, using grapes from growers to encourage them to keep tending oldest vines.

i Llevant Mall r w ★→★★★ Eleven wineries comprise this tiny, lively, island DO. Aromatic whites; intense, spicy reds. Best incl Toni Gelabert, Jaime Mesquida, Miguel Oliver and Vins Can Majoral. Exports are small, so visit and enjoy on the island.

orat Cat r w ★★→★★★★ PRI has come of age. This isolated enclave, named after the old monastery tucked under craggy cliffs, was rescued a quarter of a century ago by René Barbier of CLOS MOGADOR, ÁLVARO PALACIOS and others. Grown on *licorella* (slate) soils and terraced v'yds wines show mineral purity. After initial phase of heavy oaking, elegance and more reasonable prices are appearing. Palacios has driven introduction of "village" DOs or crus within PRI. Other top names: Celler del Pont, Cims de Porrera, Clos Erasmus, Clos de l'Obac, Clos i Terrasses, Coma Vella, Combier-Fischer-Gerin, FERRER-BOBET, MAS ALTA, Mas Doix, MAS MARTINET, SCALA DEI, Terroir al Limit, TORRES, Val·Llach.

inta Sardonia C y L r ★★★ One of glossy non-DO stars, based in Sardon de Duero, between ABADÍA RETUERTA and MAURO, launched by former colleague of Peter Sisseck at PINGUS. Member of TERRAS GAUDA group.

ventós i Blanc Pen p w ★★→★★★ Pepe Raventós made the news when he withdrew from CAVA DO, critical of its low quality standards. CONCA DEL RIU ANOIA is his alternative. V. fine rosé De Nit. Zero SO2 Extrem (no added sulphur) v. lively and textured.

caredo Pen w sp ★★→★★★ A superb CAVA producer, with also v.gd still wine. Tops is characterful, mineral *Turó d'en Mota*, from vines planted in 1940, ages brilliantly. Bio.

melluri, La Granja Nuestra Señora R Ala r w ★★→★★★ Glorious mountainous

estate. TELMO RODRIGUEZ has returned to his family property where he creat
intriguing DYA white from six varieties. Coming back to form.

Reserva Increasingly producers prefer to ignore the regulations. However – rare
the wine world – Res has actual meaning in Spain. In RIO red Res are aged f
min 3 yrs, of which 1 yr is in oak.

Rías Baixas Gal (r) w ★★→★★★★ Atlantic DO based on ALBARIÑO and grown
five subzones. Best: Adega dos Eidos, Agro de Bazán, As Laxas, Castro Cel
Fillaboa, Gerardo Méndez, VIÑA Nora, Martín Códax, PALACIO DE FEFIÑANES, Pa
de Barrantes, PAZO DE SENORANS, QUINTA do Lobelle, TERRAS GAUDA, La Val, Valmiñ
Zárate. Growing interest in longer lees-ageing, barrel-ageing.

Ribeira Sacra Gal r w ★★ Source of excellent GAL whites, from steep terrac
running dizzyingly down to river Sil. Top producers: Dominio do Bibei, Mou:
MENCÍA v. promising, eg. perfumed La Lama from Dominio do Bibei.

Ribeiro Gal (r) w ★→★★★ DYA DO in w Ourense. Fresh, light whites made fro
Treixadura, TORRONTÉS, GODELLO, LOUREIRO and Lado. Top producers incl Casal
Armán, Coto de Gomariz, VIÑA Meín, Lagar do Merens. Also speciality swe
wine, Tostado.

Ribera del Duero r p (w) ★→★★★★ Glamorous, pricey, ambitious young t
created 1982. Anything that incl VEGA SICILIA, HACIENDA MONASTERIO, PESQUE
PINGUS, AALTO has to be serious, but with 280 BODEGAS consistency is hard to fir
Too many v'yds planted in wrong places with wrong clones. DO could
extended to whites from umpteen varieties, but needs government ar
EU approval. Other top names: ALIÓN, Astrales, Cillar de Silos, Pago de
Capellanes, PÉREZ PASCUAS. *See also* neighbours ABADÍA RETUERTA, MAURO. Also
interest: Bohórquez, Emilio Moro, Matarromera, O Fournier, Protos, Sast
Tomás Postigo, Vallebueno.

Rioja r p w sp ★→★★★★★ *See* box, opposite.

Rioja Alta, La r ★★→★★★★ One of the great RIO BODEGAS back on top form, w
lovely RES, two outstanding GRAN RES. Alberdi is light, pretty, cedary; Ardan
is riper, a touch spicier but still elegant, boosted by GARNACHA. Standouts a
excellent, tangy, vanilla-edged ***Gran Res 904*** and fine, multi-layered Gran R
890, aged 6 yrs in oak. Also owns RIO ALA Torre de Oña, RÍAS BAIXAS Lagar
Cervera, RIB DEL D Àster.

Roda R Alt r ★★→★★★ Modern BODEGA nr station in HARO. Serious RES reds fro
low-yield TEMPRANILLO, backed by continued research: Roda, Roda I, Cirsión, ar
youthful Sela. More recently repeated the approach with RIB DEL D Bodegas
Horra, making Corimbo and Corimbo I. Also outstanding olive oils.

Romeo, Benjamin Rio r w ★★→★★★ Romeo (ex-ARTADI) is one of RIO's rock sta
Small production, terroiriste. Rich, ***top white Que Bonito Cacareaba***. Flagship r
Contador, "super-second" La Cueva del Contado. V. concentrated single v'yd
VIÑA de Andrés. Wines to lay down.

Rothschild & Vega Sicilia, Bodegas Rio, R Alt r ★★★ Link with Edmond
Rothschild (Bordeaux, Château Clarke) a long time in the making, with caret
research of v'yds. First wine Macan (from traditional nickname of local peopl
second is Macan Clásico. Launch vintage 09. Ripe fruit, fresh, with overt oa
Still a work in progress.

Rueda C y L w ★★→★★★ Spain's response to SAUV BL: zesty VERDEJO. Mostly D'
whites. "Rueda Verdejo" is 100% indigenous Verdejo. "Rueda" is blended wi
eg. Sauv Bl, VIURA. Too much poor quality. Best: Baluarte, ***Belondrade***, El Alb
Lurton, MARQUÉS DE RISCAL, Naia, Ossian, JOSÉ PARIENTE, Palacio de Bornos, Shay
Sitios de BODEGA, Unzu, Veracruz, Viñedos de Nieva, Vinos Sanz.

Scala Dei Pri r w ★★★→★★★★ V'yds of the "stairway to heaven" cling to crag
slopes that tower over an old monastery. One of PRI's classics, now tended

Rioja: news from the hills

Rio could so easily rest on its laurels. Attractive scenery, tasty traditional cooking, historic hill towns – it is made for wine tourism. Yet it still needs to make its case to consumers. For Rio is no longer just about oak and plenty of it, or about sweet vanilla-and-coconut American oak. Nor is it about simple cherry-fruited TEMPRANILLO. Nor are the wines tired. There is a new generation like David Sampedro and Olivier Rivière, *garagistes*. There are the newer approaches from ROTHSCHILD & VEGA SICILIA, Baigorri, Remírez de Ganuza. The prodigal sons – TELMO RODRÍGUEZ and ÁLVARO PALACIOS – have returned to revive family businesses. Finally there are the glorious classics: LA RIOJA ALTA, MUGA and LÓPEZ DE HEREDIA. Latest news is that Juan Carlos López de Lacalle of ARTADI has announced he is leaving Rio DO. Look for more top producers demanding Burgundy-style recognition for v'yds or valleys. Similar moves in CAVA. Watch this space: Rio has never been more interesting.

part-owner CODORNÍU, reducing CAB SAUV and increasing GARNACHA, to develop Pri signature wine, experimenting with concrete, clay pots and oak fermenters. Single-v'yd wines Sant'Antoni and Mas Deu show promise. GARNACHA BLANCA launching 2015.

erra Cantabria Rio r w ★★→★★★★ The Eguren family specializes in single-v'yd, minimal-intervention wines, a relatively new concept in RIO. Burgundian approach to winemaking showing intensity, elegance. All TEMPRANILLO. At Viñedos de Paganos, makes just two outstanding wines: superb El Puntido, powerful, structured La Nieta. Other properties incl Señorio de San Vicente in Rio and Teso la Monja in TORO.

erra de Gredos C y L r w Just outside VINOS DE MADRID: promising region of small producers working with old-vine GARNACHA and local white Albillo, grown on granite and schist.

montano r p w ★→★★ Cool-climate DO in Pyrénéan foothills beginning to define itself – slowly, given so many international varieties in v'yd. Opt for MERLOT, GARNACHA, GEWURZ, CHARD. Best producers: Enate, VIÑAS del Vero (owned by GONZÁLEZ BYASS) – from its high-altitude property Secastilla come old-vine GARNACHA, GARNACHA BLANCA.

ertes del Marqués Can r w ★→★★ Has rapidly become a sommeliers' and wine merchants' favourite. Its wines sold under this brand name, and the companion 7 Fuentes, showcase local grape varieties, and the unfamiliar origin of the CANARIES. Small production, Burgundian approach.

lmo Rodríguez, Compañía de Vinos r w sw ★★→★★★ Telmo Rodríguez made his name, and many fine wines, by restoring old v'yds, keeping old traditions. Now makes a wide range of excellent DO wines from all over, incl MÁLAGA (*Molino Real* MOSCATEL), RIO (Lanzaga, Matallana), RUEDA (Basa), TORO (Dehesa Gago, Gago, PAGO la Jara), *Valdeorras* (DYA Gaba do Xil GODELLO). Has returned to his family property REMELLURI in Rio to work with sister Amaia – look out for rise in quality.

rras Gauda Gal w ★★→★★★ Textured, complex ALBARIÑO blends. Also zesty, grapefruit-like La Mar, mainly from scarce grape Caiño Blanco. Same group as Pittacum (BIE) and QUINTA SARDONIA (RIB DEL D).

ro C y L r ★→★★★ Small DO w of Valladolid still finding its way. Tinta de Toro was rustic, overalcoholic; today can be boldly expressive. Try Maurodos (*see* MAURO), with dense old-vine San Román. Glamour comes with VEGA SICILIA-owned Pintia, and LVMH property Numanthia. Also: Elias Mora, Estancia Piedra, PAGO la Jara from TELMO RODRÍGUEZ, Teso la Monja.

> **Don't drink the furniture**
> Spain is at last beginning to move away from overoaking. But Spaniards
> love oak, esp the older generation – which likes nothing better than
> wine that tastes of furniture. Makes it difficult for producers to cut
> down, though some compromise by turning to more subtle French oak
> from powerful American oak. But too much is still too much.

Torres Cat, Pri, Rio r p w sw ★★→★★★★ Uniquely successful, consistent hig
quality family firm. Miguel Torres has handed over to his son Miguel
Torres; daughter Mireia is technical director. But he remains innovative wi
impressive focus on environment. Ever-reliable DYA CAT VIÑA Sol, grapey Vi
Esmeralda, silky sweet MOSCATEL. Best reds: top PEN CAB *Mas la Plana*; CONCA
BARBERÀ duo (Burgundy-like *Milmanda*, one of Spain's finest CHARDS, *Gra
Muralles* blend of local varieties) is stunning. JEAN LEÓN has v.gd offerings to
In RIB DEL D Celeste continues to improve as does RIO Ibéricos, and PRI Salmo
Also in Chile. CAVA promised.

Utiel-Requena r p (w) ★→★★ Satellite region of V'CIA forging own identity with rus
but now improving Bobal grape. Tiny Cerrogallina shows way ahead for quali

Valbuena Rib del D *See* VEGA SICILIA.

Valdeorras Gal r w ★→★★★ GALICIAN DO in nw Ourense leaving behind its co-o
based beginnings by virtue of its DYA GODELLO. Best: Godeval, RAFAEL PALACIOS,
Tapada, TELMO RODRÍGUEZ, Valdesil.

Valdepeñas C-La M r (w) ★→★★ Large DO nr Andalucían border. Gd-value RIO-i
reds. Home to market-leading Félix Solís business and its ever-popular *Vi
Albali* brand.

Valencia r p w sw ★→★★ Big exporter of table wine. Primary source of chea
fortified, sweet MOSCATEL. Most reliable producer: Murviedro. Growing intere
in inland, higher-altitude old vines and minimal-intervention winemakir
eg. *garagiste* Rafael Cambra, EL ANGOSTO, Celler del Roure, Aranleon.

**Goatskins: a 19th-century equivalent of bag-in-box – they collapse as the wine
taken out.**

Vega Sicilia Rib del D r ★★★★ Spain's perfectionist "first growth", and the on
Spanish wine to have real value in secondary auction market. Glamorous ne
winery enhances precise approach to winemaking. Wines are deep in colo
with cedarwood nose, intense and complex; long-lived. Youthful *Valbuena
TINTO FINO with a little MALBEC, MERLOT – has min 5 yrs in oak. Controlled, elega
flagship Único is aged 6 yrs in oak; RES Especial – NV blend of 3 vintages
spends up to 10 yrs in barrel. Both have some CAB SAUV, Merlot. Neighbouri
Alión shows modern take on RIB DEL D: 100% Tinto Fino aged in Nevers oak. █
2010 released: excess sediment. Now working on a white wine. TORO prope
Pintia 2009 also affected by sediment. Owns Oremus Tokaji (Hungary). T
newest project is Macan in Rio: *see* BODEGAS ROTHSCHILD & VEGA SICILIA.

Vendimia Vintage.

Viña Literally, a v'yd.

Vino de la Tierra (VDT) Table wine usually of superior quality made in a demarcat
region without DO. Covers immense geographical possibilities; catego
incl many prestigious producers, non-DO by choice to be freer of inflexi
regulation and use the varieties they want.

Yecla Mur r (p) w ★→★★ Something stirs in the isolated enclave of Yecla. Only
producers, but a real focus on reviving MONASTRELL, esp CASTAÑO.

Zárate Gal (r) w ★★→★★★ Based in Val do Salnés. Elegant, textured ALBARIÑO w
long lees ageing. Rare RÍAS BAIXAS reds from Caíño Tinto and Loureiro Tinto.

ortugal

ecent vintages

)14 A mild summer produced fresh, balanced whites and reds of great intensity – provided the latter were picked before a long spell of rain.

)13 Great for (most) whites, also reds picked before the rain; mixed results after the rain.

)12 Concentrated wines, good balance, especially whites.

)11 Well-balanced year; outstanding Douro, Alentejo reds.

)10 Good quality and quantity all round. Bairrada had another excellent year.

)09 Good overall. Bairrada and Lisboa excellent. Douro, Tejo, Alentejo: big wines, high alcohol.

)08 Almost uniformly excellent; Bairrada, Alentejo particularly. Good fruit intensity, balance, aroma.

)07 Aromatic whites; well-balanced reds with round tannins.

SPAIN / PORTUGAL

çores (Azores Atlantic archipelago of nine volcanic (and rainy) islands with three DOCS (Pico, Biscoitos, Graciosa) for *licoroso* (high-alcohol late-harvest or fortified) wines. Since 2004 VINHO REGIONAL Açores table wines permitted; promising VERDELHO, Arinto do Açores and Terrantez do Pico. Look for FITA PRETA, Insula, Curral Atlantis, Cancela do Porco.

lega A cellar or winery.

lenquer Lis r w ★★→★★★ 10 11' 12 13 14 Sheltered DOC, home to LIS best reds incl SYRAH pioneer MONTE D'OIRO, CHOCAPALHA.

lentejo (w) ★→★★★ 06 07' 08' 09 10 11' 12 13 Huge, warm, s region divided into sub-regional DOCS Borba, Redondo, Reguengos, PORTALEGRE, Evora, Granja-Amareleja, Vidigueira, Moura. VR Alentejano preferred by many top estates. Rich, ripe reds, esp from Alicante Bouschet, SYRAH, TRINCADEIRA, TOURIGA NACIONAL. Whites fast improving. CARTUXA, ESPORÃO, MALHADINHA NOVA, MOUCHÃO, MOURO, JOÃO PORTUGAL RAMOS have potency, style. Watch: Dona Maria, FITA PRETA, SÃO MIGUEL, do Rocim, Terrenus, TIAGO CABAÇO, SUSANA ESTEBAN, Explicit.

lgarve r p w sp ★→★★ A s coast VINHO REGIONAL. A ready tourist market and the heat (can mean unripe tannins) means wines fall well short of its Michelin-starred gastronomy. Organic estate Monte da Casteleja at least shows terroir.

liança, Caves Bair r p w sp ★★→★★★ Large BAIR-based firm; gd reds (esp QUINTA das Baceladas) and *sparkling* shown with art at Aliança Underground Museum. Interests in Beiras (Casa d'Aguiar), ALEN (Quinta da Terrugem), DÃO (Quinta da Garrida), DOU (Quatro Ventos).

meal, Quinta do Vin w sp sw ★★★ V.gd LOUREIRO by ANSELMO MENDES, incl age-worthy, oaked Escolha, Special Late-Harvest and ARINTO ESPUMANTE. Also a new wine tourism project.

phros Vin r p w sp ★★★ Permaculture bio estate with food forest. Top LOUREIRO (Daphne, with skin contact), Vinhão (oaked Silenus) esp food-friendly.

veleda, Quinta da Vin r p w ★→★★ DYA Home of eponymous estate-grown wines and Casal García, born 1939 and still VIN's biggest seller.

acalhoa Vinhos Alen, Lis, Set r p w sp sw ★★→★★★ Principal brand and HQ of Madeiran billionaire José Berardo's group; also owns National Monument QUINTA da Bacalhoa, which makes v.gd CAB SAUV (planted 1979). Barrels of delectable SETÚBAL MOSCATEL, incl rare Roxo, displayed alongside fine art. Modern, well-made brands: Serras de Azeitão, Catarina, Cova da Ursa (PENÍNSULA DE SETÚBAL), TINTO da Anfora (ALENTEJO).

ágeiras, Quinta das Bair r w sp ★★★→★★★★ (GARRAFEIRA r) 04' 05' 08' 09 10 Stunning, traditional *garrafeira* BAGA (r), white built to age. Res, Pai Abel (young

v'yd) and elegant new Avô Fausto are Baga with TOURIGA N. Fine, artisanal ze
dosage sparkling, ages superbly.

Bairrada r p w sp ★→★★★★ 03' 04 05' 06 07 08' 09' 10' 11 12 13 An Atlanti
influenced DOC. Traditional strengths: age-worthy sparkling, BAGA reds, no
fortified Baga. Top Baga specialists: Casa de Saima, CAVES SÃO JOÃO, FILIPA PATO, LU
PATO, Sidónia de Sousa, QUINTA DAS BÁGEIRAS. Watch: Quintas de Baixo (NIEPOOI
owned), Vadio. CAMPOLARGO, ALIANÇA, Colinas de S. Lourenço (IDEAL DRINKS), Tia
Teles bring flair to French varieties, esp CAB SAUV, PINOT N (Colinas). VINHO REGION
is Beira Atlântico.

Bairrada's suckling pig (local speciality) is the perfect foil for Baga.

Barca Velha Dou r ★★★★ 82' 83 85 91' 95' 99 00 04 Portugal's iconic red, create
in 1952 by FERREIRA. Made in exceptional yrs, it forged DOU's reputation for stell
wines. Aged several yrs pre-release. Second label, Casa Ferreirinha *Res Especie*
is v.gd, esp 01 07.

Beira Interior ★→★★ Large DOC between DÃO and Spanish border. Huge potenti
from old, high (up to 700m) v'yds, esp for white Siria, Fonte Cal. Beyra, QUINT
do Cardo, dos Currais, dos Termos impress.

Branco White.

Bussaco Bei At r w ★★★ (r) 01 04 05' 06' 07 10 *Bussaco Palace hotel's* Manueli
Gothic architecture as frothy as wines are stern; lists wines back to 40s. Re
blend BAIR BAGA/DÃO TOURIGA N, whites DÃO Encrudado with Bair MARIA GOME
Bical. VM is single v'yd: Vinha da Mata.

Bucelas Lis w ★★ Tiny DOC making tangy, racy ARINTO (aka "Lisbon Hock" in 19t
century England). Best: QUINTA DA ROMEIRA, Coteaux da Murta.

Cabaço, Tiago Alen Talented SUSANA ESTEBAN blends native and international variete
incl fruity ".beb" (from *beber* – to drink), to food-friendly ".com" (*comer* – to ea
and pun-ful flagship "blog". New: (old vine) Vinhas Velhas (r w) cuvées.

Campolargo Bair r w sp ★→★★★ Large estate; pioneer of Bordeaux varieties, PINOT
V.gd native CERCEAL, ARINTO (w), Alvareloa and Rol de Coisas blend (r).

Carcavelos Lis br sw ★★★ An excellent local initiative to revive this old DOC
toothsome apéritif and dessert wines rests on the shoulders of the new Vil
Oeiras brand.

Cartuxa, Adega da Alen r w sp ★★→★★★★ 17th-century cellars a tourist magnet b
modern winery, organic and bio v'yds produce gd-value EA reds and Cartu
RES to well-structured flagship Pêra Manca red and white (r) 97 98 01 03 05' 0
08' 09. New: Scala Coeli Res PETIT VERDOT.

Carvalhais, Quinta dos Dão r p w sp ★★→★★★ (r) SOGRAPE's pioneering DÃ
winery. Home of Duque de Viseu brand. Estate-grown flagship TOURIGA N Unic
and Encrudado v.gd.

Casal Branco, Quinta de Tej r w sp ★→★★ Large family estate. Solid entry-lev
blends (local, international grapes). Best is Falcoaria range: old-vine CASTEL
and FERNÃO PIRES (w), Alicante Bouschet.

Castro, Alvaro Dão ★★★→★★★ Highly characterful wines mostly under QUIN
names, de Saes and de Pellada. Res, Primus (w), *Pape* (r) excellent. Dens
Carrocel (TOURIGA N) needs time but Castro now releasing it after 5 yrs. New a
Caniças *vin de soif* from young Touriga N and old-vine field blends.

Chocapalha, Quinta de Lis r p w ★★ (r) Modernist blending Portuguese and Frenc
grapes incl gd-value Mar de Lisboa. TOURIGA N flagship "CH" v.gd.

Chryseia Dou r ★★→★★★★ 06 07 08' 09 11' 12' Basing Bordeaux's Bruno Prats ar
SYMINGTON FAMILY ESTATES partnership at QUINTA de Roriz has raised the quali
of this polished red. Second label: *Post Scriptum* 08 09 10 11' 12. Prazo c
Roriz gd value.

Churchill Estates Dou r p w ★★→★★★ 07 08 09′ 10 11′ 12 Fruity white, ROSADO, TOURIGA N. Best: old-vine, mineral, grippy QUINTA da Gricha, Grande Res reds.

Colares Lis r w ★★ Tiny coastal DOC. Ungrafted Ramisco vines on sand produce *tannic reds*, fresh MALVASIA whites. Fundação Oriente, Casal Santa Maria and Monte Cascas bring modern flair to ADEGA Regional de Colares' and Viuva Gomez's traditional style.

Conceito Dou ★★→★★★ Precocious talent Rita Ferreira Marques does style and substance. Strikingly labelled DOU Superior wines are modern in their clarity and finesse, trad in their use of local varieties, incl an unusual PINOT N-like Bastardo. Marques is now also making wines at QUINTA do Fojo.

Covela r p w Vin Bought from receivers, this estate nr the DOU has bounced back; Rui Cunha still winemaker. VIN from Avesso grape is star, gd ARINTO.

Crasto, Quinta do Dou r w ★★→★★★ (r) 06 07′ 08 09′ 10 11′ 12 Family-owned Cima Corgo estate. The jewel in the crown is two v. old field-blend parcels, producing Vinha da Ponte 03 04 07′ 10′ 12, María Theresa 03′ 05′ 06 07 09′ 11′; also (great-value) Res. Probably Portugal's best TINTA RORIZ. Gd Port. New: Superior BRANCO 700m v'yd.

Dão Dão r p w sp ★★→★★★ 04 05 06 07′ 08′ 09 10 11′ 12 Historic DOC. Modern pioneers CARVALHAIS, ALVARO CASTRO, DÃO SUL, QUINTAS MAIAS, ROQUES make structured, elegant, perfumed reds, textured whites. Second wave incl JÚLIA KEMPER, Casa da Passarella, CASA DE MOURAZ. Names to watch: Antonio Madeira, NIEPOORT (Quinta da Lomba), MOB, Druida. VINHO REGIONAL: Terras do Dão.

Dão Sul Dou r w sp ★★→★★★ Changes at top have seen rationalization of modern but eclectic portfolio: das Tecedeiras (DOU) sold to COVELA and do Encontro (BAIR) range pruned. Core brands: QUINTA dos Grilos, Quinta Cabriz, organic Paco dos Cunhas de Santar and CASA DE SANTAR (DÃO), Encostas do Douro (Dou), do Encontro (Bair), do Gradil (LISB), Herdade Monte da Cal (ALEN).

Denominacão de Origem Controlada (DOC) Demarcated wine region controlled by a regional commission. *See also* VR.

Doce (vinho) Sweet (wine).

Douro r p w sw ★★→★★★★ 04′ 05 06 07′ 08′ 09′ 10 11′ 12 Port country DOC for powerful, increasingly elegant table wines. Perfume, fruit, minerals typify its best reds. Top whites textured, complex. Look for BARCA VELHA, CONCEITO, CRASTO, DUAS QUINTAS, *Niepoort*, PASSADOURO, POFIRA, *Vale Dona Maria*, VALE MEÃO, VALLADO, WINE & SOUL. Watch: *Duorum*, Maritávora (w), Monte Xisto, MUXAGAT, QUINTAS DO NOVAL, da Touriga, do Fojo. VR is Duriense.

Duas Quintas Dou r w ★★★ (r) 05 06 07′ 08 09′ 10 11′ 12 Port shipper Ramos Pinto's quest for balance, finesse now entirely focused on blending two QUINTAS (dos Bons Ares, 600m; Ervamoira, 110–340m). No longer makes Ramos Pinto Collection or Res Especial.

Duorum Dou r w ★★→★★★ Joint project of JOÃO PORTUGAL RAMOS and Jose Maria Soares Franco. New O Leucura Cota 200 and 400 reds from old vines at 200 and 400m showcase the DOU's diversity of terroir. Gd-value, fruity Tons entry level from new 250 ha Castelo Melhor v'yd. V.gd Vintage Port.

Esporão, Herdade do Alen r w sw ★★→★★★ 08′ 09 10 11′ 12 13 Large estate making high-quality modern wines. Gd-value fruity, entry-level brands, esp Monte Velho. Varietal range, Esporão Res, Private Selection, GARRAFEIRA, v. limited-edition Torre 04′ 07′ has increasing complexity. New PORTALEGRE v'yd at 500m augments freshness. DOU estate too (QUINTA das Murças).

Espumante Sparkling. Not great but best from BAIR, esp BÁGEIRAS, Kompassus, Colinas São Lourenço (IDEAL DRINKS), DOURO (esp Vértice), Távora-Varosa (MURGANHEIRA) and VIN.

Esteban, Susana Alen Eponymous project of acclaimed Spanish winemaker in

Portugal since 1999. Clever blend of subregions: fresh, mineral PORTALEG
old-vine fruit with fuller-bodied Estremoz grapes. Procura flagship stunnir
Aventura gd value.

Falua Tej r p w JOÃO PORTUGAL RAMOS' TEJO outpost. Well-made export-focused Tag
Creek blends national and international grapes. Conde de Vimioso mo
traditional; gd Res. New: gd Alicante Bouschet.

Ferreira Dou r w ★→★★★★ SOGRAPE-owned Port shipper. Dizzying array of DOU win
under Casa Ferreirinha labels, from entry-level Esteva to BARCA VELHA. Top re
from QUINTA da Leda, top white (new Antónia Adelaide Ferreira), Vinha Gran
rosé from Quinta do Sairrão at 650m.

Fita Preta Alen Restless winemaker António Maçanita scored with upfront,
popular Sexy sister-brand. Fita Preta label more serious, esp Palpite and excitir
Signature Series: small-batch experimental wines with a foot in past (sk
contact, amphora ageing, revival of AÇORES native grapes).

Fonseca, José María da Lis r p w dr sw sp ★★→★★★ Historic family-own
estate. Fortified Setúbal MOSCATEL pioneer, using back catalogue to great effe
in Apoteca, 20-yr-olds Alambre and Roxo. Popular volume brands: LANCE
PERIQUITA. Of super-premium wines FSF and partially amphora-fermented Jo
de Sousa reds best; new Hexagon white impresses.

Colares' vines take root in giant (several metres deep) sand pits.

Garrafeira Label term: traditionally a merchant's "private res". Must be aged for m
2 yrs in cask and 1 yr in bottle (often aged much longer).

Horácio dos Reis Simões Set Innovative boutique producer of MOSCATEL from si
incl late-harvest and fortified (esp single-cask and Excellent). Thrilling fortifi
Bastardo and centenarian BOAL white.

Ideal Drinks Bair, Dão, Vin Founder, Swiss watch designer and businessman Carl
Dias brings experience marketing luxury goods to an ultra-ambitious ran
made with consultancy from Bordeaux's Pascal Chatonnet. Already Portuga
best CAB SAUV, still and sparkling (PINOT N) rosé (Colinas São Lourenço, BAI
From VIN, powerful LOUREIRO (Paço de Palmeira) and ALVARINHO (QUINTA da Pedra

Kemper, Júlia Dão ★★★ r w p Organically cultivated (and certified) Kemper plant
15 ha of vines at her family estate QUINTA do Cruzeiro in 2003 and restored th
original 50s winery. Stylish Encruzado/MALVASIA Fina whites, gd foot-trodde
reds. New: fresh,dry TOURIGA N ROSADO.

Lagoalva, Quinta da Tej r p w ★★ Young winemakers Diogo Campilho and Ped
Pinhão target a new generation with fruity, fresh blends of native grapes wi
CHARD, SAUV BL, SYRAH; oak can be overenthusiastic. V.gd varietal Alfrocheir
Hobby Abafado (fortified FERNÃO PIRES).

Lancers p w sp ★ JOSÉ MARÍA DA FONSECA's semi-sweet (semi-sparkling) ROSADO, nc
white, sparkling (p w) and alcohol-free versions.

Lavradores de Feitoria Dou r w ★★→★★★ Collaboration of 18 producers wi
unusual strength in whites, esp SAUV BL, Meruge (100% Viosinho). Gd reds, in
Três Bagos Res, QUINTA da Costa das Aguaneiras, elegant Meruge (mostly TIN
RORIZ from a n-facing 400m v'yd).

Lisboa Large, hilly VR around the capital with varied terroir and a muddle of loc
and international grapes. Best-known DOCS: ALENQUER (pioneering boutiq
wineries CHOCAPALHA, MONTE D'OIRO produce reds of great finesse) and tradition
BUCELAS, CARCAVELOS, COLARES. Accomplished fresh, mineral whites at Bioma
(Jampal), Casal Figueira (Vital), Casal Sta Maria (Colares, v.gd CHARD) and Va
da Capucha – organic, like QUINTA da Serradinha which, bordering DÃO and BA
focuses on Encruzado (w) and BAGA (r).

Madeira r w ★→★★★★ Island famous for fortifieds. Modest table wines (Terr

Madeirenses VR, Madeirense DOC). VERDELHO best. Look for Primeira Paixão, QUINTA do Moledo, Barbusano.

ias, Quinta das Dão ★★→★★★ Sister of QUINTA DOS ROQUES; Organic entry-level wines and varietal wines, incl Jaen, MALVASIA Fina, DÃO's only VERDELHO more characterful than flashy flagship Flor das Maias.

lhadinha Nova, Herdade da Alen r p w sw ★★★ 06 07 08' 09 10' 12 Family estate with stylish country-house hotel. Entry-level (da Peceguina) and middle-tier wines increasingly single varietal. Top blends offer better complexity, balance.

ateus Rosé r p (w) sp ★ World's bestselling, medium-dry, lightly carbonated rosé now available in white, fully sparkling (p w) or drier with no spritz. Expressions are: (MARIA GOMES/CHARD) and three rosé blends (BAGA/SHIRAZ, Baga/ MUSCAT; ARAGONEZ/ZIN).

endes, Anselmo Vin r w sw sp ★★→★★★ Fine ALVARINHOS Contacto, Muros Antigos, Muros de Melgaço, new Expressões and esp oaked Curtimenta, single-v'yd Parcela Única. Gd LOUREIRO too. Pardusco, silky and modern red VIN, is a revelation.

essias Bair r w ★→★★★ Large BAIRRADA-based firm; interests in DOURO (incl Port). Old-school reds best.

inho Vin River between n Portugal and Spain, also VR. Some leading VIN producers prefer VR Minho label.

onte d'Oiro, Quinta do Lis r w p ★★→★★★ Initial consultancy and cuttings (Syrah 24 from 60-yr-old Hermitage vines) from Chapoutier (see France) give Portugal's best SYRAH. V.gd VIOGNIER (Madrigal) and TINTA RORIZ (Tempera). Bento & Chapoutier Ex-Aequo Syrah/TOURIGA N now labelled Monte d'Oiro.

oscatel do Douro Dou The elevated Favaios region produces surprisingly fresh, fortified MOSCATEL Galego (MUSCAT à Petit Grains) to rival those of SET. Look out for: Adega Cooperativa Favaios, PORTAL, POÇAS (see Port chapter), NIEPOORT.

ouchão, Herdade de Alen r w ★★★ 03' 05' 06 07 08' 09 Leading traditional Alicante Bouschet-focused estate: museum release (Colheitas Antigas), *Tonel 3-4* (top yrs), fortified *licoroso*, grappa. Flashier Ponte das Canas Alicante Bouschet blend incl SHIRAZ. Dom Rafael (new packaging) gd value.

ouraz, Casa de Dão ★★ Modern but characterful (esp Elfa) gd-value wines from several family-owned v'yds (140-400m), certified organic 1996. Alr label is from bought-in DOU, VIN, ALEN organic grapes.

ouro, Quinta do Alen r w ★★★ Imposing reds, mostly ALEN grapes with TOURIGA N, CAB SAUV (both sometimes single variety too). Mouro Gold in top yrs 00 02 05 06' 07' 08 09. Rich, savoury Vinha do Malhó, gd Centurion. Approachable Vinha do Mouro incl new gd value white.

urganheira, Caves ★★★ Largest ESPUMANTE producer; owns RAPOSEIRA. Blends and single-varietal (native, French grapes) fizz. Best: Vintage, Grande Res, Czar rosé.

uxagat Dou His grandfather made pioneering BARCA VELHA; now Mateus Nicolau de Almeida is at the vanguard of a generation living in the DOU, growing grapes and making wines. Elevated DOU Superior organically farmed v'yds and low-intervention winemaking are the secret to minerally fresh whites and nuanced reds; gd dry ROSADO too.

Rock around the clock

If you laid all the v'yd walls in PICO (AZORES) end to end, they would encircle the globe twice. These walls, built with black basalt rocks, protect the vines from the harsh, salt Altantic winds. Basalt rules here: the vines are planted in the cracks of basalt lava fields, in soil imported from the neighbouring island of Faial. Not surprisingly it's a World Heritage Site.

Niepoort Dou r p w ★★★→★★★★ Family Port shipper and DOU wine pion
reproducing the magic elsewhere. Exceptional new wines with a scapel-l
focus on terroir and old vines incl Turris (DOU r), Poeirinho (BAIR r) and Cons
(DÃO); next Sidecar with SUSANA ESTEBAN (PORTALEGRE). Stellar core Dou rar
incl *Redoma* (r p w Res w), Tiara (w), Coche (w) and reds Vertente, Char
and Batuta. Experimental Projectos range incl Docil (VIN LOUREIRO) and ma
playthings; v'yds in QUINTAS de Baixo (Bair) and da Lomba (DÃO) show lo
term commitment.

Noval, Quinta do Dou r ★★→★★★ AXA-owned Port shipper, since 2004 maki
DOU wines (or Duriense VR with SYRAH), incl gd-value Cedro, Labrador (10
SYRAH, named after winemaker's dog), v.gd varietal TOURIGA N.

Palmela Set r w ★→★★★ CASTELÃO-focused DOC. Can be long-lived, eg. Herdade Peg
Claros, Casa Ermelinda Freitas.

Passadouro, Quinta do Dou r w ★★→★★★ Superbly concentrated estate reds, e
old-vine Res. TOURIGA N and new Touriga Franca come from QUINTA do Sib
whites from elevated granite v'yds. Entry label Passa gd value. V.gd Port.

Pato, Filipa Bair r w sp ★★★ Like her father LUÍS PATO, Filipa tests the boundari
Silky, perfumed BAGA: fruity FP Baga, amphora-aged Post Quercus (delic
vin de soif), "new" old-vine Territorio Vivo Baga, Espirito de Baga fortified a
sparkling. "Wines with no make-up" approach puts terroir centre-stage
flagship Nossa Calcario Baga and Bical (w).

Pato, Luís Bair r w sw sp ★★→★★★★ Forged his name with *seriously age-worthy, sing
v'yd Baga*: Vinhas Barrio, Pan, Barrosa. Two Pé Franco cuvées from ungraf
vines: QUINTA do Ribeirinho (sandy soils) and finer-framed Valadas (cha
clay, younger vines). For the impatient *Vinhas Velhas* is v.gd each way bet; BA
Rebel (fermented on Bical skins), wacky red FERNÃO PIRES (fermented on Ba
skins) are for drinking young. V.gd whites incl Vinhas Velhas, single-v'yd Vin
Formal, racy new Sercialinho. Of sparkling, characterful single-ferment Méto
Antigo gd value.

Pegões, Adega de Set r p w sw sp ★→★★ Dynamic co-op. Stella label and low-alcol
Nico white offer gd clean fruit. COLHEITA Seleccionada (r w) exceptional value.

Península de Setúbal Set VR Est producers (eg. Bacalhoa Vinhos, JOSÉ MARÍA FONSE
Casa Eremlinda Freitas) on Azeitão's gentle chalky slopes or mineral-rich san
soils of Sado and Tagus ivers. Newcomers lie further w and s. Watch: Herdad
da Comporta, do Cebolal and Soberanas.

Periquita Nickname for the CASTELÃO grape and successful brand name a
trademark of JOSÉ MARÍA DA FONSECA.

Poeira, Quinta do Dou r w ★★★ QUINTA DE LA ROSA's winemaker Jorge Moreir
estate. Wines from cool, n-facing slopes as intense yet softly spoken as the
maker, esp red, now released with more bottle age. White is taut, mineral, oak
ALVARINHO (VR Duriense). Classy second label Pó de Poeira (r).

Portugal's trendiest red grape is Baga. For white, Alvarinho.

Portalegre Alen r p w ★→★★★ Wine writers Richard Mayson (QUINTA do Centr
and João Afonso (Solstício/Equinócio), Lisbon chef Vitor Claro, consulta
Rui Reguinga (Terrenus), SUSANA ESTEBAN, ESPORÃO, now NIEPOORT have flock
to ALEN's n-most subregion (DOC). Elevation, granite and schist, old vin
(incl field blends), gd rainfall account for fresh, structured, mineral wine
Region to watch.

Quinta Estate (*see* under name, eg. POEIRA, QUINTA DO).

Ramos, João Portugal Alen r w Since planting his first 5 ha in ALEN (199
Ramos now works in most of Portugal's regions, both under his own nam
(eg. VIN) and other brands (FALUA, DUORUM, Foz de Arouce and Beir). His reci

for success? Wines with strong commercial appeal, invariably true to their region and offering gd value. Top wines, eg. Marqués de Borba Res, Estremus, as gd as any.

Raposeira Dou sp ★★ Classic-method fizz; flagship Velha Res, CHARD/PINOT N lees-aged 4 yrs.

Real Companhia Velha Dou r p w sw ★★→★★★ Under POEIRA's Jorge Moreira better focused, terroir-driven wines esp Vinhas Velhas QUINTA das Carvalhas (r w), new white from n-facing v'yd. Delaforce ALVARINHO, Quinta de Cidro CHARD, GEWURZ, SÉM show skill with atypical varieties.

Ex-goalkeeper André Manz now saves grapes (Lisboa's Jampal), not goals.

Romeira, Quinta da w ★★→★★★ Historic BUCELAS estate. Set to consolidate pre-eminent position under new owner Wine Ventures with CEO ex-SOGRAPE director Francisco de Sousa Ferreira, new v'yds and consultancy from ex-Carvalhais winemaker Manuel Vieira. V.gd ARINTO (Regia Premium, oaked Morgado Sta Catherina Res, gd-value Prova Regia/VR LISBOA). New: Principium French/native grape blends.

Roques, Quinta dos Dão r w sp ★★→★★★ (r) V.gd age-worthy red blends (esp Res and GARRAFEIRA) and single varietals, esp Encruzado (now more subtly oaked), TOURIGA N, Alfrocheiro Preto. New Jaen plantings reflect upswing of interest in Spain's MENCIA. Gd-value, entry-level Correio label.

Rosa, Quinta de la Dou r p w ★★★ Spick and span after winery/tourism accommodation make-over. Rich but elegant reds, esp Res, now in big formats (up to 18 litres). Gd-value DouROSA entry level. More generous Passagem from QUINTA das Bandeiras. Gd Port too.

Rosado Rosé; despite the success of MATEUS ROSÉ, a curiously unexploited category. IDEAL DRINKS' Colinas São Lourenço Principal Tête de Cuvée Rosém, Sparkling Brut Rosé set new standards.

Santar, Casa de Dão r w sp ★★→★★★ Under DÃO SUL leadership poised reds and textured but fresh Encruzado whites, esp flagship Condessa de Santar.

São João, Caves Bair r w sp ★★ →★★★ A traditional and family-owned firm, known for v.gd, old-fashioned reds, esp *Frei João*, Poço do Lobo (BAIR) and Porta dos Cavaleiros (DÃO), of which older vintages (cellared since 1963) are now being released. New management; updated range incl gd ARINTO/CHARD white and sparkling blends.

São Miguel, Herdade de Alen r p w ★★→★★★ Smart modern wines, entry-level Ciconia under screwcap; Res, firmer Montinho gd value. São Miguel label: serious, well-defined estate wines, esp Res, Dos Descobridores range, showier Private Collection.

Setúbal (r) (w) br (dr) sw ★★★ Tiny DOC s of the river Tagus. Moreish fortified MOSCATEL dessert wines incl rare red MOSCATEL Roxo; best perfumed, balanced. Main producers: BACALHOA VINHOS, JOSÉ MARIA DA FONSECA, HORÁCIO DOS REIS SIMÕES. Watch: António Saramago, Adriano Tiago.

Soalheiro, Quinta de Vin w sp ★★★ Sunny, organically cultivated ALVARINHO v'yd. Even "basic" Alvarinho is age-worthy. Best is subtly barrel-fermented old-vine Primeiras Vinhas; Res is oakier. Dócil is off-dry. New: allo Alvarinho/LOUREIRO blend.

Sogrape Vin ★→★★★★ Portugal's biggest player. MATEUS ROSÉ, BARCA VELHA jewels in the crown for contrasting reasons. Portfolio encompasses VIN (Azevedo, Gazela, Morgadio da Torre), DÃO (CARVALHAIS), ALEN (Herdade do Peso), DOU (Barca Velha, FERREIRA, SANDEMAN and OFFLEY Port). Approachable multi-regional brands incl Grão Vasco, Pena de Pato, Callabriga.

Sousa, Alves de Dou r w ★★★ Characterful range from several QUINTAS, incl rugged

Abandonado, polished Vinha de Lordelo (r); oxidative, skin-contact whites Reds are fresh; look for new white Berço (Avesso/ARINTO). Port range expanding New winery 2015.

Symington Family Estates Dou r w ★★→★★★★ Port shipper; DOU wines since 2000 incl super-premium CHRYSEIA, QUINTA do Vesúvio reds and volume Altano brand Best: Altano wines organic red and Quinta do Ataíde Res TOURIGA N, incl Block 62 in top yrs.

Tejo r w DOC and VR around the river Tagus. Quantity-to-quality shift (better soils/grapes), but little sets the pulse racing. Aptly named Encosta do Sobral's old-vine Different Red prospers on unusual schist soils. Old vines also produce gd results with stalwart FERNÃO PIRES (Casca Wines, CASAL BRANCO). Solid performers: QUINTA da Alorna, FALUA. More ambitious: QUINTA DA LAGOALVA, Pinha da Torre, Rui Reguinga (Tributo).

Tinto Red.

Trás-os-Montes Tras Mountainous inland DOC, just n of DOU; (VR Transmontano) Leading light: Valle Pradinhos.

Vale Dona Maria, Quinta do Dou r p w ★★→★★★ *V.gd plush yet elegant reds*, incl CV Casa de Casal de Loivos; also structured white VZ. Gd-value Van Zellers range from bought-in fruit. New: two single-parcel estate wines: Vinha do Rio, Vinha da Francisca and fruity entry level Rufo.

Vale Meão, Quinta do Dou r w ★★★→★★★★ A leading DOU Superior estate – once source of BARCA VELHA. V.gd second label: Meandro, now incl white. Top red rich and satisfying but balanced. The single-varietal/parcel F Olazabal Monte Meão range's finer frame is due to freshness of TOURIGA N on granite and firm TINTA RORIZ tannins.

Vallado Dou r p w ★★★ (r) Family estate gives strength in whites and persistent reds. New DOU Superior QUINTA do Orgal v'yd now onstream. Entry-level red v.gd. Strong varietal range (Sousão, TOURIGA N, dry MOSCATEL). Res and flagship Adelaide old-vine reds well-structured, mineral. Ambitious Ports incl Adelaide Vintage and Adelaide Tributa Very Old Tawny.

Vinho Regional (VR) Same status as French Vin de Pays. More leeway for experimentation than DOC.

Europe's westernmost vineyard is Casal Santa Maria (Colares), planted by Baron Bruemmer, aged 95.

Vinho Verde (Vin) r w p sp ★→★★★ The n-most coastal DOC, once just sharp fizzy wines, undergoing a renaissance with fresh but better concentrated blends Most exciting is unstoppable march of high-end, subregional, varietal QUINTA wines, esp ALVARINHO from Monção e Melgaço (eg. ANSELMO MENDES, QUINTAS DI SOALHEIRO, do Reguengo, de Melgaço, da Pedra, do Regueiro) and LOUREIRO from Lima (eg. QUINTA DO AMEAL, APHROS, NIEPOORT Docil, Paço de Palmeria), now Avesso (*see* COVELA). Red Vinhão grape is acquired taste worth a try (eg. APHROS). Large brands spritzy; DYA.

Wine & Soul Dou r w Winemaking couple Sandra Tavares' and Jorge Serôdic Borges' intense wines incl stunning Guru (w), elegant QUINTA da Manoella Vinhas Velhas and denser Pintas from neighbouring sites. V.gd second labels (r): Pintas Character, Manoella (r). Stunning 5G Very Old Tawny Port from Borges' inherited stocks.

Port, Sherry & Madeira

It takes a French word to describe the latest activity in Jerez: that of "négociant". Equipo Navazos started it when the winemaker for Valdespino and La Guita joined forces with a criminology professor to select and bottle outstanding casks (or butts). They've bottled around 10 individual casks now. Several more companies have copied, cherry-picking fine casks for limited-edition sales. Now Equipo Navazos has started to bottle Montilla in the same way.

Port is becoming less and less reliant on vintage declarations to make headlines. Typically only one in three vintages is declared and even then, production is miniscule – 2011 Vintage Port is already in scarce supply. A spate of glamorous Very Old (and v. expensive) Tawny releases has tapped into the market for Colheita; this, like (dwindling) stocks of mature Vintage, can be promoted as anniversary wine. Limited-edition Single Quinta Vintage Port magnums are also on the increase. In Madeira, efforts are underway to widen the wine's appeal beyond collectors and connoisseurs of top Frasqueira (vintage) wines. Fine 10-year-olds are accessible and attractive.

Recent Port vintages

"Declared" when the wine is outstanding and meets the shippers' highest standards. In good but not quite classic years most shippers now use the names of their quintas (estates) for single-quinta wines of great character but needing less ageing in bottle. The vintages to drink now are 1966, 1970, 1977, 1980, 1983, 1985, 1987, 1992, 1994, though I drank Warre 2011 with chocolate and loved it. Don't be scared to try.

2014 Excellent from those vineyards which ducked September's rain; production low.

2013 Mid-harvest rain made for a difficult year, especially for Touriga N.

2012 Single-quinta year. Very low-yielding, drought-afflicted. Stars: Noval, Graham dos Malvedos.

2011 Classic year, widely declared. Inky, outstanding concentration and stucture. Stars: Noval Nacional, Taylor's Quinta de Vargellas Vinha Velha, Fonseca.

2010 Single-quinta year. Hot, dry but higher yields than 2009. Stars: Vesuvio, Dow da Senhora da Ribeira.

2009 Controversial year. Declared by Fladgate, but not Symington's or Sogrape. Stars: Taylor's, Niepoort, Fonseca, Warre's.

2008 Single-quinta year. Low-yielding, powerful wines. Stars: Noval, Vesuvio, Taylor Terra Feita, Passadouro. Sandeman's LBV is v gd.

2007 Classic year, widely declared. Deep-coloured, rich but well-balanced wines. Stars: Taylor's, Vesuvio.

2006 Difficult; handful single-quintas. Stars: Vesuvio, Roriz, Barros Quinta Galeira.

2005 Single-quinta year. Stars: Niepoort, Taylor de Vargellas, Dow da Senhora da Ribeira – iron fist in velvet glove.

2004 Single-quinta year. Stars: Pintas, Taylor de Vargellas Vinha Velha, Quinta de la Rosa – balanced, elegant wines.

2003 Classic vintage year. Hot, dry summer. Powerfully ripe, concentrated wines, universally declared. Drink from 2020–30.

2001 Single-quinta year. Stars: Noval Nacional, Fonseca do Panascal, do Vale Meão – wet year; relatively forward wines.

2000 Classic year. A very fine vintage, universally declared. Rich, well-balanced wines for the long term. Drink from 2018.

Alexander Jules Sherry ★★→★★★ The US-based négociant bottling selected BUTT: Young business, with wines currently available in the USA, Japan.

Almacenista Sherry ★→★★★ Producer, literally wholesaler, selling to Sherry shipped needing extra quality and/or quantity. Often source of terrific Sherries. LUSTA: pioneered outstanding portfolio, eg. OLOROSO Pata de Gallina. Newer UK range in Pedro's Almacenista Selection.

Álvaro Domecq Sherry ★★→★★★ Founded 1998, based on SOLERAS of Pilar Aranda: JEREZ's oldest bodega. Polished, elegant wines. Gd FINO La Janda. Excellent 173(VORS series.

Alvear Mont-M ★★→★★★ Largest MONT-M producer of v.gd pale, dry FINO from PX, es Fino CB. V. fine, unctuous, raisined PX. Silky, supple SOLERA 1927.

Andresen Port ★★→★★★ Family-owned house. Excellent wood-aged Ports esp 20-y: old TAWNY, *Colheitas* (1900' 1910' still bottled on demand; 1980' 92' 97, 03' Pioneered on-trend age-dated WHITE PORTS 10-, 20-, v.gd 40-yr-old.

Barbadillo Sherry, Man ★→★★★★ A BODEGA in a former palace overlookin(Sanlúcar's old town. The range runs from reliable to some of SANLÚCAR's finest incl Solear MANZANILLA. Barbadillo was a pioneer of Manzanilla EN RAMA, with fou seasonal SACAS and distinctive bird labels. Reliquía range is top, esp AMONTILLAD(and PALO CORTADO. Treasury incl superb centenarian Amontillado. The winer: outside JEREZ makes table wines, incl Castillo San Diego, which are popula locally, from PALOMINO.

Barbeito Mad ★★→★★★★ Best known for innovative single-cask COLHEITAS, 20-, 30 40-yr-old MALVASIA. Exciting new wines draw on famous old v'yds Fajã dos Padre (Malvasia FRASQUIERA 1986) and Ribeiro Real (whose 1950s Tinta Negra bring sublime depth to 20-yr-old VERDELHO and BOAL).

Barros Almeida Port ★→★★★ Focuses on wood-aged ports. Mellifluous 20-yr-old: 40-yr-old TAWNY, COLHEITAS 74' 80', Very Old Dry White and Colheita (35) WHIT PORTS. Owned by Sogevinus (along with BURMESTER, CÁLEM, KOPKE).

Barros e Sousa Mad ★★★ Acquired by PEREIRA D'OLIVEIRA 2013 who will bottl(remaining stock but set aside no new wines for this brand. Look for rar(Bastardo Old RES and 5-yr-old Listrão.

Blandy Mad ★★→★★★★ Historic family firm, dynamic CEO. Since 2012 Chri: Blandy has acquired v'yds, moved production to modern port-side location New externally heated *estufas* optimize quality of basic wines. *Funchal lodge* showcase history, incl vast library of FRASQUEIRA (BUAL 1920', 1968', MALMSEY 1988', VERDELHO 1973', SERCIAL 1910'). V.gd 20-yr-old Terrantez and COLHEITA: (Bual 1996, Verdelho and Sercial 1998).

Borges, HM Mad ★→★★★ Sisters Helena and Isabel Borges have bottled tiny amounts of fine 1877 Terrantez demi-john from founding yr for auction. V.g(30-yr-old MALVASIA incl wine from 1930.

Bual (or Boal) Mad Classic Madeira grape: tangy, smoky, sweet wines; not as rich a: MALMSEY. Perfect with cheese and lighter desserts.

Burmester Port ★→★★★ Sogevinus-owned. Elegant wood-aged ports esp sophisticate(20-, 40-yr-old TAWNY, COLHEITAS 63' 98, age-dated WHITE PORTS, incl fine 40-yr-old Gd Single QUINTA VINTAGE PORT: Quinta do Arnozelo.

Butt Sherry 600-litre barrel of long-matured American oak used for Sherry. Fille(5/6 full, allows space for FLOR to grow. Popular in Scotland, post-Sherry use, fo adding final polish to whisky.

Cálem Port ★→★★★ Sogevinus-owned; relatively forward, fruity style. Velhotes is the main brand. V.gd COLHEITAS, 40-yr-old TAWNY, 10-yr-old WHITE PORT.

Canteiro Mad Method of naturally cask-ageing the finest Madeira in warm, humid lodges for greater subtlety/complexity than ESTUFAGEM.

César Florido Sherry ★→★★ MOSCATEL specialist, family business (one of CHIPIONA's oldest: est 1887). Succulent Moscatel Pasas, min 4 yrs old, from raisined grapes.

Chipiona Sherry The zone of production of MOSCATEL grapes required by Sherry companies. Some producers now bottle and sell their own. CÉSAR FLORIDO leads the way.

Churchill Port ★★★ Est 1981 by Johnny Graham whose family founded GRAHAM. V.gd WHITE PORT, unfiltered LBV, VINTAGE PORT 82 85 91 94 97 00 03 07' 11', incl Single-QUINTA da Gricha (11' in 1,570 limited-edition magnums only).

Cockburn Port ★★→★★★ A historic shipper bought by SYMINGTON FAMILY ESTATES in 2010. Special RES RUBY now aged longer in wood and more vibrant LBV 1 yr less. V.gd VINTAGE PORT 63 67 70 75 83' 91 94 97 00 03' 07' 11' and single-QUINTA dos Canais.

Colheita Port, Mad Vintage-dated Port or Madeira of a single yr, cask-aged at least 7 yrs for Port and 5 yrs for Madeira. Bottling date shown on the label.

Cossart Gordon Mad MADEIRA WINE COMPANY-owned brand. Drier style than BLANDY. New: 2005 MALVASIA Harvest.

Crasto, Quinta do Port The Roquette family's old vines go into some of the region's best wines and a v. concentrated VINTAGE PORT and unfiltered LBV.

Croft Port ★★→★★★ Fladgate-owned historic shipper. Return to foot-treading (2003) brings more backbone to sweet, fleshy VINTAGE PORT 66 70 75 77 82 85 91 94 00 03' 07 09' 11'; QUINTA da Roêda is lighter. Popular styles: Indulgence, Triple Crown, Distinction and pioneering Pink, a ROSÉ PORT.

Crusted Port RES RUBY-quality Port, usually non-vintage, bottled young then aged so throws a deposit/"crust" – decant. Look for GRAHAM, FONSECA, DOW, CHURCHILL and NIEPOORT.

Delgado Zuleta Sherry, Man ★→★★ Oldest (1744) SANLÚCAR firm; crisp, penetrating wines. 8-yr-old *La Goya* MANZANILLA; also Manzanilla PASADA EN RAMA XL. Monteagudo AMONTILLADO Viejo, v. original; 40-yr-old Quo Vadis? Amontillado shows terrific intensity.

Domecq Sherry Still one of great names in Sherry, former owner of HARVEY's Bristol Cream and Fundador Brandy, though its SOLERAS and family members long dispersed after takeovers. VORS wines owned by OSBORNE; *La Ina, Botaina, Rio Viejo*, Viña 25 by LUSTAU. ÁLVARO DOMECQ runs boutique BODEGA.

Douro Port The river that lends its name to region. Subregions: Baixo Corgo and, best for Port, Cima (Upper) Corgo and Douro Superior. Rises in Spain, where it is the Duero.

Dow Port ★★★→★★★★ Historic shipper owned by SYMINGTON. Drier VINTAGE PORT 66 70 72 75 77 80 83 85' 91 94 97 00' 03 07' 11', esp single-QUINTA from Bomfim

---

Catching the breeze

What determines the style of Sherry is not just the base wine but also the BODEGA: cool and humid is best. Hotter, drier bodegas produce richer, more solid wines. Bodegas facing the sea and catching the sea breeze are the most desirable: the windows on that side will be left open, but kept closed and shaded at the other end to keep the sun out. Higher roofs keep things cooler, and earth floors help humidity. FINO from one end of a bodega can taste totally different from the same wine from the other end. The hottest, driest bodegas are kept for old AMONTILLADOS and OLOROSOS.

(Senhora da Ribeira is richer). Purchase of QUINTA da Sabordela adds 30 ha to Bomfim (with new winery/visitor centre).

Duorum Port ★★→★★★★ The duo is JOÃO PORTUGAL RAMOS and ex-FERREIRA winemaker José Maria Soares Franco. V.gd dense, pure-fruited VINTAGE PORT 07 11' 12 from centenarian vines. Second label Vinha de Castelo Melhor blends old and young DOU Superior vines. Also gd table wines.

Emilio Hidalgo Sherry ★★★→★★★★ An outstanding small family BODEGA. All the wines (except PX) start by spending time under FLOR. Excellent mature (15 yrs old) La Panesa FINO, intense El Tresillo AMONTILLADO Fino, 50-yr-old Amontillado Tresillo 1874 and rare Santa Ana PX 1861. Easy mistake, HIDALGO-LA GITANA is a different company.

Equipo Navazos Sherry ★★★→★★★★ Pioneer of the négociant approach to Sherry bottling from selected BUTTS from different BODEGAS. Jesús Barquín and Eduardo Ojeda form a team (*equipo*) seeking out outstanding Sherries, numbering in a series from 1, eg. La Bota de MANZANILLA No. 42. Also MONT-M: eg. No. 46. Their quality has attracted a new generation worldwide to JEREZ. Separate Manzanilla line *"I Think"* EN RAMA. Collaborations with Perez Barquero (Montilla), Colet Navazos (sparkling; uses Sherry in *liqueur d'expedition*), Navazos-Palazzi (brandy). FLOR Power is fascinating – unfortified, *flor*-aged wine: a homage to the traditional winemaking of Jerez.

Espiritus de Jerez Sherry ★★★ →★★★★ The boutique collection of RIOJA businessman Roberto Amillo has just four exceptional wines. Presented in perfume-like bottles and taken from fine old SOLERAS.

Estufagem Mad Bulk process of slowly heating Madeiras min 3 mths for characteristic scorched-earth tang. Finer results with external heating jackets and lower max temperature (45°C/113°F), but less subtle than CANTEIRO.

Ferreira Port ★★ →★★★ SOGRAPE-owned historic Port house. Winemaker Luis Sottomayor reckons LBV now as gd as last decade's VINTAGE PORT; both categories on the up here. V.gd spicy TAWNY incl RES (Don Antónia), 10- and 20-yr-old Tawny (QUINTA do Porto, *Duque de Bragança*).

Fladgate Port Independent family-owned partnership. Owns leading Port houses TAYLOR, FONSECA, CROFT, now KROHN and the luxury hotel in VILA NOVA DE GAIA, The Yeatman.

Like Sherry? You'll love Sherry vinegar. Essential for making a real gazpacho.

Flor Sherry Spanish for "flower": refers to the layer of *Saccharomyces* yeasts that develop naturally and live on top of FINO/MANZANILLA Sherry in a BUTT 5/6 full. *Flor* consumes oxygen and other compounds (process known as "biological ageing") and protects wine from browning (oxidation). Traditional AMONTILLADO begin as Finos or Manzanillas before the *flor* dies naturally or with addition of fortifying spirit. *Flor* grows a thicker layer nearer the sea at EL PUERTO DE SANTA MARÍA and SANLÚCAR, hence lighter character of Sherry there. Most abundant in spring and autumn.

Fonseca Guimaraens Port ★★★→★★★★ FLADGATE-owned Port house, founded 1815. Voluptuous Bin 27 (Waterloo is bicentenary special edition), organic Terra Prima RES and esp VINTAGE PORT: **66' 70 75 77' 80 83 85' 92 94' 97** 00' 03' 07 09 11'. Second label Vintage Port Guimaraens if no classic declaration eg. 2012 Single-QUINTA Panascal.

Frasqueira Mad Single-yr Madeira aged min 20 yrs in wood, usually much longer for more concentration (by evaporation) and complexity (by oxidation). Date of bottling compulsory.

Garvey Sherry ★ →★★ Last remnant of the Ruiz-Mateos empire now seeking a buyer. Best known for San Patricio FINO.

> **Sherry goes dry**
> Goodbye to the alluring-sounding "OLOROSO dulce" and "sweet
> AMONTILLADO". Now, if you want to call it Sherry, it has to be dry. If it's not
> dry it's either "medium" (5–115 g/l residual sugar); or sweeter "cream"
> (115–140 g/l). Look out for phrases like "a blend of Oloroso Sherries".

González Byass Sherry ★★→★★★★ GB (founded 1845) remains a family business. Cellarmaster Antonio Flores, who inherited the job from his father, is a debonair, poetic presence. From the most famous of FINOS, *Tío Pepe*, Flores has developed a fascinating portfolio: EN RAMA and the elegant Palmas range of aged Finos (6-, 8-, 10- and 40-yr-old). Alongside are consistently polished Viña AB AMONTILLADO, Matúsalem OLOROSO, Noë PX. Also gd brandies; table wines, incl Beronia (RIOJA), Vilarnau (PENEDÈS), Viñas del Vero (Somontano); plus (not so gd) Croft Original Pale Cream. FINCA Moncloa, from Cádiz region, produces still reds; also glorious Tintilla de Rota, from eponymous grape (aka GRACIANO), revival of a historic sweet red fortified style.

Graham Port ★★★→★★★★ SYMINGTON-owned Port house. First division Ports from RES RUBY Six Grapes to VINTAGE PORT 63 66 70' 75 77' 80 83' 85' 91' 94' 97 00' 03' 07' 11', incl age-worthy single-QUINTA dos Malvedos. Exciting limited releases incl Special Old Vines Six Grapes Edition, Stone Terraces Vintage Port 11', royal anniversary COLHEITAS 52' 82 and, trumping them all, sublime Ne Oublie Very Old TAWNY, one of three 1882 casks laid down by AJ Symington.

Guita, La Sherry ★→★★★ Gd *Manzanilla*. Grupo Estévez-owned (also VALDESPINO).

Gutiérrez Colosía Sherry ★→★★★ Rare remaining riverside BODEGA in EL PUERTO DE SANTA MARÍA. Former ALMACENISTA. Excellent old PALO CORTADO.

Harvey's Sherry ★→★★★ Once-great Sherry name. Famed for Bristol Cream. Fine collection of VORS wines; some show briskness of old age.

Henriques & Henriques Mad ★★→★★★★ Madeira shipper with 11 ha of v'yd incl rare Terrantez grape. Unique extra-dry apéritif Monte Seco. Best are 20-yr-old MALVASIA and Terrantez,15-yr-old (NB *Sercial*, also Single Harvest Sercial 2001), vintage (eg. VERDELHO 1957, Terrantez 1954, Sercial 1971'). New: vanilla-edged Fine Rich Single Harvest 1997 spent 6 mths in seasoned bourbon barrels.

Herederos de Argüeso Sherry, Man ★★→★★★ One of SANLÚCAR's top producers. V.gd San León, dense and salty *San León Res* and youthful Las Medallas; also impressively lively VORS AMONTILLADO Viejo.

Hidalgo-La Gitana Sherry, Man ★★→★★★★ Historic (1792) SANLÚCAR firm fronted by Javier Hidalgo. Famed for ultra-delicate MANZANILLA La Gitana. EN RAMA is more expressive. Finest Manzanilla is intense single-v'yd *Pastrana Pasada*, verging on AMONTILLADO maturity. Outstanding VORS, incl Napoleon Amontillado, Wellington PALO CORTADO, Triana PX.

Jerez de la Frontera Sherry Centre of Sherry region, between Cádiz and Seville. "Sherry" is a corruption of the ancient name, pronounced "*hereth*". In French, Xérès. Hence DO is Jerez-Xérès-Sherry.

Justino Mad ★→★★★ The largest Madeira shipper, owned by the rum giant La Martiniquaise – makes Broadbent label. A bit four-square but Terrantez Old RES NV v.gd as are Terrantez 1978 and MALVASIA 1964,1933 FRASQUEIRAS.

Kopke Port ★→★★★ The oldest Port house (1638). Forte is spicy and structured COLHEITAS 35' 57' 64' 80' 87 89 91'; age-dated TAWNY and WHITE PORT – outstanding 40-yr-olds.

Krohn Port ★→★★★ Exceptional stocks of aged TAWNY, COLHEITA 61' 66' 67' 76' 82' 83' 87' 91 97 dating back to 1863. Now Fladgate-owned; some stock being diverted to TAYLOR eg. 1863, 1964. VINTAGE PORTS on the up, 07' 09 11.

LBV (Late Bottled Vintage) Port Robust, bright-fruited Port from a single yr, which is kept in wood for twice as long as VINTAGE PORT (around 5 yrs). Commercial styles broachable on release without decanting unlike age-worthy unfiltered versions eg. CHURCHILL, FERREIRA, NIEPOORT, QUINTA do Nova, QUINTA DO NOVAL, SANDEMAN, WARRE.

Leacock Mad Long, distinguished track record for FRASQUEIRA. Since 1981 acquisition by the MADEIRA WINE COMPANY, focused on volume with new modern label for broader appeal.

Lustau Sherry ★★★→★★★★ Renowned for a treasure trove of Sherries; launched the original ALMACENISTA collection. Explore styles of JEREZ DO with MANZANILLA Papirusa, Puerto FINO, La Ina Fino. Emilín is superb MOSCATEL, VORS PX is outstanding, carrying age and sweetness lightly. One of the few BODEGAS t release vintage Sherries, eg. profound OLOROSO AÑADA 97.

Madeira Vintners Mad Est 2012, but already making waves with idiosyncrati approach, incl plans to release small-batch, terroir-driven wines (labels ma refer to growers, says CEO Paulo Mendes), Listrão (aka PALOMINO FINO) and us of various techniques (eg. cask fermentation, fermentation on skins, micro oxygenation or ESTUFAGEM) to attain complexity and profile of 5- to 10-yr-old i 3 yrs. Watch this space.

Madeira Wine Company Mad Est 1913; an association of all 26 British Madeir companies. Owns BLANDY, COSSART GORDON, Leacock, Miles and accounts for over 50% of bottled Madeira exports. Since the Blandy family gained control, almos exclusively focused on promoting Blandy brand.

Maestro Sierra, El Sherry ★★★ *Small, traditional bodega*, brilliant quality, run b Carmen Borrego, following on from her mother Pilar Plá. Fine FINO, AMONTILLAD 1830 VORS, OLOROSO 1/14 VORS.

Malmsey (Malvasia Candida) Mad The sweetest and richest of traditional Madeir grape varieties, yet with Madeira's unique sharp tang. Perfect with rich frui chocolate puddings.

Montilla-Moriles Mont-M ★→★★★ Andalucian DO nr Córdoba. At the top end superbly rich PX, some with long ageing in SOLERA. Often great value. Also create versions of FINO with PX. Top producers: ALVEAR, PÉREZ BARQUERO, TORO ALBALÁ Important source of PX for use in JEREZ DO.

When it's gone, it's gone

So they say of supermarket deals. But it's true of Very Old TAWNY PORT too. It may be bang on trend but v. old stock is rare, and casks special enough to fly solo even rarer (hence the dizzy prices). It might be better, say some, to eke them out and add a bit of magic to more affordable 20-yr-old and 40-yr-old Tawnies instead. But less headline-grabbing....

Niepoort Port ★★★→★★★★ Small family-run Port house; great table wines too Late 80s and 90s suffered quality dip; now compelling VINTAGE PORT rang incl classic (00' 03 05' 07 09' 11'), approachable Secundum, unique *garrafeir* (aged in demijohns) and single-v'yd Bioma. Exceptional COLHEITA, TAWNY incl VW a 999-bottle Tawny blend (base component:1863). CRUSTED v.gd. Also makin white wine in JEREZ with EQUIPO NAVAZOS.

Noval, Quinta do Port ★★★→★★★★ Historic port QUINTA owned by AXA. Elegantl structured VINTAGE PORT 63' 66 67 70 75 78 82 85 87 91 94' 95 97' 00' 03' 04 07 08' 11' 12 is fraction of price of rare, compelling *Nacional* from 2.5ha ungrafte v'yd. Second vintage label: Silval. V.gd age-dated TAWNY, COLHEITAS, unfiltered LBV plush, chocolatey Noval Black RES.

Offley Port ★→★★ Principal QUINTA (Boa Vista) sold by Sogrape in 2013. Gd recent fruit-driven VINTAGE PORT and TAWNY. Apéritif/cocktail styles incl Cachuca RES WHITE PORT, ROSÉ PORT.

Osborne Sherry ★★→★★★★ Historic (1772) BODEGA at gateway to EL PUERTO DE SANTA MARÍA. FINO QUINTA and mature Coquinero Fino typical of El Puerto. Superb v. old SOLERAS incl AOS AMONTILLADO, PDP PALO CORTADO, OLOROSO Seco BC 200, PX Solera Vieja. Owns former DOMECQ VORS incl 51–1a Amontillado. Its black bull logo now recognized as a national icon. Also makes table wines in RIOJA, RUEDA, RIBERA DEL DUERO; renowned for brandies.

Passadouro Port Powerful single-QUINTA VINTAGE PORT, made by NIEPOORT 1992–2000, now WINE & SOUL's Jorge Serôdio Borges. Concentrated foot-trodden unfiltered LBV; gd RES RUBY.

What's known as Madeira cake in Britain is "English cake" in Madeira.

Paternina, Federico Sherry ★→★★★ Based on the cellars of Díez Merito. Light, young Sherries; plus fine aged VORS range: AMONTILLADO *Fino Imperial*, Victoria Regina OLOROSO, Vieja SOLERA PX.

Pedro Romero Sherry ★→★★ Leading MANZANILLA producer, esp Pasada-style Aurora. Owns v. old SOLERAS, incl from Gaspar Florido. Oldest is piercing, concentrated, from Ansar Real PALO CORTADO solera (1820). A supplier to EQUIPO NAVAZOS.

Pereira d'Oliveira Vinhos Mad ★★→★★★★ Vast stocks (1.6 million litres) of bottled-on-demand FRASQUEIRA on ullage (incl stunning 19th-century vintages, eg. Terrantez 1880, Sercial 1875). Rare 1927 Bastardo and 1875 MOSCATEL. COLHEITAS spend min 10 yrs in cask. All blends aged in ESTUFAGEM.

Pérez Barquero Mont-M ★→★★★ A leader in revival of MONT-M PX. Fine Gran Barquero FINO, AMONTILLADO, OLOROSO; plus v.gd La Cañada PX. A supplier to EQUIPO NAVAZOS.

Porto Cruz Port's largest brand, owned by La Martiniquaise. Flashy multi-media visitor centre contrasts with neighbouring lodges, as do lighter Ports aimed at a younger, broader church.

Puerto de Santa María, El Sherry One of three towns forming the "Sherry Triangle". Production now in decline; remaining BODEGAS, incl former ALMACENISTA, GUTIÉRREZ COLOSÍA, OSBORNE and TERRY. Puerto FINOS are prized as less weighty than JEREZ, not as "salty" as SANLÚCAR.

Quinta Port Portuguese for "estate". "Single-quinta" denotes VINTAGE PORTS from shipper's quinta v'yds; declared in gd, not great yrs. With more single-estate producers, increasingly made in top yrs too. Rising stars: ALVES DE SOUSA, PASSADOURO, Romaneira, Vale Meão, Vale D Maria, WINE & SOUL's Pintas.

Ramos Pinto Port ★★★ Owned by Champagne Roederer. Tweaks to VINTAGE PORT bringing greater structure. Rich single-QUINTA Vintage (de Ervamoira, DOU Superior). Concentrated TAWNY range adopts single-QUINTA approach for 10-yr-old (de Ervamoira) and 20-yr-old (do Bom Retiro, DOU Cima Corgo).

Reserve / Reserva Port Better than basic premium Ports, bottled without a vintage date or age indication. Mostly RUBY; some TAWNY and WHITE PORT.

Rey Fernando de Castilla Sherry ★★→★★★ Superb BODEGA managed by Jan Pettersen, formerly of OSBORNE. Reliable Classic collection. Terrific oxidatively-aged Antique Sherries; all qualify as VOS or VORS, though Pettersen avoids the label. Fascinating, complex, 8-yr-old Antique FINO, fortified to historically correct 17%. Also v. fine brandy and vinegar. A supplier to EQUIPO NAVAZOS.

Rosé Port Port New (2009) growing generation X category prompted by CROFT's pioneering "Pink," now made by most shippers. Quality variable. Serve chilled, on ice or, most likely, in a cocktail.

Royal Oporto Port ★→★★★ Quality renaissance coincides with arrival of technical director Jorge Moreira and outstanding 2011 vintage. Look for 2011 Real Companhia Velha, single-QUINTA das Carvalhas VINTAGE PORT, Carvalhas Memórias do Século XIX Very Old Tawny (dating back to 1867).

Rozès Port ★★★ Port shipper owned by Champagne house Vranken. VINTAGE PORT, incl LBV, sourced from DOU Superior QUINTAS (Grifo, Anibal, Canameira). Terras do Grifo Vintage is blend of all three 07 09' 11; v.gd LBV from Grifo only.

Ruby Port Youngest, cheapest Port style: simple, sweet, red; best is labelled RES.

Saca A withdrawal of Sherry for bottling. For EN RAMA wines the most common *sacas* are in *primavera* (spring) and *otoño* (autumn), when the FLOR is richest and most protective.

Sacristía AB Sherry Promising project est. 2010 by Antonio Barbadillo Mateos, one of the BARBADILLO family. Fascinating collection of mature MANZANILLAS, proving they can age well.

Sánchez Romate Sherry ★★→★★★ Old (1781) family firm with wide range. 8-yr-old *Fino Perdido*, nutty AMONTILLADO NPU, PALO CORTADO Regente, excellent VORS AMONTILLADO and OLOROSO La Sacristía de Romate, unctuous Sacristía PX. Also brandy Cardenal Mendoza.

Sandeman Sherry ★→★★ More famous for its Port than its Sherry. VOS wines are most interesting, incl Royal Esmeralda AMONTILLADO, Royal Corregidor Rich Old OLOROSO.

Sandeman Port Port ★★→★★★ V.gd age-dated TAWNY, esp 20-, 40-yr-old, but VINTAGE 63 66 70 75 77 94 97 00 03 07' 11' back on form. Second label: forward Vau Vintage. Unfiltered LBV is v.gd. New: finely honed Cask 33 Very Old Tawny (one of around 40 casks set aside in 1963).

Most expensive grapes in Iberian peninsula? Those sold for Port.

Sanlúcar de Barrameda Sherry, Man The 3rd of the Sherry triangle towns (along with JEREZ and PUERTO DE STA MARÍA), at mouth of river Guadalquivír. Humidity in low-lying cellars encourages FLOR. Sea air is said to give wines a salty character; analytically unproven but evident. Wines aged under FLOR in Sanlúcar BODEGAS qualify for DO MANZANILLA-Sanlúcar de Barrameda.

Sercial Mad Both the wine and the grape: driest of all Madeiras. *Supreme apéritif,* gd with gravad lax or sushi. *See* Grapes chapter.

Silva, C da Port ★★→★★★ Port shipper. Best is v. sophisticated Dalva Golden WHITE COLHEITA range 52' 63 71' and Colheita TAWNY.

Smith Woodhouse Port ★★★ SYMINGTON-owned small Port firm founded in 1784. Gd unfiltered LBV; some v. fine vintages (drier style): 66 70 75 77' 80 83 85 91 94 97 00' 03 07 11'. QUINTA da Madelena is single-QUINTA VINTAGE PORT.

Solera Sherry, Mad System for blending Sherry and, less commonly now, Madeira. Consists of topping up progressively more mature BUTTS with slightly younger wines of same sort from previous stage, or *criadera*. Maintains vigour of FLOR, gives consistency and refreshes mature wines. Min age for FINO, MANZANILLA is 2 yrs in solera.

Sousa, Alves de Port Long-term TAYLOR grower making DOURO wines, latterly gd Ports from family QUINTAS incl Alves de Sousa 09' 11' Baixo Corgo/Cima Corgo blend and Quinta da Gaivosa 03, 08, 12 Baixo Corgo single-quinta VINTAGE PORT. Gd 20-yr-old TAWNY and Caldas WHITE PORT.

Tawny Port Wood-aged Port (hence tawny colour), ready to drink on release. RES and age-dated (10-, 20-, 30-, 40-yr-old) wines ratchet up in complexity. COLHEITAS and Very Old Tawny Ports (min 30 yrs old but most much older – *see* TAYLOR, GRAHAM, NIEPOORT, VALLADO, WINE & SOUL, ROYAL OPORTO, SANDEMAN) cost gd deal more than VINTAGE.

Taylor, Fladgate & Yeatman (Taylor's) Port ★★→★★★★ Historic port shipper, Fladgate's

Sherry styles

Manzanilla Fashionably pale, dry, low-strength (15%): green-apple character; a popular, unchallenging introduction to the flavours of Sherry. Matured in the maritime conditions of SANLÚCAR DE BARRAMEDA where the FLOR grows more thickly, and the wine is said to acquire a salty tang. Drink cold from a newly opened bottle with tapas (or oysters). Eg. HEREDEROS DE ARGÜESO, San León RES.

Manzanilla Pasada Mature Manzanilla, where *flor* is fading; v. dry, complex. Eg. HIDALGO-LA GITANA's single-v'yd Manzanilla Pasada Pastrana.

Fino Dry; weightier than Manzanilla; 2 yrs age min (as Manzanilla). Eg. GONZÁLEZ BYASS 4-yr-old Tío Pepe. Serve as Manzanilla. Don't keep once opened. Trend for mature Finos aged 8–12 yrs, eg. FERNANDO DE CASTILLA Antique, González Byass Palmas range.

Amontillado A Fino in which the layer of protective yeast *flor* has died, allowing the wine to oxidize, creating more complexity. Naturally dry. Eg. LUSTAU Los Arcos. Commercial styles may be sweetened.

Oloroso Not aged under *flor*. Heavier, less brilliant when young, matures to nutty intensity. Naturally dry. May be sweetened with PX and sold as DULCE. Eg. EMILIO HIDALGO Gobernador (dr), Old East India (sw). Keeps well.

Palo Cortado V. fashionable. Traditionally a wine that had lost its *flor* – between Amontillado and Oloroso. Today often blended to create the style. Difficult to identify with certainty, though some suggest it has a keynote "lactic" or "bitter butter" note. Dry, rich, complex: worth looking for. Eg. BARBADILLO Reliquía, FERNANDO DE CASTILLA Antique.

Cream Blend sweetened with grape must, PX and/or MOSCATEL for an inexpensive, medium-sweet style. There are few great Creams: EQUIPO NAVAZOS La Bota No. 21 is outstanding exception; otherwise unashamedly commercial.

En Rama Manzanilla or Fino bottled from the BUTT with little or no filtration or cold stabilization to reveal full character of Sherry. More flavoursome but less stable, hence unpopular with some retailers. Back in fashion with trend for more natural wines. The *saca* or withdrawal is typically when *flor* is most abundant. Keep in fridge, drink up quickly.

Pedro Ximénez (PX) Raisined sweet, dark, from partly sun-dried PX grapes (grapes mainly from MONT-M; wine matured in JEREZ DO). Concentrated, unctuous, decadent, bargain. Overall, world's sweetest wine. Eg. Emilio Hidalgo Santa Ana 1861, Lustau VORS.

Moscatel Aromatic appeal, around half sugar of PX. Eg. Lustau Emilín, VALDESPINO Toneles. Unlike PX not required to be fortified. Now permitted to be called "Jerez".

VOS / VORS Age-dated sherries: some of the treasures of the Jerez BODEGAS. Exceptional quality at relatively low prices. Wines assessed by carbon dating to be more than 20-yrs-old are called VOS (Very Old Sherry/Vinum Optimum Signatum); those over 30-yrs-old are VORS (Very Old Rare Sherry/Vinum Optimum Rare Signatum). Also 12-yr-old, 15-yr-old examples. Applies only to Amontillado, Oloroso, Palo Cortado, PX. Eg. VOS Hidalgo Jerez Cortado Wellington. Some VORS wines are softened with PX: sadly producers can be overgenerous with the PX.

Añada "Vintage" Sherry with a declared vintage. Runs counter to tradition of vintage-blended SOLERA. Formerly private bottlings now winning public accolades. Eg. Lustau Sweet Oloroso Añada 1997.

jewel in the crown. Imposing VINTAGE PORTS 66 70 75 77' 80 83 85 92' 94 97' 00' 03' 07' 09' 11', incl single-QUINTAS (Vargellas, Terra Feita), rare Vargellas Vinha Velha from 70-yr-old+ vines. Market leader for TAWNY incl v.gd age-dated. Acquisition of KROHN stock sees 1863 follow-up to Very Old Tawny Scion; 1964 COLHEITA is first in a series of 50-yr-old wines.

Toro Albalá Mont-M ★→★★★ PX only here, and some venerable old wines in addition to the young wines. Among them lively AMONTILLADO Viejísimo and superb, treacly Don PX Gran Res.

Tradición Sherry ★★→★★★★ Est 1998, with fine pedigree. Originally focused on VOS and VORS but now also has delicate FINO. Consistently gd: salty AMONTILLADO, v. balanced PX. Vintage Sherries incl superb 70 75 OLOROSOS.

Valdespino Sherry ★★→★★★★ Famous JEREZ BODEGA producing Inocente FINO from top Macharnudo single v'yd (EN RAMA version bottled by EQUIPO NAVAZOS). Terrific dry AMONTILLADOS Tío Diego, *Coliseo VORS*; vibrant SOLERA 1842 OLOROSO VOS; remarkable 80-yr-old Toneles MOSCATEL, Jerez's best. Owned by Grupo Estévez (also owns Marqués del Real Tesoro, LA GUITA).

Vallado, Quinta da Dou Family-owned estate best known for DOU wines but Adelaide Tributa Very Old (pre-phylloxera) TAWNY Port signalled serious intent behind Port. Gd 10-, 20-, 30-, 40-yr-old Tawny and VINTAGE PORT 09 11' 12.

Verdelho Mad Style and grape of medium-dry Madeira; pungent but without the austerity of SERCIAL. Gd as an apéritif or paired with pâté. Increasingly popular for table wines.

Vesúvio, Quinta do Port ★★★★ With NOVAL, a single-QUINTA Port on par with the best VINTAGE PORT 92 94 95' 96' 97 98' 99 00' 01 03' 04 05' 06 07' 08' 09 10 11' 12. The only SYMINGTON FAMILY ESTATES Port still foot-trodden by people (not robotically). Capela da QUINTA Vesuvio 07' 11' from lower-lying parcel nr river.

Least accessible vineyard: Madeira's Fajã dos Padres. Get there by boat or cable car only.

Vila Nova de Gaia Port Town across the river DOURO from Oporto. Traditional home to the major Port shippers' lodges, though shippers increasingly moving out of the centre for modern facilities elsewhere.

Vintage Port Classic vintages are the best wines declared in exceptional yrs by shippers between 1 Jan and 30 Sept in the second yr after vintage. Bottled without filtration after 2 yrs in wood, it matures v. slowly in bottle throwing a deposit – always decant. Modern vintages broachable earlier (and hedonistic young) but best will last more than 50 yrs. Single-QUINTA Vintage Ports also drinking earlier; best can last 30+ yrs.

Warre Port ★★★→★★★★★ The oldest of British Port shippers (1670), now owned by SYMINGTON FAMILY ESTATES. V.gd, rich, age-worthy VINTAGE 63 66 70' 75 77' 80' 83 85 91 94 97 00' 03 07' 09' 11'. Elegant Single-QUINTA and 10-, 20-yr-old TAWNY Otima reflect QUINTA da Cavadinha's cool elevation. V.gd Vintage Character (Warrior) and unfiltered LBV.

White Port Port from white grapes. Ranges from dry to sweet (*lagrima*); mostly off-dry and blend of yrs. Apéritif straight or drink long with tonic and fresh mint. Growing niche: age-dated (10-, 20-, 30-, or 40-yr-old), eg. ANDRESEN, KOPKE, QUINTA de Santa Eufemia; rare COLHEITAS eg. C DA SILVA's Dalva Golden White.

Williams & Humbert Sherry ★→★★★★ BODEGA until recently known for private-label wines. Now improving, eg. vintage EN RAMA FINO 2006. Bestsellers incl Dry Sack and Winter's Tale AMONTILLADOS. V.gd mature wines incl *Dos Cortados* PALO CORTADO, *As You Like It* sweet OLOROSO, VOS Don Guido PX.

Ximénez-Spinola Sherry Small JEREZ producer specializing in fine wine from PX.

Switzerland

Abbreviations used in the text:

Aar	Aargau
Ber	Bern
Gris	Grisons
Neu	Neuchâtel
Schaff	Schaffhausen
Thur	Thurgau
Tic	Ticino
Val	Valais
Vd	Vaud
Zür	Zürich

Switzerland's bank secrecy may be crumbling, but the Swiss seem as keen as ever to maintain their other secret: their vineyards. All over the country there are growers who compensate for their dizzy slopes and sometimes extreme climate with diligence, intelligence and perfectionism. Vineyards tended like gardens, white mountains and blue skies, grazing cattle, lovely lakes and gurgling rivers – for the wine tourist, Switzerland is paradise. Unfortunately, the choice of Swiss wines available abroad has never reflected the country's potential. The best labels scarcely ever cross the border. No wonder, since the Swiss don't make enough to satisfy even half the country's thirst. They drink 99 per cent of their annual production of 100 million litres themselves – and they import another 150 million litres. The average Swiss wine-lover has plenty of expertise; the best local wine gets drunk at home.

Recent vintages

2014 Dry, sunny September saved crop; a year of classically structured wines.

2013 Up to 50% less than usual. In eastern Switzerland outstanding, wines of great freshness, purity.

2012 A winemaker's vintage. Difficult year with hail and rain.

2011 Very good vintage, from a unusually long, warm autumn.

2010 A classic vintage. Very elegant; less volume than 2009.

2009 One of the best recent years.

Older fine vintages: 2005 (all wines), 2000 (esp Pinot N, Valais reds), 1999 (Dézaley), 1997 (Dézaley), 1990 (all).

Aargau Wine-growing canton se of Basel, 400 ha, mainly PINOT N, MÜLLER-T. Good growers: Döttingen co-op, Haefliger, Hartmann, LITWAN, Meier (zum Sternen).

Aigle Vd (r) w ★★ One of the best-known communes for CHASSELAS. BADOUX' Les Murailles is famous, but can be v. light. Try Terroir du Crosex Grillé.

AOC The equivalent of French Appellation Contrôlée, but unlike in France, it is not nationally defined and every canton has its own rules. 85 AOCs countrywide.

Bachtobel, Schlossgut Thur ★★★ Refined PINOT N from slopes nr Weinfelden. Each yr's bottlings are numbered 1–4 (higher number = better wine and longer barrel-ageing).

Badoux, Henri Vd ★★ Big producer; his CHASSELAS AIGLE les Murailles (classic lizard label) is the most popular Swiss brand, though seldom convincing.

Baumann, Ruedi Schaff ★★★ 00' 03 05' 08 09 10 11 12 13 14 Leading estate at Oberhallau; berry-scented, ageable PINOT N, esp -R-, Ann Mee (Beatrice Baumann's project), Zwaa (collaboration with nearby Bad Osterfingen estate).

Bern Capital and homonymous canton. Wine villages on Lake Biel (La Neuveville, Ligerz, Schafis, Schernelz, Twann) and Lake Thun (Spiez). 240 ha, mainly CHASSELAS, PINOT N. Top growers: Andrey, Johanniterkeller, Schlössli, Steiner.

Besse, Gérald et Patricia Val ★★★ Leading VAL family estate, mostly on steep sloping terraces; range of elegant FENDANT (Les Bans), GAMAY from granite soils, powerful old-vines Ermitage (MARSANNE).

Bovard, Louis Vd ★★→★★★★ If Chasselas were PINOT N, this family estate (ten generations) could be considered Switzerland's DRC (*see* France). Textbook DÉZALEY La Médinette 99' 00 03 05' 06 07 09 11 12' lasts 10 yrs+. Now new winemaker, but *grand seigneur* Louis-Philippe Bovard continues to be active.

Bündner Herrschaft Gris r p w ★★→★★★ 05' 09' 10 11 12 13 14 BLAUBURGUNDER (PINOT N) with accentuated fruit, structure (mild s winds and cool climate from nearby mts). Individualistic growers, only four villages: FLÄSCH, Jenins, Maienfeld, MALANS.

Calamin Vd w ★★★ GRAND CRU of LAVAUX, nr EPESSES and neighbouring DÉZALEY; a tarter style of CHASSELAS. Only 16 ha, growers incl Dizerens, DUBOUX, Testuz.

Chablais Vd (r) w ★★→★★★ Wine region at the upper end of Lake Geneva, top villages: AIGLE, YVORNE, esp known for CHASSELAS. Name is derived from Latin *caput lacis*, head of the lake.

Chanton, Josef-Marie and Mario Val ★★★ Terrific Valais *spécialités*; v'yds up to 800m altitude: HEIDA, Lafnetscha, Himbertscha, Eyholzer Roter, Plantscher, Resi, Gwäss. Also gd PINOT N.

Chappaz, Marie-Thérèse Val r w sw ★★★→★★★★ Small VAL estate at Fully, famous for magnificent sweet wines (GRAIN NOBLE CONFIDENCIEL) of local grape Petite ARVINE 00 02 03 06' 09 and Ermitage (MARSANNE). Hard to find.

Cruchon, Henri Vd ★★→★★★ Bio producer of LA CÔTE, 36 ha, v. consistent, known for CHASSELAS and range of other varieties (Altesse, CHARD, SAUV BL, GAMAY, Gamaret, Servagnin aka PINOT N). Top growth is refined, age-worthy Pinot N Raissennaz.

Dézaley Vd (r) w ★★★ 90' 97 99 00 03 05' 09' 10 11 12 13 14 Celebrated LAVAUX GRAND CRU on steep slopes of Lake Geneva, 50 ha, reclaimed in the 12th century by Cistercian monks. Potent CHASSELAS develops with age. Best: *Louis Bovard*

Wine regions

Switzerland has six major wine regions: VAL, VD, GENEVA, TIC, Trois Lacs (NEU, Bienne/BER, Vully/FRIBOURG) and German Switzerland, which comprises ZÜR, SCHAFF, GRIS, AAR, St Gallen, Thur and some smaller wine cantons. And contrary to Switzerland's reputation for making white wines, 60 per cent of wines are red, mostly PINOT N.

DUBOUX, *Fonjallaz*, Monachon, Testuz, Ville de Lausanne. Try vintages back to 1976 at Georges Wenger's restaurant in Le Noirmont.

Dôle Val ★★ A traditional red blend: PINOT N plus some GAMAY. VAL's answer to Burgundy's Passetoutgrains, but lighter, less tannic and more fruity. Try BESSE, Gilliard, PROVINS and MERCIER. Lightly pink Dôle Blanche is pressed straight after harvest.

Domaine la Colombe Vd ★★→★★★ Family estate of FÉCHY, LA CÔTE, 15 ha, bio. Raymond Paccot's CHASSELAS is neither thin nor heavy, but fine and ages well, eg. La Brez.

World's smallest registered vineyard: Les Amis de Farinet in Valais. Just three vines.

Duboux, Blaise Vd (r) w ★★★ 5 ha family estate in LAVAUX. Outstanding DÉZALEY *vieilles vignes* Haut de Pierre (v. rich, but still mineral style), CALAMIN Cuvée Vincent. Also Plant Robert, a local clone of GAMAY.

Epesses Vd (r) w ★→★★★ 09 10 11' 12 13 14 Well-known LAVAUX AOC, 130 ha surrounding GRAND CRU CALAMIN: sturdy, full-bodied whites. Growers incl BOVARD, Luc Massy, DUBOUX, Fonjallaz.

Féchy Vd ★→★★★ A famous though unreliable AOC of LA CÔTE, mainly CHASSELAS. Wine-lovers with a preference for Féchy wines are said to have a Féchytism.

Federweisser / Weissherbst German-Swiss pale rosé or can also be Blanc de Noirs from BLAUBURGUNDER.

Fendant Val w ★→★★★ Full-bodied VAL CHASSELAS, ideal for fondue or raclette. Try BESSE, Domaine Cornulus, PROVINS, GERMANIER, SIMON MAYE. The name is derived from French *se fendre* (to burst) because ripe berries of the local Chasselas clone crack open if pressed between fingertips.

Fläsch Gris ★★★→★★★★ Small wine village on schist, producing the most mineral, austere PINOT N of all BÜNDNER HERRSCHAFT. Lots of gd estates, esp members of Adank, Hermann, Marugg families. *Gantenbein* is outstanding, also for CHARD.

Flétri / Mi-flétri Late-harvested grapes for sweet/slightly sweet wine.

Fribourg 115 ha on the shores of Lake Murten (Mont Vully): powerful CHASSELAS, elegant TRAMINER, round PINOT N. Try Château de Praz, Cru de l'Hôpital, Derron.

Fromm, Georg Gris ★★★ 05' 08 09' 10 11 12 13 14 Top grower in MALANS, 4 ha, known for fragrant, subtle PINOT N from a range of single v'yds: Selfi, Fidler, Schöpfi. Also in NZ under Wheeler & Fromm label.

Gantenbein, Daniel & Martha Gris ★★★★ 05 08 09' 10' 11 12 13' 14 Most famous growers in Switzerland, based in FLÄSCH. Top PINOT N from DRC clones (*see* France), RIES clones from Loosen (*see* Germany), exceptional CHARD in v. limited quantity. In 2013, only 30% of usual crop.

Geneva City and wine-growing canton, 1,400 ha, mostly remote from the lake. Ambitious growers prefer international varieties and PINOT N over GAMAY, CHASSELAS, eg. Domaine des Balisiers, Domaine Grand'Cour, Novelle, Les Hutins. Most v'yds on Lake Geneva belong to neighbouring canton VD.

Germanier, Jean-René Val r w sw ★★→★★★ Important VAL estate, best-known for reliable FENDANT Les Terrasses, elegant SYRAH Cayas, and AMIGNE from schist at Vétroz, both sweet (Mitis) and dry.

Glacier, Vin du (Gletscherwein) Val Fabled oxidized, (larch)-wooded white from rare Rèze grape of Val d'Anniviers. The town hall of Grimentz is the place to look. If you love Sherry, this is a must.

Grain Noble ConfidenCiel Val Quality label for authentic sweet wines, grown on the vine. Try Domaine du Mont d'Or, CHAPPAZ, Philippe Darioli, Dorsaz (both estates), GERMANIER, PROVINS.

Grand Cru Val, Vd Inconsistent term; some VAL communes (eg. SALGESCH for PINOT N) have local regulations. In VD "Premier Grand Cru" may be used for wide range

> **A brief history of Swiss wine**
> Wine here dates back to the Romans. Archaeologists have found vine
> knives, stakes and vine wood believed to be 1,700 yrs old. In 515AD, the
> Burgundian King Sigismund founded the abbey of St-Maurice (VAL), and
> v'yds are mentioned as part of the property. The Burgundians fostered
> viticulture around Lake Murten (FRIBOURG) and in e Switzerland, incl
> GRAUBÜNDEN. By 1000, v'yds were common in all parts of the country,
> and Swiss growers were already known as painstakingly hard-working:
> a decree dated 802 or 803 prohibits working on Sundays in the v'yds of
> the BÜNDNER HERRSCHAFT.

of single-estate wines. Switzerland has only two Grands Crus in the sense of a
classification of v'yd sites: CALAMIN and DÉZALEY.

Grisons (Graubünden) Mtn canton, mainly German-Swiss (and Rhaeto-Romanic
with a smaller Italian-speaking part s of Alps (Misox, esp MERLOT). PINOT N king
CHARD v.gd, also MÜLLER-T. See BÜNDNER HERRSCHAFT. Best growers in other areas
Cicero, Manfred Meier, VON TSCHARNER.

Grünenfelder, Irene Gris r (w) ★★★ Weingut Eichholz at Jenins, BÜNDNER HERRSCHAFT
V. limited production, delicate PINOT N and aromatic SAUV BL.

Huber, Daniel ★★→★★★★ Pioneering German Swiss immigrant to TIC, producing
subtle reds from possibly historical sites Huber reclaimed from fallow in 1981
Reliable MERLOT Fusto 4, premium label Montagna Magica 03 05' 07 08 09.

Johannisberg VAL name for SILVANER, often off-dry or sweet; great with fondue
Excellent: *Domaine du Mont d'Or*.

La Côte Vd (r) w ★→★★★ Largest VD region and AOC (2000 ha) w of Lausanne
mainly CHASSELAS of v. light, commercial style. Top growers (eg. CRUCHON, DOMAIN
LA COLOMBE) use bio methods for more depth, character. Best-known villages
Mont-sur-Rolle, FÉCHY, MORGES.

Lavaux Vd (r) w ★★→★★★★ Best region on Lake Geneva, source of rich, minera
CHASSELAS; 30 km of steep s-facing terraces e of Lausanne; UNESCO Worl¢
Heritage Site. Two GRANDS CRUS: DÉZALEY, CALAMIN and several village AOCs.

Litwan, Tom Aar ★★★ Newcomer who studied in Burgundy. Delicate, fine-grained
PINOT N Auf der Mauer ("on top of the wall") and Chalofe ("limekiln").

Malans Gris Village in BÜNDNER HERRSCHAFT. Top PINOT N producers incl Donatsch
FROMM, Liesch, Studach, Wegelin. Late-ripening local grape Completer is ar
idiosyncratic, phenolic white. Monks used to drink it with their day's last praye
(Compline). Adolf Boner is keeper of the Grail.

Maye, Simon et Fils Val r w ★★★ Perfectionist estate at St-Pierre-de-Clages, 12 ha
in 50 parcels. Dense SYRAH *vieilles vignes* 00 02 07' 08 09; spicy, powerful Païer
(HEIDA); concentrated PINOT N. FENDANT, DÔLE v.gd too.

Mémoire des Vins Suisses Association uniting 50 leading growers in effort to create
stock of Swiss icon wines, to prove their ageing capacities. Oldest wines are from
1999. One public tasting every yr.

Mercier, Anne-Catherine & Denis Val ★★★ Growers in SIERRE, only 6 ha, producing
some of the most sought-after CORNALIN 99 02 05' 09' 10 11 12 13 and SYRAH.

Möhr-Niggli Gris ★★→★★★ Young couple making fruit-driven, elegant PINOT N
(premium label Pilgrim) at Maienfeld, BÜNDNER HERRSCHAFT.

Morges Vd (r) w ★→★★ Large VD AOC on the shores of Lake Geneva,with mainly
CHASSELAS. Fruity reds.

Neuchâtel r p w ★→★★★★ 595 ha around city and lake. CHASSELAS usually v. ligh
(10–11 per cent) and slightly sparkling (mostly vinified *sur lie*). PINOT N from
local clone (Cortaillod) can be exquisite, also gd ŒIL DE PERDRIX, PINOT GR, CHARD

Growers incl Château d'Auvernier, La Maison Carrée, Porret and Tatasciore. Vintage 2013 was severely hit by hail.

on Filtré SPÉCIALITÉ from NEU: unfiltered CHASSELAS, appealing through freshness.

Eil de Perdrix Neu PINOT N rosé, allegedly the colour of a partridge's eye. Originally from NEU, now found elsewhere.

'ircher, Urs Zür ★★★→★★★★ 05' 08 09' 10 11 12 13 Top estate at Eglisau, steep s-facing slope overlooking Rhine. Stadtberger Barrique from old Swiss clones is one of the most complex and best-ageing PINOT N of Switzerland. Whites of great purity and elegance, eg. 13 PINOT GR.

'rovins Valais Val ★→★★★ Huge co-op and biggest producer: 4,000+ members, 1,500 ha. Gd oak-aged Maître de Chais range; reliable entry-level wines, now sparkling Blanc de Noirs (PINOT N/GAMAY) and ambitious Bordeaux blend Electus (under Valais Mundi label).

'ouvinez Vins Val r w ★→★★★ Well-distributed producer at SIERRE, best known for cuvées La Trémaille (w) and Le Tourmentin (r). The Rouvinez family controls also three other VAL companies: Orsat, Imesch, Charles Bonvin.

.t. Jodern Kellerei Val ★★→★★★ VISPERTERMINEN CO-OP (founded 1978) famous for HEIDA Veritas from ungrafted old vines – a unique and superb reflection of Alpine terroir.

t-Saphorin Vd (r) w ★★→★★★ 09 10 11' 12 13 14 Famous CHASSELAS AOC in LAVAUX for lighter whites than DÉZALEY, but often with the same mineral delicacy. Try Pierre Monachon's Les Manchettes.

algesch Val ★★→★★★ German-speaking village in VAL, PINOT N stronghold on calcareous soils. GRAND CRU regulations since 1988 (concerning yields and must weight). No v'yd classification. Growers incl A&D Mathier, Albert Mathier, Cave du Rhodan.

chaffhausen ★→★★★ German-Swiss canton/town on the Rhine with the famous Falls, 482 ha. BLAUBURGUNDER, MÜLLER-T and spécialitiés. Best-known village is Hallau, but be v. careful. Top growers: BAUMANN, Bad Osterfingen, Markus Ruch, Stamm. GVS is a gd co-op.

chenk SA Vd ★→★★★ Wine giant with worldwide activities, based in Rolle (VD), founded 1893. Classic wines (esp Vd and VAL); one of v. few producers with substantial exports.

chloss Salenegg Gris ★★★ Historic estate at Maienfeld, BÜNDNER HERRSCHAFT, known for delicate, refined PINOT N.

chwarzenbach, Hermann Zür r w ★★★ Leading family estate on Lake Zürich. Best-known for crisp whites that go well with freshwater fish: local variety Räuschling, MÜLLER-T. Also excellent PINOT N.

ierre Val r w ★★→★★★ Sunny resort; rich, luscious VAL wines. Best-known names: Imesch, MERCIER, ROUVINEZ, Maurice Zufferey.

ion Val r w ★★→★★★ Capital/wine centre of VAL, domicile of big producers: *Charles Bonvin Fils*, PROVINS VALAIS, Robert Gilliard, Varone.

he Swiss drink 34 litres wine/person/year – down from 50 litres in 1988.

pecialités / Spezialitäten Specialities: quantitatively minor grape varieties producing some of best Swiss wines in terms of quality, eg. Räuschling, GEWÜRZ or PINOT GR in German Switzerland, or local varieties (and grapes like JOHANNISBERG, SYRAH) in VAL.

tucky, Werner Tic ★★★→★★★★ Immigrant from German Switz to TIC (in 1981), changing MERLOT del Ticino from light and fruity to dense, oak-aged. Today, three wines: Temenos (Completer/SAUV BL), Tracce di Sassi (Merlot), Conte di Luna (Merlot/CAB SAUV). One of Stucky's best v'yds is only accessible via a funicular.

icino ★★→★★★ 05' 08 09' 10 11 12 (13) Italian-speaking s Switzerland, mainly

> **Swiss army**
> The most underrated of all Swiss wines are those made from local
> varieties. Remarkable white autochthonous grapes are: Completer
> (BÜNDNER HERRSCHAFT), Räuschling (Lake ZURICH), Petite ARVINE, AMIGNE,
> HEIDA, HUMAGNE BLANCHE (VAL). Red varieties incl Bondola (TIC), CORNALIN,
> Durize, Humagne Rouge (Val). In VISPERTERMINEN, a group of wine-lovers
> led by grape-scientist Jose Vouillamoz recently joined forces to save an
> old v'yd containing a dozen old varieties, incl Gouais Blanc – a parent of
> many European varieties.

    MERLOT. Best are well-structured, far from "international" in style, eg. Giald
HUBER, Kaufmann, Klausener, Kopp von der Crone Visini, STUCKY, Tamborin
VINATTIERI, ZÜNDEL. Also Azienda Mondò in Sementina, specializing in ol
Bondola grape.

Tscharner, Gian-Battista von r w ★★→★★★★ Family estate at Reichenau Castle
Graubünden, known for tannin-laden PINOT N to age, eg. Jeninser Tscharnergu
old vines 11'. Jeninser Blauburgunder "Mariafeld" **90'** still fresh and delightful
berry-scented.

Valais (Wallis) Largest wine canton, in dry, sunny upper Rhône Valley. Man
local varieties (eg. white AMIGNE, HUMAGNE Blanche, Petite ARVINE; red CORNALIN
Humagne Rouge), wide spectrum of soils (granite, schist, lime); styles from dr
CHASSELAS (FENDANT) to barrel-aged reds and sweet. MARSANNE, SYRAH doing v. wel
Top: BESSE, CHANTON, CHAPPAZ, Domaine Cornulus, Darioli, Dorsaz, GERMANIE
Didier Joris, SIMON MAYE, MERCIER, Domaine du Mont d'Or, PROVINS VALAIS, L
Rodeline, La Romaine, ROUVINEZ, ST. JODERN KELLEREI, Maurice Zufferey.

Vaud (Waadt) Wine canton known for conservative spirit, incl CHABLAIS, LA CÔT
LAVAUX, and small outposts at Lake Murten and Lake Neuchâtel. Important bi
producers: Hammel, Bolle, Obrist, SCHENK. CHASSELAS is main grape – but only g
terroirs justify growers' loyalty.

Switzerland's highest vineyard is at 1,100 metres.

Vinattieri Ticinesi Tic ★★→★★★★ 09' 10 11' 12 (13) Luigi Zanini (junior and senio
produce MERLOT in a decidedly international style, powerful and heavily oal
influenced. Top wine: Castello Luigi.

Visperterminen Val w ★→★★★★ Upper VAL v'yds, esp for HEIDA. One of highest v'yc
in Europe (at 1,000m+; called Riben). See it from the train to Zermatt or Saa
Fee. Try CHANTON, ST. JODERN KELLEREI.

Yvorne Vd (r) w ★★→★★★★ Top CHABLAIS AOC for rich CHASSELAS. Best v'yd sites l
on the detritus of a 1584 avalanche. Try Commune d'Yvorne, Château Maiso
Blanche, Domaine de l'Ovaille.

Zündel, Christian Tic r w ★★★→★★★★ 02 05' 09 10 11 12 13 German Swis
geologist in TIC. Pure, age-worthy MERLOT/CAB SAUV Orizzonte. Recent emphas
on wonderful cool-climate CHARD.

Zürich Largest wine-growing canton in German Switzerland, 610 ha. Main
BLAUBURGUNDER, MÜLLER-T. Räuschling a local speciality. Best growers: Gehrin
Lüthi, PIRCHER, SCHWARZENBACH, Zahner.

Austria

Abbreviations used in the text:

Burgen	Burgenland
Carn	Carnuntum
Kamp	Kamptal
Krems	Kremstal
Low A	Lower Austria
M Burg	Mittelburgenland
N'see	Neusiedlersee
N'see-H	Neusiedlersee-Hügelland
S/W/SE Sty	Styria
Therm	Thermenregion
Trais	Traisental
Wach	Wachau
Wag	Wagram
Wein	Weinviertel

AUSTRIA

Austria is a tiny player in the world of wine but punches well above its weight in terms of quality. It's a land of small growers, producing individual, hand-crafted, site-driven wines. Austria's deeply continental climate of warm summers, long autumns and cool nights allows for a winning combination of ample fruit and lively acidity. This goes for racy, light everyday wines as well as reserve and nobly sweet wines. The drive for quality continues steadily: Austria now boasts nine DACs, all produced to rigorous standards. The first was Weinviertel DAC in 2001, its latest the Wiener Gemischter Satz DAC in 2013. Lower Austria, along the Danube and its tributaries, is white wine country: home to Austria's flagship variety Grüner Veltliner and world-class Rieslings. Styria in the southeast stands for Sauvignon Blanc, while the Pannonian climate of easterly Burgenland favours reds like Blaufränkisch, Zweigelt and St-Laurent.

Recent vintages

2014 Scrupulous selection was necessary: tricky August, wet September, some hail damage. Quality meant sacrificing quantity.

2013 Hot, dry summer, rain in September; very good for sweet wines.

2012 Quantities down from 2011. Quality satisfactory or better.

2011 One of finest vintages in living memory.

2010 Hand-picking, meticulous work imperative, yields down by up to 55%.

2009 Uneven, with some outstanding whites (Lower Austria, Styria) and reds (Neusiedlersee, Middle Burgenland).

2008 The coolest year since 2004. Some outstanding results.

2007 Good in Styria and, in Burgenland, for Blaufränkisch, Zweigelt, Pinot N.

Achs, Paul N'see r (w) ★★★ 10 11 12 13 Fine GOLS producer obsessed with site expression. Quality across the board, esp BLAUFRÄNKISCH Ungerberg and elegant PINOT N.

Allram Kamp w ★★★ 10 11 12 13 Ambitious producer of GRÜNER V, RIES esp Heiligenstein, Gaisberg.

Alphart Therm w ★★→★★★ Traditional, reliable estate, gd ROTGIPFLER/ZIERFANDLER.

Alzinger Wach w ★★★★ 05 06 07 08 09 10 11 12 13 Top estate: expressive and age-worthy RIES, GRÜNER V.

Arndofer Kamp r w ★★★ Creative, talented young winemaking couple. Leidenschaf are top bottlings. Interesting oak-matured RIES.

Ausbruch PRÄDIKAT wine with high sugar levels. Min. must weight 27°KMW o 138.6°Oechsle. Made from either botrytized or dried grapes. Traditionally produced in RUST.

Ausg'steckt ("Hung out") Fresh greenery hung outside HEURIGEN or Buschenschank when open.

Beck, Judith N'see r w ★★→★★★ Rising bio winemaker. Well-crafted red blends (based on BLAUFRÄNKISCH or ZWEIGELT), *St-Laurent*.

Braunstein, Birgit N'see r w ★★★ 11 12 Gifted winemaker of BLAUFRÄNKISCH LEITHABERG, PINOT N, ST-LAURENT esp Felsenstein.

Bründlmayer, Willi Kamp r w sw sp ★★★★ 05 06 07 08 09 10 11' 12 13 World-class estate for outstanding RIES, GRÜNER V, esp Ries Heiligenstein Alte Reben, GV Käferberg. Impressive sparkling *méthode traditionelle*, esp Extra Brut.

Burgenland Burgen r (w) Province and wine region in e bordering Hungary. Warm climate for textbook BLAUFRÄNKISCH, esp in M BURG and SÜDBURGENLAND, and ideal conditions for botrytis wines around shallow NEUSIEDLER SEE (Lake Neusiedl).

Carnuntum Low A r w Dynamic region se of VIENNA now showing gd reds, often on ST-LAURENT base. Best: G Markowitsch, MUHR-VAN DER NIEPOORT, Netzl, TRAPL.

Vienna is the world's only capital with serious v'yds of its own: 612 ha.

Christ Vienna r w ★★★ Innovative VIENNA producer, instrumental in the GEMISCHTER SATZ movement. Interesting red blends.

Districtus Austriae Controllatus (DAC) Origin- and quality-based appellation system for regionally typical wines. The first, WEINVIERTEL DAC, created in 2003 marked a steep quality curve. Currently nine DACs: EISENBERG, KAMP, KREMS LEITHABERG, M BURG, N'SEE, TRAIS, Weinviertel, Wiener GEMISCHTER SATZ. Most DACs are stratified into Klassik and Res with varietal and ageing stipulations.

Domäne Wachau Wach w ★★→★★★ Excellent co-op (formerly Freie Weingärtner) producing a third of all WACH wines, quality across the board. V'yds in best sites eg. Achleiten, Kellerberg. Great tasting rooms.

Ebner-Ebenauer Wein w ★★★ Impressive, energetic newcomer. Look for GRÜNER V, CHARD, wonderful Blanc de Blancs *méthode traditionelle*.

Ehmoser Wag r w ★★★ Small individualist producer, gd GRÜNER V.

Eichinger, Birgit Kamp ★★★ Star producer of RIES, savoury GRÜNER V from single sites Gaisberg, Heiligenstein, Lamm.

Eisenberg S Burg Small DAC (since 2009), elegant BLAUFRÄNKISCH from slate soils.

Erste Lage First Growth according to ÖTW v'yd classification, currently 62 v'yds in KAMP, KREMS, TRAIS, WAGRAM.

Esterhazy Burgen r (w) ★★ Princely *schloss* in Eisenstadt (BURGEN) under ambitious new management.

Federspiel Wach Mid-level of VINEA WACHAU classification, min 11.5%, max 12.5% ABV. Elegant wines with depth rather than power; perfect food wines. Named after a falcon species.

Feiler-Artinger N'see r w sw ★★★→★★★★ 03 04 05 06 07 08 09 10 11 12 13

Outstanding RUST estate with top AUSBRUCH dessert wines *often v.gd value* for money, elegant reds. Beautiful baroque house too.

Forstreiter Krems w ★→★★ Consistent KREMSTAL producer, particularly gd RIES.

Gemischter Satz Vienna White field-blend of co-planted and co-fermented varieties. Age-old European survival, now re-est. Since 2013 DAC for VIENNA. No variety to exceed 50%. Historically a way of min frost risk to any one variety; now fashionable again. Look for CHRIST, WIENINGER.

Gesellmann, Albert & Silvia M Burg r w (sw) ★★★ Famous for BLAUFRÄNKISCH Hochberg and red blends.

Geyerhof Krems r w ★★ Organic pioneer making elegant, individual RIES, GRÜNER V.

Gols N'see r w Wine commune on n shore of LAKE NEUSIEDL. Top producers: BECK, G HEINRICH, NITTNAUS, PITTNAUER, PREISINGER.

Gritsch Mauritiushof Wach w ★★ Consistently underrated producer, esp RIES from 1000-Eimberberg, fine Gelber MUSKATELLER.

Groiss, Ingrid Wein w ★★ Quality-driven newcomer. Expressive, convincing GRÜNER V.

Gross S Sty ★★★ Perfectionist s STY producer concentrating on regional character. Esp SAUV BL.

Grosse Lage Sty Highest classification level in STY, but not in use along Danube (*see* ERSTE LAGE). For further confusion *see* Germany.

Gsellmann N'see r w ★★ Bio estate in GOLS, known for red blends, gd dry PINOT BL.

Gumpoldskirchen Therm Famous HEURIGEN village south of VIENNA, centre of THERM. Signature white varieties: ZIERFANDLER, ROTGIPFLER.

Gut Oggau N'see r w ★★→★★★ Innovative bio producer of authentic wines.

Haider N'see sw ★★★ 13 grape varieties on 13 ha, best-known for TBA (*see* Germany).

Heinrich, Gernot N'see r w dr sw ★★★ 06 07 08 09 10 11 12 13 Accomplished GOLS estate, member of PANNOBILE group. Outstanding single-v'yd red wines: Salzberg, Alter Berg.

Heinrich, J M Burg r w ★★★ 05 06 08 09 11 12 13 Leading M BURG producer. V.gd BLAUFRÄNKISCH Goldberg RES.

Heuriger Wine of most recent harvest. **Heurigen** taverns where growers by ancient decree can serve their own wines with rustic foods – integral to Vienna life.

Hiedler Kamp w sw ★★★ Consistently fine grower, concentrated wines from steep terraced v'yds.

Hirsch Kamp w ★★★ 05 06 09 11 12 13 Great bio producer. Esp fine Heiligenstein, Lamm, Gaisberg v'yds. Thrilling RIES.

Hirtzberger, Franz Wach w ★★★★ 05 06 07 08 10 11' 12 13 Stellar grower in Spitz, the narrowest part of WACH. *Highly expressive, mineral Ries*, GRÜNER V, esp from the Honivogl, Singerriedel v'yds.

Huber, Markus Trais w Quality-focused young winemaker. Pure expressions of TRAIS with elegant lightness.

Illmitz N'see sw SEEWINKEL market town and region famous for BA, TBA (*see* box, Germany). Best from KRACHER, Opitz.

Jäger Wach w ★★★ Producer of outstanding GRÜNER V at FEDERSPIEL and SMARAGD level.

Jamek, Josef Wach w ★★→★★★ Traditional estate with long-est restaurant. RIES, GRÜNER V from single WACH v'yds: Klaus, Achleiten, Hochrain.

Johanneshof Reinisch Therm r w ★★→★★★ Talented producers of reds esp PINOT N, ST-LAURENT, also ZIERFANDLER, ROTGIPFLER. Single v'yds Spiegel, Satzing, Holzspur.

Jurtschitsch Kamp w ★★★ Large but reliable KAMP estate; energetic, innovative, v.gd sparkling too.

Kamptal Low A (r) w Wine region along river Kamp north of WACH, broader in style. Top v'yds: Heiligenstein, Käferberg, Lamm. Best: Brandl, BRÜNDLMAYER, EICHINGER, HIEDLER, HIRSCH, JURTSCHITSCH, LOIMER, SCHLOSS GOBELSBURG. Kamp is DAC for GRÜNER V, RIES.

Kerschbaum, Paul M Burg ★★★ 05 06 07 08 09 11 12 A rapidly expanding BLAUFRÄNKISCH specialist, with individual and often fascinating wines.

Klassifizierte Lage Second Growth (156 v'yds) in the classification system of ÖTW. See also ERSTE LAGE.

Klosterneuburg Wag r w Main wine town of Donauland, seat of Austria's wine reserach institute and university founded in 1860. Best: Stift Klosterneuburg.

KMW An abbreviation for Klosterneuburger Mostwaage ("must level"), which is the Austrian unit denoting must weight, ie. the sugar content of grape juice. 1°KMW = 4.86°Oechsle (see Germany).

Knoll, Emmerich Wach w ★★★★ 83 86' 88 90 99' 01 03 04 05 06 07 08 09 10 11 12. Outstanding traditional estate in Loiben. *Delicate, fragrant, age-worthy and world class Ries, complex Grüner V* from Loibenberg, Schütt v'yds.

Kollwentz N'see r w ★★★ 05 06 07 08 09 10 11 12 Outstanding producer with a wide spectrum of wines.

Kracher N'see sw★★★★ 01 02 03 04 05 06 07 08 09 10 11 12 World-famous ILLMITZ producer specializing in botrytized sweet BA, TBA (see box, p.163, Germany), with and without oak.

Kremstal (r) w Wine region and DAC for GRÜNER V, RIES. Top: Buchegger, Malat, MOSER, NIGL, SALOMON-UNDHOF, WEINGUT STADT KREMS.

Krutzler S Burg r ★★★ 06 07 08 09 11' 12 13 Outstanding S BURGEN family estate. Full-bodied, velvety BLAUFRÄNKISCH, reliable at every level. Notable: Perwolff.

Lagler Wach w ★★★ Spitz-based producer of clean-cut RIES, GRÜNER V. One of few to produce Neuburger SMARAGD.

Laurenz V ★★★ Mainly internatonally marketed brand of GRÜNER V created by Laurenz Maria Moser V. Grapes from KAMP, KREM, WEIN. expressing different styles like Charming, Singing, Forbidden, etc.

Leithaberg Burgen DAC on n shore of LAKE NEUSIEDL, based on limestone and mica schist of Leithaberg mtn.

Lenikus w ★★ VIENNA newcomer, ambitious wines. Try GEMISCHER SATZ from Bisamberg.

Loimer, Fred Kamp w★★★ 05 06 07 09 11 12 13 Steadily evolving and enterprising bio producer of fine GRÜNER V, RIES (Steinmassl, Heiligenstein).

Mantlerhof Krems w ★★ →★★★ Grower expressing local loess soils v. well.

Mayer am Pfarrplatz Vienna (r) w ★★ Est producer and HEURIGE, recently much improved, esp GEMISCHTER SATZ Nussberg, also delicate PINOT N.

Mittelburgenland Burgen r Wine region on Hungarian border, with stuctured age-worthy BLAUFRÄNKISCH (also DAC). Producers incl GESELLMANN, J HEINRICH, KERSCHBAUM and WENINGER.

Moric N'see ★★★ 05 06 09 10 11 12 Wines of elegance, depth from old BLAUFRÄNKISCH vines in Lutzmannsburg and Neckenmarkt.

Biggest pest in Viennese vineyards? People – hikers, tourists – all nibbling away.

Morillon Traditional designation for CHARD in S STY.

Moser, Lenz Krems ★→★★ Austria's largest producer (2,700 ha), based nr Krems.

Muhr-van der Niepoort Carn r w ★★★ Yes, Niepoort as in Port. Outstandingly stylish reds, esp BLAUFRÄNKISCH Spitzerberg. Samt & Seide (Blaufr) and Sydhang SYRAH are also notable.

Neumayer Trais w ★★★ Top estate making powerful, focused, dry GRÜNER V, RIES.

Neumeister SE Sty ★★★ 08 09 11 12 13 Modernist, meticulous producer, esp fine SAUV BL from v'yds Klausen and Moarfeitl.

Neusiedlersee-Hügelland r w dr sw Wine region w of LAKE NEUSIEDL around RUST on the lake shores, and Eisenstadt in Leitha foothills (see LEITHABERG DAC). Best BRAUNSTEIN, FEILER-ARTINGER, KOLLWENTZ, MORIC, PRIELER, SCHRÖCK, TRIEBAUMER.

Neusiedlersee (Lake Neusiedl) Burgen Shallow BURGEN lake on Hungarian border

> **Girl power**
> It may seem outdated to highlight women in wine in this late day and age, but Austria is still socially conservative, and the association "II Frauen und Ihre Weine" (II women and their wines), is a powerhouse of quality and innovation. BECK, BRAUNSTEIN, EICHINGER, GEYERHOF and SCHRÖCK are amongst its capable and determined members.

largest steppe-lake in Europe, important nature reserve. Lake mesoclimate instrumental for botrytis. Eponymous DAC limited to ZWEIGELT.

Niederösterreich (Lower Austria) A ne region with 58 per cent of Austria's v'yds, divided in three parts: areas around the Danube (KAMP, KREM, TRAIS, WACH), the huge WEIN (ne) and s (CARN, THERM).

Nigl Krems w ★★★★ Outstanding KREM estate at Senftenberg, esp *ethereal Ries.*

Nikolaihof Wach w ★★★ 05 06 07 08 09 10 11 12 13 Bio pioneer making wines with ageing potential, often v. closed when young. Outstanding RIES Steiner Hund.

Nittnaus, Anita & Hans N'see r w sw ★★★ Bio producer of elegant wines; ageworthy BLAUFRÄNKISCH Kalk&Schiefer, LEITHABERG DAC. Also v.gd red blends for PANNOBILE (Comondor), exquisite TBA (*see* box, p.163, Germany).

Österreichische Traditionsweingüter (ÖTW) Kamp, Krems, Trais, Wag Association engaged in the classification of ERSTE LAGE v'yds around the Danube. Currently 26 members, but no WACH estates.

Ott, Bernhard Low A w ★★★ GRÜNER V specialist from WAG, expressive and savoury, esp Fass 4, Spiegel, Stein, Rosenberg.

Pannobile N'see Union of nine N'SEE growers centred on GOLS, named after the mild Pannonian climate. Pannobile bottlings may only use indigenous reds (ZWEIGELT, BLAUFRÄNKISCH, ST-LAURENT), whites only PINOTS BL, GR, CHARD. Members: ACHS, BECK, GSELLMANN, G HEINRICH, NITTNAUS, PITTNAUER, PREISINGER.

Pfaffl Wein r w ★★★ 07 08 09 11 12 Large estate, 75 ha. Top WEIN DAC RES wines, esp Hommage. Delicious, easy entry-level wines.

Pichler, Franz X Wach w ★★★★ 05 06 07 08 09 11 12 13 Great producer. Intense, *iconic Ries* (Unendlich, Loibenberg), GRÜNER V (esp Kellerberg).

Pichler, Rudi Wach w ★★★★ 05 06 09 10 11 12 13 Expressive RIES, GRÜNER V from top sites (Achleiten, Steinriegl, Hochrain).

Pichler-Krutzler Wach w ★★★ Marriage of two famous names; outstandingly pure, thrilling RIES esp from Wunderburg v'yd.

Pittnauer, Gerhard N'see r ★★★ Organic N'SEE red specialist, one of Austria's finest for ST-LAURENT; also quality entry-level Pitti.

Polz, Erich & Walter S Sty ★★→★★★ 08 09 10 11 12 13 V.gd large growers, 70 ha; top v'yd Hochgrassnitzberg: SAUV BL, CHARD.

Prager, Franz Wach w ★★★★ 05 06 07 08 09 11 12 RIES, GRÜNER V of impeccable elegance, mineral structure from top sites: Wachstum Bodenstein, Achleiten, Klaus and Steinriegl.

Preisinger, Claus N'see r ★★★ Talented young bio winemaker. PANNOBILE member.

Prieler N'see r w ★★★ Consistently fine N'SEE producer. Esp gd BLAUFRÄNKISCH Goldberg, notable PINOT BL.

Proidl, A und F Krems w ★★★ Highly individual grower of expressive RIES, GRÜNER v. Look out for late releases like 06 Ries.

Reserve Attribute for DAC and other wines of origin; min 13% ABV and prolonged (cask) ageing.

Ried Austrian term for v'yd.

Rust Burgen r w dr sw Historic, bijou town on shore of LAKE NEUSIEDL, 17th-century architecture. Look for storks nesting on chimneys. Famous for Ruster AUSBRUCH. Top: FEILER-ARTINGER, SCHRÖCK, E TRIEBAUMER.

Sabathi, Hannes S Sty w ★★★ Youthful, highly professional estate. Fine single-v'yd whites (esp SAUV BL Merveilleux).

Salomon-Undhof Krems w ★★★ Consistently gd; often outstanding and v. age worthy RIES from Kögl v'yd.

Sattlerhof S Sty w ★★★ 07 08 09 10 11' 12 Crystalline, precise SAUV BL, MORILLON from v. steep v'yds.

Schiefer, Uwe S Burg r ★★★ Ex-*garagiste;* complex BLAUFRÄNKISCH of mineral elegance

Schilcher W St Easy-drinking, thirst-quenching rosé from indigenous Blaue Wildbacher grapes, a speciality of w STY. Look for Domäne Müller, Schilchere Jöbstl and Reiterer.

Schilfwein (Strohwein) Sweet wine made from grapes dried on reeds from N'SEE *Schilf* = reed, *Stroh* = straw.

Schloss Gobelsburg Kamp r w dr sw ★★★★ 06 07 08 09 10 11 12 13 Respected estate owned by Cistercian monastery Zwettl, run by star winemaker Michae Moosbrugger. Rewarding at every level: top single-v'yd RIES, GRÜNER V; gd sparkling

Schloss Halbturn N'see r w sw ★★★ 06 09 11 12 Ambitious estate with an international approach to Austrian varieties.

Schlumberger sp Largest sparkling winemaker in Austria.

Schmelz Wach w ★★★ Fine, underrated producer, outstanding RIES Dürnsteine Freiheit, GRÜNER V Pichl Point.

Schröck, Heidi N'see (r) w sw ★★★ AUSBRUCH of great purity and focus from a thoughtful RUST grower.

Schuster, Rosi N'see r ★★★ 09 11 12 Refined BLAUFRÄNKISCH; sappy, complex ST-LAURENT

Seewinkel N'see ("Lake corner") Part of NEUSIEDLERSEE around ILLMITZ, idea conditions for botrytis.

Acacia barrels were traditional in Lower Austria: local, cheap, nicely aromatic Still used by some.

Smaragd Wach Highest category of VINEA WACHAU, min 12.5% ABV, often up to 14% dry, rich, age-worthy, expressive, like a big, dry Spätlese. Depending on produce can be botrytis-influenced. Named after local emerald (=Smaragd) lizard.

Spätrot-Rotgipfler Therm Blend of ROTGIPFLER/Spätrot = synonym for ZIERFANDLER Aromatic, weighty wines. typical for GUMPOLDSKIRCHEN. *See* Grapes chapter.

Spitz an der Donau Wach w Picturesque town at the narrowest and coolest part o WACH. Famous v'yd Singerriedel and 1000-Eimerberg. HIRTZBERGER, LAGLER.

Stadlmann Therm r w sw ★★→★★★ Producer specializing in opulent ZIERFANDLER ROTGIPFLER wines. As counterpoint try ultra-delicate Gelber MUSKATELLER.

Stadt Krems w ★★★ Consistent producer of clean-cut whites, esp RIES. from Grillenparz, Wachtberg v'yds overlooking town.

Steinfeder Wach Lightest VINEA WACHAU category for delicate, dry wines. Max 11.5% ABV. Named after the fragrant Steinfeder grass.

Stift Göttweig ★★→★★★ Baroque Benedictine monastery nr Krems. Fine single-v'yd wines, esp Silberbichl, Gottschelle.

Styria (Steiermark) Sty The s-most region of Austria, known for aromatic, fresh dry whites, esp SAUV BL. *See* SÜDSTEIERMARK, SÜD-OSTSTEIERMARK, WESTSTEIERMARK.

Südburgenland r w A small e wine region. V.gd BLAUFRÄNKISCH. Best: KRUTZLER SCHIEFER and WACHTER-WIESLER.

Süd-Oststeiermark SE Sty (r) w STY region with excellent v'yds. Best: NEUMEISTER Ploder-Rosenberg, Winkler-Hermaden.

Südsteiermark S Sty Best STY region close to Slovenian border, cool-climate whites (SAUV BL, MUSKATELLER) from steep slopes. Best growers: GROSS, POLZ, SABATHI SATTLERHOF, TEMENT, WOHLMUTH. Look for MORILLON.

Tegernseerhof Wach w ★★ Rising grower of v. interesting RIES, GRÜNER V.

Tement, Manfred S Sty w ★★★ 96 97 01 02' 03' 04 05 07 08 09' 10 11 12 12 Top producer of precise, chiselled whites, esp SAUV BL, MORILLON from Zieregg site.

Thermenregion Low A r w Region of hot springs e of VIENNA. Indigenous grapes (eg. ZIERFANDLER, ROTGIPFLER), serious reds (ST-LAURENT, PINOT N). Producers: ALPHART, Reinisch and STADLMANN.

Tinhof, Erwin Burgen r w ★★★ Meticulous producer of elegant reds, esp BLAUFRÄNKISCH Gloriette, ST-LAURENT Feuersteig. Experimental bottlings such as oxidatively aged Aperitif.

Traisental Low A Small district s of Krems on Danube. Lighter whites than WACH. Top producers: HUBER, NEUMAYER.

Trapl, Johannes Carn r ★★ Ambitious producer of elegant, poised, floral BLAUFRÄNKISCH, esp Sitzerberg. Notable SYRAH.

Triebaumer, Ernst N'see r (w) (sw) ★★★★ 05 06 07 08 09 10 11' 12 A top RUST producer; quality and bio pioneer, exquisite BLAUFRÄNKISCH (incl legendary Mariental). V.gd AUSBRUCH.

Umathum, Josef N'see r w dr sw ★★★ Top bio producer. Beautiful reds, incl PINOT N, BLAUFRÄNKISCH esp Kirschgarten. Stunning rosé Rosa.

Velich N'see w sw ★★★ Cultish producer. Powerful, creamy CHARD Tiglat. Some of top sweet wines in SEEWINKEL.

Veyder-Malberg Wach ★★★ A 2008 start-up, cultivating some of WACHAU's most labour-intensive v'yds, producing handmade wines of great purity and finesse.

Vienna (r) w Wine region with 612 ha within city limits. Ancient tradition; re-invigorated drive for quality. As of 2013 DAC GEMISCHTER SATZ for locally famous white field-blends. HEURIGEN visit a must. Best producers: CHRIST, WIENINGER, Zahel.

Vinea Wachau WACH growers association founded 1983. No v'yd classification, but strict quality charter and definition of three categories for dry wine: STEINFEDER, FEDERSPIEL, SMARAGD.

Wachau Low A World-renowned Danube region, home to some of Austria's most mineral, long-lived RIES, GRÜNER V. Top: ALZINGER, Donabaum, DOMÄNE WACHAU, HIRTZBERGER, Högl, JAMEK, KNOLL, NIKOLAIHOF, F PICHLER, R PICHLER, PICHLER-KRUTZLER, PRAGER, SCHMELZ, TEGERNSEERHOF, VEYDER-MALBERG.

Wachter-Wiesler, Weingut S Burg r ★★★ Christoph Wachter (mid-20s) is shooting star of EISENBERG DAC; fruit-driven, dense, discreetly oak-influenced BLAUFRÄNKISCH.

Wagram Low A (r) w Region w of VIENNA, incl KLOSTERNEUBURG. Mainly loess soils, GRÜNER V. Best: EHMOSER, Fritsch, Stift Klosterneuburg, Leth, OTT.

Weingut Stadt Krems Krems r w ★★→★★★ Co-op capably steered by Fritz Miesbauer, esp RIES from v'yds Grillenparz and Wachtberg, Miesbauer also vinifies for STIFT GÖTTWEIG.

Weinviertel (r) w ("Wine Quarter") Largest Austrian wine region, 13,356 ha between Danube and Czech border, eponymous DAC. No longer just simple whites: GRÜNER V in all its myriad expressions. Try: EBNER-EBENAUER, Graf Hardegg, GROISS, PFAFFL.

Weninger, Franz M Burg r (w) ★★★★ 05 06 07 08 09 11' 12 Top estate at Horitschon, *fine reds esp Blaufränkisch*, from clay- and iron-rich soils (Dürrau v'yd). Also in Hungary: Weninger-Gere.

Weststeiermark W St Small wine region specializing in SCHILCHER. Best: Klug, Lukas, Domaine Müller, Reiterer, Strohmeier.

Wien *See* VIENNA.

Wieninger, Fritz Vienna r w sp ★★★→★★★★ 07 08 09 11 12 13 Leading grower with HEURIGEN: CHARD, RIES, PINOT N, gd GEMISCHTER SATZ. Best v'yds: Nussberg, Rosengartl.

Winzer Krems Krems w Quality-oriented co-op with 1,050 growers covering 1,000 ha. Gd RIES, GRÜNER V.

Wohlmuth S Sty w ★★★ Exquisite producer of SAUV BL, esp from single-v'yds Edelschuh, Steinriegl.

England & Wales

The year 2014 was pivotal for English wine; a record harvest of ripe healthy grapes was excellent news, but just as important were tastings that convinced the press that the sparkling wines coming from a couple of dozen now established makers in the south of England have to be taken seriously. Their quality is levelling with good Champagne, while their overall style is distinctly English; bright, sharp, invigorating and full of orchard-fruit flavour. Ideally four or five years of bottle age adds to the attraction. They are no longer an eccentric choice or a long-odds bet.

Still wine quality is also on the rise, but sparkling is the story. Here we list the sparkling successes. After the relatively small 2011 and the dismal 2012 harvests, 2013 and 2014 have replenished both stocks and growers' confidence and as much wine was produced in those two years as in the previous four or five vintages. 2014 was an amazing year for both quality and quantity, and both still and sparkling wines will be excellent. We still add "and Wales" as a courtesy to the Principality; in fact only one producer is in contest; in future we'll just say "English". Abbreviations: Berkshire (Berks), Buckinghamshire (Bucks), Cornwall (Corn), East/West Sussex (E/W S'x), Gloucestershire (Glos), Hampshire (Hants), Oxfordshire (Oxf), Worcestershire (Worcs).

Bluebell Estates E S'x ★ Est large-scale producer using both Champagne varieties and SEYVAL BL. Hindleap Classic Cuvée 10; Blanc de Blancs and Rosé 10 also v.gd. Nr the Bluebell Railway.

Bolney Wine Estate W S'x ★★→★★★ Est 1972, now 2nd generation and making gd sparkling, still. Blanc de Blancs 10 with 4 yrs' bottle age and Cuvée Rosé 10 best wines. V.gd visitor facilities.

Breaky Bottom E S'x ★★→★★★ One of pioneers. Just celebrated 40th yr with same owner/winemaker. Best: Cuvée Princess Colonna 08 and SEYVAL BL-based Cuvée Koizumi Yakumo 10 (named after distant relative). Well worth a visit if you can handle a cross-country ride.

Camel Valley Corn ★★★ One of UK's biggest producers; Cornwall's only. Dozens of awards. Best wines PINOT N Rosé Brut 12, Cornwall Brut 12.

Chapel Down Kent ★★★ Huge expansion plans and successful crowd-funding share offer; set to be country's largest producer. Best: CHARD-based Blanc de Blancs 09, Champagne-varieties Three Graces 09. NV Brut, now mainly Champagne varieties, excellent value. Visitor facilities superb. Also makes gd beer.

Coates & Seely Hants Newish concern; Seely is the AXA wine boss. Fine quality, austere style. NV Brut Res is best wine to date.

Court Garden E S'x Newcomer with CHARD-based Blanc de Blancs 10. Blanc de Noirs, Classic Cuvée also worth trying.

The UK's most northerly vines: Black Hamburg, 20 vines in a polytunnel, Isle of Lewis, teetotal grower.

Davenport E S'x Organic grower, still and sparkling. Best: Limney Estate 09 (PINOT N, AUXERROIS), 10 also v.gd.

Furleigh Estate Dorset ★★ New s-coast v'yd with the three classic varieties. To watch.

Gusbourne Kent ★★★ Major Champagne-variety producer with v'yds in both Kent and W S'x; set to become one of the UK's top five. Best: Brut Res 10, Blanc de Blancs 10. Still CHARD, PINOT N also v.gd. New winery planned.

> **Chalk or no chalk?**
> Champagne boasts of its chalk hills, and England's South Downs are the same chalk, which ducks under the Channel and resurfaces in S'x – but most English v'yds aren't planted on chalk. Most are on green sandstone; clay loam, sandy soil, ancient slate…. How important is chalk to sparkling wine? Time will tell: s England is one big terroir experiment.

Hambledon Vineyard Hants England's oldest commercial v'yd now revived with big new v'yds, all Champagne varieties. Impressive gravity-powered winery. Current wine is NV Classic Cuvée. Hambledon was cradle of cricket.

Hattingley Valley Hants Impressive newcomer; s-sloping v'yds with well-equipped winery. Best wines Classic Cuvée and Rosé, both 11. Also makes wines for several other v'yds.

Henners E S'x Newcomer making v.gd wines from promising site. First wines well received. Best wines PINOT-based 10 Brut and 11 Rosé.

Herbert Hall Kent One of few organic growers making gd (if quite dry, high-acid) sparkling from Champagne varieties. Best: Brut 11.

Hush Heath Estate Kent ★★★ One of the UK's best; impressive v'yds. Champagne variety-based sparkling Balfour Brut; now new 1503 label. Best: Rosé 10, 11. Also gd cider; worth a visit.

Jenkyn Place Hants Well-sited v'yds, some gd wines. Best are subtle, toasty Brut 09 and fruity Brut Rosé 09.

Laithwaite's Berks, Bucks ★★→★★★ Major UK online wine retailer with interest in sparkling. Retails Ridgeview's South Ridge brand (p w), plus v. small volume but high-quality Theale and Wyfold v'yds. Now v'yds in Marlow and Windsor Great Park. Set to become major force.

Langham Dorset Newcomer; impressive start with Champagne varieties. Best: Classic Cuvée 10, Rosé 11, PINOT MEUNIER-based Blanc de Noirs 11.

Meonhill Hants Only v'yd in the UK started by Champagne producer, now part of HAMBLEDON business. Best: Grande Res Cuvée NV, blend of 09, 08, 01.

Nyetimber W S'x ★★★ One of England's first, best-known and best: fine tasty wines from 150 ha of vines and more being planted. Best: toasty Classic Cuvée, fruity Rosé, both 09 and excellent (but v. expensive) Tillington 09.

100 sheep graze among the vines at Nyetimber. Food and wine matching?

Plumpton College E S'x ★ The UK's only wine college, with growing influence and now its own wines. Gd still, sparkling. Best sparklers Dean Brut NV, Rosé NV.

Redfold W S'x Newcomer with Champagne varieties close to original NYETIMBER site. Sold under the Ambriel label. Best: Classic Cuvée 10.

RidgeView E S'x ★★★★ Still UK's best for consistency, range, value, although others are challenging. Cuvées named for parts of London. Best: long-lasting 100% CHARD Grosvenor 10 and super-fruity Victoria Rosé. Contract maker for other growers. Founder Mike Roberts died 2014; children continue.

Sharpham Devon Still wine producer now making gd sparkling. Best: PINOT N/PINOT BL-based Sparkling Pink 10 and PINOT GR/PINOT N/PINOT M-based Sparkling Blanc 10. Also excellent cheese.

Wiston W S'x ★★→★★★ Relative newcomer now making v.gd sparkling (v. dry) under own label and for others. All Champagne varieties; uses traditional Coquard Champagne vertical basket press. Best: Rosé 11, Blanc de Blancs NV.

Wyfold ★★★ Tiny (1-ha) Champagne variety vy'd at 120m above sea level in Chilterns, part-owned by hands-on LAITHWAITE family. Maiden vintage (2009) won prizes. Best: Wyfold Brut 10.

Central & Southeast Europe

More heavily shaded areas are the wine-growing regions.

Abbreviations used in the text:

Bal	Balaton	N Hun	North Hungary
Cri & Mar	Crişana & Maramures	N/S Pann	North/South Pannonia
Cro Up	Croatian Uplands	Pod	Podravje
Dan P	Danubian Plain	Pos	Posavje
Dalm	Dalmatia	Prim	Primorje
Dob	Dobrogea	Sl & CD	Slavonia & Croatian Danube
I & Kv	Istria & Kvarner	Thr L	Thracian Lowlands
Mold	Moldova / Moldavia	Tok	Tokaj
Mun	Muntenia & Oltenia Hills	Trnsyl	Transylvania

HUNGARY

Wine, and good wine, is key to Hungary's DNA. Tokaj (sweet and dry wines) continues to lead the march on to global wine lists, with more than 20 per cent of Michelin-starred restaurants in the USA and UK now listing wines from Hungary's only world-famous region. A set of new regulations is in place to enhance quality further – as is a marketing programme. But, it's not just about Tokaji. Hungary is increasingly gaining overdue recognition for a full range of wines from inexpensive, reliable whites through to serious dry whites and reds.

Árvay Tok w dr sw ★★ Family winery in TOK since 2009; 17 ha. Long-lived dry whites.
Aszú Tok Botrytis-affected and shrivelled grapes, and the resulting sweet wine from TOK. From 2014, legal minimum sweetness is 120 g/l residual sugar, equivalent to 5 PUTTONYOS. Producers may choose to label as 5 or 6 Puttonyos but no longer obligatory. 3 and 4 Puttonyos sweetness levels are no longer permitted (wines could be beautifully balanced at this level – but the majority weren't). The terms may appear on labels for marketing purposes provided wine meets new higher sweetness level. Gd Aszú in 05 06 07 08 09 (11) (13). Small quantities in 2014 but producers report gd quality.

Aszú Essencia Tok Still seen on pre-2010 labels but not permitted after that. Was 2nd-sweetest TOKAJI level (7 PUTTONYOS+). Do not confuse with ESSENCIA/ESZENCIA.

Badacsony Bal ★★→★★★ Volcanic slopes n of Lake BALATON; full, rich whites. Look for *Szeremley* (age-worthy KÉKNYELŰ 09' 06, SZÜRKEBARÁT) and Villa Sandahl (esp 12 Rake & Scoop, Multiplexor RIES), Villa Tolnay (esp WELSCHRIESLING 12), Laposa (Bazalt Cuvée 12).

Balaton Region, and Central Europe's largest freshwater lake. BADACSONY, Balatonfüred-Csopak (best for whites esp Béla és Bandi, Feind, Figula, Jasdi: impressive Siralomvágó OLASZRIZLING), Balatonmelléke (DR. BUSSAY), SOMLÓ to n. BALATONBOGLÁR to s.

Balatonboglár Bal r w dr ★★→★★★ Wine district, also major winery of TÖRLEY, s of Lake BAL. Gd producers: Garamvári, KONYÁRI, IKON, Légli Otto, Légli Géza, Budjosó, Pócz, Varga.

Barta Tok w dr sw ★★★ 10 11 12 (13) Highest v'yd in TOK, producing impressive dry whites (esp Öleg Király FURMINT) with top winemaker Attila Hommona. Also v.gd sweet SZAMORODNI.

Béres Tok w dr sw ★★→★★★ Gd ASZÚ 06 07 08' and dry wines: 09 11 Lőcse FURMINT, 09' Diókút HÁRSLEVELŰ.

Bikavér N Hun r ★→★★★ 07 08 09' 11' Means "Bull's Blood". PDO for EGER and SZEKSZÁRD. Egri Bikavér must be blend of three from list of specified varieties, none to exceed 50% with KÉKFRANKOS in majority, oak-aged for min 6 mths. Superior is min five varieties, 12 mths in barrel, 30–50% Kékfrankos, from restricted sites. Best for Egri Bikavér: Bolyki, DEMETER, Grof Buttler, GÁL TIBOR, ST ANDREA, Thummerer. In SZEKSZÁRD look for Eszterbauer Tüke esp 09 11', HEIMANN, Mészáros, TAKLER, Sebestyén.

Bor is "wine": *vörös* is red; *fehér* is white; *édes* is sweet, *száraz* is dry, *válogatás* is selected.

Bock, *József* S Pann r ★★→★★★ 09' 11 12 Leading family in VILLÁNY, making rich, full-bodied reds. Try: Bock Cuvée 09', Capella Cuvée 07, SYRAH 11, KÉKFRANKOS Res 12.

Bussay, Dr. Bal w ★★ 11 12 RIP, ground-breaking doctor and winemaker in Balatonmelléke, died tragically young at 57 in August 2014. Intense TRAMINI, PINOT GR, OLASZRIZLING.

Csányi S Pann r ★→★★ 09 11 (12) Ambitious large winery in VILLÁNY. Look for Kővilla Cuvée 09, Borklub Bora Cuvée 09 and Chateau Teleki MERLOT 11.

Degenfeld, Gróf Tok w dr sw ★★→★★★ Large TOK estate with luxury hotel. Sweet wines best: 6 PUTTONYOS 08, Andante 11; also pretty semi-dry DYA MUSCAT Blanc.

Demeter, Zoltán Tok w dr sw ★★★→★★★★ Elegant, intense dry wines, 11 12, esp Veres, Kakas and Lapis FURMINTS; excellent Szerelmi HÁRSLEVELŰ. 09 Eszter late-harvest also v.gd.

Dereszla Tok w dr sw ★★★ 07' 08' 09 10 11 12 Owned by d'Aulan family from Champagne. Excellent ASZÚ and *flor*-aged dry SZAMORODNI Experience. Also try Kabar and v.gd FURMINT Lapis.

Districtus Hungaricus Controllatus (DHC) Term for Protected Designation of Origin (PDO). Symbol is a local crocus and DHC on label.

Disznókő Tok w dr sw ★★→★★★★ 06 07' 08' 09 Important TOK estate, owned by French insurer AXA. Fine expressive ASZÚ, Kapi is top cru. Gd-value late-harvest.

Dobogó Tok (r) w dr sw ★★★ 06' 07' 08 09 11 (12) Impeccable small TOK estate. Benchmark ASZÚ and late-harvest Mylitta, superb Mylitta Álma, thrilling dry FURMINT, esp Betsek DŰLŐ and *pioneering Pinot N* Izabella Utca.

Dűlő Named v'yd; single site.

Duna Duna Great Plain. Districts: Hajós-Baja (try Sümegi, Koch), Csongrád (Somodi), Kunság (Frittmann: decent Cserszegi Fűszeres, KADARKA, Generosa).

Eger N Hun ★→★★★ Top red region of n and its baroque capital. Egri BIKAVÉR is most

---

Tokaj women and wine

Women play a significant role in TOK, esp compared to the rest of the country, and they make some of Tok's most exciting wines. They have also founded an association to work together and spread the word about the new face of Tokaji. Marta Wille-Baumkauf (PENDITS), Natália Demkó (Holdvölgy), Stephanie Berecz (KIKELET), Sarolta Bárdos (TOKAJ NOBILIS), Judit Bodó (Bott Pince), Angelika Árvay (ÁRVAY), Melinda Béres (BÉRES), Countess Maria Degenfeld (DEGENFELD), Erszébet Prácser (Erszébet), Katinka Kékessy (PATRICIUS) and president Edit Kulcsár (Demetervin) are just some of the female highflyers in the region. At ROYAL TOKAJI Fruzsina Ostvath is winemaker and Stéphanie Berecz consultant.

---

famous. CAB FR, PINOT N, SYRAH increasingly important; DHC for Debrői HÁRSLEVELŰ. Try: Bolyki, Gróf Buttler, DEMETER, **Gál Tibor**, Kaló Imre, KOVÁCS NIMRÓD, Pók Tamás, ST ANDREA, Thummerer.

Egri Csillag N Hun "Star of Eger". Dry white blend modelled on BIKAVÉR. Blend of at least four grapes; min 50% must be local Carpathian varieties.

Essencia / Eszencia Tok ★★★★ Syrupy, luscious free-run juice from ASZÚ grapes. Rarely bottled and typically sold by the spoonful. Residual sugar min 450 g/l (but can be 800 g/l), alcohol usually well below 5%. Reputed to have miraculous medicinal/aphrodisiac properties.

Etyek-Buda N Pann Dynamic region noted for expressive, crisp whites and fine sparklers, esp CHARD, **Sauv Bl**, PINOT GR and promising for PINOT N. Leading producers: Etyeki Kúria (esp Pinot N, SAUV BL), Nyakas (Budai label), György-Villa (premium wines from TÖRLEY), Haraszthy, Rókusfalvy, Kertész.

Gál Tibor N Hun r w ★★ Improving wines from son of late Tibor Gál, famed as winemaker at Ornellaia (see Italy). Try appealing EGRI CSILLAG DYA, PINOT N 09, BIKAVÉR Supérior 09.

Gere, Attila S Pann r (p) ★★★ 06' 07' 08 09' 11 Leading light in VILLÁNY making some of country's best reds, esp rich Solus MERLOT, intense Kopar Cuvée, top Attila barrel selection. **Cab Sauv** is gd value and ages well.

Heimann S Pann r ★★→★★★ 07 08 09' 11 12 (13) Impressive family winery in SZEKSZÁRD, esp superb Barbár and Franciscus Cuvée. V.gd KADARKA (winery collects rare Kadarka clones), selected (válogatás) KÉKFRANKOS.

Hétszőlő Tok w dr sw ★★ Historic first-growth TOK estate bought in 2009 by Michel Reibier, owner of Cos d'Estournel (Bordeaux). Noted for lighter styles of Tokaji.

Hilltop Winery N Pann r p w dr ★★ 09 11 12 13 In Neszmély. Meticulous, gd-value DYA varietals (p w). Also v.gd: ART range, v'yd selection Premium range.

Homonna Tok w dr ★★★ 09' 11 12 Fine, elegant FURMINTS, esp Határi v'yd, plus new Rány v'yd.

Ikon r w ★★ Hungary's 2013 "Winery of The Year", s of Lake BAL. Gd-value, well-made wines from majority shareholder Janos KONYÁRI and former Tihany abbey v'yds.

Kikelet Tok w dr sw ★★★ One of TOK's inspiring group of leading women winemakers. Wonderful Váti Furmint 12 and fine, pure SZAMORODNI 08.

Királyudvar Tok w dr sw sp ★★★ 06' 07' 08 Bio TOK winery in old royal cellars at Tarcal, owned by Anthony Hwang (see also Vouvray, France). Excellent FURMINT Sec 11 12, Cuvée Ilona (late-harvest), flagship 6 PUTTONYOS Lapis ASZÚ and Henye Peszgo (sparkling) since 2008.

Konyári Bal r p w dr ★★→★★★ 09' 11 (12) (13) Father and son making high-quality estate wines at BALATONBOGLÁR: esp fruity DYA rosé; consistent Loliense (r w) excellent Szárhegy (w). Top reds: Jánoshegy KÉKFRANKOS, Páva and Sessio.

Kovács Nimród Winery N Hun r p w dr ★★ 09 11' EGER producer impressing with excellent KÉKFRANKOS 11, Grand Bleu 09, tasty DYA Rosé, rich Battonage CHARD.

Kreinbacher Bal w dr ★★ 09 11 Organic methods, with focus on local grapes. Try: Juhfark, HÁRSLEVELŰ Selection.

Mád Tok Important historic town in heart of TOK region, top v'yds incl Betsek, Nyulaszo, St Tamas. Gd producers: Alana-Tokaji, BARTA, OROSZ GABOR, Demetervin (gd dry FURMINT 12, sweet Elvezet 12), Lenkey, Holdvölgy (esp SZAMORODNI 08, Meditation Furmint 09) KIKELET, ROYAL TOKAJI, SZENT TAMÁS WINERY, SZEPSY, Tok Classic.

Malatinszky S Pann r p w dr ★★★ 06' 07 08 09' 11 Certified organic from 2012. Excellent unfiltered Kúria CAB FR, CAB SAUV, Kövesföld (r), Pinot Bleu. Also tasty DYA Le Sommelier rosé and Serena (w).

Mátra N Hun ★→★★ Gd region for decent value, fresh whites and rosé. Better producers: Benedek, Gabor Karner (notable KÉKFRANKOS), NAG, Szöke Mátyás, Borpalota (Fríz label), NAGYRÉDE.

Mézes-Mály Top TOK cru in Tarcal. Try ROYAL TOKAJI and tiny but excellent Balassa.

Mór N Pann w ★→★★ Small region, famous for fiery local *Ezerjó*. Also promising for CHARD, TRAMINI, RIES. Try Maurus winery.

Nagyréde N Hun (r) p w ★ Gd-value, commercial DYA varietal wines under Nagyréde, Mátra Hill, Spice Trail labels.

Oremus Tok w dr sw ★★→★★★★ 05 06' 07 08 09 11 12 Outstanding Tolcsva winery, named for historic TOK v'yd of founding Rakóczi family, owned by Spain's Vega Sicilia: first-rate ASZÚ; v.gd dry FURMINT *Mandolás*.

Orosz Gábor Tok w dr sw ★★ 06 07 08 09 11 Small estate in MÁD with gd v'yds. Best: Király HÁRSLEVELŰ, Betsek FURMINT, 6 PUTTONYOS ASZÚ. Second label: Bodvin.

Pajzos-Megyer Tok w dr sw ★★→★★★ 06' 07 08 09 11 (12) Jointly managed TOK properties. Megyer in cooler n of region, esp dry FURMINT, MUSCAT (dr sw). Pajzos makes richer, age-worthy sweet wines only.

Pannonhalma r p w dr ★★→★★★ 12 13 800-yr-old Pannonhalma Abbey is the only notable producer in the region of the same name. Stylish, aromatic whites, esp RIES, TRAMINI and SAUV BL. Gd-value Tricollis, lovely top Hemina (w) and improving PINOT N.

Patricius Tok w dr sw ★★ 06' 07 08 09 11 12 Consistent, gd-value dry FURMINT, late-harvest Katinka, 6 PUTTONYOS ASZU.

PDO See DHC.

Pécs S Pann (r) w ★→★★ Wine region nr s city of Pécs. Known for whites, incl local CIRFANDL. Ebner PINOT N impresses.

Pendits Winery Tok w dr sw ★★ 02 03 05 06 Only Demeter-certified bio estate in Hungary. Luscious long ageing ASZÚ, pretty dry DYA MUSCAT.

Puttonyos (putts) Traditional indication of sweetness and quality in TOKAJI ASZÚ. No longer required on label from 2013 but may appear as option. Historically a *puttony* was a 25 kg bucket or hod of aszú grapes. The number of puttonyos added to a 136-litre barrel of base wine or fermenting must determined the final sweetness of the wine.

2013 superb vintage for Tokaji Aszu: Royal Tokaji Essencia has >700g/l sugar.

Royal Tokaji Wine Co Tok dr sw ★★→★★★★ 05 06 07' 08' 09 Pioneer joint-venture at MÁD that led renaissance of TOK in 1990 (I am a co-founder). Mainly first-growth v'yds. 6-PUTTONYOS single-v'yd bottlings: esp MÉZES-MÁLY, Betsek, Szent Tamás, Nyulászó plus 5 Puttonyos. Also from **2011** complex dry FURMINT, Furmint DÜLŐ-válogatás, luscious, gd-value Late Harvest (Mád Cuvée in the USA). Promising new consultant winemaker.

St Andrea N Hun r w dr ★★★ 06' 07 08 09' 11 12 Top name in EGER, leading way in modern, high-quality BIKAVÉR (Merengő, Hangács, Áldás). Excellent white blends: Napbor, Örökké, organic Boldogságos, plus v.gd PINOT N.

Sauska S Pann, Tok r p w ★★→★★★★ 07 08 09' 11' 12 Immaculate winery in VILLÁNY.

V gd KADARKA, KÉKFRANKOS, CAB FR, stunning MERLOT 11 and impressive red blends esp Cuvée 7 and Cuvée 5. Also Sauska-Tokaj with focus on v.gd dry whites, esp Cuvée 105, FURMINT Birsalmás, Medve Furmint.

Somló Bal w ★★→★★★ 09 11 (12) Dramatic volcanic hill famous for mineral-rich whites: *Juhfark* ("sheep's tail"), OLASZRIZLING, FURMINT, HÁRSLEVELŰ. Region of small producers making long-lived intense wines, esp Fekete Bela, Györgykovács Hollóvár, Royal Somló, Spiegelberg, Somlói Apátsági. Bigger Tornai (esp Top Selection range, Grofi HÁRSLEVELŰ), KREINBACHER also v.gd.

Sopron N Pann r ★★→★★★ Dynamic district on Austrian border overlooking Lake Fertő. KÉKFRANKOS most important, plus CAB SAUV, SYRAH, PINOT N. Top producer is bio *Weninger*, also try v. characterful wines of Ráspi (esp Electus ZWEIGELT). To watch: Pfneiszl, Luka, Taschner.

Szamorodni Tok Literally "as it was born"; for TOK produced from whole bunches with no separate ASZÚ harvest, sadly a declining category. Dry or sweet (*édes*) depending on proportion of Aszú grapes present. Best dry versions are *flor*-aged; try *Tinon*, DERESZLA, Karádi-Berger. Gd sweet versions KIKELET, SZEPSY, Höldvolgy.

Szekszárd S Pann r ★★→★★★ Ripe, rich reds from KÉKFRANKOS, CAB SAUV, CAB FR MERLOT. Also KADARKA being revived and BIKAVÉR. Look for: Dúzsi (rosé in all styles), Eszterbauer (esp Tüke Bikavér, Nagyapám KADARKA), HEIMANN, Mészáros Sebestyén, Szent Gaál, *Takler*, Remete-Bor (Kadarka), Vesztergombi (Csaba's cuvée, Turul), Vida (v.gd Hidaspetre KÉKFRANKOS).

Szent Tamás Winery Tok w sw ★★★ 11 12' New winery in MÁD with ISTVÁN SZEPSY Junior. V.gd FURMINT Szent Tamás, excellent Percze Furmint and Late Harvest 3909. Also name of top DŰLŐ.

Szepsy, István Tok w dr sw ★★★★ 05 06 07' 08' 09 10 11' 12 Brilliant, standard-setting TOK producer in MÁD. Superb age-worthy dry FURMINT, esp DŰLŐ Urágya Urbán, Szent Tamás, Betsek. V.gd sweet SZAMORODNI 09. Superb ASZÚ 05 06 07.

Szeremley Bal w dr sw ★★→★★★ 09 11' 12 Pioneer in BADACSONY. Intense, mineral RIES, *Szürkebarát*, (aka PINOT GR), KÉKNYELŰ, appealing sweet Zeus.

Takler S Pann r ★★ 09' 11' 12 Significant family producer in SZEKSZÁRD, making super-ripe, supple reds. Best: Res selections of CAB FR, KÉKFRANKOS, SYRAH, BIKÁVER. Gd new single-v'yd Kékfrankos Görögszó 11 and tasty DYA rosé.

Tinon, Samuel Tok w dr sw ★★→★★★ 00 01 04 05 07 Sauternais in TOK since 1991. Distinctive and v.gd Tok ASZÚ with v. long maceration and barrel-ageing. Hatari Dry FURMINT. Also superb *flor*-aged *Szamorodni*.

Tokaj / Tokaji ★★→★★★★ Tokaj is the town and wine region; Tokaji the wine. New regulations from 2014 mean all Tokaji has to be bottled within the region to qualify for PDO status. Recommended producers without standalone entry: Bott Pince, Balassa, Füleky, Holdvölgy, Erzsébet, Demetervin, Karádi-Berger.

Tokaj Kereskedőház Tok w dr sw ★→★★ Aka Crown Estates, still state-owned. Making break with past poor quality and heading up major investment project in TOK region. Major new winery, new winemaker (Karoly Áts, ex-ROYAL TOKAJ) new strategy for sourcing better grapes through working closely with growers. Older stocks audited after legal case in the US. Watch this space.

Tokaj Nobilis Tok w dr sw ★★★ Superb small producer run by Sarolta Bárdos, one of TOK's inspirational women. Top ASZÚ 07, dry Barakonyi HÁRSLEVELŰ and FURMINT.

EU honeypot: €330 million funding to 2020 to develop Tokaj; poor region, needs it.

Tolna S Pann Antinori-owned ★★ Tűzkő is most important estate. Gd TRAMINI, CHARD, Talentum (r).

Törley r p w dr sp ★→★★ Innovative large company. Chapel Hill is major brand name. Well-made, gd-value DYA international varietals (PINOT GR, CHARD, PINOT N), also local varieties IRSAI OLIVÉR, Zenit, Zefir. Major fizz producer (esp *Törley*, Gala

Hungaria labels) and v.gd classic method, esp François President Rosé Brut 10, Chard Brut NV. György-Villa for top selections (try JUHFARK, SYRAH).

Villány S Pann Most s wine region and best red zone. Noted for serious ripe Bordeaux varieties (esp CAB FR) and blends, also try juicy examples of local *Kékfrankos* and PORTUGIESER. Recent appearance of gd SYRAH, PINOT N in cooler spots. High-quality producers: *Bock*, CSÁNYI, ATTILA GERE, Tamás & Zsolt Gere, Kiss Gabor, Heumann, *Malatinszky*, *Sauska*, Tiffán, *Vylyan*, WENINGER-GERE, Wunderlich.

Maximum daily pick of aszu berries (shrivelled, sticky)/picker: just 15 kg.

Vincent, Chateau Bal sp ★★ Top Hungarian producer of bottle-fermented fizz (try Evolution Rosé 07, Fantazia Brut Natur 05). Also owns Garamvári estate, gd DYA IRSAI OLIVÉR, SAUV BL and v.gd Sinai CAB SAUV.

Vylyan S Pann r ★★→★★★ 07 08 09' Stylish Gombás PINOT N. Also try CAB FR, SYRAH, excellent v'yd-selected MERLOT Pillangó. *Duennium Cuvée* (Cab Fr, CAB SAUV, Merlot, ZWEIGELT) is flagship red.

Weninger N Hun r ★★→★★★ 08 09 11 12 Benchmark winery in SOPRON run by Austrian Franz Weninger Jr. Bio since 2006. Single-v'yd *Spern Steiner Kékfrankos* one of best in country. SYRAH, PINOT N and red Frettner blend also impressive.

Weninger-Gere S Pann r p ★★→★★★ 08 09 Austrian F Weninger Sr and ATTILA GERE joint-venture. CAB FR Selection excellent, gd-value Cuvée Phoenix, DYA fresh rosé.

BULGARIA

W inemakers are currently experimenting not only with new varieties of grapes but also reviving almost forgotten ones. There is interest in organic wines and in young wines in the Beaujolais Nouveau style. It is a lively and expanding wine scene, exploring new markets and new blends. There is also a growing domestic market for high-quality wines, some of which are now being exported.

Assenovgrad Thr L r ★→★★ Specialists and main producers of indigenous MAVRUD and RUBIN.

Bessa Valley Thr L r ★★★ Stephan von Neipperg (Canon la Gaffelière, Bordeaux) and K-H Hauptmann's winery nr Pazardjik. SYRAH by Enira 09, BV by Enira 09, Enira Res 08. Full-bodied, smooth. Only quality Bulgarian wine readily available in UK.

Bessa Valley (1,500 barriques) uses a barrique/week for topping up = 11,700 litres wine/annum.

Black Sea Gold Thr L (Pomorie) (r) w ★ Recent investment at this coastal winery has improved quality: try Villa Ponte CAB SAUV, SYRAH 09 and Arte Ante Cab Sauv 08.

Borovitsa Dan P r w ★★→★★★ An old v'yd with distinctive terroir close to Danube. Dux 06, complex, well-balanced fruit and oak, recommended. Les Amis CHARD 08, PINOT N Cuvée Enrique 09 worth trying. Interesting blend of old variety Evmolpia, MERLOT. Sensum 10 has several times been voted Bulgaria's no.1 wine.

Boyar, Domaine Thr L ★★→★★★ Big exporter, large winery at Blueridge. Boutique winery at Korten. Gd, consistent everyday wines. New ranges Deja Vu (incl excellent velvety MERLOT), Elements (wonderful summery, gooseberry, flowery SAUV BL). Korten's Merlot 12, CAB SAUV 12, SYRAH 12 are quality wines with ageing potential. Next Twenty Years Caladoc 10 is well-rounded newcomer to range.

Castra Rubra Thr L r ★★ Michel Rolland from Bordeaux advises successful young team. Award-winning Castra Rubra 09. Via Diagonalis 09 should age well. The curiously named Motley Cock Red 09 is a big, smooth, full-bodied red.

> **Bulgarian best**
> Look out for these wines:
> BOROVITSA Sensum 10; MIDALIDARE Grand Vintage MALBEC 12; MINKOVI
> BROTHERS Le Photographe SYRAH 13; TERRA TANGRA Roto 09.

Damianitza Thr L r (w) ★★ Struma Valley MELNIK specialist. Uniqato Melnik 10 elegant No Man's Land Kometa 11, ReDark 09. Single grape Volcano VIOGNIER and Volcano SYRAH 13 worth looking out for.

Dragomir Thr L r (w) ★★ Boutique winemaker. Try CAB SAUV and MERLOT Reserva 11 Pitos Merlot, Cab Sauv and RUBIN 10 and Karizma Cab Sauv, Merlot and SYRAH 10

Ivo Varbanov Thr L r (w) ★★ Concert pianist making fine wines from organic v'yd incl Marselan Late Harvest 11 and a VIOGNIER/Tamyanka blend 13.

Katarzyna Thr L r w ★★★ Winery in s to follow: impressive Le Voyage SYRAH/CAB FR 11 Question Mark 12 (stylish CAB SAUV/MERLOT); smooth, aromatic Katarzyna Estate Chopin Concerto Cab Sauv/Syrah 12. MALBEC Grand Vintage 12 recommended.

Levent Dan P (r) w ★★ Small winery in Russe, gd fresh whites, esp Levent Family Selection 12. Grand Selection CHARD 13, CAB SAUV Grand Selection 12. Levent SAUV BL 13 a taste of summer.

Logodaj Thr L r w ★→★★ Struma Valley. Hypnose Res MERLOT single-v'yd 10. Nobile MELNIK 12 worth looking out for; stylish Incantesimo SYRAH 12.

Midalidare Estate Thr L r w ★★ Boutique winery, impressive. Esp single-v'yd: Grand Vintage MALBEC 12, Mogilovo Village 11. Elegant SAUV BL/SÉM 13. Synergy Sauv Bl, PINOT GRIS 13 fresh and aromatic.

Minkovi Brothers Thr L r w ★★→★★★ International award-winning Le Photographe SYRAH 13. Oak Tree 11 is subtle, complex, balanced. Also Le Photographe RHEIN RIES 11 refreshing, aromatic, long finish.

Miroglio, Edoardo Thr L r w ★★ Italian-owned v'yds at Elenovo. Soli Invicto 10 Elenovo CAB SAUV Res 09. Miroglio Brut Metodo Classico 08 (and rosé 09 known as *Bulgaria's best fizz*, gd in any company, dry, gently sparkling. Soli Red 10 a smooth blend of Cab Sauv, CAB FR and indigenous MELNIK.

Plovdiv was built on seven hills. Now there are six: one was used for paving stones

Preslav Thr L (r) w ★→★★ Try Rubaiyat CHARD 13; plus gooseberry fresh Golden Age SAUV BL 13.

Strymon Thr L r ★→★★ Winery in the warm sw. Smooth MERLOT Res 10. Promising rosé from CAB SAUV, SYRAH 13.

Terra Tangra Thr L r w ★★ In top-rated Sakar Mtn area. Highly recommended Rot 09, complex blend of CAB SAUV/MERLOT/CAB FR/SYRAH/MAVRUD. Yatrus range has g eg.: SAUV BL 13, Cab Fr/MALBEC 12.

Val, Chateau de Dan P r ★★ Small producer of distinctive wines: Grand Claret Res 11. Cuvée Trophy Res 13.

Varna Wine Cellar Dan P (r) w ★→★★ Coastal winery, gd for moderately priced promising SAUV BL 13 and RIES/Varnenski MISKET 14.

Yamantievi Thr L r w ★★ Try Marble Land CHARD 10. SYRAH Res 10, VIOGNIER 12.

Zagreus Thr L r w ★★ Organic v'yds and wines. Vinica MAVRUD 11 is exotic, peppery unusual and recommended. Noble Mavrud is gd dessert wine. St Dimitar range is fruity, fresh, ready to drink young.

SLOVENIA

Slovenia continues to show the way in terms of quality for this part of Europe, with wines that reflect this small country's distinctive terroirs. The east is coming to the fore with vibrant, lively whites that hit the spot for today's tastes, while the west makes more full-bodied, complex whites and reds. Economically times are still hard, though.

Batič Prim w sw ★→★★ 09 11 12 Famous for "natural" wines in VIPAVA. Zaria Rosé is the top seller.

Bjana Prim sp ★★ V.gd traditional-method PENINA from BRDA, esp NV, Cuvée Prestige 08 and Brut Rosé.

Blažič Prim w ★★→★★★ 06 08 11 12 (13) From BRDA. Long-ageing, complex REBULA, SAUVIGNONASSE and white blend Blaž Belo in top yrs.

Brda (Goriška) Prim Top-quality district in PRIM. Many leading wineries, incl BJANA, BLAŽIČ, EDI SIMČIČ, Dolfo (esp sparkling Spirito 10, SIVI PINOT, Skocaj), Erzetič, JAKONČIČ, KRISTANČIČ DUSAN, MOVIA, Prinčič, ŠČUREK, SIMČIČ, Vinska Klet Goriška Brda, ZANUT and orange wines (whites fermented with skins) from Kabaj and Klinec.

Burja Prim r w ★★→★★★ 11 13 Project in VIPAVA, focus on local grapes Zelen and MALVAZIJA. Bela Burja is modern take on traditional blend. Burja Noir is one of country's best PINOT N.

Conrad Fürst Pod w ★★ 11 12 Restituted historic family v'yds nr historic Jeruzalem. Try FURMINT, Pod Stolpom.

Cotar Prim r w ★★ 05 06 08 09 11 Pioneer of long-lived "natural" wines from KRAS, esp Vitovska (w), MALVAZIJA, SAUV BL, TERAN, Terra Rossa red blend.

Cviček Pos Traditional low-alcohol, sharp, light red blend of POS, based on Žametovka grape. Try Bajnof.

Šipon: Slovenian name for Furmint, though rarely used for export labels now Hungary has put dry Furmint on the wine map.

Dveri-Pax Pod r w sw ★★→★★★ 11' 12' 13 Benedictine-owned estate nr Maribor. Crisp, mineral, v.gd-value whites in Benedict series (esp ŠAUV BL, FURMINT, RIES). V.gd Admund v'yd selections: Furmint Ilovci, Ries M, CHARD Vajgen. Also superb sweet ŠIPON straw wine.

Edi Simčič Prim r w ★★★→★★★★ 08 09 10 11 12 (13) Perfectionist in BRDA; red wine superstar with Duet Lex 06 07 09, barrel selection Kolos 04 06 09. Excellent whites: SIVI PINOT, REBULA, MALVAZIJA, Triton Lex. Superb Kozana single-v'yd CHARD.

Guerila Prim r w ★★ Bio producer in VIPAVA; benchmark local DYA PINELA and Zelen.

Heaps Good Wine Pod r w ★★ Promising newcomer. Kiwi Nick Gee and wife Marija make bright, fruit-focused PINOT N, MODRA FRANKINJA; rich PINOT GR in Štajerska.

Istenič Pos sp ★→★★ Reliable PENINA. Basic is N°1, best: Gourmet Rosé and Prestige.

Istria Coastal zone extending into Croatia; main grapes: REFOŠK, MALVAZIJA. Best: Bordon (E Vin rosé, Malvazija), Korenika & Moškon (PINOT GR, Kortinca red), Rojac (Renero, Stari d'Or), Pucer z Vrha (Malvazija), SANTOMAS, Steras (Refošk Kocinski 09), VINAKOPER.

Jakončič Prim r w sp ★★★ 09 10 11 12 V.gd BRDA producer with elegant style, esp Bela Carolina REBULA/CHARD blend, PENINA and Rdeča (r) Carolina.

Joannes Pod r w sp ★★ 09 10 11 12 13 RIES specialist nr Maribor, wines age well. Also fresh light PINOT N, pretty DYA Yellow MUSCAT.

Klet Brda Prim r w ★→★★★ 09 11 12 13 Forward-looking major winery in BRDA. Gd consistent DYA whites, esp Quercus SIVI PINOT, PINOT BL, REBULA. Bagueri is premium oaked range, Krasno Belo is v.gd unoaked blend. Excellent A+ (r w) only in best vintages.

Kogl Pod r w ★★ 11 12 13 Hilltop estate nr Ormož, dating from 1542. Mea Culpa is

main label (esp AUXERROIS, SAUV BL, Yellow MUSCAT). Appealing PINOT N Rubellus 1·
and Magna Domenica 11.

Kras Prim Small, famous district on Terra Rossa soil in PRIM. Best-known for TERAN
MALVAZIJA. Look for much improved Vinakras.

Kristančič Dusan Prim r w ★★ 11 12 13 Family winery in BRDA. Decent CHARD, CA
SAUV, MERLOT. Pavo is top label.

Kupljen Pod r w ★★ 11 12 13 Consistent dry wine pioneer nr Jeruzalem. Gd RENSK
RIZLING, SIVI PINOT, FURMINT, PINOT N. Best is White Star of Stiria.

Ljutomer Ormož Pod Famous subdistrict in POD for crisp, delicate whites and
top sweet wines. Best: CONRAD FÜRST, HEAPS GOOD WINE, P&F, KOGL, Krainz, KUPLJEN
PRA-VINO, VERUS.

Marof Pod r w ★★→★★★ 12' 13 Exciting winery in Prekmurje. DYA classic range
v.gd LAŠKI RIZLING Bodonci, RENSKI RIZLING. Barrel-fermented Breg excellent, es
CHARD 12, SAUV BL 12.

Movia Prim r w sp ★★★ ★★★★ 05 06 07 08 09 11 High-profile bio winery led b
charismatic Ales Kristančič. Excellent v. long-lived Veliko Belo (w) and Velik
Rdeče (r); v.gd MODRI PINOT. Sparkling Puro w 03, rosé 05 are showstoppers
Orange Lunar is controversial.

**Slovenia has Europe's largest accessible caves at Postojna, home to an indigenou
blind salamander.**

P&F Pod r w sp ★★ 11 12 13 Former state winery and v'yds returned to origina
Puklavec family, renamed P&F (Puklavec & Friends). Now v.gd-value, *consistent
crisp aromatic whites* in P&F range. Selected Gomila gold label wines are exceller
esp FURMINT, SAUV BL. Jeruzalem Ormož label for local market.

Penina Designation for quality sparkling wine (*charmat* or traditional method
Look for RADGONSKE GORICE (largest), ISTENIČ, BJANA, MOVIA, Vino Gaube (Gaudiur
Rosé Brut, CHARD), Dolfo (Spirito).

Podravje Region in the ne. Noted for crisp dry whites; often better value than w
Improving reds from PINOT N, MODRA FRANKINJA.

Posavje Region in the se. Best wines are sweet, esp PRUS, Šturm (★★★★ Icewine
botrytized MUSCAT).

PRA-VinO Pod w sw 06' 07 09 11 12 1970s pioneer of private wine production, sor
and grandson now in charge. World-class ★★★★ sweet wines, incl Icewine (*leden
vino*) and botrytis wines from ŠIPON, LAŠKI RIZLING, RIES. Drier styles improving.

Primorje Region in the sw from Slovenian ISTRIA to BRDA. Aka Primorska.

Prus Pos w sw Small family producer making stunning ★★★★ 06 09 11 swee
wines, esp Icewines and botrytis wines from Rumeni MUŠKAT, RIES, SAUV BL.

Pullus Pod r w ★★→★★★ 11 12 13 V.gd crisp modern whites from Ptuj winery, es
Pullus SAUV BL, RIES. Top "G" wines (notable Sauv Bl); lovely RENSKI RIZLING 09 (sw

Radgonske Gorice Pod ★ Best-selling Slovenian sparkler Srebrna (silver) PENINA
classic-method Zlata (golden) Penina, popular demi-sec black label TRAMINEC.

Slovenia's quality wines

All wines have to pass a tasting to gain quality status. *Vrhunsko vino z
zaščtenim geografskim poreklom*, or *Vrhunsko vino ZGP*, is the term for top-
quality PDO wines, though not widely used because of cost of additional
v'yd checks. *Kakovostno vino ZGP* is more common for quality wines.
Deželno vino PGO is for PGI wines. For quality sweet wines, descriptions
are: *Pozna Trgatev* (Spätlese), *Izbor* (Auslese), *Jagodni Izbor* (BA), *Suhi
Jagodni Izbor* (TBA). (*See* box, Germany p.163 for more on quality level
definitions.) *Ledeno Vino* is Icewine, *Slamno Vino* is straw wine from
semi-dried grapes, PENINA is natural sparkling wine.

Refošk The red to drink in Istria; should be nicely tannic, fruity, brusque.

Santomas Prim r w ★★→★★★ 06 09 10 12 ISTRIAN estate, some of country's best *Refošk* and REFOŠK/CAB SAUV blends: Antonius (60-yr-old vines), Mezzoforte blend.

Ščurek Prim r w sw ★★→★★★ 09 10 11' 12 13 Gd consistent BRDA producer. DYA varieties BELI PINOT, CHARD, REBULA, CAB FR. Best wines focus on local grapes, esp Stara Brajda (r w), Pikolit, Up.

Simčič, Marjan Prim r w sw ★★★→★★★★ 09 10 11 12 13 Whites, esp SIVI PINOT, SAUVIGNONASSE, REBULA, CHARD, SAUV BL Selekcija impress. V.gd Teodor blends; elegant MODRI PINOT; notable Opoka single-v'yd range (Sauv Bl, MERLOT). Sweet Leonardo is great.

Štajerska Slovenija Pod Important wine district in east since 2006. Check out Gaube (esp CHARD Kaspar), Frešer, Kušter, Valdhuber, Miro Vino (esp ŠIPON).

Steyer Pod w sw sp ★★ 10 11 12 (13) TRAMINER specialist in Štajerska: dr sp sw oak-aged.

Sutor Prim r w ★★★ 09' 10 11' Excellent producer from VIPAVA. CHARD is one of country's best, ages well. V.gd SAUV BL, fine MALVAZIJA, elegant MERLOT-based red and exciting new white blend 11.

Tilia Prim r w ★★ 11 12 13 Husband-and-wife team in VIPAVA. Appetizing Sunshine range esp SAUV BL, PINOT GR; premium Golden Tilia range esp fine PINOT N.

94 per cent of Slovenia's 30,000 growers farm less than 0.5 ha, approximately the size of a football pitch.

Valdhuber Pod r w ★ 12 13 Dry pioneer in POD. Refreshing straightforward whites.

Verus Pod r w ★★★ 11' 12' 13 Fine, focused, mineral whites, esp v.gd FURMINT, crisp SAUV BL, flavoursome PINOT GR, refined RIES. Pure, juicy PINOT N 12.

Vinakoper Prim r w ★→★★ 11 12 13 Recently improved large producer in ISTRIA. Gd-value Capris line (DYA MALVAZIJA, REFOŠK, MUSCAT); premium Capo d'Istria REFOŠK.

Vipava Prim Valley noted for cool breezes in PRIM, source of some fine wines. Also large former state winery, Vipava 1894, with new winemaker (try Prestige MALVAZIJA 13, PINELA 13, lovely sweet Pikolit 09). Producers: BATIČ, BURJA, GUERILA, Mlečnik, Štokelj (best Pinela), SUTOR, TILIA.

Vinanut Prim r w ★★ 06 08 11 12 Family winery in BRDA; excellent SAUVIGNONASSE, intense SAUV BL and in top yrs single-v'yd MERLOT Brjač.

Zlati Grič Pod w sp ★ V'yd with golf course nr Maribor. Most of range correct but uninspired. Fantastically elegant PINOT N 12 is an exception.

CROATIA

Croatia is now a fully-fledged member of the EU, but its wines remain little-known except to tourists, who are thrilled by the unexpected quality (but often stunned by the hefty prices). Tourists are the main ambassadors; meanwhile effort is going into the Vina Mosaica project, which is rebranding Croatia under four easier-to-understand regions – Istria & Kvarner, Croatian Uplands, Slavonia & Danube, Dalmatia.

Agrokor r w p ★→★★★ 09 10 11 12 13 Owns multiple wineries and has over 30 per cent market share. Best labels: Vina Laguna Festigia (v.gd MALVAZIJA, MERLOT, CAB SAUV, rosé, Castello red blend), Vina Belje (esp Goldberg GRAŠEVINA, premium CHARD).

Arman, Franc Is & Kv r w ★★ 11 12 13 A 6th-generation family winery. V.gd precise whites esp CHARD, classic MALVAZIJA, TERAN barrique 09.

Babić Rare red from stony sea-terraces at Šibenik. At best almost burgundian.

Badel 1862 r w ★★ 08 09 10 11 12 13 Group of wineries. Best: Korlat SYRAH and Cuvée from Benkovac winery. Gd-value Duravar range esp SAUV BL, GRAŠEVINA. Gd PLAVAC and Ivan Dolac from PZ Svirče.

230 |

Benvenuti Is & Kv r w ★★ ISTRIAN family winery. Gd MALVAZIJA, v.gd TERAN 11, swee Corona Grande 13.

BIBICh Dalm w ★★ 10 12 Well-regarded producer noted for local Debit grape (w esp Lučica single-v'yd and sweet Ambra.

Bodren Cro Up w sw ★★→★★★ 09 10 11 Excellent sweet and Icewines, incl CHAR TRAMINER, RIES and Triptych blend.

Bolfan Cro Up w dr ★→★★ 11 12 13 Nr Zagreb with 20 ha incl bio and "natura wines. RIES, PINOT N rosé best.

Bura-Mrgudič Dalm r ★★→★★★ 09 10 (11) One of country's best DINGAČ. Also make Benmosché Dingač.

Capo Is & Kv r w ★★ 10 11 12' 13 New quality-focused producer in ISTRIA. Try SAUV Sagittarius, CAB FR Aries, PINOT N Gemini.

Cattunar Is & Kv r w dr ★★ 11 12 13 Family-owned hilltop estate. MALVAZIJA, esp ric Collina 11, is v.gd.

Coronica Is & Kv r w ★★ 09 11 12 Notable ISTRIAN winery, esp barrel-aged Gra MALVAZIJA and benchmark Gran TERAN.

Dalmatia Rocky coastal zone and its lovely islands to s of Zadar. Idyllic climate.

Dingač Dalm 08 09' 10 11 First quality designation in 1961, now PDO, on Pelješa peninsula in s DALM. Robust full-bodied reds from PLAVAC MALI. Look for: BUR MRGUDIČ, Kiridžija, Lučič, Matuško, Madirazza, Milicic, SAINTS HILLS, Vinari Dingač (300-ha co-op with v.gd quality Dingač, Postup).

Enjingi, Ivan Sl & CD w sw ★★ Pioneer in SLAVONIJA. V.gd sweet botrytis and d whites, esp GRAŠEVINA barrique, Venje.

Galić Sl & CD r w ★★ 09 11 12 13 Promising new producer in SLAVONIJA, es GRAŠEVINA, red blend Crno 9.

Gerzinić Is & Kv r p w ★★ 11 12 13 Brothers making v.gd TERAN, MALVAZIJA, rosé, SYRA

Grgić Dalm r w ★★→★★★ 07 08 Legendary Napa Valley (USA) producer returned Croatian roots to make PLAVAC MALI, rich POŠIP on Pelješac peninsula.

Hvar Beautiful island with world's oldest continuously cultivated v'yd and UNESC protection. Noted for PLAVAC MALI, incl Ivan Dolac designation. Gd: Carič, Planči PZ Svirče, TOMIČ, ZLATAN OTOK.

Iločki Podrumi Sl & CD r w ★★ 11 12 13 Family-owned; claims to have the 2n oldest wine cellar in Europe: built 1450. Try premium GRAŠEVINA, TRAMINAC ar Principovac range.

Istria North Adriatic peninsula. MALVAZIJA is main grape. Gd also for CAB SAUV, MERL TERAN. Look for ARMAN FRANC, BENVENUTI, Clai (orange wines esp Sveti Jakov), CAP CATTUNAR, CORONICA, Cossetto (Malvazija Rustica, Mozaik), Degrassi (MUSC Terre Bianche), GERZINIČ, Kabola (esp Malvazija Amfora), KOZLOVIČ, MATOŠEV MENEGHETTI, Peršurič (Croatia's best sparkling wines, esp Misal Millenium Bru Pilato (Malvazija, PINOT BL), RADOVAN, Ritoša, ROXANICH, SAINTS HILLS, TRAPAN.

Vrhunsko vino: **premium-quality wine;** *Kvalitetno Vino:* **quality wine;** *Stolno Vir* **table wine.** *Suho:* **dry;** *Polsuho:* **semi-dry.**

Korta Katarina Dalm r w ★★★ 08 09 11 12 Modern interpretations of tradition styles from Korcula. Excellent POŠIP and PLAVAC MALI, esp Reuben's Res.

Kozlović Is & Kv w ★★→★★★ 09 11 12 13 *Benchmark Malvazija* in all its forms, e exciting, complex Santa Lucia 06 Akacia, sweet Sorbus 12. Also promisir Santa Lucia Crni.

Krauthaker, Vlado Sl & CD r w sw ★★★ 08 10 11 12 (13) Top producer from KUTJE esp CHARD Rosenberg, GRAŠEVINA Mitrovac, sweet Graševina Izborna Berba. PIN N Selekcija 11 shows promise.

Kutjevo Sl & CD Name shared by a town in SLAVONIJA and ★→★★ Kutjevo Cellars noted for gd GRAŠEVINA esp Turkovič 12.

Maraština Alias of the common MALVAZIJA of the coast; often fair refreshment.

Matošević Is & Kv r w ★★ 11 12 13 Benchmark MALVAZIJA, esp Alba Antiqua 09. Also v.gd Grimalda (r w).

Meneghetti Is & Kv r w ★★ 09 10 11 Sleek blends (r w), fine precise MALVAZIJA.

Miloš, Frano Dalm r sw ★★ 06 09 Built reputation with powerful Stagnum, but PLAVAC is more approachable.

Postup Dalm Famous v'yd designation nw of DINGAČ. Full-bodied rich red from PLAVAC MALI. Donja Banda, Miličič, Mrgudič Marija, Vinarija Dingač are noted.

Prošek Dalm Possible name confusion here: negotiations are under way with PROSECCO Consorzio in Italy to allow Croatia to continue to sell this historic sweet passito wine from DALM. Gd versions: TOMIČ Hectorovich using Bogdanuša, Maraština, Prč. Also Stina made with PLAVAC MALI and POŠIP.

Radovan Is & Kv r w ★★→★★★ 09 11 12 Impeccable whites; superb CAB SAUV, MERLOT.

Roxanich Is & Kv r w ★★→★★★ 07 08 Natural producer; powerful, intriguing amber wines (MALVAZIJA Antica, Ines U Bijelom) and impressive complex reds, esp TERAN Ré, Superistrian Cuvée, MERLOT.

Saints Hills Dalm, Is & Kv r w ★★→★★★ 08 09 10 11 Three v'yds plus two wineries; Michel Rolland consults. V.gd Nevina MALVAZIJA/CHARD from ISTRIA; richly fruity PLAVAC MALI St Roko, serious DINGAČ.

Slavonija Region in ne, famous for oak, and for whites, esp from GRAŠEVINA. Gd reds appearing now, esp PINOT N. Look for Adzič, Bartolovič, Belje, ENJINGI, GALIČ, KRAUTHAKER, KUTJEVO, Mihalj, Zdjelarevič.

Stina Dalm r w ★★ 10 11 12 13 From Brač island. Dramatic steep v'yds producing v.gd POŠIP, PLAVAC MALI, esp Majstor label. Gd Crljenak, Opol rosé and rare Vugava.

Suha Punta Dalm r w ★★→★★★ 09' (11) (12) Small exciting winery nr Primošten, co-owned by Professor Leo Gracin; country's *best Babič* from rocky, sea-facing v'yds.

Tomac Cro Up r w sp ★★ Estate nr Zagreb with 200-yr history, famous for sparkling and pioneering amphora wines.

Tomič Dalm r w ★★ 08 09 10 11 Outspoken personality on island of HVAR, with new organic PLAVAC MALI v'yd. Gd reds, esp PLAVAC Barrique, Hectorovich PROŠEK.

Trapan, Bruno Is & Kv r w ★★ 11 12 13 Try MALVAZIJA; aged Uroboros; DYA Ponento.

Zlatan Otok Dalm r w ★★→★★★ 09 10 Family winery from HVAR island with v'yds at Šibenik and Makarska too. Famous for huge reds, esp Zlatan PLAVAC Grand Cru. Also look for easier-drinking PLAVAC Šibenik, BABIČ and excellent POŠIP 12 13.

BOSNIA & HERZEGOVINA, MACEDONIA (FYROM), SERBIA, MONTENEGRO

A growing interest in quality wine means new wineries keep popping up, though it's not clear how many are financially viable. Some of the big guys are trying to move away from reliance on bulk exports and cheap mass-market wines.

Bosnia & Herzegovina now has 29 wineries on its new wine routes. The industry is mainly based on local grapes: white Žilavka and plummy red Blatina (Look for Hercegovina Produkt, Vilinka, Andrija, Crnjac & Zadro, Vukoje and Tvrdoš).

Macedonia (Republic of, or even Former Yugoslav Republic of Macedonia because of ongoing disagreements with Greece) is working hard to raise quality and get

---

Teran teacup storm

One for m'learned friends? TERAN is a PDO in Slovenia (for REFOŠK from Kras). Cross producers of Teran the grape in Croatian ISTRIA are refusing to relabel their wines.

away from reliance on cheap bulk exports. Unusually, it is the bigger wineries tha are leading the drive for quality. Giant Tikveš has a French-trained winemake and multiple academic research projects. Bela Voda and Barovo single-v'y wines impress (r 11 12, w 13'), gd Special Selection range (esp Vranec, GRENACH BLANC, Temjanika). Stobi sources only from its 600 ha of v'yds and impresse with Vranec Veritas, Žilavka, CHARD, refined PETIT VERDOT and fine SYRAH. Châtea Kamnik is the leading boutique winery, with gd CARMENÈRE, Syrah 10 barrels 10 1 Vranec Terroir (esp impressive 12), Temjanika Premium. Other wineries to loc for: Skovin (Markov Manastir Vranec, Temjanika), Ezimit (PLAVAC MALI, Vranec Popova Kula (Stanušina rosé), Popov (MALVASIA, PINOT GR, Cuvée).

Serbia has some wonderful terroir and v'yd sites, only recently showin their potential through the appearance of new quality-focused producer: Aleksandrovič impresses with Trijumf Gold and Triumf Barrique, PINOT N-base Trijumf Noir and Rodoslav. Radovanovič CAB Res is excellent, Ivanovič has take local Prokupac to a new level, while Budimir also uses Prokupac in blends to g effect in age-worthy Svb Rosa 07 and Triada. Also look for Aleksic, Janko, Ki Kovačevič, Matalj,Temet, Zvonko Bogdan.

Montenegro is now an EU candidate country. Its 4,500 ha of v'yds are divide between the coastal zone and Lake Skadar basin. 13 Jul Plantaže is th major producer with 2,310 ha in one of Europe's largest v'yds, but wines ar consistently gd (try Procorde Vranac, Vranac Barrique), also look out for seriou Vranac from the tiny Sjekloča winery.

Czech words
Jakostní víno = Quality wine; *Jakostní víno s přvlastkem* = Quality wine with attributes (equivalent to German QmP, *see* box, Germany p.163).
Pozdní sbě = late harvest.

CZECH REPUBLIC

The Czech Republic is divided into two wine regions, the tiny Bohemia (Boh) and 20-times-larger Moravia (Mor). Leading player on the market is the giant Bohemia Sekt Group: apart from the largest sparklin wine cellar near the beer capital of Pilsen (Boh) it also owns Víno Mikulo Habánské Sklepy, Château Bzenec and Pavlov winery (all in Moravia). It is followed by Vinselekt Michlovský, Znovín Znojmo, Vinné Sklepy Valtice (Valtice Wine Cellars) and Templářské Sklepy (Knights Templar), the only co-op in the country (all in Moravia).

Baloun, Radomil Mor One of first to go private in 1990. Now investing and stylish modernizing two dilapidated former wine co-ops with own (not EU) money.

Dobrá Vinice Mor Maverick inspired by Slovenia's Aleš Kristančič. Undoubtedly th best whites in the country.

Dufek, Josef Mor Award-winning, dynamic, modern family winery drawing o centuries-old tradition cultivating more than 30 organically grown grape varietie

Dva Duby Mor Dedicated terroirist, cultivating just 4 ha in Dolní Kounice Frankovka-land (BLAUFRÄNKISCH) according to Maria Thun's principles.

Lobkowicz, Bettina Boh Outstanding PINOT N and classic-method sparkling RIE Pinot N Blanc de Noirs, Cuvée CHARD/PINOT BL/PINOT GR.

Stapleton & Springer Mor Joint-venture between Jaroslav Springer and ex-U ambassador Craig Stapleton with brother Benjamin. Just four varieties, wit emphasis on PINOT N.

Tanzberg Mor Gd Pálava hills WELSCHRIESLING, PINOT N. Award-winning sparklers.

Valihrach, Josef Mor Three times winner of Winemaker of the Year title; specializes in wines for laying down.

Žernoseky Cellars Boh Best RIES, PINOT BL, MUSCAT from great Elbe River valley terroir.

SLOVAK REPUBLIC

Six wine regions: Malokarpatská (Small Carpathians), Juhoslovenská (Southern Slovakia), Nitrianska (Nitra), Stredoslovenská (Central Slovakia), Východoslovenská (Eastern Slovakia) and smallest, Tokajská (Tokaj), in the far east, adjacent to its more celebrated Hungarian namesake. They lie on the foothills of the Tatra Mountains and along the southern and eastern borders. Classic Central European varieties dominate, as well as international favourites. As in the Czech Republic, there are few signs of any crisis here, with big money continuing to flow into swanky new wineries such as Elesko (Modra, Small Carpathians), a huge facility unrivalled in Central Europe with restaurant, art gallery (Warhol originals) and money from abroad. Other notable producers are: Château Béla (Mužla, Southern Slovakia) for Riesling with Egon Müller zu Scharzhof involvement, Karpatská Perla (Šenkvice), Víno Matyšák (Pezinok), Víno Pavelka (Pezinok), Víno Rariga (Modra), Malík & Sons (Modra), Château Modra (all Small Carpathians), Juraj Zápražný (Veľký Krtíš, Central Slovakia) and JJ Ostrožovič (Veľká Tŕňa, Tokaj), while Vinárske závody Topoľčianky and JE Hubert are the largest wine and Sekt producers, respectively, in the country.

ROMANIA

Romania is still the 12th-biggest wine producer worldwide and number six in Europe, but in recent years a strong domestic market has limited exports. Lots of new vineyards planted with EU money (and several big foreign names) should boost quality, but in practice many have been planted without enough winery capacity, or any realistic way of marketing the production. Bankruptcies and consolidation look likely. A raft of small estates has appeared, which are giving the old guard a run for their money at home, and the best exporters are doing well with good-value, commercial wines: not just Pinot Noir and Pinot Grigio, but with local varieties like Fetească Neagră and Tămâioasă too.

Alira Estate Dob r ★★ 10 11 12 Premium estate owned by same team as Bulgaria's BESSA VALLEY. Now making impact with rich reds incl Alira Tribun blend, Alira and Grand Vin range.

Avincis Mun r w ★→★★ 11' 12 (13) Go-ahead revived family winery with bright young Alsace winemaker in DRĂGĂȘANI. Try Cuvee Andréi (r), MERLOT and PINOT GR/FETEASCĂ REGALĂ.

Banat Wine region in w. RECAȘ winery is major producer. Also Italian-owned PETRO VASELO estate.

Budureasca Mun r w ★→★★ 11 12 300 ha estate in DEALU MARE with UK winemaker. Consistent mid-level Budureasca (try SHIRAZ, FETEASCĂ NEAGRĂ) and top Origini label (try CAB SAUV).

Romania's three native Fetească vine varieties make up nearly 30 per cent of its *Vitis vinifera* plantings.

Cotnari DOC region in MOLD, noted for centuries for sweet wines. Now mostly medium to sweet GRASĂ, FETEASCĂ ALBĂ, TĂMÂIOASĂ and dry Frâncuşă. ★ Cotnari Winery (1,200 ha). Collection wines esp *sweet versions can be long-lived, impressive.*

Crama Girboiu Mold r w ★ Improving estate with 200 ha in Vrancea. DYA Livia whites and top Bacanta label.

Crama Oprisor Mun r w ★★→★★★ 11 12 13 V.gd producer in far sw, owned by German Reh-Kendermann. Exciting La Cetate range; also look for Caloian, Maiastru, Smerenie labels. Val Duna is commercial export label.

Crişana & Maramures Region to nw. Much-improved Wine Princess (esp 11 Stone Wine range), Nachbil based here.

Davino Winery Mun r w ★★★ 07 09' 10 11 12 13 Top producer with 68 ha in DEALU MARE. V.gd Dom Ceptura (r w), Purpura Valahica and Alba Valachia featuring local grapes. Gd new mid-range Iacob label. Flamboyant (r) 09 is superb, while Rezerva red 07 sets new quality standards for Romania.

Dealu Mare / Dealul Mare Means "The Big Hill". Historic quality zone and DOC on s-facing slopes in MUN. Location of promising new boutiques: LACERTA, Rotenberg (MERLOT, esp Menestrel, Notorius), Crama Basilescu (Merlot, FETEASCĂ NEAGRĂ).

Dobrogea Black Sea region. Incl DOC regions of MURFATLAR, Badabag and Sarica Niculitel. Historically famous for sweet, late-harvest CHARD and now also for full-bodied reds.

Domeniile Ostrov Dob r w ★ €20 million investment; 2,000 ha in DOB. Commercial DYA CAB SAUV, MUSCAT Ottonel.

Domeniile Sahateni Mun r w ★→★★ 09 11 12 13 70-ha estate in DEALU MARE. Try Artisan (r) and Artisan TĂMÂIOASĂ dry.

Domeniul Coroanei Segarcea Mun r w ★★ 11 12 13 Historic royal estate. Best for whites, incl FETEASCĂ ALBĂ, TĂMÂIOASĂ (also gd semi-sweet rosé). Decent CHARD, CAB SAUV (Minima Moralia range), PINOT N.

Around 6,000 brown bears live in Romania's Carpathian Mountains. Look ou behind you....

Drăgăşani Mun Dynamic region on river Olt. PRINCE ŞTIRBEY pioneered revival joined by AVINCIS, Isarescu, Negrini, Via Sandu and recently Bauer. Gd for aromatic crisp whites, esp local Crâmposie Selecţionată, TĂMÂIOASĂ, zesty SAUV BL. Distinctive local reds: Novac, Negru de Drăgăşani.

Halewood Romania Mun r p w ★★ 11 12 13 Impressive female winemaker has raised quality standards at this British-owned company. Best wines: Hyperion reds, Kronos PINOT N, Theia CHARD. Single-v'yd series also v.gd: La Catina Pino N, FETEASCĂ NEAGRĂ, Scurta VIOGNIER/TĂMÂIOASĂ. La Umbra is gd-value, consisten brand from DEALU MARE v'yds, Paris Street for wines from TRNSYL.

Jidvei Trnsyl w ★→★★ Romania's largest v'yd with 2,460 ha in Jidvei subregion in TRNSYL. New winery in 2014. Owner's Choice range by consultant Marc Dworkin is best (also Bulgaria's BESSA VALLEY), esp FETEASCĂ ALBĂ Maria, Mysterium TRAMINER/SAUV BL, CHARD Ana.

Lacerta Mun r w ★★ 10 11 12 13 Quality-focused estate in DEALU MARE, named afte local lizards. Try Cuvée IX red and Cuvée X white, MERLOT Rezerva.

Liliac Trnsyl w p ★★ 13' V.gd estate in TRNSYL, name means "bat". Graceful, fresh whites esp FETEASCĂ REGALĂ, FETEASCĂ ALBĂ, SAUV BL, delicious sweet Nectar Excellent PINOT N Rosé 13.

DOC

Denumire de Origine Controlată is the Romanian term for PDO. Sub-categories incl DOC-CMD for wines harvested at full maturity, DOC-CT for late-harvest and DOC-CIB for noble-harvest. *Vin cu indicatie geografică* is term for PGI.

oldova / **Moldavia** Largest wine region ne of Carpathians. Borders Republic of Moldova. DOC areas incl Bohotin, COTNARI, Huşi, Iaşi, Odobeşti, Coteşti, Nicoreşti.

untenia & Oltenia Hills Major wine region in s covering DOC areas of DEALU MARE, Dealurile Olteniei, DRĂGĂŞANI, Pietroasa, Sâmbureşti, Stefaneşti, Vanju Mare.

urfatlar Winery Dob r w ★→★★ Major domestic producer with 3,000 ha in Murfatlar region. Variable quality; best label is Trei Hectare. Also boutique winery MI Crama Atelier with Răzvan Macici (Nederburg, *see* South Africa), incl Arezan, Leat 6500 and Sable Noble ranges.

tro Vaselo Ban r w ★→★★ II I2 I3 Promising new Italian estate in BANAT. Decent Bendis sparkling, Rosu and Alb, Melgris FETEASCĂ NEAGRĂ.

ince Ştirbey Mun r p w ★★→★★★ II I2 I3 Pioneering estate in DRĂGĂŞANI. V.gd dry whites, esp local Crâmposie Selectionată, SAUV BL, FETEASCĂ REGALĂ, TĂMÂIOASĂ ROMÂNEASCĂ. Recommended local reds (Novac, Negru de Drăgăşani); gd bottle-fermented sparkling.

caş Winery Ban r w ★★→★★★ II I2 I3 Progressive British/Romanian estate in BANAT region. V.gd-value, bright varietal wines sold as Paparuda, I heart, Frunza, Castel Huniade, Terra Dacica. Excellent premium wines, esp Solo Quinta, Sole, Cuvée Uberland. Selene reds, esp FETEASCĂ NEAGRĂ, first made with Alesso Planeta (*see* Italy), are exciting.

nator Mold r w ★ Large producer with 850 ha across four regions. Monser range feaures Romanian varieties, Omnia is organic, Varius for international grapes.

ERVE Mun r w dr ★★→★★★ 09' IO II I2 I3 DEALU MARE winery founded by the late Count Guy de Poix of Corsica. Vinul Cavalerului whites and rosé gd, excellent Terra Romana range. *Cuvée Charlotte* is the benchmark for quality reds in Romania.

ansylvania Cool mtn plateau in centre of Romania. Mostly white wines with gd acidity from FETEASCĂ ALBĂ and REGALĂ, MUSCAT, TRAMINER, RIES ITALICO.

le Metamorfosis Mun r w ★★ 09 I2 I3 Antinori-owned estate in DEALU MARE with Italian winemaker. Top: Cantvs Primvs CAB SAUV 09 and new FETEASCĂ NEAGRĂ I2. V.gd Viile Metamorfosis DYA white blend, rosé and MERLOT.

la Vinea Trnsyl r w ★★ Young Italian-owned estate in TRNSYL. Gd whites, esp GEWURZ, SAUV BL, FETEASCĂ REGALĂ. Promising FETEASCĂ NEAGRĂ.

narte Winery Mun r w ★★ 09 IO II I2 I3 V.gd Italian-led investment with three estates: Villa Zorilor in DEALU MARE, Castel Bolovanu in DRĂGĂŞANI, Terase Danubiane in Vanju Mare. Best: Soare CAB SAUV, Prince Matei MERLOT. Castel Starmina is gd value, esp DYA whites and Negru de Drăgăşani.

ncon Winery Mold r w dr sw ★ Major domestic-focused producer with 1,500 ha in Vrancea.

MALTA

he whole of Malta and Gozo can only muster about I5 wineries, and a lot of growers are part time. Viticulture is not particularly g business here. Much of the everyday stuff is made on the island om imported Italian grapes. If you want something grown on Malta ok for the local grapes Gellewza and Girgentina, red and white spectively, and newly fashionable. Both are quite light: Gellewza d is more like rosé, and makes some pretty pink fizz. Both are often ended, Gellewza perhaps with Syrah, Girgentina with Chardonnay. arsovin is experimenting with Amarone-style Gellewza. Other big oducers include Delicata and Meridiana.

Greece

The economic crisis and the prolonged recession in Greece has initiated a major reshuffling of values for Greeks, especially the young. The younger generation is now less keen on rushing off to Athens or Thessaloniki, as was the case even ten years ago. Connecting with the land and continuing a family business in a remote part of Greece seems more intriguing than renting a tiny apartment in Athens and working for a multinational. This is bringing new blood into the wine industry all over the country, and it will make Greek wines even more exciting in ten years time. Abbreviations: Aegean Islands (Aeg), Central Greece (C Gr), Ionian Islands (Ion), Macedonia (Mac), Peloponnese (Pelop), Thessaloniki (Thess

Alpha Estate Mac ★★★ Impressive, highly acclaimed estate in cool-clima Amindeo. Excellent MERLOT/SYRAH/XINOMAVRO blend, pungent SAUV BL, exo MALAGOUSIA, unfiltered New-World-style Xinomavro from old, ungrafted vines one of finest expressions of the grape.

Amyntaion Mac (POP) The coolest appellation of Greece, XINOMAVRO-dominate Fresh but dense reds, excellent rosés, both still and sparkling. White sparkli not incl in POP, but can be magnificent.

Antonopoulos Pelop ★★★ Patras-based winery, with top-class MANTINIA, crisp Ad Ghis (w), burgundian Anax CHARD and CAB-based Nea Dris (stunning 04 06).

Argyros Aeg ★★★ Top SANTORINI producer; exemplary VINSANTO aged 20 yrs in ca (★★★★). Exciting KTIMA (w) that ages for a decade. Vareli (w) more elegan oaked nowadays. Try ageing rare MAVROTRAGANO (r) for 15 yrs+.

Xinomavros from the 60s are still alive and kicking. Start stocking the 2012s now

Avantis C Gr ★★★ Boutique winery in Evia with v'yds in Boetia as well. Dense SYRA Aghios Chronos Syrah/VIOGNIER, pungent SAUV BL and rich MALAGOUSIA. Top wir Rhône-like single-v'yd Collection Syrah 03 04 05 06 07 08 09.

Biblia Chora Mac ★★★ Both top quality and huge commercial success. Punge SAUV BL/ASSYRTIKO. Ovilos CAB s, Areti AGHIORGHITIKO are stunning. Ovilos (v Assyrtiko/ sÉm, could rival top white Bx at triple the price.

Boutari, J & Son ★→★★★ Historic producer with several wineries. Excellent value, e *Grande Res Naoussa* to age for decades. V. popular MOSCHOFILERO. Top SANTOR Kalisti Res (oaked), herbal Flliria (r) from GOUMENISSA.

Carras, Domaine Mac ★→★★ Pioneer estate at Sithonia, Halkidiki, with own PC (Côtes de Meliton). Chateau Carras 01 03 04 05 06 07 08, ambitious SYRAH a floral MALAGOUSIA, but LIMNIO (r) might be *best value* of all.

Cephalonia Ion Important island with three appellations: mineral ROBOLA (w), ra MUSCAT (w sw) and excellent MAVRODAPHNE (r sw). A must-visit.

Driopi Pelop ★★★ 06 07 08 09 10 11 Venture of TSELEPOS in NEMEA. Serious (e single-v'yd Res), high-octane style. Tavel-like Driopi rosé.

Economou Crete ★★★ One of the great artisans of Greece, with brilliant, esote Sitia (r). burgundian in style but Greek in essence.

Gaia Aeg, Pelop ★★★ Top-quality NEMEA- and SANTORINI-based producer. Fun Noti range. New-World-like AGHIORGHITIKO. Thought-provoking, top-class, dry wh Thalassitis Santorini and revolutionary *wild-ferment Assyrtiko*. Top wine: *Ga Estate* 99 00 01 03 04 05 06 07 08 09 10, dazzling "S" red (Aghiorghitiko wi a touch of SYRAH).

Gentilini Ion ★★→★★★ Exciting Cephalonia whites, incl *steely Robola*. V.gd d MAVRODAPHNE (r), serious SYRAH. Selection ROBOLA called Rhombus redefines t variety but not allowed an appellation, since law forbids screwcap. Eclipse (r) is rare, but worth the hunt.

erovassiliou Mac ★★★ Perfectionist miniature estate nr Salonika. Benchmark ASSYRTIKO/MALAGOUSIA, top Malagousia. Complex Avaton (r) 03 04 05 06 07 08 09 10 from rare indigenous varieties and SYRAH 01 02 03 04 05 06 07 08 09. For many, the quality leader.

oumenissa Mac (POP) ★→★★★ Oaked XINOMAVRO/Negoska (r), lighter than NAOUSSA. Esp Chatzyvaritis (silky ★★★), Aidarinis (single v'yd ★★★), BOUTARI (esp Filiria).

atzidakis Aeg ★★★ Low-tech, top-class producer redefining SANTORINI appellation. Stunning range, bordering on the experimental. Nihteri, Mylos and Louros ASSYRTIKO bottlings could age for decades. Not your average dry whites.

elios Pelop New umbrella name for Semeli, Nassiakos and Orinos Helios wines. Top Nassiakos MANTINIA, complex NEMEA Grande Res.

arydas Mac ★★★ Small family estate; amazing v'yd in NAOUSSA crafting classic, compact always refined XINOMAVRO of great breed. Age for a decade if you can.

atogi-Strofilia ★★→★★★ V'yds and wineries in Attica, Pelop and Epirus. Katogi: original cult Greek wine. Top: KTIMA Averoff (from original Katogi CAB SAUV v'yd) and Rossiu di Munte range from altitudes of 1,000m+. Charming Strofilia (w).

atsaros Thess ★★★ 03 04 05 06 07 08 Small winery on Mt Olympus. KTIMA (CAB SAUV/MERLOT), has staying power. Esoteric CHARD and broad-shouldered Merlot.

ir-Yanni Mac ★★→★★★ V'yds in NAOUSSA and Amindeo. Vibrant whites Samaropetra and Tesseris Limnes are charmers; Akakis sp a joy. Reds Ramnista, Diaporos and Blue Fox (★★★★) are trendsetting and age-worthy.

ima Estate, domaine.

azaridi, Nico Mac ★→★★★ Wineries in Drama and Kavala. Gd Château Nico Lazaridi (r w). Top wine: Magiko Vouno (CAB SAUV) enjoys cult status in Greece.

azaridis, Kostas Attica, Mac ★★★ V'yds and wineries in Drama and Attika (sold under Oenotria Land label). Popular Amethystos label. Top wine: amazing Cava Amethystos CAB SAUV 97 98 99 00 01 02 03 04 06, followed closely by Oenotria Land Cab Sauv/AGIORGITIKO. Michel Rolland consults.

raraliis Crete ★★→★★★ Producer from Heraklio with delicious range. Whites from the rare Plyto and Dafni practically saved these varieties from extinction (single-v'yd versions are extraordinary; more rare grapes to follow). Deep, complex SYRAH/Kotsifali.

anoussakis Crete ★★★ Impressive estate with Rhône-inspired blends. Delectable range under Nostos brand, led by age-worthy ROUSSANNE and SYRAH.

antinia Pelop (POP) w High altitude, cool region. Fresh, crisp, utterly charming, sometimes sparkling *Moschofilero*. Low in alcohol and high in acid and intensity – more German than Greek in style.

ercouri Pelop ★★★ One of the most beautiful family estates in Europe. V.gd KTIMA (r), delicious RODITIS, age-worthy Cava (r), classy REFOSCO (r), stunning sweet Belvedere MALVASIA and excellent sweet Hortais MAVRODAPHNE.

onemvassia-Malvasia Latest POP, allowed from 2010 on, with Monemvassia, ASSYRTIKO and Kydonitsa grapes used to re-create legendary sun-dried, sweet white wines of Middle Ages – the original Malmsey. Exciting first vintage from Tsimpidis (Monemvassia Winery).

aoussa Mac (PDO) Top-quality region for sophisticated, excellent XINOMAVRO. Best on a par (in quality, style) with Italy's Barolo, Barbaresco, can last even longer.

emea Pelop (POP) Source of top AGHIORGHITIKO wines. Huge potential for quality; styles from fresh to classic to exotic. (*see* GAIA, SKOURAS, NEMEION, PAPAÏOANNOU, HELIOS, DRIOPI, Mitravelas).

emeion Pelop ★★★ A KTIMA in NEMEA, high prices (esp Igemon red), with wines to match. Owned by Vassiliou (Attica).

> **Greek appellations**
> Terms are changing in line with other EU countries. The quality
> appellations of OPAP and OPE are now fused together into the POP (or
> PDO) category. Regional wines, known as TO, will now be PGE (or PGI).

Palyvos Pelop ★★→★★★ Excellent producer in NEMEA; modern, big-framed reds. Mul
vintage Noima (r) is one of country's most expensive, but gorgeous nevertheles

Papaïoannou Pelop ★★★ If NEMEA were Burgundy, Papaioannou would be Jaye
Classy reds; flavourful whites. A benchmark range of Nemeas: excellent val
KTIMA, Palea Klimata (old vines), Microklima (micro-single-v'yd) and top-er
Terroir (super-strict, 200%-new-oaked selection).

Pavlidis Mac ★★★ Ambitious estate at Drama. Acclaimed ASSYRTIKO/SAUV
Emphasis: varietals incl classy Assyrtiko, SYRAH and TEMPRANILLO. KTIMA (r) fro
AGHIORGHITIKO/Syrah is dazzling. Top-ranking stuff.

Peza Crete POP nr Heraklio. Vilana (w) and Mandilaria/Kotsifali (r). Unde
performing since many producers prefer alternative varieties like Vidiano.

Rapsani Thess ★★★ Historic POP from Mt Olympus. Made famous in the 199
by TSANTALIS, but new producers, such as Dougos, have different interpretation
XINOMAVRO, Stavroto and Krasato grapes.

Retsina Usually considered the nail in the coffin of Greek wine, but new Retsin
(eg. GAIA or Kechris) show that this white with added Aleppo pine resin could
a good alternative to Fino Sherry.

Samos Aeg (POP) Island famed for sweet golden MUSCAT. Esp (fortified) Anthem
and (sun-dried) Nectar. Rare old bottlings are ★★★★ in all but the price, such
the hard-to-find Nectar 75 or 80.

Santo Aeg ★★→★★★ Successful SANTORINI co-op. Vibrant portfolio; dazzling Gran
Res and rich yet crisp VINSANTOS. Standard ASSYRTIKO and Nyhteri are great valu

Santorini Aeg ★★★ Dramatic volcanic island n of CRETE and POP for white (dr sv
Luscious VINSANTO, mineral, ***bone-dry Assyrtiko***. Top producers: ARGYROS, GA
HATZIDAKIS, SIGALAS, Santo. Possibly the cheapest ★★★★ dry whites around, able
age for 20 yrs, huge export success. Reds from MAVROTRAGANO grape (not incl
POP) can be sublime as well.

Retsina: possibly perfect wine to accompany sea urchins – if you like sea urchins

Sigalas Aeg ★★★ Top SANTORINI estate. Stylish VINSANTO and excellent MOURVÈDRE-lil
MAVROTRAGANO (try 08 09 10). Nyhteri, Cavalieros dry whites out of this world.

Skouras Pelop ★★★ Innovative, incredibly consistent estate. Mineral, wild-yea
Salto MOSCHOFILERO is a game changer for variety. Top reds: high-altitude Gran
Cuvée NEMEA, Megas Oenos and solera-aged Labyrinth. V. stylish Fleva SYRAH ar
Condrieu look-alike VIOGNIER Eclectique.

Thimiopoulos Mac ★★★★ New age NAOUSSA with spectacular export success, sold
Ghi kai Ouranos, or Earth and Sky.

Tsantalis Mac ★→★★★ Long-est producer in Mac, Thrace and other areas. C
Metoxi (r), RAPSANI Res and Grande Res, gd-value organic CAB SAUV. Top of ran
monastery wines from Mount Athos, eg. excellent Avaton, cult Kormilitsa Go

Tselepos Pelop ★★★ Top-quality MANTINIA producer. Greece's best GEWURZ ar
best MERLOT (★★★★ Kokkinomylos). Others: oaky CHARD, v.gd spark Amal
astounding single-v'yd Avlotopi CAB SAUV. *See also* DRIOPI.

Vinsanto Aeg Sun-dried sweet ASSYRTIKO and Aidani from SANTORINI. Madeira-mee
Recioto in style. Deserves long ageing, in oak and bottle. Best are ★★★★ ar
practically indestructible.

Zitsa Mountainous Epirus POP. Delicate Debina (w sp) Best: Glinavos, Zoinos.

Eastern Mediterranean & North Africa

EASTERN MEDITERRANEAN

This is a very dynamic wine region: it gave the world wine culture, and is now coming back to life after 2,000 years of stagnation. The tragedy is that politics, strife and religious intolerance are holding back appreciation of the dramatic strides in quality. However, they can't take away from the fact that Israel, Lebanon and Turkey are making some pretty good wines today and Cyprus is also playing catch-up.

Cyprus

The outlook for the wine industry on Cyprus is surprisingly positive, but the economy is still struggling to recover from the banking crash. It seems this crisis has encouraged consumers to drink local to support their own producers. This is undoubtedly helped by quality being better than ever, though cheap imports and demand for ever-lower prices from all-inclusive hotels remain a challenge.

Aes Ambelis w r br ★→★★ 13 (14) Consistent, appealing XYNISTERI-based whites and rosé. V.gd modern version of COMMANDARIA.

Argyrides Estate (Vasa) r w ★★ 09 10 11 12 13 (14) Immaculate pioneering winery. Top MARATHEFTIKO, MOURVÈDRE. V.gd VIOGNIER, Agyrides blend (r). VLASSIDES consults.

Ezousa Mavri w sw ★→★★ 10 12 13 Sweet wines from late-harvest and semi-dried MUSCAT are best; dry wines lag behind.

Constantinou r w ★→★★ Self-taught winemaker in Lemesos region impressing with Ayioklima XYNISTERI DYA and SHIRAZ.

Cyprus, one of only three countries in world never affected by vine pest phylloxera.

ETKO r w br ★→★★ Former big producer, now focusing on higher quality at Olympus winery. New winemaker making positive changes from 2013 esp Lefkada (r). Noted for St Nicholas COMMANDARIA and superior Centurion 1991.

Hadjiantonas r w ★→★★ 11 12 Family winery owned by a pilot, making decent CHARD, XYNISTERI, rosé, SHIRAZ.

KEO ★ Second biggest producer, now making wine only at Mallia winery in hills. Ktima Keo range is best. Rediscovered Yiannoudi shows promise. Classic St John ★★ COMMANDARIA.

Kyperounda r w ★★→★★★ 11' 12 13 (14) Some of Europe's highest v'yds at 1,450m. Petritis is standard-setting XYNISTERI. Excellent CHARD esp new own-v'yd Epos. Reds also v.gd: SHIRAZ, Andessitis, top red Epos 09. COMMANDARIA 05 worth trying.

Vlakkas r w ★→★★ 11 12 13 Garage winery in Pafos region owned by former economist. Gd MARATHEFTIKO, SHIRAZ and tasty entry-level red and white blends.

SODAP r w p ★→★★ 12 13 (14) Largest producer, grower-owned co-op with state-

> #### Commandaria
> Possibly the most ancient wine still in production, documented as far back as 800BC. Rich, dark, sweet, and made from sun-dried XYNISTERI and MAVRO, grown in the PDO region covering 14 villages in the Troodos mtns. Traditional examples: St Barnabas (SODAP), St John (KEO), Centurion (ETKO). Modern versions now appearing esp Anama project, AES AMBELIS, KYPEROUNDA, TSIAKKAS.

> **Cyprus regions**
> Lemesos, Paphos, Larnaca, Lefkosia have regional wine status (PGI).
> PDOs cover Commandaria, Laona-Akamas, Pitsilia, Vouni-Panayias/
> Ambelitis, wine villages of Lemesos, but only two per cent of Cyprus
> wine is produced as PDO.

of-art winery in Pafos hills. DYA whites and lively rosé gd value and appetizir
Look for Kamanterena, Island Vines and Stroumbeli brands.

Tsiakkas r w p br ★★ 13 14 Banker turned winemaker. Expressive fresh whites, e
SAUV BL, XYNISTERI and vivid rosé from high-altitude vines. Also red Vamvaka
(aka MARATHEFTIKO), new modern COMMANDARIA.

Vasilikon Winery w r ★★ Family winery owned by three brothers. Gd DYA XYNISTE
and decent reds: Ayios Onoufrios 12, Methy 11.

Yiannoudi: rediscovered red vine. Found in v'yd of man named Yiannis (little Joh

Vlassides r w ★★→★★★ 11 12' 13' (14) UC Davis-trained Vlassides makes some
the island's best wines. Benchmark SHIRAZ, v.gd Lefkos white (XYNISTERI/SAUV B
CAB SAUV and excellent long-ageing Private Collection red 09.

Vouni Panayia w r p ★→★★★ 13 (14) Pioneer. Try Promara, Spourtiko, Yiannoudi.

Zambartas r p w ★★→★★★ 11' 12 13' (14) Top family winery making inten
CAB FR/LEFKADA rosé, v.gd SHIRAZ/Lefkada red, excellent MARATHEFTIKO, zes
XYNISTERI. Promising trials with local Yiannoudi.

Israel

Israeli wines have always been pretty New World in style. Lately there have been
moves to a more Old World approach. Southern-Rhône-type blends and Med
varieties are becoming more popular, and there is a big improvement in fresh
whites. Of course many, but not all, Israeli wines are kosher, which have a captive
market worldwide. Abbreviations: Galilee (Gal), Golan (Gol), Judean Hills (Jud),
Negev (Neg), Samson (Sam), Shomron (Shom); Upper Galilee (Up Gal).

Abaya Gal r Tiny terroiriste. Moon-A a compôte of flavours.

Adir Up Gal r ★★ Big, rich, well-made reds, incl peppery SHIRAZ.

Amphorae Gal r w ★→★★ Beautiful winery. New prestige Velours.

Barkan-Segal Gal, Sam r w ★→★★ Owned by Israel's largest brewery. Barkan ar
Segal are marketed separately. Israel's largest exporter. Gd Segal Argaman.

Bar Maor Shom r ★★ Wild, untamed reds. Red Moon bright, fruity, intriguing.

Binyamina Gal, Sam r w ★→★★ New, young team. Delicious sweet GEWURZ.

Bravdo Sam r w ★→★★ Big CHARD, spicy SHIRAZ and gd CAB FR-based blend Coupag

Carmel Up Gal, Shom r w sp ★★→★★★ Israel's historic winery founded by a (Lafit
Rothschild. Elegant Bordeaux style Limited Edition 05 07' 08' 09 10. Awar
winning Kayoumi v'yd SHIRAZ. Complex Mediterranean-style blend.

Château Golan Gol r (w) ★★→★★★ Geshem (r w) v.gd Mediterranean blends.

Clos de Gat Jud r w ★★★★ Classy estate exuding quality, style and individualit
Powerful Sycra SYRAH 04 06 07' 09, rare MERLOT and buttery CHARD are super
Spicy Harel Syrah and fresh entry-level Chanson (w) gd value.

Large Bronze Age wine cellar found at Tel Kabri, Galilee, 3,000 years+ old.

Cremisan Jud r w V.gd Palestinian wine: indigenous varieties, Hamdani Jandali.

Dalton Up Gal r w ★★ Pure, minerally single-v'yd SÉM. Flagship is rich Matatia.

Domaine du Castel Jud r w ★★★ Family estate in Jerusalem mtns. Set the standard
in Israel for style and quality. Characterful, supple Grand Vin 06' 07 08' 09' 1
11. Second label, Petit Castel, great value. C is CHARD. V.gd rosé.

Flam Jud, Gal r (w) ★★★→★★★★ Founded by brothers, 2nd generation winemakers. Superb, elegant Noble 08' 09 10', a Bordeaux blend. Earthy SYRAH/CAB. Classico provides excellent value. Fresh, fragrant white, rosé.

Galilee Quality region in n, esp higher-altitude Upper Galilee.

Galil Mtn Up Gal r w ★→★★ Fresh VIOGNIER best. Owned by YARDEN.

Golan Heights High-altitude plateau, with volcanic tuff and basalt soil.

Judean Hills Quality region rising towards the Jerusalem Mts.

Kosher For those observing Jewish Dietary Laws. Designation irrelevant to quality. Wines can be v.gd.

Lewinsohn Gal r w ★★★ Quality *garagiste* in a garage. Exquisite, lean CHARD. Red a chewy Mediterranean blend of SYRAH, CARIGNAN and PETITE SIRAH.

Margalit Gal, Shom r ★★★ Israel's first cult wine. Best is Bordeaux blend Enigma 08' 09 10' 11, with gd ageing potential. Father and son-owned.

Negev Desert region in s of country.

Pelter Gol r w (sp) ★★ Fresh whites with gd acidity. New KOSHER label Matar.

Recanati Gal r w ★★→★★★ Award-winning Special Res 07 08' 09' 11; complex CARIGNAN, chewy PETITE SIRAH, ripe and spicy Marselan. V.gd prestige white and entry level Yasmin.

Samson Central region incl the Judean plain and foothills, se of Tel Aviv.

Sea Horse Jud r (w) ★★ Artistic approach. James a fine old-vine CHENIN BL.

Shomron Region with v'yds mainly around Mt Carmel and Zichron Ya'acov.

Shvo Up Gal r w ★★→★★★ Non-interventionist grower-winemaker. Super-rustic Mediterranean red, characterful rosé and minerally CHENIN BL.

Sphera Jud w ★★→★★★ Only white wines. Complex White Signature (CHARD/SÊM/RIES), expressive First Page (PINOT GR/Ries/Sém), crystal-clear SAUV BL.

Tabor Gal r w sp ★★ V.gd whites: Adama SAUV BL, ROUSSANNE, entry-level Har CHARD. Gd-value MERLOT and Sufa blend.

Teperberg Jud, Sam r w sp ★→★★ Largest family winery in Israel. CAB FR, gd typicity.

Tishbi Jud, Shom r w sp Veteran grape-growing family.

Tulip Gal r (w) ★→★★ Opulent Black Tulip. Mala – exciting new project.

Tzora Jud r w ★★★ Terroir-led, talented winemaker. Shoresh minerally SAUV BL. Prestige Misty Hills 07 09 10' 11 CAB SAUV/SYRAH blend. Value Judean Hills red.

Vitkin Jud r w ★★★ Small winery specializing in rarer varieties. V.gd CARIGNAN.

Yarden Gol r w sp ★★★ Pioneering winery that brought New World technology to Israel. Wines range from rare, prestige Katzrin 03 04' 07 08' to big-selling brand Hermon Red. Superb vintage Blanc de Blancs and Brut Rosé. Luscious HeightsWine dessert.

Yatir Jud, Neg r (w) ★★★→★★★★ Desert winery with forest v'yds up to 900m elevation. Velvety, concentrated Yatir Forest 05' 06 07 08' 09 10 11. Edgy SYRAH, powerful PETIT VERDOT. Owned by CARMEL.

Lebanon

The Bekaa Valley was always the hub of vineyard activity, but enterprising new wineries are planting elsewhere, at Batroun (north), Mt Lebanon (west) and Jezzine (south). Wines are underrated. There is a lot more to Lebanon than just the iconic Musar.

Château Belle-Vue r (w) ★★★ Le Château a plush blend of Bordeaux grapes, SYRAH.

Château Ka r w ★→★★ Great-value, cherry-berry Cadet de Ka.

Château Kefraya r w ★★→★★★ Superb, ripe, concentrated, spicy *Comte de M* 07 08 09'. Light, easy-drinking Les Bretèches. Delicious Nectar fortified dessert wine.

Château Ksara r w ★★ Founded 1857. Best value is mouthfilling, fruity Res du Couvent. Le Souverain of interest (CAB SAUV and Arinarnoa). Well-balanced CHARD.

Château Marsyas r (w) ★★ Crisp CHARD, SAUV BL; deep, powerful red. Owners of complex, minerally Dom Bargylus ★★★ (Syria). Stephane Derenoncourt consults.

Chateau Musar r w ★★★→★★★★ Icon wine of the e Med; the legendary Serge Hochar died at end of 2014. CAB SAUV/CINSAULT/CARIGNAN 96 97 99 00' 01' 02 03 04 05' 06 07. *Unique recognizable style.* Best after 15–20 yrs in bottle. Indigenous Obaideh and Merwah white ages indefinitely; totally original. Though style is criticized by the conventional, it is a blessing in the globalized world of sameness. Underrated Hochar red is more modern and fruit-forward.

Clos St-Thomas r w ★★ Well-balanced ripe, plummy red wines with soft tannins.

Domaine de Baal r (w) ★★ Smoky red and floral white from organic v'yd.

Domaine des Tourelles r w ★★→★★★ Blockbuster SYRAH. Oustanding Marquis des Beys. Fragrant white. Maybe Lebanon's fastest improving winery.

Domaine Wardy r w ★→★★ Deep, rich, oaky Private Selection red blend.

IXSIR r w ★★ Beautiful winery. Modern, New World-style wines under labels Atitudes, Grand Res and prestige El.

Karam r w ★→★★ Pilot makes bright, fruity wines in Jezzine. Fragrant Cloud Nine.

Massaya r w ★★→★★★ Entry-level Classic wines v.gd value. Silver Selection (r) is complex, Rhône-style blend showing sun and spice. Prestige Gold Res is full of fruit, herbs, spice from CAB SAUV, MOURVÈDRE, SYRAH.

Turkey

Winery owners in Turkey need to be saints. It is virtually forbidden to market wines there. However, they have wines of real interest, including indigenous varieties grown in one of the birthplaces of the vine. Look for Boğazkere, Oküzgözü and Narince. Wineries investing in quality deserve support.

Büyülübag r (w) ★★ One of the new small, quality wineries. Gd CAB SAUV.

Corvus r w ★★→★★★ Boutique winery on Bozcaada island. Corpus is powerful.

Doluca r w ★→★★ Karma label blends local and classic varieties. Gd CAB SAUV/ OKÜZGÖZÜ and NARINCE/CHARD.

Kavaklidere r w sp ★→★★★ Specialist in local varieties. Best is OKÜZGÖZÜ from the Pendore estate. Gd-value entry-level Yakut. Stephane Derenoncourt consults.

Kayra r w ★→★★ Gd Imperial CAB SAUV, SHIRAZ. Rustic Buzbag from OKÜZGÖZÜ and BOĞAZKERE grapes. Californian winemaker.

Pamukkale r w ★→★★ Anfora MERLOT is smooth, full-flavoured.

Sarafin r w ★→★★ Pioneer of classic varieties in Turkey. Owned by DOLUCA.

Sevilen r w ★→★★ International variety specialist. Deep SYRAH. Aromatic SAUV BL.

Vinkara r w ★ Charming NARINCE and cherry-berry Kalecik Karasi.

NORTH AFRICA

Castel Frères Mor r p ★ Gd-value brands like Bonassia, Sahari, Halana, Larroque.

Celliers de Meknès, Les r p w ★→★★ Virtual monopoly in Morocco; Château Roslane.

Domaine Neferis Tun r p w ★→★★ Calastrasi joint venture. Selian CARIGNAN best.

Kahina Mor ★★ Occasional GRENACHE/SYRAH blend by Bernard Magrez (Bordeaux).

Lumière Mor ★★ Actor Gérard Depardieu and Bernard Magrez joint venture.

Thalvin Mor r p w ★★ Fresh whites. Raisiny Tandem SYRAH (Syrocco in the USA) ★★★ made with Alain Graillot (Rhône).

Val d'Argan Mor r p w ★→★★ At Essaouira. Gd value: Mogador. Best: Orients.

Vignerons de Carthage Mor r p w ★ Best from UCCV co-op: Magon Magnus (r).

Vin Gris ★ Pale-pink resort of the thirsty. Castel Boulaouane brand is best-known.

Volubilia r p w ★→★★ Best delicate pink *vin gris* in Morocco.

Asia & Old Russian Empire

ASIA

China's Grape Leap Forward means that it now has the 4th-largest v'yd in the world, and is the 5th-largest producer. A lot of the grapes are destined for eating, however. Most of China's c.680,000 ha are n of the Yangtze River, from the extreme nw Xinjiang province (c.22 per cent of plantings) to n-central Ningxia and Shanxi, and the e coastal provinces of Liaoning and Hebei. Annual production is around 13.2 million hl. With around 60 per cent of the total v'yd, CAB SAUV is the most widely planted, followed by MERLOT, CHARD, Cabernet Gernischt (CARMENÈRE) and SYRAH. There's some RIES, WELSCHRIESLING, UGNI BLANC, SEMILLON, PINOT N, PETIT VERDOT, GAMAY and, more recently, Marselan, PETIT MANSENG and VIDAL. One of the biggest challenges is harsh winters, when temperatures can reach -20°C/-4°F. Vines have to be buried to ensure survival. In coastal Shandong, where Château Lafite has a joint venture, wet weather and typhoons in summer are not conducive to ripening. Newer high-altitude (between 2,200 and 2,700m) v'yds in s Yunnan province (bordering Vietnam, Laos and Burma) seem more propitious for Moët-Hennessy's joint venture with Shangri-la Winery's yet-unreleased wine. Gd wines are made by Jia Bei Lan, Silver Heights, Domaine Helan Mtn (owned by Pernod Ricard) and Moët-Hennessy's Domaine Chandon. Sha Po Tou, at the foot of the Xiangshan Mtn in Ningxia, distinguishes with a 100% Cabernet Gernischt from 19-yr-old vines. Do the Chinese drink all this wine? Currently China's 1.3 billion population consumes slightly more than a litre per head annually. That figure, though, is only for wine that has paid domestic duty and does not take into account what is smuggled into the country.

In 2016, China is expected to become become world's biggest consumer of wine.

India's 114,400 ha of vines are mainly table grapes; wine v'yds total c.1,850 ha, mostly SAUV BL, CHENIN BL and VIOGNIER for white, and SHIRAZ, CAB SAUV, MERLOT and GRENACHE for red. There is some CHARD and a little TEMPRANILLO, ZIN and SANGIOVESE. The v'yds are mainly in the states of Maharashtra (capital: Mumbai), Karnataka (capital: Bangalore) and Andhra Pradesh (capital: Hyderabad). Sauv Bl remains the country's most consistently impressive wine with Sula and Grover (particularly Zampa Art Collection) delivering the best. SYRAH or Shiraz has gd, but not yet fully realized, potential while Moët-Hennessy's Domaine Chandon delivers white and rosé bubbles.

Japan Although grapes are grown from as far n as the island of Hokkaido to the isle of Kyushu in the s, Yamanashi Prefecture on Honshu is the heart of Japanese wine-growing: about 40 per cent of Japan's estimated 19,000 ha of plantings are here. It was in Yamanashi that Japan tried making its first wine back in the mid-1870s. The most planted are the hybrid MUSCAT Bailey, for light red and Koshu, the indigenous, tingling, high-acid white. Most small to mid-sized wineries produce both wine and table grapes. Large corporations dominate, however, and they also happen to be the country's largest brewers: Sapporo, Kirin and Suntory. Perhaps the biggest challenge facing the Land of the Rising Sun is that the sun doesn't hang around long enough. Instead, typhoon season runs from May to October, peaking between July and September, months so critical for grape ripening. Because of the climate, three-quarters of wines bottled here rely to some extent on imported bulk wine and concentrate. The most ambitious producers are smaller family-owned companies using 100 per cent homegrown grapes. Top producers incl Grace Wine, Aruga Branca and Lumière.

OLD RUSSIAN EMPIRE

Political instability makes the future of winemaking in the Crimea – which includes some prime vineyards known from the times of the Russian Empire – uncertain. In addition to the Crimea, other suitable areas for grape-growing are located around the Black Sea or in the valleys of the Caucasus. The continental climate makes it hard for vines, some of which have to be covered for winter. Large companies dominate, but a new wave of small local producers is on the rise. Russia, Ukraine and Moldova give priority to international grapes, while Georgia and Armenia stick to their quirky and occasionally great indigenous varieties.

Armenia vies with Georgia as a birthplace of winemaking (the most ancient winery dates back 6,100 yrs) and as a source of authentic wines. There are up to 50 indigenous varieties: red Areni can be potentially great. International consultants Michel Rolland (Tierras de Armenia), Alberto Antonini (Zorah Karasi), Emilio del Medico (ArmAs) and Paul Hobbs are already involved.

Georgian producers total around 70, but wine is made by almost every family, putting 48,000 ha of v'yds to gd use. A unique viticultural heritage spanning more than 7,000 yrs encompasses grapes, production techniques and wine styles. There are around 500 indigenous grape varieties, but red SAPERAVI (anything from easy and semi-sweet to robust and tannic) and white RKATSITELI (lively, refreshing) cover most of the v'yds. Traditional *kvevris* (amphorae), now with UNESCO World Heritage status, are a symbol of Georgian winemaking and a preferred instrument for new experiments. Most wines, though, including vast quantities of drinkable fizz, are made with modern equipment. Leading large and small producers incl GWS, Tbilvino, Badagoni, Marani (TWC), Kindzmarauli Marani, Ch Mukhrani, Pheasant's Tears, Schuchmann.

Try *kvevri* wines with a modern twist from Tbilvino, Marani (TWC), Khareba.

Moldova Fine wine was made under the Tsars; in the USSR every 2nd bottle had Moldovan origin. Now producers seek to export to Europe and the USA. There are four geographic areas. European grapes are historically grown alongside local Rara Neagră, Plavai, Galbenă, Djiharda, Bătuta Neagră, FETEASCA ALBĂ. Historic red blends Roşu de Purcari (CAB SAUV/MERLOT/MALBEC) and Negru de Purcari (Cab Sauv/ Rara Neagră/SAPERAVI) are revived by flagship Moldovan winery Vinăria Purcari. Other quality producers: Acorex Wine Holding, Vinăria Bostavan, Château Vartely, Dionysos Mereni, DK Intertrade, Lion Gri, Asconi, Cricova (sparkling).

Russia At the moment any wine bottled in Russia, be it from imported bulk or homegrown grapes, can be sold as Russian, misleading consumers. Most v'yds and wineries are in the sw; the Krasnodar region is the biggest producer. European white and red varieties are widely used: indigenous red Krasnostop and Tsimliansky are candidates for Russian authenticity. Lefkadia, with the help of consultant Patrick Leon, est itself as a premium quality leader. Other companies of note: Château le Grand Vostock, Fanagoria, Kuban Vino, Gai-Kodzor, Tsimlianskiye Vina, Abrau-Durso (Charmat and traditional method sparkling).

Ukraine Wine is grown around the Black Sea and on the border with Hungary. Natural conditions are favourable, but most production is industrial. Crimea has greatest quality potential, also proved by new wines from small growers, eg. Pavel Shvets. Historically the best (often excellent) Ukrainian wines were modelled on Sherry, Port, Madeira and Champagne. Gd fortifieds are not to be missed from historic producers, incl Massandra, Koktebel, Magarach, Solnechnaya Dolina. For traditional-method sparkling look for Novy Svet and Artyomovsk Winery. Names to watch: Veles (Kolonist), Guliev Wines.

United States

Abbreviations used in the text
see also Principal Vineyard/
Viticultural Areas p.246, p.260):

CA	California
Clark	Clarksburg, CA
Coomb	Coombsville, CA
Mad	Madera
Mend	Mendocino, CA
Mont	Monterey, CA
Oak Knoll	Oak K,CA
San LO	San Luis Obispo, CA
Santa B	Santa Barbera, CA
Santa Cz Mts	Santa Cruz Mountains, CA

Son	Sonoma, CA
CT	Connecticut
ID	Idaho
NJ	New Jersey
Tex	Texas
VA	Virginia

CALIFORNIA

The good news is that California's run of outstanding vintages continues Even better news is that wine-growers are listening to what the grapes are telling them and increasingly crafting balanced and (often) elegant wines, forsaking the knock-your-socks off model. From south to north and from the coast to the Sierra Foothills, winemakers are turning away from the super-concentrated and jammy wines that created a cult following and are crafting more supple wines with, in many cases, the ability to age. You can find almost any grape variety in Califonia these days – and you should look. There are exceptions: Napa producers focused on what are termed "luxury goods" rather than wines that aren't going to change course in a hurry. Otherwise, California is enjoying a renaissance of the classic form that won the wines so many friends a few decades ago. Well done!

Principal vineyard areas

There are over 100 American Viticultural Areas (AVAs) in California. Below are the key players.

Alexander Valley (Alex V) Sonoma. Warm region in upper RRV. Gd Sauv Bl nr river; Cab Sauv, Zin on hillsides.

Anderson Valley (And V) Mendocino. Pacific fog and winds follow Navarro River inland; gd Ries, Gewurz, Pinot N; v.gd Zin on benchlands.

Arroyo Seco Monterey. Warm AVA; gd Cab Sauv, Chard.

Calistoga (Cal) Napa. The n end of Napa V. Red wine territory, esp Cab Sauv.

Carneros (Car) Napa, Sonoma. Cool AVA at n tip of San Francisco Bay. Gd Pinot N, Chard; Merlot, Syrah, Cab Sauv on warmer sites. V.gd sparkling.

Dry Creek Valley (Dry CV) Sonoma. Outstanding Zin, gd Sauv Bl; gd hillside Cab Sauv and Zin.

Edna Valley (Edna V) San Luis Obispo. Cool Pacific winds; v.gd minerally Chard

Howell Mtn Napa. Classic Napa Cab Sauv from steep hillside v'yds.

Livermore Valley (Liv V) Alameda. Historic district mostly swallowed by suburbs but regaining some standing with new-wave Cab Sauv and Chard.

Mt Veeder Napa. High mtn v'yds for gd Chard, Cab Sauv.

Napa Valley (Napa V) Napa. Cab Sauv, Merlot, Cab Fr. Look to sub-AVAs for meaningful terroir-based wines. Note Napa V is an area within Napa County.

Oakville (Oak) Napa. Prime Cab Sauv territory.

Paso Robles (P Rob) San Luis Obispo. Excellent Zin, Rhône varieties.

Red Hills Lake County. Promising for Cab Sauv, Zin.

Redwood Valley Mendocino. Warmer inland region; gd Zin, Cab Sauv, Sauv Bl.

Russian River Valley (Russian RV) Sonoma. Pacific fog lingers; Pinot N, Chard gd Zin on benchland.

Rutherford (Ruth) Napa. Outstanding Cab Sauv, esp hillside v'yds.

Saint Helena Napa. Lovely balanced Cab Sauv.

Santa Lucia Highlands (Santa LH) Monterey. Higher elevation with gd Pinot N Syrah, Rhônes.

Santa Maria Valley (Santa MV) Santa B. Coastal cool; gd Pinot N, Chard, Viognie

Sta Rita Hills (Sta RH) Santa Barbara. Excellent Pinot N.

Santa Ynez (Santa Y) Santa Barbara. Rhônes, Chard, Sauv Bl the best bet.

Sierra Foothills (Sierra F'hills) Zin, Sauv Bl, Rhône varieties are best.

Sonoma Coast (Son Coast) Son. V. cool climate; edgy Pinot N.

Sonoma Valley (Son V) Son. Gd Chard, v.gd Zin; excellent Cab Sauv from sub-AVA Sonoma Mountain (Son Mtn). Note Sonoma V is an area within Son County

Spring Mtn Napa. Terrific Cab Sauv; v.gd Sauv Bl.

Stags Leap (Stags L) Napa. Classic Cab Sauv; v.gd Merlot.

Recent vintages

California is too big and too diverse for any neat summary to stack up. Keeping that in mind, the following assessments can be useful in a general way.

2014 Despite 3rd year of drought, quality appears high. Short growing season, mild harvest weather. Quantity down almost ten per cent from large 2013.

2013 Another large harvest with excellent quality prospects.

2012 Cab Sauv looks oustanding. Very promising for most varieties.

2011 Another difficult year, below-average crop. Those who picked later reported very good quality – Cab Sauv, Pinot N.

2010 Cool, wet. But some outstanding bottlings, esp Rhône varieties and Zin.

2009 Reds and whites good balance, ageing potential. Napa Cab Sauv excellent.

2008 Uneven quality. Acid levels low; some areas' grapes may not have ripened.

2007 Rain; results mixed, especially for Cab Sauv.

2006 Cab Sauv improving with age. Overall, above average.

2005 Cab Sauv especially good early on but fading fast.

American Viticultural Areas

Federal regulations on appellation of origin in the USA were approved in 1977. There are two categories. First is a straightforward political AVA, which incl an entire state, ie. CA, Washington, Oregon and so on. Individual counties can also be used, ie. Santa B or Son. When the county designation is used, all grapes must come from that county. The 2nd category is a geographical designation, such as Napa V or Will V, within the state. These AVAs are supposed to be based on similarity of soils, weather, etc. In practice, they tend to be inclusive rather than exclusive. Within these AVAs there can be further sub-appellations, eg. the Napa V AVA contains Ruth, Stags L and others. When these geographical designations are used, all grapes must come from that region. A producer who has met the regulatory standards can choose a purely political listing, such as Napa, or a geographical listing, such as Napa V.

---

breu Vineyards Napa V ★★★→★★★★★ 05 07 09 10 11 12 (13) Supple CAB SAUV-based wines from selected v'yds. Madrona v'yd leads the way with a powerful opening, and a long, layered finish. V.gd cellar choice for up to 15 yrs.

cacia Car ★★★ Always gd, sometimes outstanding CHARD and PINOT N from single v'yds in Napa Car. Also classic SYRAH, all smoke and fruit.

corn Vineyards Russian RV ★★→★★★ Newcomer has a way with ZIN, esp silky, seductive Alegria V'yd Heritage Vines bottling; also gd CAB FR.

lante St Helena ★★★ Low-production, outstanding CAB SAUV from a single v'yd. Gd structure with layered finish; capable of ageing.

lban Vineyards Edna V ★★★ Original rider with Rhône Rangers, still out in front. Top VIOGNIER, GRENACHE, splendid Reva Estate SYRAH capable of extended ageing.

lma Rosa Santa RH ★★★ Richard Sanford, Central Coast PINOT N master, has moved to new ground with organic v'yds and palate-pleasing *Pinot N* that is better than ever. V.gd *vin gris* of Pinot N and PINOT GR. CHARD is superb.

ltamura Vineyards Napa V ★★★ 01 03 04 05 06 07 08 09 10 (11) (12) (13) CAB SAUV built to last. Be patient and it will show gd depth and long, echoing flavours.

mador Foothills Winery Sierra F'hills ★★→★★★ Single-v'yd ZIN is a must-try; SAUV BL has bright minerality. New owners who promise to keep up gd work.

ndrew Murray Santa B ★★→★★★ It's Rhônes around the clock here and the hits keep coming. SYRAH is a favourite but don't overlook VIOGNIER, ROUSSANNE.

nthem Napa V ★★★ 10 11 12 Newcomer poised to be one of Napa's best, producing small lots of CAB SAUV and MERLOT from top v'yds. Look esp for superb Beckstoffe V'yd Las Piedras. Intense, rich Mt Veeder Merlot.

Antica Napa V ★★★ 09 10 11 12 It took a few yrs to sort out Piero Antinori's (*see* Italy Napa v'yds, but the wines are at last meeting expectations, with bright, balance CAB SAUV and rounded, zesty CHARD. Lively rosé is welcome addition.

Araujo Napa V ★★★★ 01 02 03 04 05 06 08 09 10 11 12 13 Massive, long-lasting CA SAUV from historic *Eisele v'yd*. Refreshing SAUV BL, in some yrs v.gd VIOGNIER. No owned by Artemis, ie. the Pinaults of Château Latour (Bordeaux).

Au Bon Climat Santa B ★★★→★★★★ Jim Clendenen been at top of game for decade leader in coining a distinctive Central Coast idiom for toasty burgundian-styl CHARD, rich PINOT N. Unusual bottlings under the Clendenen Family label.

Babcock Vineyards Santa Y ★★★ Central Coast pace-setter sources outstanding PINO N and v.gd CHARD, SAUV BL from cool-climate v'yds. Top choices: low productio Terroir Wines, brilliant Chard and superb Pinot N from Sta RH AVA.

Balletto Russian RV ★★★ Outstanding estate CHARD, PINOT N. Delicious *Pinot G takes the grape seriously. Gd SYRAH from estate vines.

Barnett Vineyards Napa V ★★★ Car CHARD from the Sangiocomo V'yd is a cream treat, as is spicy Tina Maria PINOT N from Russian RV. Also look for Spring Mt MERLOT and distinctive Rattlesnake V'yd from Spring Mtn.

Beaulieu Vineyard Napa V ★→★★★ 07 09 10 11 12 You might say "thanks for th memory" to this historic estate, but Georges de Latour Private Res CAB SAUV ca still hold up its head. Budget wines under Beaulieu Coastal Estate label gd gulp

Beckmann Vineyards Santa Y ★★→★★★ Outstanding Rhône varietals, esp Le Be Blanc and Cuvée Le Bec, Rhône blends that change from vintage to vintage. V.g SYRAH from Purisimia Mtn V'yd in Santa Y Valley, backed by v.gd GRENACHE ros

Bella Son ★★→★★★ 09 10 11 12 13 Focus is on ZIN from several Son v'yds, esp Th Belle Canyon Zin featuring quintessential Dry CV brambly fruit. Lily Hill Esta from Dry CV powerful counterpont. Recently, excellent PINOT N, powerful SYRA

Benovia Russian RV ★★★ Outstanding PINOT N from Cohn V'yd; gd GRENACHE fro Son Mtn; best of show is silky Russian RV CHARD.

Benziger Family Winery Son V ★★→★★★ Pioneer in bio and organic farmin Tribute, new CAB SAUV-based blend, complex and structured for ageing. Also v.g estate bottlings of Cab Sauv, MERLOT, SAUV BL.

Beringer Blass Napa ★→★★★ (CAB SAUV) 01 05 07 09 10 11 12 13 Historic winery single-v'yd Cab Sauv Res are massive, but are age-worthy. Velvety, powerf Howell Mtn MERLOT is v.gd. Founder's Estate gd bargain line.

Bernardus Mont ★★→★★★ 07 08 09 10 11 12 13 The Marinus red Bordeaux blen is superb, gd for short-term ageing but delicious as a youngster. Recently adde Ingrid's V'yd PINOT N from Carmel Valley AVA is v.gd. Also gd SAUV BL, CHARD.

Blair Vineyards Mont ★★★ Small lots of v.gd-designated PINOT N and v.gd Bordeau blend are highlights. Also unusually complex PINOT GR from Arroyo Seco.

Bodegas Paso Robles P Rob ★★→★★★ A delicious glass of Spain on the Centr Coast, incl Donna Blanca, charming GARNACHA BLANCA/MALVASIA; Vaca Negr TEMPRANILLO/MOURVÈDRE. Pure yummy. ALBARIÑO a welcome addition.

Boeger Central V ★→★★ Gd-value quaffs that are fine for the picnic table and n out of place on the dinner table. Reds are best, esp BARBERA, ZIN.

Bogle Vineyards Central V ★→★★★ Consistently gd and sometimes v.gd everyda budget wines. Old-Vine ZIN leads the way. Current favourite is Phantom, superb blend of Zin, MOURVÈDRE, PETITE SIRAH from Lodi and Sierra F'hills.

Bokisch Lodi ★★→★★★ Outstanding wine from Spanish varieties with a Californ accent. A v.gd TEMPRANILLO leads the list (why isn't this grape more planted California?) backed by superb GARNACHA and ALBARIÑO.

Bonny Doon Mont ★★★→★★★★ 08 09 10 11 12 13 (Le Cigare Volant) Since terroir

> **Looking to Lake County**
> With high-elevation v'yds and a complex web of volcanic soils, Lake County on California's North Coast is getting attention as a key wine-growing region. It has been known for some yrs as a prime ZIN and SAUV BL area but in the past few yrs it has become a top source for Rhône varieties as well as Spanish entries such as ALBARIÑO and TEMPRANILLO.

Randall Grahm sold his mass-market budget brands to concentrate on bio single v'yds, there has been a sharp improvement. Flagship *Le Cigare Volant* has moved into ★★★★ territory. Vin Gris de Cigare is one of California's top rosés. Recent addition of Contra, budget label blend of CARIGNANE and MOURVÈDRE, is a treat.

Bonterra CA *See* FETZER.

Bouchaine Car ★★★ Car pioneer keeps quality high with estate PINOT N, CHARD; recent addition of Son Coast SYRAH is excellent; v.gd RIES from Car. Rare bottling of PINOT MEUNIER is excellent.

Bronco Wine Company CA Founded by Fred Franzia, nephew of the late Ernest GALLO. Franzia uses low-cost Central Valley grapes for his famous Charles Shaw Two-Buck Chuck. There are dozens of other labels incl Napa Creek and Napa Ridge. Quality is not the point: Franzia is selling wine as a popular beverage.

Buehler Napa ★★★ 05 07 09 10 11 12 13 An underrated Napa treasure, Buehler consistently delivers balanced CAB SAUV in a pleasing brambly style with gd structure. Also look for an outstanding ZIN from Napa grapes and a v.gd CHARD from Russian RV fruit.

Burbank Ranch P Rob ★★→★★★ New Central Coast producer steps up with super MOURVÈDRE and excellent ARNEIS: a fine beginning.

Burgess Cellars Howell Mt ★★★ (CAB SAUV) 05 07 09 10 11 12 13 Powerful and age-worthy Cab Sauv from Howell Mtn grapes. Don't overlook the gd SYRAH.

Cain Cellars Spring Mtn ★★★→★★★★ 05 07 09 10 11 12 13 Cain Five, a supple, layered blend of five Bordeaux varieties from Spring Mtn, is at head of the class. Consistent and *age-worthy*. Cain Concept and Cain Cuvée, both CAB SAUV-based, are well worth a taste.

Cakebread Napa V ★★★→★★★★ 05 06 07 09 10 11 12 13 CAB SAUV is a gold standard, structured for ageing but delicious after 4 or 5 yrs in bottle. SAUV BL ranks among the best; CHARD v.gd.

Calera CA ★★★★ 07 08 09 10 11 12 13 (PINOT N) Josh Jensen, who fell in love with Pinot N while at Oxford, offers outstanding portfolio, esp Reed, Selleck. Don't miss line-up of CHARD, intense, flowery VIOGNIER and ALIGOTÉ, a rare US bottling.

Carter Cellars Napa V ★★★ 07 09 10 11 12 13 It's all about single-v'yd CAB SAUV, beginning with an outstanding To Kalon bottling. Also various Bordeaux blends, which can be v.gd.

Cass P Rob ★★→★★★ Another Central Coast specialist in Rhône varieties getting it right. SYRAH is superb with deep chocolate/coffee tones and a long finish; terrific VIOGNIER, superb ROUSSANNE, MARSANNE.

Castoro Cellars P Rob ★★★ ROUSSANNE is a super starter wine. Move on to a pleasing SYRAH and a lovely ZIN blend called Zinfusion.

Caymus Napa V ★★★→★★★★★ 01 05 06 07 09 10 11 12 13 Special Selection CAB SAUV is a Napa icon, consistently one of California's most formidable: strong, intense, slow to mature. The regular Napa bottling is no slouch. V.gd CHARD under the Mer Soleil brand from Monterey; a gd SAUV BL and MERLOT under Emmolo label; Conundrum, a second label, offers gd value.

Ceja Vineyards Napa ★★→★★★ 07 09 10 11 12 13 Line-up incl stylish Napa CAB SAUV, v.gd Car CHARD. Also SYRAH from Son Coast and red blend Vino de Casa.

Cesar Toxqui Cellars Mend ★★★ Toxqui came n from Mexico when he was 16, and landed his first job at FETZER. He makes superb PINOT N, v.gd ZIN from organic v'yds in Lake and Mend counties. Ruthless Red blend is gd starter.

Chalone Mont ★★★ Historic Mont mtn estate, intense, rich PINOT N, minerally CHARD. Broken out of Burgundian frame with v.gd estate GRENACHE, SYRAH. Look for v'yd blend of Central Coast Pinot N in a classic "come drink me" style.

Chamisal Vineyards Edna V ★★★ Chamisal has been making outstanding Central Coast CHARD, PINOT N for four decades. Recent bottlings have raised the bar, esp unoaked Chard and v.gd SYRAH.

There are 4,100 wineries in California, up from 1,870 in 2003.

Chappellet Napa V ★★★→★★★★ 03 05 06 07 08 09 10 11 12 13 Pioneer (1969) on Pritchard Hill, St Helena. *Signature label* CAB SAUV is for serious ageing; v.gd CHARD, CAB FR, MERLOT; NB *Chenin Bl*. Chappellet owns Sonoma-Loeb, offering v.gd Chard, VIOGNIER and PINOT N from Car and Russian RV.

Charles Krug Napa V ★★→★★★ Historically important winery enjoying a comeback, esp supple CAB SAUV and gd SAUV BL .

Chateau Montelena Napa V ★★★→★★★★ (CHARD) 09 10 11 12 13 (CAB SAUV) 01 03 05 06 07 09 10 11 12 13 Balanced and supple Cab Sauv for drinking young or putting away for at least a decade. Chard is outstanding, as is the supple and delicious estate ZIN.

Chateau St Jean Son V ★★→★★★ 05 06 07 09 10 11 12 13 Cinq Cépages, blend of five Bordeaux red varieties, is top card here; v.gd estate MERLOT, gd SAUV BL, CHARD.

Chimney Rock Stags L ★★★ 03 05 07 09 10 11 12 13 Underrated producer of balanced, age-worthy CAB SAUV.

Claiborne & Churchill Edna V ★★→★★★ Alsace style rules here with several bottlings of RIES and other aromatic whites. PINOT N also worth a try.

Clark-Clauden Howell Mt ★★★ 05 07 09 10 11 12 13 Eternity Res CAB SAUV gets top marks, focused fruit and lasting wraparound flavours. Also v.gd Wild Irish SAUV BL. Much *underrated* producer.

Clayhouse P Rob ★★→★★★ Old-vine PETITE SIRAH restores faith in that variety. It has it all: lovely black-cherry, chocolate, black pepper and a long finish. Look for Adobe series, incl v.gd white blend and supple ZIN.

Cliff Lede Stags L ★★★ 07 09 10 11 12 13 Brilliant Stags L CAB SAUV, featuring lean minerality; built to age; also v.gd Appellation Cab Sauv series from Howell Mtn, Diamond Mtn, Oakville. For 10–15 yrs.

Clos du Val Napa V ★★★ 05 07 09 10 11 12 13 Consistently outstanding CAB SAUVS, never overstated in style, much underrated. CHARD *is a delight*, SÉM/SAUV BL blend Ariadne is a charmer.

Clos Pegase Napa V ★★★ Look-at-me winery with outstanding MERLOT from Car v'yd. Also gd CAB SAUV.

Cobb Wines Son Coast ★★★ Story here – and it's a gd one – is Son Coast PINOT N from select v'yds. Restrained, balanced, lovely.

Conn Creek Napa V ★★★→★★★★ 03 05 06 07 09 10 11 12 13 CAB SAUV with gd structure, from several Napa V AVAs. Gd candidates for cellar, esp Ruth bottling.

Constellation CA ★→★★★ The world's biggest wine company. Produces 90+ million cases/yr. Owns wineries in California, NY, Washington State, Canada, Chile, Australia, NZ. Once a bottom-feeder, now going for the top, incl ROBERT MONDAVI, FRANCISCAN V'YD, Estancia, Mt Veeder, RAVENSWOOD, Simi, among others.

Continuum Napa V ★★★ Tim Mondavi doing what he always wanted to do, make a single wine from Bordeaux varieties. Early results more than promising. The 2011 in particular is supple and pleasing.

Corison Napa V ★★★★ 95 96 97 99 00 01 02 05 06 07 09 10 11 12 13 Cathy Corison is a national treasure. While many in Napa V follow the $iren call of powerhouse wines for big scores and little pleasure, Corison continues to make flavoursome, *age-worthy Cab Sauv*. Top choice is luscious, velvety Kronos V'yd.

Cornerstone Cellars Howell Mt ★★★ 03 05 07 09 10 11 12 13 Impressive CAB SAUV from Howell Mtn: harmony, balance; v.gd valley floor Cab Sauv; bright SAUV BL.

Cosentino N Coast ★★→★★★ Gd-value CAB SAUV, CHARD from Napa V. Impressive CAB FR from Lodi v'yd.

Cuvaison Car ★★★ 05 07 08 09 10 11 12 13 Top marks go to PINOT N, CHARD from Car estate; gd SYRAH, superb CAB SAUV from Mt Veeder.

Dashe Cellars Dry CV ★★→★★★ A happy obsession with Dry CV ZIN, with single-v'yd bottlings capturing the classic Dry CV brambly style.

David Bruce Santa Cz Mts ★★★ 09 10 11 12 13 (CHARD) Legendary mtn estate is all about silky and superb PINOT N and powerful, long-lasting CHARD.

Davis Bynum Russian RV ★★★ PINOT N specialist offering a series of v.gd clonal-select single-v'yd Pinot N from Russian RV; lean yet silky CHARD.

Dehlinger Russian RV ★★★ Series of outstanding PINOT N from estate v'yd. Also v.gd CHARD, SYRAH.

Diamond Creek Napa V ★★★★ 99 00 01 03 06 07 09 10 11 12 13 Austere CAB SAUV from hillside v'yds on Diamond Mtn: Gravelly Meadow, Volcanic Hill, Red Block Terrace. Wines age beautifully. One of Napa's jewels, overshadowed in recent yrs by more glitzy cult Cabs.

Domaine Carneros Car ★★★ Taittinger outpost in CA offering consistently gd sparklers, esp Vintage Blanc de Blancs La Rêve; v.gd NV bubbly rosé. Outstanding range of PINOT N, CHARD led by The Famous Gate Pinot.

Domaine Chandon Napa V ★★→★★★ Top bubbly is the NV Res Étoile; also v.gd rosé sparkler. Still wines incl gd Car PINOT N.

Dominus Estate Napa V ★★★★ 97 99 01 02 05 06 07 08 09 10 11 12 13 Elegantly austere winery and wine of Christian Moueix of Pomerol. One of Napa's great treasures. Don't rush it; the wine amply repays cellar time with supple layers of intense flavours, long wraparound finish.

Donkey & Goat CA ★★★ One of several artisan urban (Berkeley) wineries that have sprung up across the USA, sourcing grapes from selected v'yds. Delicious GRENACHE from El Dorado AVA in Sierra F'hills and SYRAH, CARIGNANE from Mend.

Dry Creek Vineyard Dry CV ★★→★★★ Has been a leader in the Heritage ZIN movement: v. impressive line-up of single-v'yd bottlings. V.gd SAUV BL, CHENIN BL.

Duckhorn Vineyards Napa V ★★★→★★★★ 05 06 07 08 09 10 11 12 13 (Merlot) Known for dark, tannic, plummy-ripe single-v'yd MERLOTS (esp Three Palms) and CAB SAUV-based Howell Mtn bottling. Also Golden Eye PINOT N, made in a robust style at an Anderson V winery. Excellent Russian RV CHARD, Pinot N have been added to Duckhorn's Migration label.

Three of every five bottles of wine sold in the USA are from California.

Dunn Vineyards Howell Mt ★★★★ 91 95 97 99 01 03 06 07 09 10 11 12 13 Randy Dunn makes superb and *intense Cab Sauv* from Howell Mtn estate. They age magnificently; more restrained bottlings from valley floor for short-term drinking. One of few Napa V winemakers to resist the stampede to jammy, lush wines to curry critics' favour.

Dutton-Goldfield Russian RV ★★★→★★★★ Exceptional terroir-based PINOT N, CHARD from Son Coast and Russian RV v'yds. Wines are modern CA classics. Limited bottlng of ZIN also worth a glass or two.

Edmunds St John CA ★★★ Steve Edmunds has scanned CA v'yds for decades, sourcing sometimes offbeat varieties to make v.gd wines. Recent eg. is delicious El Dorado Bone-Jolly GAMAY Noir Rosé. Also try Heart of Gold, a VERMENTINO/GRENACHE BLANC blend from Sierra F'hills.

Edna Valley Vineyard Edna V ★★★ Lovely, true-to-variety SAUV BL; crisp CHARD with generous tropical fruit. Impressive SYRAH, gd CAB SAUV.

Elizabeth Spencer N Coast ★★★ Outstanding CAB SAUV with gd ageing potential from Ruth. V.gd CHARD from Russian RV, delightful CHENIN BL from Mend and a splendid Son Coast PINOT N from hillside v'yds.

Elyse Vineyards Napa V ★★★ 05 08 09 10 11 12 13 All bases covered here; small lots of single-v'yd CAB SAUV, bright fruit, layered flavours, excellent ageing potential. V.gd old-vine ZIN. SYRAH at top of list for bottlings of Rhône varieties.

Farella Coomb ★★★ Artisan producer with vines in the cool Coomb AVA of Napa. Excellent La Luce SAUV BL, cherry-bright MERLOT, elegant CAB SAUV.

Fetzer Vineyards N Coast ★★→★★★ Pioneer in organic/sustainable viticulture. Consistent-value from least expensive range (Sundial, Valley Oaks) to brilliant Res wines. Owns BONTERRA v'yds (organic): *Roussanne and Marsanne are stars.*

Ficklin Vineyards Mad ★★★ It isn't just about sweet wines here; also impressive Iberian varieties, incl delicious TOURIGA N rosé, v.gd TEMPRANILLO.

Firestone Santa Y ★★→★★★ Reliable Central Coast producer. Splendid SAUV BL and useful *off-dry Ries.* Also a gd rosé. Top is The Ambassador, a red MERITAGE blend.

Flora Springs Wine Co Napa V ★★★ 05 06 07 09 10 11 12 13 (CAB SAUV) Sometimes-overlooked Napa gem, esp Signature series, incl Trilogy, an amazing CAB SAUV-based jewel from hillside v'yds; Soliloquy, v.gd SAUV BL from Oak AVA; fine CHARD.

Flowers Vineyard & Winery Son Coast ★★★ Son Coast pioneer (first CHARD planted in 1991), now farms organically; won praise for intense PINOT N and Chard.

Foppiano Son ★★→★★★ One of CA's grand old wine families, est 1896. Outstanding ZIN yr in, yr out. Also leads in rich, firmly structured PETITE SIRAH, known as "petty sir" among the rear guard. Also appealing CAB SAUV, lively SAUV BL, gd estate rosé.

Forman Vineyard Napa V ★★★★ 00 01 03 05 07 09 10 11 12 13 Ric Forman, a dedicated, some might say fanatic terroirist, makes elegant, age-worthy CAB SAUV-based wines from hillside v'yds. Also v.gd CHARD with a nod to Chablis.

Franciscan Vineyard Napa V ★★→★★★ Magnificant, a red Bordeaux blend, is consistently excellent; CHARD also quite gd. Now owned by Constellation brands.

Frank Family Vineyards Ruth ★★★ Gorgeous CAB SAUV hitting on all keys. Gd for early drinking but will repay a decade+ in the cellar, esp Res bottling. Winton Hill Cab Sauv, dark and brooding, is splendid. Also good SANGIOVESE.

Freeman Son Coast ★★★ Concentrates on PINOT N and CHARD from cool-climate Son Coast and Russian RV, with a nod to Burgundy. The Ryo Fu Chard ("cool breeze" in Japanese) is amazing.

Freemark Abbey Napa V ★★★→★★★★ 01 03 05 07 09 10 11 12 13 *Stylish Cab Sauv worthy of cellar time* from often-underrated classic producer. Esp single-v'yd Sycamore, Bosche bottlings.

Freestone Son Coast ★★★ Intense but balanced CHARD, PINOT N from vines only a few miles from the Pacific show gd structure, long finish, esp Chard.

Frog's Leap Ruth ★★★★ 01 02 03 05 07 09 10 11 12 13 (CAB SAUV) John Williams, a leader in the organic and bio movement, says it all starts in the v'yd and he means it. Cab Sauv is supple, balanced, capable of ageing; a toasty CHARD, zesty ZIN and lean, *minerally Sauv Bl* are all excellent.

Newcomers

There are many exceptional new wines from CA awaiting your corkscrew. Some of the best of the newcomers incl Brecon from P Rob, esp the CAB FR and ALBARIÑO; St Rose PINOT N from Russian RV; Sojurn offers a v.gd Son Coast Pinot N; Moore Family ZIN and Black Dog CAB SAUV from Lake County are worth a glass; Cenyth from Jackson Family Wines in Son debuts with an elegant Bordeaux blend.

Gallo Sonoma Son ★→★★★ Coastal outpost of Central Valley giant sources grapes from several Son v'yds. CAB SAUV can be v.gd, also the single-v'yd CHARD. Premium line of Gina Gallo signature wines are consistently ★★★.

Gallo Winery, E & J ★→★★★ CA's biggest winery is easy target for wine snobs, but Gallo has done more to open up the American palate to wine than any other company. The 60s Hearty Burgundy was groundbreaking. Continues basic commodity wines, but has created a line of regional varieties: Anapauma, Marcellina, Turning Leaf, more, all of modest quality but predictable, affordable.

Average retail price of California wine is $6.13/bottle. For Oregon, it's $15.32.

Gary Farrell Russian RV ★★★ Excellent PINOT N, CHARD from cool-climate v'yds. Rocholi v'yd Chard is superb. Don't overlook stylish ZIN, splendid SYRAH.

Gloria Ferrer Car ★★→★★★ Gd bubbly; spicy CHARD; bright, silky PINOT N. Fizz has developed a sweet tooth with the addition of Va de Vi, a blend of Pinot N, Chard, MOSCATO. Owned by Spanish Cava giant Freixenet. Royal Cuvée is superb sparkler.

Grace Family Vineyard Napa V ★★★★ 03 05 06 07 09 10 11 12 13 Stunning CAB SAUV shaped for long ageing. One of few cult wines that might be worth the price.

Grgich Hills Cellars Napa V ★★★ 05 07 08 09 10 11 12 13 CAB SAUV, now farmed bio, is outstanding; supple, age-worthy CHARD. SAUV (FUMÉ) BL and gd rustic ZIN.

Groth Vineyards Oak ★★★★ 99 00 01 05 06 07 09 10 11 12 13 Estate CAB SAUV offers supple, wraparound flavours, structured for ageing. Res Cab Sauv more tightly wound. Excellent CHARD, SAUV BL.

Hall Napa V ★★★ 07 08 09 10 11 12 13 Kathryn Hall Signature Napa CAB SAUV is outstanding: layers of flavour, gd ageing potential. Delicious, mineral SAUV BL.

Handley Cellars And V ★★★ New emphasis on PINOT N with five bottlings, incl superb estate Res and a Mend beginner's Pinot N: silky smooth and gd picnic companion. V.gd RIES plus fine limited release bubbly.

Hanna Winery Son ★★★ Son classic with outstanding SAUV BL, PINOT N from Russian RV. CAB SAUV, MERLOT from Alex V v'yds superb. New Merlot-based rosé a treat.

Hanzell Son V ★★★★ Historic artisan producer of outstanding and terroir-driven CHARD *and Pinot N* from estate vines. Both repay a few yrs' cellar time. Deserves to be ranked with the best of CA.

Harlan Estate Napa V ★★★★ 06 07 09 10 11 12 13 Concentrated, sleek cult CAB SAUV from perfectionist estate commanding luxury prices.

HdV Wines Car ★★★ Fine, complex *Chard* with a mineral edge from grower Larry Hyde's v'yd in conjunction with Aubert de Villaine of DRC (*see* France). Also a v.gd CAB SAUV and SYRAH from Hyde's v'yd.

Heitz Cellar Napa V ★★★→★★★★ 01 03 05 07 09 10 11 12 13 A lot of Napa history here and gd wine also, incl iconic Martha's V'yd CAB SAUV; recent bottlings of Trailside V'yd Cab Sauv, with its uplifted and balanced fruit, are a match for Martha. Restrained, elegant CHARD.

Heller Estate Mont ★★★ Layered and supple *Cab Sauv* is v.gd as is the charming CHENIN BL and PINOT N. V.gd MERLOT rosé, fine late-harvest RIES.

Hess Collection, The Napa V ★★★ CAB SAUV from Mt Veeder estate v'yd hits a new quality level, esp the exceptional 19 Block Cuvée, a blockbuster with gd manners; Lake County SAUV BL is v.gd. New Artezin line focuses on single-v'yd varieties incl amazing MOURVÈDRE. Make sure to see the art gallery.

Honig Napa V ★★★ 07 08 09 10 11 12 13 Consistent quality, esp Ruth CAB SAUV, rich and deeply-flavoured, should age well. SAUV BL is delicious.

Inglenook Oak ★★★★ When Francis Ford Coppola said he was going to restore Inglenook to its former glory he didn't only mean a new paint job. Rubicon, now under the Inglenook label, marks a return to classic Napa CAB SAUV – balanced, elegant and true to the great tradition. Look esp for the Cask series.

Iron Horse Vineyards Son ★★★ Joy, top-of-line NV bubbly, is amazing. Bottled in magnum, 10–15 yrs on lees, combines elegance, power. Wedding Cuvée also a winning sparkler. V.gd CHARD and PINOT N; look for Corral V'yd Chard, fresh unoaked Chard.

Ironstone Sierra F'hills ★★→★★★ Sierra F'hills destination winery is more than just a pretty face. Old-Vine ZIN is among state's best; CAB FR is v.gd, as is charming Obsession, an off-dry blend based on hybrid Symphony grape; fun and quirky.

Jordan Alex V ★★★★ (CAB SAUV) 98 99 00 01 02 05 07 09 10 11 12 13 Consistently balanced, elegant wines from showcase Alex V estate. The Cab Sauv is a homage to Bordeaux: and it lasts. Minerally, delicious CHARD ditto to Burgundy.

Drones (unmanned planes, weighing 1.3 kg) check v'yd health – or at one California hotel, deliver Champagne to your private terrace.

Jorian Hill Santa Y ★★★ Superb Rhône-inspired wines, organic v'yds. Brilliant VIOGNIER, outstanding BEEspoke (Rhône red blend); v.gd SYRAH, a refreshing rosé.

Joseph Phelps Napa V ★★★★ (Insignia) 99 00 01 03 05 06 07 08 09 10 11 12 13 A Napa "first growth". Phelps CAB SAUV, esp *Insignia* and Backus, are always nr the top, capable of long ageing. Ovation CHARD is v.gd.

Joseph Swan Son ★★★ Long-time Russian RV producer of intense old-vine ZIN and single-v'yd PINOT N. Often overlooked Rhône varieties also v.gd, esp ROUSSANNE/MARSANNE blend from Saralee's v'yd. New to the list is a gd rosé.

J Vineyards Son ★★★ Outstanding bubbly, esp creamy brut, zesty brut rosé, luscious late-disgorged vintage. Also gd PINOT N, CHARD, refreshing VIOGNIER, lively *vin gris*.

Kathryn Kennedy ★★★ 01 03 05 07 08 09 10 11 12 13 CAB SAUV specialist in cool Santa Cz Mts. Consistent, age-worthy, restrained wines have been compared to Left Bank Bordeaux. Decant younger wines, or put away for a decade.

Kendall-Jackson CA ★★ Legendary market-driven CHARD, CAB SAUV. Even more noteworthy for developing a diversity of wineries under umbrella of Jackson Family wines with an international cast from Australia, Chile, France, Italy as well as the homegrown CA and Oregon brands.

Kent Rasmussen Winery Car ★★★ Outstanding Car wines for more than a quarter-century. Look esp for minerally CHARD and full-palate lushness of PINOT N. Ramsay is an alternative label for limited bottlings of gd-quality wines at bargain prices.

Kenwood Vineyards Son ★★→★★★ (Jack London CAB SAUV) 03 05 07 08 09 10 11 12 13 Consistently gd quality at fair prices. Jack London Cab Sauv is high point. V.gd Artist Series Cab Sauv. Several v.gd bottlings of ZIN; gulpable, delicious SAUV BL. Now owned by Pernod Ricard.

Kistler Vineyards Russian RV ★★★ Specialist in cool-climate Son County CHARD, PINOT N; over a dozen v'yd-designated wines any given yr. Much in demand.

Konsgaard Napa ★★★★ An amazing CHARD from Judge V'yd that could be from the heart of Burgundy. Consistently ranks as one of CA's best.

Korbel CA ★★ Largest US producer of crowd-pleasing classic-method fizz, with focus on fruit flavours. Recently added an organic bottling and a gd Brut Rosé.

Kosta Browne Son ★★★ Intense single-v'yd PINOT N with a burgundian touch from Son Coast, Santa LH and Russian RV. Also gd CHARD.

Kunde Estate Son V ★★★ Now in 2nd century of winemaking, firmly anchored by historic Son V v'yd. Best bet here is Estate Res Century Vine ZIN, an exceptional wine from 125-yr-old vines. Also a v.gd CAB SAUV.

La Jota Howell Mt ★★★ 01 03 04 05 07 09 10 11 12 13 Supple, age-worthy CAB SAUV, MERLOT; old-vine CAB FR gd minerality, long round finish. All Howell Mtn v'yds.

Lamborn Family Vineyards Howell Mt ★★★→★★★★ 03 04 06 07 08 09 10 11 12 13 Superstar winemaker Heidi Barrett makes intense, age-worthy CAB SAUV and big full-flavoured ZIN from estate v'yd. New Mary Hana Rosé is a yummy treat.

ang & Reed Napa ★★★ CAB FR specialist offers an entry-level North Coast blend and a superb Napa V bottling. One of best of "new wave" Cab Frs.

ange Twins Lodi ★★ A pleasing SAUV BL calls for another glass. Caricature, a CAB SAUV/ZIN blend, is a delicious elbow-bender.

arkmead Napa V ★★★→★★★★ 10 11 Historic Cal estate being revived, offering *outstanding Cab Sauv*, supple and balanced, plus bright, delicious SAUV BL. New release Tocai FRIULANO is a delight.

a Rochelle Santa LH ★★→★★★ The mission here is small lots of PINOT N; Sleepy Hollow v'yd bottling best. Also v.gd Soborantes V'yd and zesty Pinot N rosé.

aurel Glen Son V ★★★★ 01 03 05 06 09 10 11 12 13 Supple, age-worthy CAB SAUV from hillside v'yd on Son Mtn has rated nr the top for three decades. Founder Patrick Campbell sold the winery in 2011, but don't despair. Every indication is that new owners are determined to maintain the standard.

ava Cap Sierra F'hills ★★→★★★ Sierra F'hills pioneer offers a solid line-up, incl excellent ZIN, v.gd SYRAH, appealing GRENACHE and a gd Battonage CHARD.

ohr, J CA ★★→★★★ One of CA's underrated treasures. Wines better every yr. The Gesture series is a homage to Rhône with outstanding SYRAH, VIOGNIER and juicy GRENACHE Rosé. Excellent CAB SAUV and first rate MERITAGE reds. Excellent PINOT N bottling from Arroyo Seco. Cypress is gd budget line.

one Madrone P Rob ★★→★★★ Best is serious, excellent NEBBIOLO with some ageing potential. CAB SAUV from York Mtn AVA gd, as is Point West Red, Rhône blend.

ong Meadow Napa V ★★★→★★★★★ 09 10 11 12 13 Destination winery in Napa, farm and restaurant. Supple, age-worthy CAB SAUV has reached ★★★★ status; lively Graves-style SAUV BL. Ranch House Red is true elbow-bender. Organic.

ouis M Martini Napa ★★★ 05 06 07 09 10 11 12 13 Napa treasure; brilliant comeback since 2002 GALLO buy-out. Gallo took hands-off approach, giving Mike Martini the tools and letting him work with the great CAB SAUV and ZIN v'yds the family had owned for decades. Look esp for Cab Sauv from **Monte Rosso** and Alex V. Son County bottling of Cab Sauv is everyday pleasure.

Uvaggio Lodi ★★★ Italian specialist, excellent BARBERA; VERMENTINO and splendid rosé. MOSCATO Secco is v.gd apéritif, PRIMITIVO is tops. Can't go wrong here.

McIntire Vineyards Santa LH ★★→★★★ McIntire family, long-time growers, now make own wines and do a fine job. Rich cherry PINOT N backed by gd acidity. Brilliant CHARD with deep minerality. The NV L'Homme Qui Ris bubbly is v.gd.

MacPhail Son Coast ★★★ Mardikian, the estate PINOT N, is excellent. Intense, tightly-wound PINOT N, gd CHARD, refreshing Pinot N rosé from selected Son Coast v'yds.

MacRostie Son Coast ★★★ Outstanding PINOT N, CHARD from Son Coast and Russian RV. Delicious Pinot N rosé.

Malk Family Vineyards Stags L ★★★ 06 07 08 09 10 11 12 13 Elegant, supple CAB SAUV is outstanding example of Stags L typicity. Will age, so get it by the case.

Marimar Torres Estate Russian RV ★★★→★★★★ Several bottlings of CHARD, PINOT N from Don Miguel estate in Green Valley. Chard is complex, ages up to a decade. Acero Chard is unoaked, *a lovely expression of Chard fruit*. Pinot N from Doña Margarita v'yd nr the ocean is intense and rich. Gd SYRAH/TEMPRANILLO blend, zesty ALBARIÑO/Chard blend. V'yds now all bio.

Turn off the tap

After three yrs of drought in CA, more and more wine-growers are turning off the tap and going back to traditional dry-farming techniques, common until the introduction of drip irrigation in the 70s. Proponents of dry-farming say they are not only saving water but are producing wines that have more depth and complexity than wines from irrigated vines. Classic CA Cabs of 50s and 60s were not irrigated.

Markham Napa V ★★★ Outstanding CAB SAUV, MERLOT made with restraint, balanc will age. Also v.gd PINOT N.

Mayacamas Vineyards Mt Veeder ★★★ For over 40 yrs Bob Travers and his wi Elionor made outstanding *Cab Sauv* to age decades from their Mt Veeder v'y Charles Banks, a former partner in cult SCREAMING EAGLE, bought Mayacamas i 2013; fans are on edge.

Meritage CA Basically a Bordeaux blend, red or white. The term was invented fe CA but has spread. It's a trademark, and users have to belong to The Meritag Alliance. It's supposed to rhyme with heritage but often doesn't.

Merriam Vineyards Son ★★→★★★ New Russian RV producer, v.gd estate CAB hitting all right notes; v.gd tightly structured Rockpile AVA CAB SAUV; gd SAUV Bl

Merry Edwards Russian RV★★★★ Salute to Burgundy with CA attitude. Single v'y PINOT N, rounded, layered with flavour and edged with dark spice.Also lovely SAL BL. Merry Edwards, who was voted into the Vintners Hall of Fame in 2013, is national treasure.

Merryvale Napa V ★★★ Outstanding CAB SAUV, MERLOT under Merryvale-Beckstoffe label. Profile line offers a balanced, luscious Cab Sauv, backed by Silhouette, rich CHARD; gd MERLOT and v.gd PINOT N. Fruit-forward line under Starmont labe

Mettler Family Wines Lodi ★★★ The Mettler family have made wine for fiv generations. They make only ZIN, CAB SAUV, PETITE SIRAH and they do it righ supple, balanced wines, a treat to drink.

Miraflores Sierra F'hills ★★★ SYRAH and ZIN from El Dorado County are v.gd, wit bright, engaging fruit. VIOGNIER is one of best in state. PINOT GR also v.gd wit excellent varietal typicity. First-rate rosé from BARBERA.

Miura CA ★★★ Master Sommelier Emmanuel Kemiji makes several single v'y wines; look esp for Williams Ranch PINOT N from And V. Cuvée Kemiji, a C/ SAUV-based blend, is v.gd.

Chardonnay is still darling of California wine, 20% share of US off-premise sales.

Morgan Santa LH ★★★ Top-end PINOT N, CHARD from organic Double L estate v'y Esp fine, unoaked CHARD, Metallico. New RIES a delight. Charming Côtes du Crov

Mt. Brave Mt Veeder ★★★07 08 09 10 11 12 13 MALBEC a superstar, CAB SAUV splendi with soft tannins but gd balance, rounded finish. Also gd MERLOT.

Mumm Napa Valley Napa V ★★★ Stylish bubbly, esp *delicious Blanc de Noirs*; ricl complex DVX single-v'yd fizz to age a few yrs in bottle; also a v.gd Brut Rosé.

Nalle Son ★★★ Doug Nalle makes balanced, delicious ZINS, a pleasure to drin young, but will age. PINOT N also excellent. Low-key CHARD is v.gd.

Navarro Vineyards And V ★★★ V.gd RIES, GEWURZ from cool-climate pioneer. Sta turn is PINOT N, in two styles: estate-bottled homage to Burgundy from And grapes; brisk, juicy bottling from bought-in grapes.

Newton Vineyards Spring Mtn ★★→★★★★03 05 06 07 09 10 11 12 13 Top of line Th Puzzle, subtle, supple Bordeaux blend consistently ★★★★. Gd ageing potentia Red Label bottlings are fruit-forward, fun to hang out with, esp the Claret.

Niebaum-Coppola Estate CA *See* Inglenook.

Oakville Ranch Oak ★★★ Sometimes overlooked jewel, this estate on Silverado Tra makes consistently gd CAB SAUV and creamy CHARD. Robert's CAB FR is superb.

Ojai Santa B ★★★ Extensive list of v.gd PINOT N, CHARD, Rhônes offered by former A BON CLIMAT partner Adam Tolmach. Rosé based on SYRAH is delicious.

Opus One Oak ★★★★05 07 09 10 11 12 13 Mondavi-Rothschild creation has mad glorious wines, though not always. *Excellent current form*, esp 2009 – drinkabl now but leave it alone for a few yrs.

Ovid Oak ★★★ Plush new estate on Pritchard Hill, St Helena. Bright, suppl Bordeaux blends are star turn but SYRAH also outstanding. Organic.

ahlmeyer Napa V ★★★ Pièce de Résistance, powerful Bordeaux blend. MERLOTS are a cut above most and have age potential. CHARD, PINOT N from Son Coast are v.gd.

atz & Hall N Coast ★★★ Excellent series of single-v'yd PINOT N, CHARD. Son Coast bottlings are tops. Pisoni V'yd Pinot N from Santa LH is v.gd as is Pinot N and Chard from Hudson V'yd in Car.

aul Hobbs N Coast ★★★ Sometimes bewildering series of single-v'yd CHARDS, PINOT NS, CAB SAUVS and a single lonely SYRAH. They have in common depth, intensity, sometimes flirting with jammy. All worth a glass.

edroncelli Son ★★ Old hand in Dry CV producing bright, elbow-bending ZIN, CAB SAUV and solid CHARD.

eju Napa V ★★★ Something of a showcase winery, but the quality is in the bottle, esp a balanced and supple CAB SAUV.

eriano Lodi ★★→★★★ Outstanding old-vine ZIN, v.gd VIOGNIER, CHARD; gd TEMPRANILLO, excellent MALBEC, all at bargain prices.

eter Michael Winery Mont, Son ★★★ Single-v'yd concept is driving force with a dozen bottlngs of excellent CHARD. PINOT N Ma Danseuse, red Bordeaux blend Les Pavots are outstanding. There is an English fortune behind this.

hilip Togni Vineyards Spring Mtn ★★★★ 97 99 00 03 05 07 09 10 11 12 13 Spring Mtn pioneer makes estate CAB SAUV that can age for decades. Tanbark Hill CAB SAUV is less expensive softer style for earlier drinking.

ine Ridge Napa V ★★★ 01 03 04 05 06 07 09 10 11 12 13 Outstanding CAB SAUV made from several Napa v'yds. The Stags L bottling is silky, graceful. Epitome, made only in best yrs, can be superb. Gd CHARD, lively rosé.

uady Winery Central V ★★ →★★★ Madera Rare in CA: a dessert winery, incl famed orangey Essensia, rose-petal-flavoured Elysium. "Port" is Starboard.

uintessa Ruth ★★★ Supple red blend from the bio Ruth estate of Agustin Huneeus shows balanced fruit in a homage to Bordeaux. Will age.

upé Santa B ★★★ A brilliant range of Rhônes, esp MARSANNE. Also v.gd CHARD from Bien Nacido v'yd. Verdad line celebrates Spanish varieties with several single-v'yd TEMPRANILLOS and ALBARIÑOS. All excellent.

afanelli, A Dry CV ★★★ The Rafanellis have made ZIN for four generations and they do it right: classic intense Zin with bright, brambly fruit will age, but it's so delightful young, why bother? Also gd CAB SAUV.

avenswood CA See CONSTELLATION.

aymond Vineyards and Cellar Napa V ★★★ 01 03 05 07 09 10 11 12 13 Understated CAB SAUV built to age. Gd CHARD, lively PINOT N rosé.

idge N Coast, Santa Cz Mts ★★★★ (CAB SAUV) 99 00 01 03 05 07 08 09 10 11 12 13 Ridge founder Paul Draper is one of key figures in modern CA wine. Supple, harmonious estate *Montebello Cab Sauv* is superb. Outstanding single-v'yd ZIN from Son, Napa V, Sierra F'hills, P Rob. Don't overlook *outstanding Chard.*

obert Keenan Wines Napa V ★★★ Often overlooked producer of supple CAB SAUV, MERLOT, CHARD from estate vines on Spring Mtn as well as from valley floor. Res Cab Sauv is consistent ★★★★ quality.

obert Mondavi Ca ★★ →★★★ 11 12 13 Returning to form with classic Napa CAB SAUV, esp the To Kalon bottling. V.gd SAUV BL.

ochioli Vineyards & Winery Son ★★★ Excellent estate PINOT N, new Pinot N rosé, brilliant CHARD, v.gd SAUV BL.

oederer Estate And V ★★★★ One of the best sparklers in CA and hands-down *the best rosé.* Owned by Champagne Roederer. The house style tends to restraint and supple elegance, esp in luxury cuvée L'Ermitage.

oger Craig Wines Napa V ★★★ 01 03 05 07 09 10 11 12 13 CAB SAUV specialist focusing on power and complexity with bottlings from Mt Veeder, Howell Mtn and Spring Mtn. ZIN from Howell Mtn is v.gd. Gd Son CHARD.

CALIFORNIA

> **Zinfandel heritage takes root**
> Even with the rush to Rhônes and the urge for Iberian grapes, CA
> wine-growers have not forsaken ZIN. A number of wineries from the
> North Coast to the Sierra F'hills are active in the Heritage Vineyard
> Project – taking cuttings from Zin vines sometimes a century old
> to plant new v'yds. The effort is worth it: a growing number of Zin
> bottlings are making the A-list.

Rosa d'Oro ★★→★★★ Long-time Lake County growers; debut with Italian varietie
from high elevation v'yds. Excellent powerful AGLIANICO; charming BARBERA.

St Clement Napa V ★★★ 99 00 01 03 05 06 07 09 10 11 12 13 Several bottling
of single-v'yd CAB SAUV, esp multi-v'yd blend Oroppas, show deep flavours; tw
excellent CHARDS from Car and Abbott's V'yd; also v.gd MERLOT, SAUV BL.

St Francis Son ★★→★★★ Fruit-friendly wines mostly from Son County grapes es
gd CHARD, VIOGNIER, CAB SAUV; outstanding old-vine ZIN.

St-Supéry Napa ★★→★★★ SAUV BL one of best in state; powerful, silky MERLO
outstanding CAB SAUV, CHARD from Dollarhide Estate V'yd.

Saddleback Cellars ★★★→★★★★ 01 05 06 07 08 10 11 12 13 Owner-winemaker Ni
Venge is a legend in Napa V. Lush ZIN, long-lived CAB SAUV. Gd SAUV BL.

Saintsbury Car ★★★ V.gd terroiristic PINOT N, CHARD from Car v'yds. Wines a
intense but balanced.

Santa Cruz Mountain Vineyard Santa Cz Mts ★★★ Splendid age-worthy singl
v'yd PINOT N from mtn grapes; v.gd CAB SAUV, GRENACHE; unusual bottling of Du
worth a glass.

Sbragia Family Wines N Coast ★★★ Ed Sbragia, former winemaker at BERINGER, no
on his own finding gd v'yds in Napa and Son to make outstanding CHARD, ZI
CAB SAUV, esp Monte Rosso V'yd bottling.

Scharffenberger Mend V.gd and affordable NV Brut Rosé. New ownership ha
revived quality here. Look for gd things to come.

Schramsberg Napa V ★★★★ J Schram, the creamy luxury cuvée, has been calle
CA's Krug. Blanc de Noirs is outstanding, as is Brut, while Res is rich, intens
Second label Mirabelle is v. agreeable. V.gd CAB SAUV, J Davies, from mtn esta
vines. Schramsberg stands the test of time.

Screaming Eagle Napa V Small lots of cult CAB SAUV at luxury prices for those wh
like and can afford that kind of thing.

Seghesio Son ★★★ Several v'yd bottlings of superb ZINS. V.gd BARBERA, SANGIOVE
and lovely ARNEIS, rare in CA.

Selene Napa V ★★★ Mia Klein makes small lots of Bordeaux varietals; they a
superb. Excellent CAB FR, fine SAUV BL. There's even a rosé, hurrah.

Sequoia Grove Napa V ★★★ Several bottlings of single-v'yd CAB SAUV, all exceller
intense, concentrated but balanced and built to last. CHARD is also v.gd.

Ser Mont ★★★ Longtime Randall Grahm associate Nicole Walsh has launche
Ser to standing ovation. CHARD is superb with intense minerality; PINOT N offe
bright fruit, gd structure.

Shafer Vineyards Napa V ★★★→★★★★ (CAB SAUV) 01 02 03 05 07 09 10 11 12
Intense Stag's L Cab Sauv, esp Hillside Select; v.gd MERLOT; fine CHARD (Car grape
a
Sierra Vista ★★★ There's a whole lot of Rhône in the Sierra F'hills, incl outstandin
MOURVÉDRE, GRENACHE. Look also for Old-Vine Own-Root unoaked CHARD.

Silverado Vineyards Car ★★★ Disney family winery. Solo CAB SAUV shows off Sta
L AVA terroir and is excellent; fine CHARD, SAUV BL. SANGIOVESE rosé is charming

Silver Oak Alex V, Napa V ★★★ 09 00 01 02 03 05 07 09 10 11 12 13 Separa
wineries in Napa V and Alex V make CAB SAUV only. Napa bottling is classic C
Sauv, Alex V is supple, can be drunk younger.

Sinskey Vineyards Car ★★★ Outstanding MERLOT; single-v'yd CAB SAUV, CHARD, PINOT N. Abraxas, a red and a white *vin de terroir* blend from Car grapes is worth a look.

Smith-Madrone Spring Mtn ★★★ Purist; superb RIES, brilliant floral minerality. V.gd powerful CAB SAUV from high-elevation v'yd. Gd CHARD. Vines not irrigated.

Sonoma-Cutrer Vineyards Son ★★★ Excellent CHARD, PINOT N from cool climate v'yds in Russian RV and Son Coast. Founders Res Chard capable of ageing.

Spottswoode St Helena ★★★★ 97 00 01 03 05 06 07 09 10 11 12 13 On short list of CA "first growths". *Outstanding Cab Sauv*, will age. Brilliant SAUV BL is a bonus.

Spring Mountain Vineyard Spring Mtn ★★★→★★★★ 01 03 04 05 07 08 09 10 11 12 13 Signature Elivette CAB SAUV blend is concentrated, layers of flavour, will age. Estate Cab Sauv v.gd, as is SAUV BL, SYRAH.

Staglin Family Vineyard Ruth ★★★★ 03 05 07 09 10 11 12 13 Philanthropic enterprise. Elegant CAB SAUV, ageing potential. Complex, mineral Estate CHARD; gd SANGIOVESE.

Stag's Leap Wine Cellars Stags L ★★★★ 00 01 03 05 07 09 10 11 12 13 Celebrated for silky, seductive CAB SAUVS (SLV, Fay, top-of-line Cask 23), MERLOTS. Gd CHARD often overlooked. Quality still gold standard since founder Warren Winiarski sold to Chateau Ste Michelle and Marchese Antinori.

Sterling Napa V ★★→★★★ Showplace 70s winery, early leader in serious MERLOT; gd CHARD, CAB SAUV.

Stony Hill Spring Mtn ★★★★ (CHARD) 97 99 00 01 03 05 06 07 09 10 11 12 13 Legendary pioneer of Incredibly long-lived Chard: graceful, supple; now CAB SAUV: restrained and balanced. Gd RIES, GEWURZ.

Sutter Home CA *See* TRINCHERO FAMILY ESTATES.

Tablas Creek P Rob ★★★ Holy ground for Rhônistas. V'yd based on cuttings from Châteauneuf; joint venture between Beaucastel (*see* France) and importer Robert Haas. Côtes de Tablas Red and White amazingly gd, as is Tablas Creek Esprit.

Talbott Vineyards Mont ★★★ Supple, engaging CHARD, PINOT N from single v'yds in Mont. Look esp for Sleepy Hollow Chard, Santa LH and estate Kali Hart Pinot N.

Terra Valentine Spring Mtn ★★→★★★ Elegant estate CAB SAUV with round flavours; v.gd RIES, VIOGNIER; excellent CAB FR.

Thomas Fogarty Santa Cz Mts ★★★ Single-v'yd bottlings of CHARD, PINOT N top list. Estate Chard is esp gd, has ageing potential.

Trefethen Family Vineyards Oak K ★★★ 03 04 05 07 08 10 11 12 13 Historic family winery in Napa. RIES is splendid and will age. Res CAB SAUV is a keeper. CHARD can be excellent, esp Harmony Res.

Trinchero Family Estates CA ★→★★★★ Long-time Napa producer (remember SUTTER HOME White ZIN) now offering a bewildering number of labels, but ahead of pack is affordable, v. pleasing CAB SAUV under Napa Wine Company label.

Truchard Car ★★★ Brilliant bottlings of TEMPRANILLO, ROUSSANNE. Also tangy, lemony CHARD; flavourful MERLOT. CAB SAUV, SYRAH v.gd too. All Car grapes.

California rarity: Tannat only officially approved in 2002; just c.200 acres in state.

Tudal St Helena ★★★ 01 03 05 07 09 10 11 12 13 Marvellous balanced, elegant CAB SAUV. Cerruti Cellars Founders Series is top of line and v. age-worthy.

Turnbull Napa V ★★★ 05 06 07 09 10 11 12 13 CAB SAUV is Napa classic, powerful yet supple, balanced. Pierra V'yd bottling should be cellared for 10 yrs+. Fortuna MERLOT is outstanding; v.gd VIOGNIER.

Viader Estate Howell Mt ★★★★ 00 01 03 05 06 07 08 09 10 11 12 13 Long-lived, powerful CAB SAUV-based blends from Howell Mtn estate; "V" is marvellous Bordeaux blend based on PETIT VERDOT. V.gd CAB FR. Look for small-lot bottlings, incl SYRAH, TEMPRANILLO under Dare label.

Vina Robles San LO ★★→★★★ Gd CAB SAUV, SAUV BL; excellent ALBARIÑO; everyday Red and White are super-affordable, bright fruit and pleasing acidity.

Volker Eisele Family Estate Napa V ★★★ →★★★★ 99 00 01 03 05 07 09 10 11 12 13
Supple, luscious CAB SAUV-based blends, esp Terzetto; new offering is Alexander, 100% Cab Sauv. Gemini is lovely, lively SAUV BL/SÉM blend. Organic grapes.

Wente Vineyards CA ★★ →★★★ After a few lacklustre decades, historic winery is back on track with v.gd CHARD and outstanding gravel-grown SAUV BL.

Value of wine tourism in California: $1.8 billion/annum.

Whitehall Lane Ruth ★★★ 05 07 09 10 11 12 13 Powerful, elegant CAB SAUV. V.gd SAUV BL.

Wine Group, The Central V ★ The 3rd-largest producer of wine in world by volume, offering a range of everyday wines, eg. Glen Ellen, also Franzia bag-in-box.

Y Rousseau N Coast ★★★ Native of Gascony now based in Napa offers marvellous rendition of COLOMBARD from old Russian RV vines. Rare bottlng (for Ca) of TANNAT is superb. Also gd CAB SAUV from Mt Veeder.

Zaca Mesa Santa B ★★★ Focus on estate Rhône varieties with gd results. Res Mesa SYRAH exceptional; also Z Three, delicious red Rhône blend, check out ROUSSANNE.

THE PACIFIC NORTHWEST

The Northwest is going from strength to strength, as it evolves from viticultural backwater to global prominence. In Oregon it's small-production, high-value Pinot Noir above all. Washington does readily available, price-friendly Cabernet and almost everything else. Both attract consumer attention and international investment. Part of the allure is that the region's northerly latitude gives more growing-season sunlight and cooler night-time temperatures than in California, resulting in wines with fresher, food-friendly flavours. There is room for discovery here. New climates are being explored, new AVAs being designated, and new grape varieties being planted. And, not unimportantly, it is a cheaper place to plant a vineyard and build a winery than most of California – at least for the moment. With the recent influx of big money from Burgundy, British Columbia and California (not to mention plenty of well-heeled romantics buying a piece of wine country prestige), its under-the-radar, boutique-y status may be under threat. Nevertheless, the winemaking focus here continues to be on quality, whether at $10 or $100.

Principal viticultural areas

Columbia Valley (Col V) Huge AVA in central and e Washington with a touch in Oregon. Quality Cab Sauv, Merlot, Ries, Chard, Syrah. Key sub-divisions incl Yakima Valley (Yak V), Red Mtn, Walla AVAs.

Columbia Gorge (Col G) Diverse AVA straddling Oregon and Washington; able to ripen cool- and warm-climate grapes.

Snake River Valley (Snake RV) ID's only AVA; partially in Oregon.

Southern Oregon (S Or) Warm-climate region incl AVAs Rogue, Applegate (App V) and Umpqua Valleys (Um V). Tempranillo, Syrah, Viognier are v.gd; lots of experimentation.

Willamette Valley (Will V) Oregon's home for cool-climate Pinot N and Pinot Gr, plus v.gd Chard and dry Ries. Important child AVAs incl Dundee Hills, Chehalem Mts, Yamhill-Carlton (Y-Car), Eola-Amity Hills.

Walla Walla Valley (Walla) Child AVA of Col V with own identity and vines in Washington and Oregon. Home of important boutique brands and prestige labels focusing on quality Cab Sauv, Merlot, Syrah.

Recent vintages

2014 One of the warmest and most bountiful of recent vintages. Focused flavours in both Washington and Oregon.

2013 Crisp Washington whites and well-balanced reds; Oregon Pinot N proving to be better than many expected.

2012 Landmark vintage in Oregon and stellar for Washington.

2011 Classic cool-climate Oregon Pinot N. In Washington, age-worthy wines.

2010 Very cool, so lower alcohol, higher-acid wines with fresh varietal character.

2009 Concentrated Washington wines. Oregon wines are ripe and pleasing.

Oregon

Abacela S Or ★★★ Spanish varieties specialist; consistent leader in TEMPRANILLO, ALBARIÑO; v.gd SYRAH, VIOGNIER. Excellent Rioja-style blend Paramour.

Adelsheim Vineyard Will V ★★★ 09 10' 11 12' (13) Leading pioneer producer with top-notch single-v'yd PINOT N, v.gd Res CHARD, Pinot N and fun AUXERROIS.

Anam Cara Cellars Will V ★★★ 09 10' 11' 12' (13) Family winery crafting PINOT N with grace and depth, esp Nicholas Estate; Dry RIES superb; new CHARD promising.

Antica Terra Will V ★★★→★★★★ 09 10 11' 12' Maggie Harrison left CA's Sine Qua Non to make Will V PINOT N that now has a cult-like following. Recently added highly touted small-batch CHARD.

Archery Summit Will V ★★★ 09' 10 11 12' Impressive PINOT N from estate v'yds in Dundee Hills, Ribbon Ridge AVAs. New whites incl concrete-fermented PINOT GR.

Argyle Will V ★★–★★★ 09 10 11 12' Versatile maker of reliably excellent and not overpriced PINOT N, CHARD, dry and sweet RIES, plus multiple styles of *v.gd bubbly*. Aussie Brian Croser involved.

Beaux Frères Will V ★★★→★★★★ 09' 10 11' 12' Prestige bio estate makes increasingly refined, collectible PINOT N. Part-owned by critic Robert M Parker, Jr.

Bergström Wines Will V ★★★→★★★★ 09' 10 11' 12' Josh Bergström's elegant PINOT NS from bio estate are a treat; also increasingly brilliant CHARD, esp small-lot Sigrid bottling.

Bethel Heights Will V ★★→★★★ 10 11' 12' (13) A 2nd-generation family winery; an Oregon legend. Spicy and sophisticated PINOT N, *v.gd Chard*, PINOTS GR and BL.

Brandborg Vineyard & Winery S Or ★★→★★★ 10 11 12' Um V PINOT N specialist (Ferris Wheel Estate has great complexity) also makes supple PINOT GR and v.gd GEWURZ, SYRAH.

Brick House Will V ★★★ 08 09' 10 11 12' Bio leader producing earthy, powerful PINOT N (esp Cuvée du Tonnelier), stylish CHARD. The true GAMAY is a fun find.

Broadley Vineyards Will V ★★★ 08 09' 10' 11' 12 Family winery; characterful PINOT N from older estate vines and selected v'yds. Basic Will V release is a steal, Claudia's Choice is top-end winner.

Brooks Winery Will V ★★★ 09 10 11' 12' (13) Leading bio producer and RIES champion with zesty dry and balanced sweet RIES winning accolades everywhere. Also superb PINOT N, esp estate Rasteban.

Chehalem Will V ★★★ 09 10 11' 12' (13) Powerhouse PINOT N producer, equally strong RIES, CHARD, PINOT GR. Ridgecrest Pinot N is age-worthy; unoaked *INOX Chard great value.*

Oregon has an official State Soil, of all things: Jory, usually planted with Pinot Noir.

Cowhorn S Or ★★★ 10 11 12' App V AVA bio purist makes knock-your-socks-off SYRAH; Spiral 36 white blend is sensational. Cult winery in the making.

Cristom Will V ★★★ 09' 10 11' 12' Steve Doerner consistently makes among best PINOT N in Oregon. Jessie V'yd, fresh savouriness; Sommers Res, truffle overtones.

Dobbes Family Estate Will V ★★→★★★ 09 10' 11' 12' Eminent winemaker Joe

> **The myth of the 45th**
> Northwest wineries have long touted their latitudinal similarity
> to Burgundy and Bordeaux, as if that alone conferred legitimacy.
> Particularly in Oregon the 45th parallel was drawn between the Will V
> and Burgundy; it even appeared on some labels. Alas, it isn't true.
> Dundee, Oregon, at the heart of Will V PINOT production, is nearly the
> exact latitude of Margaux – in Bordeaux. Ellensburg, Washington,
> deep within the Col V, is the same latitude as Beaune – in Burgundy. If
> latitude alone determined the character of a wine country (it doesn't),
> then the Will V should be growing CAB SAUV and the Col V Pinot N.

Dobbes; prestige Will V PINOT N (Meyer V'yd tops); plus SYRAH, GRENACHE BLANC from S Or. Second label Wine by Joe: great bargain Pinot N, PINOT GR.

Domaine Drouhin Oregon Will V ★★★→★★★★ 09 10 11' 12' New World branch of Burgundy's Domaine Drouhin. Consistently outstanding PINOT N, minerally CHARD. Barrel-select Laurène Pinot N is amazing. Purchase of Roserock estate in Eola-Amity Hills brings another 122 acres of Pinot N and Chard.

Domaine Serene Will V ★★★ 09 10 11 12' Premium PINOT N consistently wins critical raves. Small-production CHARD is particularly tasty.

Elk Cove Vineyards Will V ★★→★★★ 10 11 12' 13 Excellent-value wines from 2nd-generation winemaker. PINOT GR, RIES perennially tops; seven estate-v'yd PINOT NS deliver delectable array of Will V terroirs.

Erath Vineyards Will V ★★→★★★ 09 10 11 12' A founding Oregon winery now owned by Washington's Ste Michelle Wine Estates. Reliable value-priced Pinot-family wines; but rare single-v'd PINOT NS are fabulous.

Evening Land Will V ★★★→★★★★ 11 12' Prestige producer; Seven Springs Summum PINOT N, CHARD are rare, but among best on either side of Atlantic. La Source labels equally great and slightly more affordable.

Eyrie Vineyards Will V ★★★→★★★★ 09' 10 11' 12 The prophet David Lett planted the first Will V PINOT N. Today son Jason extends the legacy with terrific Pinot N in graceful, classically Oregon, age-worthy style. Also v.gd CHARD and PINOT GR.

Gran Moraine Y-Car ★★★ 12' First two PINOT NS from Oregon estate of CA's Jackson Family Wines are superb, esp lithe, polished Estate Res. One of the best new Northwest wineries.

Hyland Estates Will V ★★★ 09 10 11 12' Oregon veteran Laurent Montalieu uses some of the oldest PINOT N vines in the Will V for succulent, polished wines. Also top-notch RIES, CHARD, GEWURZ.

Ken Wright Cellars Will V ★★★ 09' 10 11' 12' Perennially popular maker of great single-v'yd PINOT N showing the range of Will V terroirs. Canary Hill is pretty, forward; Freedom Hill dense, firm; Guadalupe balanced, expressive.

King Estate Or ★★→★★★ 10 11 12' One of state's largest wineries; strong PINOT GR (speciality), PINOT N. Value at multiple price-points. NxNW label, Washington.

Lange Estate Winery Will V ★★★ 09' 10' 11 12' Venerable brand on a 2nd-generation roll with mouthwatering PINOT N (luscious Lange Estate), barrel-aged Res PINOT GR. CHARD gaining strong reputation.

Matello Will V ★★★ 11' 12' (13) Artisan winery growing in importance. Lazarus and Souris PINOT NS are superb, as well as strong PINOT GR, CHARD. Rising star.

Phelps Creek Vineyards Or ★★→★★★ 10 11 12' Quality-leading Col G producer of v.gd CHARD (oaked, unoaked); pretty PINOT N releases with Gorge fruit character. Winemaker Alexandrine Roy also makes Domaine Marc Roy in Burgundy.

Ponzi Vineyards Will V ★★★→★★★★ 09' 10' 11 12' (13) Legendary PINOT N specialist now in 2nd generation, making excellent wines. Aurora PINOT N a knockout; Res CHARD a standout. Don't miss brilliant ARNEIS.

Quady North S Or ★★→★★★ Influential S Or winemaker Herb Quady crafts delicious CAB FR from cooler Rogue Valley AVA sites, also intriguing styles of VIOGNIER, concentrated SYRAHS.

Rex Hill Will V ★★★ 10 11' 12 Bio and hand-crafting makes superb estate PINOT NS, notable CHARD. Same owner as the more popularly priced A to Z Wineworks.

Scott Paul Wines Will V ★★★ 09' 10 11' 12 PINOT N-only producer emphasizes elegance and grace with sophisticated burgundy-inspired character. Le Paulée approachable on release, Audrey gd for cellaring.

Sokol Blosser Will V ★★★ 10 11 12' A 2nd-generation maker of lovely PINOT N, PINOT GR from Dundee Hills, also inexpensive fun white blend called Evolution. Spectacular and innovative tasting venue.

Soter Vineyard Will V ★★★★ 09' 10 11' 12' CA legend Tony Soter moved to Oregon to make PINOT N. Estate *Mineral Springs Ranch Pinot N* is sublime, but don't miss the tremendous sparklers; perhaps the Northwest's best.

Spangler Vineyards S Or ★★★ V.gd warm-climate reds, esp Res CAB SAUV, PETITE SYRAH; VIOGNIER always top-notch.

Easy way to remember local pronunciation: It's Will-*A*-met, Damn it!

Stoller Family Estate Will V ★★★ 09' 10 11 12' Beautifully balanced PINOT NS exemplify Dundee Hills elegance; Cathy's Res is exceptional. Also v.gd Res CHARD.

Teutonic Wine Company Or ★★★ 10 11 12' Iconoclastic, delicious Mosel-inspired RIES, crisp white blends, Germanic-styled PINOT N. Brilliant up-and-comer.

Trisaetum Will V ★★★ 10 11 12' 13' Owner, artist, winemaker James Frey makes superb cool-climate RIES and PINOT N from Coast Range estate vines and other sources. New leader for both grapes in Northwest.

Willamette Valley Vineyards Will V ★★→★★★ 10 11 12' Popular publicly owned winery produces excellent estate PINOT NS, CHARD; v.gd inexpensive RIES.

Washington & Idaho

Andrew Will Wash ★★★ 08 09' 10 11' 12 Chris Camarda; stunning red blends from outstanding Col V v'yds. Sorella has big fruit, Ciel du Cheval more structured.

Betz Family Winery Wash ★★★→★★★★ 06 07' 08 09' 10 11 12' Master of Wine Bob Betz makes Rhône styles from top Col V v'yds. La Serenne SYRAH is extraordinary; powerhouse La Côte Patriarche comes from state's oldest Syrah vines.

Brian Carter Cellars Wash ★★★ 09 10 11' 12' Only blends made here, all masterful. Try unconventional PETIT V-driven Trentenaire, Byzance Rhône blend, or aromatic white Oriana.

Cadence Wash ★★★ Compelling Bordeaux-style blends incl powerful Coda from Red Mtn fruit and spicy CAB FR-dominant Bel Canto.

Cayuse Walla ★★★→★★★★ 06' 07 08' 09' 10 11 Cult bio winery delivering *spellbinding Syrah* (esp Cailloux) and amazing GRENACHE, but you have to be on mailing list to get any.

Charles Smith Wines Walla ★★→★★★ Marketeer/winemaker Charles Smith commands respect, publicity and demand. Powerful (too much so?), sometimes pricey reds (Royal City SYRAH is a favourite); but also inexpensive and v.gd Kung Fu Girl RIES.

Washington is 2nd-largest *vinifera* wine state in the USA, with over 800 wineries.

Chateau Ste Michelle Wash ★★→★★★★★ Flagship brand of Northwest's largest wine company offers wines in all prices/styles, from v.gd quaffers (excellent Col V Dry RIES) to TBA-style rarities (Eroica Single Berry Select). Gd-value Col V-labelled, premium Ethos Res.

THE PACIFIC NORTHWEST

Chinook Wines Col V ★★★ 08 09' 10 11 12' Husband (vines) and wife (wines) have a history of fine, value CAB FR (the rosé is delightful), MERLOT, CHARD, SAUV BL.

Cinder Wines Snake RV ★★★ Breakout ID winery making small amounts of marvellous VIOGNIER, a unique MOURVÈDRE/TEMPRANILLO blend, and v.gd SYRAH.

Coiled Snake RV ★★★ Owner/winemaker Leslie Preston helps to set pace in ID. The Coiled Dry RIES is pitch-perfect, while Sidewinder SYRAH is scrumptious.

Col Solare Col V ★★★ →★★★★ 07 08 09' 10 11' STE MICHELLE and Tuscany's Antinori join to make a single Col Solare red blend each vintage, invariably complex, long-lasting. Less-expensive Shining Hill blend more approachable.

Columbia Crest Col V ★★ →★★★ Washington's largest winery makes masses of v.gd, affordable wines under Grand Estates, H3 and Res labels. Res wines are dandy, esp Walter Clore red wine; H3 wines are all from Horse Heaven Hills AVA: succulent and great value.

Côte Bonneville Yak V ★★★ 07 08 09' 10 11 12' Kerry Shiels uses estate DuBrul V'yd fruit from steep basalt ground and wins medals for deep, sleek CAB blends, esp *Carriage House*. Don't overlook RIES, CHARD.

DeLille Cellars Wash ★★★ →★★★★ 08 09 10' 11 12' Sophisticated producer of age-worthy reds. Harrison Hill CAB SAUV from state's 2nd-oldest v'yd is penetrating; Chaleur Estate blends consistently superb; Grand Ciel is signature wine.

Almost all of Washington's vines are ungrafted; phylloxera is nearly non-existent.

Doubleback Walla ★★★ 07 08 09 10' 11 Created by football star Drew Bledsoe; signature CAB SAUV blend (by Chris Figgins) beautiful expression of Walla flavours.

Dusted Valley Vintners Walla ★★★ 10 11 12' Fast-rising star; impressive wines. Stained Tooth SYRAH; beautiful Old-Vine CHARD or any single-variety release.

Efeste Wash ★★★ 09 10 11' Brilliant boutique label for zesty RIES, racy CHARD from cool Evergreen V'yd, also v.gd SYRAHS.

Fidélitas Col V ★★★ 08' 09 10 11' Charlie Hoppes makes superior Bordeaux-style wines. Luscious Optu red blend; Ciel du Cheval V'yd CAB SAUV shows power of Red Mtn AVA fruit.

FIGGINS Walla ★★★ Chris Figgins grew up with his father's LEONETTI CELLAR, but he has est his own identity with Figgins Estate red blend and RIES. New Toil PINOT N from Oregon is a portent of things to come.

Gramercy Cellars Walla ★★★ →★★★★ 09' 10 11 12 Master sommelier-turned-winemaker Greg Harrington makes voluptuous SYRAHS. Recently added earthy TEMPRANILLO, herby CAB SAUV winners too.

Hedges Family Estate Red Mt ★★★ Venerable family winery produces polished and reliable wines, esp estate red blend and DLD SYRAH.

Hogue Cellars, The Col V ★★ →★★★ Stylish value single-variety wines under Hogue brand. Genesis- and Res-labelled wines more focused and smaller production.

Januik Wash ★★★ 10 11' 12 Artisan wines from a veteran winemaker. Cold Creek CHARD is superb, Champoux V'yd CAB SAUV is edgy and winning.

Koenig Winery Snake RV ★★ →★★★ Reliable SYRAH, MERLOT, CHARD. The CSPV is an unusual CAB SAUV/PETIT VERDOT blend.

L'Ecole No 41 Walla ★★★ 10 11 12' Everything is gd here. Grab Apogee or Perigee (each from a different v'yd) red blend for a treat, or the cultish SÉM for a remarkably bright, aromatic white.

Leonetti Cellar Walla ★★★★ 06 07' 08 09 10 11' Legendary, cult-status winery for elegant, refined, collectable CAB SAUV, MERLOT, SANGIOVESE. Founder of Walla AVA.

Long Shadows Walla ★★★ →★★★★ Allen Shoup's unique venture brings seven globally famous winemakers to Washington to make their signature variety with Col V fruit. Pedestal MERLOT by Michel Rolland is luscious, Feather CAB SAUV by California's Randy Dunn is refined. Others equally impressive.

> **Between a rock and a hard place**
> Grapes know no borders, but marketing does. "The Rocks District of
> Milton-Freewater" is a new AVA on the Oregon side of the Walla AVA.
> Composed of fields of basalt-based coarse cobblestones, the region is
> unlike any other. Ironically, its cult-like wines come from a few boutique
> wineries based in – Washington. It's a tricky one. In order to use the
> prestigious "The Rocks" AVA name, 85 per cent of the grapes must come
> from the AVA *and* the wine be fully finished within the state of the AVA –
> which is Oregon. The potential for conflict has caused the federal
> regulators to look at changing the multi-state labelling rules – a gd thing.

Maison Bleue Col V ★★★ 10 11' 12' Newish boutique turning heads, esp Upland V'yd GRENACHE and pinpoint-correct MARSANNE, VIOGNIER. Can be difficult to find.

Maryhill Winery Wash ★★→★★★ Popular Columbia Gorge AVA producer; huge range. Res ZIN and Res CAB FR are always v.gd, also RIES.

Millbrandt Vineyards Col V ★★★ Well-made value varietal wines; consistent quality from the Wahluke Slope and Ancient Lakes AVAs.

Northstar Walla ★★★→★★★★ 06 07' 08 09 10' Winemaker "Merf" Merfeld is a MERLOT maven. Recent Premier Merlot is drop-dead gorgeous, Walla Walla Merlot is sultry.

Pacific Rim Wash ★★→★★★ RIES specialist making oodles of tasty, inexpensive yet eloquent Dry and Organic. For profundity, *single-v'yd releases*, incl bio-farmed bottlings, are unbeatable.

Pepper Bridge Walla ★★★ 06' 07 08 09 10' 11' Estate Pepper Bridge and Seven Hills V'yds are among Washington's best. Winemaker Jean François Pellet's CAB SAUVS are sensuous and rich, MERLOT spicy and aromatic.

Quilceda Creek Wash ★★★★ 01 02' 03' 04' 05' 06 07 09 10 11' Extraordinary, often 100-point *Cab Sauv* and blends from one of the most lauded producers in North America: dense, intense, tremendously long-lasting. Find it if you can.

Reynvaan Family Vineyards Walla ★★★ 07 08 09 10' Family maker of Walla V, SYRAH and Rhône-style whites has developed a cult following and majestic critical scores. Wait-list winery with wonderful wines.

Ste Chapelle Snake RV ★→★★ ID's 1st and largest winery makes quaffable RIES, inexpensive bubbly and Icewines.

Sawtooth Winery Snake RV ★★→★★★ 10 11 12' Winemaker Meredith Smith is upping the quality ante at this signature ID producer, esp elegant, lean TEMPRANILLO and tight, tasty SYRAH.

Average vineyard size in Washington is 143 acres; in Oregon it's a mere 28 acres.

Seven Hills Winery Walla ★★★ 09 10 11 12' Respected esp for silky CAB SAUV (Ciel du Cheval V'yd is an age-worthy delight), though VIOGNIER is a treat too.

Sparkman Cellars Wash ★★★ 07' 08' 09 10 11 12' Remarkably well-made wines, surprisingly diverse grapes and styles. Most notable: Rainmaker CAB SAUV, new Evermore Old Vines CAB SAUV. Look for spicy Ruckus SYRAH.

Spring Valley Vineyard Walla ★★★ (Merlot) 06' 07 08 09 10' 11' Nina Lee SYRAH is lip-smacking gd; Uriah MERLOT blend deep, refined; Frederick red blend suave, polished. Superb line-up.

Syncline Wash ★★★ James Mantone makes excellent wines from Col G and Col V fruit. Subduction Red is hedonistic, GRENACHE BLANC is great.

Waterbrook Walla ★→★★ Large gd-value producer: multiple styles, many price points.

Woodward Canyon Walla ★★★→★★★★ (CAB SAUV) 02 03 04' 06 07 09 10 11 12' Impeccable wines. *Old Vines Cab Sauv* is refined, complex; Charbonneau Res blend scrumptious, ageable; estate BARBERA a silky surprise.

NORTHEAST, SOUTHEAST & CENTRAL

The world at large has not grasped the fever of planting and winemaking in the USA as a whole – but above all in the Eastern States, which until recently thought good wine by international standards was beyond them. The wrong weather, the wrong soils... none of which, we now know, is true. It started in New York State, in the Finger Lakes, spread to Long Island, now gives Virginia a new mojo and crops up everywhere from Maine to Georgia. Different climates and terroirs present different problems, but everyone is having a go and quite a few are doing it well.

Recent vintages

Extreme cold and heavy rain led to crop loss in a few areas, but overall 2014 was one of the best vintages ever seen in the East. What one Long Island vintner described as "a vintage one only reads of or dreams about". 2014 wines will be elegant, with lush, ripe flavours and alcohol levels of 14% or less.

21 Brix NY ★★★ 13 14 On shoreline of Lake Erie; young winery already garnering kudos for excellent RIES, GEWURZ, Icewine.

Alba NJ ★ Gd CHARD, RIES, GEWURZ, plus the largest PINOT N planting on the East Coast

Anthony Road Finger L ★★★ 10 13 14 Outstanding estate with some of best dry semi-dry RIES in the USA, as well as fine GEWURZ, PINOT GR, CAB FR/LEMBERGER blend

Barboursville VA ★★★ 10 12′ 13 14 Iconic VA estate founded 1976 by Italy's Zonin family on site once known to Thos Jefferson. One of best in the East, with succulent Bordeaux-style blend Octagon and excellent CAB FR; outstanding Italian varieties incl VERMENTINO, NEBBIOLO. NB rich Malvaxia Passito. Elegant inn and Tuscan-style restaurant.

Bedell Long I ★★★ 10 11 13 14 Classy LONG I winery. Influential winemaker distinctive CHARD, GEWURZ, MERLOT; superb SYRAH and CAB FR; exceptional blends Stylish Art Series labels, handsome gardens.

Boxwood VA ★★★ 12 13 14 Stylish estate specializing in high-end Bordeaux-style CAB-based blends.

Breaux VA ★ 12 13 14 Hilltop v'yd an hour from Washington DC. Gd SAUV BL VIOGNIER, MERLOT, CAB SAUV.

Casa Larga Finger L ★ 12 14 Fine family-run estate with notable RIES, GEWURZ PINOT N and VIDAL Icewine.

Channing Daughters Long I ★★★ 10 12 13 14 Creative South Fork producer with v.gd Tocai FRIULANO, PINOT GRIGIO and bevy of Italianate rosés; also gd PETIT VERDOT CAB SAUV, inspired blends.

Chester Gap VA ★★ 12 13 14 High-altitude v'yds, exceptional PETIT MANSENG and VIOGNIER, gd ROUSSANNE, MERLOT, CAB FR, PETIT VERDOT.

Chrysalis VA ★★ ★ 10 12 13 14 Benchmark VIOGNIER, native Norton; v.gd PETIT MANSENG, ALBARIÑO, TANNAT, PETIT VERDOT.

Delaplane VA ★★★ 10 12 13 14 Stunning mtn views, structured wines, incl CHARD VIOGNIER, TANNAT, William Gap and other toothsome Bordeaux-style red blends.

Finger Lakes NY Bucolic region in upstate NY with deep glacial lakes whose mass of water helps protect vines in harsh winters. Most of the 125 wineries cluster around the four major lakes. Known especially for RIES. Top wineries inc ANTHONY ROAD, FOX RUN, DR. KONSTANTIN FRANK, HEART & HANDS, HERMANN J WIEMER Kemmeter, KING FERRY, LAMOREAUX LANDING, Ravines, MCGREGOR, Red Tail Ridge Silver Thread, Swedish Hill. Up-and-coming: KEMMETER WINES.

Fox Run Finger L ★★★ 10 12′ 13 14 Noteworthy RIES, plus gd CHARD, lush GEWURZ rosé, PINOT N. Informal café overlooking Lake Seneca.

Frank, Dr. Konstantin (Vinifera Wine Cellars) Finger L ★★★★ 10 12 13 14 Pioneering estate (1961), first to plant *vinifera*. One of top US *Ries* producers; v.gd GEWURZ, CHARD; admirable RKATSITELI, PINOT N. Fine Château Frank sparkling.

Georgia More than 15 wineries: look for Wolf Mtn, Frogtown, Three Sisters, Habersham V'yds, Tiger Mtn. In Atlanta, Château Élan, a conference centre, resort and winery, produces wines based on native muscadine.

Glen Manor Vineyards VA ★★★ 10 12 13 14 V'yds on steep slopes of Blue Ridge Mtns; noteworthy SAUV BL, impressive red Bordeaux-style blend.

Grace Estate VA ★ New estate, small production incl VIOGNIER, CHARD, CAB FR, TANNAT, Bordeaux-style blends.

Hamptons, The (aka South Fork) Long I Coastal region with three wineries: CHANNING DAUGHTERS, Duckwalk and WÖLFFER ESTATE.

Heart & Hands Finger L ★★★ 12 13 14 Small estate on shores of Cayuga Lake; classic cool-climate RIES, PINOT N.

Hermann J Wiemer Finger L ★★→★★★ 12 13 14 One of East's best estates, est 1976 by German winemaker. Superb RIES; admirable CHARD, GEWURZ; fine sparkling and dessert wines.

Horton VA ★★ 12 13 14 Pioneer (est 1991); signature VIOGNIER; full-bodied TANNAT.

Hudson River Region NY Borders the scenic Hudson River 90 minutes' drive n of Manhattan. Oldest winemaking and grape-growing region in the USA, now has 42 wineries.

Kemmeter Wines Finger L ★★★ New venture; talented German winemaker formerly with ANTHONY ROAD. RIES focus.

King Family Vineyards VA ★★ 12 13 14 Serious, age-worthy MERITAGE, gd CHARD, VIOGNIER, CAB FR, luscious *vin de paille*-style PETIT MANSENG dessert wine.

King Ferry / Treleaven Wines Finger L ★★ 12 13 14 Notable dry, semi-dry and dessert RIES, also CHARD, CAB FR, MERITAGE.

n Ohio it is illegal to give alcohol to a (live) fish.

Lake Erie NY, OH, PA Tri-state AVA. Standout producers: 21 BRIX and Mazza Chautauqua Cellars. Look for RIES, PINOT G, CHARD, Icewine, high-quality eau de vie.

Lamoreaux Landing Finger L ★★★★ 10 12 13 14 Greek Revival building overlooking Lake Seneca; excellent *Chard*, v'yd-designate RIES, GEWURZ, CAB FR and Icewine.

Linden VA ★★★★ 11 12' 14 Just 65 miles w of Washington DC. One of VA's leading estates; notable high-altitude wines incl vivacious SAUV BL. Savoury PETIT VERDOT, elegant, complex Bordeaux-style red blends, succulent late-harvest PETIT MANSENG.

Long Island NY Easy access from NYC. One of earliest wine regions in the East (1st winery 1973); 53 commercial wineries, two AVAs: Long I/NORTH F and Long I/ THE HAMPTONS, aka The South Fork), most estates on North F. Leaders: BEDELL, CHANNING DAUGHTERS, MACARI, PAUMANOK, SHINN ESTATE, SPARKLING POINTE, WÖLFFER.

Macari Long I ★★★ 09 10 12 14 One of LONG I's best, with savoury CHARD and v.gd SAUV BL, outstanding CAB FR, plush MERLOT, fine Bordeaux-style reds.

McCall Long I ★★★ 12 14 One of LONG I's few PINOT N producers. Also excellent CHARD, MERLOT, Bordeaux-inspired red blends.

McGregor ★★ 12 13 14 Venerable FINGER L winery (1980), making gd CAB FR, CAB SAUV, PINOT N and RIES.

Martha Clara Long I ★ 12 13 14 Gd CHARD, MERLOT, Bordeaux-style red blends.

Maryland 64 wineries, surprisingly fine wines, from PINOT GR to Bordeaux-style reds. Black Ankle, Knob Hall, Slack, Sugarloaf, Big Cork and Bordeleau impress. Elk Run's CAB FR and other reds continue to please.

Michael Shaps / Virginia Wineworks VA ★★★ 10 12 13 14 Exceptional VIOGNIER, complex CHARD, dark, aromatic PETIT VERDOT, CAB FR, fine MERITAGE, CAB-based Port-style Raisin d'Etre. Multifaceted blend of PETIT MANSENG, RIES, Chard, Viognier.

Michigan 110 wineries now, with Bel Lago, Black Star, Boathouse, Bowers Harbor,

Brys, Chateau Fontaine, Chateau Grand Traverse, Fenn Valley, Tabor Hill, L Mawby, St Julian leading the pack with RIES, GEWURZ, PINOT N, v.gd CAB FR blends. Notable: Chateau Chantal, 45 North, Lawton Ridge, Left Foot Charley, 2 Lads, Verterra, Hawthorne, Laurentide. Up-and-coming: 12 Corners, WaterFire.

Millbrook Hudson ★★ 12 13 14 Most important HUDSON Valley winery with decent RIES, CHARD, FRIULANO, CAB FR.

Missouri The University of Missouri has a new experimental winery to test techniques and grape varieties in local conditions. Best so far: SEYVAL BL, VIDAL, Vignoles (sweet and dry) and Chambourcin. Stone Hill in Hermann produces v.gd Chardonel (frost-hardy hybrid, Seyval Bl x CHARD), Norton and gd Seyval Bl, Vidal. Hermannhof is notable for Vignoles, Chardonel, Norton. Also: St James for Vignoles, Seyval, Norton; Mount Pleasant in Augusta for rich fortified and Norton; Adam Puchta for fortifieds and Norton, Vignoles, Vidal; Augusta Winery for Chambourcin, Chardonel, Icewine; Les Bourgeois for SYRAH, Norton, Chardonel, Montelle, v.gd Cynthiana and Chambourcin.

New Jersey Leading wineries in this small state are Cape May, Unionville and ALBA. With v. little winter damage and an unusually warm, dry growing season vintners believe 2014 may be the best vintage ever, esp for PINOT N, CHARD, RIES.

New York (NY) New York State has advanced at an astounding pace in wine quality, v'yd acreage and number of wineries (141 new in 5 yrs), total 375 producers today in five official AVAs: LONG I (incl NORTH F and THE HAMPTONS) HUDSON R; FINGER L (incl Cayuga and Seneca Lakes); Niagara Escarpment; LAKE ERIE. If only NYC would embrace its local products.

North Carolina This s state now has 150 wineries, incl Biltmore, Childress, Duplin (for muscadine), Grandfather, Hanover Park, Iron Gate, Laurel Gray, McRitchie Old North State, Ragapple Lassie, RayLen, Raffaldini, Shelton. Top varieties CHARD, VIOGNIER, CAB FR and native muscadine.

North Fork Long I Ritzy summer playground for Manhattanites. Its potato fields became the first LONG I v'yds in the 1980s. Top estates incl BEDELL, CHANNING DAUGHTERS, MACARI, PAUMANOK, SHINN ESTATE, SPARKLING POINTE, WÖLFFER.

Ohio 215 wineries, five AVAs. Some exceptional PINOT GR, RIES, PINOT N, Icewine In s Ohio CAB FR. Top producers: Breitenbach, Debonné, Ferrante, Firelands Harpersfield, M Cellars, Kinkead Ridge, Markko, Paper Moon, St Joseph and Valley V'yds.

Paumanok Long I ★★★ 10 12 13 14 Venerable LONG I estate (founded 1982) with excellent RIES, CHARD, CAB SAUV, MERLOT, late-harvest. Exceptional CHENIN BL.

In Pennsylvania: buy wine from a vending machine, complete with breathalyzer.

Pennsylvania 170 wineries. Top: Blair (PINOT N, CHARD), Briar Valley (RIES, CAB FR) Allegro (red Bordeaux blend), Galen Glen (GRÜNER VELTLINER, ZWEIGELT), Galer (Bordeaux reds), Karamoor (Cab Fr, red blends), Manatawny Creek (Chard GEWURZ, PINOT GR, Cab Fr, MERITAGE), Nimble Hill (Ries, Gewurz), Penns Wood (Chard, Pinot Gr, MERLOT, Cabs), Pinnacle Ridge (Bordeaux blend, Chard), Walta (Chard, Cabs), Va La (Italian varieties).

Pollak VA ★★★ 12 13 14 Excellent CHARD, PINOT GR, CAB FR, MERLOT, VIOGNIER.

Ravines Finger L ★★★ 10 12' 13 14 Exceptional v'yd-designate and other dry *Ries* plus CAB FR, PINOT N, MERITAGE.

RdV VA ★★★ 12 13' 14 Founded in 2011 and already one of the best in the East Serious, intense, complex Bordeaux-inspired red blends.

Red Tail Ridge Finger L ★★★ 12 13 14 Highest quality; incl dry and dessert RIES CHARD, BLAUFRANKISCH, PINOT N.

Shinn Estate Long I ★★★ 10 12 13 14 Gd CHARD, SAUV BL, Bordeaux-style blends, eau de vie and grappa. Lovely little inn.

Silver Thread Finger L ★ 13 14 Specializes in RIES; gd GEWURZ, CHARD and PINOT N.

Sparkling Pointe Long I ★★→★★★ Superb sparkling, some mature and mellow, others youthful and vivacious.

Sunset Hills VA ★★ 10 13 14 Scenic winery in renovated barn; gd CHARD, VIOGNIER, CAB SAUV, outstanding Bordeaux-style red blend.

Swedish Hill Finger L ★★★ 13 14 Iconic FINGER L estate (since 1969); consistently gd CHARD, RIES, sparkling, Vidal, Vignoles late-harvest.

Iberian grapes, ie. Albariño, Touriga, heading to Maryland and Virginia. Plus ultra....

Unionville Vineyards NJ ★★ 12 14 Once the largest peach orchard in the USA; excellent CHARD, RIES, fine Bordeaux-style red.

Veritas VA ★★ 10 12 13 14 Gd sparkling, CHARD, VIOGNIER, CAB FR, MERLOT, PETIT VERDOT and Bordeaux-inspired red blend.

Villa Appalaccia VA ★★ 12 13 14 On the scenic Blue Ridge Parkway, Italian-inspired estate produces PRIMITIVO, SANGIOVESE, AGLIANICO, MALVASIA, TREBBIANO, CAB FR.

Virginia Rapidly expanding, 275 wineries. Many of best wines penetrated market in nearby Washington DC. Try VIOGNIER, PETIT MANSENG, PETIT VERDOT, CAB FR, TANNAT.

Wisconsin Best is Wollersheim Winery, with popular Prairie Fumé (SEYVAL BL) and Prairie Blush (Foch).

Wölffer Estate Long I ★★★ 12' 13 14 Superior winery on South Fork with fine CHARD, excellent rosé, praiseworthy CAB SAUV, gd MERLOT from German-born winemaker.

THE SOUTHWEST

What do you do when you have more customers than wine? More and more wineries are demanding more grapes from farmers who can't just ramp up their operation at the drop of a ten-gallon hat. The solution is to buy grapes from the West Coast and blend them in. Not everyone is doing it, but enough are that it makes sense to ask. The benefit to the consumer of all this rampant growth is that the best wineries in the Southwest are competing hard and producing extremely good wines. Unfortunately, in many cases, the only place you'll find these wines is at the winery. Why? If they sell a $20 bottle, they get $20. If they sell that same bottle through a distributor, they get about $7. So go visit.

Arizona Arizona Stronghold: ★ excellent CHARD, v.gd red blend Nachise. Bitter Creek: v.gd red blend The Fool. Caduceus Cellars: ★ owned by Tool lead singer Maynard James Keenan; top reds Sancha, Anubis, Nagual del la Naga and v.gd rosé VSC GSM. Callaghan V'yds: ★★ one of Arizona's best wineries, esp red blends Back Lot, Caitlin's, Claire's. Dos Cabezas: look for white Meskeoli, red blends La Montaña and Aguileon. Keeling Schaefer V'yds: ★ Best Friends VIOGNIER, Three Sisters SYRAH, GSM blend Partners. Lawrence Dunham V'yds: gd Viognier, v.gd PETITE SIRAH. Page Springs: ★ Rhône-style (r w), plus excellent red blends El Serrano and Ecips, v.gd Dragoon V'yd Rockpile Clone ZIN and La Flor Rosa rosé. Pillsbury Wine Company: ★ filmmaker Sam Pillsbury makes excellent Chard, Petite Sirah. Sand-Reckoner V'yds: v.gd MALVASIA, gd red blend "7". Sonoita V'yds: popular COLOMBARD, v.gd rosé Sonora Rossa.

Becker Vineyards Tex ★★★ Superb collection of interesting wines. Esp CAB SAUV Res Canada Family, Newsom Cab Sauv, VIOGNIER, Res MALBEC, rosé Provençal.

Bending Branch Tex ★ Young winery already producing a number of excellent wines, incl PICPOUL Blanc, PETITE SIRAH, TANNAT, Newsom V'yds CAB SAUV.

Brennan Vineyards Tex ★★ Excellent VIOGNIER, white Rhône blend called Lily; TEMPRANILLO; v.gd CAB SAUV, SYRAH.

> **AVA writ large**
> The largest AVA in the USA is the Upper Mississippi River Valley, est in 2009 and covering 21,914 square miles across four states: Minnesota, Iowa, Wisconsin and Illinois.

Brushy Creek Tex Owned by a nuclear physicist who likes to experiment. Wines change on an annual basis, but Rhône varietals always gd.

Cap Rock Tex ★★→★★★ Much-medalled High Plains winery with remarkable MERLOT and *Roussanne.*

Colorado Bookcliff: ★★ excellent MALBEC, Bordeaux blend Ensemble, v.gd SYRAH, RIES. Boulder Creek: ★★ excellent CAB SAUV, Syrah, v.gd Dry Rosé. Canyon Wind: excellent PETIT VERDOT, MERLOT. Creekside: ★ excellent Syrah, v.gd CHARD. Grande River: SAUV BL, CAB FR, Petit Verdot, Malbec. Guy Drew: ★★★ excellent VIOGNIER, dry RIES from Russell Vyd, unoaked Chard, Metate, Cab Fr. Infinite Monkey Theorem: ★ excellent red blend 100th Monkey, v.gd Petit Verdot and Viognier/ ROUSSANNE Blind Watchmaker White, gd line of canned wines. Jack Rabbit Hill: bio and organic, PINOT GR, M&N. Plum Creek: ★ superb Ries, v.gd Cab Sauv, Merlot. St Kathryn Cellars: huge selection of quality fruit wines, esp Peach. Two Rivers: ★ excellent Syrah, v.gd Chard. Whitewater Hill V'yds: exceptional Cab Fr. Winery at Holy Cross: ★ excellent Cab Fr, v.gd Syrah, Merlot.

Dotson Cervantes Tex ★★ Outstanding dessert wine Gotas de Oro.

Duchman ★★★ Amongst Tex's best; nr-perfect VERMENTINO, TEMPRANILLO, fresh Bianco.

Fall Creek V'yds Tex ★★★ One of Tex's oldest wineries. Gorgeous Salt Lick TEMPRANILLO and GSM, consistently excellent Bordeaux blend Meritus, v.gd Res CHARD, scrumptious off-dry CHENIN BL.

Haak Winery Tex ★★ Gd dry Blanc du Bois; exceptional "Madeira" copies.

Inwood Estates Tex ★★★ Exceptional TEMPRANILLO and v.gd PALOMINO/CHARD blend. Small but outstanding producer.

Llano Estacado Tex ★★→★★★ One of Tex's earliest and largest wineries. Excellent MALBEC. V.gd Viviana (w), Viviano (r).

Lost Oak Tex ★ V.gd VIOGNIER, TEMPRANILLO, gd MERLOT.

McPherson Cellars Tex ★★★ Some of best Rhône-variety wines in state, all at prices. Delicious Les Copains Rosé, excellent Res ROUSSANNE.

Messina Hof Wine Cellars Tex ★ Makes over 60 different wines. Excellent RIES, esp late-harvest. V.gd Papa Paolo Port-style wines.

Nevada Churchill V'yds: gd SÉM/CHARD. Pahrump Valley: v.gd PRIMITIVO, TEMPRANILLO.

Texas has over 50 wine festivals each year. Any excuse for a party?

New Mexico Black Mesa: ★★ Coyote, PINOT N, Woodnymph RIES. Casa Rondeña: 1629, blend of SYRAH, CAB SAUV, TEMPRANILLO *Gruet:* ★★★ excellent sparkling wines, esp Blanc de Noirs, also excellent CHARD, Pinot N. Heart of the Desert: v.gd Syrah, GEWURZ. Luna Rossa: ★ v.gd SHIRAZ, Tempranillo. Noisy Water: ★→★★ excellent Cab Sauv and v.gd Shiraz. Ponderosa Valley: ★ v.gd Chard and off-dry Jemez Red. Southwest Wines: ★★ esp St Clair MALVASIA Bianca and sparkling wines DH Lescombes Brut and St Clair Bellissimo.

Oklahoma Chapel Creek: ★ v.gd MUSCAT, RIES, TEMPRANILLO, Norton. Clauren Ridge: v.gd SYRAH, VIOGNIER. Redbud Ridge: ★ Syrah. Stable Ridge: v.gd Bedlam CHARD. Summerside V'yd: ★ esp v.gd Cream "Sherry". The Range V'yd: gd Jackwagon.

Pedernales Cellars Tex ★★★ Award-winning VIOGNIER Res, excellent TEMPRANILLO, GSM, Viognier and GARNACHA Dry Rosé. MERLOT is bargain of list.

Spicewood Vineyards Tex ★★→★★★ Exceptional Sancerre-like SAUV BL and v.gd SÉM.

William Chris Wines Tex ★★ Widely considered one of Tex's finest. Best buys CAB SAUV "GHV", red blends Emotion and Enchante.

Mexico

The 16th-century Spanish *conquistadors* who overan Mexico liked their daily wine, so it didn't take them long to bring in vines from Spain and kickstart the Mexican wine industry. The first winery, Hacienda San Lorenzo, was established in 1597. It's now called Casa Madero and is still going in the Parras Valley of Central Mexico. The offical wine grape acreage of Mexico is listed at 55,000, but most of those grapes from the nation's centre go for brandy production. Quality wine production is in the coastal valleys of northern Baja, especially the Guadalupe Valley southeast of Tijuana. Although the temperature can reach 38°C/100°F, cooling Pacific winds can drop the temperature by up to 16°C/61°F after sunset. In the past decades, there has been an explosion of boutique wineries, some showing good quality.

Adobe Guadalupe ★★→★★★ Baja star winemaker Hugh Acosta consults here. Wines, blends of Bordeaux varieties and others, are named after angels. V.gd quality in balanced, flavourful wines. Also restaurant, B&B.

Bibayoff Vinos ★★→★★★ Hillside vines are dry-farmed, avoiding salty taste from contaminated irrigation water found in some Baja wines. Outstanding ZIN and v.gd Zin/CAB SAUV blend. Zesty CHENIN BL.

Bodegas Santo Tomas ★★→★★★ Oldest winery in Baja, founded in 1888, has a respectable portfolio of wines. Best offerings: TEMPRANILLO, CAB SAUV, SAUV BL.

Casa de Piedra ★★→★★★ Artisan producer making Vino de Piedra, v.gd blend of CAB SAUV/TEMPRANILLO; Piedra del Sol, CHARD, three sparklers of average quality.

Many 19th-century Baja vineyards were planted by Russian immigrants.

Château Camou ★★→★★★ Top marks to Gran Vino Tinto, velvety, balanced CAB SAUV-based blend, with a supple, elegant finish. Companion wine, Gran Vino Tinto ZIN, is powerful statement of variety.

LA Cetto ★→★★★ Baja's largest winery, est 1928, offers a range from simple quaffs to more complex CAB SAUV. Dry-farmed single-v'yd ZIN is a treat. Don Luis is top of line with v.gd Cab Sauv blend and floral VIOGNIER. Visitor's centre sports a bullring. Eat your heart out, Napa.

Monte Xanic ★★→★★★ Est 1987, Monte Xanic quickly built a reputation for top quality; CAB SAUV is excellent, deeply flavoured with long finish; also v.gd MERLOT. CHENIN BL, with a dash of COLOMBARD, is a delightful apéritif.

Rognato ★★→★★★ A small new winery making excellent CAB SAUV and a super red blend, Tramonte, with layers of flavour and a lasting finish. Wines have potential for ageing.

Tres Mujeres ★★→★★★ Gd example of the new wave of artisan producers in Baja. Excellent TEMPRANILLO; v.gd GRENACHE/CAB SAUV, La Mezcla del Rancho.

Viñas de Garza ★★→★★★ Fine Bordeaux blend, Tinto del Rancho Morgorcito, outstanding CAB SAUV, MERLOT from artisan producer. Also v.gd TEMPRANILLO, ZIN.

Vinisterra ★★ New producer has taken the Rhône route, with the best offering Pedegal, a deeply flavoured blend of SYRAH and MOURVÈDRE.

Canada

It's been a decade of unprecedented growth in Canadian wine, and as young winemakers get down to the business of relating to the terroir in their vineyards the future seems even brighter. At last count there were over 700 licensed wineries from coast to coast, with many now setting up outside the traditional areas of Niagara Peninsula and Okanagan Valley. Although Canada was historically famous for Icewine, modern Canadian wine is mostly dry and fresh, reflecting the country's cool climate. More transparency, less oak, better acidity and more minerality with different blends and grapes all point to a new energy in Canadian wine. In Ontario Chardonnay, Riesling, Pinot Noir and Cabernet Franc lead the way while in British Columbia the stars are Riesling, Pinot Gris, Chardonnay, Pinot Noir, Syrah and red blends. Canadian sparkling wine is another bright spot with some very fine bottles coming out of Nova Scotia.

Ontario

Four appellations of origin, all adjacent to Lakes Ontario and Erie: Niagara Peninsula (Niag), Lake Erie North Shore, Pelee Island, Prince Edward County (P Ed). Niagara Peninsula boasts ten growing areas.

13th Street Niag r w sp ★★ 07' 10' 11 12' 13 Winemaker Jean-Pierre Colas makes critically acclaimed GAMAY, sparkling CHARD, RIES, SAUV BL and SYRAH; best are tagged Old Vines, Res, Essence.

Bachelder Niag r w ★★★ 11 12' 13 Montrealer Thomas Bachelder, ex-LE CLOS JORDANNE; pure, terroir-driven CHARD, PINOT N (purchased fruit, select Niagara sites). Watch.

Cave Spring Niag r w sw sp ★★★ 10' 11 12' 13 Winemaker Angelo Pavan's RIES, esp CSV (old vines) and Estate labels can be unearthly. Elegant, old-vines CHARD, exceptional late-harvest and Icewine.

Château des Charmes Niag r w sw ★★ 10' 11 12' 13 The 114 ha Bosc family farm is a charter member of Sustainable Winegrowing Ontario; RIES from bone-dry to Icewine, sparkling and Equuleus flagship red blend.

Clos Jordanne, Le Niag r w ★★★ 09 10' 11' 12' 13 Burgundian-born Sebastien Jacquey makes elegant, organic CHARD and PINOT N in three tiers: Village Res, Single V'yd and select parcel Le Grand Clos.

Creekside Niag r w ★★ 10 11 12' 13 Gd buzz for Broken Press and Res SHIRAZ, red blends, CHARD, excellent SAUV BL; NB organic, single-barrel Undercurrent lots.

Flat Rock Niag r w ★★ 11 12' 13 14 32 ha on Twenty Mile Bench yields modern, crisp, screwcap RIES, PINOT N, CHARD. Top: Single-block Nadja's Ries, Rusty Shed Chard.

Henry of Pelham Niag r w sw sp ★★ 10' 11 12' 13 14 Speck brothers Paul, Matt, Daniel make CHARD, RIES; Exceptional Cuvée Catherine Brut fizz, Speck Family Res (SFR), unique Baco Noir, Ries Icewine.

Canadians drink over 1 billion glasses (220 million bottles) of Canadian wine/year.

Hidden Bench Niag r w ★★★★ 10' 11 12' 13 14 Less is more at this 40 ha, artisanal Beamsville Bench producer. Outstanding Felseck: RIES, PINOT N, CHARD and signature Nuit Blanche white blend.

Inniskillin Niag r w sw ★★ 11 12' 13 14 Canada's Icewine pioneer is evolving under winemaker Bruce Nicholson. Tasty Res RIES, PINOT GR, PINOT N, super CAB FR; amazing Ries, VIDAL Icewine.

Malivoire Niag r w ★★★ 11 12' 13 14 Eco-friendly Shiraz Mottiar; four Niagara Escarpment v'yds. Excellent Tête de Cuvée GAMAY, CHARD; tasty PINOT N, GEWURZ.

Norman Hardie P Ed r w ★★★★ 10' 11' 12' 13 14 Iconic P Ed pioneer hand-crafting burgundian-style CHARD, PINOT N, v.gd RIES. Cuvée L Chard, Pinot N in best yrs.

Pearl Morissette Niag r w ★★ 10' 11 12' 13 14 François Morissette (winemaker/partner) trained under Frédéric Mugnier (*see* France) makes original RIES aged in *foudre*, CHARD, CAB FR, PINOT N with concrete eggs and *foudres*.

Ravine Vineyard Niag r w ★★★ 10' 11 12' 13 14 Organic 14 ha St David's Bench v'yd spans early Niagara River watercourse circa 1869. Top Res CHARD and CAB FR; drink-now labels are Sand and Gravel.

Stratus Niag r w ★★★ 10' 11 12' 13 14 Iconoclast JL Groux works 25 ha of Niagara Lakeshore fruit at the LEEDS-certified (ie. green) winery where blends (r w) are king; plus v.gd RIES, SYRAH.

Tawse Niag r w ★★★★ 10' 11 12' 13 14 Gold standard in eco–friendly wine production. Outstanding CHARD, RIES, high-quality PINOT N, CAB FR, MERLOT; v'yds organic and bio.

Vineland Niag r w sw ★★★ 10' 11 12' 13 14 Niagara Escarpment; 1st-class restaurant. Legacy of v. fine RIES, Icewine. Other top picks incl Res SAUV BL, CAB FR, Meritage.

British Columbia

BC has identified five appellations of origin: Okanagan Valley (Ok V), Similkameen Valley, Fraser Valley, Vancouver Island and the Gulf Islands.

Blue Mountain Ok V r w sp ★★★★ 11 12 13 (14') Matt and Christy Mavety bring next-generation energy to a sparkling programme; age-worthy PINOT N, CHARD, PINOT GR. Outstanding Res PINOT N.

Burrowing Owl Ok V r w ★★ 11 12 13 (14') Pioneer s Ok V estate; excellent CAB FR, v.gd PINOT GR, SYRAH on Black Sage Bench; acclaimed boutique hotel and restaurant.

CedarCreek Ok V r w ★★★ 11 12' 13 (14') Terrific low-alcohol aromatic RIES, GEWURZ, EHRENFELSER. High-quality PINOT N, CHARD. Platinum labels: top single-v'yd blocks.

Church & State Wines Ok V r w ★★ 11 12' 13 (14') Stylish Coyote Bowl winery in South Ok V making delicious blends Tre Bella (Rhône white), Quintessential (Bordeaux red); excellent CHARD, VIOGNIER, SYRAH.

Hester Creek Ok V r w ★★ 11 12 13 (14') Electric TREBBIANO (40-yr-old vines); flagship red blend The Judge. Aromatic PINOT GR, PINOT BL, CAB FR. Guest villa, restaurant.

Mission Hill Ok V r w ★★★ 10 11 12' 13 (14') V.gd Res varietals, esp RIES. Top Legacy series: Oculus, Perpetua, Quatrain, Compendium. Visitor centre, al fresco dining.

Nk'Mip Ok V r w ★★★ 11 12' 13 (14') Dependable quality PINOT BL, RIES, PINOT N; top-end Qwam Qwmt Pinot N, SYRAH. Part of $25 million aboriginal resort with must-see Desert Cultural Centre.

Osoyoos Larose Ok V r ★★★ 07 08 09' 10 11 12' 13 Bordeaux-based Groupe Taillan operates benchmark, 33 ha single v'yd; Top label age-worthy Le Grand Vin and earlier-drinking Pétales d'Osoyoos.

Painted Rock Ok V r w ★★★ 11 12' 13 (14') Steep-sloped Skaha Bench site; guided by Bordelais consultant Alain Sutre, v.gd SYRAH, CHARD, signature red blend Icon.

Pentâge Winery Ok V r w ★★ 12' 13 (14') 5,000-case Skaha Bench producer making fine VIOGNIER, PINOT GR, GEWURZ, Rhône-style blends (r w).

Quails' Gate Ok V r w ★★ 12' 13 (14') Winemaker Nikki Callaway has transformed Quails' Gate, mixing fruit, complexity. Excellent PINOT N, CHARD, aromatic RIES, CHENIN BL, cult-like Old-Vines Foch.

Red Rooster Ok V r w ★★ 11 12' 13 (14') Signature is fresh, aromatic Naramata Bench wines. Top value picks: CHARD, PINOT GR, RIES. Impressive Res CHARD.

Road 13 Ok V r w ★★★ 11 12' 13 (14') Winemaker JM Bouchard all about site-specific wine, selective use of oak. Premium tier led by CHENIN BL, VIOGNIER, SYRAH, PINOT N.

Stag's Hollow Ok V ★★★ 12' 13 (14') Winemaker Dwight Sick exploring new heights mid-valley in Okanagan Falls with delicious VIOGNIER, GRENACHE, PINOT N, SYRAH.

Tantalus Ok V r w ★★★★ 10 11 12' 13 (14') "New pioneers"; terroir-driven PINOT N, RIES, CHARD from oldest (1927) continuously producing Ok V v'yds.

South America

Abbreviations used in the text:

Aco	Aconcagua
Bío	Bío-Bío
Cach	Cachapoal
Casa	Casablanca
Cata	Catamarca
Cho	Choapa
Col	Colchagua
Coq	Coquimbo
Cur	Curicó
Elq	Elqui
Ita	Itata
La R	La Rioja
Ley	Leyda
Lim	Limarí
Mai	Maipo
Mal	Malleco
Mau	Maule
Men	Mendoza
Neu	Neuquén
Pat	Patagonia
Rap	Rapel
Río N	Río Negro
Sal	Salta
San A	San Antonio
San J	San Juan

Chile

The vinous map of Chile keeps changing. New vineyards near the Pacific coast, stretching from the Atacama Desert south to Itata are now producing fresh and racy Sauvignon Blanc, mineral-sharp Chardonnay, light and juicy Pinot Noir, and Syrah aromatic in Northern Rhône style. In the Central Valleys, traditional ripe and round wines are still eager to please, but you'll find new Mediterranean varieties like Grenache and Mourvèdre popping up too. This is also home to Chile's old-vine renaissance with Carignan, Malbec and even the rustic País being given their chance. On the eastern edge of Chile, vineyards are creeping higher and higher into the Andes Mountains where winemakers are looking at altitude to bring a new backbone to Chilean wine. Makers are reminding themselves that Chilean wine had personality before the oak/alcohol invasion.

Recent vintages

While still steady compared to European vintages, vintage variation is becoming more evident, especially in newer or more extreme wine regions. Vibrant fruit with good concentration is always the wow factor in South American wines, making even the youngest vintages very drinkable, but top reds need four to six years cellaring to reach their prime.

Aconcagua Traditionally home to big reds, new coastal plantations have the freshest appeal. SYRAH has star quality.

Almaviva Mai ★★★★ CONCHA Y TORO/Baron Philippe de Rothschild joint venture. Handsome – and handsomely priced – Bordeaux-style blend (mainly CAB SAUV).

Altaïr Wines Rap ★★★ Complex, precise red blend; recent vintages use less oak. Second label, Sideral, is easier drinking. Pascal Chatonnet of Bordeaux consults.

Antiyal Mai ★★→★★★ Elegant garage wines from bio specialist Alvaro Espinoza. Complex red blends of CARMENÈRE, CAB SAUV, SYRAH, PETIT VERDOT. Plus pure single-v'yd Carmenère.

Syrah is one of Chile's hottest trends, growing by almost 30% over the last 5 years.

Apaltagua ★★→★★★ Large, recently diversified portfolio from coast and Central Valley. Gd CARMENÈRE, PINOT N; value RIES.

Aquitania, Viña Mai ★★★ Sol fa Sol range has excellent CHARD, PINOT N. Chilean/ French joint venture also makes v.gd aged Lazuli CAB SAUV from Quebrada de Macul. Also small-production sparkling.

Arboleda, Viña Aco ★★ Part of the ERRÁZURIZ/CALITERRA stable; v'yds from ACO coast to Andes. Fresh SAUV BL, rich CHARD, concentrated reds.

Aristos Cach, Mai ★★★ Chileans François Massoc and Pedro Parra join Burgundian Liger-Belair (*see* France) to reinvent Cach with three must-try wines: rich, mineral Duquesa CHARD; classy Duque CAB SAUV; Baron Cab/MERLOT/SYRAH.

Bío-Bío Historic s region again rising to fame, cool enough for crisp RIES, GEWURZ, PINOT N, CHARD. Promising for fizz.

Botalcura Cur ★★ Frenchman Philippe Debrus makes big reds, incl NEBBIOLO. Try young, cheap Porfia G Res MALBEC.

Caliboro Mau ★★★ Francesco Marone Cinzano is soul of Erasmo, a refined CAB SAUV/ CAB FR/MERLOT/SYRAH blend, and a rare Torontel (MUSCAT family) Late Harvest.

Caliterra Casa, Col, Cur, Ley ★→★★ Sister winery of ERRÁZURIZ, focus on organic and sustainable farming. Gd-value whites, simple, juicy reds. Try flagship red Cenit.

Calyptra Cach ★★★ French-Chilean François Massoc makes excellent Zahir CAB SAUV, Gran Res CHARD and complex barrel-aged SAUV BL. Top Cach producer.

Carmen, Viña Casa, Col, Elq, Mai ★★→★★★ Organic pioneer; keen on CARMENÈRE. Ripe, fresh CASA CHARD Special Res; v.gd PETITE SIRAH, MERLOT, top Chilean CAB SAUV Gold Res.

Casablanca Casa Pioneering cool-climate region now in great demand: most wineries seek a Casa in their portfolio, esp CHARD, SAUV BL, PINOT N, SYRAH.

Casa Marín San A ★★★ Single-v'yd specialist with v'yds up to 4 km from coast. V.gd RIES, GEWURZ, PINOT GR, SAUV BL, late-harvest, nobly rotten RIES. Most known for its whites, but don't miss excellent Miramar SYRAH.

Casas del Bosque Casa, Mai ★★→★★★ Resident NZ winemaker; excellent SAUV BL (try Gran Res), SYRAH (Gran Res) from one of coolest parts of CASA. V.gd CHARD.

Casa Silva Col, S Regions ★★→★★★ Traditional Col family winery with big reds (v.gd CARMENÈRE) and fresher coastal whites from Paredones. Interesting PINOT N, CHARD from Chile's s-most region, Lake Ranco. Try Col SAUVIGNON Gris too.

Clos des Fous Cach, Casa, S Regions ★★→★★★ Terroir hunters, minimal-intervention winemaking. Excellent CAB SAUV/CARIGNAN-based blend; PINOT N.

Clos Ouvert Mau ★★ Frenchman Louis Antoine Luyt making "natural" wines. Focus on Chile's oddball varieties like PAÍS, CARIGNAN, CINSAULT.

Concha y Toro Central V ★→★★★★ Leading Chile in volume, category and

CHILE

Rise of Riesling

Chilean RIES used to be blowsy, but plantings in cooler zones have moved it from softly spoken to sharp tongued. Exemplary Ries is coming from coastal plantations and in s regions like BÍO. Try CASA MARÍN, Terrunyo (CONCHA Y TORO), CONO SUR, Lafken, MATETIC, Meli.

> **Cabernet with chords**
> Winemaker and music nut Juan Ledesma has been making musical
> wines in MAU and ITA for three vintages by submerging speakers into
> barrels. Consumer tastings suggest it has worked; the cynical can judge
> for themselves as the wines become available this yr.

recognition; it would take months to try the full portfolio. Don't miss Terrunyo
range for top-notch SAUV BL, v.gd RIES, CAB SAUV, CARMENÈRE, SYRAH; classic Cab
Sauv *Marques de Casa Concha* (Puente Alto) and *Don Melchor* (MAI). Also Icon
Carmenère Carmín (Peumo), subtle CHARD Amelia (CASA), remarkable Maycas
Chard and PINOT N (LIM), Series Riberas MALBEC (Col). Plus varietals and blends
Trio and Casillero del Diablo. *See also* ALMAVIVA, TRIVENTO (Argentina).

Cono Sur Casa, Col, Bio ★★→★★★ PINOT N specialist delivering value at all price
points (try 20 Barrels and top Ocio). Also v.gd CAB SAUV, RIES, late-harvest Ries.
Ocio Pinot N is top, along with new Silencio Cab Sauv. Try Single V'yds, and
Bicicleta for gd-value weekday wine.

Cousiño Macul Mai ★★→★★★ Historic Santiago winery. Reliable Antiguas Res
MERLOT; zesty SAUVIGNON Gris; top-of-range Lota is still one of top blends in Chile.

De Martino Cach, Casa, Elq, Mai, Mau, Ita ★★→★★★ Pioneering minimal-
intervention winemaking, using amphorae and no new oak. Excellent SYRAH
from 2,000m v'yd in ELQ; v.gd MUSCAT and CINSAULT from old vines in low-altitude
ITA. Legado single-v'yd range for classic CAB SAUV, CHARD, CARMENÈRE, Syrah,
MERLOT, SAUV BL from top sites around the country.

Elqui Extreme and dry n region with sea breeze at low altitude (350m) and cool
temperatures at high altitude (up to 2,200m, Chile's highest). Brilliant SYRAH,
v.gd SAUV BL, interesting PX (better known for Pisco). Astounding star gazing.

Chilean vineyard workers must be supplied with factor-30 sun cream, by law.

Emiliana Casa, Rap, Bio ★→★★★ Organic/bio specialist involving Alvaro
Espinoza (*see* ANTIYAL, Geo Wines). Complex, SYRAH-heavy G and Coyam show
almost Mediterranean-style wildness; cheaper Adobe, Novas ranges v.gd for
affordable complexity.

Errázuriz Aco, Casa ★★→★★★ Pioneer in ACO coastal region, now making
impressive wild-ferment wines (PINOT N, SAUV BL, CHARD, SYRAH). Rich and fragrant
top wines (Don Maximiliano, KAI), gd GRENACHE-based blend. *See also* ARBOLEDA,
CALITERRA, SEÑA, VIÑEDO CHADWICK.

Falernia, Viña Elq ★★→★★★ Intrepid Italian cousins, first commercial producer in
ELQ. Excellent Rhône-like SYRAH, herbaceous SAUV BL, complex reds, uncommon
PX. Labels incl Alta Tierra, Mayu.

Fournier, Bodegas O Ley, Mau ★★→★★★ Old v'yds in MAU cooled by Maule River.
V.gd red blends, CARIGNAN from Mau, top Ley SAUV BL. Small, Spanish-owned.

Garcés Silva, Viña San A ★★→★★★ The brand at this no-expense-spared operation
is Amayna; rich, ripe styles, a bit of alcohol removed for balance. SAUV BL
particularly gd.

García & Schwaderer Casa, Mau ★★ Young husband-and-wife winemakers,
exciting CASA (PINOT N, SAUV BL, SYRAH), aromatic CARIGNAN from MAU. Part of the
independent vintners movement (MOVI).

Hacienda Araucano Casa, Rap ★★→★★★ Bordeaux winemaker François Lurton's
outpost in Chile. Gran Lurton is elegant CAB SAUV, Alka top CARMENÈRE, Humo
Blanco excellent PINOT N. V.gd SAUV BL and red blends.

Haras de Pirque Mai ★★→★★★ Estate in Pirque. Character SYRAH is top, also smoky
SAUV BL, stylish CHARD, dense CAB SAUV/MERLOT. Solid red Albis (Cab Sauv/
CARMENÈRE) made with Antinori (*see* Italy).

Itata A s region being rediscovered. Rolling hillsides and some of the oldest vines in the Americas. Gd for CINSAULT, PAÍS, MUSCAT.

Lapostolle Cach, Casa, Col ★★→★★★★ Stunning bio estate in Col owned by Grand Marnier family. Rich reds, esp lush CARMENÈRE-based Clos Apalta; decisive whites (CHARD, SAUV BL). New Collection range (SYRAH, Carmenère) offers fresher interpretations from all over country. Cool Pisco from ELQ too.

Leyda, Viña Col, Mai, San A ★★→★★★ Brought the eponymous region to the limelight. Zesty and concentrated coastal whites (CHARD, SAUV BL, Sauv Gris), spicy SYRAH, juicy PINOT N (also lively rosé), gd sparkling. Try Lot range.

Limarí Between cactus plants lie v'yds in this young, arid coastal region. Limestone gives particularity to wines. Try CHARD, SAUV BL, SYRAH.

Loma Larga Casa ★★→★★★ Top Chilean MALBEC, v. different from Argentine versions; the Pacific makes the difference. Impressive CAB FR (also rosé), SYRAH.

Maipo Renowned historic region, home to some of both best and most mediocre wines of Chile. Now planting further onto hillsides. Excellent CAB SAUV from Pirque and Puente Alto.

Matetic Casa, San A ★★★ Julio Bastías is now at the helm of this bio estate straddling CASA and SAN A. Superb SYRAH, *v.gd Sauv Bl* and PINOT N. Consistent quality.

Maule One of the 1st and most widely planted regions on s tip of Central Valley. Best for old-vine CARIGNAN and PAÍS. Look for the subregions of Loncomilla and Cauquenes.

Maycas del Limarí Lim ★★→★★★ CONCHA Y TORO winemaker Marcelo Papa's passion project for company. Mineral coastal wines (v.gd SAUV BL, CHARD, PINOT N, SYRAH).

Montes Casa, Col, Cur, Ley ★★→★★★★ Feng-shui in the v'yds, angels in the cellar. Intense, complex reds (Alpha CAB SAUV, *Folly Syrah*, Purple Angel CARMENÈRE) are complemented by fresher coastal wines incl v.gd Outer Limits range (SAUV BL, PINOT N) from Zapallar and CINSAULT from ITA.

MontGras Col, Ley, Mai ★★→★★★ Fine limited-edition wines, incl SYRAH and pink ZIN. High-class flagships Ninquén CAB SAUV, Antu Ninquén SYRAH. Gd-value organic Soleus, excellent Amaral SAUV BL, CHARD from Ley

Montsecano Casa ★★★ Cool, high-altitude, small-scale, bio PINOT N made by five Chileans and Frenchman André Ostertag. Top stuff.

Morandé Casa, Mai, Mau ★★→★★★ Large producer, impressive portfolio. Skip the classics and head to Limited Edition CARIGNAN, Vigno, Gran Res (esp PINOT N) and 30 months on the lees Brut Nature NV (CHARD, Pinot N) sparkling.

Neyen Rap ★★★ Apalta project for Patrick Valette of Bordeaux; intense old-vine CARMENÈRE/CAB SAUV. Owned by VERAMONTE.

Odfjell Mai, Mau ★→★★★ French winemaker Arnaud Hereu produces v.gd red blends and single varieties incl excellent CARIGNAN from MAU.

Pérez Cruz, Viña Mai ★★★ Interesting Chaski PETIT VERDOT; Edición Limitada COT; balanced, classic Waiki CAB SAUV.

Polkura Col ★★ Independent and focused on Marchigue SYRAH; also rich MALBEC.

Quebrada de Macul, Viña Mai ★★→★★★ Ambitious winery making gd CHARD, plus excellent Domus Aurea, one of most elegant, classic CAB SAUVs from Chile.

Rapel Large, traditional Central Valley region mainly known for Col and Cach Valleys: busty reds, esp quality CARMENÈRE and SYRAH. New plantings towards the cooler coast and higher in the Andes.

> **Itata: where it's at**
> Interested in old vines (some up to 200 yrs), cool conditions with plenty of water and forgotten varieties? ITA in the far s is your region. It is home to mainly small producers, but with TORRES buying up 230 ha last yr, the big guns might be moving in.

CHILE

> **Mountains to coast**
> Chile's appellation system is split in three: Costa (Coastal), Entre Valles (Central Valley) and Andes. Classifying climates e to w (and not n to s) makes sense because Andes wines have altitude influence; Entre Valles has warmer, continental climate; Costa has cool, maritime influence.

RE Mai ★★★ Pablo Morandé Jnr: "natural" wines, clay amphorae, offbeat blends and orange wines. Unorthodox and exciting for Chile.

Ribera del Lago Mau Amazing young SAUV BL from clay soil, and Laberinto PINOT N.

San Antonio San A Large coastal region neighbouring CASA. Cooling sea breezes and dry conditions make for excellent whites; v.gd PINOT N, SYRAH. Ley is subregion.

San Pedro Cur ★→★★★ Massive Cur-based producer. 35 South (35 Sur) and Castillo de Molina are affordable, everyday wines. Best are 1865 Limited Edition reds, ELQ, SYRAH, elegant Cabo de Hornos. Same ownership as ALTAÏR, VIÑA MAR, Missiones de Rengo, Santa Helena, TARAPACÁ.

Santa Carolina, Viña ★★→★★★ Large, traditional brand with a few ventures into the less explored. Try Specialities range, esp MOURVÈDRE, CARIGNAN. Top wines are pricey but excellent Herencia (Carmenère) and VSC.

Santa Rita Mai ★★→★★★★ Large, historical MAI winery, big portfolio from around country. Try new Bougainville PETITE SIRAH, *Casa Real Cab Sauv* for classic richness, Pehuèn CARMENÈRE, Triple C (CAB SAUV/CAB FR/Carmenère), Floresta range, gd-value Medalla Real CHARD.

Seña Aco ★★★★ Originally combined effort with Robert Mondavi, now Chadwick family (ERRÁZURIZ). Seña, Bordeaux-style blend from ACO hillsides. One of best.

Tabalí ★★→★★★ Winemaker Felipe Müller has led way in refined cool-climate styles with single-v'yd range from limestone in LIM. Top CHARD, SAUV BL, PINOT N, SYRAH.

Tarapacá, Viña Casa, Ley, Mai ★★ Steadily improving historic winery, part of VSPT group. Top: Tara-Pakay (CAB SAUV/SYRAH), Etiqueta Negra Gran Res (Cab Sauv).

Torres, Miguel Cur ★★→★★★★ Spanish winemaker Miguel Torres pioneered this region in 80s; now rehabilitating the long overlooked PAÍS grape, among other efforts. Fresh whites from ITA, v.gd single-v'yd reds (esp terrific CAB *Manso de Velasco*), Beaujolais-style País (Res de Pueblo), pretty pink sparkling País Estelado.

Undurraga Casa, Ley, Lim, Mai ★→★★★ With one of the youngest head winemaker in Chile, Rafael Urrejola's TH (Terroir Hunter) range shook off Undurraga's previously dowdy image. Also try top CAB SAUV and plethora of party fizz.

Valdivieso Cur, San A ★→★★★ Major producer impressing with Res and Single V'yd range (esp CAB FR, MALBEC) from top terroirs around Chile (*Ley Chard* esp gd). V.gd sparkling NV red blend Caballo Loco, wonderful CARIGNAN-based Éclat.

Vascos, Los Rap ★→★★★ Lafite-Rothschild venture trying hard to improve its Bordeaux wannabe reds. Top: Le Dix, Grande Res.

Pipeño – young, fruity País, standard drink until 80s, trendy again in Santiago bars

Ventisquero, Viña Casa, Col, Mai ★→★★★ Ambitious winery named after a hanging glacier; most recent releases in Tara range from Chile's n-most plantings in Atacama region. Excellent Kalfu Sumpai SYRAH (Ley); try Enclave CAB SAUV (MAI).

Veramonte Casa, Col ★★ Ripe but elegant reds from Col (Primus blend is pick), fresher styles from CASA, where Ritual PINOT N, Res SAUV BL stand out.

Villard Casa, Mai ★★ Sophisticated wines made by French-born Thierry Villard. Gd MAI reds, esp PINOT N, MERLOT, Equis CAB SAUV, CASA whites.

Viñedo Chadwick Mai ★★★→★★★★ Stylish CAB SAUV improving with each vintage from v'yd owned by Eduardo Chadwick, president of ERRÁZURIZ.

Viu Manent Casa, Col ★★ MALBEC specialist (totally different from Argentine Malbec), lots more to offer. Top CARMENÈRE-based El Incidente, zesty SAUV BL from CASA.

ARGENTINA

Argentina has had a good run. Originality, simplicity (it's Malbec, dummy) and strength have made its wines recognizable and memorable – if not subtle. It seems you can't stop Malbec: it's all over the country from north to south. But there are a couple of other horses entering the race: Cabernet Sauvignon and Bonarda have long been closing in on Malbec, but it is actually Cabernet Franc that is creating a buzz for its seductively spicy characteristics and impressive body. Petit Verdot too. And then there are the whites: bold Chardonnay, spicy Torrontés and tropical Sauvignon Blanc leading the line. Where are its style-leaders going? Mainly uphill, for lower temperatures, precious cooler nights above all, and even possibly less alcohol.

Achaval Ferrer Men ★★★ MALBEC specialist using old vines for single-v'yd Altamira (Uco Valley), Bella Vista (Luján de Cuyo) and Mirador (Maipú) wines.

Aleanna Men ★★→★★★★ Break-away project from CATENA winemaker Alejandro Vigil and Adrianna Catena. Concentrated MALBEC, BONARDA, CHARD and excellent single-v'yd CAB FR under Enemigo and Gran Enemigo labels.

Alta Vista Men ★→★★★ The 1st to focus on single-v'yd wines; French-owned winery produces v.gd MALBEC, TORRONTÉS, sparkling and top *Alto* blend (Malbec/CAB SAUV).

Altocedro Men ★→★★★ Small red wine producer in La Consulta (Uco Valley). Karim Mussi makes excellent TEMPRANILLO, v.gd MALBEC and blends.

Altos las Hormigas Men ★★★ Terroir experts from Italy and Chile unite for top single-v'yd MALBECS (Appellation range), gd-value BONARDA, new sparkling Bonarda.

Antucura Men ★★→★★★ PAÍS with Michel Rolland (*see* France): boutique project focuses on Bordeaux varieties and big blends plus younger Barrandica range.

Atamisque Men ★→★★★ French-owned project with a massive estate in Uco Valley. Excellent-value reds (esp blends), v.gd CHARD, PINOT N, VIOGNIER in Catalpa, and Serbal range too.

Benegas Men ★★→★★★★ Old World-style producer in historic MEN winery; old vines for top-notch CAB FR and Meritage Benegas Lynch label. Interesting SANGIOVESE.

Bressia Men ★★→★★★ Top red blends Profundo, Conjuro, latest Última Hoja. V.gd Monteagrelo range, Lágrima Canela (CHARD/SÉM). New everyday Sylvestra range.

Callia San J ★→★★ Gd-value wines based on SYRAH in hotter SAN J region.

Canale, Bodegas Humberto Rio N ★→★★★ One of oldest wineries in Patagonia, with traditional varieties and v.gd old-vine RIES.

Carmelo Patti Men ★★ Garage winemaker Carmelo has been turning out gd CAB SAUV, MALBEC for over 20 yrs.

Caro Men ★★★★ Means "expensive" in Spanish, fittingly: joint venture by CATENA and Rothschilds of Lafite (France): seriously classy Caro and younger Amancaya.

Casa Bianchi Men ★→★★★ V. traditional winery and sparkling producer in San Rafael. Gd value. Look for Leo brand, joint venture with Lionel Messi's Foundation.

Casarena Men ★★→★★★ Luján-based producer with v.gd single-v'yd MALBEC, CAB FR; value reds. Also traditional-method cider.

Catena Zapata, Bodega Men ★★→★★★★ One of biggest and best-known wineries. Pioneered premium MALBECS 20 yrs ago. Ranges from entry-level Alamos to high-end Catena Alta. Two excellent (and expensive) CHARDS from Gualtallary (White Stones, White Bones); flagship top-end Malbec (Argentino) and blend (Nicolas Catena Zapata) still make the running.

Chacra Rio N ★★★ *Superb Pinot N* from old vines and tiny bodega owned by Piero Incisa della Rocchetta of Sassicaia (*see* Italy), top Treinta y Dos from 1932 v'yd; also lush but light Mainqué MERLOT.

Clos de los Siete Men ★★ Consistent Vistaflores (Uco Valley) blend of MALBEC,

MERLOT, SYRAH, CAB SAUV; winemaking overseen by Michel Rolland (*see* DIAMANDES and MONTEVIEJO).

Cobos, Viña Men ★★★ Flying winemaker Paul Hobbs and Marchiori & Barraud (check out own label): concentrated wines. Hobbs' CAB SAUV stands out (top Volturno, premium Bramare, entry-level Felino). V.gd MALBEC from old Marchiori v'yd.

Colomé, Bodega Sal ★★ →★★★ Seriously high-altitude wines: up to 3,100m in the Calchaquí Valley. Intense MALBEC-based reds, lively TORRONTÉS, smoky TANNAT. Owned by California's Hess Collection.

Decero, Finca Men ★★ →★★★ Lush but modern. Go for PETIT VERDOT, blended Amano.

DiamAndes Men ★★ One of CLOS DE LOS SIETE wineries, owned by Bonnie family of Château Malartic-Lagravière (Bordeaux), making solid, meaty Gran Res (MALBEC/CAB SAUV); lively VIOGNIER, CHARD; young Malbec.

Dominio del Plata Men ★★ →★★★ Susana Balbo is queen of TORRONTÉS, but try v.gd Ben Marco, Signature CAB SAUV, Nosotros MALBEC. Entry-level Crios is gd value.

Doña Paula Men ★ →★★★ Consistent and well-made wines from SANTA RITA (*see* Chile) group. Surprising RIES, v.gd single-v'yd MALBECS (Parcel range), appealing blends, new sparkling SAUV BL.

Etchart Sal ★★ Traditional, high-altitude producer. Top TORRONTÉS, gd Arnaldo B red blend. Try late-harvest Torrontés.

Fabre Montmayou Men, Rio N ★★ →★★★ French-owned, started in 90s, bought old v'yds in Luján de Cuyo, RÍO N (Infinitus); gd second label Phebus; also gd-value Viñalba, top MALBEC, CAB SAUV, Grand Vin.

Fin del Mundo, Bodega Del ★ →★★★ Big producer in Neu. Entry-level Postales, Ventus, Newen gd value. Top is Special blend; try single-v'yd Fin range (esp CAB FR).

Flichman, Finca Men ★★ →★★★ Traditional winery owned by Sogrape (*see* Portugal). Impressive SYRAH; try Dedicado, Paisaje blends. Top MALBEC Parcela 26 (Uco Valley).

Fournier, O Men ★ →★★★ Avant-garde winery in Uco Valley. TEMPRANILLO specialist (excellent Alfa Crux blend); try v.gd Urban Uco entry-level range and B Crux (esp SAUV BL). Fantastic winery restaurant. Spanish-owned; *see* Chile.

Kaikén Men ★★ →★★★ Owned by Montes (*see* Chile); top Mai MALBEC, also Ultra CAB SAUV and Malbec, Corte blend.

La Anita, Finca Men ★★ →★★★ High-class reds, esp Varúa CAB SAUV. Gd SYRAH, MALBEC, MERLOT; intriguing whites (FRIULANO, SÉM).

La Riojana La R★ →★★ Big Fairtrade producer. *Raza Ltd Edition Malbec* is top wine, but quality, value at all levels, esp TORRONTÉS.

Las Moras, Finca San J ★ →★★★ Big SAN J producer; v.gd SYRAH, gd-value entry-level lines. Top is MALBEC/BONARDA Mora Negra blend.

Luca / Tikal / Tahuan / Alma Negra Men ★★ →★★★ Family of boutique wineries owned by Nicolas CATENA's children Laura (Luca) and Ernesto (Tikal/Tahuan/Alma Negra). Excellent red blends, v.gd sparkling, sophisticated PINOT N.

Luigi Bosca Men ★★ →★★★ Large, traditional producer with wide range. Try top blend Icono (MALBEC/CAB SAUV), old-vine Finca Los Nobles field blends, v.gd Gran PINOT N and RIES. Finca La Linda range a classic.

Manos Negras Men ★★ Terroir series making site-specific wines across Argentina and Chile. V.gd MALBEC, PINOT N and TORRONTÉS. TeHo, ZaHa are related labels.

Marcelo Pelleriti Men ★★ →★★★ MONTEVIEJO winemaker's own label. Concentrated MALBEC, textural TORRONTÉS. Abremundos label: floral Malbec/CAB FR blends.

Chalk it up

Chalk is flavour of the month in MEN. Terroir studies and umpteen test pits have led Argentine winemakers to the conclusion that the best soil for MALBEC is calcareous. It's found esp in the Uco Valley, and resulting wines are often elegant, linear and will soon be v. expensive.

Masi Tupungato Men ★★→★★★ Masi (Valpolicella; *see* Italy) heads s. Passo Doble is fine *ripasso*-style MALBEC/CORVINA/MERLOT blend; Corbec is even better Amarone lookalike (Corvina/Malbec).

Matias Riccitelli Men ★★→★★★ Boutique winery makes linear single-v'yd MALBEC and gd-value varieties in Apple Doesn't Fall Far From The Tree range.

Mendel Men ★★★ Admired winemaker Roberto de la Motta makes top MALBECS (Finca Remota) and attractive Unus blend. Classy SÉM from 70-yr-old vines, and gd Lunta (Malbec, TORRONTÉS, TEMPRANILLO).

Mendoza Produces three-quarters of Argentina's wine. Divided between warmer, historic Maipú; traditional Luján de Cuyo; and high-altitude Uco Valley (incl Gualtallary, Altamira, La Consulta).

Pre-Colombian technology: Mendoza's irrigation channels were built by Huarpe people, pre-1500s.

Michel Torino Sal ★★ Historic and big Cafayate producer. Gd table wine, and finer wines under El Esteco brand (try Fincas Notables CAB SAUV).

Moët-Hennessy Argentina Men ★→★★★ Original foreign investors in Argentina. Chandon is party fizz; also traditional-method Baron B. *See* TERRAZAS DE LOS ANDES.

Monteviejo Men ★★→★★★★ Flagship winery of CLOS DE LOS SIETE estate. Superb, tiny La Violeta; Lindaflor MALBEC; v.gd Lindaflor CHARD. V.gd-value Petite Fleur range.

Nieto Senetiner, Bodegas Men ★→★★ Wide portfolio with gd-value wines in Nieto range and more concentrated Cadus range. Top BONARDA and gd sparklings.

Noemia ★★★→★★★★ Outstanding Patagonian old-vine, terroir-driven MALBEC. Also J Alberto, A Lisa (incl rosé), stylish Bordeaux blend "2" (CAB SAUV/MERLOT).

Norton, Bodega Men ★→★★★ Traditional winery, classic style and consistency. Gd-value entry-level wines, excellent single-v'yd MALBEC Lot range, top Gernot Lange blend. Lots of v.gd sparkling.

Passionate Wine Men ★★→★★★ Fresher styles and earlier harvesting in the ripe world of MEN. Sharp Agua de Roca SAUV BL, vibrant PINOT N, fresh BONARDA.

Peñaflor Men ★→★★★ Argentina's biggest wine group, incl FINCA LAS MORAS, AndLuar V'yds (SAN J), MICHEL TORINO (SAL), Santa Ana, TRAPICHE (MEN).

Piatelli Sal ★→★★ Two properties in Cafayate, MEN. Oaked TORRONTÉS, modern reds.

Piedra Negra Men ★→★★★ French winemaker François Lurton's MEN winery making classy and gd-value wines. Top is Piedra Negra MALBEC. Try aromatic whites Corte FRIULANO and PINOT GRIGIO.

Poesia Men ★★→★★★ Same owner as Clos l'Église, Bordeaux; dedicated to reds. Stylish, mouthfilling Poesia (CAB SAUV/MALBEC); fine Clos des Andes (Malbec); juicy Pasodoble Malbec/SYRAH/Cab Sauv.

Porvenir de Cafayate, El Sal ★★→★★★ Young Cafayate estate with juicy, oaky Laborum varietals, incl fine, firm TANNAT. Amauta blends also gd, elegant TORRONTÉS. Advised by flying winemaker Paul Hobbs.

Pulenta Estate Men ★★→★★★ Pulenta brothers are 3rd generation winemakers with a penchant for fast cars. Excellent CAB FR, top-notch Gran Corte and, soon, single-v'yd MALBEC. Entry-level La Flor v.gd value.

Renacer Men ★★→★★★ Chilean winery (SAUV BL from Casa). Flagship Renacer is mostly MALBEC; v.gd Punto Final (Malbec, CAB SAUV); try Amarone-style Enamore.

Riglos Men ★★★ Try Gran Corte (MALBEC/CAB SAUV/CAB FR), Cab Fr, Cab Sauv, Malbec. V.gd Quinto SAUV BL.

Río Negro Patagonia's best PINOT N. Also MALBEC, SAUV BL, SÉM, MERLOT. Watch out for dinosaur fossils.

Ruca Malén Men ★★ Don Raul is top blend (MALBEC/CAB SAUV/PETIT VERDOT), Kinean v.gd 2nd line. Try Ruca range PETIT VERDOT. Winery restaurant must-visit in MEN.

Salentein, Bodegas Men ★★→★★★ Handsome winery; attractive wines too. Try new

> **Choosing Malbec**
> Styles vary. SAL and Cata give structure and power; RÍO N and NEU give
> more elegance, with often a touch of PINOT N in the blend. MEN is still the
> main region, but the higher-altitude Uco Valley gives more freshness
> than Luján de Cuyo or other parts of Men.

top blend Gran Uco (MALBEC/CAB SAUV), Single V'yd range (formally Primus), v.gd Numina blend. El Portillo is entry-level: some of best value in Argentina.

Salta Extreme altitudes and extreme sun. Subregion Cafayate is renowned for TORRONTÉS (esp Calchaquí Valley). Intense reds.

San Juan 160 km n of MEN, SAN J is Argentina's 2nd largest wine region. Mostly SYRAH, BONARDA, VIOGNIER.

San Pedro de Yacochuya Sal ★★★ Cafayate collaboration between Michel Rolland (*see* France) and ETCHART family. Ripe but fragrant TORRONTÉS, dense MALBEC SPY, powerful Yacochuya (Malbec from oldest vines).

Schroeder, Familia Neu ★★ V.gd Saurus Select range, esp PINOT N, fragrant MALBEC. Top Familia Schroeder Pinot N/Malbec. Interesting CAB SAUV, sparkling.

Sophenia, Finca Men ★★→★★★ Large Tupungato estate, first to plant so high. Many varieties, always fresh. V.gd Synthesis line, excellent SAUV BL and now sparkling.

Tapiz Men ★★ Punchy SAUV BL (from La R), v.gd red range topped by serious Black Tears MALBEC. Owner also breeds llamas.

Terrazas de los Andes Men ★★→★★★ Still-wine sister of Chandon (MOËT-HENNESSY). Top single-v'yds in Perdriel, Las Compuertas and Altamira. Also perfumed TORRONTÉS (SAL), buttery CHARD. Joint venture with Cheval Blanc (Bordeaux) making superb ***Cheval des Andes*** blend.

Toso, Pascual Men ★★→★★★ Californian Paul Hobbs heads a team making gd-value, tasty range, incl ripe but finely structured Magdalena Toso (mostly MALBEC), Malbec/CAB SAUV single-v'yd Finca Pedregal.

Trapiche Men ★→★★★ One of biggest portfolios in country. Try single-v'yd MALBEC; Las Palmas CAB SAUV; Iscay blends, Extravaganza blends.

Trivento Men ★→★★★ Owned by CONCHA Y TORO of Chile. Eolo MALBEC is pricey flagship, but Golden Malbec, SYRAH, CHARD top value.

Val de Flores Men ★★★ Michel Rolland owns this old (and bio) MALBEC v'yd in Vistaflores. Deep, elegant, earthy, with firm tannins. For ageing. Also try Mariflor line (single varieties and excellent Camille blend).

Viña Alicia ★★★ Part-owned by LUIGI BOSCA family. Small production with seductive white blend Tiara (RIES/ALBARIÑO/SAVAGNIN) and racy NEBBIOLO among others.

ViñaVida Men ★★→★★★ Beautiful Vistaflores v'yds incl crop circle pattern in search of the perfect MALBEC. Roberto de la Mota consults.

Zorzal Men ★★★ Three winemaking Michelini brothers make fresh, dynamic wines from Gualtallary. Excellent Eggo line using no oak, just cement eggs (try SAUV BL, PINOT N, new release CAB FR).

Zuccardi Men ★→★★★ Family winery with combined energy from father-son winemakers. Excellent single-v'yd Alluvional wines, Zeta blend, v.gd Q label (try TEMPRANILLO), experimental Textual line (incl Ancellotta, Caladoc). Entry-level Santa Julia still gd value. New Uco winery to open soon.

BRAZIL

The largest country in South America, Brazil has a huge amount of land under vine but it is only in recent years that wineries have focused on quality *Vitis vinifera* and age-worthy wines. The best region is in the southern tip of the country in Serra Gaúcha, where you'll find rolling hills, cooler temperatures and a boom in Bordeaux varieties, plus an eclectic European mix (Touriga Nacional, Alicante Bouschet, Barbera, Gewurztraminer, Malvasia). Other sources include Campanha, Serra do Sudeste, Planalto Catarinense, Vale do São Francisco. Best of all in Brazil is the sparkling.

Casa Valduga ★→★★★ One of the oldest producers in Brazil. V.gd traditional-method sparklers and top MERLOT Storia.

Cave Geisse ★★ Sparkling specialist: Chilean Mario Geisse makes Brut Nature, Blanc de Noirs.

Miolo ★→★★★ Pioneer, major producer; Portuguese grapes like TINTA RORIZ, TOURIGA NACIONAL. Try Castas Portuguesas. Michel Rolland consults. Elegant sparkling.

Vale dos Vinhedos is Brazil's first appellation: go for Merlot.

Pizzato Vinhas ★→★★★ Still and sparkling producer. V.gd DNA 99 single-v'yd MERLOT from Vale dos Vinhedos. Fausto label for young varietals; Pizzato label for more depth, esp Concentus.

Quinta da Neve ★★ PINOT N from from coolest region of Santa Catarina, v. aromatic.

Salton Massive producer; quality varies. "Intenso" label: CAB FR, TEROLDEGO, Marselan.

Valmarino Vinicola ★★ Surprisingly gd CAB FR. Try Valmarino from Serra Gaucha. Sparkling too.

URUGUAY

This small country has plenty of international admirers for its wines. Reds are dominated by flagship variety Tannat: dark and tannic, with rich fruit. A new wave of lighter reds like Pinot Noir are stepping up, and fresh Albariño and Sauvignon Blanc come from near the coast, complementing some pretty rich Chardonnay.

Alto de la Ballena ★→★★ Small family project nr coast with high acid, fresh reds (CAB FR); beautifully aged whites.

Bouza ★→★★★ Boutique winery with top wines, classic cars and excellent restaurant. Try single-v'yd TANNAT Parcela Unica (A6, B6), blend Monte Vide Eu (Tannat/MERLOT/TEMPRANILLO), peachy ALBARIÑO.

Garzón ★★→★★★ Italian star Alberto Antonini consults to this small project n of Punta del Este. Don't miss TANNAT, SAUV BL, crisp ALBARIÑO.

Juanico Establecimiento ★→★★★ Largest producer in Uruguay, oldest cellar. Gd-value wines, all prices. Top red Preludio Familia Deicas (TANNAT/CAB SAUV/CAB FR/MERLOT/PETIT VERDOT/Marselan); creamy white Preludio Blanc (VIOGNIER, CHARD).

Marichal ★→★★★ Son Juan Andres heads boutique family winery in Canelones. V.gd PINOT N and still Blanc de Noirs.

Pisano ★→★★★ Traditional winery, v.gd reds and whites. Try Río de los Pájaros range.

OTHER SOUTH AMERICAN WINES

Bolivia claims highest-altitude vineyards in the world; a surprising wine producer but with steady growth in its modest way. The Tarija Valley is the most important region, with robust Bordeaux varieties (CAB SAUV, MERLOT, MALBEC), fruity whites (TORRONTÉS, CHENIN BL), interesting RIES. Try Kohlberg, Aranjuez, Campos de Solana, La Conception, Casa Grande (sparkling), Magnus, Uvairenda.

Peru While Peru does have wine vines (try Tacama Blanco de Blancos, Don Manuel, Gran Blanco Fina Res, Intipalka young MALBEC/MERLOT, Vista Alegre PINOT BL), the star of Peru's grape scene remains its famous brandy: Pisco.

Australia

Abbreviations used in the text:

Ad Hills	Adelaide Hills, SA
Beech	Beechworth, Vic
Coon	Coonawarra, SA
Kang I	Kangaroo Island, SA
Lang C	Langhorne Creek, SA
Margaret R	Margaret River, WA
McLaren V	McLaren Vale, SA
Mor Pen	Mornington Penninsula, Vic
N/S Tas	North/South Tasmania
Ruth	Rutherglen, Vic
Qld	Queensland

G rape growers don't fancy driving their tractors uphill. It's why the valley floors were always the first to see vines. Indeed, much of Australian viticulture was determined not even by farmers but by their tractors; the space between rows was never so much about the ideal, as about the width a standard tractor could safely negotiate. So for all the highbrow debate about ideal spacing and canopy-management, Australia's vine rows have been, with exceptions of course, spaced too far apart. If Australia was going to conquer the wine world it would need all it could grow. So a change to fancy Italian tractors, slim-hipped, air-conditoned, with sound systems and sat nav, gives you an idea of what's happening out there. It's a little thing but it paints a picture of Australia's changing mind-set. It wasn't just quantity the world wanted; it was style, interest, a bang for its buck. Many, if not most, Australian wine regions still grapple with the essential question: which varieties should we focus on, which grow best here – and what will the supermarkets be looking for next year? It's not quite existential angst but it might be the wine equivalent.

Many of Australia's best wines now come from green hillsides rather than brown dry valleys. The march towards "cool climate" wine-growing only started in earnest here in the early 80s and like most change it's been an ooze rather than a flood. In short, Australia is in the process of being redefined, the warm/hot regions not replaced but added to. In this rule-less, underregulated wine land, diversity of wine style and type is rampant. And we can choose: the full-on or the nicely judged.

Recent vintages

New South Wales (NSW)

2014 Hot, dry vintage for the most part, marred by spring frosts. Hunter Shiraz will be exceptional. Canberra Ries, Shiraz right up there.

2013 Short, sharp season. Rich reds and whites. Hunter Sem and Canberra Ries especially good.

2012 A wet, cold year. Sem could pull a rabbit out and perhaps Cab Sauv too, but generally disappointing.

2011 The Hunter Valley escaped the floods of further south, but it was still a cold, damp year.

2010 Regular heavy rain made for a tricky year in most districts. Lighter reds, good whites.

2009 Excellent vintage all over although reds better than whites. Generally a successful year.

Victoria (Vic)

2014 Frost damage galore but a great red vintage in most regions.

2013 Wet winter followed by a warm, dry summer. Good season all round/over.

2012 Turning out better than expected. Reds, whites very good to exceptional.

2011 Wet; disease pressure in vineyards. Generally better for whites than reds.

2010 Temperate vintage. Whites and reds should be good from most districts.

2009 Bush fire (and resultant smoke taint). Extreme heat and drought. Yarra Valley worst affected. Some surprises to be found.

South Australia (SA)

2014 Hot, low-yield year has produced generous wines, white and red.

2013 Water was a problem so yields generally well down. A streaky vintage.

2012 Yields were down but a brilliant year. Great for Ries; Cab Sauv should be a stand-out.

2011 Cool, wet. Lean whites, herbal/spicy reds. Some interesting results.

2010 Excellent. Clare, Eden Valley Ries v.gd. Shiraz from all major districts best since 05. Coonawarra Cab Sauv on song.

2009 Hot. Adelaide Hills gd whites, reds. Coonawarra reds excellent. McLaren Vale, Barossa Valley generally good for Shiraz.

Western Australia (WA)

2014 The luck continues; almost getting monotonous. Another tip-top year.

2013 Both Cab Sauv and Chard very strong. Some rain but gods were kind.

2012 The drought continued, so too the run of beautiful, warm/hot vintages.

2011 Warm, dry, early vintage. Particularly good Cab. Delicate whites less successful. WA's great run of vintages continued.

2010 Reds generally better than whites. Some were caught by late rains but mostly very good.

2009 Especially good for Margaret River red and white and Pemberton white.

AUSTRALIA

Accolade Wines Name for wines/wineries previously under HARDYS, CONSTELLATION groups. Prolonged slumber but the words "fine wine" can at least be mentioned again. Or at least whispered.

Adelaide Hills SA Best SAUV BL region: cool 450m sites in Mt Lofty ranges. CHARD, SHIRAZ best performers now. SHAW & SMITH, ASHTON HILLS, MIKE PRESS, SC PANNELL powering along.

Alkoomi Mt Barker, WA r w (RIES) 04' 05' 07' 10' 11' 12'13 (CAB SAUV) 01' 02' 05' 07' 08' Veteran maker of fine RIES; rustic, long-lived reds.

All Saints Estate Ruth, Vic br ★★ Producer with a history of great fortifieds.

Alpine Valleys Vic Geographically and varietally similar to KING V. Best producers incl MAYFORD, Ringer Reef, Billy Button. Aromatic whites, but TEMPRANILLO is region's comet.

Andevine Hunter V, NSW r w ★★★ Initial SHIRAZ, SEM and CHARD releases from mature v'yds all outstanding. A long time since such an exciting new venture began around here.

Andrew Thomas Hunter V, NSW r w ★★★ Charismatic producer: old-vine SEM; silken, lavishly oaked SHIRAZ.

Angove's SA r w (br) ★★ MURRAY V family business. Some organic offerings. Cheapies (r w) a happy hunting ground; often outgun try-hard super premiums.

Annie's Lane Clare V, SA r w Part of TWE. Gd, boldly-flavoured wines. Flagship Copper Trail (can be) excellent, esp RIES, SHIRAZ. Not exactly setting world alight.

Arenberg, d' McLaren V, SA r w (br) (sw) (sp) ★★★ Sumptuous SHIRAZ, GRENACHE. Many varieties, wacky labels (incl The Cenosilicaphobic Cat SAGRANTINO). Elton John of Oz wineries.

Arrivo Ad Hills, SA r ★ Long-maceration, tannic, minty NEBBIOLO. Dry, complex, sexy rosé. Minute quantities.

Ashton Hills Ad Hills, SA r w (sp) ★★★ (PINOT N) 04' 05' 10' 12 13' Star of the AD HILLS. Compelling Pinot N made by seminal winemaker Stephen George from 30-yr-old+ v'yds.

Bailey's NE Vic r w br ★★★ Rich SHIRAZ, magnificent dessert MUSCAT (★★★★) and TOPAQUE. Part of TWE. V'yds now grown organically. PETIT VERDOT a gd addition. Suddenly has a skip in its step.

Balgownie Estate Bendigo, Vic, Yarra V, Vic r w ★→★★ Old name for medium-bodied, well-balanced, minty CAB, BENDIGO. Separate YARRA V arm. Hits and misses.

Balnaves of Coonawarra SA r w ★★★ Grape-grower since 1975, with winery since 1996. Lusty CHARD; v.gd spicy, medium-bodied SHIRAZ, Full-bodied Tally CAB SAUV is flagship.

Bannockburn Vic r w★★★ (CHARD) 06' 08' 10' 11 (PINOT N) 05' 08' 10' 12 Intense, complex CHARD and spice-shot PINOT N. Funkified SAUV BL. In yellow-jersey form.

Banrock Station Riverland, SA r w 1,600 ha property on Murray River, massive 243 ha v'yd, owned by ACCOLADE. Once was a budget wine warrior.

Barossa Valley SA Spiritual home of blood-and-thunder Aussie red wine. Local specialities: v. old-vine SHIRAZ, MOURVÈDRE, CAB SAUV, GRENACHE. Re-invents itself regularly, but bold flavour paramount.

Bass Phillip Gippsland, Vic r ★★★ (PINOT N) 04' 10' 11 12' Ultimate outsider. Tiny amounts of variable but at times exceptional Pinot N in three quality grades. There's Oz Pinot N, and then there's Bass Phillip.

Bay of Fires N Tas r w sp ★★★ Pipers River outpost of ACCOLADE empire. Stylish table wines and Arras super-cuvée sparkler. Increasingly complex PINOT N. Heavily underpromoted.

Beechworth Vic Rugged, rock-strewn, inland high country. CHARD, SHIRAZ best-performing varieties. NEBBIOLO, SANGIOVESE in minute quantity. CASTAGNA, GIACONDA, Sorrenberg essential producers.

Bendigo Vic Hot central VIC region with dozens of small v'yds. BALGOWNIE ESTATE the stalwart but handy performers aplenty. Rich reds.

Best's Grampians, Vic r w ★★★ (SHIRAZ) 04' 05' 09' 10' 11' 12 13' Conservative family winery; *v.gd mid-weight reds.* Thomson Family Shiraz from 120-yr-old vines superb. Shiraz across the range shows many a whippersnapper how it's done.

Bindi Macedon, Vic r w ★★★→★★★★ (PINOT N) 04' 06' 10' 12 13 Ultra-fastidious, terroir-driven maker of outstanding, long-lived Pinot N, CHARD.

Blue Pyrenees Pyrenees, Vic r w sp ★ 180 ha of mature v'yds. CAB SAUV quality mildly resurgent.

Boireann Granite Belt Qld r ★★ Consistently best producer of red wines in Qld (in tiny quantities). SHIRAZ/VIOGNIER the stand-out, if you can find it.

Bortoli, De Griffith, NSW, Yarra V, Vic r w (br) dr sw ★★→★★★★ (Noble SEM) Both irrigation-area winery and leading YARRA V producer. Excellent, cool-climate PINOT N, SHIRAZ, CHARD, SAUV BL and v.gd sweet, botrytized, Sauternes-style Noble Sem. Yarra V arm is where the sparks fly.

Brand's of Coonawarra Coon, SA r w ★ Owned by MCWILLIAM'S. Custodian of 100-yr-old vines. Quality struggles at the top end but the main fighting range (CAB SAUV, SHIRAZ, CHARD) delivers gd fruit-and-oak flavour. Supermarket specialist.

Brash Higgins McLaren V, SA ★★★ Brad Hickey has degrees in English and botany and has worked as brewer, baker, sommelier and now maker of radical expressions of MCLAREN V (r w).

Bremerton Lang C, SA r w ★★ Silken CAB, SHIRAZ with mounds of flavour. Thrived since Willson sisters took over family winery.

Brokenwood Hunter V, NSW r w ★★★ (ILR Res SEM) 03' 05' 06' (Graveyard SHIRAZ) 98' 00' 06' 07' 09' 11, Cricket Pitch Sem/SAUV BL fuel sales. HUNTER V figurehead.

Aussie $ has, after a long run of highs, trended downwards. Prices could be in buyers' favour.

Brookland Valley Margaret R, WA r w ★★ Volume producer of v.gd SAUV BL, CHARD, CAB SAUV. Budget 'Verse' + Sem/Sauv Bl and Cab/Merlot (esp 12') excellent value. ACCOLADE-owned.

Brown Brothers King V, Vic r w br dr sw sp ★★ (Noble RIES) 02' 04' 05' 08 Family firm. Wide range of crowd-pleasing styles, varieties. General emphasis on sweetness. Recently bought extensive TAS PINOT N (and other) v'yds, released now under TAMAR RIDGE/Devil's Corner range.

By Farr / Farr Rising Vic r w ★★★★ 08' 09' 10' 11' 12' Gary Farr and son Nick's own labels/winery, after departure from BANNOCKBURN. CHARD, PINOT N can be minor masterpieces. Nick mostly in charge now. Quality soaring. Top of Oz tree.

Campbells Ruth, Vic r (w) br ★★ Smooth ripe reds (esp Bobbie Burns SHIRAZ); extraordinary Merchant Prince Rare MUSCAT, Isabella Rare TOPAQUE (★★★★).

Canberra District NSW Both quality and quantity on increase; site selection important; cool climate. CLONAKILLA best known. COLLECTOR, CAPITAL, Ravensworth, EDEN ROAD, Mount Majura the new guns.

Capel Vale WA r w ★ Wide range of varieties and prices. Variable quality, but when they're gd....

Cape Mentelle Margaret R, WA r w ★★★★ (CAB SAUV) 01' 07' 08' 10' 11' 12' 13' In outstanding form. Robust Cab has become a more elegant (and lower alcohol) style, CHARD v.gd; also ZIN, v. popular SAUV BL/SEM. SHIRAZ on rise. Owned by LVMH Veuve Clicquot (*see* France).

Capital Wines Canberra, NSW r w ★★ Estate's Kyeema v'yd has history of growing some of region's best. SHIRAZ (13' excellent), RIES stand-outs. V.gd MERLOT.

Casella Riverina, NSW r w ★ [Yellow Tail] is be-all and end-all of operation. Budget reds and whites, huge in the USA for over a decade, really hit the sweet spot.

Reason for Riesling
Pristine, dry RIES from the CLARE V and EDEN V has dominated the Australian Ries landscape for the past 30 yrs, and truth is that its quality is vastly underappreciated other than by those in the know. Fortunately it keeps prices down. But there's movement at the Ries station in Oz, with greater experimentation in terms of style and region. Wild yeast, time on skins, partial maturation in old neutral oak, smaller batches, dabbling with sugar levels, etc, are all being tried. TAS, S and mtn VIC, GREAT SOUTHERN are all key regional Ries players now.

Castagna Beech, Vic r ★★★★ (SYRAH) 02' **04' 05' 06' 08' 10' 12'** Filmmaker/cook/vigneron Julian Castagna leads the Oz bio brigade. Estate-grown SHIRAZ/VIOGNIER, SANGIOVESE/Shiraz excellent. Non-estate range named Adam's Rib. New growers (non-estate) wines added.

Chalkers Crossing Hilltops, NSW r w ★ Cool-ish climate wines made by French-trained Celine Rousseau; esp SHIRAZ. High alcohol levels hold it back.

Chambers Rosewood NE Vic (r) (w) br ★★★ Viewed with MORRIS as greatest maker of sticky TOPAQUE, *Muscat*. Far less successful table wines.

Chapel Hill McLaren V, SA r (w) ★★–★★★ Leading MCLAREN V producer. SHIRAZ, CAB lead way, but TEMPRANILLO and esp GRENACHE both v.gd. Range has ballooned in recent yrs.

Charles Melton Barossa V, SA r w (sp) ★★★ Tiny winery with bold, ripe reds, esp Nine Popes, an old-vine GRENACHE/SHIRAZ blend. Goes about things quietly.

Chatto Tas r ★★★ Jim Chatto's (MOUNT PLEASANT winemaker) secret s assignment. Tiny producer making PINOT N of fruit and spice and all things nice. Ultra-savoury.

Clarendon Hills McLaren V, SA r ★★ Full-monty reds (high alcohol and intense fruit) made with grapes grown on the hills above MCLAREN V. Nothing like its former prominence.

Clare Valley SA Small, pretty, high-quality area 145 km n of Adelaide. Best toured by bike, some say. Australia's most prominent RIES region. Gumleaf-scented SHIRAZ; earthen, tannic CAB SAUV. WENDOUREE, TIM ADAMS, GROSSET, MOUNT HORROCKS, Kirrihill, KILIKANOON lead way.

Clonakilla Canberra, NSW r w ★★★★ (SHIRAZ) 01' **03' 05' 06' 07'** 08 **09' 10'** 12 13' *Deserved leader of the Shiraz/Viognier brigade.* RIES, VIOGNIER excellent. Has put Canberra on wine map.

Coldstream Hills Yarra V, Vic r w (sp) ★★★ (CHARD) 05' **06' 08'** 10' 11' 12' 13' (PINOT N) **04' 06'** 10' 12 13' Est 1985 by critic James Halliday. Delicious Pinot N to drink young, *Res to age.* V.gd Chard (esp Res). Recent single-v'yd releases added sparkle. Part of TWE.

Collector Wines Canberra, NSW r ★★★ (Res SHIRAZ) **06' 07' 08' 09'** 12 Collector Wines indeed. Res Shiraz is layered, spicy, perfumed, complex.

Constellation Wines Australia (CWA) See ACCOLADE WINES.

Coonawarra SA The s-most v'yds of state: home to some of Australia's best (value and quality) CAB SAUV; successful CHARD, SHIRAZ. WYNNS the region's beating heart. BALNAVES, MAJELLA, KATNOOK, BRAND'S, LINDEMAN'S, YALUMBA, Rymill all key. Stunning red soil on an ancient bed of limestone.

Coriole McLaren V, SA r w ★★ (Lloyd Res SHIRAZ) **98' 02' 04' 06'** 09 10' To watch, esp for SANGIOVESE and old-vine Shiraz Lloyd Res. Interesting FIANO, SAGRANTINO, NERO D'AVOLA. Resurgent.

Craiglee Macedon, Vic r w ★★★ (SHIRAZ) **00' 02' 06' 08'** 10 12 A salt-of-the-earth producer. North Rhône inspired. Fragrant and peppery Shiraz, age-worthy CHARD. Shiraz/VIOGNIER a new addition.

Crawford River Heathcote, Vic w ★★★ Consistently one of Australia's best RIES from this ultra-cool region.

Cullen Wines Margaret R, WA r w ★★★★ (CHARD) 04' 08' 09' 10' 11 12 (CAB SAUV/ MERLOT) 98' 04' 05' 07' 09' 11 12 Vanya Cullen makes substantial but subtle SEM/ SAUV BL, outstanding Chard, elegant, sinewy Cab/Merlot. Bio.

Cumulus Orange, NSW r w ★ By far the largest v'yd owner and producer in Orange. Variable quality.

Curly Flat Macedon, Vic r w ★★★ (PINOT N) 05' 06' 07' 10' 11 12 Robust but perfumed Pinot N (esp impressive) on two price/quality levels. Full-flavoured CHARD. Both are age-worthy.

Dalwhinnie Pyrenees, Vic r w ★★ (CHARD) 05' 06' 07' 10' (SHIRAZ) 04' 05' 06' 07' 08' 10' Rich Chard, CAB SAUV, Shiraz. Stunning site.

Deakin Estate Vic r w ★ High-volume varietal table wines. V. low-alcohol MOSCATO. Spicy SHIRAZ, CAB SAUV. Remarkable at the budget end.

Devil's Lair Margaret R, WA r w ★★ Opulent CHARD, CAB SAUV/MERLOT. Fifth Leg long-standing second label. New 9th Chamber Chard attemps to inject some pizzazz. Part of TWE.

Domaine A S Tas r w ★★★ Swiss owners/winemakers Peter and Ruth Althaus are perfectionists; v.gd oak-matured SAUV BL. Polarizing cool-climate CAB SAUV. Charismatic, let's say.

Domaine Chandon Yarra V, Vic (r) (w) sp ★★ Cool-climate sparkling and table wine. Owned by Moët & Chandon (*see* France). Known in UK as Green Point. Hand has hovered over the excitement button for a long time without ever really threatening to push it.

Domenica Beech, Vic ★★ Flashy new producer with est v'yds. Exuberant, spicy SHIRAZ. Textural MARSANNE.

Eden Road r w ★★★★ Energetic producer making wines from Hilltops, TUMBARUMBA, CANBERRA DISTRICT regions. Exc SHIRAZ, CHARD, CAB SAUV. Keeps raising bar.

Eden Valley SA Hilly region home to HENSCHKE, TORZI MATTHEWS, Radford, Chris Ringland, PEWSEY VALE and others, cutting RIES, (perfumed, bright) SHIRAZ, CAB SAUV of top quality.

Elderton Barossa V, SA r w (br) (sp) ★★ Old vines; rich, oaked CAB SAUV, SHIRAZ. All bases covered. Some organics/bio. Keeps active.

Eldridge Estate Mor Pen, Vic r w ★★ Winemaker David Lloyd is a fastidious experimenter. PINOT N, GAMAY, CHARD worth the fuss.

Epis Macedon, Vic r w ★★★ (PINOT N) Can an ex-footballer grow/make delicate Pinot N? Not likely, but Alec Epis proves it's possible. Long-lived Pinot N and elegant CHARD. Cold climate.

Evans & Tate Margaret R, WA r w ★★ Owned by MCWILLIAM'S since 2007. Quality is better than ever. SHIRAZ, CAB SAUV, CHARD. Value too.

Faber Vineyards Swan V, WA r ★★★★ (Res SHIRAZ) 07' 08' 09' 10 11' John Griffiths is guru of WA winemaking. Home estate redefines what's possible for SWAN V Shiraz. Non-estate CHARD, CAB SAUV v.gd.

Ferngrove Vineyards Gt Southern, WA r w ★ Cattle farmer Murray Burton's 223-ha wine venture. Gd RIES, MALBEC, CAB SAUV.

Soils in Margaret River are two billion years old – some of the world's oldest.

Flametree Margaret R, WA r w ★★★ Exceptional CAB SAUV; spicy, seductive SHIRAZ; occasionally compelling CHARD.

Fraser Gallop Estate Margaret R, WA r w ★★★ A new breed of MARGARET R; concentrated CAB SAUV, CHARD, (wooded) SEM/SAUV BL. Flying.

Freycinet Tas r w (sp) ★★★ (PINOT N) 05' 08' 09' 10' 11 12' An e-coast TAS winery producing dense Pinot N, gd CHARD, excellent Radenti sparkling.

Frogmore Creek Tas r w ★★ Off-dry RIES, age-worthy CHARD, undergrowthy PINOT N. Epitome of cool-climate Australian wine.

Geelong Vic Region w of Melbourne. Cool, dry climate. Best names: BANNOCKBURN, BY FARR, LETHBRIDGE, Bellarine Estate, Clyde Park.

Gemtree Vineyards McLaren V, SA r (w) ★★ Warm-hearted SHIRAZ alongside TEMPRANILLO and other exotica, linked by quality. Largely bio.

Geoff Merrill McLaren V, SA r w ★ Ebullient maker of Geoff Merrill and Mt Hurtle brands. Strolling along.

Giaconda Beech, Vic r w ★★★★ (CHARD) 02' 05' 06' 08' 10' 11 12 (SHIRAZ) 04' 06' 08' 10' In the mid-80s Rick Kinzbrunner walked up a steep, dry, rock-strewn hill and came down a winemaking (living) legend. Arguably Australia's best CHARD producer. Excellent SHIRAZ.

Giant Steps / Innocent Bystander Yarra V, Vic ★★★ Buoyant producer. Fun and funky but serious and influential. Top single-v'yd CHARD, PINOT N. Vintages 12 13 both high points.

Glaetzer-Dixon Tas r w ★★★ GLAETZER clan famous in Australia for cuddly warm-climate SHIRAZ. Then Nick Glaetzer turned all this on its head by setting up shop in cool TAS. Euro-style RIES, Rhôney Shiraz, meaty PINOT N. Star, with a bullet.

Glaetzer Wines Barossa V, SA r ★★ Hyper-rich, unfiltered, v. ripe old-vine SHIRAZ led by iconic Amon-Ra. V.gd examples of high-octane style.

Goulburn Valley Vic Old region in temperate mid-Vic. Full-bodied, savoury table wines. MARSANNE, CAB SAUV, SHIRAZ the pick, TAHBILK, MITCHELTON mainstays. Also referred to as Nagambie Lakes.

Grampians Vic Region previously known as Great Western. Temperate region in nw Vic. High-quality spicy SHIRAZ, sparkling Shiraz. Home to SEPPELT, BEST'S, MOUNT LANGI, The Story.

Granite Belt Qld High-altitude, (relatively) cool, improbable region just n of Qld/ NSW border. Spicy SHIRAZ, rich SEM.

Grant Burge Barossa V, SA r w (br) (sw) (sp) ★★ Smooth reds and whites from best grapes of Burge's large v'yd holdings. Takeover imminent.

Great Southern WA Remote cool area; Albany, Denmark, Frankland River, Mount Barker, Porongurup are official subregions. First-class RIES, SHIRAZ, CAB SAUV.

Greenstone Vineyard Heathcote, Vic r ★★ Partnership between David Gleave MW (London), Alberto Antonini (Italy), Australian viticulturist Mark Walpole; v.gd SHIRAZ, gd SANGIOVESE.

Grosset Clare V, SA r w ★★★ (RIES) 02' 05' 10' 12' 13 14' (Gaia) 99' 04' 05' 12' Fastidious winemaker. Foremost Australian Ries, lovely CHARD, v.gd *Gaia* CAB SAUV/MERLOT. Improving PINOT N.

Hanging Rock Macedon, Vic r w sp ★★ (HEATHCOTE SHIRAZ) 00' 01' 02' 04' 06' 08' Successfully moved upmarket with sparkling MACEDON and Heathcote Shiraz. Gone quiet.

Harcourt Valley Vineyards Bendigo, Vic r ★★ Has sprung thoroughly to life in recent yrs. Dense, syrupy, seductive SHIRAZ, MALBEC, CAB SAUV, with help from American oak.

Hardys r w (sw) sp ★★★ (Eileen CHARD) 02' 04' 06' 08' 10' 12 13 (Eileen SHIRAZ) 04' 06' 10' Historic company now part of ACCOLADE. CHARD excellent. Shiraz getting there slowly. New Eileen PINOT N promising.

Heathcote Vic The region's 500-million-yr-old Cambrian soil has great potential for high-quality reds, esp SHIRAZ. Finally starting to add some runs to the board.

Heggies Eden V, SA r w dr (sw) ★ V'yd at 500m owned by S Smith & Sons; v.gd RIES, VIOGNIER. CHARD can surprise.

Henschke Eden V, SA r w ★★★★ (SHIRAZ) 90' 91' 96' 04' 06' 09 12' (CAB SAUV) 86' 88 90' 96' 02' 04' 06' 09' Pre-eminent 150-yr-old family business known for delectable Hill of Grace (Shiraz), v.gd Cab Sauv and red blends, gd whites and scary prices.

Hewitson SE Aus r (w) ★★★ *(Old Garden Mourvèdre)* 98' 99'02' 05' 09' 10 Dean Hewitson sources parcels off v. old vines. SHIRAZ and varietal release from "oldest MOURVÈDRE vines on the planet". Rock-solid.

Hollick Coon, SA r w (sp) ★ Gd CAB SAUV, SHIRAZ. Sold recently to offshore investors.

Houghton Swan V, WA r w ★★ Once-legendary winery of WA. Part of ACCOLADE. Inexpensive white blend once considered *a national classic*. V.gd CAB SAUV, SHIRAZ, etc. sourced from MARGARET R, GREAT SOUTHERN. Needs to get out more.

Howard Park WA r w★★→★★★★ (RIES) 04' 08' 11' 12'13' (CAB SAUV) 99'01' 05' 07' 09' 10' 11' Scented Ries, CHARD; earthy Cab. Second label MadFish superb value. Blossoming range; new emphasis on PINOT N.

Hunter Valley NSW Great name in NSW, sub-tropical coal-mining area 160 km n of Sydney. Mid-weight, earthy SHIRAZ and gentle SEM can live for 30 yrs. Classic terroir-driven styles. TYRRELL'S, Mount Pleasant, BROKENWOOD, ANDREW THOMAS are the pillars.

NSW bird flu outbreak caused least-expected shortage: egg whites for fining wines.

Jacob's Creek (Orlando) Barossa V, SA r w (br) (sw) sp ★★ Pioneering company, now owned by Pernod Ricard. Almost totally focused now on various tiers of uninspiring Jacob's Creek wines, covering all varieties and prices.

Jamsheed Pyrenees, Vic, Yarra V, Vic★★★ Exciting producer, esp SHIRAZ from YARRA V, GRAMPIANS, PYRENEES, BEECH. Complex, savoury, questioning expressions.

Jasper Hill Heathcote, Vic r w ★★★ (SHIRAZ)02' 04' 06' 08' 09' 10' Emily's Paddock Shiraz/CAB FR blend, Georgia's Paddock Shiraz from dry-land estate are intense, burly, long-lived. Bio.

Jim Barry Clare V, SA r w ★★★ Great v'yds provide v.gd RIES, McCrae Wood SHIRAZ, richly robed, oaked, pricey The Armagh Shiraz.

John Duval Wines Barossa V, SA r★★★ John Duval – former chief red winemaker for ꞁꞁꞁꞁꞁꞁꞁ (ꞁꞁꞁ Cꞁꞁꞁꞁꞁ) makes positively *delicious Rhône-y reds of great intensity* and character.

Kaesler Barossa V, SA r (w) ★★ Gd (in heroic, full-on style) but variable; alcohol levels often tip balance. Old vines.

Katnook Estate Coon, SA r w (sw) (sp) ★★ (Odyssey CAB SAUV) 99' 00'04' 08' 09 Pricey icons *Odyssey*, Prodigy SHIRAZ. Concentrated fruit, oak.

Kilikanoon Clare V, SA r w ★★★ RIES, SHIRAZ excellent performers in recent yrs. Luscious, beautifully made. Big end of town style-wise.

King Valley Vic Altitude between 155–860m has massive impact on varieties, styles. Around 25 brands headed quality-wise by Dal Zotto, Chrismont, PIZZINI.

Kirrihill Clare V, SA r w ★★ V.gd CAB SAUV, SHIRAZ and RIES at, often, sensationally gd prices.

Knappstein Wines Clare V, SA r w★★★ Lion is awake. Reliable RIES, CAB SAUV/MERLOT, SHIRAZ, Cab Sauv. Owned by LION NATHAN. New medium-bodied, perfumed Shiraz/MALBEC and skin-contact Ries adds charm/interest to range.

Kooyong Mor Pen, Vic r w★★★★ PINOT N, *Superb Chard* of harmony, structure. PINOT GR of charm. Single-v'yd wines. Clearly among Australia's finest.

Lake Breeze Lang C, SA r (w) ★★ Maker of succulently smooth, gutsy, value SHIRAZ, CAB SAUV. Struggles to produce top-end wine but has the mid-range licked.

Lake's Folly Hunter V, NSW r w ★★ (CHARD) 05' 07' 09' (CAB SAUV) 01' 05' Founded by Max Lake, pioneer of HUNTER V Cab Sauv. Chard often better than Cab Sauv blend. Its own beast.

Langmeil Barossa V, SA r w ★★ Owns world's oldest block of SHIRAZ (planted in 1843) plus other old v'yds, often producing opulent, full-throttle Shiraz.

Larry Cherubino Wines Frankland R, WA r w ★★★★ Intense SAUV BL, RIES, *spicy Shiraz*, polished CAB SAUV. Ambitious label now franking its early promise in full.

Leasingham Clare V, SA r w ★★ Once-important brand with v.gd RIES, SHIRAZ, CAB SAUV, Cab Sauv/MALBEC blend. Husk of former self. Brand owned by ACCOLADE.

Leeuwin Estate Margaret R, WA r w ★★★★ (CHARD) 02' 04' 05' 06' 08' 10' 11' Iconic Chard producer. Full-bodied, age-worthy Art Series *Chard*. SAUV BL, RIES less brilliant. *Cab Sauv* can be v.gd.

Leo Buring Barossa V, SA w ★★★ 02' 05' 06' 08' 13' Part of TWE. Exclusively RIES; Leonay top label, *ages superbly*. Air gone out of the brand.

Lethbridge Vic r w ★★★ Small and stylish producer of CHARD, SHIRAZ, PINOT N, RIES. Star burns bright.

Limestone Coast Zone SA Important zone, incl Bordertown, COON, Mt Benson, Mt Gambier, PADTHAWAY, Robe, WRATTONBULLY.

Lindeman's r w ★★ Owned by TWE. Low-price Bin range now its main focus, far cry from former glory. Lindeman's COON Trio reds still v.gd.

Lion Nathan NZ brewery; owns KNAPPSTEIN, PETALUMA, ST HALLETT, STONIER, TATACHILLA. Hits and misses.

Macedon and Sunbury Vic Adjacent regions: Macedon higher elevation, Sunbury nr Melbourne airport. Quality from BINDI, CRAIGLEE, CURLY FLAT, EPIS, Granite Hills and HANGING ROCK.

Mac Forbes Yarra V, Vic ★★★ Contemplative single-v'yd releases, mainly PINOT N, RIES. Slowly building enviable reputation.

McLaren Vale SA Historic, maritime region on outskirts of Adelaide. Big-flavoured reds have great appeal in the USA, but CORIOLE, CHAPEL HILL, WIRRA WIRRA, GEMTREE, Inkwell, BRASH HIGGINS, SC PANNELL, MARIUS and growing number of others show elegance as well as flavour.

McWilliam's SE Aus r w (br) (sw) ★★★ Family owned. Hanwood, EVANS & TATE, BRAND'S, Mount Pleasant are key pillars, but with assortment of other labels. Focusing increasingly on home NSW state.

Main Ridge Estate Mor Pen, Vic r w ★★★ Rich, age-worthy CHARD, PINOT N. Doyen of MOR PEN wine. Miniscule estate.

Majella Coon, SA r (w) ★★★ Opulent, crowd-pleasing, quality SHIRAZ, CAB SAUV. Super-reliable.

Margaret River WA Temperate coastal area s of Perth. Powerful CHARD, structured CAB SAUV, spicy SHIRAZ. CULLEN, LEEUWIN, MOSS WOOD, VOYAGER ESTATE, FRASER GALLOP, DEVIL'S LAIR, FLAMETREE and many others. Great touring (and surfing) region.

Marius McLaren V, SA r ★★★ Varietal SHIRAZ and blends of eye-opening concentration/quality. More finesse than frills.

Mayford NE Vic, Vic r w ★★★ Tiny v'yd in a private, hidden valley. Put Alpine Valleys on the map. SHIRAZ, CHARD, and star of the show, TEMPRANILLO.

Meerea Park Hunter V, NSW r w ★★ Brothers Garth and Rhys Eather have taken 25 yrs to be an overnight success. Age-worthy SEM, SHIRAZ.

Mike Press Wines Ad Hills, SA r w ★★ Tiny production, tiny pricing. SHIRAZ, CAB SAUV, CHARD, SAUV BL. Crowd favourite of bargain-hunters.

Mitchelton Goulburn V, Vic r w (sw) ★★ Stalwart producer of RIES, SHIRAZ, CAB SAUV, plus speciality of *Marsanne*, ROUSSANNE. Rarely reaches great heights but has renewed energy now.

Mitolo r ★★ High-quality SHIRAZ, CAB SAUV. Heroic but (often) irresistible wines.

Moorilla Estate Tas r w (sp) ★★★ Nr Hobart on Derwent River. Gd RIES, CHARD; PINOT N. Superb restaurant and extraordinary art gallery. Wine quality on steady rise.

Moorooduc Estate Mor Pen, Vic r w ★★★★ Long-term producer of stylish, sophisticated CHARD, PINOT N; no signs of any slacking off.

Moppity Vineyards Hilltops, NSW r w ★★★ Making a name for its SHIRAZ/VIOGNIER,

CAB SAUV (Hilltops) and CHARD (TUMBARUMBA). Stern, tannic, spice-drenched reds. Kicking goals from all angles.

Mornington Peninsula Vic An exciting cool coastal area 40 km se of Melbourne. Multiple high-quality boutique wineries. PINOT N, CHARD and PINOT G. Wine/surf/beach/food playground.

Morris NE Vic (r) (w) br ★★★★ RUTH producer of Australia's greatest dessert MUSCATS, Tokays/TOPAQUES.

Moss Wood Margaret R, WA r w ★★★ (CAB SAUV) 01′ 04′ 05′ 10 Makes MARGARET R's most opulent wines from its 11.7 ha. SEM and CHARD, super-smooth *Cab Sauv*. Oak-rich.

Mount Horrocks Clare V, SA r w ★★ Fine dry RIES, sweet Cordon Cut Ries; *Chard best in region.* SHIRAZ, CAB SAUV in fine form.

Mount Langi Ghiran Grampians, Vic r w ★★★★ (SHIRAZ) 04′ 05′08′ 09′ 10 12′ Rich, peppery, *Rhône-like Shiraz.* V.gd sparkling Shiraz. Excellent Cliff Edge Shiraz. Cool-climate site. Great site.

Mount Mary Yarra V, Vic r w ★★★ (PINOT N) 05′10′ 12′ (Quintet) 98′ 00′04′ 10′ 12′ The late Dr. Middleton made tiny amounts of suave CHARD, vivid PINOT N, elegant CAB SAUV blend. All age impeccably. Modern era an improvement, if anything.

Mudgee NSW Region nw of Sydney. Sizeable reds, fine SEM, full CHARD. Struggling to gain traction.

Murray Valley SA Vast irrigated v'yds. Now at centre of climate-change firestorm.

Ngeringa Ad Hills, SA r w ★★ Perfumed PINOT N and NEBBIOLO. Rhôney SHIRAZ. Savoury rosé. Constantly pushing boundaries. Bio.

Ninth Island Tas *See* PIPERS BROOK (Kreglinger).

Ochota Barrels Barossa V, SA r w ★★★ Quixotic producer making hay with (mostly) old-vine GRENACHE, SHIRAZ from MCLAREN V, BAROSSA. Hero of Oz's sommelier set.

O'Leary Walker Wines Clare V, SA r w ★★★ Low profile but excellent quality. CLARE V RIES, CAB SAUV standout. MCLAREN V SHIRAZ oak-heavy but gd.

Orange NSW Cool-climate, high-elevation region. Lively SHIRAZ (when ripe) but best suited to (intense) aromatic whites and CHARD.

> Producers in Orange are cross about "orange" (ie. skin-contact white) wines. Fruit fight?

Padthaway SA Large area developed as overspill of COON. V.gd SHIRAZ, CAB SAUV. Salinity an issue. Less prominent than it was a decade back.

Pannell, SC McLaren V, SA r ★★★ Excellent SHIRAZ (often labelled Syrah) and (esp) GRENACHE-based wines. NEBBIOLO to watch. Thoroughly ascendant. Unafraid of whole-bunch fermentation.

Paringa Estate Mor Pen, Vic r ★★★ Maker of spectacular PINOT N, SHIRAZ. Fleshy, fruity, flashy styles. CHARD not in same class. Reds irresistible.

Paxton McLaren V, SA r ★★ Australia's most prominent organic/bio grower/producer, large holdings bio v'yds. Ripe, elegant SHIRAZ, GRENACHE. Hugely influential.

Pemberton WA Region between MARGARET R and GREAT SOUTHERN; initial enthusiasm for PINOT N replaced by RIES, CHARD, SHIRAZ.

Penfolds r w (br) ★★★★ (Grange) 55′ 60′ 62′ 63′ 66′ 71′ 76′ 86′ 90′ 96′98′ 99′ 02′ 04′ 05′ 06′ 08′ 10′ (CAB SAUV Bin 707) 91′ 96′ 98′02′ 04′ 06′ 10′ 12′ Originally Adelaide, now SA. Australia's best warm-climate red wine company. Yattarna CHARD, Bin Chard now of comparable quality to reds. Dizzying prices.

Penley Estate Coon, SA r w ★ Rich, textured, fruit-and-oak CAB SAUV; SHIRAZ/Cab Sauv blend; CHARD. High alcohol.

Petaluma Ad Hills, SA r w sp ★★ (RIES) 02′ 07′ 11′ 12′ 13 (CHARD) 07′ 12′ (CAB SAUV COON) 90′ 91′ 98′ 99′ 04′ 05′ 07′ 08′ Seems to miss ex-owner/creator Brian Croser. Bought by LION NATHAN in 2002. Gd but low-key now.

The empire strikes back

South Australian wines have dominated Australia's most prominent wine award – the Jimmy Watson Trophy – for the past 40-odd yrs, but when the bounty stopped for six consecutive yrs, some wondered whether a SA wine would ever take the award again. Warm-climate reds were out; cool-climate lunatics had the keys to the asylum. Enter SC PANNELL. His AD HILLS SYRAH, from SA and incl a portion of whole bunches, proved a popular winner of the 2014 award, and restored (in some people's eyes) Australian wine to rights.

Peter Lehmann Wines Barossa V, SA r w (br) (sw) (sp) ★★★ Well-priced wines, often in substantial quantities. Luxurious/sexy Stonewell SHIRAZ among many others (r w). Peter died 2013; company sold 2014 to CASELLA (YELLOW TAIL).

Pewsey Vale Ad Hills, SA w ★★ Excellent RIES, standard and (aged-release) The Contours, grown on lovely tiered v'yd.

Piano Piano Beech, Vic w V'yd in next paddock along from GIACONDA. Powerful CHARD. Finding its feet.

Pierro Margaret R, WA r w ★★ (CHARD) 06' 08' 09' 11'12' Producer of expensive, tangy SEM/SAUV BL and ballsy Chard.

Pipers Brook Tas r w sp ★★★ (RIES) 06' 07' 09'13' (CHARD) 05' 08'09' Cool-area pioneer; gd Ries, *restrained Chard and sparkling* from Tamar V. Second label: Ninth Island. Owned by Belgian Kreglinger family.

Pirramimma McLaren V, SA r w ★ Century-old family business with large v'yds (just) moving with the times.

Pizzini King V, Vic r ★★ (NEBBIOLO) 02' 05' 10 Leads the charge towards Italian varieties in Australia. NEBBIOLO, SANGIOVESE, blends. Heartbeat of the KING V.

Plantagenet Mt Barker, WA r w (sp) ★★★ Wide range of varieties, esp rich CHARD, SHIRAZ, vibrant, potent, age-worthy CAB SAUV. 40 yrs young.

Primo Estate SA r w dr (sw) ★★★ Joe Grilli's many successes incl rich MCLAREN V SHIRAZ, tangy COLOMBARD, potent Joseph CAB SAUV/MERLOT.

Punch Yarra V, Vic r w★★★ Lance family ran Diamond Valley for decades. When they sold, they retained the close-planted PINOT N v'yd. It grows detailed, decisive, age-worthy wines.

Pyrenees Vic Central Vic region producing rich, often minty reds. DALWHINNIE, TALTARNI, BLUE PYRENEES, Mount Avoca, Dog Rock leading players.

Richmond Grove Barossa V, SA w Gd RIES at bargain prices; not much else. Owned by JACOB'S CREEK.

Riverina NSW Large-volume irrigated zone centred on Griffith.

Robert Oatley Wines Mudgee, NSW r w ★ Robert Oatley created ROSEMOUNT ESTATE. Ambition burns anew. Finisterre range gd.

Rockford Barossa V, SA r w sp ★→★★★ Small producer from old, low-yielding v'yds; reds best, also iconic sparkling Black SHIRAZ.

Rosemount Estate r w ★★ Major volumes. In doldrums for nearly a decade but making stuttering signs of a form reversal. GRENACHE, SHIRAZ esp.

Ruggabellus Barossa V, SA r★★★ Causing a stir. Funkier, more savoury version of the BAROSSA. Old oak, minimal sulphur, wild yeast, whole bunches/stems. Blends of GRENACHE, SHIRAZ, MATARO, CINSAULT.

Rutherglen & Glenrowan Vic Two of four regions in the ne Vic zone, justly famous for sturdy reds and magnificent fortified dessert wines.

St Hallett Barossa V, SA r w★★★ (Old Block) 99'02' 04' 06' 08'10' Old Block SHIRAZ is the star; the rest of range is smooth and stylish. LION NATHAN-owned. Up and about.

Saltram Barossa V, SA r w ★★★ Excellent-value Mamre Brook (SHIRAZ, CAB SAUV) and (rarely sighted) No 1 Shiraz are leaders. TWE owned. "1859" range worth a look.

Samuel's Gorge McLaren V, SA r ★★ Wild-haired Justin McNamee makes SHIRAZ, TEMPRANILLO of character and place.

Savaterre Beech, Vic r w ★★ (PINOT N) 04' 06' 08' 10' 12 Fine producer of full-bodied CHARD, meaty Pinot N; now close-planted SHIRAZ.

Seppelt Grampians, Vic r w br sp ★★★ (St Peter's SHIRAZ) 96' 97' 02' 04' 06' 08' 10' A historic name owned by TWE. Impressive array of region-specific RIES, CHARD and Shiraz.

Seppeltsfield Barossa V, SA r br ★★★ National Trust Heritage Winery bought by KILIKANOON in 2007. Fortified wine stocks date back to 1878. Table wines show increasing promise.

Sevenhill Clare V, SA r w (br) ★ Owned by the Jesuitical Manresa Society since 1851. Consistently gd, warm SHIRAZ; RIES.

Seville Estate Yarra V, Vic r w ★★★ (SHIRAZ) 04' 05' 06' 10' 12' Excellent CHARD, spicy Shiraz, delicate PINOT N. YARRA V pioneer.

Shadowfax Vic r w ★★ Stylish winery, part of historic Werribee Park. V.gd CHARD, PINOT N, SHIRAZ. Neither fanfare nor bad wines.

Shaw & Smith Ad Hills, SA (r) w ★★★ Founded by Martin Shaw and Australia's first MW, Michael Hill-Smith. Crisp *harmonious* Sauv Bl, complex barrel-fermented M3 CHARD and, surpassing them both, *Shiraz*. Daylight to PINOT N but it's improving. Savvy outfit, black turtle-necks and all.

Shelmerdine Vineyards Heathcote, Vic r w ★★ Elegant wines from estate in the YARRA V, HEATHCOTE. PINOT N, SAUV BL, SHIRAZ, CHARD can all be v.gd.

Southern NSW Zone NSW Incl CANBERRA, Gundagai, Hilltops, TUMBARUMBA.

Spinifex Barossa V, SA r w ★★★ Wonderful boutique BAROSSAN producer. Complex SHIRAZ, GRENACHE blends. Nothing over the top.

Stanton & Killeen Ruth, Vic r br ★★ The untimely death of Chris Killeen in 2007 was a major blow but his children carry on in gd style. Fortified vintage remains the star.

Stefano Lubiana S Tas r w sp ★★★ Beautiful v'yds on banks of Derwent River, 20 minutes from Hobart. Excellent PINOT N, sparkling, MERLOT, CHARD.

Stella Bella Margaret R, WA r w ★★★ Humdinger wines. CAB SAUV, SEM/SAUV BL, CHARD, SHIRAZ, SANGIOVESE/CAB SAUV. Sturdy, characterful.

Stoney Rise Tas r w ★★★ Joe Holyman was wicket keeper for TAS; holds first-class record for highest number of catches on debut; now looks after all winemaking tasks for his outstanding PINOT N, CHARD.

Said it before and must say it again: ignore Aussie Pinot Noir at your peril.

Stonier Wines Mor Pen, Vic r w ★★ (CHARD) 07' 08' 12 13' (PINOT N) 04' 06' 09' 12 13' Consistently gd; Res notable for elegance. Owned by LION NATHAN.

Sunbury Vic *See* MACEDON AND SUNBURY.

Swan Valley WA 20 mins n of Perth. Birthplace of wine in the west. Hot climate makes strong, low-acid wines. FABER V'YDS leads way.

Tahbilk Goulburn V, Vic r w ★★★ (MARSANNE) 01' 06' 08' 13 14' (SHIRAZ) 76' 02' 04' 06' 10 Historic family estate: long-ageing reds, also some of Australia's best old-vine *Marsanne*. Res CAB SAUV can be outstanding; value for money ditto. Rare 1860 Vines Shiraz.

Taltarni Pyrenees, Vic r w sp ★★ SHIRAZ, CAB SAUV in best shape in yrs. Long-haul wines but jack hammer no longer required to remove tannin from your gums.

Tamar Ridge N Tas r w (sp) 230 ha+ of vines make this a major player in TAS. Acquired in 2010 by BROWN BROTHERS. Unexciting initial releases.

Tapanappa SA r ★★★ WRATTONBULLY collaboration between Brian Croser, Bollinger,

J-M Cazes of Pauillac. Splendid CAB SAUV blend, SHIRAZ, MERLOT. Surprising *Pinot N* from Fleurieu Peninsula.

Tar & Roses Heathcote, Vic r w ★★ Affordable SHIRAZ, TEMPRANILLO, SANGIOVESE of impeccable polish, presentation. Modern success story.

TarraWarra Yarra V, Vic r w ★★★ (Res CHARD) 02' 04' 05' 06' 08' 10' 11 12' (Res PINOT N) 04' 06' 10' 12' Has moved from hefty and idiosyncratic to elegant and long. Res far better than standard. Beautiful estate.

Tasmania Cold island region with hot reputation. Outstanding sparkling, PINOT N, RIES. CHARD, SAUV BL, PINOT GR v.gd.

Tatachilla McLaren V, SA r w ★★ Significant production of whites and reds. Acquired by LION NATHAN in 2002. Mouth-to-mouth required.

Taylors Wines Clare V, SA r w ★★ Large-scale production led by RIES, SHIRAZ, CAB SAUV. Exports under Wakefield Wines brand with success.

Ten Minutes by Tractor Mor Pen, Vic r w ★★★ Wacky name, smart packaging, even better wines. *Chard, Pinot N both excellent* and will age. Cracking.

Teusner Barossa V, SA r ★★★ Old vines, clever winemaking, pure fruit flavours. Leads a BAROSSA V trend towards "more wood, no good". All about grapes.

Tim Adams Clare V, SA ★★ Ever-reliable RIES, CAB SAUV/MALBEC blend, SHIRAZ and now TEMPRANILLO.

Tolpuddle Tas ★★★ SHAW & SMITH bought this outstanding 1988-planted v'yd in the Coal River Valley in 2011. Lean (too lean?), lengthy, complex PINOT N, CHARD.

Topaque Vic Iconic RUTH sticky Tokay gains a clumsy new name thanks to the EU.

Torbreck Barossa V, SA r (w) ★★★ The most stylish of cult wineries beloved of the USA. Focus on old-vine Rhône varieties led by SHIRAZ. Rich, sweet, high alcohol. Acrimonious split lead to founder Dave Powell's departure in 2013.

Torzi Matthews Eden V, SA r ★★ Aromatic and stylish SHIRAZ. Excellent value. Torzi Schist Rock Shiraz difficult to say, politely, after a glass or two – but worth the effort.

Treasury Wine Estates (TWE) Aussie wine behemoth. Merger of Beringer Blass and Southcorp wine groups. Dozens of well-known brands, LINDEMAN'S, PENFOLDS, WYNNS, DEVIL'S LAIR, COLDSTREAM HILLS, SALTRAM, BAILEY'S among them.

Trentham Estate Vic (r) w ★ 60,000 cases of family-grown and made, sensibly priced wines from "boutique" winery on Murray River.

Tumbarumba NSW Cool-climate NSW region nestled in the Australian Alps. Sites 500–800m. CHARD the star.

Tumbarumba Chardonnay: great name, and the cool highlands of NSW give super-sleek wines.

Turkey Flat Barossa V, SA r p ★★★ Top producer of bright-coloured rosé, GRENACHE, SHIRAZ from core of 150-yr-old v'yd. Controlled alcohol and oak. New single-v'yd wines. Old but modern, in a gd way.

Two Hands Barossa V, SA r ★★ Brash SHIRAZ from PADTHAWAY, MCLAREN V, Lang C, BAROSSA V, HEATHCOTE. The whole box and dice.

Tyrrell's Hunter V, NSW r w ★★★★ (SEM) 01' 05' 08' 09' 10' 11' 13 (Vat 47 CHARD) 04' 07' 09' 10' 12 13' Australia's greatest maker of Sem, Vat 1 now joined with series of individual v'yd or subregional wines. *Vat 47*, Australia's first Chard, continues to defy the climatic odds. Outstanding old-vine 4 Acres SHIRAZ, Vat 9 Shiraz.

Vasse Felix Margaret R, WA r w ★★★★ (CAB SAUV) 99' 01 04' 07' 08' 09' 10 11 With CULLEN, pioneer of MARGARET R. Elegant Cab Sauv for mid-weight balance. Generally resurgent. Complex CHARD creating waves. Now returning to estate-grown roots.

Voyager Estate Margaret R, WA r w ★★★ Sizeable volume of (mostly) estate-grown, rich, powerful SEM, SAUV BL, CHARD, CAB SAUV/MERLOT. Ever-reliable.

Wantirna Estate Yarra V, Vic r w ★★★★ Regional pioneer showing no sign of slowing down. CHARD, PINOT N, Bordeaux blend all excellent. Tiny production; just the way they like it.

Wendouree Clare V, SA r ★★★ Treasured maker (tiny quantities) of powerful, tannic, concentrated reds, based on SHIRAZ, CAB SAUV, MOURVÈDRE, MALBEC. Recently moved to screwcap. Buy for next generation (or entirely for yourself).

West Cape Howe Denmark, WA r w ★★ The minnow that swallowed the whale in 2009 when it purchased 7,700-tonne Goundrey winery and 237 ha of estate v'yds. V.gd SHIRAZ, CAB SAUV blends.

Westend Estate Riverina, NSW r w ★ Thriving family producer of tasty bargains, esp Private Bin SHIRAZ/Durif. Recent cool-climate additions gd value.

Willow Creek Mor Pen, Vic r w ★★ Gd gear. Impressive producer of CHARD and PINOT N in particular.

Wirra Wirra McLaren V, SA r w (sw) (sp) ★★★ (RSW SHIRAZ) 02' 04' 05' 06' 10' 12' (CAB SAUV) 04' 05' 06' 09' 10' 12' High-quality wines in flashy new livery. RSW Shiraz has edged in front of Cab Sauv. The Angelus Cab Sauv named Dead Ringer in export markets.

Wolf Blass Barossa V, SA r w (br) (sw) (sp) ★★★ (Black Label CAB SAUV blend) 96' 02' 04' 05 06' 10' Owned by TWE. Not the noisy player it once was but still a volume name. Top-end wines overpriced but decent.

Woodlands Margaret R, WA r (w) ★★★ 7 ha of 35-yr-old+ CAB SAUV among the top v'yds in the region, plus younger but still v.gd plantings of other Bordeaux reds. Reds of brooding impact.

Wrattonbully SA Important grape-growing region in LIMESTONE COAST ZONE for 30 yrs; profile lifted by activity of TAPANAPPA, Peppertree.

Wynns Coon, SA r w ★★★★ (SHIRAZ) 98' 99' 04' 05' 06' 10' 12 13' (CAB SAUV) 91' 94' 96' 98' 00' 02' 04' 05' 06' 09' 10' 12 TWE-owned COON classic. RIES, CHARD, Shiraz, *Cab Sauv* all v.gd, esp Black Label Cab Sauv, *John Riddoch Cab Sauv*. Recent single-v'yd releases add lustre. In the form of its long life.

Yabby Lake Mor Pen, Vic r w ★★★ Joint venture between movie magnate Robert Kirby, Larry McKenna, Tod Dexter. Quality rose sharply with winemaker Tom Carson's arrival. Single-site CHARD, PINOT N can be sensational.

Yalumba Barossa V, SA r w sp ★★★ 163 yrs young, family-owned. *Full spectrum of high-quality wines*, from budget to elite single-v'yd. In excellent form. Entry-level Y Series v.gd value.

Yarra Valley Vic Historic area just ne of Melbourne. Growing emphasis on v. successful PINOT N, CHARD, SHIRAZ, sparkling. Deceptively gd CAB SAUV.

Yarra Yering Yarra V, Vic r w ★★★★ (Dry Reds) 93' 94 97' 99' 00' 04' 05' 06' 08' 09' 10 12' Lilydale boutique winery. Powerful PINOT N; deep, herby CAB SAUV (Dry Red No 1); SHIRAZ (Dry Red No 2). Luscious, daring flavours (r w). Much-admired founder Bailey Carrodus died in 2008. Acquired 2009 by KAESLER.

Yellow Tail NSW *See* CASELLA.

Yeringberg Yarra V, Vic r w ★★★★ (MARSANNE/ROUSSANNE) 02' 04 06' 09' 12 13' (CAB SAUV) 00' 04 05' 06' 08' 10' 12' Dreamlike historic estate still in the hands of founding family. Small quantities of v. high-quality Marsanne, Roussanne, CHARD, CAB SAUV, PINOT N.

Yering Station / Yarrabank Yarra V, Vic r w sp ★★ On the site of Vic's first v'yd; replanted after 80-yr gap. Excellent Yering Station table wines (Res CHARD, PINOT N, SHIRAZ, VIOGNIER); Yarrabank (v.gd sparkling wines in joint venture with Champagne Devaux).

Zema Estate Coon, SA r ★ One of last bastions of hand-pruning in COON. Powerful, straightforward reds.

New Zealand

Abbreviations used in the text:

Auck	Auckland
B of P	Bay of Plenty
Cant	Canterbury
N/C Ot	North/Central Otago
Gis	Gisborne
Hawk	Hawke's Bay
Hend	Henderson
Marl	Marlborough
Mart	Martinborough
Nel	Nelson
Waih	Waiheke Island
Waip	Waipara
Wair	Wairarapa

New Zealand now ranks among the 15 largest wine producers in the world. Hard on the heels of the record 2013 vintage, 2014 produced an even heavier crop, equivalent to an extra 84 million bottles of wine to sell. The good news is that Australians have fallen in love with Kiwi Sauvignon Blanc – above all Oyster Bay – and New Zealand has emerged as the second-largest supplier of wine to the UK in the £7+ category, behind only France. Unfortunately over half the country's wine is from a single grape grown in a single region – Marlborough Sauvignon Blanc – but the 1,000-odd Pinot Noirs now on the market are also internationally acclaimed. Chinese companies are investing in vineyard land, and long-established producers are being snapped up by rich American, Australian and Japanese buyers. Chardonnay, Pinot Gris, Merlot and Riesling are also planted widely, with Syrah on the rise, and interest is expanding in varieties not of French origin, particularly Grüner Veltliner, Arneis, Albariño and Verdelho.

Recent vintages

2014 A huge harvest, far bigger than the previous record. April rainfall disrupted vintage in Marlborough, Nelson, Canterbury. Hawke's Bay growers are bullish; in Marlborough, those who picked early fared best.

2013 Record crop and ripe grapes retaining freshness and acidity. Especially good in North Island, Marlborough.

2012 Racy Marlborough Sauv Bl. Best for whites in Hawke's Bay. Central Otago fine all round.

2011 Regions in the middle of the country, including Marlborough, fared best; elsewhere, a stiff test of grape-growing and winemaking skills.

Akarua C Ot r (p) (w) (sp) ★★★ Highly respected producer with consistently outstanding, perfumed, rich Bannockburn PINOT N **12** 13; v.gd drink-young style, Rua. Intense RIES; scented, full-bodied PINOT GR. Vivacious sparklings, NV, Rosé.

Allan Scott Marl w (r) (sp) (p) ★★ Medium-sized family firm. V.gd RIES; tropical-fruit-flavoured SAUV BL. New, charming, strawberry and spice-flavoured PINOT N rosé. Recent focus on organic and sparkling.

Alpha Domus Hawk r w ★★ V.gd CHARD and peachy, slightly creamy, nutty VIOGNIER. Concentrated Bordeaux-style reds, esp savoury MERLOT-based The Navigator **10**' and notably dark, rich CAB SAUV The Aviator **10**'. Top wines labelled AD (superb Noble Selection from SEM **11**'). Everyday range, The Pilot.

Amisfield C Ot r (p) (w) ★★→★★★ Fleshy, smooth PINOT GR; tense, minerally RIES (dr and sw, incl v. intense, racy, Spätlese-style Lowburn Terrace **11**'); lively, ripe SAUV BL; classy Pinot Rosé and dark, rich, savoury PINOT N (RKV Res is Rolls-Royce model). Lake Hayes is lower-tier label.

Ara Marl r w (p) ★★ Huge v'yd in Waihopai Valley; all wines estate-grown. Consistently gd since 2011 with winemaker Jeff Clarke (ex-Montana.) Weighty, dry, ripe SAUV BL; fleshy, off-dry PINOT Gr; floral, fruity PINOT N **12**. Top-tier: Resolute, followed by Select Block, then Single Estate, then Pathway. Value.

Astrolabe Marl (r) w ★★ Rich, harmonious Voyage SAUV BL (oak-aged Taihoa Sauv Bl generous, complex). Also gd, full-bodied PINOT GR; generous, dry CHENIN BL; buttery, moderately complex CHARD; powerful, firm PINOT N.

Ata Rangi Mart r (p) (w) ★★★→★★★★ Small, highly respected. Seductively fragrant, powerful, long-lived *Pinot N* **09**' **10 11** 12, is one of NZ's greatest (oldest vines planted 1980). Delicious younger-vine Crimson PINOT N 13. Notably rich, complex Craighall CHARD 13' from vines planted in 1983; off-dry Lismore PINOT GR 12.

Auckland Largest city (northern, warm, cloudy) in NZ with 1% of v'yd area. Nearby wine districts: Hend, Kumeu/Huapai/Waimauku (both longest); newer (since 1980s): Matakana, Clevedon, Waih. Stylish, savoury, MERLOT/CAB blends in dry seasons (**10**' **13**'), bold, peppery SYRAH is expanding and rivals HAWK for quality; rich, underrated CHARD.

Auntsfield Marl r w ★★ Excellent wines from site of the region's first v'yd, planted in 1873 and replanted 1999. Strong, tropical-fruit, partly barrel-fermented SAUV BL, fleshy, rich CHARD; sturdy, dense PINOT N **12** (Heritage is esp lush, powerful **10**').

Awatere Valley Marl Key subregion (pronounced *Awa-terry*); v. few wineries but huge v'yd area (more than HAWK), pioneered in 1986 by VAVASOUR. YEALANDS is key producer. Slightly cooler and drier than WAIRAU VALLEY: racy, herbaceous ("tomato stalk") SAUV BL; tight, vibrant RIES, PINOT GR; scented, often slightly herbal PINOT N.

Babich Hend r w ★★ →★★★ Sizeable family firm (1916), 3rd generation. HAWK, MARL v'yds. Refined, age-worthy, single-v'yd Irongate CHARD **10' 11** 13'; v. elegant Irongate CAB/MERLOT/CAB FR **10' 09**'. Ripe, dry Marl SAUV BL big seller. Mid-tier Winemakers Res (oak-aged Sauv Bl esp gd). Organic Sauv Bl, GRÜNER V (Headwaters Block).

Bell Hill Cant r w ★★★ Tiny, elevated v'yd on limestone, with family link to GIESEN. Rare but strikingly rich CHARD **11**' and gorgeously-scented, powerful, velvety PINOT N **10' 11**. Second label: Old Weka Pass.

Blackenbrook Nel r w ★★ Small winery; outstanding aromatic whites, esp highly perfumed, rich, Alsace-style GEWURZ 14, PINOT GR **14**' and (rarer) off-dry MUSCAT 14. Punchy SAUV BL 14; v. promising MONTEPULCIANO. Second label: St Jacques.

Borthwick Wair r w ★★ V'yd at Gladstone with Paddy Borthwick brand. Lively, tropical-fruit SAUV BL 14; rich, dryish RIES; peachy, toasty CHARD; fleshy, dry PINOT GR 13; perfumed, supple PINOT N.

Brancott Estate Marl r w (p) ★→★★★ Brand of PERNOD RICARD NZ that replaced Montana worldwide. Top wines: Letter Series (eg. "B" Brancott SAUV BL **13**). Huge-selling, lively, ripely herbaceous MARL Sauv Bl 14; floral, easy-drinking South

> **Babich's century**
>
> Not all producers in the New World are new. In 1910, at the age
> of 14, Josip ("Joe") BABICH left Croatia to join his brothers toiling
> in the gum fields of the far n of NZ. His first wine was produced
> in 1916: happy birthday.

Island PINOT N. Middle-tier Special Res range (rich Sauv Bl, PINOT GR). Living Land:
organic. Flight: plain, low-alcohol. Chosen Rows: v. classy, tight, long-lived Sauv
Bl 10'. Top value Hawk MERLOT 13'.

Brightwater Nel (r) w ★★ Impressive, gd-value whites, esp weighty, crisp, flavour-
packed SAUV BL 14'; fresh, medium-dry RIES; lively, citrus, gently oaked CHARD; rich,
gently sweet PINOT GR. PINOT N fast improving 12. Top wines: Lord Rutherford.

Cable Bay Waih r (p) w ★★ Waih-based producer, recently restructured, with v.
refined CHARD 13'; sturdy, complex VIOGNIER; bold yet stylish SYRAH. Subtle, fine-
textured MARL SAUV BL. Third label: Selection. Outstanding Res Chard 13'.

Canterbury NZ's 5th-largest wine region; most v'yds are in relatively warm,
sheltered, n Waip district. Greatest success with aromatic, vibrant RIES (since
mid-80s) and later dark, rich PINOT N. Emerging strength in Alsace-style PINOT GR.
SAUV BL also widely planted.

Carrick C Ot r w ★★★ Bannockburn winery with intense RIES (dry, medium C OT;
sweetish Josephine); tight, elegant CHARD, esp EBM 12'; densely packed PINOT N,
built to last. Delicious, drink-young Unravelled PINOT N 13'.

Central Otago (r) 10' 12 13' 14 (w) 10' 12 13' 14 Cool, low-rainfall, high-altitude inland
region (now NZ's 3rd-largest) in s of South Island. Most vines are in Cromwell
Basin. Scented, crisp RIES, PINOT GR; PINOT N (75% v'yd area) is perfumed, vibrantly
fruity, with drink-young charm; top wines mature 5 yrs+. V.gd PINOT N rosé and
traditional-method sparkling.

Chard Farm C Ot r w ★★ Pioneer winery with fleshy, oily PINOT GR; perfumed, mid-
weight, supple PINOT N (River Run: floral, charming; single-vy'd The Tiger 12 and
The Viper 12 more complex). Light, smooth Rabbit Ranch Pinot N.

Church Road Hawk r w (p) ★★→★★★ A PERNOD RICARD NZ winery; historic HAWK
roots. Rich barrel-aged CHARD 13'; ripe, partly oak-aged SAUV BL; weighty, slightly
sweet, Alsace-style PINOT GR; dark, full MERLOT/CAB SAUV (value). Impressive Grand
Res wines; superb, pricey, Bordeaux-style red TOM 09'. *McDonald Series,*
between standard and Grand Res ranges, offers eye-catching quality, value (incl
SYRAH 12).

Churton Marl r w ★★ Elevated Waihopai Valley site with subtle, bone-dry SAUV BL 13';
sturdy, creamy VIOGNIER; fragrant, harmonious PINOT N 10' 11 12 (esp The Abyss:
oldest vines, greater depth 10'). Sweet, steely, compelling PETIT MANSENG 13'.

Clearview Hawk r (p) w ★★→★★★ Coastal v'yd (also drawing grapes from inland)
renowned for hedonistic, well-oaked Res CHARD 13'; impressive oak-fermented
Res SAUV BL; dark, rich Res CAB FR, Enigma (MERLOT-based), Old Olive Block (CABS
SAUV/Fr blend). Second-tier: Beachhead, Cape Kidnappers.

Clifford Bay Marl r w ★★ Gd, affordable range from Foley Family Wines. Fresh, racy
gooseberry and lime SAUV BL, scented, vibrant PINOT GR are best.

Clos Henri Marl r w ★★→★★★ Started by Henri Bourgeois of Sancerre. Weighty,
well-rounded SAUV BL (stony soils) one of NZ's best; sturdy, ripe, firm PINOT N
(clay) 12'. Second label: Bel Echo (reverses variety/soil match). Third label Petit
Clos, from young vines. Distinctive, satisfying wines, priced right.

Cloudy Bay Marl r w sp ★★★ Large-volume but still classy SAUV BL (weighty, dry, fine,
some barrel ageing since 2010). NZ's most famous wine (14'). CHARD (robust,
complex, crisp 12), PINOT N (rich, supple 10' 11 12) both classy. Pelorus vintage
sparkling (toasty, rich), elegant, Chard-led NV. Rarer GEWURZ, Late Harvest

RIES, barrel-aged, medium-dry Ries and Te Koko (oak-aged Sauv Bl); all full of personality. Expanding involvement in C OT: Te Wahi PINOT N. Owned by LVMH.

Constellation New Zealand Auck r (p) w ★→★★ NZ's largest wine company, previously Nobilo Wine Group, now owned by US-based Constellation Brands. Strength in solid, lower-priced wines. Nobilo MARL SAUV BL (fresh, ripe, tropical) is big seller in the USA. *See* KIM CRAWFORD, Monkey Bay, SELAKS.

Cooper's Creek Auck r w ★★→★★★ Innovative medium-sized producer; well-made, gd-value wines from four regions. Excellent, high-flavoured Swamp Res CHARD 13'; gd SAUV BL, RIES; MERLOT; top-value VIOGNIER; easy-drinking PINOT N. SV (Select V'yd) range mid-tier. NZ's first: ARNEIS (2006), GRÜNER V (2008), ALBARIÑO (2011).

Craggy Range Hawk r (p) ★★★ High-profile winery with large v'yds in HAWK and MART. Stylish CHARD 13', PINOT N; excellent, rich, mid-range MERLOT and SYRAH from GIMBLETT GRAVELS; dense Sophia (Merlot), The Quarry (CAB SAUV), show-stopping SYRAH Le Sol 09' 10' 11. Latest reds more supple, refined (Te Kahu, Merlot-based blend, is gd value.)

Delegat's Auck r w ★★ V. large, listed company (two million cases/yr), still controlled by the Delegat family. V'yds in HAWK and MARL. Hugely successful OYSTER BAY brand. Delegat range revamped from 2012: tight, crisp, citrus CHARD; full-flavoured, herbaceous SAUV BL; vibrantly fruity, supple MERLOT.

Destiny Bay Waih r ★★→★★★ Expatriate Americans produce Bordeaux-style reds: at best brambly and silky. Flagship is substantial, deep, savoury Magna Praemia 08' (mostly CAB SAUV). Mid-tier: Mystae 09. Some recent disappointments. Can be classy, but v. pricey.

Deutz Auck sp ★★★ Champagne house gives name to refined sparklings from MARL by PERNOD RICARD NZ. V. popular NV is lively, citrus, yeasty (min 2 yrs on lees). Vintage Blanc de Blancs is finely scented, vivacious, piercing (10). Rosé is crisp, toasty, strawberryish. Prestige is esp classy, mostly CHARD 10' 11.

Dog Point Marl r w ★★★ Grower Ivan Sutherland and winemaker James Healy (both ex-CLOUDY BAY) make complex, minerally, oak-aged SAUV BL (Section 94); CHARD (v. elegant, citrus, age-worthy); rich, finely textured PINOT N 10' 11 12', one of region's greatest. Also larger volume, but weighty, dry, unoaked Sauv Bl 14.

Dry River Mart r w ★★★ Small pioneer winery, now US-owned. Reputation for v. elegant, long-lived CHARD, RIES 13', PINOT GR (NZ's first outstanding Pinot Gr 13'), GEWURZ 13'; late-harvest whites; floral, sweet-fruited, slowly-evolving PINOT N 09' 10 11; dense, elegant SYRAH 11.

Elephant Hill Hawk r (p) w ★★ German-owned v'yd, stylish winery at Te Awanga on coast, also draws grapes from inland. Sophisticated: scented, oily, rich VIOGNIER 13'; rich CHARD; dark, floral, concentrated SYRAH 13'.

Escarpment Mart r (w) ★★★ Known for savoury, complex, dense PINOT N, made by Larry McKenna, formerly of MARTINBOROUGH V'YD. Top label: Kupe 10' 11. Single-v'yd, old-vine reds (Kiwa 12' and Te Rehua 12' are esp gd). MART Pinot N is regional blend 10' 11. Lower-tier: The Edge.

Use for old wine barrels: skateboards, from The Paper Rain Project. Obvious, really.

Esk Valley Hawk r p w ★★→★★★ Owned by VILLA MARIA. Acclaimed MERLOT-based reds (esp Winemakers Res blend 11 10' 09'); top value Merlot/CAB SAUV/MALBEC 13'. Lovely dry Rosé 14; full-bodied CHARD; crisp CHENIN BL, VERDELHO. Flagship red: The Terraces (spicy, single-v'yd blend, MALBEC/Merlot/CAB FR 09' 06').

Felton Road C Ot r w ★★★★ Star winery at Bannockburn. Bold yet graceful PINOT N Block 3 and 5 10', 11, 12' 13' from The Elms V'yd; light, intense RIES (dr s/ sw) outstanding; rich, citrus, long-lived CHARD (esp Block 2 12'); key label is perfumed, deep, harmonious Bannockburn Pinot N 12' 13', blended from its three v'yds. Other v. fine single-v'yd Pinot Ns: Cornish Point 13', Calvert 13'.

Forrest Marl r (p) w ★★ Mid-size winery. Gd SAUV BL (full-bodied, ripe, dry) and RIES (medium-dry); gorgeous botrytized Ries; rich HAWK Newton/Forrest Cornerstone (Bordeaux red blend). Distinguished flagship range, John Forrest Collection. Popular low-alcohol (9%) Ries and Sauv Bl: The Doctors'. Impressive Otago range: Tatty Bogler.

Framingham Marl (r) w ★★ Owned by Sogrape (*see* Portugal). Strength in aromatic whites: intense, zesty RIES (esp rich Classic) from mature vines. Perfumed, lush PINOT GR, GEWURZ. Subtle SAUV BL. Scented, silky PINOT N. Rare F Series wines, full of personality.

Fromm Marl r w ★★★ Distinguished PINOT N, incl valley-floor Fromm V'yd 12 10' 09' and esp hill-grown *Clayvin* V'yd (more perfumed, supple 12' 11 10'). Also v. stylish, citrus Clayvin CHARD 11' and RIES Dry. Earlier-drinking La Strada range also v.gd. Clayvin V'yd leased to GIESEN, but Fromm will still draw grapes. Excellent dry Rosé 14.

Gibbston Valley C Ot r (p) w ★★→★★★ Pioneer winery with popular restaurant at Gibbston. Most but not all v'yds at Bendigo. Strong reputation for PINOT N, esp rich CENTRAL OTAGO blend 13' and exuberantly fruity Res 13' 12' 09'. Scented, silky Le Maitre 13' from original vines. Racy, medium-dry RIES 13', scented, full-bodied PINOT GR. Gold River Pinot N: drink-young charm.

Giesen Cant (r) w ★★ Large family winery with fast-growing emphasis on quality. Most is ripe, tangy MARL SAUV BL. Generous, medium RIES (value). Also bold The Brothers Sauv Bl and weighty, rich, barrel-fermented The August Sauv Bl 12'. Fast-improving PINOT N (esp The Brothers) and Single Vineyard bottlings. Recently leased famous Clayvin Vineyard.

Gimblett Gravels is defined entirely by soil type: surprisingly rare in the world.

Gimblett Gravels Hawk Defined area (800 ha planted), with mostly free-draining, low-fertility soils noted for rich Bordeaux-style reds (typically MERLOT-led, but stony soils suit CAB SAUV), *floral, vibrant Syrah*. Best of both are world-class. Also powerful, age-worthy CHARD, VIOGNIER. Producers increasingly promote Gimblett Gravels origin, ahead of HAWK.

Gisborne (r) 10'13' 14 (w) 14' 13' NZ's 4th-largest region, on e coast of North Island; plantings have shrunk in past five yrs but now stable. Abundant sunshine but often rainy; v. fertile soils. Key is CHARD (deliciously fragrant and soft in youth, but best mature well.) Excellent GEWURZ, VIOGNIER; MERLOT, PINOT GR more variable. Interest in ALBARIÑO (rain-resistant). Star winery: MILLTON.

Gladstone Vineyard Wair r w ★★ Tropical SAUV BL (incl barrel-fermented Sophie's Choice); weighty, smooth PINOT GR; gd med-dry RIES; classy VIOGNIER; v. graceful PINOT N under top label, Gladstone 13'; 12,000 Miles is lower-priced brand.

Grasshopper Rock C Ot r ★★→★★★ Estate-grown at Alexandra. Subregion's finest red 10'11 12': graceful, harmonious, with strong cherry and dried-herb flavours. V. age-worthy; great value.

Greenhough Nel r w ★★→★★★ One of region's top producers; immaculate RIES, SAUV BL, CHARD, PINOT N. Top label: Hope V'yd (complex, organic Chard; fleshy, old-vine PINOT BL is NZ's finest 12'; mushroomy Pinot N 10' 11).

Greystone Waip (r) w ★★★ Star producer with notably perfumed, rich aromatic whites (RIES 13, GEWURZ 13', PINOT GR 13); fast-improving CHARD 13', SAUV BL, PINOT N 12. Bought MUDDY WATER in 2011.

Greywacke Marl r w ★★→★★★ Distinguished wines from Kevin Judd, ex-CLOUDY BAY. Incisive SAUV BL 14'; weighty CHARD 12'; fleshy PINOT GR 13'; gently sweet RIES 13; silky, savoury PINOT N 12 11. Barrel-fermented Wild Sauv 12' is full of personality.

Grove Mill Marl r w ★★ Attractive whites, esp punchy SAUV BL, perfumed GEWURZ 13', slightly sweet RIES. Value lower-tier Sanctuary brand. Foley Family Wines owns.

Hans Herzog Marl r w ★★★ Warm, stony v'yd at Rapaura with powerful, long-lived MERLOT/CAB SAUV (region's greatest 05'); MONTEPULCIANO 11; PINOT 10; sturdy, dry VIOGNIER and PINOT GR; fleshy, oak-aged SAUV BL. V. rare NEBBIOLO 11. Sold under Hans brand in Europe, USA.

Hawke's Bay (r) 09'10' 13' 14' (w) 10'13' 14 NZ's 2nd-largest region. Long history of winemaking in sunny, warm climate. Prime soils are GIMBLETT GRAVELS. Rich, classy MERLOT and CAB SAUV-based reds in gd vintages; SYRAH (floral, vibrant plum and black pepper flavours) a fast-rising star; powerful, peachy CHARD; ripe, rounded SAUV BL (suits oak); NZ's best VIOGNIER. Alsace-style PINOT GR from elevated, inland districts. Central Hawk (elevated, cooler) suits PINOT N.

Highfield Marl r w sp ★★ Stunning views from Tuscan-style tower. Light, intense RIES 13, citrus CHARD 13; immaculate, racy SAUV BL and generous, savoury PINOT N 11. Elstree sparkling variable lately. Second label: Paua.

Huia Marl (r) w (sp) ★★ V. satisfying, organic SAUV BL 14'; fleshy, dry PINOT GR; bold PINOT N 10' 12. Complex Brut 09'. Gd-value, lower-priced range: Hunky Dory.

Hunter's Marl (r) (p) w (sp) ★★→★★★ Pioneer, medium-sized winery with classic, dry, tropical-fruit SAUV BL 14. Kaho Roa is ripe, oak-aged Sauv Bl 13. Vibrant, gently oaked CHARD. Excellent sparkling (*MiruMiru*). RIES, GEWURZ, PINOT GR all rewarding and value. PINOT N easy-drinking. Second label: Stoneburn.

Invivo Auck r w ★★ Fast-expanding young producer with strong, nettley, mineral MARL SAUV BL 14; full-bodied, medium-dry Marl PINOT GR 14; punchy, medium C OT RIES 14; classy C Ot CHARD 13'; weighty, rich C Ot PINOT N 12'.

Jackson Estate Marl r w ★★ Weighty, lush Stich SAUV BL is consistently excellent 13; v. attractive, citrus, peachy, nutty CHARD 12 and vibrant, fruit-packed Homestead PINOT N 13. Gd value.

Johanneshof Marl (r) w sp ★★ Small winery acclaimed for perfumed, gently sweet, soft GEWURZ (one of NZ's finest 13). Crisp, dry, lively Emmi sparkling; v.gd RIES, PINOT GR. Maybern PINOT N from cool, wet site often less exciting, but scented, complex, savoury 13' is best yet.

Jules Taylor Marl (r) (p) w ★★ Skilfully crafted MARL and GISBORNE WINOU. PINO, citrus, creamy Marl CHARD; sturdy, dry Marl PINOT GR; classy, intense Marl SAUV BL; vivacious, dry Gisborne Rosé 14; graceful, supple Marl PINOT N 13.

Julicher Mart r (w) (p) ★★ Small producer with vibrantly fruity, slightly biscuity CHARD; delicious dry Rosé 13; distinguished, savoury PINOT N 10'11. 99 Rows is 2nd tier Pinot N 12. V.gd value.

Kim Crawford Hawk ★→★★ Brand owned by CONSTELLATION NEW ZEALAND. Easy-drinking wines, incl scented, tasty MARL SAUV BL (gd quality, one million cases/yr); fresh, fruity HAWK MERLOT; light MARL PINOT N. Low alcohol range: First Pick.

Kumeu River Auck (r) w ★★★ Rich, complex Estate CHARD 10'11 12 is multi-site blend. Single-v'yd Mate's V'yd Chard (planted 1990) is more opulent 10'11 12; single-v'yd Hunting Hill Chard 10'11 12 is rising star: notably refined, tight-knit. Lower-tier Village Chard is great value. Weighty, floral PINOT GR; sturdy, earthy PINOT N.

Lake Chalice Marl (r) (p) w ★★ Medium-sized producer with vibrant, creamy CHARD; buoyantly fruity, dry PINOT GR; incisive, slightly sweet RIES; crisp, ripely herbaceous SAUV BL (esp intense, zingy The Raptor). Solid PINOT N. Lower-tier: The Nest.

Lawson's Dry Hills Marl (r) (p) w ★★→★★★ Gd-value wines. Best known for Incisive, faintly oaked SAUV BL 14 and exotically perfumed, sturdy GEWURZ 12. Dry, toasty, bottle-aged RIES, CHARD. Fast-improving PINOT N. Top-end range: The Pioneer. New Res range: weighty, rich Sauv Bl 14'.

Lindauer Auck ★→★★ Hugely popular, low-priced sparkling brand, esp bottle-fermented Lindauer Brut NV, owned by LION NATHAN. Latest batches offer lively, easy drinking, with a touch of complexity; rosé version is esp gd value.

Lowburn Ferry C Ot r ★★ PINOT N specialist. Flagship is The Ferryman Res (lovely, savoury, velvety **13'**). Also Home Block (fleshy, rich, silky **10' 12 13**); Skeleton Creek (not entirely estate-grown, but concentrated, complex **13**).

Mahi Marl r w ★★ Stylish, complex wines. Sweet-fruited, finely textured SAUV BL (part oak-aged); weighty, vibrant, gently oaked CHARD; weighty, soft, dry PINOT GR; savoury, mushroomy PINOT N **12**.

Man O' War Auck r w ★★★ Largest v'yd on Waih. Crisp, tight, penetrating CHARD; impressive, weighty, rich, medium PINOT GR **13'** (grown on adjacent Ponui Island). Dense Bordeaux-style reds (esp Ironclad **10' 11**); powerful, spicy, firm Dreadnought SYRAH **10' 11 12'**.

Marisco Marl r w ★★ Owned by Brent Marris, ex-WITHER HILLS. Fast-growing Waihopai Valley producer with two brands, The Ned and (latterly) Marisco The King's Series. Impressive, ripe, rich Marisco The King's Favour SAUV BL **13'**; fresh, punchy The Ned Sauv Bl **13'**. Gd CHARD, PINOT GR, PINOT N.

Marlborough (r) **10' 12 13' 14** (w) **13' 14** NZ's largest region (65% of plantings at top of South Island; first vines in modern era planted 1973. Warm, sunny days and cold nights give v. aromatic, crisp whites. Intense SAUV BL, from sharp, green capsicum to ripe tropical fruit (top wines are often faintly oak-influenced). Fresh medium-dry RIES (recent wave of sweet, low-alcohol wines); some of NZ's best PINOT GR, GEWURZ; CHARD is leaner than HAWK but can mature well. High-quality sparkling and botrytized Ries. PINOT N underrated, top examples (from n-facing clay hillsides) among NZ's finest. Interest stirring in GRÜNER V.

Martinborough Wair (r) **10' 13' 14** (w) **13 14** Small, prestigious district in s WAIR (foot of North Island). Warm summers, dry autumns, gravelly soils. Success with several white grapes (SAUV BL, PINOT GR widely planted), but esp acclaimed since mid-late 1980s for sturdy, rich, long-lived PINOT N (higher percentage of mature vines than other regions).

Martinborough Vineyard Mart r (p) (w) ★★★ Pioneer winery; famous PINOT N **10'** cherryish, spicy, nutty, complex. Rich, biscuity CHARD; intense RIES (dr s/sw); rich medium-dry PINOT GR. Single-v'yd Burnt Spur, drink-young Te Tera ranges (top value Pinot N). After financial problems, sold to Foley Family Wines in 2014.

Matawhero Gis r (p) w ★★ Former star GEWURZ producer of the 1980s, now with new owner and gd, fruit-driven, unoaked CHARD, Gewurz (fleshy, soft), plummy fruity MERLOT, promising ALBARIÑO, ARNEIS, GRÜNER V. Top range: Church House.

Matua Valley Auck r w ★★→★★★ Producer of NZ's first SAUV BL in 1974 (Auckland grapes). Now owned by TWE, with v'yds in four regions. Most are pleasant, easy drinking. Luxury range of Single V'yd wines, incl v. classy HAWK ALBARIÑO **14** powerful, complex Hawk CHARD **13'**; dark, dense MERLOT **13'**; SYRAH **13'**.

Mills Reef B of P r w ★★→★★★ Impressive wines from estate v'yds in GIMBLETT GRAVELS and other HAWK grapes. Top Elspeth range incl rich CHARD **13**, powerful Bordeaux-style reds and SYRAH (latest vintages more refined, supple). Res range reds can be gd value (esp dark, fragrant, rich Res MERLOT/MALBEC **13'**).

Millton Gis r (p) w ★★→★★★★ Region's top winery, esp for whites. Wines certified organic. Hill-grown single-v'yd Clos de Ste Anne range (CHARD, CHENIN BL

Riesling stars

"Jesus Drank Riesling" is the message on T-shirts worn by many NZ winemakers in love with this great grape – but few of the country's wine drinkers worship at the same altar. RIES flourishes in the coolness of the South Island, yielding classy, scented, vibrantly fruity wines, ranging from light-bodied to mouthfilling and bone-dry to super-sweet (a style variability that partly explains sluggish sales). Classic labels incl DRY RIVER Craighall V'yd, FELTON ROAD Bannockburn, NEUDORF Moutere, PEGASUS BAY, RIPPON V'YD Mature Vine and VALLI Old Vine.

VIOGNIER, SYRAH, PINOT N) is strikingly rich, complex, characterful. Long-lived, oak-aged *Chenin Bl* (distinctly honeyed in wetter vintages), is NZ's finest 14'. Lower-tier range: Crazy by Nature.

Misha's C Ot r w ★★ Large v'yd at Bendigo. Consistently classy GEWURZ 13, PINOT GR 13, RIES (dry Lyric 13' and slightly sweet Limelight 13'); sophisticated, partly oak-aged SAUV BL 13'; savoury, complex PINOT N 10' (Verismo is oak-aged longer 10').

Mission Hawk r (p) w ★★ NZ's oldest wine producer, first vines 1851; first wine sales in 1890s; still owned by Catholic Society of Mary. Solid varietals: fruit-driven SYRAH, PINOT N (MART) are top-value. Res range incl excellent MERLOT 13', CAB SAUV 13', Syrah 13', CHARD 13'. Top label: Jewelstone (classy Chard 13' and Cab/MERLOT 09'). Purchased large AWATERE VALLEY v'yd in 2012 (crisp, incisive MARL SAUV BL).

Mondillo C Ot r w ★★ Rising star at Bendigo; scented, citrus, slightly sweet RIES 13, classy Nina Late Harvest Ries 12' 14, powerful, fruity, supple PINOT N 12' 13'.

Pinot N: <10% of NZ production but 25% of total number (not volume) of wines

Mount Riley Marl r w (p) ★★ Medium-sized family firm. Punchy, gd-value SAUV BL; finely textured PINOT GR; gd drink young CHARD, easy-drinking PINOT N. Top range is Seventeen Valley (elegant, complex Chard 11 13; fleshy, barrel-fermented Sauv Bl 12; fresh, savoury Pinot N 13).

Mt Difficulty C Ot r (p) w ★★→★★★ Quality producer in warm Bannockburn. Powerful, concentrated PINOT N: Roaring Meg is lighter, Cromwell Basin blend for early consumption; single-v'yd Pipeclay Terrace dense, lasting. Classy whites (RIES, PINOT GR, v. promising CHENIN BL 12).

Muddy Water Waip r w ★★→★★★ Small high-quality producer now owned by GREYSTONE. Organic James Hardwick RIES (weighty, medium-dry, among NZ's best 13'); mineral CHARD; savoury, notably complex PINOT N (esp Slowhand, based on oldest, low-yielding vines 12').

Mud House Cant r w ★★→★★★ Large MARL-based producer of South Island wines (incl WAIP and C OT), bought in 2013 by Australian Accolade Wines. Brands incl Mud House, WAIPARA HILLS, Hay Maker (lower tier). Regional blends incl punchy Marl SAUV BL (classy and value 14); scented, oily Marl PINOT GR 14; lively, strong-flavoured, medium-dry RIES 14. Excellent Estate selection (single v'yds) and Single V'yd range (from growers).

Nautilus Marl r w sp ★★→★★★ Medium-sized, v. reliable range of distributors Négociants (NZ), owned by S Smith & Sons (*see* Yalumba, Australia). Top wines incl tight, dry SAUV BL 14; v. classy CHARD (complex, subtle 13'); sturdy, savoury PINOT N 12, Alsace-style PINOT GR; intense, yeasty NV sparkler, one of NZ's finest (min 3 yrs on lees). Mid-tier: Opawa (fruit-driven). Lower tier: Twin Islands.

Nelson (r) 10 13 14 (w) 13 14 Smallish region west of MARL; climate wetter but equally sunny. Clay soils of Upper Moutere hills (full-bodied wines) and silty WAIMEA plains (more aromatic). Strengths in aromatic whites, esp RIES, SAUV BL, PINOT GR, GEWURZ; also gd (sometimes outstanding) CHARD, PINOT N. Too often underrated.

Neudorf Nel r (p) w ★★★→★★★★ A small winery with a deservedly big reputation. Powerful, mineral *Moutere Chard* 10' 11 12 13' one of NZ's greatest; superb, savoury Moutere PINOT N 12', SAUV BL, powerful, off-dry PINOT GR 13'; RIES (dr s/sw) also top flight. Delightful dry Pinot Rosé.

Ngatarawa Hawk r w ★★ Mid-sized producer, owned by Corban family. Popular Stables Res range: mouthfilling, vibrant HAWK CHARD; sturdy, firm Hawk MERLOT/CAB; generous, supple Hawk SYRAH 13. Top range: Alwyn. Second tier: Glazebrook.

No. 1 Family Estate Marl sp ★★ Family-owned company of pioneer Daniel Le Brun, ex-Champagne. No longer owns Daniel Le Brun brand. Specialist in often v.gd sparkling wine, esp citrus, yeasty, tight-knit, NV Blanc de Blancs, Cuvée No 1.

Nobilo Marl *See* CONSTELLATION NEW ZEALAND.

Obsidian Waih r (p) w ★★–★★★ Onetangi v'yd with v. stylish Bordeaux blend (The Obsidian 10'), VIOGNIER, CHARD 13', SYRAH, TEMPRANILLO under top brand Obsidian Res (was Obsidian). Gd-value Waih reds (incl MERLOT, Syrah, MONTEPULCIANO, Tempranillo) under 2nd-tier Obsidian label (was Weeping Sands).

Oyster Bay Marl r w sp ★★ From DELEGAT'S, this is a marketing triumph. Vibrant wines with a touch of class, from MARL and HAWK. Marl SAUV BL is huge seller (punchy, passion fruit/lime), citrus, gently oaked Marl CHARD (v. popular in the USA), medium-bodied, dry, Grigio-style Hawk PINOT GR; supple, strawberryish Marl PINOT N, fragrant, smooth Hawk MERLOT, easy-drinking sparklers.

Palliser Mart r w ★★–★★★★ One of district's largest and best. Excellent, lively, tropical-fruit SAUV BL 13', CHARD 13', RIES 13, PINOT GR 13, bubbly (best in MART); perfumed, rich, v. harmonious PINOT N 10 13'. Top wines: Palliser Estate. Lower tier: Pencarrow (great value, majority of output).

Pask Hawk r w ★★ Mid-size winery; extensive v'yds in GIMBLETT GRAVELS. CAB SAUV, MERLOT, SYRAH well-priced and full-flavoured, can be green-edged. V.gd CHARD. Top Declaration range incl fleshy, rich, toasty Chard 13. Lower tier: Roys Hill.

Passage Rock Waih r w ★★ Powerful, opulent SYRAH, esp Res (Waih's most awarded wine 10' 12); non-Res also dense, fine-value 10' 12. Gd Bordeaux-style reds, whites solid (esp bold, creamy Res VIOGNIER 13').

Pegasus Bay Waip r w ★★★ Pioneer family firm with superb range: taut, slow-evolving, complex CHARD 11, SAUV BL/SEM; rich, zingy, medium RIES (big seller) 12'; lush, silky PINOT N 10' 11 12, esp mature-vine Prima Donna 10' 11 12'. Second label: Main Divide, v.gd value, esp PINOT GR.

Peregrine C Ot r w ★★ Crisp, concentrated whites (esp RIES, dry, slightly sweet Rastaburn) and fleshy, rich, v. finely balanced CHARD 13'. Scented, silky PINOT N 09' 11 12. Saddleback Pinot N gd value.

Pernod Ricard NZ Auck r (p) w sp ★–★★★ NZ's 3rd-largest producer, formerly Montana. Changes since 2010 incl withdrawal from GIS and axing of Montana brand in favour of BRANCOTT ESTATE. Wineries in AUCK, HAWK, MARL. Extensive co-owned v'yds for Marl whites, incl crisp, punchy, huge-selling Brancott Estate SAUV BL 14. Strength in sparkling, esp DEUTZ Marl Cuvée. Classy, great-value CHURCH ROAD reds, quality CHARD. Other key brand: STONELEIGH (tropical Sauv Bl).

Pisa Range C Ot r (w) ★★→★★★ Small v'yd; rich Black Poplar PINOT N 10' 12; v.gd young vine Pinot N 13: Run 245. Crisp, dryish PINOT GR and rich, dry RIES 13'.

Puriri Hills Auck r (p) ★★→★★★ Classy, silky, seductive MERLOT-based reds from Clevedon 08' 10'. Res is esp rich and plump, with more new oak. Top label is outstandingly lush, complex Pope 10'.

Pyramid Valley Cant r w ★★→★★★ Tiny elevated limestone v'yd at Waikari. Estate-grown, floral, increasingly generous PINOT N (Angel Flower, Earth Smoke 10' 12) arrestingly full-bodied CHARD 12. Classy Growers Collection wines from other regions. Not universally admired, but strong personality.

Quartz Reef C Ot r w sp ★★→★★★ Small, quality bio producer with crisp, dry PINOT GR 13; sturdy, spicy PINOT N 10' 13', Bendigo Estate esp concentrated 10' 12; intense yeasty, racy sparkling (vintage esp gd 09).

Rippon Vineyard C Ot r w ★★→★★★ Stunning pioneer v'yd on shores of Lake Wanaka; arresting wines. Scented, concentrated Rippon PINOT N 10' 12' from mature vines; Jeunesse Pinot N 12' is younger vines. Powerful, highly complex Tinker's Field Pinot N (from oldest vines 10' 12'). Slowly evolving whites, esp outstanding, steely, minerally RIES 10' 11' 12' 13.

Rockburn C Ot r (p) w ★★ Crisp, lively, slightly sweet PINOT GR, v.gd medium-sweet RIES 13', SAUV BL. Fragrant, rich PINOT N 10' 12' blended from Cromwell Basin (mostly) and Gibbston grapes, is best. Second label: Devil's Staircase.

Sacred Hill Hawk r w ★★→★★★ Mid-size producer, partly Chinese-owned

Acclaimed Riflemans CHARD 10' 13', powerful but refined, from inland, elevated site. Dark, long-lived Brokenstone MERLOT 09' 10' 11, Helmsman CAB/Merlot 09' 10' 11 and Deerstalkers SYRAH 09' 10' 12, from GIMBLETT GRAVELS. Punchy MARL SAUV BL. Halo: mid-tier. Other brands: Gunn Estate, Wild South (gd-value Marl range).

Saint Clair Marl r (p) w ★★ →★★★ Largest family-owned producer in region. Highly acclaimed for pungent SAUV BL from lower Wairau Valley: esp great-value regional blend 14, strikingly rich, slightly salty, minerally Wairau Res 14. Easy-drinking RIES, PINOT GR, CHARD, MERLOT, PINOT N. Res is top range; then a wide array of classy, 2nd-tier Pioneer Block wines (incl several classy Pinot N, Sauv Bl); then gd-value regional blends; 4th tier is Vicar's Choice. Recent investment in HAWK for reds.

Seifried Estate Nel (r) w ★★ Region's biggest winery, family-owned. Long respected for gd, medium-dry RIES 14' and GEWURZ 14'; now also gd-value, often excellent SAUV BL 14', CHARD 13'. Peachy, spicy GRÜNER V 14. Best: Winemakers Collection. Old Coach Road is 3rd tier. Whites much better than reds.

Selaks Marl r w ★→★★ Old producer of Croatian origin, now a brand of CONSTELLATION NEW ZEALAND. Solid, easy-drinking Premium Selection range. Gd Res HAWK CHARD, MERLOT/CAB, SYRAH. Revived top Founders range: esp gd SAUV BL 14',Chard 13',

Seresin Marl r w ★★ →★★★ Medium-sized; organic focus, excellent quality. Subtle, sophisticated, age-worthy SAUV BL 13' (partly barrel-fermented), is one of NZ's finest; v. tight, rich Res Sauv Bl from oldest vines 11'. Excellent CHARD, PINOTS N/GR, RIES; 2nd tier Momo (gd quality/value). Overall, complex, finely textured wines.

Royal NZ Navy banned alcohol on board: too much inappropriate behaviour, ahem.

Sileni Hawk (p) w ★★ Large producer. Top wines: powerful, rich EV (Exceptional Vintage) CHARD 10' 13', SYRAH 13'. Mid-range incl lush, buttery The Lodge Chard 13', The Triangle MERLOT, The Plateau PINOT N 13'; then Cellar Selection (gd, easy-drinking Merlot, off-dry PINOT GR). Rich, smooth MARL SAUV BL (esp The Straits).

Spy Valley Marl r (p) w ★★ →★★★ High-achieving company; extensive v'yds. Richly flavoured aromatic whites (RIES 13', GEWURZ 13', PINOT GR 13' 14), superb value; also impressive SAUV BL 14, CHARD 13', PINOT N 12. Satisfying, dry Pinot N Rosé 14. Classy top selection: Envoy (rich, subtle Chard 12, Alsace-style Pinot Gr, Mosel-like Ries, powerful, concentrated Outpost Pinot N 12'). Second label: Satellite.

Staete Landt Marl r w ★★ V'yd at Rapaura (Wairau Valley) producing refined CHARD 11 (biscuity, rounded); top-flight Annabel SAUV BL 13' (fleshy, rich, tropical, partly oak-aged); creamy, complex, dry PINOT GR; graceful PINOT N 12. V. promising VIOGNIER 13', SYRAH 11'. Second label: Map Maker (gd value).

Stonecroft Hawk r w ★★ Small winery. NZ's 1st serious SYRAH (1989), Res 10' 13'; Serine Syrah is lighter. Outstanding Old-Vine CHARD 12, v. rich Old-Vine GEWURZ 14'. Sound SAUV BL. NZ's only ZIN (medium-bodied, spicy 13).

Stoneleigh Marl r (p) w ★★ Owned by PERNOD RICARD NZ. Based on relatively warm Rapaura v'yds. Gd large-volume MARL whites, incl punchy, tropical SAUV BL 14; generous, floral, slightly sweet PINOT GR 14; full-bodied, strong RIES 13, fast improving, savoury PINOT N 13. Mid-tier range: Latitude (incl fleshy, sweet-fruited Sauv Bl). Top wines: Rapaura Series (fragrant, rich, peachy, toasty CHARD 13, sturdy, rich Pinot Gr 14', generous, silky Pinot N 13').

Stonyridge Waih r w ★★★→★★★★ Boutique winery. Famous for exceptional, CAB SAUV-based red, Larose 08' 09 10' 12, one of NZ's greatest, matures superbly. Airfield is little brother of Larose. Also powerful, dense Rhône-style Pilgrim 12 and super-charged Luna Negra MALBEC 10' 12.

Te Awa Hawk r w ★★ GIMBLETT GRAVELS v'yd; reputation for MERLOT-based reds. VILLA MARIA purchased (2012), site of key new HAWK winery. Subsequent releases (CHARD, PINOT GR, SYRAH, Merlot/MALBEC) mostly in Left Field range (low-priced, gd value).

Te Kairanga Mart r w ★★ One of district's largest wineries, but chequered history.

Bought 2011 by American Bill Foley (owner of VAVASOUR, GROVE MILL). V.gd CHARD 13', PINOT GR 13, SAUV BL 13, PINOT N 13; excellent RIES 13'. Runholder is middle-tier. Res is John Martin: weighty, rich Chard 13', dense, supple Pinot N 13'.

Te Mania Nel ★★ Small, gd-value producer with fresh, lively CHARD, GEWURZ 13', PINOT GR 13', RIES, racy SAUV BL (organic), generous, floral, supple, organic Res PINOT N 13.

Te Mata Hawk r w ★★★ →★★★★ Prestigious winery (first vintage 1895); run by Buck family since 1974. *Coleraine* (CAB SAUV/MERLOT/CAB FR blend) 98' 00 02 04 05' 06' 07' 08 09' 10' 11 13' has rare breed, great longevity; lower-priced Awatea Cabernets/Merlot 09' 10' 13' is also classy and more forward. *Bullnose Syrah* 09' 10' 13' among NZ's finest. Rich, elegant Elston CHARD 10' 11 13'. Estate V'yds (was Woodthorpe) range for early drinking (v.gd Chard, SAUV BL, GAMAY NOIR, Merlot/ Cabs 13', Syrah).

Terra Sancta C Ot r (p) (w) ★★ Bannockburn's first v'yd, founded 1991 as Olssens. V.gd value, generous, drink-young Mysterious Diggings PINOT N 13; Bannockburn Pinot N is mid-tier 12'; dense, savoury Slapjack Block Pinot N from oldest vines. Excellent RIES and lovely, vivacious Pinot N Rosé 14'.

Te Whare Ra Marl r w ★★ Label: TWR. Region's oldest vines, planted 1979. Best-known for highly perfumed, spicy, organic GEWURZ, also rich, vibrant SAUV BL 13, RIES (dry "D" and medium "M" 13'), PINOT GR 13, PINOT N 12.

Te Whau Waih ★★→★★★ Tiny, acclaimed seaside v'yd and restaurant. Classy, complex CHARD 13'; savoury, mostly CAB SAUV blend, The Point 08' 10' 12. Powerful, densely packed SYRAH 10 12.

Tiki Marl (r) w ★★ McKean family owns extensive v'yds in MARL and Waip. Punchy, vibrant SAUV BL 14 and weighty, penetrating Single V'yd Sauv Bl 13'; fleshy, smooth PINOT GR; fruity, easy-drinking PINOT N. Second label: Maui.

Tohu r w ★★ Maori-owned venture with extensive v'yds in MARL and NEL. Racy SAUV BL 14 and rich, rounded, oak-aged Mugwi Res Sauv Bl 13'; strong, dry RIES; creamy, unoaked CHARD and increasingly complex PINOT N 13'.

Trinity Hill Hawk r (p) w ★★ →★★★★ Highly regarded, innovative producer, sold in 2014 to American Charles Banks (ex-Screaming Eagle). Refined, gd-value Bordeaux-style blend, The Gimblett 09' 10 13; stylish GIMBLETT GRAVELS CHARD 13'. Exceptional Homage SYRAH: v. floral, dense 09' 10'. Impressive, plummy TEMPRANILLO. Scented, soft VIOGNIER among NZ's best. Lower-tier, "white label" range gd value.

Two Paddocks C Ot r (w) ★★ Actor Sam Neill makes light, racy, dry RIES 13' and several PINOT NS, incl single-v'yd First Paddock (more herbal, from cool, elevated Gibbston district 11), Last Chance (riper, from warmer Alexandra 12'). Purchase of Desert Heart v'yd, Bannockburn, will add another. Picnic by Two Paddocks: drink young, regional blend 13'.

Two Rivers Marl r w ★★ Convergence SAUV BL – deep, dry wine from WAIRAU and AWATERE VALLEYS 14. V.gd CHARD (mouthfilling, rich and creamy), PINOT GR, RIES 14, PINOT N (esp Tributary: v.gd depth and complexity, delicious young 13').

Valli C Ot ★★–★★★ Excellent single-v'yd PINOT N (esp Gibbston 11' 12, Bannockburn 11 12') and strikingly intense, dry Old-Vine RIES 13' (vines planted 1981). New light, racy, sweeter Waitaki Ries 13'.

Vavasour Marl r w ★★ →★★★ Planted first vines in AWATERE VALLEY in 1986. Rich creamy CHARD 11; best known for vibrant, pure, nettley SAUV BL 13'; promising PINOTS N/GR. Ownership link via Foley Family Wines to GROVE MILL, TE KAIRANGA.

Vidal Hawk r w ★★→★★★ Est 1905, owned by VILLA MARIA since 1976. Acclaimed CHARD producer, esp top Legacy (fragrant, smoky, tight-knit, long 10' 11 12 13' and excellent mid-tier Res Chard 13'. Legacy CAB SAUV/MERLOT (intense, complex 09' 10). Lower-tier: White Series. Impressive SYRAH (esp Legacy 09' 10' 11).

Villa Maria Auck r (p) w ★★ →★★★ NZ's largest fully family-owned winery, first vintage 1961, headed by Sir George Fistonich. Also owns VIDAL, ESK VALLEY, TE AWA.

Notable success in competitions, esp with HAWK CHARD, MARL PINOT N. Top ranges: Res (express regional character) and Single V'yd (reflect individual sites); Cellar Selection: mid-tier (less oak) is often excellent; 3rd-tier Private Bin wines can be v.gd and fine value (esp SAUV BL, but also GEWURZ, PINOT GR, VIOGNIER, Pinot N). Small volumes of v.gd ARNEIS, VERDELHO, GRENACHE.

Vinoptima Gis w ★★→★★★ Small GEWURZ specialist, owned by Nick Nobilo (ex-NOBILO). Top vintages (06' 08) pricey but full of power, personality. Second label: Bond Road 09. Memorable, oily Noble Gewurz 07' is NZ's most expensive wine.

Waimea Nel r (p) w ★★ One of region's largest and best white producers. Punchy SAUV BL 14', rich, rounded PINOT GR 13', GEWURZ 13', vibrant VIOGNIER 13'. V.gd RIES (Classic is honeyed, medium style 13), weighty, rich CHARD 13'. Scented, dry GRÜNER V. Full-bodied, savoury, supple PINOT N 13'. Spinyback is 2nd tier.

Waipara Hills Cant r w ★★ Brand of MUD HOUSE. Ripe passion fruit/lime MARL SAUV BL 14'. Top Equinox range from WAIP: oak-aged, generous Sauv Bl 13', fleshy, dryish PINOT GR 13', elegant CHARD 13', v. floral, supple PINOT N 12, scented, rich RIES 13'.

Waipara Springs Cant r w ★★ Small producer of strong, racy, medium RIES 13', gd drink-young PINOT N 13'. Impressive top range: Premo, incl v. rich Ries 13', fragrant, sturdy, concentrated PINOT N 10' 12 from district's oldest Pinot N vines.

Wairarapa Wair NZ's 6th-equal largest wine region (not to be confused with Waip, CANT). See MART. Also incl Gladstone subregion in n (slightly higher, cooler, wetter). Driest, coolest region in North Island; strength in whites (SAUV BL, PINOT N most widely planted) and esp PINOT N (full-bodied, warm, savoury from relatively mature vines). Strong sales in nearby capital city, Wellington.

Wairau River Marl r (p) w ★★ Gd whites: ripe, tropical fruit SAUV BL 14, full-bodied, rounded PINOT GR 14, gently sweet Summer RIES 14, strong, tangy ALBARIÑO 14. Res is top label (elegant, subtle VIOGNIER, weighty, rich PINOT N 12).

Wairau Valley Marl MARL's largest subregion (first v'yd planted 1873; modern era since 1973). Three important side valleys to the s: Brancott, Omaka, Waihopai. SAUV BL thrives on stony, silty plains; PINOT N on clay-based, n-facing slopes. Limited scope for further planting.

Waitaki Valley C Ot Slowly expanding subregion in N Ot, with cool, frost-prone climate. V. promising PINOT N (but can be leafy), crisp, vibrant, racy PINOT GR, RIES. Several producers, but only one winery.

Whitehaven Marl r (p) w ★★ Medium-sized producer. Flavour-packed, harmonious SAUV BL 13 is top value, big seller in the USA. Rich, soft GEWURZ 13; citrus, slightly buttery CHARD 13; oily-textured, dryish PINOT GR 13; strong, lemon/lime RIES 13, sturdy, savoury PINOT N 12. Gallo (see California) is part-owner. Top range: Greg.

Wither Hills Marl r w ★★ Large producer, once small and prestigious, now owned by LION NATHAN. Popular, gd-value, gooseberry/lime SAUV BL. Generous, gently oaked CHARD; fragrant, softly-textured PINOT N.

Wooing Tree C Ot r (p) w ★★ Single-v'yd, mostly reds. Bold, dark PINOT N 12 13' (Beetle Juice Pinot N less new oak 13). Less "serious", all Pinot N, incl delicious Rosé 14', Blondie (basically white 14), Tickled Pink (sweet, light, raspberry/plum 14).

Woollaston Nel r (p) w ★★ Smallish organic producer. Top Mahana range (sometimes from grapes grown at Mahana) incl concentrated, dry PINOT GR 12; mouthfilling, dry, scented RIES 13'; rich, oak-aged SAUV BL 12; muscular, dense, savoury, firm PINOT N 12. Lower-tier Nelson range: gd value. .

Yealands Marl r (p) w ★★ Sweeping estate v'yd, NZ's biggest "single v'yd", in AWATERE VALLEY. Fast-growing production, partly estate-grown, mostly MARL. Most wines not organic, but strong profile for sustainability. Estate range incl SAUV BL, vibrant, herbaceous, pure 14; RIES, refined, off-dry; v. promising, lemony, spicy, dry GRÜNER V 14'. PINOT N, generous floral, supple 13'. Classy selection of Single Block Sauv Bls. Lower-priced range: Peter Yealands.

NEW ZEALAND

South Africa

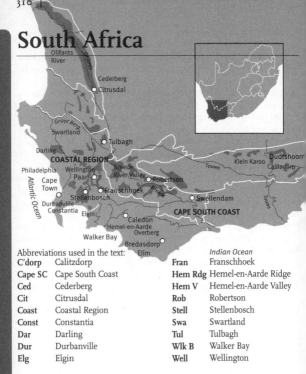

Abbreviations used in the text:

C'dorp	Calitzdorp		*Indian Ocean*
Cape SC	Cape South Coast	**Fran**	Franschhoek
Ced	Cederberg	**Hem Rdg**	Hemel-en-Aarde Ridge
Cit	Citrusdal	**Hem V**	Hemel-en-Aarde Valley
Coast	Coastal Region	**Rob**	Robertson
Const	Constantia	**Stell**	Stellenbosch
Dar	Darling	**Swa**	Swartland
Dur	Durbanville	**Tul**	Tulbagh
Elg	Elgin	**Wlk B**	Walker Bay
		Well	Wellington

Sobering. Contentious. Divisive. The landmark South Africa vs Australia "test match" was all of that. Staged in Cape Town two decades ago, just a year after SA's transition to democracy, the SAA Shield took place under the auspices of the national carrier, SA Airways. One hundred selected wines from each country were blind-tasted "to gauge relative quality and price values". Despite a dramatic trumping of the legendary Penfold's Grange by a local Syrah (Stellenzicht 94), and first places for SA in three of the II categories, the resounding overall victory by Australia – 78 points to 21 – rocked the still inward-looking domestic wine industry. Detractors decried the contest as ill-advised, or at best ill-timed. But defenders hailed it as a seminal event, one that would abet much-needed introspection and re-engagement with the wider wine world. Two decades on, the SA wine scene is transformed: a new, younger generation is locking hands with high-profile foreign investors, overseas wine-growers are crafting boutique wines in prime SA soil, locals are mentoring fledgling wine-growers in neighbouring countries, annual wine exports are up by a staggering 370 per cent and SA is being acclaimed as among the most exciting, dynamic wine countries in the world. Freed from isolation-era restrictions, new vine-growing areas are being explored (established ones revitalized), exotic grape varieties planted (forgotten ones revived) and unorthodox production techniques embraced along with innovative wine styles, even palate-stretching wine-and-beer hybrids. The role of the SAA Shield in all of this is still moot. What's less arguable is that if going in to bat today, Team SA would be confident of significantly rearranging the scoreboard.

Recent vintages

2014 Challenging year needing good judgement, timing; lighter, elegant wines.
2013 Bumper harvest, in both size and quality, with bonus of moderate alcohol.
2012 Good to very good vintage for both reds and whites; lower alcohol levels.
2011 Variable year; producer record should guide buying/cellaring decisions.
2010 Mixed bag, later-ripening varieties (reds, whites) generally performing best.
2009 SA's 350th harvest and one of its best. Stellar whites and most reds.
Note: Most dry whites are best drunk within 2 to 3 years.

AA Badenhorst Family Wines Swa r (p) w (sp) ★★→★★★ "Brand extensions" like craft beer and new CHENIN BL-based cocktail ingredient, Caperitif, epitomize serious yet playful and experimental approach of cousins Hein and Adi Badenhorst, vinifying mainly Mediterranean varieties and Chenin Bl for their AA Badenhorst and Secateurs labels.

Alheit Vineyards W Cape w ★★★→★★★★ Young HEMEL-EN-AARDE-based old-vines specialists Chris Alheit and wife Suzaan produce multiregion CHENIN BL/SÉM Cartology, various single-site wines and field-blend from home farm Hemelrand to huge acclaim.

Anthonij Rupert Wyne W Cape r (p) w (br) (sp) ★→★★★ Portfolio named for owner Johann Rupert's late brother; imposing winery nr FRAN. Anthonij Rupert flagship reds; Cape of Good Hope terroir explorations; L'Ormarins MCC sparklers and Port style; Italianate *Terra del Capo* food partners; Protea stylish everyday wines.

Anwilka W Cape r ★★★ KLEIN CONSTANTIA's red-wine-specialist sibling, partly Bordeaux-owned. Top label is modern SHIRAZ/CAB SAUV Anwilka **05 06** 07 08 09' 10 11 12. Petit Frère similar blend, lighter oak.

Ashbourne *See* HAMILTON RUSSELL.

Ataraxia Wines W Cape r w ★★★ Acclaimed CHARD, SAUV BL and Serenity red (unspecified varieties) by Kevin Grant (ex-HAMILTON RUSSELL) from own HEMEL-EN-AARDE and bought-in WLK B fruit.

Avondale Paarl r p W sp ★★→★★★ Family-owned and pioneer embracing organics, bio and science to produce impressive Bordeaux- and Rhône-style reds, rosé, white blend, CHENIN BL and MCC.

Axe Hill C'dorp r br sw ★→★★★ Noted Port-style exponent (Cape Vintage, mainly TOURIGA N **01 02' 03' 04 05'** 06 07 08 09 11' 12 13) recently also offering unfortified SHIRAZ and Port-grape blends.

Bamboes Bay Tiny (6 ha) maritime WARD in OLIFANTS RIVER REGION. Fryer's Cove first and only winery, with three bracing SAUV BL and rare w coast PINOT N.

Bayten *See* BUITENVERWACHTING.

Beaumont Wines Bot River r (p) w (br) (sw) ★→★★★ Historic family estate (with 200-yr-old working watermill), home to expressive CHENIN BL, PINOTAGE, varietal and blended MOURVÈDRE, Bordeaux red blend Ariane.

Bellingham W Cape r (p) w ★→★★★ Enduring DGB brand, with personality-packed Bernard series and larger-volume, easy-drinking Insignia, Ancient Earth and The Tree ranges.

Beyerskloof W Cape r (p) (w) (br) ★→★★★ SA's PINOTAGE champion, nr STELL. Eight versions on offer, incl varietal Diesel **06** 07' 08' 09 10 11 12, CAPE BLENDS and Port style. Also classic CAB SAUV/MERLOT Field Blend **00 01 02 03' 04 05** 07 08 09.

Black Economic Empowerment (BEE) Initiative aimed at increasing wine-industry ownership and participation by previously disadvantaged groups. Since late 90s, with pioneers New Beginnings and Fairvalley, black-owned or part-black-owned cellars have increased and now incl majors like KWV.

Boekenhoutskloof Winery W Cape r (p) w sw ★★→★★★★ Consistently excellent producer with cellars in FRAN, STELL and SWA. Spicy SYRAH **01' 02' 03 04' 05 06'**

07 08 09' 10 11 12' 13; intense CAB SAUV 01' 02' 03 04' 05 06' 07' 08' 09' 10 11' 12 13. Also *fine Sém* and Mediterranean-style red The Chocolate Block; organic SHIRAZ Porseleinberg; gd-value labels Porcupine Ridge, Wolftrap and Helderberg Wijnmakerij.

Bon Courage Estate Rob r (p) w (br) sw (s/sw) sp ★→★★★ Comprehensive family-grown range. Inkará reds, stylish trio of brut MCC, aromatic RIES, MUSCAT desserts.

Boplaas Family Vineyards W Cape r w br (sp) ★→★★★ Sixth-generation Nel family vintners at C'DORP, known for Port styles, esp Vintage Res 99' 01 03 04' 05' 06' 07' 08 09' 10 11 and Cape Tawny. Recently more emphasis on unfortified Port grapes and cooler areas eg. Upper Langkloof.

Boschendal Wines W Cape r (p) w (sw) sp ★→★★★ Famous old estate nr FRAN under DGB ownership. Calling cards: SHIRAZ, SAUV BL, Bordeaux/Shiraz Grand Res and MCC. Cool-climate expression in ELG Series.

Botanica Wines W Cape r p w ★★→★★★ Instant stardom for CHENIN BL from 50-yr-old w-coast bush vines, made by US brand owner Ginny Povall. Since joined by elegant PINOT N, Bordeaux reds and rosé from STELL and HEMEL-EN-AARDE v'yds.

Bot River *See* WALKER BAY.

Bouchard Finlayson Cape SC r w ★★→★★★★ V. fine PINOT N grower at Hermanus: Galpin Peak 01 02' 03 04 05 07 08 09 10 11 12 13; barrel selection Tête de Cuvée 99 01' 03' 05' 07 09 10 12. Impressive CHARD, SAUV BL and exotic Hannibal red.

Breedekloof Large (12,870 ha) inland DISTRICT in Breede River Valley REGION; mainly bulk wine. Notable exceptions: Bergsig, Deetlefs, Du Preez, Merwida, Opstal and US-owned Silkbush; Du Toitskloof Winery byword for gd value.

Buitenverwachting W Cape r (p) w sw (sp) ★★→★★★ Classy family v'yds, cellar and restaurant at CONST. Standout SAUV BL, CAB FR, Bordeaux red blend Christine 00 01' 02 03 04 06 07 08 09' 10 11 12 13, VIOGNIER. Labelled "Bayten" for export.

Calitzdorp DISTRICT in KLEIN KAROO REGION climatically similar to the Douro and known for Port styles. Best producers: AXE HILL, BOPLAAS, DE KRANS, Peter Bayly, Lieben/Quinta do Sul. Newer unfortified Port-grape "C'DORP Blends" and varietal bottlings show potential.

Cape Agulhas *See* ELIM.

Cape Blend Usually a red blend with proportion of PINOTAGE. Notable exponents: ASHBOURNE, BEAUMONT, BEYERSKLOOF, GRANGEHURST, KAAPZICHT, MEINERT, SPIER, WARWICK.

Cape Chamonix Wine Farm Fran r w (sp) ★★→★★★★ Recent vintages confirm excellence of these winemaker-run mtn v'yds. Distinctive PINOT N, PINOTAGE, CHARD, SAUV BL, Bordeaux-style blends (r w) and new CAB FR, all for laying down.

Cape Peninsula Maritime DISTRICT recently renamed (was "Cape Point") and enlarged to encompass entire Cape Peninsula. 454 ha, mainly SAUV BL, CAB SAUV, MERLOT, SHIRAZ. Hout Bay and CONST are WARDS.

Cape Point *See* CAPE PENINSULA.

Cape Point Vineyards W Cape (r) w (sw) ★★→★★★ Exciting, consistent producer of complex, age-worthy SAUV BL/SÉM blends, CHARD, SAUV BL, occasional botrytis dessert and new CAB SAUV; gd-value label Splattered Toad.

Cape South Coast Cool-climate "super REGION" comprising DISTRICTS of CAPE AGULHAS, ELG, Overberg, Plettenberg Bay, Swellendam and WALKER BAY, plus standalone WARDS Herbertsdale, Napier, Stilbaai East.

Cape Winemakers Guild (CWG) Independent, invitation-only association of 46 top growers. Stages benchmarking annual auction of limited premium bottlings and, via a trust, provides development aid, bursaries, mentorship for promising wine-growers.

Cederberg High-altitude standalone WARD in rugged Cederberg Mts. Mainly SHIRAZ and SAUV BL. Driehoek and CEDERBERG PRIVATE CELLAR are sole producers.

Cederberg Private Cellar Ced, Elim r (p) w (sp) ★★→★★★ Nieuwoudt family with among SA's highest (CED) and most southerly (ELIM) v'yds. Elegant intensity in SHIRAZ, CAB SAUV, SAUV BL, SÉM, CHENIN BL, rare Bukettraube and PINOT N under top-tier Five Generations, Ghost Corner, Cederberg labels.

Central Orange River Standalone inland "mega WARD" (±11,000 ha) in Northern Cape GEOGRAPHICAL UNIT. Hot, dry, irrigated; mainly white wines and fortified. Major producer is Orange River Wine Cellars.

Chamonix *See* CAPE CHAMONIX WINE FARM.

Coastal Large (±30,000 ha) REGION, incl sea-influenced DISTRICTS of CAPE PENINSULA, DAR, Tygerberg, STELL and SWA, but confusingly also inland FRAN, PAARL, TUL, WELL.

Colmant Cap Classique & Champagne W Cape sp ★★★ Exciting *méthode traditionnelle* sparkling specialist at FRAN. Brut Res, Rosé and CHARD, and newer Sec Res; all MCC, NV, well priced and excellent.

Constantia Cool, scenic WARD on Constantiaberg, SA's original fine-wine-growing area, revitalized in recent yrs by GROOT and KLEIN CONSTANTIA, Beau Constantia, BUITENVERWACHTING, Constantia Glen, CONSTANTIA UITSIG, Eagles' Nest, STEENBERG, Silvermist and others.

Constantia Uitsig Const r w br sp ★★→★★★ Premium v'yds under new owners, with high ambitions. Visitor venue and cellar planned (vinification historically at neighbour STEENBERG). Mainly white wines and MCC, carefully crafted.

Creation Wines Wlk B r w ★★→★★★ Elegant modernity in family-owned/-vinified range, showcasing Bordeaux, Rhône and Burgundy varietals and blends. Kaleidoscopic cellar-door offering worth the trip.

Crystallum W Cape r w ★★★ Burgundy-grape specialist Peter-Allan Finlayson sources from cool HEMEL-EN-AARDE and Overberg sites for excellent quartet of PINOT N and pair of CHARD. Perfumed SHIRAZ/MOURVÈDRE under Paradisum branding.

Dalla Cia Wine & Spirit Company W Cape r w ★★→★★★ Family patriarch Giorgio Dalla Cia vinifies CAB SAUV, PINOT N, Bordeaux red blend Giorgio, CHARD, SAUV BL, pricey new "Supertuscan" Teano, and advises select clients like STELL's 4G Wines.

Danie de Wet *See* DE WETSHOF.

Darling DISTRICT around eponymous w coast town. Best v'yds in hilly Groenekloof WARD. Cloof, Darling Cellars, Groote Post, Ormonde and Lanner Hill bottle under own labels; most other fruit goes into third-party brands.

David & Nadia Sadie Swa r w ★★★→★★★★ Husband-and-wife David and Nadia Sadie follow natural winemaking principles of the Swartland Independent movement for exceptional Rhône-style blends Elpidios and Aristargos, varietal Grenache Noir and CHENIN BL, mostly old vines.

De Krans W Cape r (p) w br (sw) ★→★★★★ Nel family v'yds at C'DORP noted for Port styles (esp Vintage Res 01 02 03' 04' 05' 06' 07 08' 09' 10' 11' 12' 13) and fortified MUSCATS. Growing focus on unfortified Port grapes, blended and solo.

Delaire Graff Sunrise: both a Fancy Vivid Yellow diamond and, more prosaically, a Chenin Bl-based fizz.

Delaire Graff Estate W Cape r (p) w (br) (sw) (sp) ★★→★★★ International diamantaire Laurence Graff's eyrie v'yds, winery and tourist destination nr STELL. Varied portfolio now incl trendy CHENIN BL-based MCC.

Delheim Wines Coast r (p) w sw (s/sw) ★★→★★★ Eco-minded family winery in Simonsberg foothills fringing STELL. Vera Cruz SHIRAZ and new PINOTAGE; cellar-worthy CAB SAUV Grand Res 00 01 03 04' 05 06 07' 08 09 13, scintillating Edelspatz botrytis RIES.

DeMorgenzon W Cape r (p) w (sp) ★★→★★★★ With Baroque music being piped to vines 24/7, Hylton and Wendy Appelbaum's property is not your average STELL spread. Focus on Bordeaux and Rhône varieties and blends, CHARD and CHENIN BL (incl new MCC); confident winemaking by Carl van der Merwe.

De Toren Private Cellar Stell r ★★→★★★ Consistently flavourful Bordeaux red blend Fusion V 02 03' 04 05' 06' 07 08 09' 10 11 12 13 and earlier-maturing MERLOT-based "Z"; light-styled red La Jeunesse Délicate. Newer limited-edition Book XVII (Bordeaux red blend) and Black Lion (SHIRAZ) among SA's costliest wines.

De Trafford Wines Stell r w sw ★★→★★★★ Boutique grower David Trafford with track record for bold yet harmonious wines. Bordeaux/SHIRAZ blend Elevation 393 01 03' 04 05 06 07 08 09 10 11, CAB SAUV 01 03' 04 05 06 07 08 09 10 11 12, Shiraz and Straw Wine from CHENIN BL. Characterful Sijnn (pronounced "sane") reds, whites, rosé from maritime Malgas WARD, now vinified on-site.

De Wetshof Estate Rob r w sw sp ★→★★★ Famed CHARD pioneer and exponent; nine versions, oaked/unwooded, varietal/blended, still/sparkling, in De Wetshof, Danie de Wet and Limelight tiers.

DGB W Cape Long-est producer/wholesaler based in WELL, with brands such as BELLINGHAM, BOSCHENDAL, Brampton, Douglas Green.

Diemersdal Estate W Cape r (p) w ★→★★★ DUR family farm with younger generation excelling with SAUV BL, red blends, PINOTAGE, CHARD and SA's first/only commercial GRÜNER V. Burgeoning web-inspired brand Sauvignon.com; w-coast joint-venture Sir Lambert.

Diemersfontein Wines Well r w ★→★★★ Family wine estate, restaurant and guest lodge, esp noted for full-throttle MALBEC, CHENIN BL and VIOGNIER in Carpe Diem range. Espresso-toned Diemersfontein PINOTAGE created much-emulated "coffee style". BEE brand is Thokozani.

Distell W Cape SA's biggest drinks company, seated in STELL. Owns many brands, spanning styles and quality scales. Also has interests in BEE label Earthbound, DURBANVILLE HILLS, CAPE AGULHAS estate Lomond and, via Lusan Premium Wines, various top STELL wineries.

District *See* GEOGRAPHICAL UNIT.

Durbanville Cool, hilly WARD nr Cape Town, known for pungent SAUV BL and MERLOT. Corporate co-owned DURBANVILLE HILLS and many family farms. Also thriving *garagiste* community.

Durbanville Hills Dur r (p) w (sw) ★→★★★ Maritime-cooled v'yds, restaurant and cellar-door owned by DISTELL, local growers and a staff trust. Best are V'yd Selection and Rhinofields ranges.

Edgebaston W Cape r w ★★→★★★ Finlayson family (GLEN CARLOU fame) winery nr STELL. V.gd GS CAB SAUV 05' 06 07 08 10 11 12 13, PINOT N, SHIRAZ, CHARD; classy early-drinking wines; handsomely packaged new old-vines series Camino Africana.

Eikendal Vineyards W Cape r w ★→★★★ Well-est Swiss-owned property nr STELL resurgent under winemaker/viticulturist Nico Grobler. Historic strong suits (Bordeaux red blend Classique, MERLOT, CHARD) back to form, along with newer additions eg. allsorts red Charisma.

Elgin Cool-climate DISTRICT in CAPE SC REGION recognized for SAUV BL, CHARD, PINOT N, MERLOT, Bordeaux blends. Mainly family-owned boutiques, incl organic ELG Ridge, standout Richard Kershaw and up-and-coming Spioenkop.

Elim Sea-breezy WARD in s-most DISTRICT, CAPE AGULHAS; aromatic SAUV BL, white blends and SHIRAZ. Also grape source for majors like FLAGSTONE and CEDERBERG.

Ernie Els Wines W Cape r (p) (w) ★★→★★★★ SA's star golfer's wine venture at STELL, driven by big-ticket Bordeaux red Ernie Els Signature 01 02' 03 04' 05 06 07' 08 09' 10 11 12 13. Earlier-drinking Big Easy range.

Estate Wine Official term for wine grown, made and bottled on "units registered for the production of estate wine". Not a quality designation.

Fable Mountain Vineyards W Cape, Tul r w ★★★→★★★★ Bio TUL grower and sibling of MULDERBOSCH, owned by California's Terroir Capital. Exceptional SHIRAZ (varietal and blend) and textured white blend Jackal Bird.

Fairtrade The international Fairtrade network's sustainable development and empowerment objectives are embraced by a growing list of SA producers, incl big players such as Origin, Stellar, Van Loveren.

Fairview Coast r (p) w (sw) (s/sw) ★→★★★★ Owned by dynamic, innovative Charles Back. Smorgasbord of sensibly priced varietal, blended, single-v'yd, terroir-specific bottlings: Fairview, Spice Route, Goats do Roam, La Capra, Leeuwenjacht. Also, via shareholding/partnership, Six Hats (FAIRTRADE) and Land's End.

FirstCape Vineyards W Cape r p w sp DYA Overall, the biggest-selling SA wine brand in the UK. Joint venture of five local co-ops and UK's Brand Phoenix, with entry-level wines in more than a dozen ranges, some sourced outside SA.

Flagstone Winery W Cape r w (br) ★→★★★ High-end winery at Somerset West, owned (via Accolade Wines) by Australia's CHAMP Private Equity. Sibling to mid-tier Fish Hoek and entry-level KUMALA brands. Best in Flagstone and Time Manner Place ranges.

Fleur du Cap W Cape r w sw ★→★★★ DISTELL premium label; incl v.gd Unfiltered Collection and always-stellar botrytis CHENIN BL and Bordeaux red blend Laszlo in Bergkelder Selection.

Franschhoek Valley Upscale French Huguenot-founded DISTRICT in COASTAL REGION planted with mainly CAB SAUV, CHARD, SAUV BL, SHIRAZ. Characterful portfolios incl Allée Bleue, Black Elephant, GlenWood, Holden Manz, Maison, Môreson.

Geographical Unit (GU) Largest of the four main WO demarcations. Currently five GUs: Eastern, Northern and Western Cape, KwaZulu-Natal and Limpopo. The other WO delineations (in descending size): REGION, DISTRICT and WARD.

Glen Carlou Coast r w (sw) (sp) ★→★★★ First-rate Donald Hess-owned winery, v'yds, art gallery and restaurant nr PAARL. Fine Bordeaux red blend Grand Classique and CHARD; handful of TANNAT bottlings.

Glenelly Estate Stell r w ★★→★★★ Former Château Pichon-Lalande (*see* Bordeaux) owner May-Eliane de Lencquesaing's v'yds and cellar. Impressive flagships Lady May (mainly CAB SAUV) and Grand Vin duo (Bordeaux/SHIRAZ and CHARD); readier-on-release Glass Collection.

Graham Beck Wines W Cape r (p) w sp (sw) ★→★★★ Front-ranker with 25+ labels, incl classy bubbles, varietal and blended reds/whites, topped by superb Cuvée Clive MCC, Ad Honorem CAB SAUV/SHIRAZ and Pheasants' Run SAUV BL.

Grangehurst Stell r p ★★→★★★ Small, top-notch red, rosé specialist. V.gd CAPE BLEND Nikela 98 99 00 01 02 03' 05 06 07 08; PINOTAGE 97 98 99 01 02 03' 05 06 07 08.

Groot Constantia Estate Const r (p) w (br) sw (sp) ★★→★★★ Historic property, tourist mecca in Cape's original fine-wine-growing area, with suitably serious wines esp Grand Constance, reviving CONST tradition of world-class MUSCAT desserts.

Guardian Peak *See* RUST EN VREDE ESTATE.

Hamilton Russell Vineyards Hem V r w ★★→★★★★ Cool-climate pioneer and enduring burgundian-style specialist at Hermanus, now embracing bio. Elegant PINOT N 01' 03' 04 05 06 07 08 09' 10 11 12'; *exceptional Chard*. Super SAUV BL, PINOTAGE and white blends under Southern Right and Ashbourne labels.

Hartenberg Estate Stell r w ★★→★★★★ Consistent top performer. Quintet of outstanding SHIRAZ: extrovert single-site The Stork 03 04' 05' 06 07 08 09' 10 11, savoury Gravel Hill, always serious Shiraz 01 02 03 04' 05 06 07 08 09 10 11, recent entry-level Doorkeeper; also fine MERLOT, CHARD, RIES.

Haskell Vineyards Stell r w (sw) ★★★ American-owned v'yds and cellar nr STELL receiving rave notices for pair of SYRAHS (Pillars and Aeon), red blends and CHARD. Ever-improving sibling brand Dombeya.

Hemel-en-Aarde Trio of cool-climate WARDS (Hemel V, Upper Hem, Hem Rdg) in WLK B DISTRICT; outstanding PINOT N, CHARD and SAUV BL. ALHEIT, ATARAXIA, BOUCHARD FINLAYSON, CREATION, CRYSTALLUM, HAMILTON RUSSELL, NEWTON JOHNSON are top names.

Hermanuspietersfontein Wynkelder W Cape r (p) w ★★→★★★ Leading SAUV BL and Bordeaux red blend specialist; creatively markets physical and historical connections with seaside resort Hermanus.

Iona Vineyards Elg r (p) w ★→★★★ Pioneering ELG winery co-owned by staff, its high-altitude v'yds in conversion to bio. Hailed for CHARD and SAUV BL; newer Bordeaux/Rhône red and PINOT N. Quaintly named entry range Sophie & Mr P.

J C le Roux, The House of W Cape sp ★★ SA's largest specialist bubbly house at STELL, DISTELL-owned. Best labels are PINOT N, Scintilla (CHARD/Pinot N) and Brut NV, all MCC.

Jean Daneel Wines W Cape r w ★★→★★★ Family winery at Napier; outstanding Signature series, esp Red (Bordeaux/SHIRAZ), CHENIN BL and new SAUV BL. Young home-v'yds feature under Le Grand Jardin label.

Jordan Wine Estate W Cape r (p) w sw ★★→★★★★ Family winery nr STELL offering consistency, quality, value, from entry-level Bradgate and Chameleon lines to immaculate CWG Auction bottlings. Flagship Nine Yards CHARD; Bordeaux red Cobblers Hill 00 01 03 04' 05' 06 07 08 09 10 11 12; CAB SAUV; MERLOT; SAUV BL (oaked and unwooded); RIES botrytis dessert Mellifera.

Kaapzicht Wine Estate Stell r w (br) (sw) ★★→★★★ Family winery with internationally acclaimed top range Steytler: Vision CAPE BLEND 01' 02' 03' 04 05' 06 07 08 10 12, PINOTAGE and Bordeaux red blend Pentagon. Superb new old-vines The 1947 CHENIN BL under Kaapzicht label.

Kanonkop Estate Stell r (p) ★★→★★★★ Grand local status for three decades, mainly with PINOTAGE 01 02 03' 04 05 06 07 08 09' 10' 11 12 13, Bordeaux blend Paul Sauer 01 02 03 04' 05 06' 07 08 09 10 11 12 and CAB SAUV. Second tier is Kadette (red, dry rosé and new PINOTAGE).

Ken Forrester Wines W Cape r (p) w sw (s/sw) ★→★★★ Vintner/restaurateur Ken Forrester and wine-grower Martin MEINERT collaboration based in STELL, seeking to earn as much recognition for Mediterranean reds as CHENIN BL (dry, off-dry, botrytis). Devilishly drinkable budget range, Petit.

Klein Constantia Estate W Cape r (p) w sw sp ★★→★★★★ Iconic property, revitalized by foreign owners. Luscious, cellar-worthy (non-botrytis) *Vin de Constance* 00' 01 02' 04 05 06' 07' 08 09 convincing re-creation of legendary 18th-century CONST MUSCAT dessert. Also fine Estate Red, new Metis SAUV BL with Loire's Pascal Jolivet, MCC and earlier-ready KC range, now incl PINOT N. Sibling is ANWILKA in STELL.

Kleine Zalze Wines W Cape r (p) w (sp) ★→★★★ STELL-based star with brilliant CAB SAUV, SHIRAZ, CHENIN BL, SAUV BL in Family Res and V'yd Selection ranges; tasty, affordable Cellar Selection, Foot of Africa and Zalze line-ups.

Klein Karoo Mainly semi-arid REGION known for fortified, esp Port style in C'DORP DISTRICT. Gd PINOT N, SHIRAZ and SAUV BL in higher-lying Outeniqua, Tradouw, Tradouw Highlands and Upper Langkloof WARDS.

Krone, The House of W Cape (w) sp ★★→★★★ Elegant and classic MCC, incl new semi-sweet Night Nectar, made at revitalized Twee Jonge Gezellen Estate in TUL. Also non-sparkling PINOT N/CHARD.

Kumala W Cape r (p) w (s/sw) ★ DYA Hugely successful entry-level export label and sibling brand to premium FLAGSTONE and mid-tier Fish Hoek, all owned by Sydney-based CHAMP Private Equity.

KwaZulu-Natal Province and demarcated GEOGRAPHICAL UNIT on SA's e coast; summer rain; sub-tropical/tropical climate in coastal areas; cooler, hilly central Midlands plateau home to nascent fine wine industry, led by Abingdon Estate.

KWV W Cape r (p) w (br) (sw) sp ★→★★★ Formerly the national wine co-op and controlling body, today a partly black-owned listed group based in PAARL. Extensive line-up of reds, whites, sparkling, Port styles and fortified desserts in Mentors, Cathedral Cellar, KWV Res, Laborie and Roodeberg ranges. Bonne

> **Platteland Pop**
> SA's continuing fascination with traditional varieties and techniques
> sees a small but rising number of wineries embrace *méthode ancestrale/
> rurale* style sparkling wine production (natural ferment initiated in tank,
> completed in bottle). Early versions by producers such as AA BADENHORST
> (using a blend of MUSCAT/CHENIN BL/VERDELHO), Scali (Chenin Bl) and
> Vondeling (CHARD) are promising, so expect more examples – and
> exploding experiments.

Esperance, Café Culture ("coffee" PINOTAGE, still and fizzy) and Pearly Bay are
quaffing wines targeting the pop palate.

Lamberts Bay West coast WARD (22 ha) close by Atlantic. Trenchant SAUV BL and
peppery SHIRAZ by Sir Lambert, local joint venture with DIEMERSDAL.

Lammershoek Winery Swa r (p) w ★★→★★★ Organically grown, traditionally
vinified Rhône-style blends and CHENIN BL that epitomize SWA generosity and
palate appeal. Younger-vines LAM quartet overdelivers.

La Motte W Cape r w (sw) (sp) ★★★ Showpiece winery and cellar-door at FRAN owned
by the Koegelenberg-Rupert family. ORGANIC underpin for Old-World-styled
Bordeaux and Rhône varieties and blends, CHARD, SAUV BL and MCC.

Le Riche Wines Stell r (w) ★★★ Fine CAB SAUV-based boutique wines, hand-crafted by
respected Etienne le Riche and family. Also elegant CHARD.

MCC *See* MÉTHODE CAP CLASSIQUE.

Meerlust Estate Stell r w ★★★★ Prestigious family-owned v'yds and cellar. Elegance
and restraint in flagship Rubicon 99 00 01' 03' 04 05 06 07' 08 09' 10, one of
SA's first Bordeaux-blend reds; also excellent MERLOT, CAB SAUV, CHARD, PINOT N.

Meinert Wines Elg, Stell r (p) w ★→★★★ Thoughtful producer/consultant/
collaborator Martin Meinert esp noted for fine CAPE BLEND Synchronicity. New ELG
PINOT N in Family Collection.

Méthode Cap Classique (MCC) EU-friendly name for bottle-fermented sparkling,
one of SA's major success stories. 200 labels and counting. General resurgence
of CHENIN BL spurring mini-boom in Crémant de Loire-style bubblies. Try KEN
FORRESTER, DELAIRE GRAFF, DEMORGENZON, Old Vines Cellars.

Morgenster Estate Stell r (p) w ★★→★★★ Prime Italian-owned wine and olive farm
nr Somerset West, advised by Bordelais Pierre Lurton (Cheval Blanc). Classically
styled Morgenster 00 01 03 04 05' 06' 08 09 10 11, second label Lourens River
Valley (both Bordeaux-blend reds) and newer Bordeaux-blend white. SANGIOVESE
and NEBBIOLO blends in Italian Collection. Newer young-vines NU Series 1.

Mulderbosch Vineyards W Cape r p w (sw) ★★→★★★ STELL winery owned by
California investment group Terroir Capital, with renewed focus on CHENIN
BL, SAUV BL (dry and botrytis), CHARD. Juicy CAB SAUV rosé. Co-proprietor Charles
Banks, winemaker Adam Mason and reputed chef Peter Tempelhoff collaborate
in food-friendly Yardstick standalone brand.

Mullineux & Leeu Family Wines Swa r w sw ★★★→★★★★ Star husband-and-wife team
Chris and Andrea Mullineux, with recent investment by Indian entrepreneur
Analjit Singh, specializing in smart, carefully made SYRAH, Rhône-style blends
(r w) and *Chenin Bl*. New bottling of ultra-rare Sémillon Gris for CWG Auction.

Mvemve Raats Stell r ★★★ Mzokhona Mvemve, SA's 1st university-qualified
black winemaker, and Bruwer RAATS vinify acclaimed Bordeaux red blend MR
De Compostella.

Nederburg Wines W Cape r (p) w sw s/sw (sp) ★→★★★★ Among SA's biggest (2.8
million cases) and best-known brands, PAARL-based, DISTELL-owned. Exceptional
Ingenuity Red Italian Blend 05 06 07' 08 09 10 11 and White Blend; excellent
Manor House, Heritage Heroes and II Centuries ranges. Also low-priced

quaffers, still and sparkling. Small Private Bins for annual Nederburg Auction, incl CHENIN BL botrytis *Edelkeur* 02 03' 04' 05 06 07' 08 09' 10' 11 12' 13.

Neil Ellis Wines W Cape r w ★★→★★★★ Veteran STELL-based cellar-master Neil Ellis and viticulturist/winemaker son Warren source cooler-climate parcels for site expression. Top V'yd Selection CAB SAUV 99 00' 01 03 04' 05 06 07 09 10' 11, Rhône red blend Rodanos, sensational old-vine Grenache Noir.

Newton Johnson Vineyards Cape SC r (p) w ★→★★★★ Acclaimed cellar and restaurant in scenic Upper HEM V. Outstanding *Pinot N, Chard*, SAUV BL, Rhône-blend reds, from own and partner v'yds; lovely botrytis CHENIN BL, L'illa, ex ROB; entry-level brand Felicité.

Olifants River A w coast REGION (10,000 ha). Warm valley floors, conducive to organic cultivation, and cooler, fine-wine-favouring sites in the mtn WARD of Piekenierskloof, and, nr the Atlantic, BAMBOES BAY and Koekenaap.

Outeniqua *See* KLEIN KAROO.

Paarl Town and demarcated wine DISTRICT 50km+ ne of Cape Town. Diverse styles and approaches; best results with Mediterranean varieties (r w), CAB SAUV, PINOTAGE. Est heavy hitters incl KWV, FAIRVIEW, NEDERBURG and VILAFONTÉ; up-and-coming Babylonstoren, Painted Wolf and Vondeling.

Paul Cluver Estate Wines Elg r w s/sw sw ★★→★★★★ ELG's standard bearer, Cluver family-owned; convincing PINOT N, elegant CHARD, always *gorgeous Gewurz*, knockout RIES (botrytis 03' 04 05' 06' 07 08' 09 10 11' 12 and two drier versions).

Raats Family Wines Coast r w ★★→★★★ CAB FR, pure-fruited CHENIN BL (oaked and unwooded) and newer Bordeaux blend Red Jasper, vinified by STELL-based Bruwer Raats, also a partner in boutique-scale MVEMVE RAATS.

Region *See* GEOGRAPHICAL UNIT.

Reyneke Wines W Cape r w ★★→★★★ Leading organic and bio producer nr STELL with apt Twitter handle "Vine Hugger". Limpid Res Red (SHIRAZ), CHENIN BL, Res White (SAUV BL).

Rijk's Coast r w ★★→★★★ TUL pioneer with Res, Private Cellar and Touch of Oak tiers focused on varietal and blended SHIRAZ, PINOTAGE, CHENIN BL.

Robertson Valley Low-rainfall inland DISTRICT; ±14,000 ha; lime soils; conducive climate for organic production. Historically gd CHARD, dessert styles (notably MUSCAT); more recently SAUV BL, SHIRAZ, CAB SAUV. Major cellars: BON COURAGE, DE WETSHOF, GRAHAM BECK, ROBERTSON WINERY, Rooiberg, SPRINGFIELD; also many family wineries incl new UK-owned Vierkoppen.

Robertson Winery Rob r (p) w (br) sw s/sw (sp) ★→★★ Consistency, value throughout extended portfolio. Best: No 1 Constitution Rd SHIRAZ; also v.gd V'yd Selections.

Rupert & Rothschild Vignerons W Cape r w ★★★ Top v'yds and cellar nr PAARL owned by the Rupert family and Baron Benjamin de Rothschild. Always-impressive Bordeaux red blend Baron Edmond 98 00 01 03' 04 05 07 08 09 10' 11 12 and graceful CHARD Baroness Nadine.

Rustenberg Wines W Cape r w (sw) ★→★★★★ Prestigious family winery nr STELL. Flagship is CAB SAUV Peter Barlow 99' 01' 03 04 05 06 07 08 09 10 11 12. Outstanding Bordeaux red blend John X Merriman, savoury SYRAH, single-v'yd *Five Soldiers Chard*, rare varietal ROUSSANNE.

Rust en Vrede Estate Stell r w sw ★★→★★★ Owner Jean Engelbrecht's powerful, pricey offering incl Rust en Vrede red varietals and blends; Cirrus SYRAH joint venture with California's Silver Oaks; STELL Res tribute to Stell town and its people; Donkiesbaai CHENIN BL (dry and *vin de paille*) and new PINOT N; v.gd Guardian Peak wines.

Sadie Family Wines Stell, Swa, Oliphants River r w ★★★→★★★★ Organic, traditionally made Columella (SHIRAZ/MOURVÈDRE) 01 02' 03 04 05' 06 07' 08 09' 10' 11 12 13, a Cape benchmark; complex, intriguing multi-variety white Palladius; groundbreaking Old Vines series, celebrating SA's wine heritage. Revered winemaker Eben Sadie also grows Sequillo (r w) with Cape Wine Master Cornel Spies.

Saronsberg W Cape r (p) w (sw) (sp) ★→★★★ Art-adorned TUL showpiece with awarded Bordeaux-blend reds, Rhône (r w) varieties and blends, and newer MCC in eponymous and Provenance ranges.

Saxenburg Wine Farm Stell r (p) w (sp) ★★→★★★ Swiss-owned v'yds, winery and restaurant. Roundly oaked reds, SAUV BL and CHARD in high-end Private Collection; new Drunken Fowl quaffing SHIRAZ; premium-priced flagship SHIRAZ Select **00 01 02 03' 05' 06' 07' 09**.

Secateurs *See* A A BADENHORST FAMILY.

Sequillo *See* SADIE FAMILY.

Shannon Vineyards Elg r w (sw) ★★★ Exemplary MERLOT, PINOT N, SAUV BL, SÉM and rare botrytis Pinot N, grown by brothers James and Stuart Downes, and vinified at NEWTON JOHNSON.

Sijnn *See* DE TRAFFORD WINES.

Simonsig Landgoed W Cape r w (br) (sw) (s/sw) sp ★→★★★ Malan family estate nr STELL admired for consistency, value and lofty standards throughout wide range. Merindol SYRAH **01 02' 03 04 05 06 07 08 10' 11 12**, Red Hill PINOTAGE **01 02 03' 04 05 06 07' 08 09 10 11 12**. First 40+ yrs ago with bottle-fermented bubbly (Kaapse Vonkel) and still a leader.

Solms-Delta W Cape r (p) w (br) (sp) ★→★★★ Delightfully different wines from historic FRAN estate, partly staff-owned; Amarone-style SHIRAZ, elegant dry rosé, aromatic white blend, *pétillant* SHIRAZ.

Southern Right *See* HAMILTON RUSSELL.

Spice Route Winery *See* FAIRVIEW.

Spier W Cape r w (br) (sp) ★→★★★ Large, multi-awarded winery and tourist magnet nr STELL. Flagship is brooding CAPE BLEND Frans K Smit **04 05' 06' 07 08 09 10 11**; Spier and Savanha brands, each with tiers of quality, show meticulous winegrowing. Expressive 21 Gables and *Creative Block series* worth a taste.

Springfield Estate Rob r w ★★→★★★ Cult winemaker Abrie Bruwer traditionally vinifies pairs of CAB SAUV, CHARD, SAUV BL, plus a Bordeaux-blend red and new PINOT N. All ooze class, personality.

Stark-Condé Wines Elg, Stell r w ★★→★★★★ Meticulous boutique winemaker José Conde in STELL's alpine Jonkershoek. Superb CAB SAUV and SYRAH in Three Pines and eponymous ranges; earlier-drinking Postcard Series from ELG and Overberg.

Steenberg Vineyards W Cape r (p) w sp ★→★★★★ Top CONST winery, v'yds and chic cellar-door, known for SAUV BL, Sauv Bl/SÉM blends and MCC. Fine reds incl rare varietal NEBBIOLO.

Stellenbosch University town, demarcated wine DISTRICT (±13,000 ha); heart of wine industry – the Napa of SA. Many top estates, esp for reds, tucked into mtn valleys and foothills; extensive wine tasting, accommodation and fine-dining options.

Stellenbosch Vineyards W Cape r (p) w (sp) ★→★★ Big-volume winery with impressive new Flagship PETIT VERDOT, cut-above Credo, easy-drinking Arniston Bay, Versus, Welmoed and Four Secrets ranges.

Swartland Fashionable, chiefly warm-climate DISTRICT in COASTAL region; new maritime WARD St Helena Bay; ±11,000 ha of mainly shy-bearing, unirrigated bush vines making concentrated, hearty but fresh wines. A A BADENHORST, DAVID & NADIA SADIE, LAMMERSHOEK, MULLINEUX, SADIE FAMILY, BOEKENHOUTSKLOOF-owned Porseleinberg. Increasingly source of fruit for non-locals, with some stellar results.

Thelema Mountain Vineyards W Cape r (p) w (s/sw) (sp) ★→★★★★ STELL-based pioneer of SA's modern wine revival, still top of game with *Cab Sauv* **00' 03 04 05 06 07 08 09 10**, The Mint Cab Sauv **05 06' 07 08 09 10 11** *et al*. Sutherland (ELG) v'yds broaden the repertoire (eg. new CHARD MCC).

Tokara W Cape r (p) w (sw) ★★→★★★★ Wine, food and art showcase nr STELL. V'yds also in ELG, WLK B. Gorgeous, distinctive Director's Res blends (r w); promising new GRENACHE; pure, elegant CHARD, SAUV BL. Winemaker Miles Mossop's eponymous bottlings also stellar.

Tulbagh Inland DISTRICT historically associated with white wine and bubbly, latterly also with beefy reds, some sweeter styles and organic. ±1,100 ha. FABLE, KRONE, Lemberg, RIJK'S, SARONSBERG, Waverley Hills Organic.

Twee Jonge Gezellen *See* KRONE.

Vergelegen Wines W Cape r w (sw) (sp) ★★★→★★★★ Historic mansion, immaculate v'yds and wines, stylish cellar-door at Somerset West; owned by Anglo American plc, lately advised by top French consultants. Powerful CAB SAUV "V" 01' 03 04 05 06 07 08 09' 11, sumptuous Bordeaux blend GVB Red, mineral *Sauv Bl/Sém* White, varietal SÉM.

Plettenberg Bay: expanding wine-growing area, also venue for SA's biggest high-school graduation party.

Vilafonté Paarl r ★★★ California's acclaimed Zelma Long (ex-Simi winemaker) and Phil Freese (ex-Mondavi viticulturist) partnering WARWICK's Mike Ratcliffe. Two superb Bordeaux blends: firmly structured Series C, fleshier Series M.

Villiera Wines W Cape r w (sw) sp ★★→★★★ Grier family v'yds and winery nr STELL with excellent quality/value range. Cream of crop: Bordeaux-blend red Monro; Bush Vine SAUV BL; Traditional CHENIN BL; five brut MCC bubblies (incl low-alcohol Starlight). Also boutique-scale Domaine Grier nr Perpignan, France.

Walker Bay Small (975 ha), highly reputed maritime DISTRICT, with sub-appellations HEMEL-EN-AARDE, Bot River, Sunday's Glen and Stanford Foothills. Home to some of SA's biggest names, plus gems like La Vierge, Restless River, Seven Springs, Springfontein, Sumaridge and newcomer Storm Wines. PINOT N, SHIRAZ, CHARD, SAUV BL standout.

Ward The smallest of the WO demarcations. *See* GEOGRAPHICAL UNITS.

Warwick Estate W Cape r w ★★★ Tourist-cordial Ratcliffe family farm on STELL outskirts. V. fine Bordeaux-blend red Trilogy, best-barrels CAB SAUV Blue Lady, perfumed CAB FR, opulent CHARD (wooded and unoaked).

Waterford Estate W Cape r (p) w (sw) (sp) ★→★★★ Classy family winery nr STELL, with awarded cellar-door. Savoury Kevin Arnold SHIRAZ 01 02' 03 04 05 06 07 08 09 10, elegant CAB SAUV 01 02 03' 04 05 06 07 08 09 10 11 and intricate Cab Sauv-based flagship The Jem.

Waterkloof Stell r (p) w ★→★★★ British wine-grower Paul Boutinot's bio v'yds, winery and cantilevered cellar-door nr Somerset West. Top tiers: Waterkloof, Circle of Life, Circumstance and new Seriously Cool; also gd-value False Bay and Peacock Ridge lines.

Wellington Warm-climate DISTRICT abutting PAARL with growing reputation for PINOTAGE, SHIRAZ, chunky red blends and CHENIN BL. Try Bosman/De Bos, DIEMERSFONTEIN, Doolhof, Jacaranda, organic Lazanou, Mont du Toit, Nabygelegen, Napier, Val du Charron, Welbedacht.

Wine of Origin (WO) SA's "AC" but without French cost and yield, etc. restrictions. Certifies vintage, variety, area of origin. Opt-in sustainability certification guarantees eco-sensitive production from grape to glass. *See* GEOGRAPHICAL UNIT.

Winery of Good Hope, The W Cape r w (sw) ★→★★★ Polished STELL producer as eclectic as its Australian-French-SA-UK ownership. Creative, compatible blend of styles, influences, varieties and terroirs in eponymous, Radford Dale, Vinum and Land of Hope line-ups.

Worcester DISTRICT with mostly co-ops producing bulk wine; exceptions incl Arendskloof/New Cape/Eagle's Cliff, Alvi's Drift, Conradie Family, Leipzig.

The world's greatest white grape

Why Riesling?

The short answer would be because it's the world's greatest white grape. Not the most widely grown, or the most famous, or the most useful – Chardonnay would probably win the last two accolades. But while Chardonnay is capable of making worthy wines at every quality level, and has cheered up many a dull blend, even its greatest wines do not fascinate in the way that great Riesling does (unless they're in the form of Champagne – and even then, a blend with Pinot Noir is the original – some still think essential – recipe). Chardonnay is a winemaker's wine: if you don't have a great terroir you can manipulate Chardonnay in the winery and it will obediently respond with more texture, more creaminess, more freshness or whatever you choose.

Riesling has more of a mind of its own. It doesn't do cheap wines all that well. It's fussy about where it grows. It's seldom a great blending grape. But make it happy in the vineyard, don't fiddle with it too much in the winery, and it will sing of its origins in clear, pure tones. It can be a ravishing soprano, an expressive alto, even a passionate tenor – though rarely a bass. And no other white grape responds so eloquently to maturing in bottle.

So is Riesling all about terroir? To a large degree, yes. It transmits a picture of its site – its morning or evening sun, its dry summers and wet springs – with detailed precision. You can tell at a sniff and a sip if it comes from cool vineyards in the high latitudes (Germany above all) or from nearer the noonday sun (it makes great wine in Australia too). But it's about more than just terroir and geography. Riesling is about tension. There is an invigorating, tensile line running through Riesling. It's a high-wire act: the wine pirouettes at high altitude, risking all, driving forward, even showing off; Riesling can be flamboyant too. And meditation it can do better than any other grape.

But whether it's showy or restrained, it should never be safe. Safe Rieslings don't work. Winemakers have to dare. If they daren't, they're better off making something more suitable to their temperament: Pinot Grigio, perhaps. Riesling needs to fly.

A German grape?
Riesling's heritage

The clue is in the name. Where Riesling is grown outside Germany, its names often contain a reference to the river Rhine: Rheinriesling in Austria, Riesling Renano in Italy, Ryzlink Rýnský in the Czech Republic and Slovakia, Rajnai Rizling in Hungary, Renski Riesling in Slovenia. An awful lot of people, over the years, have regarded Riesling as having come from the Rhine.

The earliest documented mention of Riesling so far unearthed is dated 1435 and is in the Rheingau, near Frankfurt; in Alsace it's first mentioned in 1477. If one assumes that it must have taken quite a while for a new seedling among many others in a vineyard to be noticed, propagated and have attracted enough attention to be given a name and planted in other vineyards, then Riesling must have been around for quite a while by then. The Rheingau seems to have been its birthplace, and the Cistercian monks of Kloster Eberbach in the Rheingau, who by 1392 were insisting that white grapes be planted instead of the previously dominant red, probably had a hand in it. In 1720–21 it started to be planted as the sole variety in some vineyards, notably that of Schloss Johannisberg – we're still in the grand estates of the Rheingau. Clearly, it was always regarded as something remarkable. In the later 1700s the dominant church estates of the Mosel planted nothing else.

It's one of Germany's greatest exports. It has been the prestige grape of Alsace for almost as long. At some point it reached Austria, and from there travelled throughout the Austrian Empire; but with

The Rheingau: where it (probably) all started

the exceptions of a few hectares in Spain (notably at Torres), Riesling
didn't head westwards.

At least, not until the New World entered the vinous picture. It
was one of the first grapes to be planted in Australia, and until 1992 it
was Australia's most widely planted white vine. In the 1960s it was all
over California, though not now: now it's New York's Finger Lakes that
are attracting attention for Riesling. It's also in Canada, New Zealand
and South Africa.

Everywhere, to some extent, it has been seen as Germanic.
When German flavours were in fashion, that was fine; when German
wine suffered its self-inflicted cataclysmic decline in the 70s and 80s,
Riesling went with it. That was why it fell from grace in California –
though longer term that was probably inevitable, since there are few
spots in California cool enough for it. It's why it has only fairly recently
been taken seriously again in Australia.

In wine, reputations can be hard to regain. Austria and Alsace
have expended a lot of time and trouble on explaining to people that
their wines are not Germanic, and marketing departments across the
world have quietly dropped the old gothic script they'd used in the past
for Riesling labels. But the association was so toxic that it has taken a
new generation to see Riesling afresh.

A new generation, and dry wines. Liebfraumilch seldom
contained any Riesling; the only similarity to Riesling was in the
sweetness. Why was Riesling sweet? *See* pp.332–33 for more on this.

Riesling's ideal climate
Cool, cooler, coolest

Here's a conundrum: a grape that doesn't like warm climates nevertheless needs to get ripe. Too much warmth and it ripens too fast and just tastes dull. Too little and it will be raw and green, with tooth-stripping acidity. California falls into the "too warm" category; Germany, for most of the 50s and 60s, was very nearly too cold.

These were chilly years in Europe. In some vintages German growers added water to the fermentation vats to dilute the acidity because the grapes were nowhere near ripe. Until the late 80s disastrous vintages were common in Germany. Climate change has brought Riesling into its comfort zone. How long that will continue is another matter; but at the moment Riesling in Germany is as happy as Larry.

So what does it have there, and how much do other regions seek to imitate German conditions? Well, the Mosel is about as far north as Riesling will grow. Riesling is pretty tough when it comes to winter chill, but it needs maximum sunshine and shelter. Slopes – and the Mosel has plenty of slopes – get more sunshine than flat land, and a slope leading down to a river, so that the water can reflect back more light, is a plus. But plant it too far down the slope and it will find itself shrouded in river mists; much above 200 metres, and it's too cold. In the slightly warmer Rheingau and Pfalz the conditions can be less stringent, but it still wants the best, sunniest spots.

New York State's Finger Lakes come into the same category: a cool climate mitigated by steep slopes and deep water. The lakes delay budding in spring and warm the vines in autumn: without them the cold would be too harsh even for Riesling.

At the other end of the temperature scale there is Australia's Clare Valley. Some parts of this topographically convoluted area are too warm for Riesling: Jeffrey Grosset goes high, up to 460 metres, to find cooler spots. He adds that Clare's clear skies, which give an average of nine hours' sunshine per day, also allow the temperature to drop dramatically at night, thus preserving acidity.

Alsace, for Riesling, has a Goldilocks climate that is just right. But even there Riesling is still the most difficult vine to get to perfect ripeness, according to Olivier Humbrecht of Zind-Humbrecht. He reckons that there's nowhere in Alsace that's too warm, but Riesling must not be too high up or too low down; it must face the right way; and be on poor soil: it's down to terroir.

Austria is the same: a Goldilocks climate, in which you have to get the terroir right. The Wachau, and Kamptal and Kremstal too, can be at the limit geographically of where Riesling will ripen (suddenly valleys narrow and the ground rises, and it's too cold for vines) the wines have body and weight. But only because they come from vineyards as punishingly steep and rocky as any in the world. Riesling doesn't like it easy.

The Abtsberg vineyard, looking down on the winery

EXTREME RIESLING:
Maximin Grünhauser Abtsberg Spätlese 2003, Ruwer, Germany

Extremely long name, extremely cold climate. If you think the Mosel is chilly, try the Ruwer. The valley in this tributary of the Mosel is narrow and draughty, and it takes a suntrap like the south-facing Abtsberg vineyard (a 70 per cent slope of easily warmed blue slate) to ripen Riesling. There have been vines here for 1,000 years.

The 2003 vintage was also extreme: extremely hot. Much of Europe made four-square, chunky wines; the Ruwer came into its own with superb ripeness and taut acidity. The wine has some residual sugar to balance its acidity, and it will last for years. I drank it recently with pheasant *à la Normande*: cooked with apples and crème fraîche. The combination was perfect.

The perfect site
Mirroring the terroir

Terroir is not just soil, of course; it encompasses exposure to the sun, altitude, climate and even the hand of the grower. For Riesling, the soil type is probably the least important of these.

Is this a surprise? Do German growers not compare the blackcurrant nuance of Piesport (clay) with the steeliness of Traben-Trarbach (blue slate)? Does not the rich wineyness of Alsace Riesling come from the basically chalky clay soils, so different from German slate? Doesn't Jeffrey Grosset's Springvale, from red loam over limestone over slate in Australia's Clare Valley, taste different to his Polish Hill, from shale and clay marl over slate?

Yes, all this is true. Riesling reflects every facet of its terroir with great faithfulness. What I mean is that it is climate, exposure and altitude that determine where Riesling will flourish. As long as soil is poor and stony it doesn't seem to matter what sort it is – which is one reason why great Rieslings are so varied. A grape that responds differently to volcanic soils, loess, gneiss, gravel, marl, quarzite, slate, sandstone, shale, limestone, granite and flint has a lot to say for itself.

I am not suggesting that in some way the vine sucks up slate or flint and transmits it to the grape, and that this is somehow transferred to the wine. Plants don't work like that. How they obtain nutrients from the soil is complicated, but certainly doesn't involve "slate flavours", whatever they might be, being transferred to the wine. It is reasonable to say, however, that different soils have different balances of nutrients and that this, together with their different drainage properties, produces different flavours in the wines. If we can recognize a characteristic smoky note in some Rieslings and say, "Ah – slate" – and be right – what we're recognizing is not the flavour of slate itself. It's the flavour that results from the sort of drainage you get on slate and the sort of micro-nutrients available to the vine; it's the flavour of morning or evening sunshine that ripens the grapes to a particular point; it's these flavour precursors in the grape that are emphasized, and not those.

Sorry. What it all comes down to is drainage, the more or less rapid run-off or run-through of water, the resulting soil temperature and the resulting ripeness. Which is dull, and not what Riesling lovers really want to spend their time talking about. We may taste drainage, but what we see are wines with the tensile strength of a steel cobweb and the clarity of rock crystal; the fatness of smoked cream and the texture of wet rock. We trace these flavours back to a particular vineyard in a particular year. And Riesling gives us a clearer mirror than any other.

TERROIR RIESLING:
Grosset Springvale 2014 and Polish Hill 2014, Clare Valley, Australia

Jeffrey Grosset is Australia's greatest exponent of Riesling. It was he who fought the authorities to ensure that "Riesling" on the label meant just that, and could not be used as a generic term for white wine – and now this pair of wines, both from Clare Valley, will demonstrate how perfectly Riesling reflects its specific site. Springvale is sappy and firm, more aromatic and floral; Polish Hill restrained, stony, even chalky, but sleek. In both wines the typical lime flavours of Clare Riesling come second to a pure minerality. Springvale is the highest and coolest vineyard in the Watervale district of Clare: it's 450 metres up and the topsoil is thin. In Polish Hill the vines struggle even more, and the bunches and berries are smaller. Grosset himself talks of "hard rock" (Polish Hill) and "soft rock" (Springvale) sites. The rest of us can only marvel.

Winemaking
Keep it simple

Could I build this up to look like an apocalyptic battle, the kind that divides families and sets parents against children, sibling against sibling? I could try, but quite honestly, the really boring news is that there's broad agreement on how Riesling should be made. New oak, as in barriques, doesn't work; it's a marriage made in hell. Okay, there are one or two.... And it doesn't benefit from blending; it's one of those relatively rare grapes that are complete in themselves, and need no help from anything else. Add something to Riesling, and you lose the essence of Riesling.

Which doesn't mean that Riesling can't offer a helping hand to other grapes in a blend. Some Riesling added to Gewurztraminer or Muscat, for example, can give the raciness that those grapes tend to lack; Pinot Blanc can also benefit from the association. But in such cases Riesling becomes a sort of Lady Bountiful, graciously extending a helping hand to the needy.

The only real argument over winemaking (and even "argument" is putting a bit strongly) is about oak – that is, big old oak vats – or steel. Germany, Alsace and Austria have a tradition of using big old oak vats (sometimes called *fuder*) for fermentation and ageing. They were the containers before steel came along; why change? Other countries, with no such heritage, automatically use stainless steel. Germany, Alsace and Austria also use stainless steel quite a lot of the time these days, offering a useful comparison between the two styles.

Oak has a slightly softening and rounding effect, and the gentle oxidation you get in *fuders* is useful, say some winemakers, for a wine that tends to be reductive. In the days before the climate started to warm up nobody bottled wine young. It was usually too acid. Ageing in big oak, even for five or ten years, mellowed it. But in the 80s and

STEEL AND WOOD:
Domaine Weinbach Schlossberg Vendange Tardive 2004 and Schlossberg 2012, Kientzheim, Alsace

Domaine Weinbach favours steel fermentation for Vendange Tardive wines, and old oak *foudres* for drier ones (where the acidity is more prominent). The Vendange Tardive from Grand Cru Schlossberg is honeyed, elegant, linear and filigree, very pure, spicy and mineral: it transcends fruit. The dry 2012 is much younger, full of citrus and white flowers, and that same bracing minerality. The winemaking is done with such a light hand that you don't think, Oh, steel, or Oh, old oak: it just feels right. Try the mature Vendange Tardive with venison and a fruity sauce; the young dry wine with fried fish.

Big old *fuders* at Domaine Weinbach

90s time became money; most winemakers turned their *fuder* into charcoal for the barbecue and instead went over to stainless steel for the crisp modernity it gave their wine. Now many winemakers use both, according to the vineyard, the style of wine and the year. If they want to emphasize crispness and brightness, they use steel. If they want a richer roundness, it's wood.

I'm doing my best to find a battle, but it's just not working, is it? Even screwcaps aren't really a battle.

But it was a bit of a skirmish, and it happened in Australia. In 2000 some Clare Valley Riesling producers got fed up. Cork taint (TCA) was a problem that showed no signs of going away, and the growers were tired of bits of tree bark ruining their wines – especially since TCA shows particularly clearly on Riesling. So they switched to screwcaps. It was the first mass migration away from cork, and it showed that on aromatic wines like Riesling screwcaps can work superbly, capturing all the vibrant freshness. In style it gives wines that are another step further along the spectrum: think of *fuder*-steel tanks-screwcaps and you'll get the picture.

Dry Riesling

Dryness rules?

That Riesling can be dry will come as a surprise to some: it's that association with German wines again. When German wines were nearly all sweet, Riesling was sweet too. As fine German wine reinvented itself in the aftermath of commercial collapse (for which the fine wines were not responsible), so it cold-shouldered sweetness. But making wine dry where it used to be sweet, or sweetish, is not just a matter of letting the fermentation run its course. Balance is more complicated than that.

Balance in a white wine comes from an equilibrium of acidity, alcohol, weight (dry extract if you want to be technical: what wine literally boils down to) and sweetness. A wine light in alcohol and weight, but high in acidity (Mosel Riesling, for example) needs sugar to balance. Ferment the rest of the sugar and you increase the alcohol; but unless you've had a warm enough summer to get ripe acidity and plenty of weight, the wine will be unbalanced.

More southerly parts of Germany do dry Rieslings spectacularly well – the Rheingau, for example, or the Pfalz, or the Nahe. The wines have the weight and the ripeness to stand unadorned. In much of Austria they do too; in Kamptal many growers are so utterly averse to any sweetness in their Rieslings that they pick quite early, for crystalline-pure wines of unbeatable precision. Australians take it for granted that Riesling should be bone-dry; in Australia, for somebody to make a Riesling that is off-dry is still a bit eccentric. Of the two main regions, Clare Rieslings are more defined by acidity and Eden is more mineral; other regions attracting notice are Tasmania and Canberra. In the USA, Oregon focuses on dry Rieslings while its neighbour Washington makes sweeter ones.

The curving flank of the Heiligenstein hill, Austria

Dry Riesling has to be very good indeed, because it has nowhere to hide. Any lack of ripeness will be exposed; any imbalance, any rawness, any shortcuts in the vineyard or the winery will announce themselves loud and clear. Those who make dry Rieslings swear that they are the clearest way of revealing the terroir of a great site. And when you're in Austria (for example) and you stare up at the Riesling terraces cut into primary rock, up and up and up, with no possibility of ever reaching those top terraces except on foot with whatever equipment you can carry on your back, you understand why the growers want to display every aspect of the vineyard they have trudged up to so many times. But they have warmer summers than the Mosel. No one would accuse Mosel growers of hiding one iota of their terroir, either. In the end the grapes and the vineyard must have the last word.

EXTREME RIESLING:
Bründlmayer Heiligenstein Riesling 2013, Kamptal, Austria

Kamptal Riesling is more about texture than fruit, and this (from a great year in Austria, and one of the country's greatest growers) has salty minerality, concentration that feels like lightness and the precision and detail of a Dürer engraving. The vines are 40–65 years old and yield wines of depth and power. Heiligenstein is Kamptal's most famous vineyard; geologically it's a freak, unlike any of the surrounding hills, and gives Riesling like taut silk.

Sweet Riesling
Still seductive?

The buzzwords of dry Riesling – minerality, saltiness – and the insidious feeling that dry Riesling is somehow more modern can blind us to the delights of sweet Riesling. Some German growers would have liked to abandon it; some Austrians won't go near it; many Australian growers would cross the road to avoid it. And yet it continues to have a hold on the UK. British lovers of German Riesling cling to it tenaciously; dry German Riesling has never yet made inroads into the British market.

Sweet doesn't have to be very sweet. It can be off-dry, or somewhere between off-dry and intensely sweet. But in any case good Riesling always has acidity to balance, so sweetish or sweet wines always have zip and zing; they always dance.

Proper sweet Riesling – the Germans prefer the term "fruity" for wines of Kabinett or Spätlese level – is sweet because the fermentation stopped before all the sugar had been used up. No sweetness is added. A German Riesling with residual sugar can be astonishingly low in alcohol – as little as 8% ABV for a Mosel Kabinett. These are among the most delicate wines you can buy, and yet they have the concentration to last for up to ten years. Feeble they are not. And their intensity of flavour means they can go incredibly well with food.

Spätlesen are riper, a little weightier; Auslesen may have a touch of noble rot; and with Beerenauslesen we are into proper noble rot territory. The acidity is still more concentrated, and the apricot and marmalade notes of *Botrytis cinerea* start to dominate the Riesling flavours. Trockenbeerenauslesen can be almost painful in their concentration, their almost bitter coffee notes. Icewine is different again: in theory it should have no noble rot, though in practice if you leave grapes on the vine until perhaps January they will tend to have a bit of noble rot. It's ignoble rot that is bad.

One or two Australian growers have ventured into Kabinett styles. Washington State versions are usually at this end of the spectrum; the taut, elegant wines of New York State's Finger Lakes also often have a touch of sweetness. Some Austrians, especially in the later-ripening Wachau, will allow a little residual sugar and a little noble rot into their Rieslings, though not usually enough to make them more than off-dry. Really sweet Rieslings, whether produced by noble rot or just by letting the berries shrivel and concentrate on the vine, can be found in Australia and New York State, in Austria and, as Icewine, in Canada. Which is not to make them sound run-of-the-mill; on the contrary, they are rare and outstanding.

So what of Alsace? There the sweetness/dryness question is alive and kicking. It is simply not possible to be certain from an Alsace label whether a wine is dry or not. Yes, Vendange Tardive, or late harvest, means it will be sweet. Sélection des Grains Nobles, from nobly rotten

Riesling, frozen for Icewine

grapes, means it will be even sweeter. But many growers routinely make wines with residual sugar, relying on their regular customers to remember which are sweet and which dry. It can drive the rest of us mad. And it's certainly a factor in the failure of Alsace wines to sell properly abroad.

EXTREME RIESLING:
Inniskillen Icewine 2012, Niagara, Ontario, Canada

The glaciers may have melted 13,000 years ago here, but it still gets pretty cold in the winter. In 2012 it was late January before a freeze set in properly, but then temperatures sank to the -10°C (14°F) that Inniskillen likes. The alcohol is just 9.5%, the residual sugar a massive 266 g/l, with acidity to balance; and the palate is intensely citrus and spicy, with mandarin and lemon flavours plus apricot and peach. Not subtle, but powerful.

Riesling likes to punish its growers by demanding scarily steep slopes and forbiddingly stony landscapes, but it's far more forgiving of its consumers. Climate change has helped too. It used to be the case that German Rieslings needed some years to come round: even Kabinett needed two or three years, and Spätlese needed five or six.

That's not the case any more. Riper wines are drinkable earlier; there's no reason why you shouldn't drink Kabinett as soon as it's released. Great ones at this age give you something like an electric shock – but it's up to you. It will change and develop with bottle age, and a Kabinett of three or four years old may well be more rewarding than an infant, but much depends on the style you prefer. As for Auslesen, they can take so long to grow up that most people have simply never tasted a fully mature one. Thirty years is a good time to keep them, sometimes 40. By this time they are no longer sweet. There's no exact word for what they are.

Austrians, for example, love to drink Riesling young. The growers despair of this national habit; they would love to persuade their customers to tuck some bottles away for later. Austrian Riesling ages brilliantly, losing none of its salty minerality, and gaining typical Riesling honey. It goes through a closed patch between about three

Riesling: shrugs off the dust of age

and seven years, but then it emerges rich and powerful, and set for the long haul. There's no hurry to drink Riesling.

Why does Riesling age so well? Ask producers and they shrug, and say, "It just does". Sooner or later some researcher will come up with a theory, no doubt, and it will probably centre on Riesling's particular balance of acidity and weight. It's not just acidity that enables wines to age, because some wines with low acidity, like Gewürztraminer, can age well. It's certainly not alcohol: Kabinett of just 8% ABV ages well. It's not sugar, because dry wines age well too, though it's true that some sweet ones seem immortal. A mysterious creaminess comes over them with age.

German Riesling may set the pace when it comes to ageing, but it's not alone. Rieslings from Alsace, Australia and the Finger Lakes can all see out a decade and more with great ease.

Then there's the petrol factor. Others say kerosene. Actual petrol notes are now considered a fault; honey is okay, petrol is not. Either way, there is no doubt that Rieslings develop a unique scent as they age. With cold-climate examples it can take years and emerge as an element in marvellously convoluted complexity. In most warmer-climate examples it is there from the start: one of the most telltale varietal sniffs of all.

Table manners
Riesling with food

Salmon with a creamy mushroom sauce:
time for a Rheingau Spätlese.

If you believe the first duty of wine is to be red you are not going to
try Riesling with your dinner. If you think the main thing about white
is a slurp with a bit of a sting you can stick to Sauvignon Blanc – and
welcome. If the sting puts you off, Pinot Gris. But if you like flavours,
relish the difference between the brown meat of a crab and the white,
crab and lobster, whiting and red mullet, pheasant and partridge, you
will soon cotton on to the things that Riesling can do.

Flavours, as we all know, can contrast or complement, go with
the grain or go across it. There is an argument (pretty weak, in my
view) for detecting, let's say, a hint of strawberry flavour in a wine and
drinking it with strawberries. Follow this line and you wash down
bananas with Beaujolais. No; a peach doesn't call for a peachy wine –
or even any wine at all. Don't bother sipping Riesling with fruit, pud...
anything of that sort.

There are natural affinities no one will deny. Red wines with their
tannins ask for high-protein, meaty foods. Oysters want acidic whites
with some body to stand up to their pungent flavours. The great virtue
of Riesling is its refreshing purity and its persistent memory of the
grape. "Fruity" doesn't really say it; even a potent mature Riesling still
carries the fresh crunch of its mother-fruit in its fan of flavours.

Why do we enjoy redcurrant jelly with lamb, cranberry with
turkey, sauce Béarnaise with beef, tartare sauce with sole, chutney with
so many things? Our palates are grateful for the contrasting freshness
or acidity of fruit. This is the Riesling message. It makes Mosel magic
with lobster, big savoury Rieslings from Deidesheim or Forst with
ham or venison, the snappy stony Rieslings of Victoria with all that
Southern Ocean seafood. I'm not saying you won't want to follow it up
with a steak and the fireside comfort of a mellow red, but there's the
glory of wine: the grape can give you both pleasures. Recently I drank
a 20-year-old Mosel Auslese with Stilton. Bonanza for both.

A little learning...

A few technical words

The jargon of laboratory analysis is often seen on back-labels. It creeps menacingly into newspapers and magazines. What does it mean? This hard-edged wine-talk, unsympathetic as it is to most lovers of wine, is very briefly explained below.

Acidity is both fixed and volatile. Fixed acidity: mostly tartaric, malic and citric acids, all from the grape, and lactic and succinic acids, from fermentation. Acidity may be natural or (in warm climates) added. Volatile acidity (VA): acetic acid, formed by bacteria in the presence of oxygen. A touch of VA is inevitable and can add complexity. Too much means vinegar. Total acidity is fixed and VA combined.

Alcohol content (mainly ethyl alcohol) is expressed as per cent (%) by volume of the total liquid. (Also known as "degrees".) Table wines are usually between 12.5%–14.5%; too many wines go as high as 16% these days.

Amphorae the fermentation vessel of the moment, and the last 7,000 years. Remove lid, throw in grapes, replace lid, return in six months. Risky: can be wonderful or frankly horrible.

Barriques Small (225 litre) oak barrels, as used in Bordeaux and across the world for fermentation and/or ageing. The newer the barrel the stronger the smell and taste of oak influence; French oak is more subtle than American. The fashion for overpowering wine of all sorts with new oak has waned: oak use is now far more subtle across most of the globe.

Biodynamic (bio) viticulture uses herbal, mineral and organic preparations in homeopathic quantities, in accordance with phases of the moon and movements of the planets. Sounds like voodoo, but some top growers swear by it. NB: "bio" in French means organic as well, but in this book it means biodynamic.

Malolactic fermentation occurs after the alcoholic fermentation, and changes tart malic acid into softer lactic acid. Can add complexity to red and white alike. Often avoided in hot climates where natural acidity is low and precious.

Micro-oxygenation is a widely used bubbling technique allowing controlled contact with oxygen during maturation. Softens flavours and helps to stabilize wine.

Minerality a tasting term to be used with caution: fine as a descriptor of chalky/stony/salty flavours; often wrongly used to imply transference of minerals from soil to wine, which is impossible.

Natural wines are undefined, but start by being organic or biodynamic, involve minimal intervention in the winery and as little SO2 as possible; sometimes none. Can be excellent and characterful, or oxidized and/or dirty. An element of Emperor's New Clothes may creep in.

Old vines give deeper flavours. No legal definition: some "vieilles vignes" turn out to be c.30 years. Should be 50+ to be taken seriously.

Orange wines are tannic whites fermented on skins, perhaps in amphorae. Caution: like natural wines, some are good, some not.

Organic viticulture prohibits most chemical products in the vineyard; organic wine prohibits added sulphur and must be made from organic grapes.

pH is a measure of acidity: the lower the pH the sharper the acidity. Wine is normally 2.8–3.8. High pH can be a problem in hot climates. Lower pH gives better colour, helps stop bacterial spoilage and allows more of the SO2 to be free and active as a preservative. So low is good in general.

Residual sugar is that left after fermentation has ended or been stopped, measured in grams per litre (g/l). A dry wine has almost none, though a gram or two might help balance.

Sulphur dioxide (SO2) is added to prevent oxidation and other accidents in winemaking. Some of it combines with sugars etc and is "bound". Only "free"